shelling but kept hostage by the
date and silence the media and o

threats and actions, including the use of white vans to abduct and to make
people disappear.

The Government shelled on a large scale in three consecutive No Fire
Zones, where it had encouraged the civilian population to concentrate, even
after indicating that it would cease the use of heavy weapons. It shelled
the United Nations hub, food distribution lines and near the International
Committee of the Red Cross (ICRC) ships that were coming to pick up the
wounded and their relatives from the beaches. It shelled in spite of its knowledge of the impact, provided by its own intelligence systems and through
notification by the United Nations, the ICRC and others. Most civilian casualties in the final phases of the war were caused by Government shelling.

The Government systematically shelled hospitals on the frontlines. All
hospitals in the Vanni were hit by mortars and artillery, some of them were
hit repeatedly, despite the fact that their locations were well-known to the
Government. The Government also systematically deprived people in the
conflict zone of humanitarian aid, in the form of food and medical supplies,
particularly surgical supplies, adding to their suffering. To this end, it pur-
posefully underestimated the number of civilians who remained in the conflict zone. Tens of thousands lost their lives from January to May 2009, many
of whom died anonymously in the carnage of the final few days.

The Government subjected victims and survivors of the conflict to further
deprivation and suffering after they left the conflict zone. Screening for suspected LTTE took place without any transparency or external scrutiny. Some of
those who were separated were summarily executed, and some of the women
may have been raped. Others disappeared, as recounted by their wives and
relatives during the LLRC hearings. All IDPs were detained in closed camps.
Massive overcrowding led to terrible conditions, breaching the basic social
and economic rights of the detainees, and many lives were lost unnecessar-
ily. Some persons in the camps were interrogated and subjected to torture.
Suspected LTTE were removed to other facilities, with no contact with the
outside world, under conditions that made them vulnerable to further abuses.

Despite grave danger in the conflict zone, the LTTE refused civilians
permission to leave, using them as hostages, at times even using their presence as a strategic human buffer between themselves and the advancing Sri
Lanka Army. It implemented a policy of forced recruitment throughout the
war, but in the final stages greatly intensified its recruitment of people of
all ages, including children as young as fourteen. The LTTE forced civilians to dig trenches and other emplacements for its own defences, thereby
contributing to blurring the distinction between combatants and civilians
and exposing civilians to additional harm. All of this was done in a quest to
pursue a war that was clearly lost; many civilians were sacrificed on the altar
of the LTTE cause and its efforts to preserve its senior leadership.

From February 2009 onwards, the LTTE started point-blank shooting of civilians who attempted to escape the conflict zone, significantly adding to the death toll in the final stages of the war. It also fired artillery in proximity to large groups of internally displaced persons (IDPs) and fired from, or stored military equipment near, IDPs or civilian installations such as hospitals. Throughout the final stages of the war, the LTTE continued its policy of suicide attacks outside the conflict zone. Even though its ability to perpetrate such attacks was diminished compared to previous phases of the conflict, it perpetrated a number of attacks against civilians outside the conflict zone.

Thus, in conclusion, the Panel found credible allegations that comprise five core categories of potential serious violations committed by the Government of Sri Lanka: (i) killing of civilians through widespread shelling; (ii) shelling of hospitals and humanitarian objects; (iii) denial of humanitarian assistance; (iv) human rights violations suffered by victims and survivors of the conflict, including both IDPs and suspected LTTE cadre; and (v) human rights violations outside the conflict zone, including against the media and other critics of the Government.

The Panel's determination of credible allegations against the LTTE associated with the final stages of the war reveal six core categories of potential serious violations: (i) using civilians as a human buffer; (ii) killing civilians attempting to flee LTTE control; (iii) using military equipment in the proximity of civilians; (iv) forced recruitment of children; (v) forced labour; and (vi) killing of civilians through suicide attacks.

Accountability

Accountability for serious violations of international humanitarian or human rights law is not a matter of choice or policy; it is a duty under domestic and international law. These credibly alleged violations demand a serious investigation and the prosecution of those responsible. If proven, those most responsible, including Sri Lanka Army commanders and senior Government officials, as well as military and civilian LTTE leaders, would bear criminal liability for international crimes.

At the same time, accountability goes beyond the investigation and prosecution of serious crimes that have been committed; rather it is a broad process that addresses the political, legal and moral responsibility of individuals and institutions for past violations of human rights and dignity. Consistent with the international standards mentioned above, accountability necessarily includes the achievement of truth, justice and reparations for victims. Accountability also requires an official acknowledgment by the State of its role and responsibility in violating the rights of its citizens, when that has occurred. In keeping with United Nations policy, the Panel does not advocate a "one-size-fits-all" formula or the importation of foreign models for accountability; rather it recognizes the need for accountability processes to be defined based on national assessments, involving broad citizen participation, needs and aspirations. Nonetheless, any national process must still meet international standards. . . .

The Government has stated that it is seeking to balance reconciliation and accountability, with an emphasis on restorative justice. The assertion of a choice between restorative and retributive justice presents a false dichotomy. Both are required. . . . The Government's two-pronged notion of accountability, as explained to the Panel, focusing on the responsibility of past Governments and of the LTTE, does not envisage a serious examination of the Government's decisions and conduct in prosecuting the final stages of the war or the aftermath, nor of the violations of law that may have occurred as a result.

The Panel has concluded that the Government's notion of accountability is not in accordance with international standards. Unless the Government genuinely addresses the allegations of violations committed by both sides and places the rights and dignity of the victims of the conflict at the centre of its approach to accountability, its measures will fall dramatically short of international expectations.

The Lessons Learnt and Reconciliation Commission

The Government has established the Lessons Learnt and Reconciliation Commission as the cornerstone of its policy to address the past from the ceasefire agreement in 2002 to the end of the conflict in May 2009. The LLRC represents a potentially useful opportunity to begin a national dialogue on Sri Lanka's conflict; the need for such a dialogue is illustrated by the large numbers of people, particularly victims, who have come forward on their own initiative and sought to speak with the Commission.

Nonetheless, the LLRC fails to satisfy key international standards of independence and impartiality, as it is compromised by its composition and deep-seated conflicts of interests of some of its members. The mandate of the LLRC, as well as its work and methodology to date, are not tailored to investigating allegations of serious violations of international humanitarian and human rights law, or to examining the root causes of the decades-long ethnic conflict; instead these focus strongly on the wider notion of political responsibility mentioned above, which forms part of the flawed and partial concept of accountability put forth by the Government. . . .

In sum, the LLRC is deeply flawed, does not meet international standards for an effective accountability mechanism and, therefore, does not and cannot satisfy the joint commitment of the President of Sri Lanka and the Secretary-General to an accountability process.

International role in the protection of civilians

During the final stages of the war, the United Nations political organs and bodies failed to take actions that might have protected civilians. Moreover, although senior international officials advocated in public and in private with the Government that it protect civilians and stop the shelling of hospitals and United Nations or ICRC locations, in the Panel's view, the public use of casualty figures would have strengthened the call for the protection of civilians while those events in the Vanni were unfolding. In addition, following the end of the war, the Human Rights Council may have been acting on incomplete information when it passed its May 2009 resolution on Sri Lanka.

Recommendation 4: United Nations

Considering the response of the United Nations to the plight of civilians in the Vanni during the final stages of the war in Sri Lanka and the aftermath:

A. The Human Rights Council should be invited to reconsider its May 2009 Special Session Resolution (A/HRC/S-11/L.1/Rev. 2) regarding Sri Lanka, in light of this report.

B. The Secretary-General should conduct a comprehensive review of actions by the United Nations system during the war in Sri Lanka and the aftermath, regarding the implementation of its humanitarian and protection mandates.

Even by the gruesome standards of the literature on human rights violations and government duplicity, this was strong stuff. For the United Nations, its own credibility was now at stake. The Secretary-General set up an internal review panel led by Charles Petrie, which submitted a comprehensive, admirably frank (and unequivocally damning) report, widely known as the Petrie Report, in November 2012. We shall focus here only on the principal paragraphs concerning the United Nations itself and related recommendations:

REPORT OF THE SECRETARY-GENERAL'S INTERNAL REVIEW PANEL ON UNITED NATIONS ACTION IN SRI LANKA[14]

United Nations failure

75. *Cultural challenges:* The UN can face significant challenges in retaining the essential support of a Government to help in delivering assistance while at the same time responding to serious violations of international law that may require the UN to issue criticism of the same Government.

---

[14] United Nations, Report of the Secretary-General's Internal Review Panel on United Nations action in Sri Lanka, November 2012, available at: http://www.un.org/News/dh/infocus/Sri_Lanka/The_Internal_Review_Panel_report_on_Sri_Lanka.pdf

In the case of Sri Lanka, a number of UN Country Teams (UNCT) and UN Headquarters (UNHQ) senior staff perceived these challenges as dilemmas or as conflicting responsibilities: (i) choosing not to speak up about Government and LTTE broken commitments and violations of international law was seen as the only way to increase UN humanitarian access; (ii) choosing to focus briefings to the Security Council on the humanitarian situation rather than on the causes of the crisis and the obligations of the parties to the conflict was seen as a way to facilitate constructive engagement by the Secretariat with Member States; and (iii) UN support in the establishment of internment camps was seen as the only option for the UN to assist internally displaced persons (IDPs) emerging from the Wanni, even if the IDPs were deprived of freedom of movement and the UN had limited access to them. Decisions at UNHQ and in the field were affected by an institutional culture of trade-offs. The tendency to see options for action in terms of dilemmas frequently obscured the reality of UN responsibilities. In fact, with its multiplicity of mandates and areas of expertise, the UN possessed the capabilities to simultaneously strive for humanitarian access while also robustly condemning the perpetrators of killings of civilians. It should have been able to push further for respect for international norms in the delivery of assistance to IDPs and avoid accusations of complicity in the detention of IDPs.

76. There was a continued reluctance among UNCT institutions to stand up for the rights of the people they were mandated to assist. In Colombo, some senior staff did not perceive the prevention of killing of civilians as their responsibility—and agency and department heads at UNHQ were not instructing them otherwise. Seen together, the failure of the UN to adequately counter the Government's under-estimation of population numbers in the Wanni, the failure to adequately confront the Government on its obstructions to humanitarian assistance, the unwillingness of the UN in UNHQ and Colombo to address Government responsibility for attacks that were killing civilians, and the tone and content of UN communications with the Government on these issues, collectively amounted to a failure by the UN to act within the scope of institutional mandates to meet protection responsibilities.

77. The tone, content and objectives of UNHQ's engagement with Member States regarding Sri Lanka were heavily influenced by what it perceived Member States wanted to hear, rather than by what Member States needed to know if they were to respond. Reflection on Sri Lanka by UNHQ and Member States at the UN was conducted on the basis of a mosaic of considerations among which the grave situation of civilians in Sri Lanka competed with extraneous factors such as perceptions of the role of the Secretariat in its relations with Member States and frequently inconclusive discussions on the concept of the Responsibility to Protect. In particular, the Security Council was deeply ambivalent about even placing on its agenda a situation that was

not already the subject of a UN peacekeeping or political mandate; while at the same time no other UN Member State mechanism had the prerogative to provide the political response needed, leaving Sri Lanka in a vacuum of inaction.

78. *Framework of action*: The overall framework for UN action in Sri Lanka was not well-adapted to the Organization's responsibilities, given the situation. Over the past 15 years, Member States and the UN system have agreed that peace, development and the protection of basic rights are deeply intertwined and mutually reinforcing and that they must be tackled together. Under UN auspices, Member States have adopted a range of interlinked standards that define UN protection responsibilities in situations such as armed conflict. These include: the international human rights law framework of civil and political and economic, social and cultural rights; the adoption of the Responsibility to Protect; and numerous resolutions by the Security Council on protecting civilians in armed conflict through the protection of international human rights and humanitarian law. All UN entities, whether in the Secretariat or UNCT, are expected to support follow-up and implementation of these standards and UN action in Sri Lanka was being measured partly on this basis. And yet, the tools with which the UN can meet its responsibilities vary widely across different country-situations ranging from, on the one hand, Security Council-mandated missions designed for complex political and armed conflict situations to, on the other hand, the UN's infrastructure in Sri Lanka consisting of a UNCT and Resident coordinator (RC) designed primarily to support development. Although additions were made to the UNCT infrastructure in Sri Lanka to help it respond to the conflict, most notably the addition of the Humanitarian Coordinator role and the significant support of UN Office for the Coordination of Humanitarian Affairs (OCHA), the staffing composition and structural posture of the UNCT and UNHQ relative to Sri Lanka nevertheless remained largely unchanged. While the UN's infrastructure remained static, the worsening situation was drastically changing both the UN's responsibilities and the expectations of the UN's role. The UN's development and humanitarian branches were unsuited to the situation and unable to fully address the UN's political and human rights and humanitarian law responsibilities; while it was these same responsibilities that became most fundamental to the survival of civilians.

79. Above all, UN action in Sri Lanka was not framed by Member State political support. In the absence of clear Security Council backing, the UN's actions lacked adequate purpose and direction. Member States failed to provide the Secretariat and UNCT with the support required to fully implement the responsibilities for protection of civilians that Member States had themselves set for such situations.

80. *Systemic failure*: The primary responsibility for killings and other violations against the estimated 360,000 or more civilians trapped during the final stages of the conflict in the Wanni lies with the Government of Sri Lanka and the LTTE. Under very difficult conditions, the UN succeeded in transporting some humanitarian assistance in convoys into the Wanni, in providing a degree of emergency shelter and relief to almost 280,000 survivors who were able to leave the conflict zone, and in positively influencing some aspects of Government plans for IDPs; exceptional attention was devoted to the situation by some senior UNHQ officials, including the Under Secretary General (and Emergency Relief Coordinator) for the Office for the Coordination of Humanitarian Affairs (USG-Humanitarian Affairs); and the Panel was inspired to find how far many individual staff in the field have gone in their efforts to uphold the principles of the Organisation. Nevertheless, the Panel's report concludes that events in Sri Lanka mark a grave failure of the UN to adequately respond to early warnings and to the evolving situation during the final stages of the conflict and its aftermath, to the detriment of hundreds of thousands of civilians and in contradiction with the principles and responsibilities of the UN. The elements of what was a systemic failure can be distilled into the following: (i) a UN system that lacked an adequate and shared sense of responsibility for human rights violations; (ii) an incoherent internal UN crisis-management structure which failed to conceive and execute a coherent strategy in response to early warnings and subsequent international human rights and humanitarian law violations against civilians, and which did not exercise sufficient oversight for UN action in the field; (iii) the ineffective dispersal of UNHQ's structures to coordinate UN action and to address international human rights and humanitarian law violations across several different UNHQ entities in Geneva and New York with overlapping mandates; (iv) a model for UN action in the field that was designed for a development rather than a conflict response; (v) the most senior position in the field graded at a D1 seniority that was below the heavy responsibilities required of the position, and a corps of senior staff that did not sufficiently include the armed conflict, political, human rights and international humanitarian law and related management experience to deal with the challenge Sri Lanka presented, and who were given insufficient support; (vi) inadequate political support from Member States as a whole, notwithstanding bilateral efforts from all regions, and inadequate efforts by the Secretariat to build such support; and (vii) a framework for Member State engagement with international human rights and humanitarian law protection crises that was outdated and often unworkable, in part because it did not enable Member States to reach a sufficiently early and full political consensus on the situation and the UN response.

IV. RECOMMENDATIONS REGARDING UNITED NATIONS ACTION TO RESPOND EFFECTIVELY TO SIMILAR SITUATIONS OF ESCALATED CONFLICT

A. Reference points

86. .... The recommendations have been framed by reflection on the political character of human rights crises and the role of UN Member States regarding such situations. All Member States regret and would wish to prevent situations where there is a large-scale loss of human life.

The single most effective UN action to protect civilians from gross human rights violations is early and robust political consensus among UN Member States in favour of protection: the combined political will alone of the international community has dramatically positive effects in encouraging parties on the ground to change their conduct and protect civilians. But, conversely, the single most significant factor that limits the UN's ability to adequately address such situations is the difficulty Member States have, especially at the Security Council, in reaching an early and qualitatively adequate political consensus on a situation. The difficulty in reaching consensus is caused by Member States' concerns that the UN actions they are asked to agree upon may have philosophical or practical consequences for national sovereignty or broader national political or economic implications. Reaching early and full political consensus among Member States is vital to improving protection of civilian lives: without firm political support the impact of UN actions is severely weakened and delayed; and without early UN action, situations quickly deteriorate creating ever-greater challenges for the Security Council that ultimately have a far greater impact on the separate concerns of Member States than would an early and light set of UN actions. Approaches need to be identified to allow UN Member States to more easily reach the necessary political consensus. These could include providing Member States with earlier and better information, and offering them new models of UN action which protect the human rights of civilians but which also have minimal impact on the wider concerns of Member States. In addition, although many Member States still have serious concerns regarding some interpretations and implications of the Responsibility to Protect, in practice possibly the greatest contribution of this concept would be as a process to help facilitate the emergence among Member States of early political consensus on human rights protection.

B. Recommendations

87. The Panel submits the following recommendations for the Secretary-General's consideration. The recommendations seek to support profound changes in how the UN approaches similar situations in the future. The recommendations are nevertheless intended to be politically feasible and to be largely resource neutral:

a) Renew a vision of the United Nations: The Secretary-General should renew a vision of the UN's most fundamental responsibilities regarding large-scale violations of international human rights and humanitarian law in crises, with a particular emphasis on the responsibility of senior staff.

1. The vision should help frame strategy and policy responses, at senior levels of the organization, to situations of massive human rights violations.

2. The vision should be introduced by the Secretary-General through a suitable opportunity. The vision should also be shared with all staff in various ways, such as: asking staff members to sign a letter to the Secretary-General re-committing themselves to upholding the principles and values of the UN when starting a new assignment; establishing mandatory, short refresher briefings on the UN's principles and values, with an emphasis on how these can be reflected in each staff member's work; incorporating these elements into appointments and performance appraisals for senior staff, and into training programmes and job descriptions for all staff.

3. Senior staff should be accountable for implementation of the vision in the UN response to relevant crises. At the most senior levels of the organization, the vision should include an obligation to fully inform Member States and the public of the realities of ongoing violations, and should help frame strategy and policy responses to crises in which civilians are at risk.

b) Embed a United Nations human rights perspective into United Nations strategies: In order to strengthen UNHQ capacity it will be essential to include international human rights, humanitarian and criminal law perspectives in overall UN analysis and strategy in relevant situations, while also strengthening UNHQ capacity to build political support from Member States for advocacy and action to address grave concerns.

1. The EOSG's internal staffing should include additional, suitably senior staff with strong international human rights and humanitarian law experience as well as understanding of UN action in mission and non-mission settings. These additional staff should strengthen EOSG analysis and liaison with the UNOCC, DPA, OHCHR and other UN departments and agencies, and Member States.

2. There must be much clearer lines of responsibility in the UNHQ response to ongoing situations of international human rights and humanitarian law violations, and improved capacity to brief the Secretary-General and Member States, and work through the UNOCC. To this end: (i) OHCHR

should be given an explicit UNHQ/NY oversight role for the international human rights and humanitarian law aspects of UN crisis response, and should be held accountable for fulfilling this responsibility, in accordance with OHCHR's General Assembly mandate to coordinate all such activities; (ii) OHCHR's staffing presence in UNHQ/NY should be significantly strengthened; (iii) to make more efficient use of limited resources and reduce duplication in monitoring and high-level situation briefings, the Secretary-General should consolidate UNHQ/NY staffing capacity on international human rights, humanitarian and criminal law violations (such as genocide, mass atrocities, and war crimes) within OHCHR's New York office; (iv) day-to-day collaboration between DPA and OHCHR at management and working levels should be strengthened, including through joint teams and reporting, and extended staff exchanges.

3. In relevant crisis situations, every UNCT should include staff with expertise in political analysis, human rights and, where relevant, international humanitarian law. UNCT planning tools must include complete and honest analysis of the human rights situation; and "protection" should be centred on ensuring respect for international human rights and humanitarian law.

4. Recognizing the constraints on UNCTs facing an emerging crisis, the Secretary-General should consider introducing new UN models of Secretariat action to ensure that the UN meets its international human rights and humanitarian law protection responsibilities during crises, including, for instance, "light-touch, high impact" teams deployable in support of a UNCT and which would be small in size of up to 20 staff, be of short deployment of a few months, have low visibility and would collaborate closely with host authorities and regional States.

c) **Strengthen the management of the whole-of-United Nations crisis response:** To ensure coherent UNHQ oversight for UN strategy and action, the Secretary-General should strengthen management of the UN response to international law crises that present large-scale risks to civilians.

1. Oversight for UN crisis response should ideally be exercised through one senior official who has direct overall responsibility. Increased use could be made of Special Envoys or Special Representatives, serving as the Senior Official. However, every effort should be made to avoid creating additional, parallel, ad hoc support structures; in this regard, the senior official should be linked to the UNOCC "Crisis Response Manager" framework. Depending on the context, appointees could cover more than one country and issue.

2. To strengthen coordination, and also to make more efficient use of resources, reduce duplication and gaps, and increase accountability, consideration should be given to reducing the number of UNHQ inter-departmental/agency coordination mechanisms in favour of action through a single mechanism per crisis situation. The mechanism should be directly linked to, and ideally managed by, the Senior Official and Crisis Response Manager. The

Policy Committee should be a forum of genuine discussion, based on complete information.

3. In situations of grave international human rights and humanitarian law violations, the UN must always be ready to present in UNHQ the best available information, and publicly release such information at appropriate moments. Where access is denied, monitoring should be conducted from UNHQ. Monitoring, reporting and presentation of international human rights and humanitarian law information should be led by OHCHR which, when it has no field presence, should be able to draw on credible information from other sources.

4. The field-level coordinator of UN action during crises should ideally have political, human rights and, where applicable, international humanitarian law expertise. Preference should be given to RC candidates who have had exposure across several UN departments, agencies and programmes. RCs should be evaluated in part on their political analysis and human rights performance. The field-level coordinator in a crisis should be managed by, and should report through, a UNHQ entity with suitable political and, where relevant, armed conflict operational and protection expertise; this could be the UN's Senior Official on the crisis.

5. In the light of the assessment section and the recommendations in this report, the useful concept of a "Policy on Special Circumstances in Non-mission Settings", as adopted by the Policy Committee in January 2012, should be developed further. This should ensure that the Secretary-General's declaration of such circumstances leads to improved UN action.

6. The UN should continue to roll out the new "programme criticality" approach to security, under which management-level decisions on evacuation and other security measures take full account of programme needs, with the understanding that "programmes" must be defined as including the full scope of UN responsibilities.

d) Promote accountability and responsibility:
1. UN departments and agencies both in headquarters and the field should adopt minimum commitments to "due diligence", including that they regularly request from OHCHR information on serious human rights concerns within countries where they operate, and that they give consideration to such information in internal strategy and policy meetings.

2. Conduct a limited internal review of UN action in every acute crisis that presents large-scale risks to the protection of civilians.

e) Improve United Nations engagement with Member States and build political support: For every relevant crisis, the Secretary-General must have an array of options that will permit him to inform Member States of the full breadth of the situation and to suggest actions. The Secretary-General cannot be in a situation where he is unable to speak about situations of grave urgency, and the Secretariat must be able to present to Member States, including regional groups, the best available information. Member States must be in the best position possible to make decisions on what response to pursue through the UN to such crises.

1. Possibly as a standard practice, regarding all situations of major international law crisis, the Secretary-General should invite interested Member States, especially regional States, to joint briefings systematically given by the heads of DPA, OHCHR and OCHA.

2. As an additional option, the Secretary-General should make more regular and explicit use of his Security Council convening authority under Article 99 of the Charter.

3. The Secretary-General should work with Member States to suggest new models through which they could convene, and begin consideration of a crisis much earlier, possibly pre-empting, through prevention, the need to take a situation to the Security Council. New models of Member State action or Secretariat briefing and deployment would pay particular attention to the role of regional States.

4. The Secretary-General should use the Responsibility to Protect (R2P) as a "convening" initiative to invite Member States to receive and consider information on the human rights aspects of a relevant crisis situation; and in this regard, DPA and OHCHR should be jointly tasked with managing its use and fulfilling the Secretariat's own responsibilities under the concept.

5. The Secretariat should make use of updated methods of briefing Member States on crises, including video and other digital media and briefings from field-based staff.

f) **Better address violations of privileges and immunities:**   The Secretary-General should review options for inviting Member States to consider what actions they could take in response to situations where one Member State engages in sustained actions against UN personnel and institutions, including violations of UN privileges and immunities, and which are having a serious impact on the UN's ability to meet its responsibilities. Further consideration should also be given to the UN's support to staff under threat.

g) **Follow-up:**   the Panel strongly urges that: (i) its report be made public; (ii) follow-up be given to the report's recommendations, that the process be led by an official within the Executive Office of the Secretary-General (EOSG), and that an implementation road-map be set out; (iii) the report be taken into consideration in other related processes, such as development of the UNOCC, programme criticality, special circumstances and change management; and (v) the UN offer to engage with the Government of Sri Lanka regarding those elements of the report that are applicable to ongoing UN action in Sri Lanka.

In response to the internal review panel's report, the Secretary-General, on 17 December 2013, launched the "Rights Up Front" initiative, after considerable internal debate within the United Nations. Chapter 16 of this volume, on Accountability in Practice, looks at that initiative and the United Nations' response to earlier failures to heed unfolding crises, in Rwanda and Srebrenica.

QUESTIONS

12. Can you think of particular factors that made the Sri Lanka case a difficult one for: (a) the Security Council; (b) the UN Human Rights Council; (c) the Secretary-General?
13. The Petrie report, although sympathetic at times, is categorical on UN mistakes in the run-up to and during the climax of the fighting. Were all of these mistakes avoidable?
14. Among the recommendations of the Petrie report, which three strike you as the most important? And which three would be easiest to implement?
15. Should such reports lead to resignations of leadership and/or staff directly implicated? Why? Or why not?

HYPOTHETICAL A

On 1 January 2015, the UN Secretary-General, not fully satisfied by the work and ideas advanced in 2013 and 2014 to craft SDGs, targets, and goals, turns to you, a staffer in his office, and asks you to develop a normative framework of principles that should govern the SDG exercise, including the rationale used for their selection, in a paper not exceeding three pages.

With or without reference to the material in this chapter, please draft such a memorandum.

HYPOTHETICAL B

You are the Secretary-General's Chief of Staff. On receipt of the Petrie Report he asks you to prioritize among the report's recommendations. Can you do so, justifying your suggestions, in a memorandum not exceeding three pages?

Further Reading

Sustainable Development Goals

Berry, Albert, "Growth, Inclusion and Society." In *International Development: Ideas, Experience and Prospects*, Bruce Currie-Alder, David M. Malone and Rohinton Medhora (eds). Oxford and New York: Oxford University Press, 2014 (text available at www.developmentideas.info).

Cornea, Giovanni Andrea and Richard Jolly (eds). *Adjustment with a Human Face (Vol. 1): Protecting the Vulnerable and Promoting Growth*; Oxford: Oxford University Press, 1987.

Davis, Kevin and Maria Mota Prado, "Law, Regulation and Development." In *International Development: Ideas, Experience and Prospects*, Bruce Currie-Alder, David M. Malone and Rohinton Medhora (eds), Oxford and New York: Oxford University Press, 2014 (text available at www.developmentideas.info).

Hagman, Lotta and David M. Malone, "The North-South Divide at the United Nations: Fading at Last?" *Security Dialogue*, Vol. 33, No. 4, December 2002, pp. 399–414.

Jolly, Richard, "Underestimated Influence: UN Contributions to Development Ideas, Leadership, Influence and Impact," *International Development: Ideas, Experience and Prospects*, Bruce Currie-Alder, David M. Malone and Rohinton Medhora (eds). Oxford and New York: Oxford University Press, 2014 (text available at www.developmentideas.info).

Leipziger, Danny, "The Role of International Financial Institutions." In *International Development: Ideas, Experience and Prospects*, Bruce Currie-Alder, David M. Malone and Rohinton Medhora (eds). Oxford and New York: Oxford University Press, 2014 (text available at www.developmentideas.info).

Williamson, John, "A Short History of the Washington Consensus," International Institute of Economics Paper commissioned for a conference "From the Washington Consensus towards a new Global Governance," September 24–25, 2004, available at: http://www.iie.com/publications/papers/williamson0904-2.pdf.

Sri Lanka

Hargreaves, Caroline, Martin Karlsson, Surabhi Agrawal, Jonathan Hootnick and Katherine Tengtio, *International Dimensions of the Sri Lankan Conflict*, Centre for Peace and Security Studies, 2012, available at: http://www.academia.edu/1565798/International_Dimensions_of_the_Sri_Lankan_Conflict.

United Nations, The Report of the Secretary-General's Panel of Experts on Accountability in Sri Lanka, 31 March 2011, available at: http://www.un.org/News/dh/infocus/Sri_Lanka/POE_Report_Full.pdf.

United Nations, Report of the Secretary-General's Internal Review Panel on United Nations action in Sri Lanka, November 2012, available at: http://www.un.org/News/dh/infocus/Sri_Lanka/The_Internal_Review_Panel_reporton_Sri_Lanka.pdf.

Part Two **Capacity**

chapter four
....

Legal Status

What *is* the United Nations? Is it a place where representatives of governments meet to discuss their interests and "harmonize their actions"? Is it an instrument of some or all of those governments, acting as an agent to carry out their will? Is it an autonomous actor, able to act independently of the collective will of the states that created the organization? Or is it a supranational authority, with the power to impose binding obligations on all states? The answer is all of the above, but it is important to understand what parts of the United Nations play which role, and under what circumstances.

The Peace of Westphalia, declared in 1648, made clear the position of states as sole actors in international law. In the era following the American and French revolutions in the eighteenth century, states replaced the Universal Church and multinational empires as the principal actors in international relations. For centuries, there was no question of equal recognition being extended to other, lesser entities. Individuals, groups, corporations, etc., were entitled to rights and duties solely under municipal legal systems. International organizations, such as the United Nations or its predecessor, the League of Nations, were inventions of the twentieth century.

Once set up, however, they came to acquire international legal status, thereby fitting uncomfortably into the paradigm of the legal system established by the Peace of Westphalia. At the time of the League of Nations, it was already recognized that such a "universal" organization of states must have an international legal personality, separate from that of its members. This, however, was not necessarily a status equivalent to that which the law accorded to states. For example, it was not clear, at first, whether the international organization enjoyed independent legal capacity with respect to nonmembers of the Organization.

With the establishment of the United Nations, the question of legal personality was finally addressed, in an advisory opinion given by the International Court of Justice (ICJ) in the *Reparations* case. Today other supranational organizations and nongovernmental organizations vie for similar status. It is now generally understood that, even with limited legal personality, these organizations have the capacity to enter into legally binding relations with nonmember states, and that member states by joining the organization may assume legal obligations not only to other members but also to the organization, as such.

If the United Nations has international legal personality, the next question is: How much? What legal powers does it possess? The *Reparations* case (extracts below) established that it has the capacity to enter into legal proceedings in order to bring independent claims on behalf of its agents. The *Reparations* case also affirms that the United Nations has the capacity to enter into treaties, for example headquarters agreements with host countries, and contracts, for example to rent cars and buildings. These flow from the nature of the United Nations functions—without these powers it would not be able to engage in these activities effectively. Beyond that, what are the scope and limits of an international organization's legal powers?

There are three schools of thought on this question. The first is the doctrine of attributed powers: an international organization (IO) has only those powers that are explicitly attributed to it in its constituent instrument. This follows from the idea that an IO is an agent of its member states and can only engage in activities that are explicitly delegated to it by those states. A second school of thought, at the other end of the spectrum, is the doctrine of inherent powers: there are some rights and duties enjoyed by every IO. This is sometimes called "objective legal personality," in the sense that there are certain powers all IOs have by virtue of the fact that they are IOs—as Jan Klabbers puts it, powers that inhere in "organizationhood" (analogous to the powers that inhere in "statehood").[1] It does not depend on the "subjective" will of the member states or the constituent instrument, but rather is bestowed by international law. The "implied powers" school occupies the middle ground: it holds that legal capacities are granted implicitly by the functions to be performed. One must look at the constituent instrument and the general purposes of the organization, from which its legal powers can be inferred.

After presenting extracts from the *Reparations* case and other cases on legal personality and the implied powers doctrine, this chapter turns to a range of issues associated with the scope and limits of the United Nations' legal powers. It considers who interprets the Charter, and the related question of whether there are any checks on how it is interpreted, including the possibility of judicial review. It then looks at two recent illustrations of how the Security Council has stretched the limits of its legal authority: quasi-judicial and quasi-legislative acts. The chapter concludes with three sections on lawmaking by the General Assembly, by some of the specialized agencies, and through the operational activities of the United Nations.

---

[1] Jan Klabbers, *Introduction to International Institutional Law* (2nd edn Cambridge: Cambridge University Press, 2009), pp. 49 and 67–68.

4.1 Legal Personality

The *Reparations* case arose in the form of a request by the General Assembly to the ICJ for an advisory opinion, provision for which is made in Chapter IV of the Statute of the Court and Article 96 of the UN Charter. In this request the Court was asked to determine the legality of a claim brought by the United Nations against Israel for reparations for the killing in Jerusalem of Count Bernadotte, a Swedish national, who had been the chief UN Truce Negotiator in the former Palestinian mandate. At that time, Israel was not yet a member of the United Nations, only being admitted on 11 May 1949, one month after the Court rendered its opinion. The ICJ ultimately decided that such a claim was permissible, and Israel paid $54,628 in compensation in 1950.[2]

GENERAL ASSEMBLY RESOLUTION 258(III) (1948): REQUEST FOR ADVISORY OPINION

The General Assembly,
   Decides to submit the following legal questions to the International Court of Justice for an advisory opinion:
   I. In the event of an agent of the United Nations in the performance of his duties suffering injury in circumstances involving the responsibility of a State, has the United Nations, as an Organization, the capacity to bring an international claim against the responsible *de jure* or *de facto* government with a view to obtaining the reparation due in respect of the damage caused (a) to the United Nations, (b) to the victim or to persons entitled through him?
   II. In the event of an affirmative reply on point I (b), how is action by the United Nations to be reconciled with such rights as may be possessed by the State of which the victim is a national?

In its opinion, the Court affirmed the legal personality of the United Nations; its ability to accord protection to its agents in a manner similar, though not directly analogous, to the right of states to offer diplomatic protection to their nationals; and its ability to bring claims against states.

---

[2] See http://unispal.un.org/UNISPAL.NSF/0/06356649E81BD0E385256D9D0066E966.

REPARATION FOR INJURIES SUFFERED IN THE SERVICE OF THE
UNITED NATIONS (ADVISORY OPINION) (1949)
ICJ REPORTS 174

The questions asked of the Court relate to the "capacity to bring an international claim"; accordingly, we must begin by defining what is meant by that capacity and consider the characteristics of the Organization, so as to determine whether, in general these characteristics do, or do not, include for the Organization a right to present an international claim. . . .

[T]he Court must first enquire whether the Charter has given the Organization such a position that it possesses in regard to its Members, rights which it is entitled to ask them to respect. In other words, does the Organization possess international personality? This is no doubt a doctrinal expression, which has sometimes given rise to controversy. But it will be used here to mean that if the Organization is recognized as having that personality, it is an entity capable of availing itself of the obligations incumbent upon its Members.

To answer this question which is not settled by the actual terms of the Charter, we must consider what characteristics it was intended thereby to give to the Organization.

The subjects of law in any legal system are not necessarily identical in their nature or in the extent of their rights, and their nature depends upon the needs of the community. Throughout its history, the development of international law has been influenced by the requirements of international life, and the progressive increase in the collective activities of States has already given rise to instances of action upon the international plane by certain entities which are not States. This development culminated in the establishment in June 1945 of an international organization whose purposes and principles are specified in the Charter of the United Nations. But to achieve these ends the attribution of international personality is indispensable.

The Charter has not been content to make the Organization created by it merely a centre "for harmonizing the actions of nations in the attainment of these common ends" (Article I, para. 4). It has equipped that centre with organs, and has given it special tasks. It has defined the position of the Members in relation to the Organization by requiring them to give it every assistance in any action undertaken by it (Article 2, para. 5), and to accept and carry out the decisions of the Security Council; by authorizing the General Assembly to make recommendations to the Members; by giving the Organization legal capacity and privileges and immunities in the territory of each of its Members; and by providing for the conclusion of agreements between the Organization and its Members. Practice—in particular the conclusion of conventions to which the Organization is a party—has confirmed this character of the Organization, which occupies a position in certain respects in detachment from its Members, and which is under a duty to remind them, if need be, of certain obligations. It must be added that the Organization is a political body, charged with political tasks of an important character, and covering a wide field namely, the maintenance of international peace and security, the development of friendly relations among nations, and the achievement of international co-operation in the solution of problems of an economic, social, cultural or humanitarian character (Article 1); and in dealing with its Members it employs political means. The "Convention on the Privileges and Immunities of the United Nations" of 1946 creates rights and duties between each of the signatories and the Organization (see, in particular, Section 35). It is difficult to see how such a convention could operate except upon the international plane and as between parties possessing international personality.

In the opinion of the Court, the Organization was intended to exercise and enjoy, and is in fact exercising and enjoying, functions and rights which can only be explained on the basis of the possession of a large measure of international personality and the capacity to operate upon an international plane. It is at present the supreme type of international organization, and it could not carry out the intentions of its founders if it was devoid of international personality. It must be acknowledged that its Members, by entrusting certain functions to it, with the attendant duties and responsibilities, have clothed it with the competence required to enable those functions to be effectively discharged.

Accordingly, the Court has come to the conclusion that the Organization is an international person. That is not the same thing as saying that it is a State, which it certainly is not, or that its legal personality and rights and duties are the same as those of a State. Still less is it the same thing as saying that it is "a super-State," whatever that expression may mean. It does not even imply that all its rights and duties must be upon the international plane, any more than all the rights and duties of a State must be upon that plane. What it does mean is that it is a subject of international law and capable of possessing international rights and duties, and that it has capacity to maintain its rights by bringing international claims.

The next question is whether the sum of the international rights of the Organization comprises the right to bring the kind of international claim described in the Request for this Opinion. That is a claim against a State to obtain reparation in respect of the damage caused by the injury of an agent of the Organization in the course of the performance of his duties. Whereas a State possesses the totality of international rights and duties recognized by international law, the rights and duties of an entity such as the Organization must depend upon its purposes and functions as specified or implied in its constituent documents and developed in practice. The functions of the Organization are of such a character that they could not be effectively discharged if they involved the concurrent action, on the international plane, of fifty-eight or more Foreign Offices, and the Court concludes that the Members have endowed the Organization with capacity to bring international claims when necessitated by the discharge of its functions. ...

. . .

The Charter does not expressly confer upon the Organization the capacity to include, in its claim for reparation, damage caused to the victim or to persons entitled through him. The Court must therefore begin by enquiring whether the provisions of the Charter concerning the functions of the Organization, and the part played by its agents in the performance of those functions, imply for the Organization power to afford its agents the limited protection that would consist in the bringing of a claim on their behalf for reparation for damage suffered in such circumstances. Under international law, the Organization must be deemed to have those powers which, though not expressly provided in the Charter, are conferred upon it by necessary implication as being essential to the performance of its duties. ...

Having regard to its purposes and functions already referred to, the Organization may find it necessary, and has in fact found it necessary, to entrust its agents with important missions to be performed in disturbed parts of the world. Many missions, from their very nature, involve the agents in unusual dangers to which ordinary persons are not exposed. For the same reason, the injuries suffered by its agents in these circumstances will sometimes have occurred in such a manner that their national State would not be justified in bringing a claim for reparation on the ground of diplomatic protection, or, at any rate, would not feel disposed to do so. Both to ensure the efficient and independent performance of these missions and to afford effective support to its agents, the Organization must provide them with adequate protection. ...

Upon examination of the character of the functions entrusted to the Organization and of the nature of the missions of its agents, it becomes clear that the capacity of the Organization to exercise a measure of functional protection of its agents arises by necessary intendment out of the Charter. ...

The question remains whether the Organization has the "capacity to bring an international claim against the responsible *de jure* or *de facto* government with a view to obtaining the reparation due" ... or whether, on the contrary, the defendant State, not being a member, is justified in raising the objection that the Organization lacks the capacity to bring an international claim. On this point the Court's opinion is that fifty States, representing the vast majority of the members of the international community, had the power, in conformity with international law, to bring into being an entity possessing objective international personality and not merely personality recognized by them alone, together with the capacity to bring international claims. ...

FOR THESE REASONS,

The Court is of opinion

On Question I (*a*):

(*i*) unanimously,

That, in the event of an agent of the United Nations in the performance of his duties suffering injury in circumstances involving the responsibility of a Member State, the United Nations as an Organization has the capacity to bring an international claim against the responsible *de jure* or *de facto* government with a view to obtaining the reparation due in respect of the damage caused to the United Nations.

(*ii*) unanimously,

That, in the event of an agent of the United Nations in the performance of his duties suffering injury in circumstances involving the responsibility of a State which is not a member, the United Nations as an Organization has the capacity to bring an international claim against the responsible *de jure* or *de facto* government with a view to obtaining the reparation due in respect of the damage caused to the United Nations.

On Question I (*b*):

(*i*) by eleven votes against four,

That, in the event of an agent of the United Nations in the performance of his duties suffering injury in circumstances involving the responsibility of a Member State, the United Nations as an Organization has the capacity to bring an international claim against the responsible *de jure* or *de facto* government with a view to obtaining the reparation due in respect of the damage caused to the victim or to persons entitled through him.

(*ii*) by eleven votes against four,

That, in the event of an agent of the United Nations in the performance of his duties suffering injury in circumstances involving the responsibility of a State which is not a member, the United Nations as an Organization has the capacity to bring an international claim against the responsible *de jure* or *de facto* government with a view to obtaining the reparation due in respect of the damage caused to the victim or to persons entitled through him.....

Dissenting Opinion of Justice Hackworth

The conclusion that power in the Organization to sponsor private claims is conferred by "necessary implication" is not believed to be warranted under rules laid down by tribunals for filling lacunae in specific grants of power.

There can be no gainsaying the fact that the Organization is one of delegated and enumerated powers ... Powers not expressed cannot freely be implied. Implied powers flow from a grant of expressed powers, and are limited to those that are "necessary" to the exercise of powers expressly granted. No necessity for the exercise of the power here in question has been shown to exist ... The employees are still nationals of their respective countries and the customary methods of handling such claims are still available in full vigour. The prestige and efficiency of the Organization will be safeguarded by an exercise of its undoubted right under point I (*a*) *supra*.

Thus the *Reparations* case firmly established that the United Nations has legal personality, that one of the incidents of legal personality is the ability to bring claims on behalf of its agents, and that it probably has other powers that are "essential to the performance of its duties." What other powers do the United Nations, and its various organs and entities possess? The ICJ has had occasion to weigh in on this a number of times since the *Reparations* case. These cases demonstrate that, although the implied powers may be broad given the open-textured language of the UN Charter and the constituent instruments of its specialized agencies, they are not unlimited.

The *Certain Expenses* case arose when France and the Soviet Union withheld funding on the grounds that the General Assembly had acted ultra vires by establishing peacekeeping operations on the Sinai peninsula (UNEF I in 1956) and the Congo (ONUC in 1960). The General Assembly did so on the basis of the Uniting for Peace resolution, which dates back to the Korea crisis in 1950. Although the ICJ was not asked to give an Advisory Opinion on the Uniting for Peace resolution in 1950, it was in 1962. (The *Certain Expenses* case is considered in more detail in Chapter 7.)

CERTAIN EXPENSES OF THE UNITED NATIONS (ARTICLE 17, PARAGRAPH 2, OF THE CHARTER) (ADVISORY OPINION) (1962) ICJ REPORTS 151

The argument rests in part upon the view that when the maintenance of international peace and security is involved, it is only the Security Council which is authorized to decide on any action relative thereto. It is argued further that since the General Assembly's power is limited to discussing, considering, studying and recommending, it cannot impose an obligation to pay the expenses which result from the implementation of its recommendations. This argument leads to an examination of the respective functions of the General Assembly and of the Security Council under the Charter, particularly with respect to the maintenance of international peace and security.

Article 24 of the Charter provides:

"In order to ensure prompt and effective action by the United Nations, its Members confer on the Security Council primary responsibility for the maintenance of international peace and security ..."

...

The Charter makes it abundantly clear, however, that the General Assembly is also to be concerned with international peace and security. Article 14 authorizes the General Assembly to "recommend measures for the peaceful adjustment of any situation, regardless of origin, which it deems likely to impair the general welfare or friendly relations among nations, including situations resulting from a violation of the provisions of the present Charter setting forth the purposes and principles of the United Nations". The word "measures" implies some kind of action, and the only limitation which Article 14 imposes on the General Assembly is the restriction found in Article 12, namely, that the Assembly should not recommend measures while the Security Council is dealing with the same matter unless the Council requests it to do so. Thus while it is the Security Council which, exclusively, may order coercive action, the functions and powers conferred by the Charter on the General Assembly are not confined to discussion, consideration, the initiation of studies and the making of recommendations; they are not merely hortatory. ...

The Court considers that the kind of action referred to in Article 11, paragraph 2, is coercive or enforcement action. This paragraph, which applies not merely to general questions relating to peace and security, but also to specific cases brought before the General Assembly by a State under Article 35, in its first sentence empowers the General Assembly, by means of recommendations to States or to the Security Council, or to both, to organize peacekeeping operations, at the request, or with the consent, of the States concerned This power of the General Assembly is a special power which in no way derogates from its general powers under Article 10 or Article 14, except as limited by the last sentence of Article 11, paragraph 2. This last sentence says that when "action" is necessary the General Assembly shall refer the question to the Security Council. The word "action" must mean such action as is solely within the province of the Security Council ... The "action" which is solely within the province of the Security Council is that which is indicated by the title of Chapter VII of the Charter, namely "Action with respect to threats to the peace, breaches of the peace, and acts of aggression". If the word "action" in Article II, paragraph 2, were interpreted to mean that the General Assembly could make recommendations only of a general character affecting peace and security in the abstract, and not in relation to specific cases, the paragraph would not have provided that the General Assembly may make recommendations on questions brought before it by States or by the Security Council. Accordingly, the last sentence of Article 11, paragraph 2, has no application where the necessary action is not enforcement action. ...

In determining whether the actual expenditures authorized constitute "expenses of the Organization within the meaning of Article 17, paragraph 2, of the Charter", the Court agrees that such expenditures must be tested by their relationship to the purposes of the United Nations in the sense that if an expenditure were made for a purpose which is not one of the purposes of the United Nations, it could not be considered an "expense of the Organization".

The purposes of the United Nations are set forth in Article 1 of the Charter. The first two purposes as stated in paragraphs 1 and 2, may be summarily described as pointing to the goal of international peace and security and friendly relations...

The primary place ascribed to international peace and security is natural, since the fulfilment of the other purposes will be dependent upon the attainment of that basic condition. These purposes are broad indeed, but neither they nor the powers conferred to effectuate them are unlimited. Save as they have entrusted the Organization with the attainment of these common ends, the Member States retain their freedom of action. But when the Organization takes action which warrants the assertion that it was appropriate for the fulfilment of one of the stated purposes of the United Nations, the presumption is that such action is not *ultra vires* the Organization.

Many years later, the ICJ had another opportunity to comment on the implied powers doctrine when the World Health Organization requested an Advisory Opinion on the threat or use of nuclear weapons. For reasons set out below, the ICJ declined to give such an opinion. However it did respond positively to a similar request from the General Assembly.[3]

LEGALITY OF THE USE BY A STATE OF NUCLEAR WEAPONS IN ARMED CONFLICT (ADVISORY OPINION) (1996) ICJ REPORTS 679

21. Interpreted in accordance with their ordinary meaning, in their context and in the light of the object and purpose of the WHO Constitution, as well as of the practice followed by the Organization, the provisions of its Article 2 may be read as authorizing the Organization to deal with the effects on health of the use of nuclear weapons, or of any other hazardous activity, and to take preventive measures aimed at protecting the health of populations in the event of such weapons being used or such activities engaged in.

The question put to the Court in the present case relates, however, *not to the effects* of the use of nuclear weapons on health, but to the *legality* of the use of such weapons *in view of their health and environmental effects*. Whatever those effects might be, the competence of the WHO to deal with them is not dependent on the legality of the acts that caused them. Accordingly, it does not seem to the Court that the provisions of Article 2 of the WHO

---

[3] Legality of the Threat or Use of Nuclear Weapons (Advisory Opinion) (1996) ICJ Reports 226.

Constitution, interpreted in accordance with the criteria referred to above, can be understood as conferring upon the Organization a competence to address the legality of the use of nuclear weapons, and thus in turn a competence to ask the Court about that.

22. .... In the view of the Court, none of these functions has a sufficient connection with the question before it for that question to be capable of being considered as arising "within the scope of [the] activities" of the WHO. The causes of the deterioration of human health are numerous and varied; and the legal or illegal character of these causes is essentially immaterial to the measures which the WHO must in any case take in an attempt to remedy their effects. In particular, the legality or illegality of the use of nuclear weapons in no way determines the specific measures, regarding health or otherwise (studies, plans, procedures, etc.), which could be necessary in order to seek to prevent or cure some of their effects. Whether nuclear weapons are used legally or illegally, their effects on health would be the same. Similarly, while it is probable that the use of nuclear weapons might seriously prejudice the WHO's material capability to deliver all the necessary services in such an eventuality, for example, by making the affected areas inaccessible, this does not raise an issue falling within the scope of the Organization's activities within the meaning of Article 96, paragraph 2, of the Charter. The reference in the question put to the Court to the health and environmental effects, which according to the WHO the use of a nuclear weapon will always occasion, does not make the question one that falls within the WHO's functions.

25. The Court need hardly point out that international organizations are subjects of international law which do not, unlike States, possess a general competence. International organizations are governed by the "principle of speciality", that is to say, they are invested by the States which create them with powers, the limits of which are a function of the common interests whose promotion those States entrust to them. The Permanent Court of International Justice referred to this basic principle in the following terms:

> "As the European Commission is not a State, but an international institution with a special purpose, it only has the functions bestowed upon it by the Definitive Statute with a view to the fulfillment of that purpose, but it has power to exercise these functions to their full extent, in so far as the Statute does not impose restrictions upon it." (*Jurisdiction of the European Commission of the Danube, Advisory Opinion, P. C.I.J., Series B, No. 14*, p. 64.)

26. .... It follows from the various instruments mentioned above that the WHO Constitution can only be interpreted, as far as the powers conferred upon that Organization are concerned, by taking due account not only of the general principle of speciality, but also of the logic of the overall system contemplated by the Charter. If, according to the rules on which that system is based, the WHO has, by virtue of Article 57 of the Charter, "wide international responsibilities", those responsibilities are necessarily

restricted to the sphere of public "health" and cannot encroach on the responsibilities of other parts of the United Nations system. And there is no doubt that questions concerning the use of force, the regulation of armaments and disarmament are within the competence of the United Nations and lie outside that of the specialized agencies. Besides, any other conclusion would render virtually meaningless the notion of a specialized agency; it is difficult to imagine what other meaning that notion could have if such an organization need only show that the use of certain weapons could affect its objectives in order to be empowered to concern itself with the legality of such use. It is therefore difficult to maintain that, by authorizing various specialized agencies to request opinions from the Court under Article 96, paragraph 2, of the Charter, the General Assembly intended to allow them to seize the Court of questions belonging within the competence of the United Nations.

For all these reasons, the Court considers that the question raised in the request for an advisory opinion submitted to it by the WHO does not arise "within the scope of [the] activities" of that Organization as defined by its Constitution.

QUESTIONS

1. How would you describe the United Nations? Is it more like a forum, an instrument, an actor, or a supranational authority?
2. In the *Reparations* case, the ICJ provides an incomplete definition of the term "international personality" insofar as it applies to the United Nations, mentioning only that it has rights and duties on the international plane, and that these include the capacity to bring international claims. It accepts also that the rights and duties associated with such international personality differ for states and international organizations. Which characteristics of the legal personality of states[4] should apply to international organizations and why?
3. Does the capacity to bring international claims flow directly from the possession of international personality? Are there organizations that have

---

[4] Grigory Tunkin defined the full legal personality of states as including the following characteristics: (1) rights and duties under international law; (2) sovereignty, which means supreme power over states' respective territories and population; (3) sovereign equality of all states; (4) privileges and immunities of states and their organs; (5) the capacity to participate in the process of creating norms of international law; (6) the capacity to participate in international legal relations; (7) the capacity to bring international claims; (8) the capacity to take enforcement actions under international law; and (9) the capacity to bear international responsibility: Grigory Tunkin, "International Law in the International System," *Receuil des cours*, vol. 147(1) (1975), pp. 201–202.

limited international personality that does not include the capacity to bring international claims?

4. The Court's 1949 opinion in the *Reparations* case indicates that an international organization may bring a claim against a state for injury to its own national, if such national is an agent of the Organization. Should this be viewed as an intrusion upon the internal sovereignty of a state? What public policy justifies according a right to the United Nations to bring claims against the state of which a UN civil servant is a national?

5. Why did Judge Hackworth dissent in the *Reparations* case?

6. By stating in *Certain Expenses* that any action that can be tied to one of the purposes of the United Nations should be presumed to be *intra vires*, does the ICJ go beyond the position it took in the *Reparations* case?

7. Does the ICJ's denial of the World Health Organization's request for an Advisory Opinion represent a step back from the implied powers doctrine? If so, is this a positive development?

4.2 Who Interprets the Charter?

The United Nations Conference on International Organization was convened in San Francisco in 1945 for the purposes of drafting the Charter of the United Nations. The work was divided among four Commissions that were further divided into twelve technical Committees, each of which was responsible for preparing a separate portion of the Charter.

Among the issues raised for discussion during the course of this Conference was "how and by what organ or organs of the Organization should the Charter be interpreted." This question, originally presented by the Belgian Delegation to Committee II/2, was thereafter referred to Committee IV/2 and was debated upon on 28 May and 7 June 1945.

STATEMENT OF COMMITTEE IV/2 OF THE SAN FRANCISCO CONFERENCE, REPORT OF COMMITTEE IV/2 OF THE UNITED NATIONS CONFERENCE ON INTERNATIONAL ORGANIZATION, SAN FRANCISCO, 12 JUNE 1945[5]

In the course of the operations from day to day of the various organs of the Organization, it is inevitable that each organ will interpret such parts of the Charter as are applicable to its particular functions. The process is inherent

---

[5] UNCIO Doc. 933, IV/2/42(2), p. 7; 13 UNCIO Documents, p. 703, at 709–710.

in the functioning of any body which operates under an instrument defining its functions and powers. It will be manifested in the functioning of such a body as the General Assembly, the Security Council or the International Court of Justice. Accordingly it is not necessary to include in the Charter a provision either authorizing or approving the normal operation of this principle. . . .

Difficulties may conceivably arise in the event that there should be a difference in opinion among the organs of the Organization concerning the correct interpretation of a provision of the charter. Thus, two organs may conceivably hold and may express or even act upon different views. Under unitary forms of national government the final determinations of such a question may be vested in the highest court or in some other national authority. However, the nature of the Organization and of its operation would not seem to be such as to invite the inclusion in the Charter of any provision of this nature. If two member states are at a variance concerning the correct interpretation of the Charter, they are of course free to submit the dispute to the International Court of Justice as in the case of any other treaty. Similarly, it would always be open to the General Assembly or to the Security Council, in appropriate circumstances, to ask the International Court of Justice for an advisory opinion concerning the meaning of a provision of the Charter. Should the General Assembly or the Security Council prefer another course, an ad hoc committee of jurists might be set up to examine the question and report its views, or recourse might be had to a joint conference. In brief, the members or the organs of the Organization might have recourse to various expedients in order to obtain appropriate interpretation. It would appear neither necessary nor desirable to list or to describe in the Charter the various possible expedients.

It is to be understood, of course, that if an interpretation made by any organ of the Organization or by a committee of jurists is not generally acceptable it will be without binding force. In such circumstances, or in cases where it is desired to establish an authoritative interpretation as a precedent for the future, it may be necessary to embody the interpretation in an amendment to the Charter.

Thus in San Francisco it was decided that "each United Nations organ interprets such parts of the Charter as are applicable to its functions." The Security Council or General Assembly can ask the International Court of Justice for an Advisory Opinion on interpretation of the Charter, including on their competence (as the GA did in the *Southwest Africa*[6] and *Certain Expenses*[7] cases), but otherwise, each organ decides for itself what it can and cannot do.

---

[6] *South West Africa* cases. (*Ethiopia v. South Africa; Liberia v. South Africa*), Judgment of 21 December 1962: I.C.J. Report; 1962.
[7] *Certain expenses of the United Nations (Article 17, paragraph 2, of the Charter)*, Advisory Opinion of 20 July 1962: I.C.J. Reports 1962.

The implication is that the ICJ was not given the power to pass judgment on whether another UN organ misinterpreted the Charter, nor was it given the authority to declare that the Council or General Assembly acted *ultra vires*, or beyond their competence.

QUESTION

8. Why do you suppose the founders of the United Nations did not want to give the ICJ the power of judicial review?

The principle of auto-interpretation and the absence of a power of judicial review did not cause much controversy during the Cold War, as the Security Council was hamstrung by the superpower rivalry, and neither the General Assembly nor Secretary-General had sufficient authority to take actions that might have raised the hackles of a large or influential portion of the UN membership. With the end of the Cold War, the situation changed. Most notably, the Security Council has been defining "threat to the peace" in Article 39 more expansively and, once that Chapter VII threshold is crossed, has been dealing with the threat in innovative ways that were not contemplated by the UN founders.

This raises two questions: Are there any limits on what falls within the ambit of the Security Council's competence? Once it is decided that a matter falls within the SC's competence, are there any limits on what it can do to address the matter?

The language of the UN Charter itself purports to impose limits. Article 24(1) states that the Council has primary responsibility for the maintenance of international peace and security, implying it does not have responsibility in other areas (in contrast to Article 10, which grants to the General Assembly the authority to discuss "any matter within the scope of the Charter"). Thus, for example, the Security Council is not responsible for promoting economic and social cooperation. If a member state wants the Security Council to act in that area, it must make the case that the action is for the purpose of maintaining international peace and security.

The Council's expanding definition of a threat to international peace and security began at the Security Council summit in 1992, when it declared that it would include nonmilitary sources of instability. In early 2000, the Council held a meeting on HIV/AIDS, in effect declaring AIDS to be a security concern. So far the Council has not acted under Chapter VII to counter an environmental threat, or extreme social inequity, but it did meet on climate change in early 2007 and again in 2011, and it acted to address the Ebola crisis in 2014. This expansive interpretation makes some UN members nervous—and they point to the language of the Charter as a constraint.

Even more troubling to some is what the Council can do when the Article 39 "threat to the peace" threshold has been crossed. To list a few of the far-reaching measures it has taken, some of which are discussed later in this chapter and elsewhere in the volume:

- it created ad hoc international criminal tribunals in the former Yugoslavia and Rwanda[8];
- it adopted unprecedented measures in the aftermath of the 1991 Gulf War, ordering the dismantlement of Iraq's weapons of mass destruction programs and setting up a highly intrusive monitoring system;[9]
- it has authorized UN peace operations to use force to protect civilians and, in one case, to undertake offensive combat operations to neutralize and disarm armed groups;[10]
- it has established international transitional administrations in two places, giving the United Nations full governing powers for a transitional period;[11]
- it authorized coercive intervention in Libya[12] and, more ambiguously, in Cote d'Ivoire,[13] under the banner of the "responsibility to protect";
- it has created a sanctions regimes that penalizes individuals alleged to be associated with terrorist organizations;[14]
- it has adopted resolutions that impose binding obligations on all states in a broad issue area for an indefinite period.[15]

This rather expansive list prompts one to ask whether there are any limits at all on what the Council can do to restore international peace and security. Surely it cannot authorize torture in the name of counterterrorism, or coercive ethnic separation in the name of peace? Although it can and has ordered that all weapons of mass destruction be removed from Iraq, it has not and probably cannot order the complete conventional disarmament of a country (thereby depriving it of the capacity to act in self-defense).

Fortunately, there is some Charter language to reinforce those common sense intuitions. Article 24(2) states that "in discharging these duties, the Security Council shall act in accordance with the Purposes and Principles of the United Nations." The purposes and principles are enumerated in the

---

[8] SC Res. 827 (1993) and SC Res. 955 (1994) respectively.
[9] SC Res. 687 (1991) on Iraq.
[10] SC Res. 2147 (2014) on MONUSCO.
[11] SC Res. 1244 (1999) on Kosovo and SC Res. 1272 (1999) on East Timor.
[12] SC Res. 1973 (2011) on Libya.
[13] SC Res. 1975 (2011) on Ivory Coast.
[14] SC Res. 1267 (1999) Establishing the Sanctions Committee
[15] SC Res. 1373 (2001) on Terrorism; SC Res. 1540 (2004) on the Establishment of 1540 Resolution Committee, and SC Res. 2178 (2014) on Foreign Fighters.

preamble and Articles 1 and 2. They may also be gleaned from elsewhere, for example Article 51 on self-defense and Article 55 on human rights. It seems, therefore, that there are some Charter limits—even if those limits are articulated in vague and potentially contradictory terms.

One can ask similar questions about the General Assembly (or the Secretary-General). Can it establish peacekeeping missions? The ICJ in the *Certain Expenses* case said it could. Can it authorize enforcement action or impose binding economic sanctions? Probably not, because Article 11(2) stipulates that *coercive* action can only be taken by the Security Council. Can the General Assembly suspend or expel a member because the majority does not approve of its social policies? Probably not—see Articles 5 and 6, which spell out the criteria for suspension and expulsion. So it seems there are some Charter limits there as well.

That brings us back to our central question: Who sets the limits? Who judges whether the Council or any other organ of the United Nations has exceeded its competence? And what is the effect of that judgment? We have determined that the ICJ was not given the power of judicial review in San Francisco, nor for that matter were the other organs of the United Nations given the power to second-guess each other. But the ICJ has hinted in two cases that it could assert a power of judicial review, just as the US Supreme Court did in *Marbury v. Madison*. Similarly, regional and national courts have engaged in what may be termed "indirect judicial review" of the Council. José Alvarez has written of variegated forms of review, suggesting that entities other than courts may comment on the propriety of Security Council action (or inaction).[16]

Lockerbie is the first ICJ case where the issue of judicial review arose. The case involved the bombing of Pan Am Flight 103 on 21 December 1988 over Lockerbie, in Scotland. The United States indicted two Libyan nationals on the charge of having placed a bomb on board that flight, and demanded they be extradited for prosecution in US courts. In the Security Council resolution 731 (1992) was passed, under Chapter VI of the UN Charter.

SECURITY COUNCIL RESOLUTION 731 (1992)

The Security Council, . . .

Deeply concerned over results of investigations which implicate officials of the Libyan Government and which are contained in Security Council documents that include the requests addressed to the Libyan authorities by France, the United Kingdom of Great Britain and Northern Ireland and the United States of America in connection with the legal procedures related to the attacks carried out against Pan Am flight 103 and UTA flight 772 . . .

---

[16] Jose Alvarez, "Judging the Security Council", *American Journal of International Law*, Volume 90 (Jan. 1996), pp. 1–39.

3. *Urges* the Libyan Government immediately to provide a full and effective response to those requests so as to contribute to the elimination of international terrorism . . .

Libya instituted proceedings against the United States at the ICJ, claiming that the matter fell under Article 14, paragraph 1 of the Convention for the Suppression of Unlawful Acts Against the Safety of Civil Aviation[17] (the "Montreal Convention"). Both states were parties to the Convention, which provides that "any dispute between two or more contracting states concerning the interpretation or application of this convention which cannot be settled through negotiation, shall, at the request of one of them, be submitted to arbitration. If within six months of the date of the request for arbitration the parties are unable to agree on the organization of the arbitration, any one of those parties may refer the dispute to the International Court of Justice by request in conformity with the Statute of the Court." Although under Article 8, the requested state on whose territory the offender was found was not under a duty to extradite in the absence of an extradition treaty if it had made such extradition conditional upon the existence of such a treaty, Article 7 provided that in such a case, that state would "be obliged, without exception whatsoever and whether or not the offence was committed in its territory, to submit the case to its competent authorities for the purpose of prosecution." Claiming breach of these provisions by the United States, Libya brought this matter before the ICJ. Fearing both economic and military sanctions to force compliance, Libya also requested that the ICJ order "urgent provisional measures" to prevent them. In other words, it requested the ICJ to freeze the situation pending resolution of the case.

The United States contended that the ICJ should refrain from exercising jurisdiction, as the Security Council was already seized of the matter. After the close of oral proceedings but before the ICJ had announced its decision, the Security Council passed resolution 748 (1992).

SECURITY COUNCIL RESOLUTION 748 (1992)

The Security Council, . . .
   Acting under Chapter VII,
   1. *Decides* that the Libyan Government must now comply without any further delay with [resolution 731 (1992)] . . .
   7. *Calls upon* all States, including States not members of the United Nations, and all international organizations, to act strictly in accordance with the

---

[17] 974 UNTS 178, no. 14118 (1971).

provisions of the present resolution, notwithstanding the existence of any rights or obligations conferred or imposed by any international agreement or any contract entered into or any licence or permit granted prior to 15 April 1992.

The ICJ subsequently invited comments from both parties on the significance of this resolution. Libya argued that the resolution did not prejudice Libya's right to request the Court to indicate provisional measures as there is no hierarchy between the ICJ and the Security Council, and therefore the risk of contradiction between the resolution and the request for provisional measures did not render the latter inadmissible. The United States claimed that resolution 748 (1992) was framed as a binding decision, and irrespective of the right claimed by Libya under the Montreal Convention, Libya had a Charter-based duty to carry out the decisions in the resolution.

QUESTIONS OF INTERPRETATION AND APPLICATION OF THE 1971 MONTREAL CONVENTION ARISING FROM THE AERIAL INCIDENT AT LOCKERBIE (LIBYAN ARAB JAMAHIRIYA v. UNITED STATES OF AMERICA) (PROVISIONAL MEASURES) (1992) ICJ REPORTS 114

42. .... [B]oth Libya and the United States, as Members of the United Nations, are obliged to accept and carry out the decisions of the Security Council in accordance with Article 25 of the Charter; whereas the Court, which is at the stage of proceedings on provisional measures, considers that prima facie this obligation extends to the decision contained in resolution 748 (1992); and whereas, in accordance with Article 103 of the Charter, the obligations of the Parties in that respect prevail over their obligations under any other international agreement, including the Montreal Convention;

43. .... [T]he Court, while thus not at this stage called upon to determine definitively the legal effect of Security Council resolution 748 (1992), considers that, whatever the situation previous to the adoption of that resolution, the rights claimed by Libya under the Montreal Convention cannot now be regarded as appropriate for protection by the indication of provisional measures;

44. .... [F]urthermore, an indication of the measures requested by Libya would be likely to impair the rights which appear prima facie to be enjoyed by the United States by virtue of Security Council resolution 748 (1992).

45. ... [I]n order to pronounce on the present request for provisional measures, the Court is not called upon to determine any of the other questions which have been raised before it in the present proceedings, including the question of its jurisdiction to entertain the merits of the case; and whereas the decision given in these proceedings in no way prejudges any such question, and leaves unaffected the rights of the Government of Libya and the Government of the United States to submit arguments in respect of any of these questions;

46. ... The Court by eleven votes to five, [f]inds that the circumstances of the case are not such as to require the exercise of its power under Article 41 of the Statute to indicate provisional measures.

In the above order, the Court did not directly answer the contention of the United States that resolution 748 (1992) had displaced its jurisdiction over the matter. Its position was somewhat clearer in the judgment on preliminary objections, delivered on 27 February 1998.

QUESTIONS OF INTERPRETATION AND APPLICATION OF THE 1971 MONTREAL CONVENTION ARISING FROM THE AERIAL INCIDENT AT LOCKERBIE (LIBYAN ARAB JAMAHIRIYA v. UNITED STATES OF AMERICA) (PRELIMINARY OBJECTIONS) (1998) ICJ REPORTS 115

36. In the present case, the United States has contended ... that even if the Montreal Convention did confer on Libya the rights it claims, those rights could not be exercised in this case because they were superseded by Security Council resolutions 748 (1992) and 883 (1993) which, by virtue of Articles 25 and 103 of the United Nations Charter, have priority over all rights and obligations arising out of the Montreal Convention ...

37. The Court cannot uphold this line of argument. Security Council resolutions 748 (1992) and 883 (1993) were in fact adopted after the filing of the Application on 3 March 1992. In accordance with its established jurisprudence, if the Court had jurisdiction on that date, it continues to do so; the subsequent coming into existence of the above-mentioned resolutions cannot affect its jurisdiction once established ...

40. ... The United States further contends that if the Court should see fit to "assert [its] jurisdiction to examine on the merits, by way of objection, the validity of Security Council resolutions 731 (1992), 748 (1992) and 883 (1993), the Libyan Application should nonetheless be dismissed at the preliminary objections stage because it is not admissible." ...

43. ... The date, 3 March 1992, on which Libya filed its Application, is in fact the only relevant date for determining the admissibility of the Application. Security Council resolutions 748 (1992) and 883 (1993) cannot be taken into consideration in this regard, since they were adopted at a later date. As to Security Council resolution 731 (1992), adopted before the filing of the Application, it could not form a legal impediment to the admissibility of the latter because it was a mere recommendation without binding effect, as was recognized moreover by the United States. Consequently, Libya's Application cannot be held inadmissible on these grounds. ...

45. The Court will now consider the third objection raised by the United States. According to that objection, Libya's claims have become moot because Security Council resolutions 748 (1992) and 883 (1993) have rendered them without object; any judgment which the Court might deliver on the said claims would thenceforth be devoid of practical purpose. ...

47. ... What Libya contends is that this objection ... falls within the category of those which Article 79, paragraph 7, of the Rules of Court characterizes as objections "not possess[ing], in the circumstances of the case, an exclusively preliminary character." ...

49. The Court must therefore ascertain whether ... the United States objection considered here contains "both preliminary aspects and other aspects relating to the merits" or not.

That objection relates to many aspects of the dispute ... [B]y requesting such a decision, the United States is requesting, in reality, at least two others ... on the one hand a decision establishing that the rights claimed by Libya under the Montreal Convention are incompatible with its obligations under the Security Council resolutions; and, on the other hand, a decision that those obligations prevail over those rights by virtue of Articles 25 and 103 of the Charter.

The Court therefore has no doubt that Libya's rights on the merits would not only be affected by a decision not to proceed to judgment on the merits, at this stage in the proceedings, but would constitute, in many respects, the very subject-matter of that decision. ...

The Court concludes from the foregoing that the objection of the United States according to which the Libyan claims have become moot as having been rendered without object does not have "an exclusively preliminary character" within the meaning of that Article.

Subsequently, negotiations among Libya, the United States, and Britain resulted in the suspects being handed over and put on trial under Scottish law in a special court in The Hague (a compromise reached in 1998). One was convicted and the other acquitted. The suspect who was convicted appealed, and lost in March 2002. Meanwhile, Libya indicated that it was prepared to pay compensation to the families of the victims and to acknowledge some responsibility. With some twists and turns along the way, Security Council economic sanctions against Libya were suspended and then finally lifted in September 2002. A joint notification was issued by Libya and the United States on 9 September 2003 communicating their decision to discontinue the proceedings initiated by Libya. The ICJ was therefore not called upon to decide whether Libya's rights under the Montreal Convention were indeed superseded by its obligations under the Security Council resolutions. The deeper question of what complications could arise if the ICJ were to rule that they were not superseded—that is, that Libya's rights prevailed over its obligations to the Security Council—remained unanswered.

Another incident that highlights the possible conflict of jurisdiction between the Security Council and the ICJ was the application, filed by Bosnia and Herzegovina, claiming that Yugoslavia (Serbia and Montenegro) was committing acts of genocide in its territory. One of the issues raised pertains directly to the power of the ICJ to interpret and review resolutions of the Security Council.

In September 1991 the Security Council in resolution 713 (1991) had imposed a general and complete embargo on all deliveries of weapons and military equipment to Yugoslavia. Resolution 727 (1992) reaffirmed this arms embargo and clarified that it was applicable to all areas that had been part of Yugoslavia.

Bosnia and Herzegovina, one of the constituent parts of the former Yugoslavia, asked the Court to declare that it could, "as a member of the United Nations and as a party to the Genocide Convention, invoke the right of self-defense under Article 51 of the UN Charter and thereby demand the assistance of the international community in stopping the violations." In this context it claimed also that resolution 713 (1991), adopted by the Security Council pursuant to its powers under Chapter VII of the Charter, should be construed as not applicable to it because the resolution violated Bosnia and Herzegovina's Charter-based and "inherent" right of self-defense.

Note that the following is an *application to the Court by one of the parties*, not a decision by the Court.

APPLICATION OF THE REPUBLIC OF BOSNIA AND HERZEGOVINA IN CASE CONCERNING APPLICATION OF THE CONVENTION ON THE PREVENTION AND PUNISHMENT OF THE CRIME OF GENOCIDE (*BOSNIA AND HERZEGOVINA v. SERBIA AND MONTENEGRO*), 20 MARCH 1993

112. .... Pursuant to United Nations Charter Article 51, Bosnia and Herzegovina has the right to seek and receive support from the other 179 Member States of the United Nations ... including ... from the armed

attacks, armed aggressions and acts of genocide currently being perpetrated by Yugoslavia (Serbia and Montenegro) and its agents and surrogates in gross violation of the Genocide Convention as well as of its solemn obligations found in Article 2, paragraphs 2, 3 and 4, and in Article 33, paragraph I, of the United Nations Charter.

115. ... [S]o far the United Nations Security Council has not yet taken effective measures necessary to maintain international peace and security with respect to it and its People within the meaning of United Nations Charter Article 51. Therefore, Bosnia and Herzegovina's inherent right of individual and collective self-defence against the armed attack and armed aggressions by Yugoslavia (Serbia and Montenegro) and its agents and surrogates remains intact. ...

122. Therefore, all subsequent Security Council resolutions that routinely reaffirmed the arms embargo imposed upon the former Yugoslavia by paragraph 6 of resolution 713 (1991), paragraph 5 of resolution 724 (1991), and paragraph 6 of resolution 727 (1992) cannot properly be construed to apply to the Republic of Bosnia and Herzegovina. Rather, all such Security Council resolutions must be construed in a manner consistent with Article 51 of the United Nations Charter. Thereunder, the Republic of Bosnia and Herzegovina has and still has the inherent right of individual and collective self-defence, including the right immediately to seek and receive from other States military weapons, equipment, supplies, troops and financing necessary in order to defend Itself and its People from the armed attacks, armed aggressions, and acts of genocide that have been and are continuously being perpetrated upon Us by Yugoslavia (Serbia and Montenegro) and its agents and surrogates.

123. Therefore, none of these numerous Security Council resolutions imposing or routinely reaffirming an arms embargo upon the former Yugoslavia under Chapter VII of the Charter can be properly interpreted to apply to the Republic of Bosnia and Herzegovina. To do otherwise would "impair the inherent right of individual or collective self-defence" of the Republic of Bosnia and Herzegovina, and thus violate United Nations Charter Article 51, and furthermore render these Security Council resolutions *ultra vires*: "*Nothing* in the present Charter shall impair the inherent right of individual or collective self defence. ..." (Emphasis added.)

124. Furthermore, United Nations Charter Article 24, paragraph 2, provides:

2. In discharging these duties [maintaining international peace and security] the Security Council shall act in accordance with the Purposes and Principles of the United Nations. The specific powers granted to the Security Council for the discharge of these duties are laid down in Chapters VI, VII, VIII, and XII

Therefore, even when it acts under Chapter VII of the Charter, the Security Council must "act in accordance with the Purposes and Principles of the

United Nations" that are set forth in Chapter I, which consists of Articles I and 2 of the Charter.

125. Bosnia and Herzegovina claims that the arms embargo imposed upon the former Yugoslavia by the Security Council in resolution 713 (1992) and its successors legally did not apply and could not apply to the Republic of Bosnia and Herzegovina at any time. Otherwise, the Security Council would not be acting "in accordance with the Purposes and Principles of the United Nations" and thus would be in breach of Charter Article 24 (2). Such an improper interpretation of resolution 713 (1991) and its successors would render resolution 713 (1991) *ultra vires* the Security Council under both Article 24 (2) and Article 51 of the Charter.

126. In order to avoid these results, Bosnia and Herzegovina claims that this Court must interpret Security Council resolution 713 (1991) and its successors to mean that there is not, has never been, and is still not as of today, a mandatory arms embargo applicable to Bosnia and Herzegovina under Chapter VII of the Charter. This is a straightforward question of interpreting the terms of the United Nations Charter that clearly falls within the powers, competence, and purview of the Court. Indeed, no other organ of the United Nations but this Court can clarify this matter and thus vindicate the "inherent right" of Bosnia and Herzegovina under Article 51. According to Charter Article 92, it is the Court—not the Security Council or the General Assembly—that is "the principal judicial organ of the United Nations."

127. Unless and until this Court definitively rules against its claims, Bosnia and Herzegovina remains free under Article 51 and customary international law to defend itself notwithstanding the terms of any Security Council resolutions adopted so far. Thus, Bosnia and Herzegovina has the basic right under international law to immediately seek and receive from other States military weapons, equipment, supplies, troops and financing in order to defend Itself from armed attacks, armed aggressions, and acts of genocide that are currently being perpetrated upon Us by Yugoslavia (Serbia and Montenegro) and its agents and surrogates, continuously from our date of independence as a sovereign State on 6 March 1992 until today and beyond.

The Court did not make any direct reference to this request. In its Order of 13 September 1993—following a further request for provisional measures by Bosnia and Herzegovina, including that it "must have the means" to prevent the commission of genocide and to defend its people against genocide, and "must have the ability to obtain military weapons, equipment, and supplies" from the other parties to the Genocide Convention—the Court stated that it was evident that the intention of the Applicant in requesting these measures was to obtain a declaration of what rights it could invoke before the Security Council. The Court held that this request was outside the scope of the provisional measures that could be granted under Article 41 of the Statute.

The request relating to the lifting of the arms embargo was not included in the memorial submitted by Bosnia and Herzegovina on 15 April 1994, although it reserved the right to re-invoke various elements of its initial request, including those relating to the lifting of the arms embargo. The ICJ has not since been called upon to address this issue.

The embargo was subsequently lifted in three stages in 1995–1996[18] and then reimposed in 1998, following the crises in Kosovo.[19] Resolution 1367 (2001) finally brought this embargo to an end.

Commenting on the *Lockerbie* and *Bosnia Genocide* cases, José Alvarez doubts the ICJ will ever declare the Council's actions to be ultra vires, but sees it engaging in an "expressive mode of review"—a sort of ongoing dialogue with the Council.[20] Arguably, that is what the Court did in *Lockerbie*. The opinions of some of the judges constitute "warnings" or "cues" to the Council "to exercise care in undertaking similar action in the future." Moreover, Alvarez thinks the Court is not the only institution capable of commenting on Council action. The General Assembly or Human Rights Council could do it. The Secretary-General and the High Commissioner for Human Rights have done it, subtly. The International Criminal Tribunal for Yugoslavia did it, by deciding in one of its first rulings that the Security Council's powers, *"while not unlimited,"* encompassed the creation of a judicial tribunal under Article 41 of the Charter.[21]

Most dramatically, the European Court of Justice (ECJ) engaged in what may be called indirect judicial review of a Security Council sanctions regime in the *Kadi* case. This concerned a challenge to a targeted financial sanctions regime and will be considered in Chapter 10. For present purposes, it is enough to note that the European Court of First Instance (now the General Court) and ECJ were called to rule on the legality of EU regulations that were adopted in order to implement Security Council-imposed sanctions on Al-Qaeda, the Taliban, and their associates. The listing regime was seen as tantamount to criminal penalties, with no due process afforded to those put on the list. In a series of decisions, the Courts ruled that the regulations violated fundamental human rights embodied in the EU constitutional order and struck them down. Eventually the Security Council introduced new procedural rights, including mechanisms to be taken off the list if the evidence suggests a mistake was made. Though the Security Council was

---

[18] UNSC Res. S/RES/1021 of 22 November 1995 on Former Yugoslavia.
[19] UNSC Res. S/RES/1160 of 31 March 1998 on Kosovo.
[20] José Alvarez, "Judging the Security Council," *American Journal of International Law*, vol. 90 (Jan. 1996), pp. 28–36.
[21] *Prosecutor v. Tadic*, Case IT-94-1-T of 17 May 1997, Decision on Jurisdiction.

not acting in direct response to the ECJ ruling, it was an indirect response to what was in effect indirect judicial review.

QUESTIONS

9. The conclusions of the San Francisco Drafting Committee indicate that all UN organs have the capacity to interpret the provisions of the Charter. Does this also enable these organs to engage in lawmaking by way of formulating rules guiding their own functioning as well as relations with the other organs and international entities? Does it enable them to make rules at least governing their own procedures? Does the overall scheme represent a good approach?

10. How is Article 103 of the UN Charter relevant (or not) to the implementation of decisions of the UN Security Council? What is the effect of Article 25 of the UN Charter?

11. If you conclude that Security Council resolutions must get priority over other treaty obligations, does this imply that these resolutions are an independent "source of law"? (Compare Article 38(1) of the ICJ Statute.)

12. In the *Lockerbie* case, given that the Court has no power to enforce its decisions and must look to the Council for this purpose, what would have been the outcome had the decision gone in Libya's favor?

13. Does the Court, by rejecting the preliminary objections to its jurisdiction advanced by the United States, imply that it has the power to decide whether a resolution of the Security Council exceeds the Council's power under the Charter? As that question was not to be determined finally until the merits phase—not reached due to the agreement of the parties to settle the case out of court—you are free to speculate as to what the Court might have done with this difficult issue. Should the Court exercise judicial review over Council resolutions?

14. Do you agree with Bosnia's submission that resolution 713 (1992) and its successors were ultra vires? Can the ICJ rule upon such a matter? In other words, does the Court have a right to "review" Security Council resolutions? Should it?

4.3. Quasi-judicial Action by the Security Council

Legal challenges to targeted financial sanctions suggest possible limits on Security Council powers. They also illustrate another controversial post–Cold War trend: quasi-judicial action taken by the Council. The Council has long been involved in dispute settlement, which is one of the enumerated functions in Chapter VI of the Charter, but it normally does this in a non-binding way—for example by calling on parties to settle their disputes by one of the means listed in Article 33. The Council also plays a quasi-judicial role when it determines a situation constitutes a threat to the peace within the meaning of Article 39 of the UN Charter, the threshold for action under Chapter VII.

The Council went further in resolution 687—the Gulf War ceasefire resolution following Iraq's invasion of Kuwait—by holding Iraq financially liable for losses resulting from its invasion and occupation of Kuwait, and declaring that Iraq must respect the border set out in Agreed Minutes of 1963.[22] These pronouncements are in effect findings of law—decisions that would normally be left to a court. Did the Council exceed its authority by doing this?

Applying the Article 24(2) test—that it must act in accordance with the purposes and principles of the UN Charter—the Council seems to be on solid legal grounds. Regarding the border demarcation, Iraq sought to justify its invasion on the premise that Kuwait was historically an Iraqi province, so finally settling the border between them was necessary to restore peace and security in the region. Moreover, the act of demarcation was regarded by the Council as a purely technical exercise: the border had already been delimited—all the Commission would do was draw the line on a map and erect pillars on the ground. Demarcating the maritime boundary was a less straightforward exercise, but the Council did not act arbitrarily or punitively in dealing with the border issue. If it had lopped off a piece of Iraqi territory to punish Saddam Hussein for his sins, arguably it would not be acting in accordance with the purposes and principles of the United Nations. The same considerations apply to the compensation scheme. The scheme was carefully calibrated not to cripple the Iraqi economy, imposing liability only for direct losses (not indirect losses caused by the sanctions, for example) and only up to 30 percent of oil revenues per year. That figure corresponds to a fair estimate of Iraq's military expenditures, and so the burden was one it could reasonably bear.

QUESTION

15. Although a good legal case can be made that the Security Council did not act ultra vires in demarcating the border or making a finding of liability, as a matter of institutional policy and practice, is it prudent for the Security Council to do this? Should it be making what are essentially judicial determinations? Is there a way of involving the ICJ in these sorts of situations?

---

[22] Ian Johnstone, *Aftermath of the Gulf War* (Boulder CO: Lynne Rienner Publishers, 1994).

4.4 Special Courts and Tribunals

Another Security Council innovation, which can be characterized as both quasi-judicial and quasi-legislative, is the creation of ad hoc criminal tribunals. In 1993 the Council used its Chapter VII powers to establish the International Criminal Tribunal for former Yugoslavia (ICTY), an ad hoc judicial forum empowered to prosecute "serious violations of international humanitarian law committed in the territory of the former Yugoslavia between 1 January 1991 and a date to be determined by the Security Council."[23] In 1994, it established a similar International Criminal Tribunal for Rwanda (ICTR).[24]

The establishment of a permanent International Criminal Court had been on the agenda of the United Nations for more than four decades. A 1948 resolution of the General Assembly had called upon the UN International Law Commission to "to study the desirability and possibility of establishing an international judicial organ for the trial of persons charged with genocide."[25] The efforts of the ILC however, bore fruit only in 1998, with the adoption of the Rome Statute of the International Criminal Court, which came into force in 2002.

Both resolutions 827 (1993) and 955 (1994) asserted that the actions being taken were exceptional, necessitated by the "particular circumstances" in these two cases, and the constitutive statutes were thus carefully drafted to limit the material and temporal jurisdiction of the two tribunals. At the same time, for matters falling within their jurisdiction the two tribunals were given primacy over national courts, a feature that has not been repeated in the Rome Statute.

What set the Yugoslav and Rwandan Tribunals apart was that they were established solely by a mandatory resolution of the Security Council. Even though the establishment of the ICTR was preceded by a request for a criminal tribunal from Rwanda,[26] its consent to the actually proposed structure was not required, and indeed resolution 955 (1994) was passed despite Rwanda's vote against it—cast in part because the tribunal was denied the option of imposing the death penalty on convicted offenders. The duty to cooperate was also imposed upon all the other member states of the United Nations.

These two tribunals have been followed by a number of other international bodies of limited jurisdiction,[27] including one that was established

---

[23] UNSC Res. S/RES/827 of 25 May 1993 on the Establishment of the ICTY.
[24] UNSC Res. S/RES/955 of 8 November 1994 on the Establishment of the ICTR.
[25] GA Res. 260(III) (1948).
[26] UN Doc. S/1994/1115 (1994).
[27] Even after its establishment, the ICC has jurisdiction only to prosecute international crimes committed after 1 July 2002: Statute of the International Criminal Court, art. 11.

by the SC under Chapter VII. The Special Court for Lebanon was set up to try those suspected of assassinating former Lebanese prime minister Rafik Hariri. The original idea was to establish the Hariri Tribunal on the basis of an agreement between the United Nations and government of Lebanon, but the parties in the coalition government in Beirut could not agree, so the Security Council did it through a Chapter VII resolution. Five countries abstained on the controversial resolution: China, Indonesia, Qatar, Russia, and South Africa.

The other special courts and tribunals, such as the Special Court of Sierra Leone, the Iraqi Special Tribunal, and the Extraordinary Chambers for the Prosecution under Cambodian Law of Crimes Committed during the Period of Democratic Kampuchea, have been established either through agreement between the United Nations and the state government or by decision of occupying powers. Moreover, these bodies possess a more hybrid character, mingling international judges and personnel with judges who are citizens of the state whose nationals are being brought to trial.

The following excerpts highlight some important provisions of the Statute of the International Criminal Tribunal for Rwanda.

SECURITY COUNCIL RESOLUTION 955 (1994), ANNEX: STATUTE OF THE INTERNATIONAL TRIBUNAL FOR RWANDA

Article 1—Competence of the International Tribunal for Rwanda

The International Tribunal for Rwanda shall have the power to prosecute persons responsible for serious violations of international humanitarian law committed in the territory of Rwanda and Rwandan citizens responsible for such violations committed in the territory of neighbouring States, between 1 January 1994 and 31 December 1994, in accordance with the provisions of the present Statute. . . .

Article 6—Individual Criminal Responsibility

1. A person who planned, instigated, ordered, committed or otherwise aided and abetted in the planning, preparation or execution of a crime referred to in articles 2 to 4 of the present Statute, shall be individually responsible for the crime.

2. The official position of any accused person, whether as Head of State or Government or as a responsible Government official, shall not relieve such person of criminal responsibility nor mitigate punishment.

3. The fact that any of the acts referred to in articles 2 to 4 of the present Statute was committed by a subordinate does not relieve his or her superior of criminal responsibility if he or she knew or had reason to know that the subordinate was about to commit such acts or had done so and the superior failed to take the necessary and reasonable measures to prevent such acts or to punish the perpetrators thereof.

4. The fact that an accused person acted pursuant to an order of a Government or of a superior shall not relieve him or her of criminal responsibility, but may be considered in mitigation of punishment if the International Tribunal for Rwanda determines that justice so requires...

Article 8—Concurrent Jurisdiction

1. The International Tribunal for Rwanda and national courts shall have concurrent jurisdiction to prosecute persons for serious violations of international humanitarian law committed in the territory of Rwanda and Rwandan citizens for such violations committed in the territory of neighbouring States, between 1 January 1994 and 31 December 1994.

2. The International Tribunal for Rwanda shall have primacy over the national courts of all States. At any stage of the procedure, the International Tribunal for Rwanda may formally request national courts to defer to its competence in accordance with the present Statute and the Rules of Procedure and Evidence of the International Tribunal for Rwanda. ....

Article 15—The Prosecutor

1. The Prosecutor shall be responsible for the investigation and prosecution of persons responsible for serious violations of international humanitarian law committed in the territory of Rwanda and Rwandan citizens responsible for such violations committed in the territory of neighbouring States, between 1 January 1994 and 31 December 1994.

...

Article 17—Investigation and Preparation of Indictment

1. The Prosecutor shall initiate investigations ex-officio or on the basis of information obtained from any source, particularly from Governments, United Nations organs, intergovernmental and non-governmental organizations.

The Prosecutor shall assess the information received or obtained and decide whether there is sufficient basis to proceed. ....

Article 26—Enforcement of Sentences

Imprisonment shall be served in Rwanda or any of the States on a list of States which have indicated to the Security Council their willingness to accept convicted persons, as designated by the International Tribunal for Rwanda. Such imprisonment shall be in accordance with the applicable law of the State concerned, subject to the supervision of the International Tribunal for Rwanda. . . .

Article 28—Cooperation and Judicial Assistance

1. States shall cooperate with the International Tribunal for Rwanda in the investigation and prosecution of persons accused of committing serious violations of international humanitarian law.

2. States shall comply without undue delay with any request for assistance or an order issued by a Trial Chamber, including, but not limited to:
    (a) The identification and location of persons;
    (b) The taking of testimony and the production of evidence;
    (c) The service of documents;
    (d) The arrest or detention of persons;
    (e) The surrender or the transfer of the accused to the International Tribunal for Rwanda.

The resolution establishing the International Tribunal for Rwanda was followed by statements from members of the Security Council explaining the reasons for their positions. All members with the exception of Rwanda and China voted in favor of the resolution. China abstained; Rwanda voted against it, in part because the court could not impose the death penalty. Many members clarified that they voted for the ICTR because they viewed it as an *ad hoc* measure justified only by the exceptional nature of the circumstances and the urgency required by the situation in Rwanda. A number stressed that the setting up of this Tribunal and the Tribunal for Yugoslavia should not be seen as constituting precedent for the future.

QUESTION

16. In the International Criminal Court, established in 2002, the principle of complementarity applies, meaning that the ICC only has jurisdiction if the relevant national courts are unable or unwilling to handle the case. In the ICTR and ICTY, the opposite approach was taken (see Article 8(2) of the ICTR statute). Which approach is better, and why?

4.5 Lawmaking by the Security Council

Although the Security Council was not set up to be a legislative body, with powers analogous to a parliament or legislature, it does have a lawmaking function. Article 25 of the Charter says "the Members of the UN agree to accept and carry out the *decisions* of the Security Council in accordance with the present Charter." That means that, for those subject to them, Security Council decisions are binding law.

Usually it is clear when the Security Council has made an Article 25 decision rather than a recommendation. Resolutions 660, 661, and 678 on Iraq (discussed in Chapter 3), for example, were all binding decisions adopted under Chapter VII of the UN Charter.

What about action not taken under Chapter VII? Can those resolutions impose binding obligations as well? In 1970, the Security Council adopted resolution 276, which declared the continued presence of the South African authorities in Southwest Africa (Namibia today) to be illegal, and "called upon" all states to refrain from any dealings with South Africa that were inconsistent with that declaration (para. 5). Is that a binding decision? In a request for an Advisory Opinion, the Security Council put the question to the ICJ in the following terms: "What are the legal consequences for States of the continued presence of South Africa in Namibia, notwithstanding Security Council resolution 276?" In its response, the Court rejected the view that Article 25 applies only to measures adopted under Chapter VII—it applies to all decisions adopted in accordance with the Charter.

How does one know whether the Security Council has made a *decision* as opposed to recommendation or request? In resolution 276, the operative words were "calls upon," not "decides" or "demands." On this issue, the ICJ stated:

> In view of the nature of the powers under Article 25, the question whether they have been in fact exercised, is to be determined in each case, having regard to the terms of the resolution to be interpreted, the discussions leading to it, the Charter provisions invoked and, in general all circumstances that might assist in determining the legal consequences of the resolution of the Security Council.[28]

In other words, to know whether the Security Council has made a "decision," look not only at the language of the resolution, but all the circumstances surrounding its adoption.

---

[28] *Legal Consequences for States of the Continued Presence of South Africa in Namibia (South West Africa) notwithstanding Security Council Resolution 276 (1970) (Advisory Opinion)* (1971) ICJ Rep 16, para 114.

In addition to ambiguous resolutions, the Council on occasion makes declarations that look like neither decisions nor recommendations. For example, at the first ever Security Council Summit meeting in January 1992, the Security Council stated: "the proliferation of all weapons of mass destruction constitutes a threat to international peace and security."[29] Since then it has acquired the habit of holding meetings on general themes rather than particular crises: children in armed conflict, the protection of civilians, conflict prevention, humanitarian action, and the role of women in peace processes. At the end of these meetings the Council often—though not always—adopts a statement or declaration.

These determinations do not purport to impose compulsory obligations, but are in effect interpretations of what constitutes a "threat to the peace" within the meaning of Article 39 of the UN Charter. If nothing else, these normative statements may later be invoked by a member of the Council in calling for action—or resisting calls for action—when a particular case implicating the norm arises.

With the adoption of resolution 1373, the Security Council took its lawmaking role to a new level, following the attacks on the World Trade Center in New York and the Pentagon in Washington, DC, on 11 September 2001. Resolution 1373 is like a sanctions resolution, in that it imposes obligations on every state in the world. But it is not related to a particular incident or limited in time. It does not seek to enforce a decision against a particular state, but rather imposes general obligations on all states in a broad issue area for an indefinite period.[30] There is no precedent for this. This is qualitatively different from the Council's normal crisis management role and its declaratory powers. In adopting resolution 1373, the Council is acting like a legislature. It did it again in April 2004 with the adoption of resolution 1540, and then in 2014 with the adoption of 2178.

Resolution 1373 (2001) reaffirms the need to combat threats to international peace and security caused by terrorist acts and sets out a number of steps States must take to meet that threat.

SECURITY COUNCIL RESOLUTION 1373 (2001)

The Security Council, ...
   Acting under Chapter VII of the Charter of the United Nations,
   1. *Decides* that all States shall:
   (a) Prevent and suppress the financing of terrorist acts;

---

[29] UN Document S/23500, 31 January 1992.
[30] Ian Johnstone, "Legislation and Adjudication in the United Nations Security Council: Bringing Down the Deliberative Deficit," *American Journal of International Law*, vol. 102 (2008) p. 275. *See also* Stephan Salmon, "The Security Council as World Legislature," *American Journal of International Law*, vol. 99 (2005), p. 175.

(b) Criminalize the wilful provision or collection, by any means, directly or indirectly, of funds by their nationals or in their territories with the intention that the funds should be used, or in the knowledge that they are to be used, in order to carry out terrorist acts;

(c) Freeze without delay funds and other financial assets or economic resources of persons who commit, or attempt to commit, terrorist acts or participate in or facilitate the commission of terrorist acts; of entities owned or controlled directly or indirectly by such persons; and of persons and entities acting on behalf of, or at the direction of such persons and entities, including funds derived or generated from property owned or controlled directly or indirectly by such persons and associated persons and entities;

(d) Prohibit their nationals or any persons and entities within their territories from making any funds, financial assets or economic resources or financial or other related services available, directly or indirectly, for the benefit of persons who commit or attempt to commit or facilitate or participate in the commission of terrorist acts, of entities owned or controlled, directly or indirectly, by such persons and of persons and entities acting on behalf of or at the direction of such persons;

2. *Decides also* that all States shall:

(a) Refrain from providing any form of support, active or passive, to entities or persons involved in terrorist acts, including by suppressing recruitment of members of terrorist groups and eliminating the supply of weapons to terrorists;

(b) Take the necessary steps to prevent the commission of terrorist acts, including by provision of early warning to other States by exchange of information;

(c) Deny safe haven to those who finance, plan, support, or commit terrorist acts, or provide safe havens;

(d) Prevent those who finance, plan, facilitate or commit terrorist acts from using their respective territories for those purposes against other States or their citizens;

(e) Ensure that any person who participates in the financing, planning, preparation or perpetration of terrorist acts or in supporting terrorist acts is brought to justice and ensure that, in addition to any other measures against them, such terrorist acts are established as serious criminal offences in domestic laws and regulations and that the punishment duly reflects the seriousness of such terrorist acts;

(f) Afford one another the greatest measure of assistance in connection with criminal investigations or criminal proceedings relating to the financing or support of terrorist acts, including assistance in obtaining evidence in their possession necessary for the proceedings;

(g) Prevent the movement of terrorists or terrorist groups by effective border controls and controls on issuance of identity papers and travel documents, and through measures for preventing counterfeiting, forgery or fraudulent use of identity papers and travel documents;

3. *Calls upon* all States to:

(a) Find ways of intensifying and accelerating the exchange of operational information, especially regarding actions or movements of terrorist persons or networks; forged or falsified travel documents; traffic in arms, explosives or sensitive materials; use of communications technologies by terrorist groups; and the threat posed by the possession of weapons of mass destruction by terrorist groups;

. . .

(d) Become parties as soon as possible to the relevant international conventions and protocols relating to terrorism, including the International Convention for the Suppression of the Financing of Terrorism of 9 December 1999;

(e) Increase cooperation and fully implement the relevant international conventions and protocols relating to terrorism and Security Council resolutions 1269 (1999) and 1368 (2001);

Next came resolution 1540 (2004), passed in response to concerns over the proliferation of nuclear, chemical, and biological weapons, in particular their acquisition by nonstate actors posing terrorist threats.

SECURITY COUNCIL RESOLUTION 1540 (2004): NON-PROLIFERATION OF WEAPONS OF MASS DESTRUCTION

The Security Council, . . .

Acting under Chapter VII of the Charter of the United Nations,

1. *Decides* that all States shall refrain from providing any form of support to non-State actors that attempt to develop, acquire, manufacture, possess, transport, transfer or use nuclear, chemical or biological weapons and their means of delivery;

2. *Decides also* that all States, in accordance with their national procedures, shall adopt and enforce appropriate effective laws which prohibit any non-State actor to manufacture, acquire, possess, develop, transport, transfer or use nuclear, chemical or biological weapons and their means of delivery, in particular for terrorist purposes, as well as attempts to engage in any of the foregoing activities, participate in them as an accomplice, assist or finance them;

3. *Decides also* that all States shall take and enforce effective measures to establish domestic controls to prevent the proliferation of nuclear, chemical, or biological weapons and their means of delivery, including

by establishing appropriate controls over related materials and to this end shall:

(a) Develop and maintain appropriate effective measures to account for and secure such items in production, use, storage or transport;

(b) Develop and maintain appropriate effective physical protection measures;

(c) Develop and maintain appropriate effective border controls and law enforcement efforts to detect, deter, prevent and combat, including through international cooperation when necessary, the illicit trafficking and brokering in such items in accordance with their national legal authorities and legislation and consistent with international law;

(d) Establish, develop, review and maintain appropriate effective national export and trans-shipment controls over such items, including appropriate laws and regulations to control export, transit, trans-shipment and re-export and controls on providing funds and services related to such export and trans-shipment such as financing, and transporting that would contribute to proliferation, as well as establishing end-user controls; and establishing and enforcing appropriate criminal or civil penalties for violations of such export control laws and regulations;

. . .

5. *Decides* that none of the obligations set forth in this resolution shall be interpreted so as to conflict with or alter the rights and obligations of State Parties to the Nuclear Non-Proliferation Treaty, the Chemical Weapons Convention and the Biological and Toxin Weapons Convention or alter the responsibilities of the International Atomic Energy Agency or the Organization for the Prohibition of Chemical Weapons; . . .

. . .

8. *Calls upon* all States:

(a) To promote the universal adoption and full implementation, and, where necessary, strengthening of multilateral treaties to which they are parties, whose aim is to prevent the proliferation of nuclear, biological or chemical weapons;

(b) To adopt national rules and regulations, where it has not yet been done, to ensure compliance with their commitments under the key multilateral nonproliferation treaties;

(c) To renew and fulfil their commitment to multilateral cooperation, in particular within the framework of the International Atomic Energy Agency, the Organization for the Prohibition of Chemical Weapons and the Biological and Toxin Weapons Convention, as important means of pursuing and achieving their common objectives in the area of non-proliferation and of promoting international cooperation for peaceful purposes;

Resolution 1540 was harder to negotiate than 1373, for two reasons. First, the political climate had changed: negotiated immediately after the attacks of 11 September 2001, resolution 1373 could be seen as a "reaction" to 9/11 and therefore consistent with traditional Security Council crisis-management functions. Moreover, all Council members were under instructions from their capitals to be helpful to the United States at that time. It is not even clear that all knew the unprecedented nature of what they were doing. By the time of 1540, the far-reaching implications of the Security Council "legislating" had begun to sink in; many member states objected to or were deeply uncomfortable with this mode of Council decision-making.

Second, Resolution 1373 takes elements of existing international law (mainly the Convention for the Suppression of Financing of Terrorism and the Convention on the Suppression of Terrorist Bombings) and in effect makes those obligations binding on all states, even those that did not sign or ratify the conventions. Resolution 1540 goes further than 1373 by "filling gaps" in existing law. In that sense, the former creates new law in the way the latter does not, and it encroaches more deeply on existing treaty-making bodies and regimes than 1373. This was of particular concern to Pakistan and India, as non-signatories to the Nuclear Non-Proliferation Treaty (Brazil, Algeria, and others had similar concerns).

With the change in political winds, the Security Council stayed out of the business of legislating for many years. It was surprising, therefore, to see the adoption of another quasi-legislative resolution in September 2014, prompted by the rise of the Islamic State in Iraq and Syria.

SECURITY COUNCIL RESOLUTION 2178 (2014): THREATS TO INTERNATIONAL PEACE AND SECURITY CAUSED BY TERRORIST ACTS

The Security Council, . . .

Acting under Chapter VII of the Charter of the United Nations,

2. Reaffirms that all States shall prevent the movement of terrorists or terrorist groups by effective border controls and controls on issuance of identity papers and travel documents, and through measures for preventing counterfeiting, forgery or fraudulent use of identity papers and travel documents, underscores, in this regard, the importance of addressing, in accordance with their relevant international obligations, the threat posed by foreign terrorist fighters, and encourages Member States to employ evidence-based traveller risk assessment and screening procedures including collection and analysis of travel data, without resorting to profiling based on stereotypes founded on grounds of discrimination prohibited by international law; . . .

4. *Calls upon* all Member States, in accordance with their obligations under international law, to cooperate in efforts to address the threat posed by foreign terrorist fighters, including by preventing the radicalization to terrorism and recruitment of foreign terrorist fighters, including children, preventing foreign terrorist fighters from crossing their borders, disrupting and preventing financial support to foreign terrorist fighters, and developing and implementing prosecution, rehabilitation and reintegration strategies for returning foreign terrorist fighters;

5. Decides that Member States shall, consistent with international human rights law, international refugee law, and international humanitarian law, prevent and suppress the recruiting, organizing, transporting or equipping of individuals who travel to a State other than their States of residence or nationality for the purpose of the perpetration, planning, or preparation of, or participation in, terrorist acts or the providing or receiving of terrorist training, and the financing of their travel and of their activities;

6. Recalls its decision, in resolution 1373 (2001), that all Member States shall ensure that any person who participates in the financing, planning, preparation or perpetration of terrorist acts or in supporting terrorist acts is brought to justice, and decides that all States shall ensure that their domestic laws and regulations establish serious criminal offenses sufficient to provide the ability to prosecute and to penalize in a manner duly reflecting the seriousness of the offense:

8. Decides that, without prejudice to entry or transit necessary in the furtherance of a judicial process, including in furtherance of such a process related to arrest or detention of a foreign terrorist fighter, Member States shall prevent the entry into or transit through their territories of any individual about whom that State has credible information that provides reasonable grounds to believe that he or she is seeking entry into or transit through their territory for the purpose of participating in the acts described in paragraph 6, including any acts or activities indicating that an individual, group, undertaking or entity is associated with Al-Qaida, as set out in paragraph 2 of resolution 2161 (2014), provided that nothing in this paragraph shall oblige any State to deny entry or require the departure from its territories of its own nationals or permanent residents; . . .

12. Recalls its decision in resolution 1373 (2001) that Member States shall afford one another the greatest measure of assistance in connection with criminal investigations or proceedings relating to the financing or support of terrorist acts, including assistance in obtaining evidence in their possession necessary for the proceedings, and underlines the importance of fulfilling this obligation with respect to such investigations or proceedings involving foreign terrorist fighters;

QUESTIONS

17. Is there any legal prohibition against the Security Council "legislating" in this way? What are the implications of Article 2(7) of the UN Charter?
18. Even if it is within the Security Council's legal competence, what are the policy arguments for and against the Council acting in a quasi-legislative manner?

4.6 Lawmaking by the General Assembly

Like the Security Council, the General Assembly, ECOSOC, and other UN organs were not set up as legislative bodies. Indeed, other than on internal matters such as the budget and elections, the General Assembly and its subsidiary organs do not have the power to make decisions that are directly binding on member states. Nevertheless, they have acted like legislatures, as have the specialized agencies, though not in the same way as the Security Council.

The most obvious way they have done so is by adopting multilateral treaties. As the demand for international law rose, states turned to international organizations (especially the United Nations) as convenient venues for the negotiations of treaties. Typically the process begins with a state or group of states introducing a proposal in the General Assembly, ECOSOC, or a subsidiary organ. It is then sent to a drafting body, where the sponsor's draft becomes the subject of negotiations. It then goes back to the adopting organ, where it is finalized and adopted, ideally by consensus. Although that marks the end of the negotiating process, the treaty does not come into force until signed and ratified or acceded to by the requisite number of states.

An interesting feature of this process is that all member states of the United Nations or relevant specialized agency have the right to participate in the negotiation and adoption of the treaty. Additionally, nonstate actors, especially nongovernmental organizations (NGOs), tend to have more access, IO personnel play a significant role, and expert bodies such as the International Law Commission often play a role in treaty-drafting. This, according to José Alvarez, signifies the "democratization" of lawmaking.[31]

Another noteworthy feature of the treaty-making process is that some treaties are seen to "codify" or "crystallize" customary law, thereby rendering obligations in the treaty binding even on nonparties. Some treaties are explicitly designed to codify customary law, for example the Vienna Convention on the Law of Treaties. For others, the negotiating process has

---

[31] José Alvarez, *International Organizations as Lawmakers* (Oxford: Oxford University Press, 2005), p. 273.

the effect of crystallizing the law. In the process itself, which may drag on for decades, it becomes clear that what is being negotiated is already accepted as law—even if not all states sign and ratify the treaty. An example is the twelve-mile territorial sea rule in the Law of the Sea Convention, which is now seen as customary law, binding even on nonparties to the Convention.

A more contested way in which the General Assembly has contributed to the development of international law is by the adoption of resolutions that are not intended to become treaties, but purport to declare principles of international law. Examples include the Universal Declaration of Human Rights, the Declaration on the Granting of Independence to Colonial Peoples, the Declaration on Principles of International Law concerning Friendly Relations and Cooperation among States, and the multiple declarations on illegality of the threat or use of nuclear weapons. They all purport to elaborate major principles of international law, and all have been cited by governments, the ICJ, and intergovernmental committees and commissions as evidence of the law.

Lawyers disagree about the legal weight these declarations should be given. It depends in part on the clarity of intention by participating states: Is the declaration meant to reflect a refinement or codification of international law? It also depends on how much support the declaration receives: Is the vote unanimous? Did key states vote against it? The most revealing question is whether the declaration itself is ever enough to create new law. Must there also be evidence of state practice outside the General Assembly supporting the proposition that the declaration is regarded as the law?

The Declaration on the Inadmissibility of Intervention in the Domestic Affairs of States and the Protection of Their Independence and Sovereignty, passed in 1965, was born out of the concern within the General Assembly at the increasing armed intervention and direct and indirect forms of interference by some states threatening the sovereignty and political independence of others.

GENERAL ASSEMBLY RESOLUTION 2131(XX) (1965): DECLARATION ON THE INADMISSIBILITY OF INTERVENTION IN THE DOMESTIC AFFAIRS OF STATES AND THE PROTECTION OF THEIR INDEPENDENCE AND SOVEREIGNTY

The General Assembly . . . solemnly declares:
   1. No State has the right to intervene, directly or indirectly, for any reason whatever, in the internal or external affairs of any other State. Consequently, armed intervention and all other forms of interference or attempted threats

against the personality of the State or against its political, economic and cultural elements, are condemned.

2. No State may use or encourage the use of economic, political or any other type of measures to coerce another State in order to obtain from it the subordination of the exercise of its sovereign rights or to secure from it advantages of any kind. Also, no State shall organize, assist, foment, finance, incite or tolerate subversive, terrorist or armed activities directed towards the violent overthrow of the regime of another State, or interfere in civil strife in another State.

3. The use of force to deprive peoples of their national identity constitutes a violation of their inalienable rights and of the principle of non-intervention. . . .

6. All States shall respect the right of self-determination and independence of peoples and nations, to be freely exercised without any foreign pressure, and with absolute respect for human rights and fundamental freedoms. Consequently, all States shall contribute to the complete elimination of racial discrimination and colonialism in all its forms and manifestations.

The principles embodied in this resolution have subsequently been recognized as customary international law (in the 1986 *Nicaragua* case on the use of force[32]), but it is debatable whether the states that voted it into existence had visualized it as creating law. To quote the representative of the United States: "[We] view this declaration as a statement of attitude and policy, as a political declaration with a vital political message, not as a declaration or elaboration of the law governing non-intervention . . . the Special Committee of the Assembly on the Principles of International Law concerning Friendly Relations and Cooperation among States has been given the precise job of enunciating that law. Thus, we leave the precise definition of law to the lawyers, and our vote on this resolution is without prejudice to the definition of the law we shall make in the Special Committee."[33]

Rosalyn Higgins, later a judge on the ICJ, saw the resolution as an example of lawmaking by the General Assembly,[34] but many others, including Judge Stephen M. Schwebel, who reviewed her book, disagreed.[35]

Interestingly, while the Declaration had been adopted by an almost unanimous vote, with only Britain abstaining, the efforts to give the principles embodied in this declaration greater legal standing met with opposition

---

[32] *Military and Paramilitary Activities in and against Nicaragua (Nicaragua v. United States of America)*. Judgment. I.C.J. Reports 1986.
[33] United Nations General Assembly, Twentieth Session, First Committee, Verbatim Record of the 143rd Meeting, A/C.1/PV. 1423, p. 12.
[34] Rosalyn Higgins, *The Development of International Law through the Political Organs of the United Nations* (Oxford: Oxford University Press, 1963).
[35] Stephen M. Schwebel, "Book Review," *Yale Law Journal*, vol. 75 (1966), p. 677.

even within the Special Committee, and negotiations proved unsuccessful for years afterward.[36]

The ICJ has had several opportunities to comment on the weight to be given to General Assembly resolutions. In the *Nicaragua* case, it stated about the Declaration on Principles of International Law concerning Friendly Relations and Co-operation among States: "the effect of consent to the text of such resolutions cannot be understood as merely that of a 'reiteration or elucidation' of the treaty commitment undertaken in the Charter. On the contrary, it may be understood as an acceptance of the validity of the rule or set of rules declared by the resolution by themselves."[37] It elaborated in the *Nuclear Weapons* Advisory Opinion.

LEGALITY OF THE USE BY A STATE OF NUCLEAR WEAPONS IN ARMED CONFLICT (ADVISORY OPINION) (1996) ICJ REPORTS 679

68. According to certain States, the important series of General Assembly resolutions, beginning with resolution 1653 (XVI) of 24 November 1961, that deal with nuclear weapons and that affirm, with consistent regularity, the illegality of nuclear weapons, signify the existence of a rule of international customary law which prohibits recourse to those weapons. According to other States, however, the resolutions in question have no binding character on their own account and are not declaratory of any customary rule of prohibition of nuclear weapons; some of these States have also pointed out that this series of resolutions not only did not meet with the approval of all of the nuclear-weapon States but of many other States as well. ....

70. The Court notes that General Assembly resolutions, even if they are not binding, may sometimes have normative value. They can, in certain circumstances, provide evidence important for establishing the existence of a rule or the emergence of an *opinio juris*. To establish whether this is true of a given General Assembly resolution, it is necessary to look at its content and the conditions of its adoption; it is also necessary to see whether an *opinio juris* exists as to its normative character. Or a series of resolutions may show the gradual evolution of the *opinio juris* required for the establishment of a new rule

71. Examined in their totality, the General Assembly resolutions put before the Court declare that the use of nuclear weapons would be a direct violation

---

[36] See Robert Rosenstock, "The Declaration of Principles of International Law Governing Friendly Relations: A Survey," *American Journal of International Law*, vol. 65 (1971), p. 713.

[37] *Nicaragua* case.

of the Charter of the United Nations; and in certain formulations that such use "should be prohibited". The focus of these resolutions has sometimes shifted to diverse related matters; however, several of the resolutions under consideration in the present case have been adopted with substantial numbers of negative votes and abstentions; thus, although those resolutions are a clear sign of deep concern regarding the problem of nuclear weapons, they still fall short of establishing the existence of an *opinio juris* on the illegality of the use of such weapons.

72. The Court further notes that the first of the resolutions of the General Assembly expressly proclaiming the illegality of the use of nuclear weapons, resolution 1653 (XVI) of 24 November 1961 (mentioned in subsequent resolutions), after referring to certain international declarations and binding agreements, from the Declaration of St. Petersburg of 1868 to the Geneva Protocol of 1925, proceeded to qualify the legal nature of nuclear weapons, determine their effects, and apply general rules of customary international law to nuclear weapons in particular. That application by the General Assembly of general rules of customary law to the particular case of nuclear weapons indicates that, in its view, there was no specific rule of customary law which prohibited the use of nuclear weapons; if such a rule had existed, the General Assembly could simply have referred to it and would not have needed to undertake such an exercise of legal qualification.

QUESTIONS

19. Are General Assembly resolutions sources of law? Does article 38(1) of the Statute of the International Court of Justice provide any guidance?
20. Judge Schwebel and others worry about the creation of so-called "instant custom." They claim that votes in the General Assembly are not taken seriously, and even when adopted unanimously can represent a "fake" consensus. How serious are these concerns? What are the counterarguments?

4.7 Lawmaking by the Specialized Agencies

Some specialized agencies have developed specialized lawmaking processes, designed to streamline the enterprise. They make it easier to create new law without compromising the fundamental principle that states are bound only by rules to which they have consented.

The International Labour Organization is one example. Membership in the ILO is tripartite: not only do government representatives participate, but worker and employer groups do as well. They are equal participants in the negotiations on labor conventions, and they all get a vote when a convention is adopted. No reservation clauses are allowed because governments could attach them without the consent of the worker and employer representatives. Instead, there are flexibility clauses written into the ILO Conventions themselves and therefore negotiated by all three groups.

Another distinctive feature of the ILO lawmaking process is that it has an element of peer pressure built into it. All ILO members have an obligation to bring labor conventions to the attention of competent domestic authorities for appropriate action. Thus for example, they are required to submit the treaty to their national legislatures for consideration if that is the constitutional process in a given country. This is a positive obligation that applies even to ILO members who voted against the convention. If action is not taken, members must report that back to the ILO and explain the position of their government in regard to matters that fall within the scope of the Convention.

CONSTITUTION OF THE INTERNATIONAL LABOR ORGANIZATION

. . .

5. In the case of a Convention:

(a) the Convention will be communicated to all Members for ratification;

(b) each of the Members undertakes that it will, within the period of one year at most from the closing of the session of the Conference, or if it is impossible owing to exceptional circumstances to do so within the period of one year, then at the earliest practicable moment and in no case later than 18 months from the closing of the session of the Conference, bring the Convention before the authority or authorities within whose competence the matter lies, for the enactment of legislation or other action;

(c) Members shall inform the Director-General of the International Labour Office of the measures taken in accordance with this article to bring the Convention before the said competent authority or authorities, with particulars of the authority or authorities regarded as competent, and of the action taken by them;

(d) if the Member obtains the consent of the authority or authorities within whose competence the matter lies, it will communicate the formal ratification of the Convention to the Director-General and will take such action as may be necessary to make effective the provisions of such Convention;

(e) if the Member does not obtain the consent of the authority or authorities within whose competence the matter lies, no further obligation shall rest upon the Member except that it shall report to the Director-General of the International Labour Office, at appropriate intervals as requested by the Governing Body, the position of its law and practice in regard to the matters dealt with in the Convention, showing the extent to which effect has been given, or is proposed to be given, to any of the provisions of the Convention by legislation, administrative action, collective agreement or otherwise and stating the difficulties which prevent or delay the ratification of such Convention.

The WHO Constitution has similar provisions geared to apply some peer pressure on members to ratify treaties. It also contains tacit consent/opt out procedures for regulations. These rules can be adopted by simple majority and yet are binding on all members of the organizations unless they explicitly opt out.

CONSTITUTION OF THE WORLD HEALTH ORGANIZATION

Article 2

In order to achieve its objective, the functions of the Organization shall be: . . .

(k) to propose conventions, agreements and regulations, and make recommendations with respect to international health matters and to perform such duties as may be assigned thereby to the Organization and are consistent with its objective; . . .

Article 19

The Health Assembly shall have authority to adopt conventions or agreements with respect to any matter within the competence of the Organization. A two-thirds vote of the Health Assembly shall be required for the adoption of such conventions or agreements, which shall come into force for each Member when accepted by it in accordance with its constitutional processes.

Article 20

Each Member undertakes that it will, within eighteen months after the adoption by the Health Assembly of a convention or agreement, take action relative to the acceptance of such convention or agreement. Each Member shall notify the Director-General of the action taken, and if it does not accept such convention or agreement within the time limit, it will furnish a statement of the reasons for non-acceptance. In case of acceptance, each Member agrees to make an annual report to the Director-General in accordance with Chapter XIV.

Article 21

The Health Assembly shall have authority to adopt regulations concerning:

(a) sanitary and quarantine requirements and other procedures designed to prevent the international spread of disease;

(b) nomenclatures with respect to diseases, causes of death and public health practices;

(c) standards with respect to diagnostic procedures for international use;

(d) standards with respect to the safety, purity and potency of biological, pharmaceutical and similar products moving in international commerce;

(e) advertising and labeling of biological, pharmaceutical and similar products moving in international commerce.

Article 22

Regulations adopted pursuant to Article 21 shall come into force for all Members after due notice has been given of their adoption by the Health Assembly except for such Members as may notify the Director-General of rejection or reservations within the period stated in the notice. . . .

The International Civil Aviation Organization (ICAO) has the power to adopt "international standards" on air traffic. They come into effect after a designated period if adopted by two-thirds of the 33-member ICAO Council, unless before that period expires, a majority of the ICAO members disapprove. Article 38 explains how a member may opt out of a standard that has come into force.

CONVENTION ON INTERNATIONAL CIVIL AVIATION, SIGNED AT CHICAGO, 7 DECEMBER 1944 (CHICAGO CONVENTION)

Article 38. Departures from international standards and procedures

Any State which finds it impracticable to comply in all respectswith any such international standard or procedure, or to bring its own regulations or practices into full accord with any international standard or procedure after amendment of the latter, or which deems it necessary to adopt regulations or practices differing in any particular respect from those established by an international standard, shall give immediate notification to the International Civil Aviation Organization of the differences between its own practice and that established by the international standard. In the case of amendments to international standards, any State which does not make the appropriate amendments to its own regulations or practices shall give notice to the Council within sixty days of the adoption of the amendment to the international standard, or indicate the action which it proposes to take. In any such case, the Council shall make immediate notification to all other states of the difference which exists between one or more features of an international standard and the corresponding national practice of that State.

QUESTIONS

21. What are the advantages of the ILO lawmaking process over normal treaty-making? Are there other issues on which this process could be effective?
22. What are the advantages and disadvantages of the tacit consent/opt-out procedures used in the WHO and ICAO? Can it be reconciled with the principle that states are bound only by rules to which they have consented?

4.8 Lawmaking through Operational Activities

An even more contested proposition is the notion that international law has developed from operational activities of international organizations.[38] Operational activities are to be distinguished from the more explicit normative activities, such as negotiating resolutions and treaties. They include peacekeeping, development assistance, election monitoring, and the delivery of humanitarian relief.

The argument holds that these operational activities do not create new law, but give content to vague and inchoate norms. Put otherwise, soft law can harden through these operational activities.[39] How does this work? The operational activities are often undertaken against the backdrop of widely acknowledged but not well-specified norms; in carrying out those activities, international organizations typically act in a manner that conforms to the norm; these activities trigger reactions from affected governments, and the discourse that accompanies the action and reactions can cause

---

[38] Ian Johnstone, "Law-Making through the Operational Activities of International Organizations," *George Washington International Law Review*, vol. 40 (2008) p. 87.
[39] On soft law generally see Judith Goldstein et al. (eds), *Legalization and World Politics* (Cambridge MA: MIT Press, 2001); Dinah Shelton (ed), *Commitment and Compliance: The Role of Non-binding Norms in the International Legal System* (Oxford and New York: Oxford University Press, 2000); Jan Klabbers, "The Redundancy of Soft Law," *Nordic Journal of International Law*, vol. 65 (1996), p. 167.

soft law to harden. Examples where such hardening *could* take place in the United Nations include the hardening of the right to political participation through electoral assistance activities; the hardening of some of the Guiding Principles on Internal Displacement through humanitarian action by the United Nations High Commissioner for Refugees (UNHCR) and other agencies, the impact of UNICEF activities on rights of the child, the impact of WHO and World Bank activities on the "right to health", and the impact of United Nations Educational, Scientific and Cultural Organization (UNESCO) and UNICEF programs on the "right to education." Although these activities originate from mandates given by member states, this is a highly attenuated form of delegation in that the mandate is often very broad; the specifics emerge through the practices of the organization, underpinned by general support of the membership for them.

The general point is that much international law builds up as a body of practice that sets precedents and ultimately becomes a more generalized rule. The traditional place to look for that practice is states—that is how customary law is made. But increasingly the practices of IOs themselves have an impact on the development of international law.

They do not fall neatly into any of the sources of law identified in Article 38 of the Statute of the ICJ, but neither are they entirely inconsistent with the Statute. Some of these practices may simply be seen as authoritative interpretation of a treaty. Alternatively, one could argue that "general principles of international law" include not only the principles common to national legal systems but also the practice of IOs. They could even be seen as a kind of customary law formation, one step removed from state consent.

To the extent that this hardening process occurs, it highlights the autonomous powers of international organizations—they are more than just vehicles where member states cooperate. If nothing else, these practices contribute to the diffuse normative process, in which claims are made, challenged, defended, and elaborated in the course of interactions within the United Nations and between the United Nations, governments, and affected peoples.

HYPOTHETICALS

A

Suppose global negotiations on climate change have ground to a halt. Meanwhile, the United States and China continue to build on the bilateral agreement they reached in November 2014, drawing the United Kingdom into those discussions, as well as India and Brazil, who have been elected non-permanent members of the Security Council. Those four countries introduce a draft resolution in the Council, under Chapter VII, requiring all members of the United Nations to adopt measures—commensurate with the "common but differentiated responsibilities"—to limit greenhouse gas emissions. The draft specifies a long-term goal of "net zero" emissions by the year 2050, meaning any lingering emissions would have to be offset by other measures such as planting forests. The draft resolution requires all states to develop national plans on how they will meet that goal, with yearly targets. The plans are to be reviewed by a committee established by the Security Council. The Committee will have a mandate to enter into consultations with laggard governments on what more they must do to meet the 2050 goal. The President of the Security Council convenes an open meeting to discuss the draft. As your country's permanent representative to the United Nations, you plan to participate in the meeting. Develop a position on the following issues that are likely to arise at the meeting: (1) Would the Security Council be acting ultra vires by adopting a Chapter VII resolution on climate change?; (2) Would the Security Council be acting ultra vires by adopting a "quasi-legislative" resolution?; (3) If the resolution is deemed to be *intra vires*, would it be wise for the Security Council to act in this manner?; and (4) If you determine the resolution would be both *intra vires* and wise, what steps would you propose to ensure it is effective?

B

The Security Council has, to date, directly addressed two health-related crises: HIV/AIDS and the ebola outbreak. It passed two resolutions on the former (in 2000 and 2011) and, by declaring the latter a threat to international peace and security in 2014, paved the way for deployment of the United Nations Mission for Emergency Ebola Response—the UN's first "health-keeping" mission. Suppose that a number of SC members have decided that infectious disease is a particularly dangerous threat that requires more systematic national and international action. As President of the Security Council, one of those members convenes an open meeting to discuss the matter. In a non-paper circulated prior to the meeting, the concerned states sets out a non-exhaustive list of issues that could be addressed in a Chapter VII binding resolution:

- National bio-security regulations that would identify and limit the export of dangerous biological agents
- More robust national implementation of the surveillance and reporting requirements in the International Health Regulations
- Guarantees of timely access to sites of an outbreak for inter-governmental and non-governmental agencies with expertise

As your country's permanent representative to the United Nations, you plan to participate in the meeting. Develop a position on the following issues that are likely to arise: (1) Would the Security Council be acting *ultra vires* by adopting a quasi-legislative Chapter VII resolution on infectious disease?; (2) If the resolution is deemed to be *intra vires*, would it be wise for the Security Council to act in this manner?; and (3) If you determine the resolution would be both *intra vires* and wise, what steps would you propose to ensure it is effective?

Further Reading

Alvarez, José. *International Organizations as Lawmakers.* Oxford: Oxford University Press, 2006.

Boyle, Alan and Christine Chinkin. *The Making of International Law.* Oxford: Oxford University Press, 2007.

Collins, Richard and Nigel White. *International Organizations and the Idea of Autonomy: Institutional Independence in the International Legal Order.* New York: Routledge Taylor and Francis Group, 2013.

de Wet, Erika. *The Chapter VII Powers of the United Nations Security Council.* Oxford: Hart Publishing, 2004.

Dunnoff, Jeff and Mark Pollack (eds). *Interdisciplinary Perspectives on International Law and International Relations: The State of the Art.* New York: Cambridge University Press, 2013.

Einsiedel, Sebastian, David Malone, and Bruno Ugarte (eds). *The United Nations Security Council in the 21st Century.* Boulder CO: Lynne Reinner, 2015.

Hurd, Ian. *International Organizations: Politics, Law and Practice.* 2nd edn. Cambridge: Cambridge University Press, 2013.

Johnstone, Ian. *The Power of Deliberation: International Law, Politics and Organization.* New York: Oxford University Press, 2011.

Klabbers, Jan. *An Introduction to International Organizations Law.* 3nd edn. Cambridge: Cambridge University Press, 2015.

Liivoja, Rain and Jarna Petman (eds). *International Law-Making: Essays in Honor of Jan Klabbers.* New York: Routledge Taylor and Francis, 2013.

Nijman, Janne Elisabeth. *The Concept of International Legal Personality: An Inquiry into the History and Theory of International Law.* The Hague: TMC Asser, 2004.

Sands, Philippe and Pierre Klein. *Bowett's Law of International Institutions.* 6th edn. London: Sweet & Maxwell, 2009.

Sarooshi, Dan. *International Organizations and Their Exercise of Sovereign Powers.* Oxford: Oxford University Press, 2007.

Schermers, Henry and Niels Blokker. *International Institutional Law.* 5th edn. Leiden: Brill Publishers, 2011.

chapter five
....

The Secretary-General and the Secretariat

The UN Charter defines the Secretary-General as the "chief administrative officer" of the United Nations Organization, a capacity in which he or she serves the Security Council, the General Assembly, and the Economic and Social Council, as well as performing "such other functions as are entrusted to him by these organs."[1] At the same time, the Secretary-General is granted significant institutional and personal independence: the Secretariat he or she leads is itself a principal organ of the United Nations; the Secretary-General and the staff serve as international officials responsible only to the Organization; and member states undertake "to respect the exclusively international character of the responsibilities of the Secretary-General and the staff and not to seek to influence them in the discharge of their responsibilities."[2]

In practice, then, the Secretary-General and the Secretariat are set up to play two distinct roles. One is as a service staff to facilitate the effective functioning of the United Nations as a continuously operating conference of governments. The other function is to run the Organization in such a way as to give effect to its stated goals—which at any moment may or may not coincide with the interests of particular member states. These separate functions, combined in a single principal organ of the United Nations, create a dynamic tension. This chapter explores that tension through the original conception of the role of Secretary-General, the process by which he or she is appointed, and the evolution of a key power—that of bringing matters to the attention of the Security Council. The chapter concludes with an examination of the independence of the Secretary-General and the Secretariat.

---

[1] UN Charter, arts. 97–98.
[2] UN Charter, art. 100.

5.1 Secretary or General?

The Secretary-General of the United Nations is a unique figure in world politics. At once the world's senior diplomat, servant of the UN Security Council
(and member states more generally), and notional commander-in-chief of up
to a 100,000 peacekeepers, he or she depends on states for both the legitimacy and resources that enable the United Nations to function. The tension
between these roles—of being secretary or general—has challenged every
incumbent. The first, the Norwegian Trygve Lie (1946–1952), memorably welcomed his successor to New York's Idlewild Airport with the words: "The
task of the Secretary-General is the most impossible job on earth."[3]

Even before the United Nations was formally established, it was clear that
the role of Secretary-General would be a complex one.

REPORT OF THE PREPARATORY COMMISSION OF THE
UNITED NATIONS, 23 DECEMBER 1945[4]

8. The principal functions assigned to the Secretary-General, explicitly or
by inference, by the Charter, may be grouped under six headings: general
administrative and executive functions, technical functions, financial functions, the organization and administration of the International Secretariat,
political functions and representational functions.

9. Many of the Secretary-General's duties will naturally be delegated, in
greater or lesser degree, to members of his staff and particularly to his higher
officials. But the execution of these duties must be subject to his supervision
and control; the ultimate responsibility remains his alone.

10. The Secretary-General is the "chief administrative officer of the
Organization" (Article 97) and Secretary-General of the General Assembly,
the Security Council, the Economic and Social Council and the Trusteeship
Council (Article 93). Certain specific duties of a more narrowly administrative character derived from these provisions are indicated in the Charter
(for example, in Articles 12 and 20, and in Article 98, the last sentence of
which requires the Secretary-General to present an annual report to the

---

[3] Trygve Lie, *In the Cause of Peace: Seven Years with the United Nations*
(New York: MacMillan, 1954), p. 417.
[4] Report of the Preparatory Commission of the United Nations (23 December 1945),
Chapter VIII, section 2, paras. 8–17, reprinted in Simon Chesterman (ed), *Secretary
or General? The UN Secretary-General in World Politics* (Cambridge: Cambridge
University Press, 2007), pp. 243–245.

General Assembly on the work of the Organization) and in the Statute of the International Court of Justice (Articles 5 and 15).

11. Further specific duties falling under this head, many of which will no doubt be defined in the Rules of Procedure of the various principal organs concerned and their subsidiary bodies, relate to the preparation of the agenda and the convocation of sessions, the provision of the necessary staff, and the preparation of the minutes and other documents.

12. The Secretary-General also has administrative and executive duties of a wider character. He is the channel of all communication with the United Nations or any of its organs. He must endeavour, within the scope of his functions, to integrate the activity of the whole complex of United Nations organs and see that the machine runs smoothly and efficiently. He is responsible, moreover, for the preparation of the work of the various organs and for the execution of their decisions, in cooperation with the Members.

13. The last-mentioned functions of the Secretary-General have technical as well as administrative aspects. More particularly as regards the work of the Economic and Social Council and the Trusteeship Council, the expert technical assistance which the Secretary-General is able to provide, and which he himself must control, will clearly affect the degree in which these organs can achieve their purposes.

14. Under the Charter, the Secretary-General has wide responsibilities in connexion with the financial administration of the United Nations; and it may be assumed that, under the financial regulations which will be established by the General Assembly, he will be made primarily responsible for preparing the budget, for allocating funds, for controlling expenditure, for administering such financial and budgetary arrangements as the General Assembly may enter into with specialized agencies, for collecting contributions from Members and for the custodianship of all funds.

15. The Secretary-General is the head of the Secretariat. He appoints all staff under regulations established by the General Assembly (Article 101, paragraphs 1 and 5), and assigns appropriate staff to the various organs of the United Nations (Article 101, paragraph 2). He alone is responsible to the other principal organs for the Secretariat's work; his choice of staff—more particularly of higher staff—and his leadership will largely determine the character and the efficiency of the Secretariat as a whole. It is on him that will mainly fall the duty of creating and maintaining a team spirit in a body of officials recruited from many countries. His moral authority within the Secretariat will depend at once upon the example he gives of the qualities prescribed in Article 100, and upon the confidence shown in him by the Members of the United Nations.

16. The Secretary-General may have an important role to play as a mediator and as an informal adviser of many governments, and will undoubtedly be called upon from time to time, in the exercise of his administrative duties, to take decisions which may justly be called political. Under Article

99 of the Charter, moreover, he has been given a quite special right which goes beyond any power previously accorded to the head of an international organization, viz: to bring to the attention of the Security Council any matter (not merely any dispute or situation) which, in his opinion, may threaten the maintenance of international peace and security. It is impossible to foresee how this Article will be applied; but the responsibility it confers upon the Secretary-General will require the exercise of the highest qualities of political judgement, tact and integrity.

17. The United Nations cannot prosper, nor can its aims be realized, without the active and steadfast support of the peoples of the world. The aims and activities of the General Assembly, the Security Council, the Economic and Social Council and the Trusteeship Council will, no doubt, be represented before the public primarily by the Chairmen of these organs. But the Secretary-General, more than anyone else, will stand for the United Nations as a whole. In the eyes of the world, no less than in the eyes of his own staff, he must embody the principles and ideals of the Charter to which the Organization seeks to give effect.

The basic functions of the Secretary-General as they evolved over time can be grouped more simply into two broad categories: administrative and political.

In terms of administrative responsibilities, the Secretary-General supports the work of the other principal organs (with the exception of the International Court of Justice). In addition, the Secretary-General must manage the Secretariat itself—including decisions on personnel and oversight of the budget. A third area is what we might term the documentary functions of the Secretary-General: this comprises both the preparation of reports requested by the various parts of the UN system as well as the important function he or she serves as the depositary for international treaties.

The political functions of the Secretary-General stem from three sources. First, Article 98 allows the principal organs to entrust him or her with "other functions." In practice, these functions routinely include political aspects and have expanded far beyond what could have been foreseen in 1945—including, among other things, peacekeeping and administration of territory. Second, Article 99 (discussed below) clearly grants a measure of discretion in determining which situations "in his opinion" threaten international peace and security. Third, various Secretaries-General have also asserted an ability to exercise an independent political role that goes beyond the limited scope of Article 99. This last aspect has sometimes overlapped with the status of the Secretary-General as the public face of the United Nations—at times encompassing a normative role in interpreting as well as implementing the Charter.

QUESTIONS

1. How might one define the job description of the position of Secretary-General? How does it differ from that of a foreign minister or a head of state?
2. The Secretary-General fulfills many of the ceremonial functions of a head of state, together with the policymaking and administrative functions of a head of government. Would it be possible and desirable to divide these functions between different positions? Kofi Annan, in his second term, tried to move in this direction by appointing a Deputy Secretary-General to be in charge of the administrative structure of the Secretariat. Would you expect such a reform to succeed?
3. The Secretary-General serves as the "face" of the United Nations. What pressure does this place on the office in terms of what is said and done? It has been used by several Secretaries-General as a license to lead debate and press for action from the other UN organs and states. Is this appropriate? How independent can and should the Secretary-General be?
4. Should the Secretary-General be more of a "secretary" or more of a "general"?

5.2 Appointment

Article 97 of the UN Charter provides that the Secretary-General "shall be appointed by the General Assembly upon the recommendation of the Security Council." The Council has only ever recommended one person and the Assembly has always accepted that recommendation. (The sole exception was during the 1950 Security Council deadlock when it made no recommendation; in a majority vote the General Assembly decided to extend the term of the first Secretary-General, Trygve Lie.)[5]

In one of its earliest resolutions, adopted on 24 January 1946, the General Assembly had outlined the basic terms of appointment and process for selecting the Secretary-General. The Assembly historically embraced a very limited role for itself, but this may be changing as rumblings of discontent among the wider membership are rife over the Council's outsize role in this critical process ahead of the selection of a new Secretary-General in 2016.

---

[5] GA Res. 492(V) (1950).

GENERAL ASSEMBLY RESOLUTION 11(I) (1946)

Terms of Appointment of the Secretary-General

The General Assembly resolves that, in view of the heavy responsibilities which rest upon the Secretary-General in fulfilling his obligations under the Charter:

1. The terms of the appointment of the Secretary-General shall be such as to enable a man of eminence and high attainment to accept and maintain the position.

2. The Secretary-General shall receive a salary of an amount sufficient to bring him in a net sum of $20,000 (US),[6] together with representation allowance of $20,000 (US), per annum. In addition, he shall be provided with a furnished residence, the repairs and maintenance of which, excluding provision of household staff, shall be borne by the Organization.

3. The first Secretary-General shall be appointed for five years, the appointment being open at the end of that period for a further five-year term.

4. The following observations contained in paragraphs 18–21 of section 2, chapter VIII of the Preparatory Commission's Report be noted and approved:

(a) There being no stipulation on the subject in the Charter, the General Assembly and the Security Council are free to modify the term of office of future Secretaries-General in the light of experience.

(b) Because a Secretary-General is a confident [*sic*] of many governments, it is desirable that no Member should offer him, at any rate immediately on retirement, any governmental position in which his confidential information might be a source of embarrassment to other Members, and on his part a Secretary-General should refrain from accepting any such position.

(c) From the provisions of Articles 18 and 27 of the Charter, it is clear that, for the nomination of the Secretary-General by the Security Council, an affirmative vote of [nine][7] members, including the concurring votes of the permanent Members, is required; and that for his appointment by the General Assembly, a simple majority of the members of that body present and voting is sufficient, unless the General Assembly itself decides that a two-thirds majority is called for. The same rules apply to a renewal of appointment as to an original appointment; this should be made clear when the original appointment is made.

(d) It would be desirable for the Security Council to proffer one candidate only for the consideration of the General Assembly, and for debate on the nomination in the General Assembly to be avoided. Both nomination and

---

[6] Approximately $260,000 in 2014 dollars.

[7] Prior to expansion of the Security Council in 1965, decisions of the Council adopted under Article 27 required seven votes.

appointment should be discussed at private meetings, and a vote in either the Security Council or the General Assembly, if taken, should be by secret ballot.

Five days after the General Assembly resolution was passed, the Security Council met to discuss the appointment.

COMMUNIQUÉ, FOURTH MEETING OF THE UN SECURITY COUNCIL, 29 JANUARY 1946

The Security Council held a private meeting on 29 January 1946, at which it was unanimously agreed to recommend to the General Assembly the name of Mr Trygve Lie, Foreign Minister of Norway, for the post of Secretary-General.

The President of the Security Council, Mr Makin (Australia), is communicating urgently with Mr Lie in order to ascertain whether he would be prepared to accept this nomination.

Three days later, the General Assembly considered the recommendation. Rule 141 of the rules of procedure of the General Assembly provides that:

When the Security Council has submitted its recommendation on the appointment of the Secretary-General, the General Assembly shall consider the recommendation and vote upon it by secret ballot in private meeting.

During the meeting, however, the President of the Assembly proposed holding the secret ballot in a *public* meeting. This met with general approval and Trygve Lie was duly appointed with a short statement adopted:

On the recommendation of the Security Council, the General Assembly appointed as the first Secretary-General of the United Nations: His Excellency Mr Trygve Lie.[8]

Current practice now takes the form of a resolution, typically adopted by acclamation (without objection and without a vote, but a round of applause).

---

[8] UN Doc A/64 (1946).

GENERAL ASSEMBLY RESOLUTION 61/3 (2006)

The General Assembly,
  Having considered the recommendation contained in Security Council res-
olution 1715 (2006) of 9 October 2006,
  Appoints Mr. Ban Ki-moon Secretary-General of the United Nations
for a term of office beginning on 1 January 2007 and ending on 31
December 2011.

The inclusion of a start date and end date is noteworthy. The Charter does
not specify the term of office of the Secretary-General, but the provisions
of paragraph three of resolution 11(I) (1946)—which was limited to the *first*
Secretary-General—have been applied to most subsequent holders of the
office.

  A further consideration in the appointment of the Secretary-General is
the region from which he or she hails. The first two Secretaries-General were
Western European: Trygve Lie (Norway, 1946–1952) and Dag Hammarskjöld
(Sweden, 1953–1961). The third Secretary-General was Asian—U Thant
(Burma, 1961–1971)—followed by another Western European: Kurt Waldheim
(Austria, 1972–1981).

  Beginning in the 1980s the principle of regional rotation came to be
invoked as a criterion for selection of the Secretary-General. This was cham-
pioned by Latin American states, leading to the appointment of Javier Pérez
de Cuéllar (Peru, 1982–1991), and then African states, leading to the appointment of Boutros Boutros-Ghali (Egypt, 1992–1996). When it became clear
that Boutros-Ghali would not be appointed for a second term, it was generally accepted that his successor should also be from Africa, and Kofi Annan
(Ghana, 1997–2006) was duly appointed. He was followed by the Asian Ban
Ki-moon (South Korea, 2007–2016).

  There has yet to be a Secretary-General from the Eastern European group,
though after the end of the Cold War this region has been less coherent as an
entity—not least because eleven of its twenty-three members are now part of
the European Union, and four others are candidates for membership.

  The General Assembly appeared to endorse the principle of regional rotation in a resolution adopted in 1997, much of which was repeated in a similar
resolution in 2006.[9]

---

[9] GA Res. 60/286 (2006).

GENERAL ASSEMBLY RESOLUTION 51/241 (1997)

56. The process of selection of the Secretary-General shall be made more transparent.

57. The General Assembly shall make full use of the power of appointment enshrined in the Charter in the process of the appointment of the Secretary-General and the agenda item entitled "Appointment of the Secretary-General of the United Nations".

58. The duration of the term or terms of appointment, including the option of a single term, shall be considered before the appointment of the next Secretary-General.

59. In the course of the identification and appointment of the best candidate for the post of Secretary-General, due regard shall continue to be given to regional rotation and shall also be given to gender equality.

60. Without prejudice to the prerogatives of the Security Council, the President of the General Assembly may consult with Member States to identify potential candidates endorsed by a Member State and, upon informing all Member States of the results, may forward those results to the Security Council.

61. In order to ensure a smooth and efficient transition, the Secretary-General should be appointed as early as possible, preferably no later than one month before the date on which the term of the incumbent expires.

The fact that regional rotation is included in the same sentence as gender equality is of interest. Though regional rotation is frequently discussed and occasionally asserted as a normative principle, the same cannot be said of gender equality. To date only three formal candidates for the office have been women,[10] though that number will certainly increase.

In the course of 2015, a range of member states considered possible changes in both the selection process and other features of the appointment of the Secretary-General. This was encouraged by a group of former leaders known as "The Elders," which included past Secretary-General Kofi Annan. Its report "A UN Fit for Purpose," launched at the Munich Security Conference of February 2015, advocated "a more independent Secretary-General," calling for the recommendation of more than one candidate by the Council to the General Assembly, and only "after a timely, equitable and transparent search for the best qualified candidates irrespective of gender or region." In addition, the report called for a single, nonrenewable seven-year term for the next Secretary-General in order to create greater independence for the incumbent, implicitly from P-5 pressure.

---

[10] Vijaya Lakshmi Pandit (India, 1953). Gro Harlem Brundtland (Norway, 1991), Vaira Viķe-Freiberga (Latvia, 2006).

At the time of writing, in spite of considerable ferment among member states at the United Nations in New York, it is impossible to predict whether any of these, or any other, proposals for serious reform of the selection process will be adopted in 2016. China, the Russian Federation, and the United States have each made clear their opposition to any such sweeping change. Britain and France proved somewhat more flexible, entertaining such ideas as an open session or sessions of the Council to audition serious candidates. (This general approach had been improvised just beyond the United Nations to a degree by the International Peace Institute, a nongovernmental research organization working alongside the United Nations in 2006 during the election process, although few of the candidates departed from a very "prudent" path.)

QUESTIONS

5. Why did the General Assembly suggest that it would be desirable that the Security Council recommend only one candidate for Secretary-General? What other methods of selection might be possible?
6. Given the way in which decisions are made in the UN Security Council, who actually chooses the Secretary-General in practice?
7. The term of office of the Secretary-General is usually five years, with the possibility of a second term of the same length. Would it help protect the independence of the incumbent if his or her term were longer (say, seven years) and not renewable? Why, or why not?
8. Is the principle that the Secretary-General should be chosen from different regions of the world a normative requirement? Should it be?

5.3 Article 99 Powers

Article 99 is the provision in the Charter that highlights most explicitly the political role that the Secretary-General was expected to play. It is striking, however, that in the history of the United Nations it has only been invoked directly on only two occasions: the Congo in 1960, and the Tehran Hostages situation in 1979. These are the only cases in which the Secretary-General formally did "bring to the attention of the Security Council [a] matter which in his opinion may threaten the maintenance of international peace and security." Nevertheless, Article 99 has also been used to justify various implicit powers that the Secretary-General has exercised over the years, the better to carry out this potential function. In addition, much of the Secretary-General's work is carried out *in*formally, through consultations and lobbying.

On its face, Article 99 resembles other parts of the Charter—but with some key differences. Compare the following three provisions:

UN CHARTER

Article 11(3)

The General Assembly may call the attention of the Security Council to situations which are likely to endanger international peace and security. . . .

Article 35(1)

Any Member of the United Nations may bring any dispute, or any situation of the nature referred to in Article 34, to the attention of the Security Council or of the General Assembly. . . .

Article 99

The Secretary-General may bring to the attention of the Security Council any matter which in his opinion may threaten the maintenance of international peace and security.

There are several differences between the three provisions, the most important of which is that Article 99 does not grant powers to member states or a group of member states but to the Secretary-General him- or herself.

The first occasion on which a Secretary-General explicitly invoked Article 99 was in 1960 when Dag Hammarskjöld received cables from the President and Prime Minister of the Republic of the Congo requesting the urgent dispatch of UN military assistance.[11] He wrote on the same day to the President of the Security Council.

LETTER DATED 13 JULY 1960 FROM THE SECRETARY-GENERAL ADDRESSED TO THE PRESIDENT OF THE SECURITY COUNCIL[12]

I wish to inform you that I have to bring to the attention of the Security Council a matter which, in my opinion, may threaten the maintenance of international peace and security. Thus, I request you to call an urgent meeting of the Security Council to hear a report of the Secretary-General on a demand for United Nations action in relation to the Republic of the Congo.

May I suggest that the meeting is called for tonight at 8.30 p.m.

Accept, etc.

(Signed) Dag Hammarskjöld

---

[11] UN Doc S/4382.
[12] UN Doc S/4381.

The following day, the Security Council passed resolution 143 (1960), launching the UN Operation in the Congo (ONUC).[13]

Hammarskjöld later highlighted the importance of Article 99 in an oft-cited speech on the "international civil servant," which he delivered less than four months before his death in a plane crash in 1961.

DAG HAMMARSKJÖLD, "THE INTERNATIONAL CIVIL SERVANT IN LAW AND IN FACT", 30 MAY 1961[14]

It is Article 99 more than any other which was considered by the drafters of the Charter to have transformed the Secretary-General of the United Nations from a purely administrative official to one with an explicit political responsibility. Considering its importance, it is perhaps surprising that Article 99 was hardly debated: most delegates appeared to share [former South African Prime Minister Jan] Smuts' opinion that the position of the Secretary-General "should be of the highest importance and for this reason a large measure of initiative was expressly conferred." Legal scholars have observed that Article 99 not only confers upon the Secretary-General a right to bring matters to the attention of the Security Council but that this right carries with it, by necessary implication, a broad discretion to conduct inquiries and to engage in informal diplomatic activity in regard to matters which "may threaten the maintenance of international peace and security."

It is not without some significance that this new conception of a Secretary-General originated principally with the United States rather than the United Kingdom. It has been reported that at an early stage in the preparation of the papers that later became the Dumbarton Oaks proposals, the United States gave serious consideration to the idea that the Organization should have a President as well as a Secretary-General. Subsequently, it was decided to propose only a single officer, but one in whom there would be combined both the political and executive functions of a President with the internal administrative functions that were previously accorded to a Secretary-General. Obviously, this is a reflection, in some measure, of the American political system, which places authority in a chief executive officer who is not simply subordinated to the legislative organs but who is constitutionally responsible alone for the execution of legislation and in some

---

[13] See also Chapter 4, section 4.1, and Chapter 7, section 7.1.
[14] Delivered at Oxford University and available on the UN website at http://www.un.org/Depts/dhl/dag/docs/internationalcivilservant.pdf.

respects for carrying out the authority derived from the constitutional instrument directly.

The fact that the Secretary-General is an official with political power as well as administrative functions had direct implications for the method of his selection. Proposals at San Francisco to eliminate the participation of the Security Council in the election process were rejected precisely because it was recognized that the role of the Secretary-General in the field of political and security matters properly involved the Security Council and made it logical that the unanimity rule of the permanent Members should apply. At the same time, it was recognized that the necessity of such unanimous agreement would have to be limited only to the selection of the Secretary-General and that it was equally essential that he be protected against the pressure of a Member during his term in office. Thus a proposal for a three-year term was rejected on the ground that so short a term might impair his independent role. . . .

To sum up, the Charter laid down these essential legal principles for an international civil service:

- It was to be an international body, recruited primarily for efficiency, competence and integrity, but on as wide a geographical basis as possible;
- It was to be headed by a Secretary-General who carried constitutionally the responsibility to the other principal organs for the Secretariat's work;
- And finally, Article 98 entitled the General Assembly and the Security Council to entrust the Secretary-General with tasks going beyond the *verba formalia* of Article 97—with its emphasis on the administrative function—thus opening the door to a measure of political responsibility which is distinct from the authority explicitly accorded to the Secretary-General under Article 99 but in keeping with the spirit of that article.

The second occasion on which a Secretary-General invoked Article 99 was in 1979 during the Iranian occupation of the US embassy in Tehran, Iran. The United States had written to the Security Council asking for help in securing the release of diplomatic personnel, but on 13 November 1979 Iran sent a letter to Secretary-General Kurt Waldheim outlining various grievances of its own against the United States. Two weeks later, Waldheim wrote to the Council himself.

LETTER DATED 25 NOVEMBER 1979 FROM THE SECRETARY-GENERAL ADDRESSED TO THE PRESIDENT OF THE SECURITY COUNCIL[15]

I wish to refer to the grave situation which has arisen in the relations between the United States and Iran. The Government of the United States is deeply disturbed at the seizure of its Embassy in Teheran and the detention of its diplomatic personnel, in violation of the relevant international conventions. The Government of Iran seeks redress for injustices and abuse of human rights which, in its view, were committed by the previous regime. The international community is increasingly concerned that the dangerous level of tension between these two countries threatens peace and stability in the region and could have disastrous consequences for the entire world.

In my opinion, therefore, the present crisis poses a serious threat to international peace and security. Accordingly, in the exercise of my responsibility under the Charter of the United Nations, I ask that the Security Council be convened urgently in an effort to seek a peaceful solution of the problem in conformity with the principles of justice and international law.

(Signed) Kurt Waldheim

The Security Council duly met and, among other things, requested the Secretary-General to lend his good offices in addressing the situation.

SECURITY COUNCIL RESOLUTION 457 (1979)

The Security Council,

Having considered the letter from the Secretary-General dated 25 November 1979,

Deeply concerned at the dangerous level of tension between Iran and the United States of America, which could have grave consequences for international peace and security, ...

1. *Urgently calls upon* the Government of Iran to release immediately the personnel of the Embassy of the United States of America being held at Teheran, to provide them with protection and to allow them to leave the country;

2. *Further calls upon* the Governments of Iran and of the United States of America to take steps to resolve peacefully the remaining issues between

---

[15] UN Doc S/13646.

them to their mutual satisfaction in accordance with the purposes and principles of the United Nations;

3. *Urges* the Governments of Iran and of the United States of America to exercise the utmost restraint in the prevailing situation;

4. *Requests* the Secretary-General to lend his good offices for the immediate implementation of the present resolution and to take all appropriate measures to this end;

5. *Decides* that the Council will remain actively seized of the matter and requests the Secretary-General to report urgently to it on developments regarding his efforts.

"Good offices" refers primarily to mediating and diplomatic functions intended to resolve conflicts between or within states, but can also include investigation and reporting on human rights abuses as well as fact-finding in conflict situations. It is now generally accepted that the Secretary-General can offer such services not only when specifically requested to do so (under Article 98 of the Charter) but also of his or her own volition, implicitly under Article 99.

The following document, prepared by the current Secretary-General Ban Ki-moon, is representative of how Article 99 is used in this way to justify wider engagement in actual and potential threats to international peace and security.

PREVENTIVE DIPLOMACY: DELIVERING RESULTS (REPORT OF THE SECRETARY-GENERAL), 26 AUGUST 2011[16]

16. My mandate for conflict prevention originates in Article 99 of the Charter, which provides that the Secretary-General may bring to the attention of the Security Council any matter which, in his opinion, may threaten the maintenance of international peace and security. Successive Secretaries-General have used their good offices to help parties find solutions to problems at the earliest possible stage. The effectiveness of the good offices is often a function of how much political space the Secretary-General has in which to act. In my own experience, the most difficult scenario is when international interest is strong but conflicted, because the parties know that there is no unity of vision. As a custodian of the Charter, I also have the duty to speak out in certain situations, an obligation which may or may not enhance mediation efforts. At times, public advocacy in full view of the media is necessary; more

---

[16] UN Doc S/2011/552 (footnote omitted).

often, however, good offices are deployed behind the scenes. Irrespective of the approach, the key is to practise diplomacy that is as determined as it is flexible.

17. The Department of Political Affairs serves as the main operational arm for the conduct of my good offices. With regular and extrabudgetary support from the Member States, the Department was strengthened over the past three years to play its lead role in preventive diplomacy within the United Nations system more effectively. It has enhanced its analytical capacities, its technical expertise in key areas such as electoral assistance, its partnerships and its ability to learn lessons, distil best practices and facilitate system-wide responses. As a result, it is becoming better geared towards rapid response and, through its reinforced regional divisions and Mediation Support Unit, can assist good offices and mediation initiatives worldwide, whether undertaken by the Organization or its partners. Its standby team of mediation experts is able to deploy within 72 hours to assist negotiators on peace process design, security arrangements, constitution-making, gender, power-sharing and wealth-sharing. A dedicated mechanism, supported by voluntary contributions, provides more flexible financing for rapid response.

QUESTIONS

9. What role does the Secretary-General play in resolving conflicts? Can he or she create, mold, or enhance political will on the part of other states to resolve conflicts?

10. An argument for an interpretation of Article 99 that allows for the good offices role of the Secretary-General is "the greater includes the lesser." If the Secretary-General has the authority to take the dramatic step of bringing a matter to the attention of the Security Council for action at that level, he or she should have the lesser authority to deal with the matter quietly him/herself. Do you agree with that logic?

11. The Secretary-General, by virtue of Article 99 of the UN Charter, has the power to initiate discussions within the Security Council and, arguably, to recommend action. The Charter is silent as to the authority of the Secretary-General to *discourage* or *prevent* action by the Council, which he or she regards as unwise policy, or inadequately resourced. Can and should the Secretary-General ever say no to a task the Security Council or General Assembly intend to assign to him or her?

12. Article 99 allows the Secretary-General to bring to the attention of the Council any matter that "in his opinion" may threaten the maintenance of international peace and security. It would make sense for this opinion to be an informed one, but successive efforts to expand the analytical capacity of the Executive Office of the Secretary-General or the Department of Political Affairs have been resisted by member states. Why?

HYPOTHETICAL A

You are the legal adviser to the Secretary-General, who has just received a credible warning of an impending genocide in the fictional state of Ruritania. Weapons are being stockpiled, and registers of the Ruritanian population have been issued, highlighting the names and addresses of all those of a particular ethnicity. It is well known that the Chinese government has strong economic ties to Ruritania, and that the United States has extensive intelligence assets in the region.

The Secretary-General has asked you to come up with options as to how to respond to this warning, along with your recommendation as to the preferred course of action. What do you advise?

5.4 Independence of the Secretary-General and the Secretariat

Though the Secretary-General is its most prominent officer, it is the Secretariat rather than the Secretary-General that is a principal organ of the United Nations. Now numbering in excess of 40,000 personnel, the Secretariat's headquarters are in New York, but significant presences are maintained in Addis Ababa, Bangkok, Beirut, Geneva, Nairobi, Santiago, and Vienna.

The main organizational divisions are as follows:

- Executive Office of the Secretary-General (EOSG)
- Office of Internal Oversight Services (OIOS)
- Office of Legal Affairs (OLA)
- Department of Political Affairs (DPA)
- Office for Disarmament Affairs (ODA)
- Department of Peacekeeping Operations (DPKO)
- Department of Field Support (DFS)
- Office for the Coordination of Humanitarian Affairs (OCHA)
- Department of Economic and Social Affairs (DESA)
- Department for General Assembly and Conference Management (DGACM)
- Department of Public Information (DPI)
- Department of Safety and Security (DSS)
- Department of Management (DM)

Representatives of the Secretariat enjoy a degree of legal *immunity*, which will be considered in Chapter 15 of this volume. Linked to that status, Article 100 of the Charter also provides that the Secretary-General and the staff should operate *independently* of member states.

UN CHARTER

Article 100

1. In the performance of their duties the Secretary-General and the staff shall not seek or receive instructions from any government or from any other authority external to the Organization. They shall refrain from any action which might reflect on their position as international officials responsible only to the Organization.

2. Each Member of the United Nations undertakes to respect the exclusively international character of the responsibilities of the Secretary-General and the staff and not to seek to influence them in the discharge of their responsibilities.

Article 101

1. The staff shall be appointed by the Secretary-General under regulations established by the General Assembly.

2. Appropriate staffs shall be permanently assigned to the Economic and Social Council, the Trusteeship Council, and, as required, to other organs of the United Nations. These staffs shall form a part of the Secretariat.

3. The paramount consideration in the employment of the staff and in the determination of the conditions of service shall be the necessity of securing the highest standards of efficiency, competence, and integrity. Due regard shall be paid to the importance of recruiting the staff on as wide a geographical basis as possible.

Given the fact that the United Nations must routinely rely on member states to supply personnel, the question of independence has been problematic throughout its history. In some cases it is helpful to have officials who can draw on contacts in member state governments. It is no coincidence, for example, that the key positions of Under-Secretary General for Peacekeeping, Under-Secretary-General for Political Affairs, and UN Humanitarian Coordinator (also at Under-Secretary-General level) are typically held by nationals of a permanent member of the Security Council—a state of affairs increasingly resented by other member states. But in theory, at least, the individual's loyalty is meant to be to the Organization.

Such issues are typically limited to political questions, but occasionally assume a legal dimension. The *Chinese Translators* case is an interesting example of this, where the question of actual and perceived independence of the Secretariat had to be considered by the UN Administrative Tribunal (UNAT).

Established by the General Assembly in 1949, the UNAT is an independent organ competent to hear and pass judgment upon applications alleging nonobservance of contracts or terms of employment by staff members of the UN Secretariat. The *Chinese Translators* case dealt with the question of reappointment of three Chinese Verbatim Reporters ("the Applicants") employed in the Department of Conference Services (DCS). The three Applicants had been recruited for five-year terms beginning in September 1984. Their contracts stated as a special condition that they were "on secondment from the Government of China." During these five years, they had "very good" or higher performance reports and had been promoted one level. On 1 May 1989, the Administrative Officer of the DCS had requested the Office of Human Resources Management (OHRM) to grant "probationary appointments" to the Applicants (laying the ground for them to achieve permanent status as UN employees). On 11 August 1989, the Secretary-General instead submitted a request to the Chinese government to grant the Applicants a two-year extension. The Chinese government replied on 23 August 1989 that they would extend the three Applicants' secondment only until 31 December 1989, after which successors proposed by the Chinese government would take over the posts.

In October 1989 the Applicants submitted requests to be considered for career appointments in accordance with General Assembly resolutions 37/126 (1982) and 38/232 (1983), which provide for "reasonable consideration upon completion of five years of continuing good service" and recommend that in such cases "the organizations normally dispense with the requirement of a probationary appointment as a precondition for a career appointment." The Secretary-General denied these requests.

The Applicants had taken part in protests against events in China (the Tiananmen Square incident of 4 June 1989) and stated that they were afraid to return to their home country. To this end, they offered to resign from any posts they may have held in their home country. The Applicants wrote to the Secretary-General stating that the Chinese government had interfered in the administration of the international civil service, and added that China had been forcing them to hand over part of their salaries to the government. They argued that their application for tenured appointment had not been reviewed by the Secretary-General with due consideration for their qualifications.

On 15 January 1990 the Office of the Secretary-General informed the Applicants that during the review all the factors in favor of their appointment had been duly noted:

> On the other hand, it was also necessary to take into account the interests of the Organization and in particular its functional needs. In this connection, it was important to ensure that the Chinese language services continued to function effectively and efficiently. Since the primary users of those services are representatives of the Government of the People's Republic of China, it is of critical importance for the effectiveness of the services that those

representatives have confidence that their statements, both oral and written, will be objectively and fairly rendered, interpreted or reported. Furthermore, the efficient functioning of the Chinese language services would not be possible in a situation where staff members were antagonistic to each other because of expressly stated political animosities.

It would also not be in the interests of the Organization to disrupt the rotational system for the staffing of the Chinese language services, which has proven to be most effective. This system has enabled the establishment of a specialized language training programme at the Beijing Institute for Foreign Languages, the termination of which would make it immensely difficult to recruit language staff with the specific qualifications required to fill vacancies appropriately and expeditiously.[17]

The communication also informed the Applicants that the Secretary-General was conducting an examination of the alleged deductions from the salaries of the staff members of the United Nations.

On 28 February 1990 the Applicants filed their appeals with the Administrative Tribunal on the grounds that: (1) the Secretary-General failed to discharge his obligations under Article 100 and 101(3) of the Charter and General Assembly resolutions 37/126 and 38/232 to give the Applicants every reasonable consideration for a career appointment; (2) under Article 100 staff members do not serve their governments but the United Nations, and do not have to agree with the policies of governments in order to carry out their duties with impartiality; (3) the Secretary-General's decision was based on illegal considerations; and (4) the establishment of a training institute does not derogate from Articles 100 and 101 of the Charter or the Staff regulations and rules.

THE *CHINESE TRANSLATORS* CASE: *QIU, ZHOU, AND YAO v. SECRETARY-GENERAL OF THE UNITED NATIONS* (UNITED NATIONS ADMINISTRATIVE TRIBUNAL JUDGMENT NO. 482, 25 MAY 1990)[18]

Judgment

VII. .... The Tribunal notes that no details concerning the nature and conditions of the employment with the Chinese government from which the

---

[17] UN Doc. AT/DEC/482 (1990), p. 10.
[18] UN Doc. AT/DEC/482 (1990).

Applicants were seconded are given in the letters of appointment submitted by the Administration.

VIII. Neither has the Administration produced any agreement concluded with the Chinese Government ... concerning the secondment of the Applicants nor any document in which the competent authorities define the Applicants' situation in writing and specify the conditions of secondment ... no details are given concerning the Applicants' posts in their own country nor of the conditions governing their reintegration into those posts ... if such agreement did exist, it was not brought to the Applicants, for their consent.

IX. The Applicants have duly taken and signed the oath required of every United Nations staff member:

> ... to exercise in all loyalty, discretion and conscience the functions entrusted to me as an international civil servant of the United Nations, to discharge these functions and regulate my conduct with the interests of the United Nations only in view, and not to seek or accept instructions in regard to the performance of my duties from any Government or other authority external to the organization. ...

XIV. The three Applicants gave complete satisfaction in the performance of their functions in the UN ... there was no allegation of any sign of antagonism towards other colleagues, certainly not Chinese colleagues. There was no sign of political animosity. ...

XXIII. The Tribunal finds that the conditions laid down for an official to be on secondment are not fulfilled in this case ... The Applicants were not on genuine secondment within the meaning given to that term ... established in Judgment No 92, Higgins (1964): "... the term 'secondment' implies that the staff member is posted away from his establishment of origin but has the right to revert to employment in the establishment at the end of the period of secondment and retains the right to promotion and retirement benefits ..."

XXIV. ... [I]t is only when these conditions are fulfilled that "the Secretary-General of the United Nations as the administrative head of the Organization, is obliged to take into account the decision of the Government."

XXV. ... Accordingly the Tribunal considers that it was not for the Respondent either to request authorization of, or to comply with the decision of the Government in order to renew the Applicant's contracts. This being so, the Tribunal finds that the decision not to renew the Applicants' fixed term contracts was vitiated by extraneous reasons contrary to the interests of the United Nations, incompatible with Article 100 of the Charter. ...

XXIX. More generally, the Tribunal considers that the limits of the Secretary-General's discretionary powers are governed by the principle established by the Tribunal's consistent case law: the Secretary-General may not legally take a decision which is contrary to the Charter, in particular to Articles 100 and 101, or to the provisions of the Staff Rules and Regulations.

XXX. ... [T]he Secretary-General has the right to consult Governments of Member States, provided such consultation does not contravene the principle referred to in the preceding paragraph ... [I]n the present case, by accepting the position advocated by the Government the Secretary-General has not acted in conformity with the foregoing principles.

XXXI. Nevertheless, the Tribunal does not hold that the Secretary-General could not, in proper circumstances, take into consideration the requirements of the efficient functioning of the Beijing Institute of Foreign Languages. The Secretary-General stressed, in his letter of 15 January 1990, that the termination of the specialized language training programme "would make it immensely difficult to recruit language staff with the specific qualifications required to fill vacancies appropriately and expeditiously." As the Tribunal shows below, in this case, the alleged adverse effect on the efficient functioning of the Institute and on recruitment is pure speculation. It appears to the Tribunal also, that there might be other sources for the recruitment of qualified language staff.

XXXII. The Tribunal notes that there is no evidence in the files to support the existence of a threat to suppress the programme in question if the Applicants receive career appointments. ...

XXXIII. In keeping with the wishes expressed by the Chinese Mission, there is nothing to prevent the maintenance of a rotation system. The Tribunal considers that a rotation system is not unlawful *per se*. ... But in the opinion of the Tribunal, the rotation system must be established on a precise legal basis—through secondment in accordance with the terms governing secondment and without ruling out career appointments pursuant to GA Resolution 37/126.

XXXIV. Accordingly, the Tribunal can only reject the Respondent's contention that the mere existence of the rotation system would prohibit career appointments.

XXXV. The Tribunal appreciates the Administration's concern that "it is of critical importance ... that [the] representatives [of China] have full confidence that their statements both oral and written, will be objectively and fairly rendered, interpreted or reported."

XXXVI. But the Tribunal notes that during the period when the career appointments of the Applicants were considered ... no complaint was levelled against them concerning their performance. The reason invoked by the Administration for denying appointments to the Applicants is based on inaccuracy, if not an error.

XXXVII. The Tribunal has also taken into account the terms of the letter addressed to the Applicants on 15 January 1990, on behalf of the Secretary-General, by the Acting Under-Secretary-General for Administration and Management:

> The efficient functioning of the Chinese language services would not be possible in a situation where staff members were antagonistic to each other because of expressly stated political animosities.

But the Tribunal notes that no act of this nature has been alleged against the Applicants. It notes moreover that the Applicants have never failed to maintain the discretion incumbent upon them as international civil servants. Even during 1989, no such complaint against them was made by their Government. Lastly, the Tribunal notes that nothing has been shown to indicate the possibility of such a problem arising in the future.

XXXVIII. In the opinion of the Tribunal, the Respondent's assumptions in this respect lack any factual basis. The Applicants' record as international civil servants, as recognized by the Administration itself, shows that they are devoid of any substance. They constitute arbitrary suspicions on the future conduct of the Applicants. The Applicants are being disciplined by the denial of appointments, for potential misconduct. The Tribunal considers that the Applicants are being tried for their imputed intentions. An attitude of irresponsibility is ascribed to international civil servants who, during many years of service, have not given the slightest justification for such a charge.

XXXIX. The Tribunal moreover recalls that the Secretary-General has the necessary powers to prevent any irresponsible conduct on the part of the staff under his authority.

XL. The Respondent acknowledges that discussions took place with representatives of the Chinese Mission throughout the period beginning on 1 May 1989. The Tribunal takes note that following those discussions, the Secretary-General denied the Applicants career appointments on 12 December 1989.

XLI. The Tribunal finds that the Secretary-General accepted the Chinese Mission's position that the Applicants should be denied an extension of their fixed-term contracts or be offered career appointments.

The Tribunal has shown that, in the absence of the necessary criteria for secondment consistent with case-law, it was not permissible for the Secretary-General to take into account the Chinese Mission's opposition to the renewal of the fixed-term contracts.

As regards career appointments, the Tribunal considers that these were withheld because of the Chinese Mission's position concerning the rotation system. The Tribunal notes that, in the opinion of the Chinese Mission, the rotation system categorically ruled out career appointments. The Tribunal considers that the Secretary-General could not defer to this opposition by the Chinese Mission without being in breach of his obligations under the Charter and the Staff Rules and Regulations, as well as under General Assembly resolutions 37/126 and 38/232 (see para. XXXIII).

XLII. Consequently, the Tribunal finds that the Secretary-General's decision to refuse the Applicants' request for career appointments exceeds the limits of his discretion. His decision is based on reasons which are contrary to the interests of the United Nations, erroneous or inaccurate as to fact, and specious. It ignores the basic principles of the international civil service, as enunciated in Articles 100 and 101 of the Charter. . . .

XLIII. The Tribunal considers that the Secretary-General wrongly refused the Applicants career appointments, contrary to GA Resolutions 37/126 and 38/232. . . .

XLVIII. For these reasons, the Tribunal: . . .

2. Rescinds the decision taken by the Secretary-General on 12 December 1989, and confirmed on 15 January 1990, not to grant the Applicants career appointments in the circumstances provided for in General Assembly resolutions 37/126 and 38/232, and decides that they should be granted such appointments as from 1 February 1990.

3. Fixes the compensation to be paid to each of the Applicants at three years' net base salary of the Applicants as at the date of their separation from service, if the Secretary-General decides, within 30 days of the notification of the Judgment, in the interest of the United Nations, not to grant the Applicants career appointments.

Declaration by Jerome Ackerman, First Vice President

Having signed the Judgment in this case, of course, I agree with it entirely. I should like to note, in addition, that had the Tribunal thought it necessary to address the Applicants' contentions concerning the procedure established by the Administration . . . I would have deemed it axiomatic that such a procedure must observe the requirements of due process including the absence of discrimination . . . I believe that the Applicants were not accorded the due process to which they were entitled.

In my view it is also regrettable, to put it mildly, that there should be even so much as an appearance that this entire affair might be related to humanitarian pleas made by them.

After the end of the Cold War, the issue of secondment largely lost its controversial nature. Member states, notably Russia and China, that used to insist on secondment of their nationals have since changed their practice fundamentally and now permit permanent appointments.[19]

A different kind of problem emerged during the 1990s, which was the provision of gratis personnel. A response to budgetary constraints at a time of increased activity, the provision of personnel to the Organization at no cost was initially accepted, but soon raised questions about the ability of such personnel to work independently and impartially. A related concern

---

[19] Christian Ebner, "Article 100", in Bruno Simma et al. (eds), *The Charter of the United Nations: A Commentary*, 3rd edn (Oxford: Oxford University Press, 2012), 2022, 2037–2038.

was that such personnel disproportionately came from a small number of developed countries.

The UN Special Commission (UNSCOM) that was created to conduct weapons inspections in Iraq included a significant number of gratis personnel, leading to allegations that its members were not able to carry out their duties objectively.[20] When the Security Council created a successor institution, the UN Monitoring, Verification and Inspection Commission (UNMOVIC), it sought to ensure that UN officials were responsible only to the United Nations.

SECURITY COUNCIL RESOLUTION 1284 (1999)

The Security Council, . . .

1. *Decides* to establish, as a subsidiary body of the Council, the United Nations Monitoring, Verification and Inspection Commission (UNMOVIC) which replaces the Special Commission established pursuant to paragraph 9 (b) of resolution 687 (1991); . . .

5. *Requests* the Secretary-General, within 30 days of the adoption of this resolution, to appoint, after consultation with and subject to the approval of the Council, an Executive Chairman of UNMOVIC who will take up his mandated tasks as soon as possible, and, in consultation with the Executive Chairman and the Council members, to appoint suitably qualified experts as a College of Commissioners for UNMOVIC which will meet regularly to review the implementation of this and other relevant resolutions and provide professional advice and guidance to the Executive Chairman, including on significant policy decisions and on written reports to be submitted to the Council through the Secretary-General;

6. *Requests* the Executive Chairman of UNMOVIC, within 45 days of his appointment, to submit to the Council, in consultation with and through the Secretary-General, for its approval an organizational plan for UNMOVIC, including its structure, staffing requirements, management guidelines, recruitment and training procedures, incorporating as appropriate the recommendations of the panel on disarmament and current and future ongoing monitoring and verification issues, and recognizing in particular the need for an effective, cooperative management structure for the new organization, for staffing with suitably qualified and experienced personnel, who would be regarded as international civil servants subject to Article 100 of the Charter of the United Nations, drawn from the broadest possible

---

[20] Simon Chesterman, *One Nation under Surveillance: A New Social Contract to Defend Freedom without Sacrificing Liberty* (Oxford: Oxford University Press, 2011), 176–179.

geographical base, including as he deems necessary from international arms control organizations, and for the provision of high quality technical and cultural training . . .

The fact that the Secretariat is independent of national jurisdictions meant that the United Nations needed to create its own procedures for resolving internal disputes. The UNAT, which decided the *Chinese Translators* case was later replaced by a two-tier system that included a right of appeal and became operational in 2009.[21] This now comprises the UN Dispute Tribunal and the UN Appeals Tribunal.

The operations of this dispute resolution system can be seen in the case of Robert Hepworth, who joined the UN Environment Program (UNEP) in 2000 as Deputy Director of the Division of Environmental Conventions in Nairobi, Kenya. In 2004 he accepted an appointment as Acting Executive Secretary at the Executive Office of the Convention on Migratory Species (CMS). The CMS office is located in Bonn, Germany, so he relocated with his family. He successfully applied for the Executive Secretary position in 2005 and was appointed for a two-year term, which was renewed in 2007. In 2009 he was not offered a further extension but was reassigned back to Nairobi. He alleged that this was due to interference by the German government.

The Tribunal ultimately[22] held that Hepworth had a legitimate expectation that his contract would be renewed, and then turned to the question of whether the decision not to renew it was based on extraneous or irrelevant factors.

HEPWORTH v. SECRETARY-GENERAL OF THE UNITED NATIONS, UNITED NATIONS DISPUTE TRIBUNAL, 29 NOVEMBER 2013[23]

59. The Applicant alleges unlawful extraneous motivation for the Non-renewal Decision in the form of political pressure from Germany in relation to his role as Executive Secretary of CMS. In this regard the letter

---

[21] UNAT has provided for review of judgments by way of an ICJ advisory opinion, but this was regarded as not having "proved to be a constructive or useful element in the adjudication of staff disputes within the Organization." GA Res. 50/54 (1995), preamble.

[22] For earlier proceedings, see *Hepworth* UN Dispute Tribunal Judgment No.: UNDT/2010/193 and *Hepworth* UN Appeals Tribunal Judgment No. 2011-UNAT-178, available at: http://www.un.org/en/oaj.

[23] UN Dispute Tribunal Case No.: UNDT/NBI/2012/009, Judgment No. UNDT/2013/151, available at: http://www.un.org/en/oaj.

from the State Secretary of [the German Environment Ministry (BMU)] to the Executive Director dated 2 July 2008 is most telling and revealing. The letter alleged that, following the letter from the Ministry to the Applicant raising concerns about the outcomes of the 32nd meeting of the CMS Standing Committee, staff members of the CMS Secretariat were forbidden from communicating with the Ministry. The letter from BMU also accused the Applicant of beginning an "extensive campaign in which he accused Germany/the [Ministry]—and voiced those accusations to other Contracting Parties—of breaking various UN rules ... and of violating rules of protocol". It further provided:

> The latest incident, [the Applicant's] mail of 23 April 2008, which you have also seen, shows the behaviour of the Executive Secretary to be absolutely unacceptable. ...
> You will appreciate that Germany cannot tolerate the Executive Secretary damaging the international reputation of Germany and the UN city of Bonn, as has repeatedly happened over the past few weeks at least among the Parties to the Convention.
> I am turning to you, Executive Director, in order to avert permanent damage to the Convention on the Conservation of Migratory Species of Wild Animals. ...
> It is our wish to find a solution to this problem as quickly as possible which is satisfactory and constructive for all concerned.

60. By letter dated 13 August 2008, the Executive Director[24] wrote to the Applicant referring to the letter from BMU and the allegations contained therein. The Executive Director described the letter from BMU as raising "serious complaints against ... your conduct as the Executive Secretary of the CMS and refers to unacceptable insinuations made by yourself". The Executive Director also asked the Applicant "to refrain from any contact or communication with the Government of Germany in this respect".

61. The strength of the words used in the letter from BMU to the Executive Director of UNEP is striking and the message was couched in no uncertain terms: the German Government was unhappy with the Applicant and clearly expressed the desire to "find a solution to this problem as quickly as possible". Whilst a Member State may express opinions to the United Nations, it is impermissible for the Administration to yield to a demand by a Member State when to do so is not in the interests of economy and efficiency and of the Organization ... Article 100.1 of the Charter explicitly prohibits United Nations staff from receiving instructions from any government. Allowing a government to influence an internal staffing decision would constitute an improper exercise of discretion and an impermissible extraneous motivation.

---

[24] Achim Steiner, himself a German (and Brazilian) national. (footnote added.)

62. The question then is whether there is evidence that the Non-renewal Decision was influenced by pressure from the German Government. Just because the German Environment Ministry conveyed a desire for the "problem" of the Applicant to be dealt with does not mean that the Executive Director acted on it. In this connection the Executive Director very candidly explained at the hearing that national governments regularly raise issues and express concerns about situations. According to the Respondent, general concerns about management or direction of environmental entities are frequently expressed.

63. The Applicant testified that he had a tense relationship with BMU but not with the other branches of the German Government. He testified that at the beginning of 2009 he was elected chairman of all United Nations agencies in Germany and that the German Government reacted quite positively to his election, unlike BMU. If at all, the main source of the problem was the tense relationship between BMU and the Applicant and not between him and the German Government. In his letter to the Applicant dated 13 August 2008, the Executive Director requested a meeting with the Applicant on 4 September 2008 at UNEP Headquarters in Nairobi. The Applicant was not able to fly to Nairobi for the meeting due to health reasons.

64. On 17 February 2010, the Tribunal requested that the Respondent provide a copy of the response by the Executive Director to the 2 July 2008 letter. UNEP replied to that request stating that after discussions between the Federal Environment Ministry and the Executive Director on 22 August 2008 at UNEP Headquarters, "the necessity for a direct response in writing ... became obsolete". At the hearing of this case, the Executive Director testified that UNEP and the Federal Environment Ministry had agreed to "de-escalate" the matter without a formal response. The proposal was for a meeting to take place between the Applicant, possibly other CMS members, and the Federal Environment Ministry where issues could be addressed openly. The Executive Director testified that if no resolution could be found, he had agreed to respond formally to Germany's letter. No meeting ever took place between the Applicant and the Federal Environment Ministry, nor was an official response provided to Germany by UNEP.

65. That no formal response was provided to a letter raising serious allegations by a Member State about a UNEP staff member strikes the Tribunal as odd. Even if the matter was resolved informally as the Respondent claims, the Tribunal has seen no evidence that the Applicant had any meaningful involvement in this process.

66. In addition to the letters, the Tribunal had the benefit of the testimony of Mr. Müller-Helmbrecht, former Executive Secretary of the CMS, who performed a small amount of work for the Secretariat in 2008. Mr. Müller-Helmbrecht provided evidence that BMU knew of the Applicant's departure from Bonn before the Conference of the Parties in 2008. In a memorandum dated 18 May 2010, Mr. Müller-Helmbrecht claimed that

he had an informal meeting with a staff member of BMU in Bonn on 10 September 2008. He claimed that the staff member spoke exclusively about the Ministry's concerns about the Applicant relating to recruitment of staff for the CMS Secretariat, possible aversion to Germans and the decentralisation of the CMS Secretariat.

67. Mr. Müller-Helmbrecht further claimed that on 8 March 2010 he bumped into a former colleague who was then working for the Ministry. That colleague allegedly informed Mr. Müller-Helmbrecht that his Head of Department had mentioned in an internal routine meeting in November 2008 that the Applicant would be returning to Nairobi to take over another United Nations post. The Applicant claims that this evidence shows that the decision to transfer the Applicant was made, and conveyed to the Ministry, at least three months before it was raised with the Applicant himself.

68. The evidence of Mr. Müller-Helmbrecht on the attitude of the German Government towards the Applicant consists only of hearsay. Evidence of hearsay is not by itself inadmissible before the Tribunal. If this were the case the Tribunal would lose the benefit of crucial relevant and probative evidence. The weight of such evidence should however carefully be considered given its nature. Great care should be exercised before placing any weight on such evidence when the hearsay evidence seeks to establish serious allegations or grave concerns against an individual, an institution or a national government.

69. Bearing the need for cautious treatment of hearsay evidence in mind, the Tribunal finds that Mr. Müller-Helmbrecht's testimony is direct evidence of what he was told by a member of the BMU. Although Mr. Müller-Helmbrecht was uncertain of the specific date of the conversation, he was extremely specific about the event at which it occurred. What Mr. Müller-Helmbrecht was told was also pinpointed relative to a major event. Indeed, it was the very sequence of events that made it memorable to Mr. Müller-Helmbrecht and his interlocutor. The Tribunal has no reason to believe that either Mr. Müller-Helmbrecht or his interlocutor simply fabricated this information. No good reason exists on the state of the evidence for such a conclusion.

70. The lack of reasons for the Non-renewal Decision (and the resulting burden of proof on the Respondent), together with the circumstantial evidence described above has led the Tribunal to find that the Non-renewal Decision was vitiated by improper motivation, namely a desire to move the Applicant out of Bonn to placate the German Federal Environment Ministry. The circumstantial evidence of particular pertinence is: the personal allegations made by the German Environment Ministry against the Applicant and a clearly expressed desire to deal with the "problem"; the timing around the advertising of the Special Advisor position (see below); the lack of any formal response to the allegations made by Germany in relation to the Applicant; the Applicant's resistance to the transfer; the Applicant's strong performance

reviews as Executive Secretary of the CMS; and the absence of an immediate replacement.

71. The Tribunal concludes on the issue of absence of reasons that the burden resting on the Respondent to establish on a preponderance of probabilities that he was not motivated by extraneous factors in not renewing the contract of the Applicant was not met. Given the tense relationship between BMU and the Applicant, the Respondent should have offered reasons for the Non-renewal Decision in order to allay any concerns about improper motivation. ...

114. The Applicant has successfully shown that the Non-renewal Decision was based on unlawful grounds. The Tribunal is satisfied that he suffered harm to his career in that the Non-renewal Decision deprived him of his livelihood at a time when he was near the mandatory retirement age. The Tribunal therefore orders as follows:

a. Since the Applicant was two years from retirement age and had, for most of his time with the Organization, been granted two-year renewals of his fixed-term appointment, the Respondent must pay the Applicant all the Applicant's retirement benefits calculated as if the Applicant had retired from the Organization at the age of 62;

b. The Respondent must pay the Applicant compensation in the amount of one year's net base salary; and

c. All other pleas are rejected.

QUESTIONS

13. Does the impartiality of the Secretariat require that its personnel be hired without any regard for the opinion of the state of their nationality regarding their suitability or political acceptability? Is that what the UN Administrative Tribunal decided?

14. Did the UNAT interpret correctly the requirements of the UN Charter in the *Chinese Translators* case? Does its decision make for good policy? Does UN service require only that its civil servants be impartial, or that they also be seen to be impartial by the member states?

15. Does the Secretary-General have a right to require his or her staff to maintain a discreet silence as to controversial political issues arising in their home states? Why, or why not?

16. Based on your reading of the *Hepworth* decision, how should the United Nations respond when a host government (or a relevant ministry) objects to the performance of a senior official?

Further Reading

Annan, Kofi. *Interventions: A Life in War and Peace*. New York: Penguin, 2012.

Bailey, Sydney D. *The Secretariat of the United Nations*. New York: Carnegie Endowment for International Peace, 1962.

Boutros-Ghali, Boutros. *Unvanquished: A US-UN Saga*. New York: Random House, 1999.

Chesterman, Simon (ed). *Secretary or General? The UN Secretary-General in World Politics*. Cambridge: Cambridge University Press, 2007.

Franck, Thomas M. "The Secretary-General's Role in Conflict Resolution: Past, Present and Pure Conjecture." *European Journal of International Law*, vol. 6 (1995), p. 360.

Franck, Thomas M. and Georg Nolte. "The Good Offices Function of the UN Secretary-General." In Adam Roberts and Benedict Kingsbury (eds), *United Nations, Divided World: The UN's Roles in International Relations* 2nd edn. Oxford: Clarendon Press, 1993, p. 143.

Froehlich, Manuel. *Political Ethics and the United Nations: Dag Hammarskjöld as Secretary-General*. New York: Routledge, 2008.

Gordenker, Leon. *The UN Secretary-General and Secretariat*. 2nd edn. New York: Routledge, 2013.

Hammarskjöld, Dag. "The International Civil Servant in Law and in Fact (Lecture Delivered to Congregation at Oxford University, 30 May 1961)." In Wilder Foote (ed), *Servant of Peace: A Selection of the Speeches and Statements of Dag Hammarskjöld, Secretary-General of the United Nations 1953–1961*. New York: Harper and Row, 1962, pp. 329–349.

Johnstone, Ian. "The Role of the UN Secretary-General: The Power of Persuasion Based on Law." *Global Governance*, vol. 9 (2003), p. 441.

Newman, Edward. *The UN Secretary-General from the Cold War to the New Era: A Global Peace and Security Mandate*. New York: Palgrave Macmillan, 1998.

Ramcharan, Bertrand G. *Humanitarian Good Offices in International Law: The Good Offices of the United Nations Secretary-General in the Field of Human Rights*. The Hague: Martinus Nijhoff, 1983.

Schwebel, Stephen M. *The Secretary-General of the United Nations: His Political Powers and Practice*. Cambridge, MA: Harvard University Press, 1952.

Szasz, Paul C. "The Role of the UN Secretary-General: Some Legal Aspects." *New York University Journal of International Law and Politics*, vol. 24 (1991), p. 161.

Thant, Myint-U and Amy Scott. *The UN Secretariat: A Brief History*. New York: International Peace Academy, 2007.

Traub, James, *The Best Intentions: Kofi Annan and the UN in the Era of American World Power*. New York: Farrar, Straus & Giroux, 2006.

Urquhart, Brian, *Hammarskjöld*. New York: Knopf, 1972.

Viñuales, Jorge E. *The UN Secretary General between Law and Politics: Towards an Analytical Framework for Interdisciplinary Research*. Geneva: Graduate Institute of International Studies, 2005.

chapter six
. . . .

Membership

Membership is a basic constitutional characteristic of any intergovernmental organization. Is the organization open to all states, or to some only? If the latter, is it limited by geography, function, religious or historical association, or in some other way? Who decides whether the criteria for membership have been met, and how? The United Nations aspires to universal membership and is a multipurpose organization in the sense that its mandate covers almost every area of international activity. That does not mean, however, that every state is entitled to join. There are conditions for membership, set out in Articles 4–6 of the UN Charter.

Article 4(1), on admission, reads:

> Membership in the United Nations is open to all other peace-loving states which accept the obligations contained in the present Charter and, in the judgment of the Organization, are able and willing to carry out these obligations.

Article 5, on suspension, states:

> A Member of the United Nations against which preventive or enforcement action is taken by the Security Council may be suspended from the exercise of the rights and privileges of membership...

Article 6, on expulsion, provides that:

> A Member of the UN which has persistently violated the Principles contained in the present Charter may be expelled from the Organization...

In all cases of admission, suspension, and expulsion, decisions are to be taken by the General Assembly upon the recommendation of the Security Council—so the veto applies. In the early years of the United Nations admission was a major issue, with each side in the Cold War opposing candidates of the other for political reasons. The situation changed in the mid-1970s, and since then few admissions cases have been contested. There are exceptions, of course—notably Palestine and Taiwan—but the debates around those cases rarely turn on whether the criteria in Article 4 have been met.

Meanwhile, mainly because of the veto threat, there has never been a case of formal suspension or expulsion from the United Nations.

As a result, some of the most interesting cases to be discussed here did not involve membership per se, but rather denial of the right to participate in the organization in some other way. Most of these cases are either about succession (when a UN member state breaks apart) or rival claimants (when two governments insist they are the rightful occupants of a state's seat). The cases are interesting from a legal point of view because the UN Charter offers little direct guidance on how to address them. They are interesting from a policy point of view because they illustrate how restrictions on participation can be used as a kind of sanction, registering disapproval of a regime or its policies. This in turn raises interesting questions about the evolving nature of sovereignty: In its membership policy, does and should the UN engage with any government that has effective authority over territory, or should it ask questions about how that government came to power, and how it governs?

6.1 Admission

In the early years of the Cold War, the Soviet Union and its allies, badly outnumbered in the General Assembly by Western states, tried in various ways to prevent the voting majority from blocking its own candidates for membership. Among other things, it used its veto power in the Security Council to block any new Western-sponsored states, threatening to continue doing so unless candidates from the Eastern (Soviet) bloc were also admitted as members.

By its insistence that no new states would be admitted unless all applicants entered together in a "package deal," the Soviet Union precipitated the first crisis regarding membership. In an effort to break the deadlock, the General Assembly referred the matter to the International Court of Justice (ICJ) for an advisory opinion. The Court was asked to consider whether the criteria listed in Article 4(1) were exhaustive—or may a member state, when called upon to vote on an application for membership, make its consent dependent on conditions not expressly provided for in that article? In particular, could a state make its support for the membership of one state conditional on other states also being allowed to join the United Nations?[1]

---

[1] The exact question before the Court was as follows: "Is a Member of the United Nations which is called upon, in virtue of Article 4 of the Charter, to pronounce itself by its vote, either in the Security Council or in the General Assembly, on the admission of a State to membership in the United Nations, juridically entitled to make its consent to the admission dependent on conditions not expressly provided by paragraph 1 of the said Article? In particular, can such a Member, while it recognizes the conditions set forth in that provision to be fulfilled by the State concerned, subject its affirmative vote to the additional condition that other States be admitted to membership in the United Nations together with that State?"

The Court answered both questions by a majority of nine votes to six—a division that reflected the political split in the General Assembly.

CONDITIONS OF ADMISSION OF A STATE TO MEMBERSHIP IN THE UNITED NATIONS (ADVISORY OPINION), 1948 ICJ REPORTS 57

The requisite conditions are five in number: to be admitted to membership in the United Nations an Applicant must 1) be a State; 2) be peace-loving; 3) accept the obligations of the Charter; 4) be able to carry out these obligations; and 5) be willing to do so.

All these conditions are subject to the judgment of the Organization. The judgment of the Organization means the judgment of the two organs mentioned in paragraph 2 of Article 4, and in the last analysis, that of its Members. The question put is concerned with the individual attitude of each Member called upon to pronounce itself on the question of admission.

Having been asked to determine the character, exhaustive or otherwise of the conditions stated in Article 4, the Court must in the first place consider the text of that Article ... The text of this paragraph, by the enumeration which it contains and the choice of its terms, clearly demonstrates the intention of its authors to establish a legal rule which, while it fixes the conditions of admission, determines also the reasons for which admission may be refused; for the text does not differentiate between these two cases and any attempt to restrict it to one of them would be purely arbitrary.

... The natural meaning of the words used [in both the English and the French texts] leads to the conclusion that these conditions constitute an exhaustive enumeration and are not merely stated by way of guidance or example. The provision would lose its significance and weight, if other conditions, unconnected with those laid down, could be demanded. The condition stated in paragraph 1 of Article 4 must therefore be regarded not merely as the necessary conditions, but also as the conditions which suffice.

Nor can it be argued that the conditions enumerated represent only an indispensable minimum, in the sense that political considerations can be superimposed upon them, and prevent the admission of an applicant which fulfils them. Such an interpretation would be inconsistent with the terms of paragraph 2 of Article 4, which provide for the admission of ... "any *such* State." It would lead to conferring upon Members an indefinite and practically unlimited power of discretion in the imposition of new conditions. Such a power would be inconsistent with the very character of paragraph 1 of Article 4, which, by reason of the close connection it establishes between membership and the observance of the principles and obligations of the

Charter, clearly constitutes a legal regulation of the question of the admission of new States. ....

It does not, however, follow from the exhaustive character of Article 4 that an appreciation is precluded of such circumstances of fact as would enable the existence of the requisite conditions to be verified.

Article 4 does not forbid the taking into account of any factor which it is possible reasonably and in good faith to connect with the conditions laid down. The taking into account of such factors is implied in the very wide and very elastic nature of the prescribed conditions; no relevant political factor—that is to say, none connected with the conditions of admissions—is excluded. ....

The second part of the question, concerns a demand on the part of a Member making its consent to the admission of an applicant, dependent on the admission of other applicants.

Judged on the basis of the rule which the Court adopts in its interpretation of Article 4, such a demand constitutes a new condition, since it is entirely unconnected with those prescribed in Article 4. It is also in an entirely different category from those conditions, since it makes admission dependent, not on the conditions required of applicants, qualifications which are supposed to be fulfilled, but on an extraneous consideration concerning States other than the applicant State.

The provisions of Article 4 necessarily imply that every application for admission should be examined and voted on separately and on its own merits; otherwise it would be impossible to determine whether a particular applicant fulfils the necessary conditions. To subject an affirmative vote for the admission of an applicant State to the condition that other States be admitted would prevent Members from exercising their judgment in each case with complete liberty, within the scope of the prescribed conditions. Such a demand is incompatible with the letter and spirit of Article 4 of the Charter.

Dissenting Opinion of Judges Basdevant, Winiarski, Sir Arnold McNair, and Read

The provisions of paragraph 2 of Article 4, which fix the respective powers of the General Assembly and the Security Council in this matter, do not treat the admission of new Members as a mere matter of the routine application of rules of admission ... In the working of this system the Charter requires the intervention of the two principal political organs of the United Nations, one for the purpose of making a recommendation and then the other for the purpose of effecting the admission. It is impossible by means of interpretation to regard these organs as mere pieces of procedural machinery like the Committee for Admissions established by the Security Council. . .

The resolutions which embody either a recommendation or a decision in regard to admission are decisions of a political character; they emanate from political organs; by general consent they involve the examination of political factors, with a view to deciding whether the applicant State possesses the qualifications prescribed by paragraph 1 of Article 4; they produce a political effect by changing the condition of the applicant State in making it a Member of the United Nations. Upon the Security Council, whose duty it is to make the recommendation, there rests by the provisions of Article 24 of the Charter "primary responsibility for the maintenance of international peace and security"... The admission of a new Member is pre-eminently a political act, and a political act of the greatest importance. The main function of a political organ is to examine questions in their political aspect, which means examining them from every point of view. It follows that the Members of such an organ who are responsible for forming its decisions must consider questions from every aspect, and, in consequence, are legally entitled to base their arguments and their vote upon political considerations. That is the position of a member of the Security Council or of the General Assembly who raises an objection based upon reasons other than the lack of one of the qualifications expressly required by paragraph 1 of Article 4.

That does not mean that no legal restriction is placed upon this liberty. We do not claim that a political organ and those who contribute to the formation of its decisions are emancipated from all duty to respect the law. The Security Council, the General Assembly and the Members who contribute by their votes to the decisions of these bodies are clearly bound to respect paragraph 1 of Article 4, and, in consequence, bound not to admit a State which fails to possess the conditions required in this paragraph. ....

In our opinion, while the Charter makes the qualifications specified in paragraph 1 of Article 4 essential, it does not make them sufficient. If it had regarded them as sufficient, it would not have failed to say so. The point was one of too great importance to be left in obscurity...

A consideration based on the desire that the admission of the State should involve the contemporaneous admission of other States is clearly foreign to the process of ascertaining that the first State possesses the qualifications laid down in Article 4, paragraph 1; it is a political consideration. If a Member of the United Nations is legally entitled to make its refusal to admit depend on political considerations, that is exactly what the Member would be doing in this case.

As the advisory opinion noted, Article 4 includes five criteria: (1) statehood,[2] (2) being peace-loving, (3) acceptance of the obligations of the Charter, (4) ability to carry out those obligations, and (5) willingness to do so. It ruled that rejecting admission on purely political grounds was impermissible—that only criteria set out in Article 4(1) should be applied.

---

[2] According to the 1933 Montevideo Convention on the Rights and Duties of States, the criteria for statehood are: (1) permanent population, (2) defined territory, (3) government, and (4) capacity to enter into relations with other states.

In a number of cases, these criteria were invoked to deny membership, even though the real motivation may have been political. In 1971, for example, China blocked the admission of Bangladesh (formerly East Pakistan). It had political reasons for doing so, but its legal case was plausible: by not complying with Security Council resolution 307 demanding the repatriation of prisoners of war, Bangladesh was evincing an unwillingness to accept or carry out Charter obligations.

When Angola applied for admission in 1976, the United States blocked it on the grounds that it did not meet the requirements of Article 4. Given the presence of Cuban troops, three possible arguments could be and were made: (1) Angola was not "peace-loving"; (2) Cuban influence was such that Angola was not really an independent government able to carry out its Charter obligations; and (3) Angola was demonstrating unwillingness to carry out its Charter obligations to settle international disputes peacefully (Article 2(3) and Article 33). In the end, the United States gave up the fight "out of respect for sentiments expressed by our African friends," and Angola joined later that year.

QUESTIONS

1. An Advisory Opinion rendered by the Court is not binding on the requesting organ of the United Nations or on any other organ. Article 65 of the Statute of the ICJ makes provision for the Court's jurisdiction to give such opinions and to render its "advisory functions" (art. 68). Must the court accede to such a request? May there be circumstances in which it would be wise to refuse to provide such advice? Was it useful for the Court to render the 1948 opinion on conditions of admission? As states do not have to explain their votes in the principal political organs (the General Assembly and the Security Council), what would be the likely effect of the opinion given by the Court?

2. The deadlock over admissions was resolved in 1955 by an agreement between the Western and the Soviet blocs to admit sixteen nations simultaneously, by the very "package deal" rejected by the Court.[3] Was this a violation of the Charter, or was it a sensible interpretation of the rules by the members of the Security Council? What is the legal effect of such a "reinterpretation" of the Charter by the members of the Security Council?

3. Would it be acceptable for a state to vote against the admission of an applicant on the ground that it is not democratic? Is it plausible that a non-democratic state be presumed not to be "peace-loving"?

---

[3] UN Doc. S/13509 (1955); GA Res. 995(X) (1955).

The question of the admission of Palestine as a member has been on the agenda of the United Nations for many years. In 1974 the Palestine Liberation Organization (PLO) was granted observer status—before then, only non-member *states* and intergovernmental organizations had that status. As an observer "entity," the PLO was granted the right to participate in the work of the General Assembly and international conferences convened by the General Assembly or other UN organs.[4] As with other observers, this meant it had access to meetings but not the right to speak or vote. In 1988 the General Assembly changed its designation from PLO to Palestine, and granted it the right to circulate documents.[5] In 1998, its status was upgraded again to allow it to participate fully in the organization, but not to vote. The vote on the 1998 resolution was 124 in favor, four opposed (Israel, United States, Marshall Islands, and Micronesia) and 10 abstentions (a mix of states).

GENERAL ASSEMBLY RESOLUTION 52/250 (1998): PARTICIPATION OF PALESTINE IN THE WORK OF THE UNITED NATIONS

The General Assembly, . . .

Aware also that general democratic Palestinian elections were held on 20 January 1996 and that the Palestinian Authority was established on part of the occupied Palestinian territory,

Desirous of contributing to the achievement of the inalienable rights of the Palestinian people, thus attaining a just and comprehensive peace in the Middle East,

1. *Decides* to confer upon Palestine, in its capacity as observer, and as contained in the annex to the present resolution, additional rights and privileges of participation in the sessions and work of the General Assembly and the international conferences convened under the auspices of the Assembly or other organs of the United Nations, as well as in United Nations conferences . . .

ANNEX

The additional rights and privileges of participation of Palestine shall be effected through the following modalities, without prejudice to the existing rights and privileges:

1. The right to participate in the general debate of the General Assembly.

---

[4] GA Res. 3237(XXIX) (1974) on observer status for the Palestine Liberation Organization.
[5] GA Res. 43/177 (1988) on the question of Palestine.

2. Without prejudice to the priority of Member States, Palestine shall have the right of inscription on the list of speakers under agenda items other than Palestinian and Middle East issues at any plenary meeting of the General Assembly, after the last Member State inscribed on the list of that meeting.

3. The right of reply.

4. The right to raise points of order related to the proceedings on Palestinian and Middle East issues, provided that the right to raise such a point of order shall not include the right to challenge the decision of the presiding officer.

5. The right to co-sponsor draft resolutions and decisions on Palestinian and Middle East issues. Such draft resolutions and decisions shall be put to a vote only upon request from a Member State.

6. The right to make interventions, with a precursory explanation or the recall of relevant General Assembly resolutions being made only once by the President of the General Assembly at the start of each session of the Assembly. . . .

8. Palestine shall not have the right to vote or to put forward candidates.

In September 2011, Palestine applied for full membership to the United Nations.

LETTER RECEIVED ON 23 SEPTEMBER 2011 FROM THE PRESIDENT OF PALESTINE TO THE SECRETARY-GENERAL[6]

I have the profound honour, on behalf of the Palestinian people, to submit this application of the State of Palestine for admission to membership in the United Nations.

This application for membership is being submitted based on the Palestinian people's natural, legal and historic rights and based on United Nations General Assembly resolution 181 (II) of 29 November 1947 as well as the Declaration of Independence of the State of Palestine of 15 November 1988 and the acknowledgement by the General Assembly of this Declaration in resolution 43/177 of 15 December 1988.

In this connection, the State of Palestine affirms its commitment to the achievement of a just, lasting and comprehensive resolution of the Israeli-Palestinian conflict based on the vision of two-States living side by side in peace and security, as endorsed by the United Nations Security Council and General Assembly and the international community as a whole and based on international law and all relevant United Nations resolutions.

(*Signed*) Mahmoud Abbas
President of the State of Palestine

---

[6] UN Doc A/66/371–S/2011/592 (2011), Annex.

Declaration

In connection with the application of the State of Palestine for admission to membership in the United Nations, I have the honour, in my capacity as the President of the State of Palestine and as the Chairman of the Executive Committee of the Palestine Liberation Organization, the sole legitimate representative of the Palestinian people, to solemnly declare that the State of Palestine is a peace-loving nation and that it accepts the obligations contained in the Charter of the United Nations and solemnly undertakes to fulfill them.

The matter was referred to the Security Council's Committee on the Admission of New Members in accordance with Article 59 of the provisional rules of procedure. The job of this committee is to consider before reporting back to the Council whether an applicant meets the eligibility requirements for membership. It is composed of the entire Council membership and operates by simple majority vote—in other words, the veto power does not apply. The following document is a summary of discussions in the Committee.

REPORT OF THE COMMITTEE ON THE ADMISSION OF NEW MEMBERS CONCERNING THE APPLICATION OF PALESTINE FOR ADMISSION TO MEMBERSHIP IN THE UNITED NATIONS[7]

3. [T]he Presidency of the Security Council for the month of October (Nigeria) convened five informal meetings of the Committee, four of which were held at the expert level, to carefully consider whether Palestine met the ... criteria for statehood, was a peace-loving State, and was willing and able to carry out the obligations contained in the Charter.

4. In the course of the meetings of the Committee, differing views were expressed. The view was expressed that the applicant fulfills all the criteria set out in the Charter ...

5. It was stated that the criteria set out in Article 4 of the Charter were the only factors that could be taken into consideration in the Committee's deliberations. In support of this position, reference was made to the Advisory Opinion of 28 May 1948 of the International Court of Justice, on the Conditions of Admission of a State to Membership in the United Nations (Article 4 of the Charter).

---

[7] UN Doc S/2011/705 (2011).

6. It was also asserted that the Committee's work, whatever its outcome, should be mindful of the broader political context...

7. It was stated that the Committee's work should not harm the prospects of the resumption of peace talks, particularly in the light of the Quartet statement on 23 September 2011 that had set out a clear timetable for the resumption of negotiations. Similarly, it was stated that the prospect of negotiations should not delay the Security Council's consideration of Palestine's application. It was stated that Palestine's application was neither detrimental to the political process nor an alternative to negotiations. It was also stated that the Palestinian application would not bring the parties closer to peace. It was further stated that the question of the recognition of Palestinian statehood could not and should not be subject to the outcome of negotiations between the Palestinians and Israelis, and that, otherwise, Palestinian statehood would be made dependent on the approval of Israel, which would grant the occupying Power a right of veto over the right to self-determination of the Palestinian people, which has been recognized by the General Assembly as an inalienable right since 1974...

15. With regard to the requirement that an applicant be "peace-loving", the view was expressed that Palestine fulfilled this criterion in view of its commitment to the achievement of a just, lasting and comprehensive resolution of the Israeli-Palestinian conflict. It was further stated that Palestine's fulfillment of this criterion was also evident in its commitment to resuming negotiations on all final status issues on the basis of the internationally endorsed terms of reference, relevant United Nations resolutions, the Madrid principles, the Arab Peace Initiative and the Quartet road map.

16. Questions were raised as to whether Palestine was indeed a peace-loving State, since Hamas refused to renounce terrorism and violence, and had the stated aim of destroying Israel. Reference was made, on the other hand, to the Advisory Opinion of the International Court of Justice on Namibia, of 1971, which stated that the only acts that could be attributable to a State were those of the State's recognized authority.

17. With regard to the requirement that an applicant accept the obligations contained in the Charter and be able and willing to carry out those obligations, the view was expressed that Palestine fulfilled these criteria, as was evident, inter alia, from the solemn declaration to this effect contained in its application. It was recalled that in 1948, when considering the application of Israel for membership, it had been argued that Israel's solemn pledge to carry out its obligations under the Charter was sufficient to meet this criterion.

18. The view was also expressed that the Charter required more than a verbal commitment by an applicant to carry out its Charter obligations; an applicant had to show a commitment to the peaceful settlement of disputes and to refrain from the threat or the use of force in the conduct of its

international relations. In this connection, it was stressed that Hamas had not accepted these obligations.

19. The view was expressed that the Committee should recommend to the Council that Palestine be admitted to membership in the United Nations. A different view was expressed that the membership application could not be supported at this time and an abstention was envisaged in the event of a vote. Yet another view expressed was that there were serious questions about the application, that the applicant did not meet the requirements for membership and that a favourable recommendation to the General Assembly would not be supported.

20. Further, it was suggested that, as an intermediate step, the General Assembly should adopt a resolution by which Palestine would be made an Observer State.

21. In summing up the debate at the 110th meeting of the Committee, the Chair stated that the Committee was unable to make a unanimous recommendation to the Security Council.

The Committee did not need to be unanimous to make a recommendation, but given the certainty of a US veto and possible vetoes by Britain and France, the matter was not put to a vote in the Security Council. Instead, in a deal brokered by the European Union, Palestine shifted tactics and opted to seek upgraded status to "non-member observer state" in the United Nations—a decision that could be made in the General Assembly without Security Council involvement. This would not give it any new rights and privileges, such as the right to vote, without a separate General Assembly decision. But it would have important symbolic and practical consequences. The United Nations does not "recognize" states: that is a matter for each state to decide on its own, and 122 UN members had done so with respect to Palestine by 2012. But a General Assembly resolution affirming its status as a state by a substantial majority would likely give Palestine a boost in the context of its ongoing negotiations. Moreover, it could make it easier for Palestine to join other international organizations (such as the UN specialized agencies) and accede to treaties that are open only to states. As the depository of treaties, it would be up to the Secretary-General to decide whether to accept the instrument of ratification. In so doing, he would follow the practice of the General Assembly, which "is to be found in unequivocal indications from the Assembly that it considers a particular entity to be a State . . . such indications are to be found in GA resolutions."[8] For that reason, Israel was deeply

---

[8] UN's Summary of Practice of the Secretary-General as Depositary of Multilateral Treaties, paras. 82–83. https://treaties.un.org/doc/source/publications/practice/summary_english.pdf. For further discussion, see ICG Report No.112, "Curb Your Enthusiasm: Israel and Palestine after the UN" 12 September 2011.

opposed, and others were on the fence. In the end, the General Assembly granted the upgraded status on 29 November 2012 by a vote of 138 in favor, 9 against (including Israel, the United States, and Canada) and 41 abstentions.

GENERAL ASSEMBLY RESOLUTION 67/19 (2012): STATUS OF PALESTINE IN THE UNITED NATIONS

The General Assembly,

Reaffirming its commitment, in accordance with international law, to the two-State solution of an independent, sovereign, democratic, viable and contiguous State of Palestine living side by side with Israel in peace and security on the basis of the pre-1967 borders,

Recognizing that full membership is enjoyed by Palestine in the United Nations Educational, Scientific and Cultural Organization, the Economic and Social Commission for Western Asia and the Group of Asia-Pacific States and that Palestine is also a full member of the League of Arab States, the Movement of Non-Aligned Countries, the Organization of Islamic Cooperation and the Group of 77 and China,

Taking note of the 11 November 2011 report of the Security Council Committee on the Admission of New Members,

Reaffirming the principle of universality of membership of the United Nations,

1. *Reaffirms* the right of the Palestinian people to self-determination and to independence in their State of Palestine on the Palestinian territory occupied since 1967;

2. *Decides* to accord to Palestine non-member observer State status in the United Nations, without prejudice to the acquired rights, privileges and role of the Palestine Liberation Organization in the United Nations as the representative of the Palestinian people, in accordance with the relevant resolutions and practice;

3. *Expresses the hope* that the Security Council will consider favourably the application submitted on 23 September 2011 by the State of Palestine for admission to full membership in the United Nations; . . .

6. *Urges* all States and the specialized agencies and organizations of the United Nations system to continue to support and assist the Palestinian people in the early realization of their right to self-determination, independence and freedom;

As noted in the preamble to resolution 67/19, Palestine was a member of UNESCO by the time the Assembly vote was taken. Each specialized agency has its own admissions rules, some by simple majority and others by two-thirds majority vote, without any veto powers. Membership in UNESCO is open to all UN member states, as well as those voted in by two-thirds majority. Palestine first applied in 1989, but failed. Instead, UNESCO decided "to provide for the closest possible participation of Palestine in the action of UNESCO, in particular through its various programs, participation in meetings ... and access to the participation programme"[9] Palestine sought full admission in UNESCO every year after that. In 2011, it succeeded first in the Executive Board, then the plenary body.

REQUEST FOR THE ADMISSION OF PALESTINE TO UNESCO— EXECUTIVE BOARD OF UNESCO[10]

After considering this item, the Executive Board adopted the following decision, by a vote taken by roll-call, with 40 votes in favour, 4 votes against and 14 abstentions, the United States of America voting against ...

The Executive Board,

1. Considering the request for the admission of Palestine to UNESCO submitted in 1989, and reiterated at each General Conference,

2. Having noted that Palestine accepts UNESCO's Constitution and is ready to fulfil the obligations which will devolve upon it by virtue of its admission and to contribute towards the expenses of the Organization,

3. Noting that the status of Palestine is the subject of ongoing deliberations at the United Nations in New York, ...

5. Recommends that the General Conference admit Palestine as a member of UNESCO.

The vote in the General Conference was 107 in favor, 14 against, and 52 abstentions, with 21 absent or having lost their right to vote because membership dues were unpaid.

---

[9] UNESCO Res. 25 of 16 October 1989—Request for the admission of Palestine to UNESCO.
[10] UNESCO, 187 EX/SR.6 of 30 November 2011.

UNESCO GENERAL CONFERENCE RESOLUTION 76 (2011): ADMISSION OF PALESTINE AS A MEMBER OF UNESCO[11]

The General Conference, ...
Also having noted that in 187 EX/Decision 40 the Executive Board recommended the admission of Palestine to membership of UNESCO,
Decides to admit Palestine as a Member of UNESCO

Due to US legislation adopted during the 1990s, as a result of this vote, Washington was obligated to stop paying its dues to UNESCO, thus losing its own vote there in 2013. This precipitated a major budget crisis at UNESCO deepening consistently over the ensuing years, not only due to the foregone US assessed contribution to the regular UNESCO budget but also considerable voluntary funding adding up to much more in the aggregate than the United States' assessed 22 percent share.

QUESTIONS

4. Was the 2012 General Assembly resolution upgrading the status of Palestine to "non-member observer state" status an appropriate compromise?
5. After Palestine was admitted to UNESCO, why do you think it did not apply to other UN specialized agencies?
6. If Kosovo applied for membership in the United Nations now, what would the likely outcome be? Should it apply for "non-member Observer State" status like Palestine?

After achieving upgraded status in the United Nations in 2011, Palestine bided its time before taking any further steps. Then, in April 2014, it deposited instruments of ratification for sixteen treaties, including the ICCPR, the ICESCR (International Convention on Economic, Social, and Cultural Rights), the Torture Convention, and the Geneva Conventions.[12] For reasons explained below, the Statute of the International Criminal Court was not

---

[11] UNESCO, 36 C/Res.76 of 10 November 2011.
[12] Note to Correspondents in response to questions asked at noon concerning Palestinian letters for accession to international conventions and treaties. New York 2 April 2014. For a list of the treaties, see http://www.un.org/sg/offthecuff/index. asp?nid=3372.

among the sixteen. The response of the UN Secretary-General, who is the depository of most of these treaties (the Swiss government is the depository of the Geneva Conventions), is embodied in a note to correspondents released on 7 January 2015

SECRETARY-GENERAL, NOTE TO CORRESPONDENTS—ACCESSION OF PALESTINE TO MULTILATERAL TREATIES, 7 JANUARY 2015[13]

Many reporters have been asking about the documents transmitted by the Permanent Observer of Palestine to the United Nations relating to the accession of Palestine to 16 multilateral treaties in respect of which the Secretary-General is the depository, including the Rome Statute of the International Criminal Court.

In conformity with the relevant international rules and his practice as a depositary, the Secretary-General has ascertained that the instruments received were in due and proper form before accepting them for deposit, and has informed all States concerned accordingly through the circulation of depositary notifications. The information is public and posted on the website of the UN Treaty Section (https://treaties.un.org/pages/CNs.aspx).

This is an administrative function performed by the Secretariat as part of the Secretary-General's responsibilities as depositary for these treaties.

It is important to emphasize that it is for States to make their own determination with respect to any legal issues raised by instruments circulated by the Secretary-General.

The ICC Statute was not among the sixteen because it was likely to generate more opposition. Palestine's relationship with the ICC goes back to 22 January 2009, when the Palestinian National Authority (PNA) sought to confer jurisdiction on the ICC pursuant to Article 12(3) of the Statute of the Court, by lodging a declaration with the Registrar. This provision allows states to accept the jurisdiction of the Court on an ad hoc basis without formally becoming members, which in turn would lead the Prosecutor to open an investigation into a situation—in that case "acts committed on the territory of Palestine since 1 July 2002." The PNA was prompted by Operation "Cast Lead," the Israeli bombing campaign on the Gaza Strip between 27 December 2008 and 17 January 2009. As Article 12(3) allows only states to accept the jurisdiction of the Court, the declaration raised the question of whether Palestine was a "state" for the purposes of the Article. The Office of the Prosecutor did not respond to the Palestinian bid until April 2012.

---

[13] http://www.un.org/sg/offthecuff/index.asp?nid=3786.

DECISION OF THE OFFICE OF THE PROSECUTOR OF THE INTERNATIONAL CRIMINAL COURT, 3 APRIL 2012

Situation in Palestine . . .

3. The first stage in any preliminary examination is to determine whether the preconditions to the exercise of jurisdiction under article 12 of the Rome Statute are met. Only when such criteria are established will the Office proceed to analyse information on alleged crimes as well as other conditions for the exercise of jurisdiction as set out in articles 13 and 53(1).

4. The jurisdiction of the Court is not based on the principle of universal jurisdiction: it requires that the United Nations Security Council (article 13(b)) or a "State" (article 12) provide jurisdiction. Article 12 establishes that a "State" can confer jurisdiction to the Court by becoming a Party to the Rome Statute (article 12(1)) or by making an ad hoc declaration accepting the Court's jurisdiction (article 12(3)).

5. The issue that arises, therefore, is who defines what is a "State" for the purpose of article 12 of the Statute? In accordance with article 125, the Rome Statute is open to accession by "all States", and any State seeking to become a Party to the Statute must deposit an instrument of accession with the Secretary-General of the United Nations. In instances where it is controversial or unclear whether an applicant constitutes a "State", it is the practice of the Secretary-General to follow or seek the General Assembly's directives on the matter. This is reflected in General Assembly resolutions which provide indications of whether an applicant is a "State". Thus, competence for determining the term "State" within the meaning of article 12 rests, in the first instance, with the United Nations Secretary General who, in case of doubt, will defer to the guidance of General Assembly. The Assembly of States Parties of the Rome Statute could also in due course decide to address the matter in accordance with article 112(2)(g) of the Statute.

6. In interpreting and applying article 12 of the Rome Statute, the Office has assessed that it is for the relevant bodies at the United Nations or the Assembly of States Parties to make the legal determination whether Palestine qualifies as a State for the purpose of acceding to the Rome Statute and thereby enabling the exercise of jurisdiction by the Court under article 12(1). The Rome Statute provides no authority for the Office of the Prosecutor to adopt a method to define the term "State" under article 12(3) which would be at variance with that established for the purpose of article 12(1).

7. The Office has been informed that Palestine has been recognised as a State in bilateral relations by more than 130 governments and by certain international organisations, including United Nation bodies. However, the current status granted to Palestine by the United Nations General Assembly is that of "observer", not as a "Non-member State". The Office understands that on 23 September 2011, Palestine submitted an application for admission to the United Nations as a Member State in accordance with article 4(2) of the

United Nations Charter, but the Security Council has not yet made a recommendation in this regard. While this process has no direct link with the declaration lodged by Palestine, it informs the current legal status of Palestine for the interpretation and application of article 12.

8. The Office could in the future consider allegations of crimes committed in Palestine, should competent organs of the United Nations or eventually the Assembly of States Parties resolve the legal issue relevant to an assessment of article 12 or should the Security Council, in accordance with article 13(b), make a referral providing jurisdiction.

As we have seen, in November 2012 the General Assembly upgraded Palestine's status to "non-member observer state" in resolution 67/19 (2012). That is where matters stood until 31 December 2014, the day the Security Council rejected a draft resolution that would have called for Israelis and Palestinians to strike a peace deal within a year, and for Israelis to withdraw to its 1967 borders within three years. On that day, Palestine filed another Article 12(3) declaration accepting the jurisdiction of the ICC. Two days later, on 2 January 2015, it acceded to the Rome Statute. On 6 January 2015 the Secretary-General accepted the instrument of ratification.

DEPOSITARY NOTIFICATION—REFERENCE: C.N.13.2015. TREATIES-XVIII.10

ROME STATUTE OF THE INTERNATIONAL CRIMINAL COURT ROME, 17 JULY 1998

STATE OF PALESTINE: ACCESSION

The Secretary-General of the United Nations, acting in his capacity as depositary, communicates the following:

The above action was effected on 2 January 2015.

The Statute will enter into force for the State of Palestine on 1 April 2015 in accordance with its article 126 (2) which reads as follows:

"For each State ratifying, accepting, approving or acceding to this Statute after the deposit of the 60th instrument of ratification, acceptance, approval or accession, the Statute shall enter into force on the first day of the month after the 60th day following the deposit by such State of its instrument of ratification, acceptance, approval or accession."[14]

---

[14] https://treaties.un.org/doc/Publication/CN/2015/CN.13.2015-Eng.pdf.

The Office of the Prosecutor of the ICC followed up the next day, on 7 January 2015.

THE PROSECUTOR OF THE INTERNATIONAL CRIMINAL COURT, FATOU BENSOUDA, OPENS A PRELIMINARY EXAMINATION OF THE SITUATION IN PALESTINE[15]

On 2 January 2015, Palestine deposited its instrument of accession to the Rome Statute with the UNSG. As outlined in the Summary of Practice of the Secretary-General as Depositary of Multilateral Treaties, "the Secretary-General, in discharging his functions as a depositary of a convention with an 'all States' clause, will follow the practice of the [General] Assembly in implementing such a clause [. . .]." The practice of the UNGA "is to be found in unequivocal indications from the Assembly that it considers a particular entity to be a State." In accordance with this practice and specifically UNGA Resolution 67/19, on 6 January 2015, the UNSG, acting in his capacity as depositary, accepted Palestine's accession to the Rome Statute, and Palestine became the 123rd State Party to the ICC. It was welcomed as such by the President of the Assembly of States Parties to the Rome Statute.

Likewise, on 7 January 2015, the Registrar of the ICC informed President Abbas of his acceptance of the article 12(3) declaration lodged by the Government of Palestine on 1 January 2015 and that the declaration had been transmitted to the Prosecutor for her consideration.

The Office considers that, since Palestine was granted observer State status in the UN by the UNGA, it must be considered a "State" for the purposes of accession to the Rome Statute (in accordance with the "all States" formula). Additionally, as the Office has previously stated publicly, the term "State" employed in article 12(3) of the Rome Statute should be interpreted in the same manner as the term "State" used in article 12(1). Thus, a State that may accede to the Rome Statute may also lodge a declaration validly under article 12(3).[16]

---

[15] International Criminal Court, Reference Number ICC-OTP-20150116-PR1083.
[16] http://www.icc-cpi.int/en_menus/icc/press%20and%20media/press%20releases/Pages/pr1083.aspx.

QUESTION

7. Was the manner in which the Secretary-General and Office of the Prosecutor dealt with the matter appropriate? What are the implications?

6.2 Succession (I): The Soviet Union

The formal process of disintegration of the Soviet Union was initiated in Minsk on 8 December 1991, with the signing of the Declaration by the Heads of State of the Republic of Belarus, the Russian Soviet Federative Socialist Republic, and Ukraine, and the Agreement Establishing the Commonwealth of Independent States. These instruments declared that the Soviet Union no longer existed as a subject of international law and a geopolitical reality; they also proclaimed the establishment of the Commonwealth of Independent States (CIS). The CIS constituted by the three signing states would be open for accession to all member states of the Soviet Union, as well as to other states sharing the purposes and principles of the founding agreement.

These instruments, commonly referred to as the Minsk Agreements, were of questionable legality, however, for although the participating states had the right to withdraw from the Soviet Union and to set up another association of sovereign states, they could not, as only three of the twelve states that comprised the Soviet Union declared that it had ceased to exist.[17]

Soon after, on 21 December 1991, eight other states (Azerbaijan, Armenia, Kazakhstan, Kyrgyzstan, Moldova, Tajikistan, Turkmenistan, and Uzbekistan) met with the signatories to the Minsk Agreements at Alma Ata and issued a declaration supporting the establishment of the CIS and demise of the Soviet Union. The Alma Ata Declaration[18] provided that with the establishment of the CIS, the Soviet Union would cease to exist. As Ukraine, Russia, and Belarus were among the founder members of the United Nations, and as Ukraine and Belarus had maintained their membership, the Council of the Heads of State of the CIS also took a decision to support Russia's succession to the Soviet Union's seat at the United Nations, including permanent membership on the Security Council and the right to exercise the Soviet veto.

---

[17] See Sergei A. Voitovich, "The Commonwealth of Independent States: An Emerging Institutional Model," *European Journal of International Law*, vol. 4 (1993), p. 403.
[18] UN Doc. A/47/60-S/23329 (1991), Annex II.

DECISION BY THE COUNCIL OF HEADS OF STATE OF
THE COMMONWEALTH OF INDEPENDENT STATES,
21 DECEMBER 1991[19]

The States participating in the Commonwealth, referring to article 12 of the Agreement establishing the Commonwealth of Independent States,

Proceeding from the intention of each State to discharge the obligations under the Charter of the United Nations and to participate in the work of that Organization as full Members,

Bearing in mind that the Republic of Belarus, the Union of Soviet Socialist Republics and Ukraine were founder Members of the United Nations,

Expressing satisfaction that the Republic of Belarus and Ukraine continue to participate in the United Nations as sovereign independent States,

Resolved to promote the strengthening of international peace and security on the basis of the Charter of the United Nations in the interests of their peoples and of the entire international community,

Have decided that:

1. The States of the Commonwealth support Russia's continuance of the membership of the Union of Soviet Socialist Republics in the United Nations, including permanent membership of the Security Council, and other international organizations.

2. The Republic of Belarus, [Russia] and Ukraine will extend their support to the other States of the Commonwealth in resolving issues of their full membership in the United Nations and other international organizations.

LETTER FROM PRESIDENT OF THE RUSSIAN FEDERATION
BORIS YELTSIN TO THE SECRETARY-GENERAL OF THE
UNITED NATIONS, 24 DECEMBER 1991

I have the honour to inform you that the membership of the Union of Soviet Socialist Republics in the United Nations, including the Security Council and all other organs and organizations of the United Nations system, is being continued by the Russian Federation (RSFSR[20]) with the support of the countries of the Commonwealth of Independent States. In this connection, I request that the name "Russian Federation" should be used in the United Nations in place of the name "the Union of Soviet Socialist Republics."

---

[19] UN Doc. A/47/60-S/23329 (1991), Annex V.
[20] Russian Soviet Federative Socialist Republic.

The Russian Federation maintains full responsibility for all the rights and obligations of the USSR under the Charter of the United Nations, including the financial obligations.

I request that you consider this letter as confirmation of the credentials to represent the Russian Federation in United Nations organs for all the persons currently holding the credentials of representatives of the USSR to the United Nations.

Although there was some handwringing behind the scenes, the process by which Russia assumed the seat of the Soviet Union was smooth. None of the P5 wanted to open the Pandora's Box of Security Council reform by challenging Russia's right to the seat, nor, fortunately, did any other member of the Council. Nevertheless, despite the Commonwealth Accord of December 1991, there was some concern one or more of the former Soviet republics would challenge this, creating a row in the General Assembly. To avoid that, the matter was orchestrated in the Security Council. At the first Council meeting in January 1992 the nameplate of the Soviet Union was replaced by the nameplate of Russia. When the Russian representative took his seat, no other member said a word. By the time the General Assembly first met, it was treated as a *fait accompli*. Within most of the Specialized Agencies, the same happened: Russia continued the Soviet membership, without an explicit decision. Only in the ILO was there a formal decision.

Although this transition had been smooth politically, there were some questions raised about the legality of the course adopted. Yehuda Z. Blum argued that "with the demise of the Soviet Union itself, its membership in the United Nations should have automatically lapsed and Russia should have been admitted to membership in the same way as the other newly-independent republics." The issue was not merely of a change in name, or system of government; it was the termination of the Soviet Union as a legal entity.[21] According to his analysis, the lack of objections by the UN Secretary-General or member states is probably explained by the fact that the elimination of Soviet (and subsequently Russian) membership on the Security Council would have created a constitutional crisis for the United Nations.

Rein Mullerson, Michael Scharpf, and others argue that the succession was legitimate, for the following reasons: first, Russia remains one of the largest states in the world geographically, comprising three-quarters of the territory of the former Soviet Union; second, it had the seat of government, more than half of the population, and most of the resources of the USSR; third, Soviet Russia after 1917 and the Soviet Union after 1922 were treated

---

[21] Yehuda Z. Blum, "Russia Takes Over the Soviet Union's Seat at the United Nations," *European Journal of International Law*, vol. 3 (1992), p. 360.

as continuing the state that existed under the Russian Empire; and fourth, Russia's continuity of the legal personality of the Soviet Union was recognized by third states.[22]

The Vienna Convention on Succession of States in Respect of Treaties was not in force at this time. In any event it does not appear to envisage a situation where one of the constituent states of a larger entity takes over its identity after its dissolution.

6.3 Succession (II): The Socialist Federal Republic of Yugoslavia

In contrast to the relative smoothness of the Russian transition, the succession of the Federal Republic of Yugoslavia (Serbia and Montenegro) to the seat of the former Socialist Federal Republic of Yugoslavia (SFRY), was a complicated and bitterly contested affair. The Federal Republic of Yugoslavia (FRY) consisting of two of the SFRY's six republics claimed a right to succeed to its membership of the United Nations, particularly because the breakaway republics of Slovenia, Bosnia and Herzegovina, and Croatia had already been admitted to membership on 22 May 1992 by General Assembly resolutions 236, 237, and 238 respectively. The Security Council, however, opposed this request as did the other constituent units of the former Yugoslavia. Instead on 19 September 1992 the Council passed resolution 777 (1992) by a vote of twelve in favor, with China, India, and Zimbabwe abstaining.

SECURITY COUNCIL RESOLUTION 777 (1992)

The Security Council, ...

1. *Considers* that the Federal Republic of Yugoslavia (Serbia and Montenegro) cannot continue automatically the membership of the former Socialist Federal Republic of Yugoslavia in the United Nations; and therefore recommends to the General Assembly that it decide that the Federal Republic of Yugoslavia (Serbia and Montenegro) should apply for membership in the United Nations and that it shall not participate in the work of the General Assembly; ...

---

[22] See, e.g., Rein Mullerson, "The Continuity and Succession of States, by Reference to the Former USSR and Yugoslavia," *International & Comparative Law Quarterly*, vol. 42(3) (1993), p. 473.

At the Security Council meeting held to pass this resolution, various members explained why they had chosen to support the resolution or to abstain.

PROVISIONAL VERBATIM RECORD OF THE MEETING
HELD AT HEADQUARTERS, NEW YORK, ON SATURDAY,
19 SEPTEMBER 1992, AT 12.55 PM, S/PV.3116

Mr. Vorontsov (Russian Federation) (interpretation from Russian):

[Russia] is ready to support the draft resolution ... on the basis of the prevailing view in the international community that none of the republics that have emerged in the place of the former [SFRY] can claim automatic continued membership in the United Nations. We agree that the [FRY], like other former Yugoslav republics, will have to apply for membership in the United Nations, and we will support such an application.

At the same time, we were unable to agree with the proposal, put forward by some States, that the FRY should be excluded, formally or de facto, from membership in the United Nations. We are convinced that such a decision would have negative consequences for the process of the political settlement of the Yugoslav crisis ... and would also be counterproductive with regard to the London Conference, since the United Nations, through its Secretary-General, is among the leaders of that process.

The compromise that has been reached—that the FRY should not participate in the work of the General Assembly—may seem unsatisfactory to some. Frankly, we would have preferred not to have recourse to such a measure to influence the FRY, because it is already experiencing sufficient pressure from the international community in the form of economic sanctions. But we agree to this gesture of condemnation by the world community on the understanding that in order to make a full contribution to the solution of the world problems discussed in the General Assembly, the FRY must take all possible measures to bring about an early cessation of the fratricidal conflict in its region. It must effectively cooperate to promote national reconciliation and cooperation between the various ethnic groups.

At the same time, the decision to suspend the participation of the FRY in the work of the General Assembly will in no way affect the possibility of participation by the FRY in the work of other organs of the UN, in particular the Security Council, nor will it affect the issuance of documents to it, the functioning of the Permanent Mission of the FRY to the UN or the keeping of the nameplate with the name Yugoslavia in the General Assembly Hall and the rooms in which the Assembly's organs meet.

Mr. Gharekhan (India):

Regarding the constitutional aspect ... any action by the Council should be in strict conformity with the provisions of the Charter...

The draft resolution ... does not conform to either Article 5 or Article 6 of the Charter, the only two Articles that deal with the issue it is attempting to address.

The Security Council, under the Charter, is competent to recommend either suspension or expulsion of a State. Nowhere in the Charter has the Security Council been given the authority to recommend to the General Assembly that a country's participation in the Assembly be withdrawn or suspended. That authority belongs to the General Assembly, which does not need any recommendation to that effect from the Security Council. Indeed, the General Assembly is under no legal obligation to act on any such recommendation, just as the Security Council is under no legal obligation to comply with the General Assembly's recommendations.

For these reasons, my delegation will not be in a position to support the draft resolution.

Mr. Mumbengegwi (Zimbabwe):

It is significant that the text of the draft resolution before us makes no reference to any provisions of the Charter under which this action is being taken. Strict adherence to the provisions of the Charter has always been a source of protection for small States, and the increasing disregard for, or mutation of, Charter provisions causes us great concern. It would seem that the Charter's provisions are consistently ignored or applied selectively in the deliberations of our Council. My delegation has on previous occasions cautioned against the tendency to equate a majority vote in this Council as constituting international law. This tendency is bound to undermine the prestige and the moral authority of the Security Council. ...

For these reasons, my delegation will not be able to support the draft resolution before us. ...

Mr. Merimee (France) (interpretation from French):

This text responds both to the requirements of the Charter and the needs of the moment. Indeed, it respects the apportioning of competence established by the Charter between the Security Council and the General Assembly. Furthermore, it adopts a pragmatic approach in keeping with the political situation following upon the London Conference. In this respect, it confirms and translates into reality the international community's rejection of the automatic continuation in the United Nations of the former SFRY by the FRY. ...

Mr. Watson (United States of America):

For the first time, the UN is facing the dissolution of one of its Members without agreement by the successor States on the status of the original

UN seat. Moreover none of the former republics of the former Yugoslavia is so clearly a predominant portion of the original State as to be entitled to be treated as the continuation of that State. For these reasons, and in the absence of agreement among the former republics on this issue ... we cannot accept Serbia and Montenegro's claim to the former Yugoslavia's UN Seat.

I would like to comment on the provision of the resolution that Serbia and Montenegro shall not participate in the work of the General Assembly. This provision flows inevitably from the determination by the Council and the General Assembly that Serbia and Montenegro is not the continuation of the former Yugoslavia and must apply for membership in the United Nations. To state the obvious, a country which is not a member of the United Nations cannot participate in the work of the General Assembly.

The resolution's call to have the Security Council review the matter once again before the end of the fall session of the General Assembly simply refers to a willingness on the part of the Council to consider an expected application from Serbia and Montenegro. The resolution makes it clear that, in the view of the Council, Serbia and Montenegro, like any other new state must apply for membership in the United Nations and should be held to the criteria in the United Nations Charter if it does so. The criteria require that the applicant be both willing and able to fulfil United Nations obligations, including compliance with Chapter VII Security Council resolutions.

Following the Security Council resolution, the General Assembly was faced with the questions of admission and of FRY's participation in its work. The following resolution was passed on the 21 September 1992 by a vote of 127 in favor, six against, and twenty-six abstentions. A further nineteen members were absent.

GENERAL ASSEMBLY RESOLUTION 47/1 (1992)

The General Assembly,

Having received the recommendation of the Security Council of 19 September 1992 ...

1. *Considers* that the Federal Republic of Yugoslavia (Serbia and Montenegro) cannot continue automatically the membership of the former

Socialist Federal Republic of Yugoslavia in the United Nations; and therefore *decides* that the Federal Republic of Yugoslavia (Serbia and Montenegro)
should apply for membership in the United Nations and that it shall not
participate in the work of the General Assembly;

2. *Takes note* of the intention of the Security Council to consider the matter again before the end of the main part of the forty-seventh session of the
General Assembly.

These actions led to considerable confusion as to the actual status of the FRY
in the United Nations. The following clarification was issued by the UN
Legal Counsel:

UN LEGAL COUNSEL'S OPINION ON GENERAL ASSEMBLY RESOLUTION 47/1 (1992), ADDRESSED TO THE PERMANENT REPRESENTATIVES OF BOSNIA AND HERZEGOVINA AND CROATIA, 29 SEPTEMBER 1992[23]

General Assembly resolution 47/1 deals with a membership issue which is
not foreseen in the Charter of the United Nations. . .

The only practical consequence that the resolution draws is the [FRY]
shall not participate in the work of the General Assembly. It is clear therefore
that the representatives of the [FRY] can no longer participate in the work of
the General Assembly, its subsidiary organs, nor conferences and meetings
convened by it. . . .

[T]he Resolution neither terminates nor suspends Yugoslavia's membership in the Organization. Consequently the seat and the nameplate remain
as before but in Assembly bodies representatives of the [FRY] cannot sit
behind the sign "Yugoslavia". Yugoslav missions at the United Nations
Headquarters and offices may continue to function and may receive and circulate documents. At Headquarters, the Secretariat will continue to fly the
flag of the old Yugoslavia as it is the last flag used by the Secretariat. The
Resolution does not take away the right of Yugoslavia to participate in the
work of organs other than Assembly bodies. The admission to the United
Nations of a new Yugoslavia under Article 4 of the Charter will terminate
the situation created by resolution 47/1.

---

[23] UN Doc. A/47/485 (1992), Annex.

The FRY underwent a radical shift in governance with the popular uprising against the Milosevic regime in 2000. The new government decided to abandon the previous claim of automatic succession and to apply for membership in the United Nations. This was granted with General Assembly resolution 55/12 on 1 November 2000. Nevertheless, the status of the FRY during the intervening period (1992–2000) has been the subject of litigation in the ICJ. Only member states of the United Nations, ordinarily, are eligible to be parties to a case before the ICJ. The FRY was, nevertheless, a respondent in one case[24] and applicant in another.[25] In the course of these proceedings the Court had the occasion to comment on FRY's status during that period.

In the first case, when FRY was a respondent, the question of its status between 1992 and 2000 arose in the course of an Application for Revision of a 1996 Judgment of the ICJ. In that Judgment the Court had ruled against the FRY's objections to the Court's jurisdiction and the admissibility of the application made by Bosnia invoking the Genocide Convention. The FRY, which in 2003 adopted the name Serbia and Montenegro, applied for revision of the judgment on the basis that it had not been a signatory to the Statute of the International Court of Justice or a signatory to the Genocide Convention prior to its accession to the UN Charter in 2000, and thus, that the Court did not have jurisdiction. It claimed this was a "new fact" on the basis of which the judgment was open to revision as per Article 61 of the ICJ Statute. In its 2003 judgment on the Application for Revision, the Court declared it had jurisdiction—that its successful application to the United Nations in 2000 did not retroactively change its status in 1996 (there was no "new fact" that would cause the Court to revise its earlier position on jurisdiction).[26]

In the second case, when FRY was the applicant, it filed a genocide action against the member states of the North Atlantic Treaty Organization (NATO), alleging illegal use of force and perpetration of genocide against the Serbs in the Kosovo intervention of 1999.[27] In 2000, while the case was underway, Yugoslavia was admitted to the United Nations as a new state, but it did not withdraw the case. In the course of this decision the ICJ gave another opinion on the status of FRY in the years between 1992 and 2000, and also discussed its claim vis-à-vis membership in the Genocide Convention.

---

[24] *Case concerning the Application of the Convention on the Prevention and Punishment of the Crime of Genocide*, brought against the Federal Republic of Yugoslavia by Bosnia Herzegovina on 20 March 1993.

[25] *Case concerning Legality of Use of Force*, brought against certain members of the North Atlantic Treaty Organization by the Federal Republic of Yugoslavia on 29 April 1999.

[26] Application for Revision of the Judgment of 11 July 1996 in the *Case concerning Application of the Convention on the Prevention and Punishment of the Crime of Genocide (Bosnia and Herzegovina v. Yugoslavia) (Preliminary Objections)* (International Court of Justice, Judgment of 3 February 2003

[27] This incident is discussed in Chapter 2 of this volume.

LEGALITY OF USE OF FORCE (SERBIA AND MONTENEGRO v. UNITED KINGDOM) (INTERNATIONAL COURT OF JUSTICE, JUDGMENT OF 15 DECEMBER 2004)

44 ... As the Court observed earlier ..., the question whether Serbia and Montenegro was or was not a party to the Statute of the Court at the time of the institution of the present proceedings is fundamental; for if it were not such a party, the Court would not be open to it under Article 35, paragraph 1, of the Statute...

50. [Whether Serbia and Montenegro was a party to the Statute comes down to whether or not it] was a Member of the United Nations at the time when it instituted proceedings in the present case. ...

62. ... [I]t is the view of the Court that the legal situation that obtained within the United Nations during that eight-year period concerning the status of the Federal Republic of Yugoslavia ... remained ambiguous and open to different assessments. This was due, *inter alia*, to the absence of an authoritative determination by the competent organs of the United Nations defining clearly the legal status of the Federal Republic of Yugoslavia vis-à-vis the United Nations. ...

72. It must be stated that th[e] qualification of the position of the Federal Republic of Yugoslavia as "*sui generis*," which the Court employed to describe the situation during this period of 1992 to 2000, is not a prescriptive term from which certain defined legal consequences accrue; it is merely descriptive of the amorphous state of affairs in which the Federal Republic of Yugoslavia found itself during this period. No final and definitive conclusion was drawn by the Court from this descriptive term on the amorphous status of the Federal Republic of Yugoslavia vis-à-vis or within the United Nations during this period. The Court did not commit itself to a definitive position on the issue of the legal status of the Federal Republic of Yugoslavia in relation to the Charter and the Statute in its pronouncements in incidental proceedings, in the cases involving this issue which came before the Court during this anomalous period ...

73. This situation, however, came to an end with a new development in 2000 [when FRY applied for and was admitted to the UN]...

75. ... This action on the part of the Federal Republic of Yugoslavia signified that it had finally decided to act on Security Council resolution 777 (1992) by aligning itself with the position of the Security Council as expressed in that resolution. Furthermore the Security Council confirmed its own position by taking steps for the admission of the Federal Republic of Yugoslavia as a new Member of the United Nations, which, when followed by corresponding steps taken by the General Assembly, completed the procedure for the admission of a new Member under Article 4 of the Charter, rather than pursuing any course involving recognition of continuing membership of the Federal Republic of Yugoslavia in the United Nations.

76. This new development effectively put an end to the *sui generis* position of the Federal Republic of Yugoslavia within the United Nations, which, as the Court has observed in earlier pronouncements, had been fraught with "legal difficulties" throughout the period between 1992 and 2000 ... The Applicant thus has the status of membership in the United Nations as from 1 November 2000. However, its admission to the United Nations did not have, and could not have had, the effect of dating back to the time when the Socialist Federal Republic of Yugoslavia broke up and disappeared; there was in 2000 no question of restoring the membership rights of the Socialist Federal Republic of Yugoslavia for the benefit of the Federal Republic of Yugoslavia. At the same time, it became clear that the *sui generis* position of the Applicant could not have amounted to its membership in the Organization.

77. In the view of the Court, the significance of this new development in 2000 is that it has clarified the thus far amorphous legal situation concerning the status of the Federal Republic of Yugoslavia vis-à-vis the United Nations. It is in that sense that the situation that the Court now faces in relation to Serbia and Montenegro is manifestly different from that which it faced in 1999. If, at that time, the Court had had to determine definitively the status of the Applicant vis-à-vis the United Nations, its task of giving such a determination would have been complicated by the legal situation, which was shrouded in uncertainties relating to that status. However, from the vantage point from which the Court now looks at the legal situation, and in light of the legal consequences of the new development since 1 November 2000, the Court is led to the conclusion that Serbia and Montenegro was not a Member of the United Nations, and in that capacity a State party to the Statute of the International Court of Justice, at the time of filing its Application to institute the present proceedings before the Court on 29 April 1999. ...

The majority decision was criticized by seven judges, who issued a joint declaration in the same case:

LEGALITY OF USE OF FORCE, JOINT DECLARATION OF VICE-PRESIDENT RANJEVA, JUDGES GUILLAUME, HIGGINS, KOOIJMANS, AL-KHASAWNEH, BUERGENTHAL, AND ELARABY

10. We would first observe that the question whether Yugoslavia was a Member of the United Nations and as such a party to the Statute between 1992 and 2000, remained a subject of debate during that period. The Court declined to settle the issue, both in 1993 [in the *Genocide* case] ... and in 1999 when issuing its Order on Provisional Measures [in the present case] ... It

then confined itself to stating that the solution adopted in this respect by Security Council resolution 757 and General Assembly resolution 47/1 was "not free from legal difficulties" ...

Subsequent to the admission of Serbia and Montenegro to the United Nations on 1 November 2000, the Court had to consider the question whether that admission clarified the previous position. The Court then found, in its Judgment of 3 February 2003, that "Resolution 47/1 did not *inter alia* affect the Federal Republic of Yugoslavia's right to appear before the Court or to be a party to a dispute before the Court under the conditions laid down by the Statute" ... The Court added that "General Assembly resolution 55/12 of 1 November 2000 cannot have changed retroactively the *sui generis* position which the Federal Republic of Yugoslavia found itself in vis-à-vis the United Nations over the period 1992 to 2000, or its position in relation to the Statute of the Court" ... The Court thus previously found in 2003 that the Federal Republic of Yugoslavia could appear before the Court between 1992 and 2000 and that this position was not changed by its admission to the United Nations ...

12. ... Nothing has occurred, in the series of cases concerning Kosovo, since the Court's last judgment in 2003, to suggest that the grounds previously chosen have now lost legal credibility. Further, the grounds today selected by the Court are less certain than others open to it. The Court has determined that the admission of the Applicant to the United Nations in November 2000 "did not have and could not have had, the effect of dating back to the time when the Socialist Federal Republic of Yugoslavia broke up and disappeared" (para. 76). The Court has also stated that "the significance of this new development in 2000 is that it has clarified the thus far amorphous legal situation concerning the status of the Federal Republic of Yugoslavia vis-à-vis the United Nations" (para. 77). Without specifying whether this "clarification" refers to the period 1992–2000, the Court asserts that it has now become "clear that the *sui generis* position of the Applicant could not have amounted to its membership in the Organization." We find this proposition far from self-evident and we cannot trace the steps of the reasoning. Such grounds seem to us to be less legally compelling and therefore less certain, and more open to different points of view, than the grounds relied upon by the Court thus far and which are now set aside by the Court. ...

As the joint declaration warned, dismissing the *Legality of the Use of Force* case in this way cast a shadow over the ongoing *Genocide* case. To follow the ruling in the former would mean finding that over a decade of proceedings in the latter was, essentially, a waste of time. To ignore the ruling would directly contradict one of its own decisions. The Court ultimately held in the *Genocide* case that the jurisdiction issue was res judicata—that is, it had already been decided. The implication is that, despite the ruling in the *Legality of the Use of Force* that FRY was not a member of the United Nations and therefore not a party to the Statute in 1999 (and therefore could not push its claim against the NATO countries), it nevertheless was subject to the jurisdiction of the Court in the *Genocide* case, which had begun earlier, because the Court had earlier made that determination and it could not be relitigated.

QUESTIONS

8. Does the Council have the power to do what it purported to do in resolution 777 (1992)? What would have been the effect if the Council had omitted from the quoted section the words "and that it shall not participate in the work of the General Assembly"?
9. Could Yugoslavia have been suspended from the United Nations under Article 5 of the UN Charter? If it had been suspended, would the practical effect have been any different from what happened? Why do you think this approach was not taken?
10. The fact that Yugoslavia was engaged in an armed conflict with the other former Yugoslav republics was a strong political reason for not allowing FRY to occupy the Yugoslav seat, but is it legally relevant?
11. The Court's 2004 decision in the *Legality of the Use of Force* case, brought by the FRY, may seem to contradict its own 2003 decision in the *Genocide* case, by removing the ambiguity on the FRY's status between 1992 and 2000. Should the Court have perpetuated this "ambiguous" status of quasi-membership, or was it right to determine that the ambiguity never existed—that is, that the FRY had never been allowed to take up the UN membership of its predecessor, the SFRY?

6.4 Credentials

Because suspension and expulsion from the United Nations is very difficult, the credentials procedure has been used as a way of denying some states the right to participate—despite the fact the granting of credentials is meant to be a routine matter. Each delegation appointed to represent a state at the General Assembly is required to present its credentials to the Secretary-General. These documents are then passed on to a "Credentials Committee," of nine members appointed by the Assembly on the proposal of the President at each session. The Committee studies these credentials and reports to the Assembly. The acceptance or rejection of credentials does not signify recognition or nonrecognition of any particular government. Nevertheless, there have been instances where the acceptance of credentials from one of two rival claimants to governance of a country has been used to indicate which one is considered legitimate.

The China-Taiwan issue is such a case. From 1949 (the date of the Communist revolution in China) to 1971, representatives of the Kuomintang government based in Taiwan continued to occupy the UN seat. Attempts by the Soviet Union and its allies to dislodge it by means of votes in the credentials committee and the General Assembly were resisted by the United States and its allies. In 1950, Trygve Lie, first UN Secretary-General, proposed a test designed to break the deadlock. By way of analogy he drew on the Article 4(1) requirement that a state must be "able and willing to carry out obligations of membership" and asked "which of the two [rival] Governments in fact is in a position to employ the resources and direct the people of the State in fulfilment of the obligations of membership. In essence, this means an inquiry as to whether the new government exercises effective authority within the State and is habitually obeyed by the bulk of the population."[28] This test would be applied irrespective of whether individual members of the United Nations recognize the state in their national capacities. Later that year, the General Assembly adopted a resolution (GA resolution 396) that stated simply: "Whenever more than one authority claims to be the government entitled to represent a Member State in the United Nations . . . it should be considered in light of the purposes and principles of the Charter and the circumstances of each case."[29]

Taiwan continued to occupy the seat until 1971, when the tide finally turned. The General Assembly adopted a resolution unseating the representatives of Taiwan and replacing them with those of the People's Republic of China[30]—mainly because US policy toward China changed, but also because the nonaligned majority in the United Nations increased. The matter was not dealt with as an admission or expulsion issue but rather a representation one—that is, with rival claimants from the same country. As a result, Articles 4 and 6 were not relevant and so the matter was dealt with in the General Assembly, where the Security Council veto does not apply.

HYPOTHETICAL A

Given that the governments of both China and Taiwan formally adhere to a policy of reunification, the latter has avoided applying for membership in the United Nations.[31] Instead, it has sought other ways of participating in the work of the Organization—to no avail. If Taiwan were to seek admission to

---

[28] U.N.Doc S/1466 (1950).

[29] GA Res. 396 (V), Dec. 14, 1950.

[30] GA Res. 2758, October 25, 1971.

[31] An exception was the year 2007 when President Chen of the Republic of China (ROC) changed course by sending a letter to the Secretary-General applying for full membership (rather than asking allies to introduce a resolution seeking "meaningful participation.") Secretary-General Ban Ki-Moon refused to accept the letter,

membership today, would it be eligible? Would it be likely to succeed? If not, what other mechanisms for participation would you propose, if any?

In addressing these questions, put yourself in the position of representatives of Taiwan, China, the Secretary-General, President of the General Assembly, and other key member states.

Another case of rival claimants concerned Cambodia in 1978. Following the invasion of Democratic Kampuchea by Vietnam, resulting in the ouster of the Khmer Rouge, an attempt by the new People's Republic of Kampuchea to occupy the UN seat was challenged.[32] The United States resisted the idea of recognizing the credentials of the new Vietnam-installed government. Others claimed that the new Kampuchean government "had full control and effective power" in the territory and therefore should occupy the seat. India's representative proposed that the seat be left vacant. In the end, the General Assembly reseated Pol Pot's representative by a vote of seventy-one in favor, thirty-five opposed, and thirty-four abstentions. That is where things remained until 1989 when Vietnam announced it would pull its troops out of Cambodia. The seat was left vacant in 1990 and then taken over by the representative of the new transitional government (Supreme National Council) in 1991, following negotiation of the Paris Peace accords.

QUESTION

12. Applying Trygve Lie's test, would the People's Republic of China have been seated in 1950? Would the People's Republic of Kampuchea have been seated in 1979? What about the Taliban, which prior to September 2001 controlled more than 90 percent of Afghanistan, yet the delegation of former president Burhanuddin Rabbani continued to occupy the seat? As noted, the General Assembly never formally adopted the Trygve Lie test. Is it appropriate approach? Are the criteria set out in resolution 396 better?

---

citing GA resolution 2758 (the one China policy). The next year, two referendums in the ROC to support joining the United Nations failed. Meanwhile, on 17 September 2008 the UN subcommittee once again ruled against the application of its allies for "meaningful participation." In 2009, for the first time in seventeen years, Taiwan dropped the bid altogether.

[32] Colin Warbrick, "Kampuchea—Representation and Recognition," *International and Comparative Law Quarterly*, vol. 30 (1981), p. 234.

A third credentials case did not involve rival claimants. In 1974, the General Assembly rejected the credentials of the delegation of South Africa, thereby denying it the right to speak and vote in the General Assembly for as long as the state, under the regime of apartheid, denied its nonwhite citizens most of the rights of participation in governance.[33]

As the following statement by the UN Legal Counsel indicates, this use of credentials was not envisaged by the UN Charter or the Rules of Procedure of the General Assembly.

STATEMENT BY THE LEGAL COUNSEL: SCOPE OF CREDENTIALS IN RULE 27 OF THE RULES OF PROCEDURE OF THE GENERAL ASSEMBLY, 1970[34]

3. Thus credentials for the General Assembly may be defined as a document issued by the Head of State or Government or by the Minister for Foreign Affairs of a State Member of the UN submitted to the Secretary-General designating the persons entitled to represent that Member at a given session of the General Assembly. Unlike the acceptance of credentials in bilateral relations, the question of recognition of the government of a member state is not involved, and substantive issues concerning the status of Government do not arise except as examined in the following paragraph. . . .

5. Questions have . . . been raised in the Credentials Committee with respect to the Representatives of certain Members, notably South Africa and Hungary, where there was no rival claimant. There has, however, been no case where the representatives were precluded from participation in the meetings of the General Assembly. The General Assembly in the case of Hungary from the eleventh to the seventeenth session and in the case of South Africa at the twentieth session decided to take no action on the credentials submitted on behalf of the representatives of Hungary and South Africa. Under rule 29, any representative to whose admission a Member has made objection is seated provisionally with the same rights as other representatives until the Credentials Committee has reported and the General Assembly has given its decision.

6. Should the General Assembly, where there is no question of rival claimants, reject credentials satisfying the requirements of rule 27 for the purpose of excluding a member state from participation in its meetings, this would

---

[33] A/PV.2281, pp. 76, 86 (1974).

[34] Scope of "Credentials" in Rule 27 of the Rules of Procedure of the General Assembly: Statement by the Legal Counsel Submitted to the President of the General Assembly at his Request, 25 UN GAOR, Agenda Item 3, at 1 n.1, UN Doc. A/8160 (1970).

have the effect of suspending a member state from the exercise of rights and privileges of membership in a manner not foreseen by the Charter. ... The participation in the meetings of the General Assembly is quite clearly one of the important rights and privileges. Suspension of this right through the rejection of credentials would not satisfy the requirements [of Article 5 of the Charter] and would therefore be contrary to the Charter.

The UN Legal Counsel's opinion regarding challenges to South Africa's credentials was, itself, soon challenged. At the twenty-fifth session, a Member requested the Credentials Committee to consider the credentials of the South African delegation to the General Assembly and to make a special report on the matter. The Credentials Committee examined the credentials of South Africa and approved them, deciding, however, to reflect in its report that some delegations had objected. In the Assembly's plenary meeting, two amendments to the draft resolution of the Credentials Committee were proposed: the first to add the words "except with regard to the credentials of the representatives of the Government of South Africa"; the second to note that "notwithstanding the authenticity of the credentials of the representatives of the Government of South Africa, the authorities of South Africa who issued those credentials do not represent a large segment of the population of South Africa which the said authorities claim to represent." A request to vote first on the second amendment was rejected by sixty-one votes to one, with twenty-one abstentions.[35]

At the request of one representative, the President gave his opinion on the implications of the first amendment proposed.

STATEMENT BY THE PRESIDENT OF THE GENERAL ASSEMBLY, MR. EDVARD HAMBRO, 25TH SESSION, 1901ST PLENARY MEETING, A/PV.1901 (1970)

286 ... I reach the conclusion that a vote in favour of the Amendment would mean, on the part of this Assembly, a very strong condemnation of the policies pursued by the Government of South Africa. It would also constitute a warning to that Government as solemn as any such warning could be. But that, apart from that, the amendment as it is worded at present would not seem to me to mean that the South African delegation is unseated or cannot continue to sit in this Assembly; if adopted it will not affect the right and privileges of membership of South Africa. That is my understanding.

---

[35] See http://legal.un.org/repertory/art9/english/rep_supp5_vol1-art9_e.pdf

The first amendment proposed was adopted by sixty votes to forty-two, with twelve abstentions; the second amendment was withdrawn.

Further developments ensued. At the twenty-ninth session, in 1974, a proposal was adopted in the Credentials Committee itself to accept all the credentials submitted except those of South Africa by five votes to three, with one abstention. The Committee presented its report to the General Assembly, which approved it by ninety-eight votes to twenty-three, with fourteen abstentions.[36]

A member state requested that the President of the General Assembly explain the effect of the resolution just adopted.

RULING BY THE PRESIDENT OF THE GENERAL ASSEMBLY, MR. ABDELAZIZ BOUTEFLIKA, 29TH SESSION, 2281ST PLENARY MEETING, A/PV.2281 (1974)

153 ... I am asked to state here my interpretation of the General Assembly's decision to reject the credentials of the delegation of South Africa. ...

158. That text [of rule 29] perhaps does not indicate with sufficient clarity what should happen once the General Assembly has taken a decision confirming the objection to the admission of a representative or a delegation. Now, year after year, the General Assembly has decided, by ever-larger majorities, not to recognize the credentials of the South African delegation, and during this session the Credentials Committee itself took the initiative of rejecting those credentials. It has not been necessary for the Assembly to adopt an amendment along these lines to the report submitted by the Credentials Committee.

159. It would therefore be a betrayal of the clearly and repeatedly expressed will of the General Assembly to understand this to mean that it was merely a procedural method of expressing its rejection of the policy of *apartheid*. On the basis of the consistency with which the General Assembly has regularly refused to accept the credentials of the South African delegation, one may legitimately infer that the General Assembly would in the same way reject the credentials of any other delegation authorized by the Government of the Republic of South Africa to represent it, which is tantamount to saying in explicit terms that the General Assembly refuses to allow the South African delegation to participate in its work.

160. Thus it is, as President of the twenty-ninth session of the General Assembly, that I interpret the decision of the General Assembly, leaving open the question of the status of the Republic of South Africa as a Member of the United Nations which, as we all know, is a matter requiring a

---

[36] GA Res. 3206(XXIX) (1974).

recommendation from the Security Council. My interpretation refers exclusively to the position of the South African delegation within the strict framework of the rules of procedure of the General Assembly. . .

Response by Mr. Scali, Representative of the United States of America

162. There is also an obvious conflict, Mr. President, between your ruling and the Legal Opinion given to this Assembly on 11 November 1970 at the 25th Session. Further there is a conflict between your ruling and the practice that the General Assembly has consistently followed since [1970] . . . during the twenty ninth session, South Africa was allowed to vote without objection after the Assembly's decision on its credentials was made.

163. The legal opinion given at the 25th Session remains as valid today, in our view as it was then. It affirms that under the Charter the Assembly may not deprive a Member of any of the rights of membership. The Assembly may be master of its rules of procedure but no majority, no matter how large, can ignore or change the clear provisions of the Charter in this way. We consider it to be a violation of the rules of procedure and of Articles 5 and 6 of the Charter for the assembly to attempt to deny a Member State of the United Nations its right to participate in the Assembly, through this type of unprecedented action . . . The Assembly is not empowered to deprive a Member of the rights and privileges of membership other than in accordance with Articles 5, 6 and 19 of the Charter. In our view, none of these circumstances applies in this case. . . .

The ruling of the President was challenged and upheld by ninety-one votes to twenty-two, with nineteen abstentions.[37]

QUESTIONS

13. South Africa's credentials were accepted finally in 1994, after apartheid was abolished, and the country's first nonracial elections were held resulting in the installation of Nelson Mandela as president on 10 May 1994. Did the Assembly's exclusion of South Africa from participation in its work contribute to this outcome? Would this precedent have constituted a better way to have dealt with the Federal Republic of Yugoslavia from 1992 to 2000? What is the effect of these precedents on Article 5 and 6 and, by implication, on the prerogatives of the Security Council as set out in those articles?

---

[37] A/PV.2281.

14. For better or worse, the UN credentials process has gone from being a purely technical exercise to a means of registering disapproval of a government and limiting its right to participate in the United Nations. Is this a positive development? What are the implications for the constitutional order embodied in the UN Charter, including the division of labor between the Security Council and General Assembly? What does it tell us about the evolution of sovereignty? In what circumstances, if any, should the credentials process be used in this way?

Further Reading

Fox, Gregory H. "The Right to Political Participation in International Law." *Yale Journal of International Law*, vol. 17 (1992), p. 539.

Griffin, Matthew. "Accrediting Democracies: Does the Credentials Committee of the United Nations Promote Democracy through Its Accreditation Process, and Should It?" *New York University Journal of International Law and Politics*, vol. 32 (2000), p. 725.

International Crisis Group, Report No.112, "Curb Your Enthusiasm: Israel and Palestine after the UN" 12 September 2011.

Klabbers, Jan. *An Introduction to International Organizations Law*, 3rd edn. Cambridge: Cambridge University Press, 2015.

Ratliff, Suellen. "UN Representation Disputes: A Case Study of Cambodia and a New Accreditation Proposal for the Twenty-First Century." *California Law Review*, vol. 87 (1999), p. 1207.

Roth, Brad R. *Governmental Illegitimacy in International Law*. Oxford: Clarendon Press, 1999.

Scharf, Michael P. "Musical Chairs: The Dissolution of States and Membership in the UN." *Cornell International Law Journal*, vol. 28 (1995), pp. 29–69.

Sands, Philip and Pierre Klein. *Bowett's Law of International Institutions*, 6th edn. London: Sweet and Maxwell, 2009.

chapter seven

Structure, Financing, and Administration

The United Nations began with a fairly simple structure, but Chapters IX and X of the Charter[1] laid the foundations for expansion. Institutional development rapidly blossomed. The International Labour Organization, founded in 1919 became the United Nations' first "specialized agency" in 1946; the International Postal Union, created in 1874, joined two years later. Soon, however, the United Nations began to create its own subsidiary machinery: several of today's largest agencies, funds, and programs (the UN Development Program, UNICEF, the World Food Program (WFP), the Food and Agriculture Organization (FAO) and the World Health Organization (WHO)) were established in the years following the United Nations' creation. The United Nations' specialized agencies are independent organizations that have entered into an Article 63 relationship agreement with the United Nations. The Funds, Programs and Offices are creations of the UN General Assembly or of ECOSOC.

A perusal of the United Nations' organizational chart (provided at the end of this volume's introduction) provides an idea of the institutional sprawl that ensued. Each major agency, fund, and program generated its own governance structure—more or less subordinate to General Assembly decisions, but often fairly autonomous. The World Bank and International Monetary Fund (IMF) belong to the UN system only in the most formal sense, having carved out virtually complete independence from the United Nations (although still implementing Security Council mandatory decisions under Chapter VII of the Charter). They subsequently acquired resources far outstripping those of the UN system, due primarily to the Bank's ability to borrow and the IMF's ability to leverage limited capital and "on call" resources, as well as governance models that gave overwhelming clout to the funders rather than the principal clients of these institutions. (Both the Bank and the IMF have, in recent years, undergone considerable administrative and

---

[1] Discussed in Chapter 3 of this volume.

staffing compression in order to favor needs of clients and out of deference to funders in straitened circumstances.)

As is often the case with bureaucratic sprawl, issues of overlap also rapidly arose. In the quest for expansion, often through voluntary contributions, the agencies, funds, and programs (and to some extent the UN Secretariat itself) soon set about poaching activity from what appeared to be the mandate of others. Most UN agencies, for example, soon claimed to be promoting both economic and social development. When donor countries turned their attention to matters of humanitarian concern after the end of the Cold War, UN actors stampeded to stake out their colors on humanitarian ground (too readily forgetting that the International Red Cross system, with its own international conventions and complex decision-making and implementation machinery, had hitherto been primarily responsible for humanitarian action—and rather good at it).

The United Nations was soon competing in the humanitarian and development fields with a myriad of other international actors ranging from regional development banks to humanitarian NGOs, many of them remarkably capable, some surpassing the United Nations in funding capacity and effectiveness on the ground.

In this way, the United Nations evolved into a seemingly unmanageable, ever-growing organism, which the French president Charles de Gaulle referred to it as *"le machin"*—roughly translatable as "the thingummy." More troublingly, it has also competed, often not to its own advantage, with other international actors for funding and for glory, occasionally reaping ignominy instead.

This phase of wildcat growth eventually slowed and took on new forms. Donor governments, for example, started creating new bodies to cater to their latest enthusiasms, typified particularly by multi-stakeholder global programs that provide earmarked funding for specified purposes, sometimes known as "vertical funds," of which the most notable has been the Global Fund to Fight AIDS, Tuberculosis and Malaria. Launched early in the new millennium and spending roughly $4 billion annually, it was quite successful in combating AIDS but has done less well on tuberculosis and disappointingly on malaria. At the same time, it diverted resources and capacity from the World Health Organization, a point that came dramatically to light during the 2014–2015 Ebola crisis in several West African countries.

Meanwhile, many of the traditional donor countries entered a period of deep financial and economic crisis in 2008. Soon, they were casting about for ways to contain the costs of their international obligations, for example by privately calling in 2014, for the United Nations to cap its peacekeeping spending at $8 billion (without necessarily taking account of that notional ceiling in their decision-making).

Member states are not always consistent in pursuing their goals. Efforts to streamline the UN system's structure, for example by merging underfinanced research and training institutions, foundered on resistance among member states, several of which had a vested interest in a distinct identity for each of these. The UN Secretariat has grown considerably in recent decades, some of it further to targeted donor funding, which many member states oppose as distorting approved UN priorities, and the number of senior positions has also grown considerably.

In a reality check for the organization, its biennial[2] budget shrank marginally for the first time in both nominal and real terms in 2015–2016. Some of the agencies are reaching the outer limits of their capacity to meet established staff salaries and benefits while delivering any meaningful programming. Member states of the UN Education, Science and Cultural Organization (UNESCO) brought a full-scale budget crisis on itself by voting in favor of full membership of Palestine in 2011,[3] despite warnings from the United States that this would, under US congressional strictures, result in the end of US regular and voluntary contributions—which make up $150 million annually, or 22 percent of the overall budget. UNESCO, amid drastic cuts in personnel and programs, has been struggling to manage ever since.

Emerging powers such as China, India, and Brazil could arguably shoulder a greater share of the burden, but tend to shield themselves behind their official "developing country" identity. This leaves the lion's share of the burden on the traditional donor countries.

One important consequence of sprawl and fierce competition for funding (as well as a sharp instinct for turf infighting) is that actual coordination among UN actors is difficult and rare, notwithstanding many initiatives to heighten cooperation (e.g. UN Country Teams and the UN Development Group). In order to promote it, Secretary-General Kofi Annan converted the Administrative Committee on Coordination into a Chief Executives Board for Coordination that gathers major agency heads and several coordinating under-secretaries-general (for example, responsible for humanitarian action and UN-wide management). One of Secretary-General Ban Ki-moon's successes was to have induced the participation and active cooperation of the Executive Heads of the IMF, the World Bank, and the World Trade Organization (WTO)—noteworthy because the WTO is not formally affiliated with the United Nations, like the International Organization for Migration, which also attends. The High Commissioners for Human Rights and Refugees do often elicit cooperation from UN colleagues, in part through their personal authority and credibility.

The *Certain Expenses* case of the International Court of Justice, also discussed in Chapter 4, is an example of how member states have sought to use financial obligations as leverage when they disapprove of an activity. The current chapter first sets out the legal framework for UN financing and then returns to the *Certain Expenses* case, which unfolded from late 1961 to

---

[2] The UN budget operates on a two-year cycle, sometimes confusing those engaged in research on its financial status.

[3] See Chapter 6 of this volume.

mid-1962. The chapter then describes the regular budget, assessment of contributions, administrative oversight within the Organization, and some of the challenges that it has confronted. The chapter concludes with a brief discussion of alternative financing arrangements.

QUESTIONS

1. Can you think of ways to rationalize the United Nations' structure: (a) on merit, or (b) to save money?
2. In arguing in favor of these ways of rationalizing UN structure, can you think of factors that would enhance prospects of their adoption by the General Assembly?
3. Bearing in mind how legislatures (and executives) in member states discipline themselves on spending when in financial distress, can you think of means, temporary or permanent, that the United Nations could adopt to constrain or limit in absolute terms the spending of the regular budget, on peacekeeping, and of the UN system as a whole? Please detail how these would work in practice.

7.1 The Legal Framework

The annual UN budget is modest when the scope of activities are considered, spanning from the deployment of 100,000 peacekeepers to a range of responses to large-scale humanitarian emergencies around the globe, in addition to its extensive development programming. In spite of this, the United Nations has teetered on the brink of financial crisis for most of the last fifty years.[4] The reason is that although domestic expenses are urgent from the perspective of electorates and other internal constituencies, international financial obligations often strike legislatures and governments as being of a more contingent nature. Late payment of dues is endemic, a problem not helped by the fact that peacekeeping dues come in at irregular intervals (often for quite small sums of money) and all the problems that complicated exchange rates can create.

Financial reform has thus long been a key issue on the agenda of the United Nations.

Articles 17–19 of the Charter set out the legal framework for the Organization. It is noteworthy that the "power of the purse" is lodged not

---

[4] See Wilfred Koschorreck, "Article 17," in Bruno Simma (ed), *The Charter of the United Nations: A Commentary*, 2nd edn. Oxford: Oxford University Press, 2002. vol. 1, p. 348, para. 89.

in the Security Council but in the General Assembly, where every state has an equal voice. Articles 17(1) and (2) give the General Assembly the power to approve the budget for the United Nations, and to apportion its expenses among the member states. Article 18(2) specifies the requirement of a two-thirds majority to decide budgetary questions. Article 19 provides that any member of the United Nations two years in arrears of payment of its financial contribution to the United Nations shall not be allowed to vote in the General Assembly, unless the Assembly decides otherwise. These provisions together constitute the basic fiscal law of the Organization.[5]

The General Assembly acts on budgetary matters largely through its Fifth Committee. As reaffirmed by General Assembly resolution 45/248B (1990), this is the committee with principal jurisdiction over administrative and budgetary matters. It is a "committee of the whole," meaning that every member state is entitled to representation. In practice, two smaller committees, the Advisory Committee on Administrative and Budgetary Questions (ACABQ) and the Committee on Contributions (established by resolution 14(I) (1946)), are the critical decision-makers. The Contributions Committee advises the General Assembly on the apportionment of expenses among members, assessments for new members, appeals by members for a change of assessment, and the application of Article 19 in cases of arrears in the payment of assessments. Its membership has been expanded a number of times and now stands at eighteen.[6] The ACABQ will be discussed in greater detail in section 7.4 below.

The UN System is financed from two sources: the assessment of member states and voluntary contributions. Assessments are supposed to be based on the "capacity to pay"—that is, taking into account several factors, primarily the wealth of each state as measured by its Gross National Income (GNI) as a proportion of the global total. The application of this policy has been modified in two principal respects. The first is the ceiling for contributions, currently applicable only to the United States, whose assessment once amounted to one-third of the budget and was later set at 25 percent, lowered in 2001 to 22 percent. The second is a reduction for countries below a specified income threshold. In 2015, the United States remained the largest contributor, followed by Japan, Germany, France, Britain, China, Italy, Canada, Spain, and Brazil. But these rankings remain subject to significant change in the future, especially if the discount for rapidly developing countries (such as China) is differentiated from that for lower income countries. In that event, China's share would rise to second or third rank, while India would likely jump into the above list, possibly with Spain or Canada falling off. China is now the world's second-largest economy by any measure, with India rapidly climbing in the rankings, particularly in purchasing power parity terms.

---

[5] Ibid., p. 334, para. 1.
[6] See, most recently, GA Res. 31/96 (1976).

Expenditures of peacekeeping operations are assessed separately, through a scale that provides larger discounts to poorer countries and adds a premium to the permanent members of the Security Council. Expenditures for the International Criminal Tribunals for the former Yugoslavia and Rwanda are assessed through a scale that is the average of the regular budget and peacekeeping scales of assessment.

Assessed contributions also support the UN Specialized Agencies (such as the WHO, UNESCO, and the FAO) but these are generally supplemented by voluntary contributions that may exceed the assessed contributions. The UN Programmes, Funds, and other organs[7] rely almost solely on voluntary contributions. In 2012–2013, for example, the UN regular budget was $5.56 billion,[8] the peacekeeping budget was $7.383 billion,[9] the Specialized Agencies received $2.7 billion in assessed contributions[10] and $4.5 billion in voluntary contributions,[11] while the programs and funds received a further $22.7 billion in voluntary contributions.[12]

In the *Certain Expenses* case, the International Court of Justice was asked in 1961 for its opinion on whether certain expenditures authorized by the General Assembly to cover the costs of the UN Operation in the Congo (ONUC) and of the UN Emergency Force in the Middle East (UNEF), "constitute 'expenses of the Organization' within the meaning of Article 17, paragraph 2, of the Charter of the United Nations." The issue arose because two members (France and the Soviet Union) refused to pay their assessed share of these two UN peacekeeping missions—initiatives that were authorized by the General Assembly over the opposition of two permanent members of

---

[7] These include UNCDF (United Nations Capital Development Fund) since 1973, UNDP (United Nations Development Programme), UNEP (United Nations Environment Program) since 1973, UNFPA (United Nations Population Fund), UNHCR (Office of the United Nations High Commissioner for Refugees), UNICEF (United Nations Children's Fund), UNIDO (United Nations Industrial Development Organization) until 1986, UNITAR (United Nations Institute for Training and Research), UNRWA (UN Relief & Works Agency for Palestinian Refugees in the Near East), UNU (United Nations University) since 1975, and WFP (World Food Program).

[8] GA Res. 68/245 A-B (2013) on the Programme Budget for the biennium 2012–2013.

[9] For the period 1 July 2012–30 June 2013, UN Doc: A/68/731: "Overview of the financing of the United Nations peacekeeping operations: budget performance for the period 1 July 2012 to 30 June 2013 and budget for the period from 1 July 2014 to 30 June 2015."

[10] Figures are for 2013 from data compiled from Table 2, UN Doc: General Assembly: A/69/305, 12 August 2014, "Budgetary and financial situation of the organizations of the United Nations system." For specialized agencies the figure includes IAEA but does not include the IMF or World Bank.

[11] Ibid.

[12] Ibid.

the Security Council. (When the Security Council had deadlocked, the states seeking authorization for a mission transferred the issue to the General Assembly, in which authorization was obtained.) France and the Soviet Union argued that these operations were ultra vires—that is, beyond the power of the General Assembly to authorize.[13]

CERTAIN EXPENSES OF THE UNITED NATIONS (ARTICLE 17, PARAGRAPH 2, OF THE CHARTER) (ADVISORY OPINION) 1962 ICJ REPORTS 151

[I]t should be noted that at least three separate questions might arise in the interpretation of paragraph 2 of this Article. One question is that of identifying what are "the expenses of the Organization"; a second question might concern apportionment by the General Assembly; while a third question might involve the interpretation of the phrase "shall be borne by the Members." It is the second and third questions which directly involve "the financial obligations of the Members," but it is only the first question which is posed by the request for the advisory opinion. . . .

If the Court finds that the indicated expenditures are such "expenses," it is not called upon to consider the manner in which, or the scale by which, they may be apportioned. The amount of what are unquestionably "expenses of the Organization within the meaning of Article 17, paragraph 2" is not in its entirety apportioned by the General Assembly and paid for by the contributions of Member States, since the Organization has other sources of income. . . .

The text of Article 17, paragraph 2, refers to "the expenses of the Organization" without any further explicit definition of such expenses. It would be possible to begin with a general proposition to the effect that the "expenses" of any organization are the amounts paid out to defray the costs of carrying out its purposes, in this case, the political, economic, social, humanitarian and other purposes of the United Nations. The next step would be to examine, as the Court will, whether the resolutions authorizing the operations here in question were intended to carry out the purposes of the United Nations and whether the expenditures were incurred in furthering these operations. Or, it might simply be said that the "expenses" of an organization are those which are provided for in its budget. . . .

It is perhaps the simple identification of "expenses" with the items included in a budget, which has led to linking the interpretation of the word "expenses" in paragraph 2 of Article 17, with the word "budget" in paragraph

---

[13] See further the discussion of the Uniting for Peace procedure in Chapter 9, section 9.2.

1 of that Article; in both cases, it is contended, the qualifying adjective "regular" or "administrative" should be understood to be implied. Since no such qualification is expressed in the text of the Charter, it could be read in only if such qualification must necessarily be implied from the provisions of the Charter considered as a whole, or from some particular provision thereof which makes it unavoidable to do so in order to give effect to the Charter.

In the first place, concerning the word "budget" in paragraph 1 of Article 17, it is clear that the existence of the distinction between "administrative budgets" and "operational budgets" was not absent from the minds of the drafters of the Charter, nor from the consciousness of the Organization even in the early days of its history. In drafting Article 17, the drafters found it suitable to provide in paragraph 1 that "The General Assembly shall consider and approve the budget of the Organization." But in dealing with the function of the General Assembly in relation to the specialized agencies, they provided in paragraph 3 that the General Assembly "shall examine the administrative budgets of such specialized agencies" ... Moreover, had it been contemplated that the Organization would also have had another budget, different from the one which was to be approved by the General Assembly, the Charter would have included some reference to such other budget and to the organ which was to approve it.

Similarly, at its first session, the General Assembly in drawing up and approving the Constitution of the International Refugee Organization, provided that the budget of that Organization was to be divided under the headings "administrative," "operational" and "large-scale resettlement"; but no such distinctions were introduced into the Financial Regulations of the United Nations which were adopted by unanimous vote in 1950 ...

Actually, the practice of the Organization is entirely consistent with the plain meaning of the text. The budget of the Organization has from the outset included items which would not fall within any of the definitions of "administrative budget" which have been advanced in this connection. Thus, for example ... the annual budget of the Organization contains provision for funds for technical assistance [etc]. ...

It is a consistent practice of the General Assembly to include in the annual budget resolutions, provision for expenses relating to the maintenance of international peace and security. Annually, since 1947, the General Assembly has made anticipatory provision for "unforeseen and extraordinary expenses" arising in relation to the "maintenance of peace and security." ...

It is notable that the 1961 Report of the Working Group of Fifteen on the Examination of the Administrative and Budgetary Procedures of the United Nations ... records that the following statement was adopted without opposition:

22. Investigations and observation operations undertaken by the Organization to prevent possible aggression should be financed as part of the regular budget of the United Nations.

In the light of what has been stated, the Court concludes that there is no justification for reading into the text of Article 17, paragraph 1, any limiting or qualifying word before the word "budget." ...

Turning to paragraph 2 of Article 17, the Court observes that, on its face, the term "expenses of the Organization" means all the expenses and not just certain types of expenses which might be referred to as "regular expenses." An examination of other parts of the Charter shows the variety of expenses which must inevitably be included within the "expenses of the Organization" just as much as the salaries of staff or the maintenance of buildings.

For example, the text of Chapters IX and X of the Charter with reference to international economic and social cooperation, especially the wording of those articles which specify the functions and powers of the Economic and Social Council, anticipated the numerous and varied circumstances under which expenses of the Organization could be incurred and which have indeed eventuated in practice.

Furthermore, by Article 98 of the Charter, the Secretary-General is obligated to perform such functions as are entrusted to him by the General Assembly, the Security Council, the Economic and Social Council, and the Trusteeship Council. Whether or not expenses incurred in his discharge of this obligation become "expenses of the Organization" cannot depend on whether they be administrative or some other kind of expenses.

The Court does not perceive any basis for challenging the legality of the settled practice of including such expenses as these in the budgetary amounts which the General Assembly apportions among the Members in accordance with the authority which is given to it by Article 17, paragraph 2. ...

... [I]t has been argued before the Court that one type of expenses, namely those resulting from operations for the maintenance of international peace and security, are not "expenses of the Organization" within the meaning of Article 17, paragraph 2, of the Charter, inasmuch as they fall to be dealt with exclusively by the Security Council, and more especially through agreements negotiated in accordance with Article 43 of the Charter.

The argument rests in part upon the view that when the maintenance of international peace and security is involved, it is only the Security Council which is authorized to decide on any action relative thereto. It is argued further that since the General Assembly's power is limited to discussing, considering, studying and recommending, it cannot impose an obligation to pay the expenses which result from the implementation of its recommendations. This argument leads to an examination of the respective functions of the General Assembly and of the Security Council under the Charter, particularly with respect to the maintenance of international peace and security. ...

... [Under Article 24] the responsibility conferred is "primary," not exclusive ... it is the Security Council which is given a power to impose an explicit obligation of compliance if for example it issues an order or command to an aggressor under Chapter VII. It is only the Security Council which can require enforcement by coercive action against an aggressor.

The Charter makes it abundantly clear, however, that the General Assembly is also to be concerned with international peace and security. Article 14 authorizes the General Assembly to "recommend measures for the peaceful adjustment of any situation, regardless of origin, which it deems likely to impair the general welfare or friendly relations among nations, including situations resulting from a violation of the provisions of the present Charter setting forth the purposes and principles of the United Nations." The word "measures" implies some kind of action, and the only limitation which Article 14 imposes on the General Assembly is the restriction found in Article 12, namely, that the Assembly should not recommend measures while the Security Council is dealing with the same matter unless the Council requests it to do so. Thus while it is the Security Council which, exclusively, may order coercive action, the functions and powers conferred by the Charter on the General Assembly are not confined to discussion, consideration, the initiation of studies and the making of recommendations; they are not merely hortatory. Article 18 deals with "decisions" of the General Assembly "on important questions." These "decisions" do indeed include certain recommendations, but others have dispositive force and effect. Among these latter decisions, Article 18 includes suspension of rights and privileges of membership, expulsion of Members, "and budgetary questions." In connection with the suspension of rights and privileges of membership and expulsion from membership under Articles 5 and 6, it is the Security Council which has only the power to recommend and it is the General Assembly which decides and whose decision determines status; but there is a close collaboration between the two organs. Moreover, these powers of decision of the General Assembly under Articles 5 and 6 are specifically related to preventive or enforcement measures.

By Article 17, paragraph 1, the General Assembly is given the power not only to "consider" the budget of the Organization, but also to "approve" it. The decision to "approve" the budget has a close connection with paragraph 2 of Article 17, since thereunder the General Assembly is also given the power to apportion the expenses among the Members and the exercise of the power of apportionment creates the obligation, specifically stated in Article 17, paragraph 2, of each Member to bear that part of the expenses which is apportioned to it by the General Assembly ... The provisions of the Charter which distribute functions and powers to the Security Council and to the General Assembly give no support to the view that such distribution excludes from the powers of the General Assembly the power to provide for the financing of measures designed to maintain peace and security.

The argument supporting a limitation on the budgetary authority of the General Assembly with respect to the maintenance of international peace and security relies especially on the reference to "action" in the last sentence of Article 11, paragraph 2. ...

The Court considers that the kind of action referred to in Article 11, paragraph 2, is coercive or enforcement action. This paragraph, which applies not merely to general questions relating to peace and security, but also to specific cases brought before the General Assembly by a State under Article 35, in its first sentence empowers the General Assembly, by means of recommendations to States or to the Security Council, or to both, to organize peacekeeping operations, at the request, or with the consent, of the States concerned. This power of the General Assembly is a special power which in no way derogates from its general powers under Article 10 or Article 14, except as limited by the last sentence of Article 11, paragraph 2. This last sentence says that when "action" is necessary the General Assembly shall refer the question to the Security Council. The word "action" must mean such action as is solely within the province of the Security Council. It cannot refer to recommendations which the Security Council might make, as for instance under Article 38, because the General Assembly under Article 11 has a comparable power. The "action" which is solely within the province of the Security Council is that which is indicated by the title of Chapter VII of the Charter, namely "Action with respect to threats to the peace, breaches of the peace, and acts of aggression." If the word "action" in Article 11, paragraph 2, were interpreted to mean that the General Assembly could make recommendations only of a general character affecting peace and security in the abstract, and not in relation to specific cases, the paragraph would not have provided that the General Assembly may make recommendations on questions brought before it by States or by the Security Council. Accordingly, the last sentence of Article 11, paragraph 2, has no application where the necessary action is not enforcement action. . . .

The Court accordingly finds that the argument which seeks, by reference to Article 11, paragraph 2, to limit the budgetary authority of the General Assembly in respect of the maintenance of international peace and security is unfounded. . . .

It has further been argued before the Court that Article 43 of the Charter constitutes a particular rule, a *lex specialis*, which derogates from the general rule in Article 17, whenever an expenditure for the maintenance of international peace and security is involved. . . .

The argument is that agreements [under Article 43] were intended to include specifications concerning the allocation of costs of such enforcement actions as might be taken by direction of the Security Council, and that it is only the Security Council which has the authority to arrange for meeting such costs.

With reference to this argument, the Court will state at the outset that, for reasons fully expounded later in this Opinion, the operations known as UNEF and ONUC were not enforcement actions within the compass of Chapter VII of the Charter and that therefore Article 43 could not have any applicability to the cases with which the Court is here concerned. However, even if Article 43 were applicable, the Court could not accept this interpretation of its text for the following reasons.

There is nothing in the text of Article 43 which would limit the discretion of the Security Council in negotiating such agreements . . . If, during negotiations under the terms of Article 43, a Member State would be entitled (as it would be) to insist, and the Security Council would be entitled (as it would be) to agree, that some part of the expense should be borne by the Organization, then such expense would form part of the expenses of the Organization and would fall to be apportioned by the General Assembly under Article 17. It is difficult to see how it could have been contemplated that all potential expenses could be envisaged in such agreements concluded perhaps long in advance. . . .

Moreover, an argument which insists that all measures taken for the maintenance of international peace and security must be financed through agreements concluded under Article 43, would seem to exclude the possibility that the Security Council might act under some other Article of the Charter. The Court cannot accept so limited a view of the powers of the Security Council under the Charter. It cannot be said that the Charter has left the Security Council impotent in the face of an emergency situation when agreements under Article 43 have not been concluded.

Articles of Chapter VII of the Charter speak of "situations" as well as disputes, and it must lie within the power of the Security Council to police a situation even though it does not resort to enforcement action against a State. The costs of actions which the Security Council is authorized to take constitute "expenses of the Organization within the meaning of Article 17, paragraph 2." . . .

. . . [T]he Court agrees that such expenditures must be tested by their relationship to the purposes of the United Nations in the sense that if an expenditure were made for a purpose which is not one of the purposes of the United Nations, it could not be considered an "expense of the Organization."

The purposes of the United Nations are set forth in Article I of the Charter. The first two purposes as stated in paragraphs 1 and 2, may be summarily described as pointing to the goal of international peace and security and friendly relations. The third purpose is the achievement of economic, social, cultural and humanitarian goals and respect for human rights. The fourth and last purpose is: "To be a center for harmonizing the actions of nations in the attainment of these common ends."

The primary place ascribed to international peace and security is natural, since the fulfillment of the other purposes will be dependent upon the attainment of that basic condition. These purposes are broad indeed, but neither they nor the powers conferred to effectuate them are unlimited. Save as they have entrusted the Organization with the attainment of these common ends, the Member States retain their freedom of action. But when the Organization takes action which warrants the assertion that it was appropriate for the fulfilment of one of the stated purposes of the United Nations, the presumption is that such action is not *ultra vires* the Organization.

If it is agreed that the action in question is within the scope of the functions of the Organization but it is alleged that it has been initiated or carried out in a manner not in conformity with the division of functions among the several organs which the Charter prescribes, one moves to the internal plane, to the internal structure of the Organization. If the action was taken by the wrong organ, it was irregular as a matter of that internal structure, but this would not necessarily mean that the expense incurred was not an expense of the Organization. Both national and international law contemplate cases in which the body corporate or politic may be bound, as to third parties, by an *ultra vires* act of an agent.

In the legal systems of States, there is often some procedure for determining the validity of even a legislative or governmental act, but no analogous procedure is to be found in the structure of the United Nations. Proposals made during the drafting of the Charter to place the ultimate authority to interpret the Charter in the International Court of Justice were not accepted; the opinion which the Court is in the course of rendering is an advisory opinion. As anticipated in 1945, therefore, each organ must, in the first place at least, determine its own jurisdiction. If the Security Council, for example, adopts a resolution purportedly for the maintenance of international peace and security and if, in accordance with a mandate or authorization in such resolution, the Secretary-General incurs financial obligations, these amounts must be presumed to constitute "expenses of the Organization."

The Financial Regulations and Rules of the United Nations, adopted by the General Assembly, provide:

> Regulation 4.1: The appropriations voted by the General Assembly shall constitute an authorization to the Secretary-General to incur obligations and make payments for the purposes for which the appropriations were voted and up to the amounts so voted.

Thus, for example, when the General Assembly in resolution 1619 (XV) included a paragraph reading:

> 3. Decides to appropriate an amount of $100 million for the operations of the United Nations in the Congo from 1 January to 31 October 1961

this constituted an authorization to the Secretary-General to incur certain obligations of the United Nations just as clearly as when in resolution 1590 (XV) the General Assembly used this language:

> 3. Authorizes the Secretary-General ... to incur commitments in 1961 for the United Nations operations in the Congo up to the total of $24 million ...:

On the previous occasion when the Court was called upon to consider Article 17 of the Charter, the Court found that an award of the Administrative Tribunal of the United Nations created an obligation of the Organization and with relation thereto the Court said that:

> the function of approving the budget does not mean that the General Assembly has an absolute power to approve or disapprove the expenditure proposed to it; for some part of that expenditure arises out of obligations already incurred by the Organization, and to this extent the General Assembly has no alternative but to honor these engagements. (*Effects of awards of compensation made by the United Nations Administrative Tribunal, I.C.J. Reports 1954, p. 59*)

Similarly, obligations of the Organization may be incurred by the Secretary-General, acting on the authority of the Security Council or of the General Assembly, and the General Assembly "has no alternative but to honour these engagements."

The obligation is one thing: the way in which the obligation is met —that is from what source the funds are secured—is another. The General Assembly may follow any one of several alternatives ... it is of no legal significance whether, as a matter of book-keeping or accounting, the General Assembly chooses to have the item in question included under one of the standard established sections of the "regular" budget or whether it is separately listed in some special account or fund. The significant fact is that the item is an expense of the Organization and under Article 17, paragraph 2, the General Assembly therefore has authority to apportion it.

The reasoning which has just been developed, applied to the resolutions mentioned in the request for the advisory opinion, might suffice as a basis for the opinion of the Court. The Court finds it appropriate, however, to take into consideration other arguments which have been advanced. ...

The expenditures enumerated in the request for an advisory opinion may conveniently be examined first with reference to UNEF and then to ONUC. In each case, attention will be paid first to the operations and then to the financing of the operations.

In considering the operations in the Middle-East, the Court must analyze the functions of UNEF as set forth in resolutions of the General Assembly. ...

[The Court considered General Assembly resolution 998 (ES-I), resolution 1000 (ES-I), paragraphs 9, 10, and 12 of the second and final report of the Secretary-General on the plan for an Emergency International Force of 6 November, and resolution 1001 (ES-I).]

It is not possible to find in this description of the functions of UNEF, as outlined by the Secretary-General and concurred in by the General Assembly without a dissenting vote, any evidence that the Force was to be used for purposes of enforcement. Nor can such evidence be found in the subsequent operations of the Force, operations which did not exceed the scope of the functions ascribed to it. . . .

On the other hand, it is apparent that the operations were undertaken to fulfil a prime purpose of the United Nations, that is, to promote and to maintain a peaceful settlement of the situation. This being true, the Secretary-General properly exercised the authority given him to incur financial obligations of the Organization and expenses resulting from such obligations must be considered "expenses of the Organization within the meaning of Article 17, paragraph 2."

Apropos what has already been said about the meaning of the word "action" in Article 11 of the Charter, attention may be called to the fact that resolution 997 (ES-I), which is chronologically the first of the resolutions concerning the operations in the Middle East mentioned in the request for the advisory opinion, provides in paragraph 5:

> *Requests* the Secretary-General to observe and report promptly on the compliance with the present resolution to the Security Council and to the General Assembly, for such further *action as they may deem appropriate in accordance with the Charter.*

The italicized words reveal an understanding that either of the two organs might take "action" in the premises. Actually, as one knows, the "action" was taken by the General Assembly in adopting two days later without a dissenting vote, resolution 998 (ES-I) and, also without a dissenting vote, within another three days, resolutions 1000 (ES-I) and 1001 (ES-I), all providing for UNEF.

The Court notes that these "actions" may be considered "measures" recommended under Article 14, rather than "action" recommended under Article 11. The powers of the General Assembly stated in Article 14 are not made subject to the provisions of Article 11, but only of Article 12. Furthermore, as the Court has already noted, the word "measures" implies some kind of action. So far as concerns the nature of the situations in the Middle East in 1956, they could be described as "likely to impair . . . friendly relations among nations," just as well as they could be considered to involve "the maintenance of international peace and security." Since the resolutions of the General Assembly in question do not mention upon which article they are based, and since the language used in most of them might imply reference to either Article 14 or Article 11, it cannot be excluded that they were based upon the former rather than the latter article. . . .

The financing of UNEF presented perplexing problems and the debates on these problems have even led to the view that the General Assembly never, either directly or indirectly, regarded the expenses of UNEF as "expenses of the Organization within the meaning of Article 17, paragraph 2, of the Charter." With this interpretation the Court cannot agree. . . .

In an oral statement to the plenary meeting of the General Assembly on 26 November 1956, the Secretary-General said:

> I wish to make it equally clear that while funds received and payments made with respect to the Force are to be considered as coming outside the regular budget of the Organization, the operation is essentially a United Nations responsibility, and the Special Account to be established must, therefore, be construed as coming within the meaning of Article 17 of the Charter.

At this same meeting, after hearing this statement, the General Assembly in resolution 1122 (XI) noted that it had "provisionally approved the recommendations made by the Secretary-General concerning the financing of the Force." It then authorized the Secretary-General "to establish a United Nations Emergency Force Special Account to which funds received by the United Nations, outside the regular budget, for the purpose of meeting the expenses of the Force shall be credited and from which payments for this purpose shall be made." . . .

[The Court then analysed paragraph 15 of the second and final report of the Secretary-General on the plan for an emergency international Force of 6 November 1956 and a series of General Assembly resolutions concerning UNEF]

The Court concludes . . . that from year to year the expenses of UNEF have been treated by the General Assembly as expenses of the Organization within the meaning of Article 17, paragraph 2, of the Charter. . . .

The operations in the Congo were initially authorized by the Security Council in the resolution of 14 July 1960 which was adopted without a dissenting vote . . . However, it is argued that that resolution has been implemented in violation of provisions of the Charter inasmuch as under the Charter it is the Security Council that determines which States are to participate in carrying out decisions involving the maintenance of international peace and security, whereas in the case of the Congo the Secretary-General himself determined which States were to participate with their armed forces or otherwise. . . .

In the light of . . . a record of reiterated consideration, confirmation, approval and ratification by the Security Council and by the General Assembly of the actions of the Secretary-General in implementing the resolution of 14 July 1960, it is impossible to reach the conclusion that the operations in question usurped or impinged upon the prerogatives conferred by the Charter on the Security Council. The Charter does not forbid the Security Council to act through instruments of its own choice: under Article 29 it "may establish such subsidiary organs as it deems necessary for the performance of its functions"; under Article 98 it may entrust "other functions" to the Secretary-General.

It is not necessary for the Court to express an opinion as to which article or articles of the Charter were the basis for the resolutions of the Security Council, but it can be said that the operations of ONUC did not include a use of armed force against a State which the Security Council, under Article 39, determined to have committed an act of aggression or to have breached the peace. The armed forces which were utilized in the Congo were not authorized to take military action against any State. The operation did not involve "preventive or enforcement measures" against any State under Chapter VII and therefore did not constitute "action" as that term is used in Article 11.

For the reasons stated, financial obligations which, in accordance with the clear and reiterated authority of both the Security Council and the General Assembly, the Secretary-General incurred on behalf of the United Nations, constitute obligations of the Organization for which the General Assembly was entitled to make provision under the authority of Article 17, paragraph 2, of the Charter. . . .

In relation to ONUC, the first action concerning the financing of the operation was taken by the General Assembly on 20 December 1960 . . . This resolution 1583 (XV) of 20 December referred to the report of the Secretary-General on the estimated cost of the Congo operations from 14 July to 31 December 1960, and to the recommendations of the Advisory Committee on Administrative and Budgetary Questions. It decided to establish an ad hoc account for the expenses of the United Nations in the Congo. It also took note of certain waivers of cost claims and then decided to apportion the sum of $48.5 million among the Member States "on the basis of the regular scale of assessment" subject to certain exceptions. It made this decision because in the preamble it had already recognized:

> that the expenses involved in the United Nations operations in the Congo for 1960 constitute "expenses of the Organization" within the meaning of Article 17, paragraph 2, of the Charter of the United Nations and that the assessment thereof against Member States creates binding legal obligations on such States to pay their assessed shares.

By further resolutions [GA Res. 1619(XV) (1961) and GA Res. 1732(XVI) (1961)] the Genieral Assembly authorized the Secretary-General "to incur commitments [for additional periods and to limited extents] . . ."

The conclusion to be drawn . . . is that the General Assembly has twice decided that even though certain expenses are "extraordinary" and "essentially different" from those under the "regular budget," they are none the less "expenses of the Organization" to be apportioned in accordance with the power granted to the General Assembly by Article 17, paragraph 2. . . .

At the outset of this opinion, the Court pointed out that the text of Article 17, paragraph 2, of the Charter could lead to the simple conclusion that "the expenses of the Organization" are the amounts paid out to defray the costs of carrying out the purposes of the Organization. It was further indicated that the Court would examine the resolutions authorizing the expenditures referred to in the request for the advisory opinion in order to ascertain whether they were incurred with that end in view. The Court has made such an examination and finds that they were so incurred. The Court has also analyzed the principal arguments which have been advanced against the conclusion that the expenditures in question should be considered as "expenses of the Organization within the meaning of Article 17, paragraph 2, of the Charter of the United Nations," and has found that these arguments are unfounded. Consequently, the Court arrives at the conclusion that the questions submitted to it in General Assembly resolution 1731 (XVI) must be answered in the affirmative.

The opinion of the ICJ, though accepted by the General Assembly, was repudiated by France and the Soviet Union, who refused to pay their respective contributions. Even so, the loss-of-vote sanction provided under Article 19 to deal with nonpayment of dues was not applied, as many members were uncomfortable with the idea of two major powers being excluded from voting.[14] Indeed, many other states, including members of the Communist bloc and other countries from Latin America, Asia, and Africa, also refused to pay their assessed shares. When France and the Soviet Union approached the two-year default level—which would have disqualified them from voting under Article 19—the General Assembly members agreed to avoid bringing any matter to a vote, proceeding solely by consensus. Eventually, even the United States gave way and the General Assembly resolved the issue by way of a compromise formula under which the shortfalls caused by the refusals of some of the members were compensated for by voluntary contributions.[15]

To prevent the sort of situation that arose in the *Certain Expenses* case—primarily due to expenditures being incurred despite the objection of some of the permanent members of the Security Council—the normal practice tends to be consensus-based decision-making (as opposed to the affirmative vote of a two- thirds majority present and voting mandated by Article 18) to ensure money generated through assessed contributions is directed toward only "legitimate expenses."

Nevertheless, a recurrent problem for the United Nations is the withholding or threat of withholding contributions unless certain policies are followed. The United States has been the most prominent actor in this regard,

---

[14] Frederic L. Kirgis, "United States Dues Arrearages in the United Nations and Possible Loss of Vote in the UN General Assembly," *ASIL Insight*, July 1998, available at: http://www.asil.org/insights/insigh21.htm.
[15] Francesco Franscioni, "Multilateralism à la Carte: The Limits to Unilateral Withholdings of Assessed Contributions to the UN Budget," *European Journal of International Law*, vol. 11 (2000), p. 52.

its practice having initially been justified by reference to the Soviet and French position in the *Certain Expenses* case.

Because arrears were extensive during the 1990s, and because nonpayment frequently occurred, a pattern of bloated UN budgeting emerged, particularly in the peacekeeping field, so that spare cash was generated in order to avoid absolute default. Thus, a perverse Secretariat practice grew up as a response to the vices of member states, all of it contributing to a lack of transparency in UN budgeting that even the experts only fitfully penetrate.

QUESTIONS

4. Are member states of the United Nations justified in withholding funds from the organization to protest ultra vires actions?
5. The *Certain Expenses* case related to peacekeeping operations undertaken with the consent of the host state. Would the same reasoning apply to a General Assembly resolution recommending that states enforce an embargo on sale of material supporting a nuclear program, and providing funds to defray costs of member states enforcing such an embargo within their own territory? Why, or why not?
6. Given that the United Nations has no authority to borrow commercially, what are some of the potential consequences of nonpayment by member states? Given the reality of extensive arrears and frequent nonpayment of dues by member states, why has the United Nations never had to shut down? What does this tell us about apparently absolute requirements laid down in the Charter (and decisions by the ICJ)?

7.2 The Regular Budget

The United Nations' financial figures are frequently confusing. When speaking of UN finances, some people think of the regular budget and the peacekeeping budget, leaving aside the agencies, funds, and programs—but not always. To shed some light on the funding of the latter, we include here a table (up to date in early 2015 by UN standards, in other words, four years out of date) of revenue for the major funds, agencies, and programs broken down by sources (assessed or voluntary), although even these are misleading. The UN University, for example, is the beneficiary of a large endowment and draws about 20 percent of its resources from endowment income, raising the rest on a "voluntary" basis. This is not reflected accurately in the table below. And although the UN Secretariat budgets on a biennial basis, the table below is drawn up on an annual basis.

Table 2 Total Revenue by Organization (2012–2013)[16]
(in thousands of United States dollars)

	Fiscal year 2012				
	Revenue categories				
Organization	Assessed contributions	Voluntary contributions, not specified	Voluntary contributions, specified	Revenue from other activities	Totals
United Nations	2 412 020		1 387 715	165 143	3 964 878
United Nations peacekeeping	7 923 213	32 351	67 893		8 023 457
FAO	511 620		774 508	47 142	1 333 269
IAEA	428 924		208 530	3 973	641 426
ICAO	84 496		112 675	15 770	212 941
IFAD		580 158	75 522		655 680
ILO	430 810		271 345	19 300	721 458
IMO	46 861		12 886	19 109	78 856
IOM	41 694	9 231	1 089 321	95 607	1 235 852
ITC	40 490	13 352	19 861	1 123	74 826
ITU	120 166		11 025	64 484	195 675
PAHO	106 245		778 855	31 879	916 980
UN-Habitat	12 227	10 950	135 680	12 649	171 506
UNAIDS		217 420	30 454	5 671	253 544
UNDP		884 357	3 856 822	348 174	5 089 353
UNEP	181 791		371 328	8 241	561 360
UNESCO	352 971		391 039	48 191	792 201
UNFPA		437 500	533 600	9 000	980 100
UNHCR	11 856	699 011	1 712 425	13 573	2 436 865
UNICEF		1 208 296	2 702 678	76 443	3 987 417
UNIDO	101 562		189 555	1 912	293 029
UNITAR		309	19 711	1 309	21 329
UNODC		31 586	320 965	10 335	362 886
UNOPS				683 160	683 160
UNRWA		544 075	375 847	46 183	966 105
UNU			51 208	17 965	69 203
UN-Women	7 235	144 086	93 676	5 144	220 141
UNWTO	14 631	697	5 381	2 559	23 267
UPU	38 463		20 928	9 127	68 518
WFP		497 615	3 551 627	162 165	4 211 407
WHO	474 609	130 200	1 572 821	116 236	2 293 867
WIPO	19 264		11 416	342 116	372 795
WMO	71 629		27 375	3 770	102 774
WTO	214 891		24 081	2 430	241 402
TOTAL	13 647 667	5 411 193	20 906 334	2 389 881	42 355 075

[16] UN Doc: General Assembly: A/69/305, 12 August 2014, "Budgetary and financial situation of the organizations of the United Nations system." Table 2.

Fiscal year 2013

Revenue categories

Assessed contributions	Voluntary contributions, not specified	Voluntary contributions, specified	Revenue from other activities	Totals
2 606 141		1 439 693	79 418	4 125 252
7 257 894		30 274	47 045	7 335 213
511 620		743 558	78 512	1 333 689
451 550		227 310	4 263	683 122
81 952		132 035	14 796	228 783
	379 142	97 477		476 619
430 834		281 184	14 500	726 518
49 868		7 691	20 252	77 810
42 873	7 462	1 066 005	113 029	1 229 368
38 977	17 442	26 164	1 234	83 817
123 687		19 498	79 050	222 235
106 245		953 874	7 444	1 067 563
11 965	8 560	173 124	12 851	206 501
	231 555	45 786	3 127	283 469
	932 902	3 897 010	316 046	5 145 958
185 153		440 309	5 448	630 910
358 616		369 513	56 129	784 258
	460 000	504 300	49 000	1 013 300
38 996	716 453	2 389 066	20 077	3 164 591
	1 106 378	3 588 431	158 359	4 853 168
105 573		157 190	1 448	264 210
	348	19 942	1 666	21 955
	33 792	281 791	3 224	318 807
		5 966	711 170	717 136
	573 378	548 357	56 766	1 178 501
		46 037	37 056	83 093
8 004	156 958	118 465	5 077	288 505
16 621	812	2 951	3 527	23 911
39 504		21 494	9 374	70 372
	285 710	4 095 143	154 996	4 535 849
474 641	132 390	1 928 575	78 812	2 614 417
19 787		10 474	367 922	398 183
73 592		33 058	3 948	110 599
220 404		23 666	55 702	299 772
13 254 495	5 046 282	23 759 968	2 571 266	44 632 011

Because the budget extends over a two-year period, multiple adjustments and supplementary budgets are voted on throughout that period—for example to cover the United Nations' response to Ebola in West Africa in 2014 and 2015. As a result, budgets that initially are cast as representing a cutback in overall levels of funding may actually *increase*, the amount depending on what happens during the budget cycle. It takes expert knowledge to sort out any matter of fact relating to UN budgeting at any given time.

The regular budget now takes the form of a biennial program budget, beginning with an even year, a practice that was started in 1974–1975. To improve accountability within the Organization, the United Nations since 2000 has also followed a system of results-based budgeting,[17] which focuses on the expected accomplishments, before, during, and after implementation to measure and evaluate the effectiveness of expenditures.

To illustrate the changes in budgeting over the years, the budgetary arrangements for 1946 and for the 2014–2015 biennium are excerpted below.

GENERAL ASSEMBLY RESOLUTION 14(I) (1946): BUDGETARY AND FINANCIAL ARRANGEMENTS

A

The permanent budgetary and financial arrangements of the United Nations should be so designed as to promote efficient and economical administration and command the confidence of Members.

Therefore the General Assembly resolves that:

1. Arrangements be made on the basis of the general principles set out in Section 2 of Chapter IX of the Report of the Preparatory Commission and of the provisional financial regulations, for budgetary procedures, the collection and custody of funds, the control of disbursements and the auditing of accounts.

2. To facilitate the consideration of administrative and budgetary questions by the General Assembly and its Administrative and Budgetary Committee, there be appointed at the beginning of the second part of the first session of the General Assembly, an Advisory Committee on Administrative and Budgetary Questions of nine members (instead of seven as laid down in rule 37 of the provisional rules of procedure) with the following functions:

(a) To examine and report on the budget submitted by the Secretary-General to the General Assembly;

(b) To advise the General Assembly concerning any administrative and budgetary matters referred to it;

---

[17] First suggested in the Report of the Secretary-General on "Renewing the United Nations" UN Doc. A/51/950, which was endorsed by the General Assembly in GA Res. 55/231 (2000).

(*c*) To examine on behalf of the General Assembly the administrative budgets of specialized agencies and proposals for financial arrangements with such agencies;

(*d*) To consider and report to the General Assembly on the auditors report on the accounts of the United Nations and of the specialized agencies.

The Committee shall deal with personnel matters only in their budgetary aspects, and representatives of the staff shall have the right to be heard by the Committee.

3. A standing expert Committee on Contributions of ten members (instead of seven as laid down in rule 40 of the provisional rules of procedure) be appointed with instructions to prepare a detailed scale of apportionment of expenses, based on the principles set out in paragraph 13 of section 2 of chapter IX of the Report of the Preparatory Commission for consideration at the second part of the first session.

B

With a view to the integration of the administrative and budgetary planning of the Organization,

the General Assembly:

4. *Recommends* that the Secretary-General appoint at an early date a small advisory group of experts, as described in paragraphs 23–26 of section 2 of chapter IX of the Report of the Preparatory Commission to perform the functions suggested by the Preparatory Commission in paragraphs 23–26 of section 2 of chapter IX of its Report, including those specified in the provisional financial regulations.

C

Having made a general examination of the draft provisional financial regulations submitted by the Preparatory Commission,

the General Assembly:

5. *Adopts* the provisional financial regulations, as amended and reproduced in annex I to this report.

D

The opportunities of members to participate in the activities of the United Nations should be equalized as far as possible.

Therefore the General Assembly resolves that:

6. The actual travelling expenses of representatives and their alternates to and from meetings of the General Assembly shall be borne by the United Nations budget provided that the number of persons whose expenses will be so paid is limited to five in all per member. The maximum travelling allowances shall be restricted to the equivalent of first-class accommodation by recognized public transport *via* an approved route from the capital city of the member to the place where the General Assembly is meeting, and shall not include the payment of subsistence, except where this is included as an integral part of the

regular posted schedule for first class accommodation for recognized public transport. Actual travelling expenses to and from the meetings of the General Assembly of representatives or their alternates shall be reimbursed to each Member by means of an adjustment in the Member's annual contribution.

E

The General Assembly resolves that:

7. The Secretary-General after consultation with the Advisory Group referred to above, should be prepared to recommend to the General Assembly during the second part of the first session necessary action on administrative and budgetary questions, including the following:

(*a*) the form of the budget;

(*b*) procedure for the examination of the budget by the Advisory Committee on Administrative and Budgetary Questions and for submission of the Committee's report to the General Assembly;

(*c*) machinery for the control of expenditure;

(*d*) means of meeting extraordinary expenditure;

(*e*) provision of working capital;

(*f*) character and scope of special funds; and

(*g*) scope and method of audit of accounts and the procedure for the submission of the auditor's report to the Advisory Committee and the General Assembly.

F

The General Assembly:

8. *Notes* the observations made in paragraphs 5, 10 and 11 of section 2 of chapter IX of the report of the Preparatory Commission dealing with the formulation, presentation and execution of the budget, the collection and management of funds and the currency of the account and transmits them to the Secretary-General for his information and consideration.

G

The General Assembly resolves that:

9. An amount of $21,500,000 is hereby appropriated for the following purposes:

Section I—For expenses of the General Assembly and the Councils: US$1,500,000

Section II—For expenses of the Secretariat: US$16,510,750

Section III—For expenses of the International Court of Justice: US$617,250

Section IV—For unforeseen expenses: US$2,000,000

Section V—For the expenses of the Preparatory Commission and the cost of convening the General Assembly for the first part of the first session: US$872,000

10. The above amounts are available for the payment of obligations incurred prior to 1 January 1947. The Secretary-General may transfer by written order credits among or within the above listed classifications.

H

The General Assembly resolves that:

11. A working capital fund is established at the amounts of $25,000,000 (US)

12. Members shall make advances to the working capital fund in accordance with [a provisional] scale which is merely a matter of convenience and in no sense a precedent for the assessment of contributions.

13. These advances shall be readjusted at the time of the second part of the first session of the General Assembly in accordance with the scale to be adopted by the General Assembly for contribution of members to the first annual budget.

14. Except for any readjustments which may result from a revision of the scale referred to in paragraph 3, advances to the working capital fund shall not be offset against contribution of members to the first annual budget.

15. The General Assembly at the second part of its first session (September 1946) shall determine the amount at which the working capital fund should be maintained and the method and timing of consequential set-offs against contributions or other adjustments.

GENERAL ASSEMBLY RESOLUTION 67/248 A-C (2013): PROGRAMME BUDGET FOR THE BIENNIUM 2014–2015

Budget Appropriations for the Biennium 2014–2015

The General Assembly

Resolves that, for the biennium 2014–2015:

1. Appropriations totalling 5,530,349,800 United States dollars are hereby approved for the following purposes:

Part I. Overall policymaking, direction and coordination

1. Overall policymaking, direction and coordination $117 599 800
2. General Assembly and Economic and Social Council affairs and conference management $673 012 400

Part II. Political affairs

3. Political affairs $1 197 957 200
4. Disarmament $24 729 600
5. Peacekeeping operations $113 454 400
6. Peaceful uses of outer space $8 160 600

Part III. International justice and law

7. International Court of Justice $52 344 800
8. Legal affairs $47 809 200

Part IV. International cooperation for development

9. Economic and social affairs $163 049 600
10. Least developed countries, landlocked developing countries and small island developing States $11 579 100
11. United Nations support for the New Partnership for Africa's Development $17 000 300
12. Trade and development $147 132 500
13. International Trade Centre $39 913 900
14. Environment $34 963 500
15. Human settlements $23 260 700
16. International drug control, crime and terrorism prevention and criminal justice $43 883 000
17. UN-Women $15 328 500

Part V. Regional cooperation for development

18. Economic and social development in Africa $151 633 600
19. Economic and social development in Asia and the Pacific $103 764 400
20. Economic development in Europe $71 706 300
21. Economic and social development in Latin America and the Caribbean $116 669 900
22. Economic and social development in Western Asia $70 189 500
23. Regular programme of technical cooperation $58 449 700

Part VI. Human rights and humanitarian affairs

24. Human rights $174 785 600
25. International protection, durable solutions and assistance to refugees $91 496 800
26. Palestine refugees $55 227 500
27. Humanitarian assistance $31 581 400

Part VII. Public information

28. Public information $188 443 900

Part VIII. Common support services

29. Management and support services $657 782 400

Part IX. Internal oversight

30. Internal oversight $40 552 300

Part X. Jointly financed administrative activities and special expenses

31. Jointly financed administrative activities $11 357 800

32. Special expenses $143 660 200

Part XI. Capital expenditures

33. Construction, alteration, improvement and major maintenance $75 268 700

Part XII. Safety and security

34. Safety and security $241 370 100

Part XIII. Development Account

35. Development Account $28 398 800

Part XIV. Staff assessment

36. Staff assessment $486 831 800

Total $5 530 349 800

2. The Secretary-General shall be authorized to transfer credits between sections of the budget, with the concurrence of the Advisory Committee on Administrative and Budgetary Questions;

3. In addition to the appropriations approved under paragraph 1 above, an amount of 75,000 dollars is appropriated for each year of the biennium 2014–2015 from the accumulated income of the Library Endowment Fund for the purchase of books, periodicals, maps and library equipment and for such other expenses of the Library at the Palais des Nations in Geneva as are in accordance with the objects and provisions of the endowment.

7.3 Assessment of Contributions

Contributions to the regular budget are determined by reference to a scale of assessments approved by the General Assembly on the basis of advice from the Committee on Contributions. In 2000, following the United Nations Millennium Declaration, the Assembly revised this scale substantially, to ensure timely availability of resources to the Organization:

GENERAL ASSEMBLY RESOLUTION 55/5 (2001): SCALE OF ASSESSMENTS FOR THE APPORTIONMENT OF THE EXPENSES OF THE UNITED NATIONS

B

The General Assembly,

1. *Decides* that the scale of assessments for the period 2001–2003 shall be based on the following elements and criteria:

(*a*) Estimates of the gross national product;

(*b*) Average statistical base periods of six and three years;

(c) Conversion rates based on market exchange rates, except where that would cause excessive fluctuations and distortions in the income of some Member States, when price-adjusted rates of exchange or other appropriate conversion rates should be employed, taking due account of General Assembly resolution 46/221 B of 21 December 1991;

(d) The debt-burden approach employed in the scale of assessments for the period 1995–1997;

(e) A low per capita income adjustment of 80 per cent, with the threshold per capita income limit of the average per capita gross national product of all Member States for the statistical base periods;

(f) A minimum assessment rate of 0.001 per cent;

(g) A maximum assessment rate for the least developed countries of 0.01 per cent;

(h) A maximum assessment rate of 22 per cent;

2. *Decides also* that the elements of the scale of assessments contained in paragraph 1 above will be fixed until 2006[18], subject to the provisions of resolution C below, in particular paragraph 2 of that resolution, and without prejudice to rule 160 of the rules of procedure of the General Assembly;

3. *Notes* that the application of the methodology outlined in paragraph 1 above will lead to a substantial increase in the rate of assessment of some Member States;

4. *Decides* to apply transitional measures to address those substantial increases; . . .

8. *Resolves* also that:

(a) Notwithstanding the terms of financial regulation 5.5, the Secretary-General shall be empowered to accept, at his discretion and after consultation with the Chairman of the Committee on Contributions, a portion of the contributions of Member States for the calendar years 2001, 2002 and 2003 in currencies other than United States dollars;

(b) In accordance with financial regulation 5.9, States which are not Members of the United Nations but which participate in certain of its activities shall be called upon to contribute towards the 2001, 2002 and 2003 expenses of the Organization on the basis of the following rates:

Holy See: 0.001
Switzerland[19]: 1.274

These rates represent the basis for the calculation of the flat annual fees to be charged to non-member States in accordance with General Assembly resolution 44/197 B of 21 December 1989.

---

[18] Surprisingly, this has not been changed since, although the scales of assessment were being re-examined in the fall of 2015.

[19] Switzerland became a member of the United Nations in 2002.

C

The General Assembly, ...

1. *Establishes,* as from 1 January 2001, a reduced ceiling of 22 per cent for the assessed contribution of any individual Member State;

2. *Decides* to review the position at the end of 2003 and, depending on the status of contributions and arrears, to determine all appropriate measures to remedy the situation, including adjustments of the ceiling in keeping with its resolution 52/215 A to D of 22 December 1997;

3. *Stresses* that the reduction of the maximum assessment rate referred to in paragraph 1 of resolution B above shall apply to the apportionment of the expenses of the United Nations and should have no automatic implication for the apportionment of the expenses of the specialized agencies or the International Atomic Energy Agency.

The methodology underpinning the scale of assessments was to remain fixed only until 2006. However, it has also been used for every scale period since then. Consequently, the same methodology has been applied for fifteen years, from 2001 to 2015. In recent years, tensions have increased as a result of differing views regarding the need to update the methodology and, if so, in what way. Some member states have expressed the view that the current methodology does not accurately reflect a country's ability to pay, and in particular, does not sufficiently account for shifting economic realities. Much of the concern relates to the relief that is provided to low per capita income countries, some of which have very sizable economies. In adopting the 2013–2015 scale of assessments, the General Assembly noted that changes in member states' shares in world gross national income result in changes in relative capacity to pay, which should be more accurately reflected in the scale of assessments, and recognized that the current methodology can be enhanced, bearing in mind the principle of capacity to pay.

Setting aside any problems with the methodology, it should be noted that the scale of assessments suffers from an inherent delay in update. The scale is based on economic data with a two-year time lag, and is only updated every three years. Therefore, the 2016–2018 scale of assessments will be decided in December 2015 using data up to the year 2013. In today's fast-changing financial climate, this inherent delay, although largely accepted as unavoidable, has nevertheless resulted in frustrations regarding the slow pace of updates to the scale to reflect the economic reality.

Since 1992, the peacekeeping budget has surpassed the UN regular budget. In 2003, the peacekeeping budget equaled 67 percent of the assessments available to the United Nations, which are routed in part through the regular budget and in part through special accounts. This led to a greater strain upon the resources of the United Nations and brought it closer to financial

Share of UN Regular Budget (%) & Ranking by Year

Rank	Country	2012[20]	Country	2013–2015[21]
1	United States of America	22.000	United States of America	22.000
2	Japan	12.530	Japan	10.833
3	Germany	8.018	Germany	7.141
4	United Kingdom	6.604	France	5.593
5	France	6.123	United Kingdom	5.179
6	Italy	4.999	China	5.148
7	Canada	3.207	Italy	4.448
8	China	3.189	Canada	2.984
9	Spain	3.177	Spain	2.973
10	Mexico	2.356	Brazil	2.934
11	Republic of Korea	2.260	Russian Federation	2.438
12	Australia	1.933	Australia	2.074
13	Netherlands	1.855	Republic of Korea	1.994
14	Brazil	1.611	Mexico	1.842
15	Russian Federation	1.602	Netherlands	1.654

crisis, as formerly the peacekeeping account was always in surplus and the Secretary-General was able to use these funds to cross-subsidize other activities. The 1990s saw the United Nations falling into severe arrears in repayment to troop contributing countries for peacekeeping operations (PKOs), as expenditures on peacekeeping increased from $490 million in 1991 to $3.1 billion in 1993. Another source of strain has been the rapid growth of the number (and sometimes size) of Special Political Missions (SPMs), a nonmilitary counterpart to PKOs, which by late 2014 amounted to between 20 and 25 percent of the regular budget. The slow-moving pace of regular budget adjustments is ill-suited to the financing of missions that are meant to be fleet, and have the ability to cope rapidly with changing circumstances on the ground. A review of UN peace missions in 2015 made recommendations on how SPMs could be funded more rationally, perhaps along the lines of PKO budgeting.[22]

[20] UN Doc ST/ADM/SER.B/853 "Assessment of Member States' contributions to the United Nations Regular Budget for 2012," 27 December 2011.
[21] GA Res. 67/238 (2013) on the scale of assessments for the apportionment of expenses of the United Nations.
[22] See the "HIPPO" report, extracted in Chapter 9, section 9.7.

GENERAL ASSEMBLY RESOLUTION 55/235 (2000): SCALE OF ASSESSMENTS FOR THE APPORTIONMENT OF THE EXPENSES OF UNITED NATIONS PEACEKEEPING OPERATIONS

The General Assembly,

I

1. *Reaffirms* the following general principles underlying the financing of United Nations peacekeeping operations:

(*a*) The financing of such operations is the collective responsibility of all States Members of the United Nations and, accordingly, the costs of peacekeeping operations are expenses of the Organization to be borne by Member States in accordance with Article 17, paragraph 2, of the Charter of the United Nations;

(*b*) In order to meet the expenditures caused by such operations, a different procedure is required from that applied to meet expenditures under the regular budget of the United Nations;

(*c*) Whereas the economically more developed countries are in a position to make relatively larger contributions to peacekeeping operations, the economically less developed countries have a relatively limited capacity to contribute towards peacekeeping operations involving heavy expenditures;

(*d*) The special responsibilities of the permanent members of the Security Council for the maintenance of peace and security should be borne in mind in connection with their contributions to the financing of peace and security operations;

(*e*) Where circumstances warrant, the General Assembly should give special consideration to the situation of any Member States which are victims of, and those which are otherwise involved in, the events or actions leading to a peacekeeping operation;

2. *Recognizes* the need to reform the current methodology for apportioning the expenses of peacekeeping operations;

3. *Notes with appreciation* voluntary contributions made to peacekeeping operations and, without prejudice to the principle of collective responsibility, invites Member States to consider making such contributions;

II

4. *Decides* that assessment rates for the financing of peacekeeping operations should be based on the scale of assessments for the regular budget of the United Nations, with an appropriate and transparent system of adjustments based on levels of Member States, consistent with the principles outlined above;

5. *Decides also* that the permanent members of the Security Council should form a separate level and that, consistent with their special responsibilities

for the maintenance of peace and security, they should be assessed at a higher rate than for the regular budget;

6. *Decides further* that all discounts resulting from adjustments to the regular budget assessment rates of Member States in levels C through J shall be borne on a pro rata basis by the permanent members of the Security Council;

7. *Decides* that the least developed countries should be placed in a separate level and receive the highest rate of discount available under the scale;

8. *Decides also* that the statistical data used for setting the rates of assessment for peacekeeping should be the same as the data used in preparing the regular budget scale of assessments, subject to the provisions of the present resolution;

9. *Decides further* to create levels of discount to facilitate automatic, predictable movement between categories on the basis of the per capita gross national product of Member States; . . .

11. *Decides also* that Member States will be assigned to the lowest level of contribution with the highest discount for which they are eligible, unless they indicate a decision to move to a higher level;

12. *Decides further* that for purposes of determining the eligibility of Member States for contribution in particular levels during the 2001–2003 scale period, the average per capita gross national product of all Member States will be 4,797 United States dollars and the per capita gross national product of Member States will be the average of 1993 to 1998 figures;

13. *Decides* that transitions as specified above will occur in equal increments over the transition period as designated above;

14. *Decides also* that after 2001–2003, transition periods of two years will apply to countries moving up by two levels, and that transition periods of three years will apply to countries moving up by three levels or more without prejudice to paragraph 11 above;

15. *Requests* the Secretary-General to update the composition of the levels described above on a triennial basis, in conjunction with the regular budget scale of assessment reviews, in accordance with the criteria established above, and to report thereon to the General Assembly;

16. *Decides* that the structure of levels to be implemented from 1 July 2001 shall be reviewed after nine years;

17. *Decides also* that Member States may agree upon adjustments to their assessment rates under the ad hoc scale in the light of the special transitional circumstances applying during the period 1 January to 30 June 2001.

In short, the Assembly decided to adopt a new set of ten levels (A–J) for member states for the purposes of apportioning the costs of peacekeeping, to be implemented on a phased basis from 1 July 2001. The apportionments range from a premium payable by permanent members of the Security Council (Level A) to a 90 percent discount for least developed countries (Level J). General Assembly resolution 55/236 (2000) noted the voluntary movement of a number of states to higher levels than had been indicated in the previous dispensation. The system of financing for PKOs generally has been well accepted, although member states continue to grapple with the question of the discount to be afforded, if any, to those countries that have been traditionally considered as developing countries, but whose economic data reflect a high per capita income.

The table below contains the top fifteen contributing countries to the peacekeeping budget by ranking and share of the budget from 2012 to 2015. Like the regular budget scale of assessments, the peacekeeping scale of assessments can be based on data up to five years old,which creates considerable frustration among those seeking to pay less in contributions.

Perhaps the biggest current challenge in the financing of peacekeeping operations relates to the overall size of the peacekeeping budget. In 2014, the peacekeeping budget grew to $7.8 billion (see A/C.5/68/21), and with the approval of resources for two new peacekeeping missions at the end of 2014, the peacekeeping budget will exceed $8 billion for the first time. With a budget of $8.5 billion (see A/C.5/69/17), peacekeeping operations now account for 75 percent of the resources available to the UN Secretariat

Share of UN Peacekeeping Budget (%) & Ranking by Year[23]

Rank	Country	2012	Country	2013	Country	2014-15
1	United States of America	27.1415	United States of America	28.3835	United States of America	28.3626
2	Japan	12.5300	Japan	10.883	Japan	10.883
3	UK	8.1474	France	7.2159	France	7.2105
4	Germany	8.0180	Germany	7.1410	Germany	7.1410
5	France	7.5540	UK	6.6817	UK	6.6817
6	Italy	4.9990	China	6.6417	China	6.6368
7	China	3.9343	Italy	4.4480	Italy	4.4480
8	Canada	3.2070	Russian Federation	3.1454	Russian Federation	3.1431
9	Spain	3.1770	Canada	2.9840	Canada	2.9840
10	Republic of Korea	2.2600	Spain	2.9730	Spain	2.9730
11	Russian Federation	1.9764	Australia	2.0740	Australia	2.0740
12	Australia	1.9330	Republic of Korea	1.9940	Republic of Korea	1.9940
13	Netherlands	1.8550	Netherlands	1.6540	Netherlands	1.6540
14	Switzerland	1.1300	Switzerland	1.0470	Switzerland	1.0470
15	Belgium	1.0750	Belgium	0.9980	Belgium	0.9980

[23] UN Doc: General Assembly, A/67/224/Add.1, "Implementation of General Assembly Resolutions 55/235 and 55/236 Report of the Secretary General, Annex," 27 December 2012.

through assessments. The growth in the number of active missions, the size of the related budget, the delay in payment of assessed contributions, and the perception of over-budgeting have all contributed to an increased focus on the speedy return of surplus cash once a mission's mandate ends.

7.4 The Advisory Committee on Administrative and Budgetary Questions (ACABQ)

The ACABQ has a key role to play in the budgetary allocations within the United Nations, and its specialized agencies. Initially, it was proposed as a body that would supervise the Secretary-General's financial management. General Assembly resolution 14(I) (1946), quoted earlier, established the Committee and outlined four functions for it. The ACABQ's specific program of work is determined by the requirements of the General Assembly and the other legislative bodies to which the Committee reports. Its membership has been expanded since it was first established and presently stands at sixteen.

As General Assembly resolution 32/103 (1977) indicates, the Committee's work involves a detailed, comprehensive, and continuous assessment of the Organization's budget, to the point that it, and the Fifth Committee (Administrative and Budgetary), which it advises, have occasionally been criticized for "micro-management."

The membership of the ACABQ entered into public discussion in 1996 when, for the first time, a national of the United States was denied a place on the Committee. This was seen by many as a sign of United Nations condemnation of the selective withholding of assessed contributions by the United States. The measure may have been conducive to the Clinton administration's promising to pay back-dues, conditional on being given their "usual" seat the next time. However, as it turned out, the $819 million repayment package was vetoed on 21 October 1998 by President Clinton, and the US candidate failed to find a seat on the Committee in the elections held on 6 November 1998. On 5 November 1999, the United States was restored to its near permanent seat on the Committee. Soon afterward the United States agreed to repay a part of its arrears to the United Nations.

This episode casts doubt on the independence of the ACABQ members, who are supposed to be appointed in their individual capacity. That states have a direct interest in having their citizens appointed to the Committee was apparent from comments such as those of Bill Richardson, at the time US Permanent Representative to the United Nations: "The US considers the work of the ACABQ to be critical to the efforts to make more efficient use of UN resources and to improve the performance of UN programs. Membership of an American on the ACABQ is vitally important for maintaining US confidence in the financial management of the United Nations."[24] It is clear also from the proposals for UN reform in the Senate Report on the Foreign Affairs Reform and Restructuring Act of 1997, which included the creation of a permanent position for a US representative on the ACABQ, or allotment of membership based on the level of contribution.[25] The US position underscores the important role played by the ACABQ in administrative and budgetary matters in the United Nations.

In September 2005, the Committee was again in the news following the arrest of its Chairman Vladimir Kuznetsov, on charges of money laundering.[26] Among other charges, Kuznetsov was alleged to have connections with the Oil-for-Food scandal.[27] In March 2007 he was found guilty of helping to launder more than $300,000 in bribes.[28]

The ACABQ, often divided between positions of donor countries and those of developing countries, remains an important, if opaque body.

7.5 Financial Challenges and Alternatives

As we have seen, despite its relatively small budget the United Nations has faced financial crises with depressing regularity. The primary reason for this is, of course, that the Organization has no resources of its own and must depend upon member states for contributions. These have not always been forthcoming as member states have withheld both assessed and voluntary contributions on different pretexts. The most significant defaulter in this regard has been the United States, which is responsible for more than a fifth

---

[24] United States Mission to the United Nations Announces its Candidate for Membership on UN Budget Committee, 12 March 1998, USUN Press Release No. 45 (98), available at: http://www.un.int/usa/98_45.htm.

[25] Sec. 2231 (5), Senate Report 105-028—Foreign Affairs Reform and Restructuring Act of 1997 states: "The United States must have a seat on the United Nations Committee on Administrative and Budgetary Questions (ACABQ). Until 1997, the United States has served on this committee since the creation of the United Nations. This committee is key to the budgetary decisions at the United Nations and the United States, as the largest contributing nations, should have a seat on this Committee."

[26] Daily Press Briefing by the Office of the Spokesman for the Secretary-General, 02/09/2005, http://www.un.org/News/briefings/docs/2005/db050902.doc.htm. See also Statement by Ambassador John R. Bolton, US Permanent Representative to the United Nations, on the Arrest of the Chairman of the ACABQ Vladimir Kuznetsov, at the Security Council Stakeout, 2 September 2005, USUN Press Release No. 154 (05), 02/09/2005, available at: http://www.un.int/usa/05_154.htm.

[27] Betsy Pisik, "FBI Arrests Russian Envoy in UN Corruption Probe," *Washington Times*, 3 September 2005.

[28] Warren Hoge, "United Nations: Russian Ex-Diplomat Guilty in Bribe Case," *New York Times*, 8 March 2007.

of the UN Budget. For example, at the heart of the *Certain Expenses* case discussed in Chapter 4, the Soviet Union and France refused to honor their assessments for a peacekeeping operation in the Congo authorized by the UN General Assembly in the early 1960s.

The size of its share has allowed the United States to try to impose its own political agenda and policies upon the United Nations. In the past, this has included putting pressure on UN activities seen as benefiting the Palestine Liberation Organization or the South West Africa People's Organization, as well as programs for Libya, Iran, Cuba, and for certain communist countries identified in section 620(f) of the Foreign Assistance Act of 1961. That pressure has typically taken the form of withholding funds from the agencies involved. The US Congress has also denied contributions for UN funds budgeted for the "Second Decade to Combat Racism and Racial Discrimination" and for implementation of General Assembly resolution 3379(XXX) (1975) (the "Zionism is racism" resolution); for the construction of a $73,500,000 conference center in Addis Ababa, Ethiopia; for the Economic Commission for Africa; for the UN "post adjustment allowance" for employees; and for the Department of Public Information, which was accused of bias. The US government has withheld contributions for the Preparatory Commission implementing the 1982 Law of the Sea Convention and for alleged "inadequacies" in the UN system to equalize the effect of US income taxation on the salaries of US members of the UN staff.[29]

In June 2005, the UN Reform Act[30] was passed in the US Congress, which provided for the withholding of up to 50 percent of its dues, unless the United Nations committed itself to attaining its ends.

The UN's financial situation has also been affected by the great expansion in its mandate, as well as the mandates of many of its specialized agencies. Claims of mismanagement and wasteful expenditure have also been made by several countries.

During the Millennium Outcome Summit in September 2005, many states called for greater reforms in the management, accountability, and oversight in the UN Secretariat. Secretary-General Kofi Annan issued a follow-up report entitled *Investing in the United Nations: For a Stronger Organization Worldwide*. The report discusses, inter alia, some of the reasons for the financial problems of the United Nations, pointing out factors such as the inflexible budget implementation process that limits the ability of the United Nations to allocate funds strategically for operational needs, coupled with the highly restricted authority of the Secretary-General to shift resources to

---

[29] José Alvarez, "Legal Remedies and the United Nations a la Carte Problem," *Michigan Journal of International Law*, vol. 12 (1991), pp. 235–237.
[30] H.R. 2745, available at: http://wwwa.house.gov/international_relations/109/HR2745.PDF.

meet emerging needs; the lack of a single, coherent, and commonly under-stood notion of accountability for programm performance; cumbersome practices emerging from the Financial Rules and Regulations; and insuffi-cient transparency and availability of relevant financial information to pro-vide clear guidance either to member states or to Secretariat managers on the Organization's financial picture.

A number of proposals for alternative or supplementary means for financ-ing the UN System have been made by independent organizations and think tanks. These mainly include taxing the activities that link people and enter-prises involved in worldwide operations. Included are currency transaction taxes, email taxes, energy taxes, and aviation fuel taxes.[31]

It has been suggested that currency and email levies could be imposed on those involved in international transactions facilitated by UN System activi-ties. Global currency trade amounts to approximately $1.3 trillion per day. At least 80 percent of this is exchange rate speculation in the form of short- or long-term speculation. Cross-border purchase of goods and services accounts for only 2 percent. About 17 percent of foreign exchange trading takes place as a result of hedging against future exchange rate fluctuations. A tax of only 0.25 percent on these transactions could generate about $300 billion, twenty-five times the 2001 UN system-wide budget of $12 billion. An email or Internet duty would tax the amount of data sent through the Internet. A person sending 100 emails a day, each containing a ten-kilobyte document, might pay a tax of $0.01. The UNDP Human Development Report 1999 claimed that such a tax would have yielded $70 billion in 1996, almost six times the 2001 UN System Budget.[32] However, these hypothetical sources of revenue for the United Nations or its objectives came to naught, meeting considerable resistance in the industries and among potential governments involved.

Other suggestions include aviation fuel and energy taxes on those responsible for global carbon emissions. Another idea is to tax carbon diox-ide emissions from the combustion of fossil fuels. This proposal would tax carbon emissions from the burning of coal, oil, and natural gas. The European Union, in 2012, launched a tax on aviation emissions as part of its overall plan to control the phenomenon (which was fiercely resisted by the United States and in Asia, and is now the subject of discussions within the International Civil Aviation Organization). This followed an initiative by France as of 2005 joined by a number of other countries to tax airline tick-ets, with revenues benefiting UNITAID, a vehicle housed within the World Health Organization to fund greater access to treatments and diagnostics for HIV/AIDS, malaria, and tuberculosis in low-income countries.

---

[31] See, e.g., sources available from www.globalpolicy.org.
[32] Chadwick F. Alger, *The UN System: A Reference Handbook* (Santa Barbara, CA: ABC-CLIO, 2006), pp. 39–40.

QUESTIONS

7. What are the arguments for and against making the United Nations less dependent on state contributions and giving it access to direct funding through various direct taxation schemes?
8. Should UN members have to pay for operations to which they are opposed?

7.6 Mobility of Staff

Kofi Annan had served as Comptroller of the United Nations but in other areas turned out to have little interest in UN management as Secretary-General (making his mark in other ways). Ban Ki-moon, on the other hand, took the management dimension of his position very seriously; his legacy includes, among other things, greatly increasing the number of women appointed to top UN jobs—roughly a third of the total in 2015.

Rather bravely, he also tackled the rigidity of the UN staffing system. In the past, this system promised job security for life to those fortunate enough to be hired into a permanent position that they "owned" until they switched to or were promoted into another. Predictably, it also made for a great deal of accumulating deadwood as the years went on. Secretary-General Boutros Boutros-Ghali was once asked how many people worked at the United Nations and reportedly answered "about half." Another long-time observer of the United Nations estimated that 30 percent of the staff, working heroically, kept the ship afloat, and 30 percent did no harm, while 40 percent were inveterate and inventive troublemakers. The United Nations obviously deserves better.

Ban Ki-moon moved to reform and streamline the employment contract system, to shorten lengthy recruitment processes, and to promote greater competition for UN positions when they came available. This was not popular in all quarters and may have introduced new distortions into a very complex system. But he eventually went further, seeking to navigate the "third rail" of mobility by challenging the basis for immovability of staff from headquarters duties while so many colleagues toil in difficult missions in the field. The move was hotly opposed by those committed to spending their lives commuting agreeably among New York, Geneva, and Vienna. Younger, newer staff members are generally much more open to serving in the field, but worry that "lifers" in the major UN headquarters cities were unlikely to make room for them when it came time to serve there themselves.

The emphasis on greater competition for available positions was strongly supported by member states, who saw permanency of employment (with staff members moving seamlessly from one position to another over long careers) as closing off options that should be available, on a competitive basis, to external as well as internal candidates, not least member state delegates themselves.

The Secretary-General faces challenges at several levels: making sure he or she retains enough staff of long-standing to provide institutional memory, while also seeking to make sure that the United Nations employs the best candidates in any given position.

Earlier attempts had been made to encourage mobility. In 2006, the United Nations' Joint Inspections Unit reported on their lack of success.

JOINT INSPECTIONS UNIT: STAFF MOBILITY IN THE UNITED NATIONS (2006)[33]

Executive Summary—Conclusions and Recommendation

A. Staff mobility is a key element for the Secretariat to develop its activities properly and to adapt its wide range of programmes and activities to a constantly changing global environment. It is also a critical factor for staff, since it has a major influence on their professional and private lives.

Mobility is a multidimensional issue; and any mobility policy, if it is to be viable, must take this fundamental principle into account by matching coherently the organizational requirements with those of the staff.

B. There is a consensus that for human resources management to be effective the mobility of staff needs to be ensured, both within the Secretariat, funds and programmes, and between organizations of the common system. Given the complexity of the issue from a system-wide perspective, and especially because of time constraints, this report deals only with the mobility policy within the Secretariat. There is also a consensus that mobility of staff is essential to creating a more versatile, multi-skilled and experienced international civil service capable of fulfilling both the requirements of Headquarters programmes as well as the complex mandates of field activities, thus helping the Organization to increase its flexibility and responsiveness. The Inspectors who carried out the present review believe that there is a need to further develop staff mobility within the United Nations.

C. While recognizing that staff mobility is a crucial element in effective human resources management and that the Organization is evidently in need of an enhanced mobility system, the Inspectors firmly believe that other considerations should also be pondered, in particular, the need for

---

[33] United Nations, Joint Inspection Unit, "Staff Mobility in the United Nations," JIU/REP/2006/7, Geneva, 2006.

specialized staff, the preservation of institutional memory, and the costs involved.

D. The majority of the staff members interviewed and surveyed are not fully convinced about the effectiveness of the current mobility policy: 40.9% of respondents to the survey indicated that they are "not very satisfied" with the current policy, while 31.7% are "very dissatisfied". Finally, only 12.8% find the policy "encouraging", whereas 32.9% find it "not encouraging at all". The Inspectors do not see this as an expression of opposition to the mobility policy per se, but rather as an expression of a general concern and uncertainty about the viability of the policy and its implementation. They believe that the current policy does not contain enough incentives for the staff to move and that more needs to be done to carry out the mandate of General Assembly resolution 55/258.

E. The Inspectors believe that if the Secretariat is to undertake effectively its work in a challenging and fast-changing environment, there will have to be increased movement of staff.

They fully support the principles set out by the Secretary-General in his mobility policy. However, they believe that the current implementation of the policy needs to be further adjusted to fully comply with these principles and with mandates of the General Assembly. Based on the above, the Inspectors conclude that major challenges or obstacles for the further implementation of the mobility policy may be as many as the following:

- The current mobility policy does not fully address the General Assembly requests in many aspects; (see paragraphs 12, 13, 14, 15, 22, 26, 27, 37, 57, 58, 67, 69, 70 and 84);
- Despite the efforts made, there is an obvious lack of organization-wide culture of mobility, which is essential to the implementation of the mobility policy (see paragraphs 22 to 28);
- A comprehensive strategic mobility plan is not in place with quantified objectives that identify, inter-alia, the locations targeted, the type and volume of staff movement and associated indicators to measure progress in the implementation of mobility (see paragraphs 37 and 38);

No forecast for the financial implications of the implementation of the mobility policy has been made (see paragraphs 70 to 75);

- Despite current and planned initiatives, there are no mechanisms in place for knowledge management and knowledge sharing to prevent the potential loss of institutional memory due to increased mobility (see paragraphs 67 to 69);
- Lack of a clear analysis of the Organization's needs regarding mobility to determine what type of skills, when and where they are required, coupled with a detailed inventory of current staff skills and competencies available by location (see paragraphs 37 and 38);

- There are no simple and coherent staff contractual arrangements in place for the implementation of the mobility policy, the proposed harmonization of contracts has not yet happened (see paragraphs 57 to 60);
- Possible legal implications regarding the further implementation of the mobility policy (see paragraphs 59 and 60);
- There are no specific mechanisms in place to cope with a potential increase of cases due to increased mobility that can provide an efficient administration of justice, ensuring a fair treatment of staff regarding the implementation of mobility (see paragraphs 59 and 84 to 86);
- Despite certain initiatives planned or being put in place, there are no [sic] enough incentive mechanisms to encourage staff to move (see paragraph 87);
- Regardless of some actions taken, no effective measures have been taken to improve work/life conditions in some of the duty stations, which are the major concern for the staff and for the Organization in respect of the implementation of the mobility policy (see paragraphs 88 to 90); and
- In spite of the consultations held, more consultations between management and staff are required (see paragraphs 22 to 28).

F. Since the Secretariat is currently undergoing a complex reform process—about which Member States have considerably diverging views—and taking into account the challenges and obstacles set out above, the Inspectors would like to caution against the possible risks of further implementing the mobility policy. Meanwhile, concrete measures should be taken for mapping out a comprehensive strategic plan for further implementing the mobility policy. In the meantime, efforts should be made to take concrete measures for mapping out a comprehensive strategic plan for further implementing the mobility policy by taking into account all the elements of the mobility policy so as to make the Organization better equipped for its further implementation.

The Inspectors, therefore, would like to make the following recommendation, which they expect to ensure and enhance the effectiveness of the mobility policy.

Recommendation

The General Assembly should request the Secretary-General to resolve the challenges and obstacles identified in the present report (see paragraph E) before further implementing phase 4 of the mobility policy so as to better equip the Organization for the fuller implementation of mobility in the near future and to report to the General Assembly, at its sixty-second session, on the progress made in implementing the present recommendation.

Objective: To provide the General Assembly with an independent, external assessment of the viability, usefulness, cost-effectiveness and impact of the Organization's current mobility policy in the light of the principles and goals stated by the Secretary-General and the related policy directives issued by the General Assembly

In 2013, Ban Ki-moon took on the General Assembly on this sensitive issue.

REPORT OF THE SECRETARY-GENERAL: OVERVIEW OF HUMAN RESOURCE MANAGEMENT REFORM: TOWARDS A GLOBAL, DYNAMIC AND ADAPTABLE WORKFORCE—MOBILITY[34]

Introduction

1. . . . [T]he overall objective of human resources reform in the United Nations is to develop and retain a workforce that is global, dynamic and adaptable in order to ensure that the Organization is able to deliver on the diverse and complex mandates entrusted to it by Member States. [T]he Secretary-General, in consultation with staff representatives, has developed a proposed mobility and career development framework for staff in the Professional category and above, as well as the Field Service category, that aims to deliver his vision . . .

2. The framework set out . . . is based on the principle that, with few exceptions, all internationally recruited staff should move at regular intervals and that staff should be able to make choices that meet their mobility and career development aspirations. The framework . . . establishes maximum position occupancy limits, ranging from three to seven years depending on the hardship classification of the duty station. Staff would be expected to apply for positions before reaching the maximum position occupancy limit. Staff could apply to any position for which they are qualified in the same or in another duty station. To encourage geographic and functional mobility, priority in selection would be given to internal staff applying to a different duty station or to a different job family. Staff who have not moved to other positions after reaching their maximum position occupancy limit would be reassigned by the Organization.

II. Context

11. The present staff selection system has fostered staff mobility since 2007 by requiring two lateral moves for all staff in order to be eligible for posts at the P-5 level. The system also provides incentive to staff movement to

---

[34] UN Doc A/67/324/Add.1.

areas where vacancy rates are higher by requiring only one lateral move when a staff member has served in the Professional category in Nairobi or a regional economic commission other than the Economic Commission for Europe, or any duty station with a hardship classification of A, B, C, D or E for one year or longer, or when a staff member is applying for a P-5 position at those duty stations from another duty station. The requirement for lateral moves is waived entirely for staff who have served for one year or longer in a non-family mission or duty station (see ST/AI/2010/3, para. 6.3).

III. Current mobility patterns

12. Mobility is currently taking place in the Organization, but it is with little or no management and is unevenly distributed... Research on human resources has also shown that job satisfaction and involvement tends to peak in the first four years in a job and plateau or drop thereafter...

13. The Organization continues to face challenges in its staffing. Despite improvements in the overall vacancy rate in the field, certain missions, for example the United Nations Assistance Mission in Afghanistan, where the vacancy rate as of 30 June 2012 was 22.6 per cent, face chronic difficulties in filling their international positions. There are also disproportionately high vacancy rates in certain duty stations and categories of staff ...

14. As the system does not ensure regular exposure of staff to new career opportunities and challenges, the Organization does not reap the full benefits of a more widely experienced staff, which is critical for a global Organization that is increasingly field-oriented and operational. Nor does the current system meet the aspirations of staff ...

IV. Key elements of the mobility and career development framework

17. The Staff Management Committee agreed that the mobility and career development framework had three main objectives:

(a) It should enable the Organization to better retain and deploy a dynamic, adaptable and global workforce that can effectively meet current and future mandates and evolving operational needs;

(b) It should provide staff with broader opportunities for career development and contribution to the Organization and enable the further acquisition of new skills, knowledge and experience within and across departments, functions and duty stations;

(c) It should ensure that staff members have equal opportunities for service across the United Nations and, for relevant functions, a fair sharing of the burden of service in difficult duty stations.

These objectives would contribute to ensuring the Organization's global relevance, enhancing its credibility, and furthering the goal of serving as one United Nations.

18. ... The result is a framework that would allow mobility requirements to be tailored to the needs of each functional area. The proposed framework also strikes a balance between a purely voluntary and a fully centrally managed system. Staff would choose when and where to apply for positions, according to their own preferences and requirements, within the minimum and maximum position occupancy limits ...

This is a change from the current situation where individual hiring managers make selection decisions about individual positions on a case-by-case basis.

Scope

19. The proposed mobility framework would apply to all internal staff of the Secretariat in the Professional category and above up to and including the D-2 level, as well as to staff in the Field Service category, holding fixed-term, continuing and permanent appointments, except those on non-rotational positions.

21. Staff members within five years of the mandatory age of separation could choose to be exempted from geographic mobility. In order to recognize staff members who have already undertaken significant geographic mobility, those staff members who have undergone at least seven geographic moves of one year or longer would be able to choose if they want to be geographically mobile (subject to the requirements of the relevant job network).

Tremendous resistance was mounted to these proposals. The Secretary-General eventually received acceptance of their main thrust in April 2014 in General Assembly Resolution 68/265, one of his toughest battles, with implementation slated for 2016. Member states appear to have feared that mobility would simply lead to a game of musical chairs among existing staff members rather than opening up the house to renewal of human resources. (There was even a move by some to mandate preference for external candidates over internal ones. As noted above, many delegation members aspire to join the Secretariat, where some of them have done excellent work.) Further, they were worried about costs of moving staff around the world to a greater extent than had been the case previously. Promises of greater attention to equitable geographic representation were clearly not credited by all.[35]

---

[35] That said, some member states, for example Japan, are underrepresented in part for other reasons. Although most Japanese working for the United Nations perform remarkably well and bravely in the field, many highly qualified Japanese prefer to stay at home, or to work in the international private sector, leading to frustration both of the Japanese government and UN staff recruiters that more candidacies have not been forthcoming.

Other challenges include overstaffing of some departments and agencies (the Secretariat's Department of Economic and Social Affairs—a major one—spends nearly 90 percent of its budget on staff costs,[36] for example) and under-resourcing of others with rapidly expanding workloads. Because shifts of positions (if not loans of individuals) need to be approved by intergovernmental machinery, the human resources system is slow to adapt to the changing needs of the Organization, to the frustration of all concerned. In effect, like many international organizations, the United Nations is over-regulated in some respects, with staff spending too much time on reporting (in often repetitive or formulaic ways) to the membership, and members spending too much time slightly updating resolutions from earlier years and rehearsing well-established positions formulated decades ago on issues that have often ceased to be relevant. The result is a tremendous misallocation of human resources relative to meaningful results, and a great deal of disgruntlement all around.

QUESTIONS

9. Does the Mobility Framework advanced by Secretary-General Ban Ki-moon strike you as helpful to the UN's effectiveness?
10. Is the Mobility Framework fairer than the regime that pertained earlier, at headquarters and in the field? Why?
11. For the Secretary-General, was it worth investing so much time and credibility in the Mobility Framework, given that in order to succeed on this, he had to prioritize this over other objectives and reform proposals? Why?

Further Reading

Alvarez, José. "Legal Remedies and the United Nations a la Carte Problem." *Michigan Journal of International Law*, vol. 12 (1991), p. 229.
Bezanson, Keith, Paul Isenman and Alex Shak. "Learning from the Experience of Vertical Funds,"2012 available at: http://www.ifpri.org/sites/default/files/publications/focus19_18.pdf.

---

[36] In fact, staff costs account for between 46–48 percent of the UN regular budget and 68–71 percent of the regular budget where special political missions are excluded for the same period. See Table II,2, "Staff Costs as a Percentage of the United Nations Regular Budget, including Case-Study Departments (2010–2015) in A/69/5 (Vol. 1)," "Financial Report and Audited Financial Statements for the Biennium ended 31 December 2013 and Report of the Board of Auditors.' United Nations, New York, 2014.

Cardenas, Emilio J. "Financing the United Nations' Activities: A Matter of Commitment." *University of Illinois Law Review*, vol. 1995 (1995), p. 147.

Chesterman, Simon, "Articles 97–99." Bruno Simma, Daniel-Erasmus Khan, Georg Nolte and Andreas Paulus (eds), *The Charter of the United Nations: A Commentary*, 3rd edn. Oxford: Oxford University Press, 2012, pp. 1991–2021.

Ebner, Christian, "Article 100," Bruno Simma, Daniel-Erasmus Khan, Georg Nolte and Andreas Paulus (eds), *The Charter of the United Nations: A Commentary*, 3rd edn. Oxford: Oxford University Press, 2012, pp. 2022–2052.

Mangone, Gerard J. and Anand K. Srivastava. "Budgeting for the United Nations." *International Organization*, vol. 12 (1958), p. 473.

Ortiz, Even Fontaine and Tadanori Inomata. "Evaluation of Results-Based Budgeting in Peacekeeping Operations". Report of the Joint Inspection Unit, JIU/REP/2006/1, available at: https://www.unjiu.org/en/reports-notes/archive/JIU_REP_2006_1_English.pdf

Stöckl, Wolfgang, "Article 101," Bruno Simma, Daniel-Erasmus Khan, Georg Nolte and Andreas Paulus (eds), *The Charter of the United Nations: A Commentary*, 3rd edn. Oxford: Oxford University Press, 2012, pp. 2053–2088.

Part Three **Practice**

chapter eight
....

Counterterrorism and Nuclear Nonproliferation

Terrorism and nuclear proliferation have risen high on the agenda of the United Nations in recent years. In 2014, more than half of the press statements coming out of the Security Council were on terrorist-related activities.[1] In that same year the Council adopted new resolutions on Iran and North Korea, formally adding the latter to the Security Council agenda for the first time. What is striking is that this comes at a time when the Council is more divided on most issues than it has been since the Cold War. Terrorism and weapons proliferation seem to be among the few areas where the five permanent members (P5) have been able to find common ground. Indeed, the P5 have tended to be out ahead of the UN membership as a whole on these issues. In the field of peace operations and the responsibility to protect, the Council is often criticized for too little action; on terrorism and nuclear proliferation, the criticism is as likely to be for trying to do too much.

In this chapter terrorism and proliferation are discussed separately. The logic for combining them in one chapter is not only that there are some substantive areas of convergence, such as Security Council resolution 1540, but also because the role of the United Nations in respect of each has some common features. First is the point above about the shared interests of the P5. Second is the fact that although the United Nations is the center of action on neither, its work is an important part of the context in which efforts to counter terrorism and proliferation play out. Third, innovative non-UN approaches to tackling both are being experimented with, which could either complement UN efforts or undermine them. Thus the role of the United Nations in these areas sheds light on broader questions about the future of the organization in multilateral efforts to address contemporary security challenges.

---

[1] Highlights of Security Council Practice, 2014; available at: http://www.un.org/en/sc/inc/pages/pdf/highlights/2014.pdf

The chapter begins with a review of attempts to define terrorism, the familiar "one person's terrorist is another person's freedom fighter" challenge. It then moves on to the General Assembly's counterterrorism strategy adopted in 2006. The following section looks at the instruments the Security Council has brought to bear on terrorism: sanctions and quasi-legislative acts (see Chapters 10 and 4 as well). We then consider military action against terrorism, focusing on the contested doctrine of pre-emption based on an expansive reading of Article 51 of the UN Charter. The second part of the chapter begins with an overview of the nuclear nonproliferation regime, followed by two sections on that regime in action: first against Iraq, then Iran and North Korea. We conclude with a discussion of the future of nonproliferation efforts in light of recent successes and setbacks.

8.1 Defining Terrorism

The United Nations has been an important venue for the adoption of multilateral treaties that relate to terrorism. As of mid-2015, thirteen such global treaties are in force (along with several regional treaties), most of which were adopted by the General Assembly or one of the specialized agencies, such as the International Civil Aviation Organization and the International Maritime Organization. The earliest of these dates back to 1963—the Convention on Offences and Certain other Acts Committed on Board Aircraft. The most recent is the Convention for the Suppression of Acts of Nuclear Terrorism (which came into force in 2007).

None is a comprehensive convention against terrorism. Instead, they criminalize specific acts—such as hijacking an aircraft or seizing a ship on the high seas—and impose obligations on parties either to prosecute or extradite those responsible. The measures are largely in the nature of collaborative law enforcement, rather than the threat or use of armed force against the terrorists and those who support them.

The inability to agree on a definition of terrorism is the main reason a comprehensive convention has never been achieved. The League of Nations did draft a treaty that defined terrorism as "all criminal acts directed against a State and intended or calculated to create a state of terror in the minds of particular persons, or a group of persons, or the general public," but it never had enough ratifications to come in to force. Subsequent attempts at definition have been variations on that phrase, without the qualification that the terrorist acts must be "against a state."

Immediately after the 11 September 2001, attacks on the United States, a working group of the General Assembly tried once again to come up with a comprehensive convention, but that effort had foundered by the end of 2001. The latest attempt at a global definition came from the 2004 Secretary-General's High Level Panel on Threats Challenges and Change. This followed the intervention in Iraq in 2003, the political fallout of which brought the United Nations to a "fork in the road" in the Secretary-General's words, which prompted him to establish the panel to point the way forward. The Panel's lengthy report included the following definition of terrorism:

> any action, in addition to actions already specified by the existing conventions on aspects of terrorism, the Geneva Conventions and Security Council resolution 1566 [see below] that is intended to cause death or serious bodily harm to civilians or non-combatants, when the purpose of such an act, by its nature or context, is to intimidate a population, or to compel a government or an international organization to do or abstain from doing any act.[2]

In April 2005, the Secretary-General produced his own report that combined elements of the High Level Panel and another report on implementation of the Millennium Development Goals for discussion at the World Summit later that year. In *In Larger Freedom*, the Secretary-General recommended endorsement of the High Level Panel's definition of terrorism; it was the subject of intensive discussion leading to the Summit, but agreement on a definition proved to be as elusive as ever.

WORLD SUMMIT OUTCOME DOCUMENT, GA RES. 60/1 (2005)

Terrorism

81. We strongly condemn terrorism in all its forms and manifestations, committed by whomever, wherever and for whatever purposes, as it constitutes one of the most serious threats to international peace and security.

82. We welcome the Secretary-General's identification of elements of a counterterrorism strategy. These elements should be developed by the General Assembly without delay with a view to adopting and implementing a strategy to promote comprehensive, coordinated and consistent responses, at the national, regional and international levels, to counter terrorism, which also takes into account the conditions conducive to the spread of terrorism. In this context, we commend the various initiatives to promote dialogue, tolerance and understanding among civilizations.

83. We stress the need to make every effort to reach an agreement on and conclude a comprehensive convention on international terrorism during the sixtieth session of the General Assembly.

85. We recognize that international cooperation to fight terrorism must be conducted in conformity with international law, including the Charter and relevant international conventions and protocols. States must ensure

---

[2] UN Doc. A/59/565 (2004), para 164(d).

that any measures taken to combat terrorism comply with their obligations under international law, in particular human rights law, refugee law and international humanitarian law.

86. We reiterate our call upon States to refrain from organizing, financing, encouraging, providing training for or otherwise supporting terrorist activities and to take appropriate measures to ensure that their territories are not used for such activities.

QUESTIONS

1. The High Level Panel's definition was resisted by various constituencies at the World Summit for different reasons: some objected to the fact that is does not cover a state's use of armed force against civilians; others objected to the fact that it considers attacks on people only, not buildings; others were concerned it captures all nonstate parties to civil conflicts, complicating efforts to bring these wars to an end; and others still want to distinguish self-determination struggles from other forms of armed conflict. What are the merits of these objections? Can they be overcome?
2. Is a definition of terrorism needed? Are there acts that are allowed or cannot be prosecuted because of the lack of such a definition? Is this more of a legal or a political problem?

8.2 The General Assembly's Counterterrorism Strategy

The Security Council became the center of action in the "war on terrorism" in the immediate aftermath of 9/11. But precisely because not all states believed waging war was the best approach, the General Assembly adopted a more comprehensive strategy in 2006. The strategy was based on a report written by the Secretary-General in April of that year, which in turn built on the five components of an effective approach that he had identified in the lead-up to the World Summit:

- dissuading people from resorting to terrorism or supporting it;
- denying terrorists the means to carry out an attack;
- deterring States from supporting terrorism;
- developing State capacity to defeat terrorism; and
- defending human rights.[3]

---

[3] Report of the Secretary-General, "Uniting against terrorism: recommendations for a global-counter-terrorism strategy." A/60/825, 27 April 2006.

The report included an inventory of all the activities UN entities were engaged in each of the five areas and set out proposals for the future. The Assembly responded with a multifaced plan of action.

THE UNITED NATIONS GLOBAL COUNTER-TERRORISM STRATEGY, GA RES. 60/288 (20 SEPTEMBER 2006)

Plan of Action

We, the States Members of the United Nations, resolve: . . .

2. To take urgent action to prevent and combat terrorism in all its forms and manifestations and, in particular:

(a) To consider becoming parties without delay to the existing international conventions and protocols against terrorism, and implementing them, and to make every effort to reach an agreement on and conclude a comprehensive convention on international terrorism;

(b) To implement all General Assembly resolutions on measures to eliminate international terrorism and relevant General Assembly resolutions on the protection of human rights and fundamental freedoms while countering terrorism;

(c) To implement all Security Council resolutions related to international terrorism and to cooperate fully with the counter-terrorism subsidiary bodies of the Security Council in the fulfilment of their tasks, recognizing that many States continue to require assistance in implementing these resolutions;

3. To recognize that international cooperation and any measures that we undertake to prevent and combat terrorism must comply with our obligations under international law, including the Charter of the United Nations and relevant international conventions and protocols, in particular human rights law, refugee law and international humanitarian law. . . .

II. Measures to prevent and combat terrorism

We resolve to undertake the following measures to prevent and combat terrorism, in particular by denying terrorists access to the means to carry out their attacks, to their targets and to the desired impact of their attacks:

1. To refrain from organizing, instigating, facilitating, participating in, financing, encouraging or tolerating terrorist activities and to take appropriate practical measures to ensure that our respective territories are not used for terrorist installations or training camps, or for the preparation or organization of terrorist acts intended to be committed against other States or their citizens;

2. To cooperate fully in the fight against terrorism, in accordance with our obligations under international law, in order to find, deny safe haven and bring to justice, on the basis of the principle of extradite or prosecute, any person who supports, facilitates, participates or attempts to participate in the financing, planning, preparation or perpetration of terrorist acts or provides safe havens;

3. To ensure the apprehension and prosecution or extradition of perpetrators of terrorist acts, in accordance with the relevant provisions of national and international law, in particular human rights law, refugee law and international humanitarian law. We will endeavour to conclude and implement to that effect mutual judicial assistance and extradition agreements and to strengthen cooperation between law enforcement agencies; . . .

5. To strengthen coordination and cooperation among States in combating crimes that might be connected with terrorism, including drug trafficking in all its aspects, illicit arms trade, in particular of small arms and light weapons, including man-portable air defence systems, money-laundering and smuggling of nuclear, chemical, biological, radiological and other potentially deadly materials; . . .

III. Measures to build States' capacity to prevent and combat terrorism and to strengthen the role of the United Nations system in this regard

. . .

7. To encourage the United Nations Office on Drugs and Crime, including its Terrorism Prevention Branch, to enhance, in close consultation with the Counter-Terrorism Committee and its Executive Directorate, its provision of technical assistance to States, upon request, to facilitate the implementation of the international conventions and protocols related to the prevention and suppression of terrorism and relevant United Nations resolutions;

8. To encourage the International Monetary Fund, the World Bank, the United Nations Office on Drugs and Crime and the International Criminal Police Organization to enhance cooperation with States to help them to comply fully with international norms and obligations to combat money-laundering and the financing of terrorism;

9. To encourage the International Atomic Energy Agency and the Organization for the Prohibition of Chemical Weapons to continue their efforts, within their respective mandates, in helping States to build capacity to prevent terrorists from accessing nuclear, chemical or radiological materials, to ensure security at related facilities and to respond effectively in the event of an attack using such materials;

10. To encourage the World Health Organization to step up its technical assistance to help States to improve their public health systems to prevent and prepare for biological attacks by terrorists;

12. To encourage the International Maritime Organization, the World Customs Organization and the International Civil Aviation Organization to strengthen their cooperation, work with States to identify any national shortfalls in areas of transport security and provide assistance, upon request, to address them;

The counterterrorism strategy is reviewed every two years by the General Assembly. A Counter-Terrorism Implementation Task Force, composed of twenty-nine UN entities, is charged with overseeing it. As the threat of Al-Qaeda morphed into threats of violent extremism form multiple offshoots of Al-Qaeda, the Islamic State, Boko Haram, and other groups, Secretary-General Ban Ki-moon announced a new initiative at a G7 meeting in June 2015:

> Later this year, I will present a "United Nations Global Plan of Action to Prevent Violent Extremism" to the General Assembly. The Plan will propose ways to address the causes of violent extremism, including intolerance, governance failures and political, economic and social marginalization.... Addressing violent extremism demands a proactive, "all-of-society" approach that includes minorities, women and youth as partners ... Undoubtedly, security measures and even military action may be necessary to address the real threats posed by violent extremists. But when counter-terrorism efforts ignore the rule of law and violate fundamental rights—which they do far too often—they not only betray the values they seek to uphold, but can also end up further fuelling violent extremism.... Missiles may kill terrorists. But I am convinced that good governance is what will kill terrorism.[4]

QUESTION

3. The strategy adopted by the General Assembly calls on many parts of the UN system to join the fight against terrorism. For some the role is obvious, such as the UN Office for Drugs and Crime and Interpol. For others it is not so obvious, such as the World Bank and World Health Organization. What are the pros and cons of drawing these entities into efforts to counterterrorism and violent extremism?

---

[4] Secretary-General Ban Ki Moon, "Remarks at G7 Working Session on Terrorism," 8 June 2015.

8.3 Security Council Sanctions and Quasi-legislation

Before 9/11, the UN Security Council had responded to particular acts of terrorism in three cases, primarily by imposing sanctions. As discussed in Chapter 4, the first was in 1992, against Libya (resolution 748). The primary goal was to get Libya to hand over two suspects in the Lockerbie bombings. Libya eventually complied, in part due to the sanctions and other forms of diplomatic pressure.

The Council also imposed sanctions against Sudan in 1996, in respect of the assassination attempt on President Hosni Mubarak of Egypt (resolutions 1054 and 1070). Although the sanctions did not have much practical impact, they did send a signal that the Council was willing and able to become more engaged in this area.

The third case was the sanctions on the Taliban in 1999, following the bombing of US embassies in Kenya and Tanzania, for which Osama Bin Laden was deemed responsible (resolution 1267). The resolution demanded that the Taliban end its support for terrorism and extradite bin Laden. After 9/11, the Taliban regime was removed from power in Afghanistan, but financial sanctions against the Taliban, Al-Qaeda, and their associates remained in place. The 1267 sanctions regime and the legal challenges to it are covered in Chapters 4 and 10.

All three cases preceded 9/11 and, although Washington was the driving force behind all of them, it found willing partners among the other P5. As noted above, although echoes of the Cold War have been heard in Council chambers in recent years, terrorism is an area where the P5 have found much common ground. In the post 9/11 era, that common ground opened the door to a new type of Security Council action, described in Chapter 4 as "quasi-legislation".

The first of these, resolution 1373, obliges states to take a wide range of measures to prevent future terrorist acts. Most of the substantive content of 1373 comes from the Conventions on the Suppression of Terrorist Bombings and the Suppression of Financing of Terrorism. The effect of the resolution is to make those obligations binding on all states, including those that did not sign or ratify the conventions. Implementation of resolution 1373 is through the Counter-Terrorism Committee (CTC).[5] The principal job of the Committee, composed of all fifteen members of the Security Council, is to monitor compliance with the resolution by reviewing reports states submit on steps they have taken to meet their obligations.

---

[5] For details on the Counter-Terrorism Committee, see http://www.un.org/en/sc/ctc/.

Although it had a decent record of success in the early years, the CTC began to run out of steam in late 2003 and implementation lagged. So resolution 1535 was adopted early in 2004 to "revitalize" the work of the CTC. The reforms were designed to give the Committee a more proactive compliance-monitoring role, to enhance dialogue with governments through site visits, and to facilitate technical assistance to states in legislative drafting, counterterrorism investigation, border control, and law enforcement. The first chairman of the CTC, British ambassador Jeremy Greenstock, described the committee as a "switchboard," brokering deals between states needing technical assistance and those that could provide it.[6] The most innovative structural reform was a new Counter-Terrorism Executive Directorate (CTED), a body of twenty experts to help the CTC carry out its strategic and policy decisions. The CTED was created in March 2004 but not declared operational until the end of 2005. The proposal for an executive directorate generated considerable controversy, reflected in a row over whether it should report directly to the CTC or through the Secretary-General. The controversy stemmed from a concern that the Directorate could undermine the Secretariat and authority of the Secretary-General by creating a new structure accountable to the Security Council (and, by implication, its most powerful members) only. The end result was a compromise in which the CTED would operate under the "policy guidance" of the CTC, but the Executive Director would be appointed by and report through the Secretary-General, and its staff members would be subject to Article 100 of the UN Charter, the cornerstone of an independent international civil service.

Resolution 1540 was the next quasi-legislative act of the Security Council. Its main purpose is to prevent weapons of mass destruction from falling into the hands of terrorists, although it has a broader nonproliferation mandate. As discussed in Chapter 4, resolution 1540 was harder to negotiate than 1373 because the political climate had changed: it came a year after the US-led intervention in Iraq in 2003, not in the immediate aftermath of 9/11. In the end, the Security Council managed to adopt it by unanimous vote because it could be characterized as essentially a counterterrorism rather than nonproliferation resolution. A committee was established with a mandate similar to that of the CTC to oversee implementation of resolution 1540.[7] In 2006, the 1540 Committee's mandate was extended by resolution 1673.

---

[6] Report by the Chair of the Counter-Terrorism Committee on the Problems Encountered in the Implementation of Security Council resolution 1373 (2001), UN Doc. S/2004/70, annex at 8 (26 January 2004).

[7] For details on the 1540 Committee, see http://www.un.org/en/sc/1540/.

SECURITY COUNCIL RESOLUTION 1673 (2006)

The Security Council,

Noting that the full implementation of resolution 1540 (2004) by all States, including the adoption of national laws and measures to ensure the implementation of these laws, is a long-term task that will require continuous efforts at national, regional and international levels,

Acting under Chapter VII of the Charter of the United Nations, . . .

5. *Decides* that the 1540 Committee shall intensify its efforts to promote the full implementation by all States of resolution 1540 (2004) through a work programme which shall include the compilation of information on the status of States' implementation of all aspects of resolution 1540 (2004), outreach, dialogue, assistance and cooperation, and which shall address in particular all aspects of paragraphs 1 and 2 of that resolution, as well as of paragraph 3 which encompasses (a) accountability, (b) physical protection, (c) border controls and law enforcement efforts and (d) national export and trans-shipment controls including controls on providing funds and services such as financing to such export and trans-shipment, and in that regard:

(a) *encourages* the pursuit of the ongoing dialogue between the 1540 Committee and States on the full implementation of resolution 1540 (2004), including on further actions needed from States to that end and on technical assistance needed and offered;

(b) *invites* the 1540 Committee to explore with States and international, regional and sub-regional organizations experience-sharing and lessons learned in the areas covered by resolution 1540 (2004), and the availability of programmes which might facilitate the implementation of resolution 1540 (2004);

The 1540 Committee was extended for another ten years by resolution 1977 in April 2011:

SECURITY COUNCIL RESOLUTION 1977 (2011)

The Security Council, . . .

5. *Decides* to continue to provide the 1540 Committee with the assistance of experts, and to this end:

(a) *Requests* the Secretary-General to establish, in consultation with the 1540 Committee, a group of up to eight experts ("group of experts"), acting under the direction and purview of the Committee, composed of individuals with the appropriate experience and knowledge to provide the Committee with expertise . . .

12. *Requests* the 1540 Committee, with the support of the group of experts, to identify effective practices, templates and guidance, with a view to develop a compilation, as well as to consider preparing a technical reference guide about resolution 1540 (2004), to be used by States on a voluntary basis in implementing resolution 1540 (2004), and in that regard, encourages the 1540 Committee, at its discretion, to draw also on relevant expertise, including, civil society and the private sector, with, as appropriate, their State's consent;

As discussed in Chapter 4, by the time resolution 1540 was adopted many member states already had concerns about the Security Council acting in a quasi-legislative manner. Although resolution 1540 was extended in 2011, it was ten years after that original resolution before the Council was able to adopt another quasi-legislative resolution, in the context of the Syria crisis. By 2014, Syria had been the subject of three years of virtual paralysis of the Security Council, with China and Russia vetoing four resolutions. The emergence of ISIS changed the equation and, in August 2014, the Council adopted resolution 2170, which imposed sanctions on extremists groups in Iraq and Syria. This was followed by resolution 2178, which, looked beyond Iraq and Syria to the problem of foreign terrorist fighters everywhere.

SECURITY COUNCIL RESOLUTION 2178 (2014)

The Security Council, ...
   Acting under Chapter VII of the Charter of the United Nations,
   1. *Condemns* the violent extremism, which can be conducive to terrorism, sectarian violence, and the commission of terrorist acts by foreign terrorist fighters, and demands that all foreign terrorist fighters disarm and cease all terrorist acts and participation in armed conflict;
   2. *Reaffirms* that all States shall prevent the movement of terrorists or terrorist groups by effective border controls and controls on issuance of identity papers and travel documents, and through measures for preventing counterfeiting, forgery or fraudulent use of identity papers and travel documents, underscores, in this regard, the importance of addressing, in accordance with their relevant international obligations, the threat posed by foreign terrorist fighters, and encourages Member States to employ evidence-based traveller risk assessment and screening procedures including collection and analysis of travel data, without resorting to profiling based on stereotypes founded on grounds of discrimination prohibited by international law;
   3. *Urges* Member States, in accordance with domestic and international law, to intensify and accelerate the exchange of operational information

regarding actions or movements of terrorists or terrorist networks, including foreign terrorist fighters ...

4. *Calls* upon all Member States, in accordance with their obligations under international law, to cooperate in efforts to address the threat posed by foreign terrorist fighters, including by preventing the radicalization to terrorism and recruitment of foreign terrorist fighters, including children, preventing foreign terrorist fighters from crossing their borders, disrupting and preventing financial support to foreign terrorist fighters, and developing and implementing prosecution, rehabilitation and reintegration strategies for returning foreign terrorist fighters;

5. *Decides* that Member States shall, consistent with international human rights law, international refugee law, and international humanitarian law, prevent and suppress the recruiting, organizing, transporting or equipping of individuals who travel to a State other than their States of residence or nationality for the purpose of the perpetration, planning, or preparation of, or participation in, terrorist acts or the providing or receiving of terrorist training, and the financing of their travel and of their activities;

6. *Recalls* its decision, in resolution 1373 (2001), that all Member States shall ensure that any person who participates in the financing, planning, preparation or perpetration of terrorist acts or in supporting terrorist acts is brought to justice, and *decides* that all States shall ensure that their domestic laws and regulations establish serious criminal offenses sufficient to provide the ability to prosecute and to penalize in a manner duly reflecting the seriousness of the offense:

No new committee was established to oversee the implementation of resolution 2178. Instead, the committees established under resolutions 1267 and 1373 were given that task.

As to the issue of how to define terrorism, none of resolutions 1373, 1540, or 2178 provide a definition. However, Security Council was able to do so in response to an attack on a school in the town of Beslan, North Ossetia, that led to the death of 385 people, including 187 children. Resolution 1566, adopted in October 2004, contained the following language:

> ... Recalls that criminal acts, including against civilians, committed with the intent to cause death or serious bodily injury, or taking of hostages, with the purpose to provoke a state of terror in the general public or in a group of persons or particular persons, intimidate a population or compel a government or an international organization to do or to abstain from doing any act, which constitute offences within the scope of and as defined in the international conventions and protocols relating to terrorism.[8]

---

[8] Security Council Resolution 1566 (2004).

QUESTIONS

4. How problematic is the lack of a definition of terrorism in resolutions 1373, 1540 and 2178? Does it leave open the possibility of abuse of human rights, for example? Can the various committees established to oversee implementation of the resolutions help to alleviate that concern? Why, in adopting resolution 2178, did the Council not employ the definition it had agreed to in 1566?

5. Ambassador Jeremy Greenstock, the first chairman of the 1373 committee, understood that these quasi-legislative resolutions, though adopted under Chapter VII, could not be enforced coercively. Instead he promoted a dialogic approach that relied on persuasion and leadership by example. Is it realistic to expect compliance with these resolutions via a dialogic approach? What factors, if not coercive enforcement, may induce states to comply with international law?

8.4 Military Action against Terrorism

Article 51 of the UN Charter allows for individual or collective self-defense in the event of an "armed attack." When the United States launched attacks against Al-Qaeda and the Taliban in Afghanistan on 7 October 2001, it announced it was doing so on the basis of self-defense in connection with the events of 9/11. The legal justification the United States gave is set out in a letter it sent to the President of the Security Council on the day the military action began.

LETTER OF PERMANENT REPRESENTATIVE OF US TO PRESIDENT OF THE SECURITY COUNCIL, UN DOC S/2001/946, 7 OCTOBER 2001

Since 11 September, my Government has obtained clear and compelling information that the Al-Qaeda organization, which is supported by the Taliban regime in Afghanistan, had a central role in the attacks. There is still much we do not know. Our inquiry is in its early stages. We may find that our self-defense requires further actions with respect to other organizations and other States.

The attacks on 11 September 2001 and the ongoing threat to the United States and its nationals posed by the Al-Qaeda organization have been made possible by the decision of the Taliban regime to allow the parts of Afghanistan that it controls to be used by this organization as a base of operation. Despite every effort by the United States and the international community, the Taliban regime has refused to change its policy. From the territory of Afghanistan, the Al-Qaeda organization continues to train and support agents of terror who attack innocent people throughout the world and target United States nationals and interests in the United States and abroad.

In response to these attacks, and in accordance with the inherent right of individual and collective self-defense, United States armed forces have initiated actions designed to prevent and deter further attacks on the United States. These actions include measures against Al-Qaeda terrorist training camps and military installations of the Taliban regime in Afghanistan.

A year later, in September 2002, the United States adopted a new national security strategy that addressed and—in the view of some—sought to rewrite the law of self-defense for a post-9/11 world.

THE NATIONAL SECURITY STRATEGY OF THE UNITED STATES 2002

For centuries, international law recognized that nations need not suffer an attack before they can lawfully take action to defend themselves against forces that present an imminent danger of attack. Legal scholars and international jurists often conditioned the legitimacy of preemption on *the existence of an imminent threat*—most often a visible mobilization of armies, navies, and air forces preparing to attack.

We must adapt the concept of imminent threat to the capabilities and objectives of today's adversaries. Rogue states and terrorists do not seek to attack us using conventional means. They know such attacks would fail. Instead, they rely on acts of terror and, potentially, the use of weapons of mass destruction—weapons that can be easily concealed, delivered covertly, and used without warning. . . .

The United States has long maintained the option of preemptive actions to counter a sufficient threat to our national security. The greater the threat, the greater is the risk of inaction—and the more compelling the case for taking anticipatory action to defend ourselves, even if uncertainty remains as to the time and place of the enemy's attack. To forestall or prevent such hostile acts by our adversaries, the United States will, if necessary, act preemptively.

The doctrine of pre-emption was not invoked expressly to justify the intervention in Iraq in March 2003, but it was an important part of the backdrop of Security Council deliberations that led to it. The explicit legal claim for military action that the United States made was reflected in the letter it sent to the President of the Council a day before the intervention began, which is quoted in Chapter 2, section 2.1 of this volume.

As noted above, the 2003 war and its aftermath prompted the establishment of the High Level Panel on Threats Challenges and Change, which among other things considered the legality and propriety of the doctrine of preemption.

REPORT OF THE SECRETARY-GENERAL'S HIGH LEVEL PANEL ON THREATS, CHALLENGES AND CHANGE ENTITLED "A MORE SECURE WORLD: OUR SHARED RESPONSIBILITY." A/59/565, 2 DECEMBER 2004

188. . . . a threatened State, according to long established international law, can take military action as long as the threatened attack is imminent, no other means would deflect it and the action is proportionate. The problem arises where the threat in question is not imminent but still claimed to be real: for example the acquisition, with allegedly hostile intent, of nuclear weapons-making capability.

189. Can a State, without going to the Security Council, claim in these circumstances the right to act, in anticipatory self-defence, not just pre-emptively (against an imminent or proximate threat) but preventively (against a non-imminent or non-proximate one)? Those who say "yes" argue that the potential harm from some threats (e.g., terrorists armed with a nuclear weapon) is so great that one simply cannot risk waiting until they become imminent, and that less harm may be done (e.g., avoiding a nuclear exchange or radioactive fallout from a reactor destruction) by acting earlier.

190. The short answer is that if there are good arguments for preventive military action, with good evidence to support them, they should be put to the Security Council, which can authorize such action if it chooses to. If it does not so choose, there will be, by definition, time to pursue other strategies, including persuasion, negotiation, deterrence and containment—and to visit again the military option.

A more recent test case for the law of self-defense is the targeted killing of insurgents and suspected terrorists by unarmed aerial vehicles, or drones. The strikes began under the George W. Bush administration and accelerated under President Obama, especially against Al-Qaeda and the Taliban in Pakistan. Reportedly, the Pakistani government has acquiesced to the strikes, but has never explicitly consented for fear of a domestic backlash. Without consent of the host government or Security Council authorization, the only possible legal justification for the strikes is self-defense, in which case they would still have to comply with the laws of armed conflict and human rights standards.

In May 2010, the UN Human Rights Council's Special Rappporteur on extrajudicial, summary, or arbitrary executions Philip Alston presented a report on the legal issues surrounding targeted kitlings generally , and about the use of drones for such killings specifically.[9] Although most of his analysis focused on human rights and humanitarian law, he did raise questions about whether these killings could be justified as a matter of self-defense.

The Bush administration never offered a public justification for the strikes. The Obama administration was equally circumspect initially, until State Department legal adviser Harold Koh who—more than two years into President Obama's first term—set out the administration's legal position in a speech to the American Society of International Law (ASIL). In this speech he stated that "lethal operations conducted with the use of unmanned armed vehicles comply with all applicable law, including the laws of war." The United States was in an "ongoing armed conflict with al-Qaeda, the Taliban and associated forces in response to 9/11 and may use force consistent with its inherent right to self-defense. In targeting decisions, the principles of distinction and proportionality are respected."[10]

US attorney-general Eric Holder elaborated in a speech he gave at Northwestern University on 5 March 2012. He said lethal force against Al-Qaeda and associated forces was permissible because the United States was in an "armed conflict" with them and they presented an "imminent threat of violent attack." Moreover it is not restricted to Afghanistan because the enemy is stateless and is directing attacks against the United States from other countries. The United States can act in these other places either with the consent of the nation involved, or if the nations is "unable and unwilling" to deal effectively with the threat to the United States. Holder added that the test of imminence depends on "the relevant window of opportunity

---

[9] Special Rappporteur on extrajudicial, summary or arbitrary executions, "Study on Targeted Killings," A/HRC/14/24/Add.6, 28 May 2010.
[10] Harold Koh, "The Obama Administration and International Law," Annual Meeting of the American Society of International Law, 25 March 2010; available at: http://www.state.gov/s/l/releases/remarks/139119.htm.

to act, the possible harm that missing the window would cause civilians, and the likelihood of heading off future disastrous attacks against the US."[11]

QUESTIONS

6. In what ways is the application of Article 51 to the US-led military action in Afghanistan a stretch of the concept of self-defense? Is this interpretation of Article 51 justifiable? Was it accepted by the international community? To what evidence can one point to suggest it was or was not accepted? What does this tell us about Charter interpretation?
7. Could the self-defense argument be extended to justify intervention in Iraq eighteen months later? Was that argument accepted by the international community? To what evidence can one point to suggest it was or was not accepted?
8. Which is better law, the position taken in the 2002 US National Security Strategy or the 2004 UN High Level Panel? Which is better policy?
9. Do you find the US justification for the legality of the drone strikes on the basis of self-defense to be persuasive? Is the legal justification for strikes in Pakistan equally applicable to strikes in Somalia, Yemen and elsewhere? What policy issues are raised by the use of drones to combat terrorism?

8.5 The Nuclear Nonproliferation Regime

Although terrorism and nuclear nonproliferation are distinct issues, in the UN context they are linked by several factors. To reiterate points made in the introduction to this chapter, one is the menacing risk of nuclear weapons falling into the hands of terrorists. Second, these are both areas where the P5 have common interests, making Security Council action possible though not easy. Third, both threats have created direct challenges to the regimes designed to deal with them: the UN Charter rules on the use of force on the one hand, and the Nuclear Non-Proliferation Treaty on the other. These challenges have prompted unorthodox responses in both fields, which seek to compensate for the weaknesses of orthodox approaches but may in the process weaken them further.

The centerpiece of the nuclear nonproliferation regime is the Treaty on the Non-Proliferation of Nuclear Weapons, in force since 1970. As of mid-2015,

---

[11] "Attorney General Eric Holder Speaks at Northwestern University School of Law," 5 March 2012; available at: http://www.justice.gov/opa/speech/attorney-general-eric-holder-speaks-northwestern-university-school-law.

it had 188 or 189 adherents (depending on whether one counts North Korea, a state that purported to withdraw from the treaty but whose withdrawal was never formally accepted) including all five declared nuclear weapon states: China, France, Russia, the United Kingdom, and the United States. The only countries that are not parties are India, Israel, Pakistan, and, de facto, North Korea.

The Non-Proliferation Treaty (NPT) has two types of parties: nuclear weapons states and nonnuclear weapon states. The main obligation on the nonnuclear powers is to refrain from acquiring, manufacturing, or possessing such weapons. The nuclear powers in turn commit not to transfer nuclear weapons or devices to any recipient, while agreeing to assist in the peaceful development of nuclear energy by sharing of nuclear equipment, materials, and technology. To further balance the equation between nuclear haves and have-nots, the former also undertook to pursue negotiations in good faith toward nuclear disarmament. Thus the three pillars of the NPT are nonproliferation, disarmament, and peaceful nuclear energy. The NPT parties see it as a "grand bargain" between the two types of states. The holdouts see it as "discriminatory," because it creates two classes of international citizen.

To verify that nonnuclear states are complying with their obligations, they must accept safeguards administered by the International Atomic Energy Agency (IAEA), a UN-affiliated organization that was originally formed in 1957, but came to occupy a central role in nonproliferation efforts with the entry into force of the NPT. Broadly, the twin aims of the IAEA are to promote the safe use of nuclear power and to ensure that any nuclear assistance is not used to further a military purpose.

Because the IAEA failed to detect Iraq's clandestine nuclear program before 1991, its Board of Governors endorsed more vigorous implementation of the safeguards system, including "special inspections" of undeclared facilities on short notice. The strengthened verification system is now embodied in an Additional Protocol to the standard safeguards agreements all NPT parties must sign. This Additional Protocol, adopted in 1997, gives the IAEA authority to inspect countries more broadly, particularly for undeclared nuclear facilities. It is designed to ensure that a state's declaration of its nuclear facilities is "complete" as well as "correct" (i.e., that it is not engaged in clandestine activities). As of May 2015, 146 states had signed the Additional Protocol, and it was in force for 125 of them.

Both the UN General Assembly and the International Court of Justice are also part of the nuclear nonproliferation regime. The General Assembly has adopted a series of resolutions, starting in 1961, declaring that the use of nuclear weapons would be a violation of the Charter and a crime against humanity. The International Court of Justice (ICJ) examined the impact of these resolutions in its *Advisory Opinion on the Legality of the Threat or Use of Nuclear Weapons*, concluding that because of negative votes cast and abstentions, they did not signify binding customary law, but they did represent "a clear sign of deep concern regarding the problem of nuclear weapons." The main finding of the ICJ is that the threat or use of nuclear weapons would generally be contrary to humanitarian law, but—by a vote of seven to seven (the deciding vote in favor being cast by the President)—"the Court cannot conclude definitively whether the threat or use would be lawful or unlawful in an extreme circumstance of self-defense in which the very survival of the state would be at stake."

In addition to the basic NPT obligations described above, several provisions of the treaty have been the subject of legal and political contestation.

NUCLEAR NON-PROLIFERATION TREATY, 1970

Article I

Each nuclear-weapon State Party to the Treaty undertakes not to transfer to any recipient whatsoever nuclear weapons or other nuclear explosive devices or control over such weapons or explosive devices directly, or indirectly; and not in any way to assist, encourage, or induce any non-nuclear-weapon State to manufacture or otherwise acquire nuclear weapons or other nuclear explosive devices, or control over such weapons or explosive devices.

Article III

1. Each non-nuclear-weapon State Party to the Treaty undertakes to accept safeguards, as set forth in an agreement to be negotiated and concluded with the International Atomic Energy Agency in accordance with the Statute of the International Atomic Energy Agency and the Agency's safeguards system, for the exclusive purpose of verification of the fulfilment of its obligations assumed under this Treaty with a view to preventing diversion of nuclear energy from peaceful uses to nuclear weapons or other nuclear explosive devices...

Article IV

1. Nothing in this Treaty shall be interpreted as affecting the inalienable right of all the Parties to the Treaty to develop research, production and use of nuclear energy for peaceful purposes without discrimination and in conformity with articles I and II of this Treaty.

2. All the Parties to the Treaty undertake to facilitate, and have the right to participate in, the fullest possible exchange of equipment, materials and scientific and technological information for the peaceful uses of nuclear energy. Parties to the Treaty in a position to do so shall also co-operate in contributing alone or together with other States or international organizations to the further

development of the applications of nuclear energy for peaceful purposes, especially in the territories of non-nuclear-weapon States Party to the Treaty, with due consideration for the needs of the developing areas of the world. . . .

Article VI

Each of the Parties to the Treaty undertakes to pursue negotiations in good faith on effective measures relating to cessation of the nuclear arms race at an early date and to nuclear disarmament, and on a Treaty on general and complete disarmament under strict and effective international control. . . .

Article X

1. Each Party shall in exercising its national sovereignty have the right to withdraw from the Treaty if it decides that extraordinary events, related to the subject matter of this Treaty, have jeopardized the supreme interests of its country. It shall give notice of such withdrawal to all other Parties to the Treaty and to the United Nations Security Council three months in advance. Such notice shall include a statement of the extraordinary events it regards as having jeopardized its supreme interests.

QUESTIONS

10. Some argue that—despite Article IV—Iran could be denied the right to enrich uranium and/or reprocess plutonium, because its behavior had manifest an intention to use these sensitive proliferation-prone technologies for weapons rather than peaceful purposes. Is there merit to this interpretation of Article IV?

11. Article VI requires nuclear states "to pursue negotiations in good faith" to end their arms race "at an early date," and to achieve complete nuclear disarmament, with no time frame specified for the latter. What does this imprecise obligation require of nuclear weapon states? Have the five NPT nuclear states fulfilled their obligations?

12. Article X grants a right to withdraw from the NPT on three months' notice. When North Korea announced its intention to withdraw first in March 1993, then again in January 2003, the other parties did not formally accept (as of July 2015, the DPRK was still listed as a party to the NPT). Is Article X simply a procedural requirement to provide notification of withdrawal? Or can the other parties to the Treaty and the Security Council question the substance of a claim that "extraordinary events have jeopardized the supreme interests of the country"?

8.6 Nonproliferation and Iraq

An important part of the Iraq story touched on in Chapter 2 but warranting further attention here concerns the disarmament obligations of resolution 687. They require Iraq to accept the destruction and long-term monitoring of its nuclear, chemical, biological, and long-range ballistic missile programs. In some ways, resolution 687 is even more significant for the UN Charter-based order than the 1991 Gulf War itself because it imposed a highly intrusive inspection regime that sought to constrain the *future* behavior of Iraq. The demands made on Iraq illustrate how innovative the Security Council can be when it is unified—and how difficult it can be to sustain that unity over an extended period.

The IAEA was assigned primary responsibility for overseeing dismantlement of Iraq's nuclear programs. Because no comparable body existed for chemical and biological weapons, or ballistic missiles, the Security Council created the UN Special Commission (UNSCOM). UNSCOM was established as a subsidiary organ of the Security Council under Article 29 of the Charter. It reported directly to the Security Council, not the Secretary-General, and therefore was an unusual kind of organization composed of staff that worked directly for the members of the Security Council (unlike peace operations for example).

SECURITY COUNCIL RESOLUTION 687 (1991)

The Security Council, ...

Conscious of the need to take the following measures acting under Chapter VII of the Charter, . . .

8. *Decides* that Iraq shall unconditionally accept the destruction, removal, or rendering harmless, under international supervision, of [chemical and biological weapons, and ballistic missiles with a range of more than 150 kilometers]. . .

9. *Decides*, for the implementation of paragraph 8 above, the following:

(a) Iraq shall submit to the Secretary-General, within fifteen days of the adoption of the present resolution, a declaration of the locations, amounts and types of all items specified in paragraph 8 and agree to urgent, on-site inspection as specified below;

(b) The Secretary-General, in consultation with the appropriate Governments and, where appropriate, with the Director-General of the World Health Organization, within forty-five days of the passage of the present resolution, shall develop, and submit to the Council for approval, a plan calling for the completion of the following acts within forty-five days of such approval:

(i) The forming of a Special Commission, which shall carry out immediate on-site inspection of Iraq's biological, chemical and missile capabilities, based on Iraq's declarations and the designation of any additional locations by the Special Commission itself;

(ii) The yielding by Iraq of possession to the Special Commission for destruction, removal or rendering harmless, taking into account the requirements of public safety, of all items specified under paragraph 8 (a) above, including items at the additional locations designated by the Special Commission under paragraph 9 (b) (i) above and the destruction by Iraq, under the supervision of the Special Commission, of all its missile capabilities, including launchers, as specified under paragraph 8 (b) above;

(iii) The provision by the Special Commission of the assistance and cooperation to the Director-General of the International Atomic Energy Agency required in paragraphs 12 and 13 below;

10. *Decides* that Iraq shall unconditionally undertake not to use, develop, construct or acquire any of the items specified in paragraphs 8 and 9 above and requests the Secretary-General, in consultation with the Special Commission, to develop a plan for the future ongoing monitoring and verification of Iraq's compliance with this paragraph, to be submitted to the Security Council for approval within one hundred and twenty days of the passage of this resolution; ...

12. *Decides* that Iraq shall unconditionally agree not to acquire or develop nuclear weapons or nuclear-weapons-usable material or any subsystems or components or any research, development, support or manufacturing facilities related to the above; to submit to the Secretary-General and the Director-General of the International Atomic Energy Agency within fifteen days of the adoption of the present resolution a declaration of the locations, amounts, and types of all items specified above; to place all of its nuclear-weapons-usable materials under the exclusive control, for custody and removal, of the International Atomic Energy Agency, with the assistance and cooperation of the Special Commission as provided for in the plan of the Secretary-General discussed in paragraph 9 (b) above; to accept, in accordance with the arrangements provided for in paragraph 13 below, urgent on-site inspection and the destruction, removal or rendering harmless as appropriate of all items specified above; and to accept the plan discussed in paragraph 13 below for the future ongoing monitoring and verification of its compliance with these undertakings;

13. *Requests* the Director-General of the International Atomic Energy Agency, through the Secretary-General, with the assistance and cooperation of the Special Commission as provided for in the plan of the Secretary-General in paragraph 9 (b) above, to carry out immediate on-site inspection of Iraq's nuclear capabilities based on Iraq's declarations and the designation of any additional locations by the Special Commission; to

develop a plan for submission to the Security Council within forty-five days calling for the destruction, removal, or rendering harmless as appropriate of all items listed in paragraph 12 above; to carry out the plan within forty-five days following approval by the Security Council; and to develop a plan, taking into account the rights and obligations of Iraq under the Treaty on the Non-Proliferation of Nuclear Weapons of 1 July 1968, for the future ongoing monitoring and verification of Iraq's compliance with paragraph 12 above . . .

QUESTION

13. Did the Security Council's authority to impose this disarmament regime come from the Nuclear Non-Proliferation Treaty? If not, where does the authority come from?

Iraq's cooperation with both UNSCOM and the IAEA was always grudging, and there were a number of serious standoffs when the inspectors were denied access to suspect sites. The most serious incident began in November 1997, which started a chain of events leading the Secretary-General to negotiate a Memorandum of Understanding (MOU) with Saddam Hussein setting out some "special procedures" for inspection of so-called Presidential sites: more advance notice would be given and some senior diplomats appointed by the Secretary-General could accompany the UNSCOM and IAEA experts to those sites. The MOU was endorsed by the Security Council in resolution 1154 on 2 March 1998.

Iraq let the inspectors in, but after six months, more Iraqi obstructionism eventually provoked the United States and United Kingdom to launch air strikes in December 1998, in what was called Operation Desert Fox. The air strikes did not compel Saddam Hussein to readmit the inspectors, and the United States and United Kingdom did not have the appetite to force him to do so. Serious splits began to emerge in the Council, with the United States and United Kingdom on one side, Russia and China on the other, and France leaning toward Russia and China. The Secretary-General proposed a "comprehensive review" of Iraq's compliance with resolution 687. The review was prompted in part by allegations that the Executive-Director of UNSCOM (Richard Butler) was colluding with the Central Intelligence Agency in a manner that went well beyond the sharing of information that was needed to carry out effective inspections.[12]

---

[12] David Malone, "Weapons Inspector: UNSCOM, UNMOVIC and the Disarming of Iraq," *The International Struggle over Iraq: Politics in the UN Security Council 1990–2005*, Oxford: Oxford University Press, 2006, pp. 152–184.

Based on that review, the Security Council began to negotiate a new inspections regime in May 1999. The Council negotiations continued for seven months, finally ending with the adoption of resolution 1284 in December. That resolution established the United Nations Monitoring, Verification and Inspection Commission (UNMOVIC) to replace UNSCOM. The vote was eleven for and four abstentions, with China, France, Malaysia, and Russia abstaining.

SECURITY COUNCIL RESOLUTION 1284 (1999)

The Security Council, ...
   Acting under Chapter VII of the Charter of the United Nations ...
   2. *Decides also* that UNMOVIC will undertake the responsibilities mandated to the Special Commission by the Council ... that UNMOVIC will establish and operate ... a reinforced system of ongoing monitoring and verification, ... and will identify, as necessary in accordance with its mandate, additional sites in Iraq to be covered by the reinforced system of ongoing monitoring and verification;
   3. *Reaffirms* the provisions of the relevant resolutions with regard to the role of the IAEA in addressing compliance by Iraq with paragraphs 12 and 13 of resolution 687 (1991) and other related resolutions.
   4. ... *decides* in particular that Iraq shall allow UNMOVIC teams immediate, unconditional and unrestricted access to any and all areas, facilities, equipment, records and means of transport which they wish to inspect in accordance with the mandate of UNMOVIC, as well as to all officials and other persons under the authority of the Iraqi Government whom UNMOVIC wishes to interview so that UNMOVIC may fully discharge its mandate;
   6. *Requests* the Executive Chairman of UNMOVIC, within 45 days of his appointment, to submit to the Council, in consultation with and through the Secretary-General, for its approval an organizational plan for UNMOVIC, including its structure, staffing requirements, management guidelines, recruitment and training procedures, incorporating as appropriate the recommendations of the panel on disarmament and current and future ongoing monitoring and verification issues, and recognizing in particular the need for an effective, cooperative management structure for the new organization, for staffing with suitably qualified and experienced personnel, who would be regarded as international civil servants subject to Article 100 of the Charter of the United Nations, drawn from the broadest possible geographical base, including as he deems necessary from international arms control

organizations, and for the provision of high quality technical and cultural training;

QUESTION

14. What is the significance of paragraph 6 of resolution 1284?

Despite the reformed inspections regime, Saddam Hussein was not persuaded to cooperate and would not allow the inspectors back—neither UNMOVIC nor IAEA. So between December 1998 and November 2002, there were no weapons inspections at all in Iraq.

In the summer of 2002, the United States began signaling it was ready to take much more assertive action. President George W. Bush went to the UN General Assembly on September 12 and made a speech suggesting the United States was prepared to act militarily, but wanted to build a coalition to do so. He in effect challenged the Security Council to enforce its own resolutions against Iraq, or become irrelevant. Some hard negotiations followed, which led to resolution 1441, adopted on 7 November by a vote of fourteen to zero (with Syria absent).

SECURITY COUNCIL RESOLUTION 1441 (2002)

The Security Council, ...
    Acting under Chapter VII of the Charter of the United Nations ...
    5. *Decides* that Iraq shall provide UNMOVIC and the IAEA immediate, unimpeded, unconditional, and unrestricted access to any and all, including underground, areas, facilities, buildings, equipment, records, and means of transport which they wish to inspect, as well as immediate, unimpeded, unrestricted, and private access to all officials and other persons whom UNMOVIC or the IAEA wish to interview in the mode or location of UNMOVIC's or the IAEA's choice pursuant to any aspect of their mandates; further decides that UNMOVIC and the IAEA may at their discretion conduct interviews inside or outside of Iraq, may facilitate the travel of those interviewed and family members outside of Iraq, and that, at the sole discretion of UNMOVIC and the IAEA, such interviews may occur without the presence of observers from the Iraqi Government ...

7. *Decides further* that, in view of the prolonged interruption by Iraq of the presence of UNMOVIC and the IAEA and in order for them to accomplish the tasks 4 S/RES/1441 (2002) set forth in this resolution and all previous relevant resolutions and notwithstanding prior understandings, the Council hereby establishes the following revised or additional authorities, which shall be binding upon Iraq, to facilitate their work in Iraq:

– UNMOVIC and the IAEA shall determine the composition of their inspection teams and ensure that these teams are composed of the most qualified and experienced experts available; . . .

– UNMOVIC and the IAEA shall have unrestricted rights of entry into and out of Iraq, the right to free, unrestricted, and immediate movement to and from inspection sites, and the right to inspect any sites and buildings, including immediate, unimpeded, unconditional, and unrestricted access to Presidential Sites equal to that at other sites, notwithstanding the provisions of resolution 1154 (1998) of 2 March 1998; . . .

– UNMOVIC and the IAEA shall have the right to declare, for the purposes of freezing a site to be inspected, exclusion zones, including surrounding areas and transit corridors, in which Iraq will suspend ground and aerial movement so that nothing is changed in or taken out of a site being inspected;

Two weeks after the adoption of resolution 1441, the IAEA and UNMOVIC were back in the country for the first time in four years. They submitted a few reports to the Security Council that noted some lack of cooperation and compliance on the part of Iraq, but never explicitly declared Iraq to be in "material breach" of its obligations. The heads of the two organizations, Hans Blix and Mohamed ElBaradei, thought it was the job of the Security Council to make that determination. The job of the IAEA and UNMOVIC was to report the facts.

The United States and United Kingdom in particular were not satisfied with the level of Iraq's cooperation. Following failed efforts to negotiate a resolution that would explicitly authorize military action, they intervened in March 2003. The IAEA and UNMOVIC pulled out just before the military action began.

QUESTION

15. What lessons can/should be learned from the Iraq weapons inspection regime? To what extent is it a precedent that could be applied elsewhere? In your response, please consider both the experiences of UNSCOM/UNMOVIC and that of the IAEA.

8.7 Nonproliferation, Iran, and North Korea

The Nuclear Non-Proliferation Treaty itself is silent on enforcement, but the reference in Article III to IAEA safeguards provides a channel through which violations can be referred to the UN Security Council.

STATUTE OF THE IAEA

Article XII

. . .

C. The staff of inspectors shall ... report any non-compliance [with the safeguards agreement] to the Director General who shall thereupon transmit the report to the Board of Governors. The Board shall call upon the recipient State or States to remedy forthwith any non-compliance which it finds to have occurred. The Board shall report the non-compliance to all members and to the Security Council and General Assembly of the United Nations. In the event of failure of the recipient State or States to take fully corrective action within a reasonable time, the Board may take one or both of the following measures: direct curtailment or suspension of assistance being provided by the Agency or by a member, and call for the return of materials and equipment made available to the recipient member or group of members. The Agency may also, in accordance with article XIX, suspend any non-complying member from the exercise of the privileges and rights of membership.

Although violations of safeguards are to be reported to the Security Council by the IAEA, neither the NPT nor the IAEA Statute stipulate whether and how the Security Council is to respond. It is up to the Security Council to decide, on a case- by-case basis.

Iraq is not a case of NPT enforcement per se because the intervention there was prompted by the invasion of Kuwait, not by a violation of the Treaty or safeguards system. In fact referrals to the Security Council by the IAEA have been rare—Iran and North Korea are the only two cases. The story of Iran's referral is interesting. In December 2002, the United States announced concern that Iran (an NPT party) was building two new nuclear sites capable of producing highly enriched uranium (i.e., weapons-grade). Iran admitted to building these sites, but claimed they were designed to produce low-enriched uranium for nuclear power plants. The IAEA did some inspections and the Director-General expressed suspicions in spring 2003, to which

Iran objected. In September 2003, the IAEA Board of Governors adopted a resolution that gave Iran until October 31 to "remedy all failures identified by IAEA," namely failures to report material, facilities, and activities as required by safeguards agreement. Implicitly, the IAEA resolution signaled that if Iran did not respond, the matter would be referred to the Security Council.

Iran agreed in October 2003 to suspend enrichment, to cooperate fully with IAEA, and to sign and ratify the Additional Protocol to Safeguards Agreement. But suspicions about its compliance did not end. The IAEA Board of Governors responded with a series of resolutions designed to keep pressure on Iran while leaving room for talks led by the E-3 (France, Germany, and the United Kingdom) and Russia.

In August 2005, Iran resumed its nuclear enrichment activities, claiming it had a right to do so under the NPT. A month later, the IAEA Board declared Iran to be in violation of its safeguards agreement and the Agency statute. The Board did not formally refer the matter to the Security Council, but signaled that it was prepared to do so. The vote on that resolution was twenty-two for, one against, and 12 twelve abstentions (Russia, China, Brazil, Pakistan, South Africa, and Nigeria were among the abstainers).

IAEA BOARD OF GOVERNORS RESOLUTION, "IMPLEMENTATION OF THE NPT SAFEGUARDS AGREEMENT IN THE ISLAMIC REPUBLIC OF IRAN", GOV/2005/77, 24 SEPTEMBER 2005

1. Finds that Iran's many failures and breaches of its obligations to comply with its NPT Safeguards Agreement, as detailed in GOV/2003/75, constitute non-compliance in the context of Article XII.C of the Agency's Statute;

2. Finds also that the history of concealment of Iran's nuclear activities referred to in the Director General's report, the nature of these activities, issues brought to light in the course of the Agency's verification of declarations made by Iran since September 2002 and the resulting absence of confidence that Iran's nuclear programme is exclusively for peaceful purposes have given rise to questions that are within the competence of the Security Council, as the organ bearing the main responsibility for the maintenance of international peace and security; . . . .

4. In order to help the Director General to resolve outstanding questions and provide the necessary assurances, urges Iran: . . .

(ii) To re-establish full and sustained suspension of all enrichment-related activity, as in GOV/2005/64, and reprocessing activity;

(iii) To reconsider the construction of a research reactor moderated by heavy water;

(iv) Promptly to ratify and implement in full the Additional Protocol;

(v) Pending completion of the ratification of the Additional Protocol to continue to act in accordance with the provisions of the Additional Protocol, which Iran signed on 18 December 2003;

The next step came in January 2006, when the Foreign Ministers of the United States, United Kingdom, France, Germany, Russia, and China (later known as the P5 plus one) issued a statement calling for the IAEA to report Iran's noncompliance to the Security Council, but the Council should wait until March before acting. The Council took up the matter for the first time and, on 29 March, adopted a Presidential Statement expressing serious concern about the Iran situation (S/PRST/2006/15). It called on Iran to take steps required by the IAEA Board of Governors, including "full and sustained suspension of all enrichment-related activities."

In July 2006, the Security Council adopted a resolution that threatened sanctions (resolution 1696). Then in December 2006, it imposed sanctions targeted on material related to its nuclear program (resolution 1737). This was followed by three further rounds of sanctions, in resolution 1747 (March 2007), 1803 (March 2008), and 1929 (June 2010). Meanwhile non-Security Council authorized sanctions were imposed by the United States and European Union, including on Iran's oil program.

Intensive diplomatic efforts by the P5+1 (sometimes called the E3 ı 3) accompanied the sanctions. These accelerated in 2013, leading to a historic nuclear deal on 14 July 2015. The deal limits Iran's most sensitive, proliferation-prone activities and puts in place a rigorous IAEA inspections regime. In return, sanctions would be lifted progressively.[13] On 20 July 2015, the Security Council endorsed the deal by unanimous vote in resolution 2231.

QUESTION

16. Diplomatic efforts and Security Council sanctions on Iran were two elements of multilateral efforts that led to the nuclear deal. Other elements included IAEA inspections, bilateral diplomacy, the evolving situation in the Middle East (including the rise of the Islamic State), and the threat of force. What, in your view, were the most important factors? How did the various elements fit together? How important was the role of the Security Council?

---

[13] For a brief overview of the deal, see Kelsey Davenport and Daryl Kimball, "An Efficient, Verifiable, Nuclear Deal with Iran," Arms Control Association, Iran Nuclear Policy Brief, 15 July 2015.

In both Iran and North Korea, the Security Council went further than imposing targeted sanctions, by authorizing interdiction of suspicious vessels on the high seas or forcing them into port. Below are key extracts from the North Korea resolution:

SC RESOLUTION 1874 (2009)

The Security Council,

Acting under Chapter VII of the Charter of the United Nations, and taking measures under its Article 41, . . .

11. *Calls upon* all States to inspect, in accordance with their national authorities and legislation, and consistent with international law, all cargo to and from the DPRK, in their territory, including seaports and airports, if the State concerned has information that provides reasonable grounds to believe the cargo contains items the supply, sale, transfer, or export of which is prohibited by paragraph 8 (a), 8 (b), or 8 (c) of resolution 1718 or by paragraph 9 or 10 of this resolution, for the purpose of ensuring strict implementation of those provisions;

12. *Calls upon* all Member States to inspect vessels, with the consent of the flag State, on the high seas, if they have information that provides reasonable grounds to believe that the cargo of such vessels contains items the supply, sale, transfer, or export of which is prohibited by paragraph 8 (a), 8 (b), or 8 (c) of resolution 1718 (2006) or by paragraph 9 or 10 of this resolution, for the purpose of ensuring strict implementation of those provisions;

13. *Calls upon* all States to cooperate with inspections pursuant to paragraphs 11 and 12, and, if the flag State does not consent to inspection on the high seas, *decides* that the flag State shall direct the vessel to proceed to an appropriate and convenient port for the required inspection by the local authorities pursuant to paragraph 11.

Similar language exists in in SC resolution 1929 (2010) on the interdiction of Iranian vessels.

QUESTION

17. Does resolution 1874 impose any binding obligations on states? What if a flag state refused to comply with paragraph 13? Can force be used to compel it to comply?

8.8 The Future of Nonproliferation

The successful extension of the NPT in 1995 generated momentum that carried into the NPT 2000 Review Conference. Among other things, the so-called "13 steps" were adopted, which were labeled practical steps toward implementation of Article VI of the NPT on disarmament by the nuclear weapon states—including measures such as "urgent" ratification of the Comprehensive Test Ban Treaty, and an "unequivocal undertaking" to accomplish total elimination of nuclear weapons.

However, the atmosphere had soured by the 2005 NPT review conference. A consensus declaration came out of that meeting, but it contained no substantive agreement on any of the major issues dividing the parties. The World Summit Outcome document issued later that year did not have a word about nonproliferation and disarmament. Seven carefully drafted and negotiated paragraphs were removed from the text on the last day of the Summit. The only way either of these events could be described as a success is that there was no formal rollback of the agreements reached in 1995 and 2000. At the World Summit, the view of eighty or so like-minded states was that weak language in the outcome document would have been worse than no language at all.

When President Obama took office in 2008, he made nonproliferation a priority. His first big step was a speech in Prague in April 2009, envisioning a world free of nuclear weapons, picking up on a theme that George Schultz, William Perry, Henry Kissinger, and Sam Nunn have been advocating in some widely read op-ed pieces. He then chaired a Security Council summit meeting in 2009, out of which came resolution 1887.

SECURITY COUNCIL RESOLUTION 1887 (2009)

The Security Council, . . .

1. *Emphasizes* that a situation of non-compliance with non-proliferation obligations shall be brought to the attention of the Security Council, which will determine if that situation constitutes a threat to international peace and security, and emphasizes the Security Council's primary responsibility in addressing such threats; . . .

5. *Calls upon* the Parties to the NPT, pursuant to Article VI of the Treaty, to undertake to pursue negotiations in good faith on effective measures relating to nuclear arms reduction and disarmament, and on a Treaty on general and complete disarmament under strict and effective international control, and calls on all other States to join in this endeavour; . . .

7. *Calls upon* all States to refrain from conducting a nuclear test explosion and to sign and ratify the Comprehensive Nuclear Test Ban Treaty (CTBT), thereby bringing the treaty into force at an early date; . . .

11. *Encourages* efforts to ensure development of peaceful uses of nuclear energy by countries seeking to maintain or develop their capacities in this field in a framework that reduces proliferation risk and adheres to the highest international standards for safeguards, security, and safety;

12. *Underlines* that the NPT recognizes in Article IV the inalienable right of the Parties to the Treaty to develop research, production and use of nuclear energy for peaceful purposes without discrimination and in conformity with Articles I and II, and recalls in this context Article III of the NPT and Article II of the IAEA Statute; . . .

15. *Affirms* that effective IAEA safeguards are essential to prevent nuclear proliferation and to facilitate cooperation in the field of peaceful uses of nuclear energy, and in that regard:

a. *Calls upon* all non-nuclear-weapon States party to the NPT that have yet to bring into force a comprehensive safeguards agreement or a modified small quantities protocol to do so immediately,

b. *Calls upon* all States to sign, ratify and implement an additional protocol, which together with comprehensive safeguards agreements constitute essential elements of the IAEA safeguards system, . . .

16. *Encourages* States to provide the IAEA with the cooperation necessary for it to verify whether a state is in compliance with its safeguards obligations, and affirms the Security Council's resolve to support the IAEA's efforts to that end, consistent with its authorities under the Charter;

17. *Undertakes* to address without delay any State's notice of withdrawal from the NPT, including the events described in the statement provided by the State pursuant to Article X of the Treaty, while noting ongoing discussions in the course of the NPT review on identifying modalities under which NPT States Parties could collectively respond to notification of withdrawal, and affirms that a State remains responsible under international law for violations of the NPT committed prior to its withdrawal; . . .

21. *Calls for* universal adherence to the Convention on Physical Protection of Nuclear Materials and its 2005 Amendment, and the Convention for the Suppression of Acts of Nuclear Terrorism;

24. *Calls upon* Member States to share best practices with a view to improved safety standards and nuclear security practices and raise standards of nuclear security to reduce the risk of nuclear terrorism, with the aim of securing all vulnerable nuclear material from such risks within four years;

26. *Calls upon* all States to improve their national capabilities to detect, deter, and disrupt illicit trafficking in nuclear materials throughout their territories, and calls upon those States in a position to do so to work to enhance international partnerships and capacity building in this regard;

27. *Urges* all States to take all appropriate national measures in accordance with their national authorities and legislation, and consistent with international law, to prevent proliferation financing and shipments, to strengthen export controls, to secure sensitive materials, and to control access to intangible transfers of technology;

28. *Declares* its resolve to monitor closely any situations involving the proliferation of nuclear weapons, their means of delivery or related material, including to or by non-State actors as they are defined in resolution 1540 (2004), and, as appropriate, to take such measures as may be necessary to ensure the maintenance of international peace and security ...

Although the NPT and IAEA are still at the center of the nuclear nonproliferation regime, a number of nontraditional approaches are being experimented with. At the risk of oversimplifying, the traditional approach to nonproliferation is to negotiate a multilateral treaty whose goal is universal adherence, to establish a verification mechanism to monitor compliance with the treaty, and ultimately to count on the Security Council to enforce it. This approach has scored some important successes over the years: South Africa, Ukraine, Belarus, and Kazakhstan have renounced nuclear weapons; Argentina, Brazil, and Libya have abandoned nuclear intentions; there are still only nine known nuclear states (including North Korea); IAEA safeguards have been strengthened; and there was a successful NPT Review conference in 2010, regaining some of the lost ground from 2005.

But the regime has also suffered some setbacks: discovery that Iraq was cheating on safeguards in 1991, nuclear tests by India and Pakistan in 1998, North Korea's withdrawal from NPT and its nuclear tests, the Iran crisis, and growing concerns about the security of nuclear facilities and the fear of nuclear terrorism. Concerns about the viability of the regime took a further blow at the 2015 NPT Review Conference. Amidst rising frustration among the nonnuclear states about failure of the nuclear states to fulfil their part of the "grand bargain," and the enhanced risk of several additional states, notably in the wider Middle East, "going nuclear" in years ahead, the NPT conference failed to adopt a concluding document. These events have put the regime under stress, perhaps even in jeopardy.

If one feature characterizes the new approaches, it is that they are less than universal—at least at their inception. An example is resolution 1540. Another is the nuclear security summits, three of which have been held outside the UN context since 2010. A third is the Proliferation Security Initiative (PSI): an arrangement whereby states agree to interdict ships suspected of carrying WMD or WMD-related material through their territorial waters. It started out as an arrangement among 11 states and now numbers almost 100. It is not embodied in a treaty, and there is no institution to oversee it. As part of the PSI, the United States has entered into ship-boarding agreements with a number of key "flag of convenience states": Liberia, Panama, and the Marshall Islands. The United States is allowed to board those vessels if they are suspected of carrying WMD-related material.

An interesting question is whether these new approaches complement and reinforce the existing regime, or whether they will undermine and perhaps replace it. Arguably resolution 1540 and the PSI fill gaps in the regime—gaps that would not be filled quickly enough if traditional approaches to multilateral decision-making were pursued. On the other hand, the NPT is based on a carefully calibrated set of bargains and compromises. These new approaches, although useful on their own terms, might throw that delicate balance off, leading to complete collapse of nuclear nonproliferation norms and institutions.

A similar tension exists in the field of counterterrorism. The traditional approach has been to address terrorism primarily as a collaborative law enforcement problem, with the Security Council stepping in from time to time to impose sanctions. More coercive action, including drone strikes, has had some notable successes but may also undermine broader multilateral efforts.

QUESTIONS

17. Will the new approaches to nuclear nonproliferation reinforce or undermine the existing regime?
18. Is the United Nations the best forum in which to address terrorism and proliferation?

HYPOTHETICAL

In 2009, many were worried that the nuclear nonproliferation regime was unraveling. Security Council resolution 1887, a US initiative, was an attempt to address some of the concerns. Although the initiative was generally welcomed, it was met with some suspicion from the nonaligned group at the United Nations, who doubt the Security Council is well placed to take the lead on this topic given that the P5 also happen to be the five declared nuclear powers. Although the adoption of resolution 1887 was followed by a successful NPT review conference in 2010, the participants in the 2015 conference were unable to reach consensus on an outcome text. Imagine the new President of the General Assembly seeks to convene a summit meeting with the goal of shoring up the nuclear nonproliferation regime. Students shall be assigned roles as representatives of four different groups of countries: the five permanent members of the Security Council, other nuclear powers, parties to the NPT who are generally supportive of the regime, and parties to the NPT who are skeptical about the regime. Seek to negotiate a consensus document.

Further Reading

Allison, Graham. *Nuclear Terrorism: The Ultimate Preventable Catastrophe,* New York: Holt Paperbacks, 2005.

Bianchi, Andre (ed). *Enforcing International Law Norms against Terrorism.* Oxford: Oxford University Press, 2004.

Boulden, Jane, Ramesh Thakur and Tom Weiss (eds). *The UN and Nuclear Orders.* New York: United Nations University, 2009.

Brown, Michael E. et al. (eds). *Going Nuclear: Nuclear Proliferation and International Security in the 21st Century.* Cambridge, MA: MIT Press, 2010.

Cirincione, Joe. *Bomb Scare: The History and Future of Nuclear Weapons.* New York: Columbia University Press, 2007.

Duffy, Helen. *The "War on Terror" and the Framework of International Law.* 2nd edn. Cambridge: Cambridge University Press, 2015.

James Fry, *Legal Resolution of Nuclear Non-proliferation Disputes.* Cambridge: Cambridge University Press, 2013.

Johnstone, Ian. *The Power of Deliberation: International Law, Politics and Organizations.* New York. Oxford University Press, 2011, ch. 5–6.

Joyner, Daniel. *Interpreting the Nuclear Non-Proliferation Treaty.* New York: Oxford University Press, 2013.

Levi, Michael. *On Nuclear Terrorism.* Cambridge, MA: Harvard University Press, 2009.

Malone, David M. *The International Struggle over Iraq: Politics in the UN Security Council 1990–2005,* Oxford: Oxford University Press, 2006, ch. 6.

Romaniuk, Peter. *Multilateral Counterterrorism: The Global Politics of Cooperation and Contestation.* New York: Routledge, 2010.

Sagan, Scott and Kenneth Waltz, *The Spread of Nuclear Weapons: An Enduring Debate.* 3rd edn. New York: W.W. Norton, 2012.

Salinas de Frias, Ana Maria, Katjia Samuel and Nigel White. *Counter-Terrorism and International Law.* Oxford: Oxford University Press, 2012.

Saul, Ben (ed). *Research Handbook on International Law and Terrorism.* Northampton MA: Edward Elgar, 2014.

Van den Herk, Larissa and Nico Schrijver (eds). *Counter-terrorism Strategies in a Fragmented International Legal Order: Meeting the Challenge.* Cambridge: Cambridge University Press, 2015.

Weller, Mark (ed). *The Oxford Handbook on the Use of Force in International Law.* Oxford: Oxford University Press, 2015.

chapter nine
....

Peace Operations

The UN Charter foresees activities mandated by the Security Council to maintain peace and security, but says little about the form such activities should take. Chapter VI envisages diplomacy and mediation principally, although Article 38, premised on the consent of all relevant member states, provides a degree of latitude to the Council in addressing threats to the peace through unspecified "recommendations." In Chapter VII, the most attention is paid to sanctions (Article 41) or the use of force by member states (Article 42). Military action was to be taken by member states that committed forces pursuant to "special agreements" negotiated with the Security Council under Article 43, overseen by the Military Staff Committee created by Articles 46 and 47. Due to Cold War dynamics, none of these provisions functioned as intended. Proposals to revive Article 43 and to create a serious role for the Committee never gained traction. Instead, the Security Council has improvised.

Seeking to stem hostilities in Jammu and Kashmir, the Security Council set up a Commission under resolution 39 (1948) to investigate and mediate the dispute between India and Pakistan.[1] In its resolution 47 (1948), the Council decided to enlarge the Commission in a manner that eventually led to the creation of the UN Military Observer Group in India and Pakistan (UNMOGIP), charged with monitoring ceasefire violations, also still on the ground.[2] Later in 1948, it established a Truce Commission for Palestine, under resolution 48 (1948) that soon evolved into the UN Truce Supervisory Organization (UNTSO), still deployed as an observer force with headquarters in Jerusalem.[3] UNTSO's activities initially related to assistance in supervising observation of a truce between Israeli and Arab forces. These developments were linked to the appointment of high-level UN Representatives or Envoys resident in the field, one of whom, Count Folke Bernadotte, was assassinated in Jerusalem on 17 September 1948.[4]

---

[1] SC Res. 39 (1948).
[2] SC Res. 47 (1948).
[3] SC Res. 48 (1948); SC Res. 50 (1948).
[4] This was the basis for the *Reparations* case, discussed in Chapter 4 of this volume.

These small, unarmed observer missions were early steps in what has come to be the UN's most high-profile activity. The first armed peacekeeping mission, the United Nations Emergency Force (UNEF I), was deployed in 1956. This launched the first "golden age" of peacekeeping, which ran to 1974, during which ten operations were established. The years 1974 to 1988 saw a lull, with only one new peacekeeping mission in that period. Enthusiasm for peacekeeping has waxed and waned since the end of the Cold War, from irrational exuberance in the early 1990s to disillusionment in the mid-1990s, followed by an unprecedented surge in the year 1999 that leveled off by 2010 and has remained steady since. In April 2015 there were about 107,000 UN peacekeeping troops, military observers, and police deployed in sixteen missions, plus another 19,000 civilians (local and international). The approved budget for the year July 2014–2015 was US$8.5 billion. There were another eleven UN political and peacebuilding missions, with 3,500 personnel (mainly civilians). Meanwhile, the North Atlantic Treaty Organization (NATO), the African Union (AU), the European Union (EU), the Economic Community for West African States (ECOWAS), the Organization for Security and Cooperation in Europe (OSCE), and the Organization of American States (OAS) have all deployed operations.

In the period 2000 to 2015, peace operations have also became more complex and more militarily robust. The line between peacekeeping and war is blurring (as it did in the early 1990s), and many of the operations have expansive peacebuilding or state-building mandates that aim to transform the societies where they are deployed. These operations provide a lens through which we can examine some larger conceptual issues in international affairs, ranging from the evolution of sovereignty to the claim that these are really exercises in neocolonialism, where external actors rebuild in their own image societies destroyed by war. Those normative questions in turn have direct policy and operational significance, best characterized by the debate between a light and heavy footprint: Should outsiders adopt a minimalist or maximalist approach to post-conflict intervention? Thus, although there is a broad consensus that peace operations are important tools for the management of international peace and security, there is considerable contestation over when and how to use the tools.

The next section of this chapter looks briefly at the Charter framework for peacekeeping, identifying a number of issues that are addressed more fully in subsequent sections on five different types of peace operation. In those sections, we describe the main characteristics of each type and provide illustrative examples to show how the practice and doctrine of peacekeeping has evolved. The penultimate section of the chapter takes a closer look at recent peace operations doctrine, as embodied in a series of landmark reports issued by the United Nations, starting with the highly influential Brahimi Report of 2000.

The chapter concludes by considering four contemporary challenges for peace operations: the protection of civilians, the threat of violent extremism, gender and peace operations, and the dilemmas of state-building.

9.1 The UN Charter Framework

Peace operations have been classified in different ways by different scholars.[5] None of the classification schemes is ideal because there are gray areas between the various types, and some missions combine elements of more than one. We are especially wary of references to "generations" of peacekeeping, as the evolution is only roughly chronological. For analytical reasons we find it useful to break them down into five types: traditional peacekeeping, multidimensional peacekeeping, robust peacekeeping, international transitional administrations, and political missions.

One way of distinguishing the five types is to consider where they fit in the framework of the UN Charter. The term "peacekeeping" is nowhere to be found. A flexible tool, it was described by former Secretary-General Dag Hammarskjold as "Chapter VI and a half," falling somewhere between the peaceful dispute settlement mechanisms set out in Chapter VI and the enforcement provisions of Chapter VII. Chapter VI action is largely based on consent, whereas action under Chapter VII is typically coercive—or at least does not require the full consent of all the relevant actors. In addition to the techniques of peaceful settlement listed in Article 33, consent-based peacekeeping falls within this chapter, as do political missions engaged in preventive diplomacy and mediation.

Chapter VII action can be taken if the Security Council determines that a situation constitutes a threat to the peace, breach of the peace, or act of aggression (Article 39). Full-scale war against the perpetrators would be legally justified in those circumstances (Article 42), but this is rare for the United Nations. More often one sees resolutions with elements of Chapter VII. Thus robust peacekeeping straddles Chapters VI and VII, or sometimes blends the two. It is not unusual for resolutions to authorize peace operations primarily under Chapter VI, but with one or more paragraphs under Chapter VII. Nor is it unusual for the Council to authorize peace operations entirely under Chapter VII, but with the expectation that most of their activities will be undertaken with the consent and cooperation of the major actors.

In addition to UN operations, the Charter ascribes a role to regional organizations under Chapter VIII. Article 52 stipulates that nothing in the Charter shall preclude "the existence of regional arrangements or agencies for dealing

---

[5] See, e.g., Alex Bellamy and Paul Williams, *Understanding Peacekeeping*, 2nd edn, (Cambridge: Polity Press, 2010).

with such matters relating to the maintenance of international peace and security as are appropriate for regional action." Article 53(1) provides that "the Security Council shall, where appropriate, use such regional arrangements or agencies for enforcement under its authority. But no enforcement action shall be taken under a regional arrangement or by regional agencies without the authorization of the Security Council." Article 54 says all activities undertaken by regional organizations should be reported to the Security Council.

QUESTIONS

1. How can UN peace operations, whether Chapter VI, VII, or a combination of the two, be reconciled with Article 2(7) of the UN Charter?
2. Must the Security Council authorize all peace operations undertaken by regional organizations?

9.2 Traditional Peacekeeping

Traditional peacekeeping involves the monitoring of a ceasefire, troop withdrawal, and/or buffer zone between the parties to a conflict. These operations typically involve the deployment of troops or observers along a well-defined ceasefire line between the regular armies of two states. These missions are conducted under Chapter VI of the Charter. Traditional peacekeepers do not bring peace or impose peace, but rather try to provide a calming presence that will enable a peace process to go forward.

As noted, the origins of these traditional operations go back to unarmed observer missions, then expanded when the first armed operation was deployed between Israel and Egypt in the aftermath of the Suez Canal crisis of 1956. Because of Cold War politics, UNEF I was established not by the Security Council but by the General Assembly. The General Assembly's rather expansive interpretation of its own power eventually prompted an Advisory Opinion of the International Court of Justice (ICJ). The Charter stipulates that the General Assembly can "discuss" any matter, including peace and security, but its powers to act are limited to recommendations (Articles 10 and 14). Unlike the Security Council, it cannot adopt decisions binding on the member states other than on internal or administrative matters, such as the budget. Article 11(2) states that "any question on which action is necessary should be referred to the Security Council." However, in the midst of the Korea crisis, the General Assembly decided via the *Uniting for Peace* resolution of 1950 that:

... if the Security Council, because of lack of unanimity of the permanent members, fails to exercise its primary responsibility for the maintenance of international peace and security, the General Assembly shall consider the matter ... with a view to making appropriate recommendations to members for collective measures.[6]

Given the context, this seems to imply that the General Assembly can authorize even enforcement action, that is, it can authorize a "coalition of the willing" to engage in enforcement—which is essentially what happened in Korea when the Security Council was paralyzed by the threat of a Soviet veto. Less controversial is an interpretation of the resolution that allows the General Assembly to establish peacekeeping missions. In 1956, when the Council was again paralyzed, the *Uniting for Peace* resolution was invoked to establish UNEF I and then again in 1960 to take over authority for the UN Operation in the Congo (ONUC). The latter provoked the Soviet Union and France to withhold their UN dues on the grounds that the General Assembly did not have authority to do this. Asked to give an Advisory Opinion, the ICJ ruled that the General Assembly could mandate a peacekeeping operation. To make that determination, it interpreted "action" in Article 11(2) to mean "coercive" action, and held that setting up a peacekeeping mission is a "recommendation," because no UN member is forced to participate—neither the troop contributors nor the host country. See Chapters 4 and 7 for extracts of the *Certain Expenses* case.

ONUC is not a traditional peacekeeping operation, but UNEF is. It was established to supervise the ceasefire in the Middle East after Israel, Britain, and France invaded the Suez. Soon after the crisis broke out, Canadian foreign minister Lester B. Pearson suggested the need for "a truly international peace and police force ... large enough to keep these borders at peace while a political settlement is being worked out."[7] The proposal that Secretary-General Dag Hammarskjöld later submitted to the General Assembly did not specifically mention the use of force, but stated "there was no intent in the establishment of the Force to influence the military balance in the current conflict, and thereby the political balance affecting efforts to settle the conflict."[8] UNEF was later described as a "plate-glass window"— not capable of withstanding assault, but nonetheless "a lightly armed barrier that all see and tend to respect."[9]

---

[6] GA Res. 377(V) (1950).

[7] Brian Urquhart, *Ralph Bunche: An American Life* (New York: W.W. Norton, 1993), p. 265.

[8] Report of the Secretary-General on Basic Points for the Presence and Functioning in Egypt of the United Nations Emergency Force, UN Doc. A/3302 (1956).

[9] Finn Seyersted, *United Nations Forces in the Law of Peace and War* (Leyden: A.W. Sijthoff, 1966), p. 48.

GENERAL ASSEMBLY RESOLUTION 1000(ES-I) (1956)

The General Assembly,

Having requested the Secretary-General, in its resolution 998 (ES-I) of 4 November 1956, to submit to it a plan for an emergency international United Nations Force, for the purposes stated, . . .

1. *Establishes* a United Nations Command for an emergency international Force to secure and supervise the cessation of hostilities in accordance with all the terms of General Assembly resolution 997 (ES-I) of 2 November 1956;

2. *Appoints*, on an emergency basis, the Chief of Staff of the United Nations Truce Supervision Organization, Major-General E. L. M. Burns, as Chief of the Command;

3. *Authorizes* the Chief of the Command immediately to recruit, from the observer corps of the United Nations Truce Supervision Organization, a limited number of officers who shall be nationals of countries other than those having permanent membership in the Security Council, and further authorizes him, in consultation with the Secretary-General, to undertake the recruitment directly, from various Member States other than the permanent members of the Security Council, of the additional number of officers needed;

4. *Invites* the Secretary-General to take such administrative measures as may be necessary for the prompt execution of the actions envisaged in the present resolution.

GENERAL ASSEMBLY RESOLUTION 1001(ES-I) (1956)

The General Assembly,

Noting with appreciation the second and final report of the Secretary-General on the plan for an emergency international United Nations Force as requested in General Assembly Resolution 998 (ES-I), and having examined that plan,

1. *Expresses* its approval of the guiding principles for the organization and functioning of the emergency international United Nations Force as expounded in paragraphs 6 to 9 of the Secretary-General's report; . . .

3. *Invites* the Secretary-General to continue discussions with Governments of member-States concerning offers of participation in the Force, toward the objective of its balanced composition;

4. *Requests* the Chief of the Command, in consultation with the Secretary-General as regards size and composition, to proceed forthwith with the full organization of the Force; . . .

6. *Establishes* an Advisory Committee composed of one representative from each of the following countries: Brazil, Canada, Ceylon, Colombia, India, Norway and Pakistan, and requests this Committee, whose Chairman shall be the Secretary-General, to undertake the development of those aspects of the planning for the Force and its operation not already dealt with by the General Assembly and which do not fall within the area of the direct responsibility of the Chief of the Command;

7. *Authorizes* the Secretary-General to issue all regulations and instructions which may be essential to the effective functioning of the Force, following consultation with the Committee aforementioned, and to take all other necessary administrative and executive action; . . .

9. *Decides* that the Advisory Committee, in the performance of its duties, shall be empowered to request, through the usual procedures, the convening of the General Assembly and to report to the Assembly whenever matters arise which, in its opinion, are of such urgency and importance as to require consideration by the General Assembly itself;

UNEF I came to an end in 1967 when, amidst much tension between Israel and its Arab neighbors, Egyptian President Nasser demanded its withdrawal, a demand with which UN Secretary-General U Thant complied. The "Six Days War" of May 1967, during which Israel seized control of the Sinai, ensued.

QUESTION

3. Why did U Thant conclude he had no choice but to withdraw UNEF I when Egypt withdrew its consent? Was he correct as a matter of policy? As a matter of law?

The guiding principles referenced in paragraph 1 of resolution 1001 (ES-I) were elaborated in 1958 in a Secretary-General study on the establishment and operation of the UNEF I.[10] Together the Secretary-General reports laid the foundation for what have come to be known as the traditional principles of peacekeeping ("the holy trinity"): consent, impartiality, and the nonuse of force except in self-defense. Although not articulated quite this way in those reports, traditional peacekeeping operations are set up with

---

[10] Summary study of the experience derived from the establishment and operation of the Force: report of the Secretary-General, A/3943, 9 October 1958.

the consent of the parties to the conflict, and they depend for their success on the continuing cooperation of the parties on the ground. The peace-keepers are deployed to provide reassurance to each party that the other will not cheat on the ceasefire or other agreements they may have reached. Peacekeepers are meant to show complete impartiality in the exercise of their functions. They do not take sides or seek to alter the military balance on the ground. Originally, the word "neutrality" was used interchange-ably with impartiality, but no longer in peacekeeping circles (for reasons elaborated below). Traditional peacekeepers are unarmed or only lightly armed. They do not use force except to the minimum extent necessary and only in self-defense.

These principles were reiterated in 1973 with the establishment of UNEF II, but the notion of self-defense was expanded to include "defense of the mandate."

REPORT OF THE SECRETARY-GENERAL ON THE IMPLEMENTATION OF SECURITY COUNCIL RESOLUTION 340 (1973)[11]

3. Three essential conditions must be met for the Force to be effective. Firstly, it must have at all times the full confidence and backing of the Security Council. Secondly, it must operate with the full co-operation of the parties concerned. Thirdly, it must be able to function as an integrated and efficient military unit.

4. Having in mind past experience, I would suggest the following guide-lines for the proposed Force: . . .

(d) The force will be provided with weapons of a defensive character only. It shall not use force except in self-defence. Self-defence would include resis-tance to attempts by forceful means to prevent it from discharging its duties under the mandate of the Security Council. The Force will proceed on the assumption that the parties to the conflict will take all the necessary steps for compliance with the decisions of the Security Council.

(e) In performing its functions, the Force will act with complete impartial-ity and will avoid actions which could prejudice the rights, claims or posi-tions of the parties concerned. . . .

---

[11] UN Doc S/11052/Rev.1.

QUESTION

4. In traditional operations, "defense of the mandate" tends to be interpreted narrowly by commanders in the field. Why?

Although UNEF I and UNEF II were not easy missions, the application of the traditional principles was fairly straightforward. The United Nations Interim Force in Lebanon (UNIFIL)—also deployed as a "traditional" mission—had much more difficulty applying those principles.

When the civil war broke out in Lebanon in 1975, the dominant force in the South was the Palestinian Liberation Organization (PLO). On 11 March 1978, PLO forces seized an Israeli bus south of Haifa. In the ensuing confrontation with Israeli security forces, thirty-seven Israeli citizens were killed and seventy-six wounded. In retaliation, Israeli forces invaded Lebanon, and within a few days occupied the entire region south of the Litani River, except the city of Tyre, which was controlled by the PLO. The Lebanese government protested to the Security Council and disavowed any responsibility for the presence of Palestinian bases in southern Lebanon or the commando raids. The Security Council met on 17 March to consider the Lebanese complaint. On 19 March, the United States submitted a proposal that led to the adoption of resolution 425.

SECURITY COUNCIL RESOLUTION 425 (1978)

1. *Calls for* strict respect for the territorial integrity, sovereignty and political independence of Lebanon within its internationally recognized boundaries;

2. *Calls upon* Israel immediately to cease its military action against Lebanese territorial integrity and withdraw forthwith its forces from all Lebanese territory;

3. *Decides,* in the light of the request of the Government of Lebanon, to establish immediately under its authority a United Nations interim force for Southern Lebanon for the purpose of confirming the withdrawal of Israeli forces, restoring international peace and security and assisting the Government of Lebanon in ensuring the return of its effective authority in the area, the Force to be composed of personnel drawn from Member States;

4. *Requests* the Secretary-General to report to the Council within twenty-four hours on the implementation of the present resolution.

Twenty-four hours later, the Secretary-General submitted an implementation plan, which was approved in resolution 426. UNIFIL, a force of 6000, was thus born.

To provide a sense of the complexity of implementing those resolutions, consider the many actors UNIFIL has contended with over the years of its deployment: the fractious government of Lebanon and the Lebanese Armed Forces, which had virtually no authority in the South when the mission began; the Israeli Defense Forces (IDF); the PLO; the Syrian Army, which had troops north of the Litani River for many years; Amal, an anti-Israeli Shi-ite militia supported by Syria; Hezbollah, an anti-Israeli Shi-ite militia supported by Iran (and later Syria) that emerged in 1982; the De Facto Forces (DFF), a Christian militia established by Israel that served as its proxy when Israel first withdrew in June 1978; and the South Lebanon Army (SLA), which succeeded the DFF in 1984 as Israel's proxy until Israel's second withdrawal in 2000. None of these actors was enthusiastic about UNIFIL—and at one point or another all of them contested its mandate and/or area of operations. UNIFIL was continually subject to harassment, denials of freedom of movement, direct attacks, and demands from one group or another that it ought to be doing either more or less to fulfill its mandate.

In 1978, the IDF withdrew from Southern Lebanon as required by resolutions 425/426, but instead of relinquishing its positions to UNIFIL, it turned them over to the DFF. Meanwhile, the Lebanese Army was not able to deploy to the south—also required by the resolution—because both the IDF/DFF and PLO were opposed. In June 1982, following an attack on an Israeli diplomat in Paris for which Israel held the PLO responsible, Israel invaded Lebanon again, brushing the 6000 UNIFIL forces aside. This time, Israeli forces went all the way to Beirut.

In 1983, Israel began its withdrawal from Lebanon, but it did not leave entirely. From then until 2000, the IDF continued to control a 'security zone' in Southern Lebanon, with the help of the SLA. Thus for many years UNIFIL was not able to implement its mandate: it could not confirm the Israeli withdrawal, there was no "peace and security" in the region, and the Lebanese government was unwilling and unable to assert effective authority in Southern Lebanon.

QUESTIONS

5. What does consent mean in the context of a situation such as Lebanon? Consent to what? By whom? At what point does lack of cooperation with a mission amount to the de facto withdrawal of consent?

6. Prior to 2000, the environment in Lebanon did not lend itself to application of the traditional principles, yet there was no political will for peace

> enforcement. Should UNIFIL have withdrawn? Or was a traditional oper-
> ation better than no operation at all?

Things changed in April 2000, when Israel unilaterally withdrew from Southern Lebanon, certified by the United Nations (after several fraught months). The situation on the border became relatively stable but tense. The fear was that any provocation from the Lebanese side (primarily Hezbollah) would be met with a fierce response from Israel, provoking an all-out war. Lebanese administrators, police, security, and army personnel functioned throughout the South, but near the Blue Line, the Lebanese government left control to Hezbollah.

At the beginning of 2001, the Secretary-General reported that UNIFIL had essentially completed two out of three parts of its original mandate: the withdrawal of Israeli forces and, *to the extent it could*, the return of Lebanese authorities to the area. What remained was "restoration of international peace and security." That would depend on a comprehensive Middle East peace. UNIFIL was steadily downsized to 2000 troops and assumed the functions of a monitoring mission.

In 2006, the situation took a dramatic turn for the worse. Hostilities between Israel and Hezbollah broke out on 12 July, which escalated into a major conflict, ultimately involving Israeli ground troops penetrating southern Lebanon while Israeli air strikes destroyed infrastructure and Hezbollah targets throughout the South and sections of Beirut. About 1200 Lebanese and 160 Israelis died, while hundreds of thousands were displaced. The war ended with the adoption of resolution 1701.

SECURITY COUNCIL RESOLUTION 1701 (2006)

The Security Council,

Determining that the situation in Lebanon constitutes a threat to international peace and security,

1. *Calls for* a full cessation of hostilities based upon, in particular, the immediate cessation by Hizbollah of all attacks and the immediate cessation by Israel of all offensive military operations;

2. Upon full cessation of hostilities, *calls upon* the Government of Lebanon and UNIFIL as authorized by paragraph 11 to deploy their forces together throughout the South and calls upon the Government of Israel, as that deployment begins, to withdraw all of its forces from southern Lebanon in parallel; ...

11. *Decides*, in order to supplement and enhance the force in numbers, equipment, mandate and scope of operations, to authorize an increase in the

force strength of UNIFIL to a maximum of 15,000 troops, and that the force shall, in addition to carrying out its mandate under resolutions 425 and 426 (1978):

(a) Monitor the cessation of hostilities;

(b) Accompany and support the Lebanese armed forces as they deploy throughout the South ...

(d) Extend its assistance to help ensure humanitarian access to civilian populations and the voluntary and safe return of displaced persons; ...

(f) Assist the Government of Lebanon, at its request, to implement paragraph 14; ...

12. *Acting* in support of a request from the Government of Lebanon to deploy an international force to assist it to exercise its authority throughout the territory, authorizes UNIFIL to take all necessary action in areas of deployment of its forces and as it deems within its capabilities, to ensure that its area of operations is not utilized for hostile activities of any kind, to resist attempts by forceful means to prevent it from discharging its duties under the mandate of the Security Council, and to protect United Nations personnel, facilities, installations and equipment, ensure the security and freedom of movement of United Nations personnel, humanitarian workers and, without prejudice to the responsibility of the Government of Lebanon, to protect civilians under imminent threat of physical violence; ...

14. *Calls upon* the Government of Lebanon to secure its borders and other entry points to prevent the entry in Lebanon without its consent of arms or related materiel and *requests* UNIFIL as authorized in paragraph 11 to assist the Government of Lebanon at its request;

QUESTIONS

7. After the adoption of resolution 1701, was UNIFIL a traditional peace-keeping operation?
8. Does it have a Chapter VI or Chapter VII mandate? Does it matter? What are the political and operational implications?

9.3 Multidimensional Peacekeeping

A second type of operation is multidimensional peacekeeping. These operations are also based on consent, but the scope of their activities is more complex than traditional peacekeeping. The purpose is to monitor and support the implementation of a comprehensive peace agreement—not just a cease-fire and buffer zone. Successful versions from the early 1990s include operations in Namibia, El Salvador, and Mozambique.

These operations are composed of police and civilians as well as military, and involve governmental, intergovernmental, and nongovernmental partners that traditional peacekeepers rarely deal with. The range of functions includes disarmament and demobilization, humanitarian relief, refugee repatriation, and human rights monitoring. It also includes elements of peacebuilding, such as elections, security sector and justice sector reform, building administrative capacity, and the coordination of economic rehabilitation. Rather than just maintaining a peaceful environment pending a political settlement, the peacekeepers seek to get at the root causes of the conflict, which often means a substantial transformation of the societies where they are deployed.

A representative multidimensional operation in the early post–Cold War era was in El Salvador. ONUSAL (UN Observer Mission to El Salvador) was deployed following a long period of negotiations between the government and the Frente Farabundo Martí para la Liberación Nacional (FMLN) to bring an end to that country's civil war, which was fueled by external involvement on both sides. The twelve-year war (from 1980 to 1992) was brought to an end in the early 1990s with the adoption of six UN-brokered agreements. Secretary-General Boutros-Ghali later called the peace process in El Salvador a "negotiated revolution." In a nutshell, the peace accords brought an end to the war by drawing the FMLN into the political system in exchange for extensive institutional and legal reforms designed to demilitarize Salvadoran society.

ONUSAL was an operation of about 1000 civilian, police, and unarmed military personnel, plus 900 observers for the 1994 elections. It was succeeded by a series of smaller missions until 1997, when a support unit of four people housed in the UNDP was left behind to see through implementation of the lingering aspects of the peace accords. Its mandate was to verify implementation of the six peace agreements.

EL SALVADOR, ONUSAL—MANDATE (UN WEBSITE)[12]

By adopting resolution 693 (1991) of 20 May 1991, the Security Council decided to establish ONUSAL "to monitor all agreements between the two parties, whose initial mandate in its first phase as an integrated peacekeeping operation will be to verify the compliance by the parties with the Agreement on Human Rights signed at San Jose on 26 July 1990". At that stage, the tasks of the Mission included actively monitoring the human rights situation in El Salvador; investigating specific cases of alleged human rights violations; promoting human rights in the country; making

---

[12] http://www.un.org/en/peacekeeping/missions/past/onusalmandate.html.

recommendations for the elimination of violations; and reporting on these matters to the Secretary-General and, through him, to the United Nations General Assembly and Security Council.

By adopting resolution 729 (1992) of 14 January 1992, the Security Council decided to enlarge the mandate of ONUSAL to include the verification and monitoring of the implementation of "all the agreements once these are signed" at Mexico City between the Government of El Salvador and FMLN, in particular the Agreement on the Cessation of the Armed Conflict and the Agreement on the Establishment of a National Civil Police.

By adopting resolution 832 (1993) of 27 May 1993, the Security Council decided to enlarge ONUSAL's mandate to include observation of the electoral process, and requested the Secretary-General to take the necessary measures to this effect.

Thus ONUSAL's mandate began as human rights verification but came to include monitoring the ceasefire and redeployment of forces on both sides; monitoring reform, reduction, and purge of the army; overseeing the conversion of the FMLN into a political party; helping to create a new civilian police force; monitoring human rights and helping to reform the justice system; observing elections and helping to reform the electoral system; and overseeing a program to transfer land to ex-combatants (a vehicle for reintegration). ONUSAL was not an unmitigated success by any means, but it is generally regarded as one of the more effective post–Cold War UN operations. What is especially interesting is that the United Nations' role, though technically limited to "verification," was necessarily more proactive and complex than that term would seem to imply.

QUESTION

9. Consent in the context of multidimensional peacekeeping operations is quite different from traditional operations. How so? Multidimensional peace operations are in many ways an exercise in managing consent. How can this be done?

A contemporary example of a multidimensional operation is the UN Mission in Liberia (UNMIL). It took over from an ECOWAS-led mission in October 2003, with an authorized force of 15,000 military personnel and 1,115 civilian police officers (including formed units), as well as a large civilian component. UNMIL's mandate is entirely under Chapter VII, giving it the authority to act robustly, which it nevertheless used sparingly. In essence UNMIL is a long-term, consent-based mission with expansive peacebuilding functions.

SECURITY COUNCIL RESOLUTION 1509 (2003)

The Security Council,
   Acting under Chapter VII of the Charter of the United Nations, ...
   3. *Decides* that UNMIL shall have the following mandate:
   Support for Implementation of the Ceasefire Agreement:
   (a) to observe and monitor the implementation of the ceasefire agreement and investigate violations of the ceasefire; ...
   (d) to observe and monitor disengagement and cantonment of military forces of all the parties; ...
   (f) to develop, as soon as possible ... an action plan for the overall implementation of a disarmament, demobilization, reintegration, and repatriation (DDRR) programme for all armed parties; with particular attention to the special needs of child combatants and women...;
   (g) to carry out voluntary disarmament and to collect and destroy weapons and ammunition as part of an organized DDRR programme; ...
   (i) to provide security at key government installations, in particular ports, airports, and other vital infrastructure;
   Protection of civilians:
   (j) to protect United Nations personnel, facilities, installations and equipment, ensure the security and freedom of movement of its personnel and, without prejudice to the efforts of the government, to protect civilians under imminent threat of physical violence, within its capabilities;
   Support for Humanitarian and Human Rights Assistance:
   (k) to facilitate the provision of humanitarian assistance, including by helping to establish the necessary security conditions;
   (l) to contribute towards international efforts to protect and promote human rights in Liberia ...
   Support for Security Reform:
   (n) to assist the transitional government of Liberia in monitoring and restructuring the police force of Liberia, consistent with democratic policing, to develop a civilian police training programme, and to otherwise assist in the training of civilian police ...
   (o) to assist the transitional government in the formation of a new and restructured Liberian military ...
   Support for Implementation of the Peace Process:
   (p) to assist the transitional Government, in conjunction with ECOWAS and other international partners, in reestablishment of national authority

throughout the country, including the establishment of a functioning administrative structure at both the national and local levels;

(q) to assist the transitional government in conjunction with ECOWAS and other international partners in developing a strategy to consolidate governmental institutions, including a national legal framework and judicial and correctional institutions;

(r) to assist the transitional government in restoring proper administration of natural resources;

(s) to assist the transitional government, in conjunction with ECOWAS and other international partners, in preparing for national elections scheduled for no later than the end of 2005;

The mandate of the mission has been adjusted on several occasions since 2003, most recently in 2014.

SECURITY COUNCIL RESOLUTION 2190 (2014)

The Security Council, . . .

10. *Decides* that the mandate of UNMIL shall be the following, in priority order:

(a) Protection of Civilians

(i) To protect, without prejudice to the primary responsibility of the Liberian authorities, the civilian population from threat of physical violence, within its capabilities and areas of deployment;

(b) Humanitarian Assistance Support

(i) To facilitate the provision of humanitarian assistance, including in collaboration with the Government of Liberia, and those supporting it, and by helping to establish the necessary security conditions . . .

(c) Reform of Justice and Security Institutions

(i) To assist the Government of Liberia in developing and implementing, as soon as possible and in close coordination with bilateral and multilateral partners, its national strategy on Security Sector Reform; . . .

(iii) To assist the Government of Liberia in extending national justice and security sector services throughout the country through capacity-building and training; . . .

(d) Electoral Support

(i) To assist the Government of Liberia with the Senatorial Elections by providing logistical support . . . coordinating international electoral assistance and supporting Liberian institutions and all Liberian stakeholders, including political parties, in creating an atmosphere conducive to the conduct of peaceful elections . . . ;

(e) Human Rights Promotion and Protection

(i) To carry out promotion, protection and monitoring activities of human rights in Liberia, with special attention to violations and abuses committed against children and women, notably sexual- and gender-based violence; . . .

11. *Decides* that UNMIL, in accordance with paragraphs 4, 5, 6 and 10 (c) above, shall put renewed focus on supporting the Government of Liberia to achieve a successful transition of complete security responsibility to the [Liberian National Police] by strengthening its capacity to manage existing personnel and to improve training programs to expedite their readiness to assume security responsibilities throughout Liberia;

In April 2015, the Security Council set the stage for UNMIL's long-delayed drawdown. The mandate would no longer include electoral support. The Council also reaffirmed its expectation that the government of Liberia "will assume fully its complete security responsibilities from UNMIL no later than 30 June 2016 and also reaffirms its intention to consider the continued and future reconfiguration of UNMIL accordingly."

QUESTION

10. As of June 2015, UNMIL had been in Liberia for twelve years. What are the implications of such a lengthy deployment? Does UNMIL have an exit strategy? Is the strategy a good one?

9.4 Robust Peacekeeping

A distinctive feature of ONUSAL and some other early post–Cold War missions such as those in Mozambique and Namibia is that they took place in environments when there was considerable willingness among the parties to carry through on their commitments and ultimately make peace. Most post–Cold War conflicts have been messier, and peace operations have been deployed when there is no reliable peace to keep. In extreme cases, they are in so-called "failed states," where there is a complete breakdown in law and order and no functioning government whatsoever. The peace operations had to be more robust. Sometimes called peace enforcement, they fall between the consent-based operations described above and, and enforcement action such as the 1991 Gulf War. They are typically deployed fully or partially under Chapter VII of the Charter.

The Security Council acknowledged the changed environment for peace-keeping at its first ever Summit meeting in early 1992 when it adopted a declaration asking the Secretary-General to present recommendations on how to strengthen the United Nations' capacity for peace operations. This was the genesis of Secretary-General Boutros-Ghali's *Agenda for Peace,* an ambitious document that offered new conceptions of what peace operations were meant to be.

AN AGENDA FOR PEACE: PREVENTIVE DIPLOMACY, PEACEMAKING AND PEACEKEEPING (REPORT OF THE SECRETARY-GENERAL), 17 JUNE 1992[13]

8. In the course of the past few years the immense ideological barrier that for decades gave rise to distrust and hostility—and the terrible tools of destruction that were their inseparable companions—has collapsed. Even as the issues between States north and south grow more acute, and call for attention at the highest levels of government, the improvement in relations between States east and west affords new possibilities, some already realized, to meet successfully threats to common security. . . .

11. [H]owever, fierce new assertions of nationalism and sovereignty spring up, and the cohesion of States is threatened by brutal ethnic, religious, social, cultural or linguistic strife. Social peace is challenged on the one hand by new assertions of discrimination and exclusion and, on the other, by acts of terrorism seeking to undermine evolution and change through democratic means. . . .

15. [O]ur aims must be:

To seek to identify at the earliest possible stage situations that could produce conflict, and to try through diplomacy to remove the sources of danger before violence results;

Where conflict erupts, to engage in peacemaking aimed at resolving the issues that have led to conflict;

Through peacekeeping, to work to preserve peace, however fragile, where fighting has been halted and to assist in implementing agreements achieved by the peacemakers;

To stand ready to assist in peace-building in its differing contexts: rebuilding the institutions and infrastructures of nations torn by civil war and strife; and building bonds of peaceful mutual benefit among nations formerly at war . . .

17. The foundation-stone of this work is and must remain the State. Respect for its fundamental sovereignty and integrity are crucial to any common international progress. The time of absolute and exclusive sovereignty,

---

[13] UN Doc. A/47/277-S/24111 (1992).

however, has passed; its theory was never matched by reality. It is the task of leaders of States today to understand this and to find a balance between the needs of good internal governance and the requirements of an ever more interdependent world...

20. ... Peace-keeping is [defined as] the deployment of a United Nations presence in the field, hitherto with the consent of all the parties concerned, normally involving United Nations military and/or police personnel and frequently civilians as well. Peace-keeping is a technique that expands the possibilities for both the prevention of conflict and the making of peace. ...

44. Cease-fires have often been agreed to but not complied with, and the United Nations has sometimes been called upon to send forces to restore and maintain the cease-fire. This task can on occasion exceed the mission of peacekeeping forces and the expectations of peacekeeping force contributors. I recommend that the Council consider the utilization of peace-enforcement units in clearly defined circumstances and with their terms of reference specified in advance. Such units from Member States would be available on call and would consist of troops that have volunteered for such service. They would have to be more heavily armed than peacekeeping forces ... Deployment and operation of such forces would be under the authorization of the Security Council and would, as in the case of peacekeeping forces, be under the command of the Secretary-General. ...

50. The nature of peacekeeping operations has evolved rapidly in recent years. The established principles and practices of peacekeeping have responded flexibly to new demands of recent years, and the basic conditions for success remain unchanged: a clear and practicable mandate; the cooperation of the parties in implementing that mandate; the continuing support of the Security Council; the readiness of Member States to contribute the military, police and civilian personnel, including specialists, required; effective United Nations command at Headquarters and in the field; and adequate financial and logistic support.

QUESTION

11. Based on the above passages, what is the Secretary-General's stance on the traditional principles of peacekeeping?

In paragraph 44, the Secretary-General introduced the notion of peace enforcement units that would occupy a halfway house between peacekeeping and enforcement action, with a mission to perform limited but unquestionably coercive functions. No "peace enforcement units" as such were created at the time, but in the early 1990s "peacekeepers" were performing the functions that these peace enforcement units were conceived for. The

UN operations in Bosnia and Somalia are the best examples of that, both of which ended in failure. Rwanda is an example of the opposite: a peace-keeping operation that was ordered not to engage in robust action as geno-cide unfolded around it. Chapter 16 addresses those failures in more depth. However, because they had a significant impact on thinking about robust peacekeeping, a few words about each are useful here.

The UN Protection Force (UNPROFOR) was originally deployed in 1992 in Croatia, where the Yugoslav wars broke out. Its first mandate in Bosnia was to take control of the Sarajevo airport and keep open a security cor-ridor to Sarajevo for the delivery of humanitarian aid. From that point on UNPROFOR's mandate expanded, and force levels grew year by year, along-side that of NATO, which was tasked with enforcing sanctions and a flight ban. In what proved to a momentous decision, in April/May 1993 the Council declared Srebrenica, Sarajevo, Bihac, Tuzla, Zepam and Gorazde to be "safe areas" (resolutions 819 and 824). Shortly thereafter it expanded the mandates of UNPROFOR and NATO to "ensure respect" for the safe areas (the word "protection" never appears in the resolution).

SECURITY COUNCIL RESOLUTION 836 (1993)

The Security Council, . . .
   Acting under Chapter VII . . .
   4. *Decides* to ensure full respect for the safe areas referred to in resolution 824 (1993);
   5. *Decides* to extend to that end the mandate of UNPROFOR in order to enable it, in the safe areas referred to in resolution 824 (1993), to deter attacks against the safe areas, to monitor the cease-fire, to promote the withdrawal of military or paramilitary units other than those of the Government of the Republic of Bosnia and Herzegovina and to occupy some key points on the ground, in addition to participating in the delivery of humanitarian relief to the population . . .
   9. *Authorizes* UNPROFOR, in addition to the mandate defined in reso-lutions 770 (1992) of 13 August 1992 and 776 (1992), in carrying out the mandate defined in paragraph 5 above, acting in self-defence, to take the necessary measures, including the use of force, in reply to bombardments against the safe areas by any of the parties or to armed incursion into them or in the event of any deliberate obstruction in or around those areas to the freedom of movement of UNPROFOR or of protected humanitarian convoys;
   10. *Decides* that . . . Member States, acting nationally or through regional orga-nizations or arrangements, may take, under the authority of the Security Council and subject to close coordination with the Secretary-General and UNPROFOR,

all necessary measures, through the use of air power, in and around the safe areas in the Republic of Bosnia and Herzegovina, to support UNPROFOR in the performance of its mandate set out in paragraph 5 and 9 above;

The Secretary-General recommended a force of 34,000 troops to implement the mandate; the Security Council approved a "light option" of 7,600 troops. The deterrent effect was meant to be provided by the threat of NATO air support.

After an attack by Serb forces on a Sarajevo market place in February 1994 that left fifty-eight people dead, NATO declared a weapons exclusion zone around the capital. Any heavy weapons not removed from the area or put under UNPROFOR control by a set date would be subject to air strikes. Air strikes could also be launched against any artillery or mortar positions near Sarajevo that attacked civilian targets. The exclusion zones were later extended to the five other safe areas. Air strikes are different from close air support: the latter were to defend UN personnel under attack, the former were for pre-emptive or punitive purposes. A "dual key" formula for initiating the close air support and air strikes was put in place, requiring both NATO and UN approval for either to be launched.

On several occasions between March 1994 and mid-1995, Serb attacks met with NATO close air support or air strikes; on some of those occasions, the Serbs responded by taking UNPROFOR peacekeepers hostage until the strikes ended. Thus by the time of the Serb march on Srebrenica in July 1995, the dual key formula was not working well. The commander of the small Dutch contingent of 600 requested air power on three occasions; it was approved on the third of those, but deferred because night fell. On the morning of 11 July, two bombs were dropped in close air support, but when the Dutch Minister of Defense requested that they be called off, they were.

When another Serb shell landed in a Sarajevo marketplace on 28 August, killing thirty-seven people, NATO launched a two-week air campaign against Bosnian Serb targets. Simultaneously, a rapid reaction force of French, British, and Dutch troops under nominal UN command began heavy bombardment of Serb positions around Sarajevo. Meanwhile, the Croatian army had launched Operation Storm against the Serbs in Croatia, and Bosnian and Croat units were attacking the Serbs in West and North Bosnia. As the military tide turned, US envoy Richard Holbrooke aggressively pursued diplomatic efforts, resulting in the Dayton Agreement, signed on 14 December 1995 in Paris. Slobodan Milošević (President of FRY at the time) signed on behalf of the Bosnian-Serbs, whose leaders (Radovan Karadžić and Mladić) had been indicted by the ICTY. UNPROFOR was replaced by the NATO-led Implementation Force (IFOR) on 20 December 2005, a mission of 60,000 troops that included a substantial number of US forces, unlike its predecessor, which was composed mainly of Europeans and Canadians.

QUESTION

12. Was the whole concept of safe areas as applied in Bosnia flawed, or was the fall of Srebrenica due to flawed execution of the policy?

Reflecting on the experiences of Bosnia (and Somalia), the Secretary-General issued the *Supplement to an Agenda for Peace* in 1995. Although ostensibly not a revision of *Agenda for Peace*, it does represent considerable backtracking from the ambition of the earlier document.

SUPPLEMENT TO AN AGENDA FOR PEACE: POSITION PAPER OF THE SECRETARY-GENERAL ON THE OCCASION OF THE FIFTIETH ANNIVERSARY OF THE UNITED NATIONS, 3 JANUARY 1995[14]

12. The new breed of intra-state conflicts ... are usually fought not only by regular armies but also by militias and armed civilians with little discipline and with ill-defined chains of command. They are often guerrilla wars without clear front lines. Civilians are the main victims and often the main targets. Humanitarian emergencies are commonplace...

13. Another feature of such conflicts is the collapse of state institutions, especially the police and judiciary, with resulting paralysis of governance, a breakdown of law and order, and general banditry and chaos...

19. This has led, in Bosnia and Herzegovina and in Somalia, to a new kind of United Nations operation. Even though the use of force is authorized under Chapter VII of the Charter, the United Nations remains neutral and impartial between the warring parties, without a mandate to stop the aggressor (if one can be identified) or impose a cessation of hostilities. Nor is this peace-keeping as practised hitherto, because the hostilities continue and there is often no agreement between the warring parties on which a peace-keeping mandate can be based. The "safe areas" concept in Bosnia and Herzegovina is a similar case. It too gives the United Nations a humanitarian mandate under which the use of force is authorized, but for limited and local purposes and not to bring the war to an end....

33. ... the last few years have confirmed that respect for certain basic principles of peacekeeping are essential to its success. Three particularly important principles are the consent of the parties, impartiality and the non-use of

---

[14] UN Doc. A/50/60-S/1995/1 (1995).

force except in self-defence. Analysis of recent successes and failures shows that in all the successes those principles were respected and in most of the less successful operations, one or the other of them was not. . . .

35. . . . The logic of peace-keeping flows from political and military premises that are quite distinct from those of enforcement; and the dynamics of the latter are incompatible with the political process that peace-keeping is intended to facilitate. To blur the distinction between the two can undermine the viability of the peace-keeping operation and endanger its personnel.

36. . . . peacekeeping and the use of force (other than in self-defence) should be seen as alternative techniques and not just as adjacent points on a continuum, permitting easy transition from one to another.

QUESTION

13. Based on your reading of the *Supplement to an Agenda for Peace*, what was the principal doctrinal lesson the UN Secretariat learned from the experiences of Bosnia and Somalia?

The *Supplement* reflects thinking of the UN Secretariat and among many Member States in early 1995. Having been badly stung by the experiences in Somalia and Bosnia in the mid-1990s, few were advocating development of a new UN doctrine of "peace enforcement."

While the Bosnia tragedy was unfolding, the mission in Somalia was also failing. The United Nations Operation in Somalia (UNOSOM II)—ended with an ill-fated attempt to capture General Mohamed Aideed, the Somali National Alliance (SNA) leader who was held responsible for ambushing a Pakistani contingent on the way back from inspecting a weapons storage near Mogadishu. In that ambush, twenty-four peacekeepers were killed and fifty-six wounded; about the same number of Somalis died. The Security Council responded by authorizing the arrest of those responsible for the attacks. When four US soldiers were killed by landmines two months later, the United States sent 400 Rangers plus some Delta Force commandos to Somalia to help with the arrest of Aideed.

On 3 October 1993, the Rangers launched a raid on an SNA house. Twenty-four SNA leaders were apprehended, but two Blackhawk helicopters were shot down and trapped. Eighteen Rangers were killed, ninety other soldiers were injured, and one US pilot was captured. Approximately a thousand Somalis died. This mission was a US operation, planned and initiated from US Central Command in North Carolina. UN officials knew nothing about it in advance, other than the American Deputy Force Commander of UNOSOM II, who was told about the raid forty minutes before it was launched. On 7 October 1993, the United States announced it would leave Somalia by March 1994. European contingents soon announced they would follow suit. Pakistanis and others stayed, but the mission was severely depleted. The arrest warrant for Aideed was suspended in November 1993. In March 1995 the mandate of UNOSOM II was terminated.

As UNOSOM II was winding down, the Rwanda genocide took place. Fighting between the Hutu-led coalition government in Kigali and the Rwandan Patriotic Front, a mainly Tutsi group that was based in Uganda at the time, ended with a comprehensive peace agreement signed in August 1993. UNAMIR (UN Assistance Mission for Rwanda) was established three months later as a consent-based multidimensional peacekeeping operation to assist in the implementation of the accords, which would include monitoring of the ceasefire and integration of the army, performing humanitarian tasks, and observing elections in 1995. It was too small for the job (2500 troops), under-equipped and slow to deploy. From the start, the parties to the Arusha Accords did not cooperate with each other, the transitional government was never formed, and steadily the security situation deteriorated.

There were warnings of genocide in 1993 and early 1994. A report of the UN Commission of Human Rights' Special Rapporteur on Extrajudicial, Summary or Arbitrary Executions, Bacre Ndiaye, was largely ignored. A cable sent by Force Commander Romeo Dallaire to the UN Department of Peacekeeping Operations in January 1994 warned that evidence might exist of mass killings being planned, and sought authority to raid arms caches. He was instructed not to—on the grounds that that would exceed UNAMIR's mandate. Instead the information in the cable was shared with the president of Rwanda (who may not have known what the extremists were planning) and with the Ambassadors of the United States, France, and Belgium in Kigali. None took effective action to counter the threat.

The event that sparked the genocide was the shooting down of a plane carrying the presidents of both Rwanda and Burundi. Over a period of about a hundred days starting 6 April 6 1994, as many as 800,000 Rwandese were killed. Most were Tutsis; some were moderate Hutus. The principal architects were a group known as Hutu Power, with most of the killing being done by the Armed Forces of Rwanda (FAR), the Interahamwe, and other militia groups.

The reaction of the Security Council was to reduce UNAMIR to 270 personnel on 21 April after the violent death of ten Belgian peacekeepers. At the time, the situation was seen (or said to be seen) by the United States, France, and others as a civil war, not genocide, and that all the United Nations could do was try to mediate an end to the war. In mid-May, the Security Council authorized ramping up to 5,500 troops with a Chapter VII mandate, but few countries volunteered, and no new troops actually got to Rwanda until after the genocide was over.

QUESTION

14. Why did the international community, acting through the United Nations, not do more to prevent or halt the genocide in Rwanda? What more could it have done?

In 1999 and 2000, three important reports were released on the "failures" of UN peace operations in Srebrenica and Rwanda (one by the United Nations and one by the Organization of African Unity (OAU)). Extracts from these reports appear in Chapter 16. A critical point made in all of them is that there are fundamental problems with the doctrine of peacekeeping, or at least how it was applied in the two cases. Errors of judgment were made in the field, at UN Headquarters, and among capitals because officials believed (or acted as if they believed) that application of the guiding principles of impartiality, consent, and the nonuse of force could be made to work even when confronted with attempted genocide, or in the case of Rwanda, genocide that was willfully not viewed as such. Those reports fed into thinking embodied in the Brahimi Report discussed below. But even before then the United Nations had begun to re-engage in "robust peacekeeping," starting with Sierra Leone.

In February 1998, a coup against the government of Sierra Leone by a rebel group called the Revolutionary United Front (RUF) and disaffected army officers was overturned by Economic Community of West African States Monitoring Group (ECOMOG) (a West African operation led by Nigeria). Nevertheless, fighting between government forces and the RUF continued until May 1999, when the Lome Peace Agreement was signed. To help with implementation, the Security Council established the UN Assistance Mission in Sierra Leone (UNAMSIL), a peace operation of 6000 troops.

SECURITY COUNCIL RESOLUTION 1270 (1999)

The Security Council, . . .

Affirming the commitment of all States to respect the sovereignty, political independence and territorial integrity of Sierra Leone, . . .

Determining that the situation in Sierra Leone continues to constitute a threat to international peace and security in the region,

. . . .

4. *Calls upon* the RUF, the Civil Defence Forces, former Sierra Leone Armed Forces/Armed Forces Revolutionary Council (AFRC) and all other armed groups in Sierra Leone to begin immediately to disband and give up

their arms in accordance with the provisions of the Peace Agreement, and to participate fully in the disarmament, demobilization and reintegration programme; . . .

6. *Deplores* the recent taking of hostages, including UNOMSIL and ECOMOG personnel, by rebel groups and calls upon those responsible to put an end to such practices immediately. . . ;

7. *Reiterates* its appreciation for the indispensable role which ECOMOG forces continue to play in the maintenance of security and stability in and the protection of the people of Sierra Leone, and approves the new mandate for ECOMOG. . . ;

8. *Decides* to establish the United Nations Mission in Sierra Leone (UNAMSIL) with immediate effect for an initial period of six months and with the following mandate:

(a) To cooperate with the Government of Sierra Leone and the other parties to the Peace Agreement in the implementation of the Agreement;

(b) To assist the Government of Sierra Leone in the implementation of the disarmament, demobilization and reintegration plan;

(c) To that end, to establish a presence at key locations throughout the territory of Sierra Leone, including at disarmament/reception centres and demobilization centres; . . .

(g) To facilitate the delivery of humanitarian assistance;

(h) To support the operations of United Nations civilian officials, including the Special Representative of the Secretary-General and his staff, human rights officers and civil affairs officers;

(i) To provide support, as requested, to the elections, which are to be held in accordance with the present constitution of Sierra Leone; . . .

11. *Commends* the readiness of ECOMOG to continue to provide security for the areas where it is currently located, in particular around Freetown and Lungi, to provide protection for the Government of Sierra Leone . . .

14. *Acting* under Chapter VII of the Charter of the United Nations, *decides* that in the discharge of its mandate UNAMSIL may take the necessary action to ensure the security and freedom of movement of its personnel and, within its capabilities and areas of deployment, to afford protection to civilians under imminent threat of physical violence, taking into account the responsibilities of the Government of Sierra Leone and ECOMOG;

QUESTION

15. UNAMSIL is primarily mandated under Chapter VI of the UN Charter, with one paragraph under Chapter VII. Why did the Security Council do this? What are the political and operational implications? Is it a good compromise?

As specified in resolution 1270, implementation of the peace agreement was to be overseen by ECOMOG and the United Nations working together. But at the end of 1999, Nigeria, Guinea, and Ghana decided to withdraw ECOMOG for lack of funding. Thus UNAMSIL grew to 11,000 and its mandate was expanded to include ECOMOG's old responsibilities, which were the more militarily demanding Chapter VII tasks. As the UNAMSIL contingents replaced the West African troops and started moving into rebel-controlled diamond areas, the RUF attacked them and took several hundred hostage. At a moment of crisis in May 2000, there was talk of UNAMSIL withdrawing altogether, with memories of what happened in Bosnia and Somalia balanced against a sense of guilt for abandoning Rwanda.

Instead of withdrawing, the deployment of 800 British paratroopers to Freetown (ostensibly to secure the airports in order to enable evacuation of their own people) deterred further provocations by the RUF and bought time for the UNAMSIL to expand in numbers with a more robust mandate. A firefight between the UK troops and a local criminal gang, the West Side Boys, which decimated the latter, served as a warning against attacks on UNAMSIL. This brought the violence to an end and put the peace process back on track. Disarmament was completed, successful elections were held in April 2002, and UNAMSIL began a process of "gradual, phased and deliberate" drawdown, linked to five key benchmarks: capacity-building for the army and police, reintegration of ex-combatants, restoration of government control over diamond-mining, consolidation of state authority, and progress toward ending the conflict in Liberia. In June 2005, UNAMSIL's mandate was extended for a final six months. A follow-on political mission was established, and then in 2007 it became one of the first "clients" of the Peacebuilding Commission.

9.5 International Transitional Administrations

A fourth type of peace operation is like multidimensional peacekeeping in the sense that these missions are designed to bring about a comprehensive peace, but their functions are both more expansive and more intrusive. UN missions in Kosovo and East Timor are the main exemplars of this, although there were partial precedents: the United Nations Transitional Assistance Group (UNTAG) in Namibia, the United Nations Transitional Administration in Cambodia (UNTAC), and the United Nations Transitional Authority in Eastern Slavonia (UNTAES).

The relevant parts of UNTAC's mandate are described on the UN website as follows.

CAMBODIA—UNTAC—BACKGROUND[15]

The Supreme National Council was declared the unique legitimate body and source of authority in which, throughout the transitional period, the sovereignty, independence and unity of Cambodia are enshrined. . . .

The SNC would delegate to the United Nations all powers necessary to ensure the implementation of the Agreement. SNC would offer advice to UNTAC, which would comply provided there was consensus among the members of SNC and provided the advice was consistent with the objectives of the Agreement. In the absence of consensus, the Chairman of SNC would be entitled to make the decision on what advice to offer to UNTAC, taking fully into account the views expressed in SNC. Should the Chairman be unable to make such a decision, his power of decision would transfer to the Secretary-General's Special Representative, who would make the final decision, taking fully into account the views expressed in SNC. Similar provisions applied to any power to act regarding the implementation of the Agreement. In all cases, the Secretary-General's Special Representative or his delegate would determine whether the advice or action of SNC was consistent with the Agreement.

Administrative agencies, bodies and offices which could directly influence the outcome of elections would be placed under direct United Nations supervision or control . . . The Special Representative of the Secretary-General was given power to issue directives to those agencies, bodies and offices, with binding effect and to install United Nations personnel with unrestricted access to information and administrative operations, and to remove existing officers or reassign them. The civil police was to operate under UNTAC supervision and control . . .

In consultation with SNC, UNTAC was to establish a system of laws, procedures and administrative measures necessary for the holding of a free and fair election in Cambodia . . . Existing laws which could defeat the objectives and purposes of the Agreement would be nullified.

Thus UNTAC was a "transitional authority" in the sense that it had the authority to make decisions when the Supreme National Council (SNC) could not do so, to issue binding directives, and to organize elections. But formally, "sovereignty" resided in the SNC, a creation of the peace process consisting of representatives of all four factions.

Timor-Leste and Kosovo are covered in more depth in Chapters 2, 12, and 14. For present purposes, they serve as illustrations of how far the Security

---

[15] Available at: http://www.un.org/en/peacekeeping/missions/past/untacbackgr2. html.

Council has gone in authorizing missions to assume expansive governance functions. In Kosovo, sovereignty technically resided with the Yugoslav government, but for all intents and purposes, that sovereignty was suspended for the life of the transition. In East Timor, the Indonesians had withdrawn following the vote for independence in August 1999, so there was no sovereign authority at all. UNMIK (UN Mission in Kosovo) and UNTAET (UN Traditional Administration in East Timor) had full governing powers in each territory, for a transitional period. Resolution 1272 on East Timor states "All legislative and executive power, including the administration of justice, is vested in UNTAET and is exercised the SRSG." That language is not in the resolution establishing UNMIK (1244), but rather in the first regulation UNMIK adopted, which is extracted in section 14.3 of Chapter 14 of this volume.

QUESTIONS

16. Does the Security Council have the authority to create these transitional administrations?
17. Are we likely to see such a transitional administration again elsewhere? In what circumstances?

9.6 Political Missions

A fifth category of peace operation is, in UN parlance, "special political missions." All peace operations are political in the sense that they are driven by an overarching political imperative—self-sustaining peace—and all of their functions, from security to human rights to development are (or should be) harnessed to that goal.[16] But this relatively new category is worth separating from the others, because in many ways it is an alternative to large-scale peacekeeping. These are small missions though often with broad mandates. They are comprised primarily of civilian personnel (with some military and police advisers), and their main activity is political process management: political engagement with governments, parties, and civil society aimed at averting, mitigating, or stopping conflict.[17] Many have mediation

---

[16] Ian Martin, "All Peace Operations Are Political: A Case for Designer Missions and the Next UN Reform," *Review of Political Missions 2010* (New York: Center on International Cooperation, 2010).

[17] Lakhdar Brahimi and Salman Ahmed, "The Seven Deadly Sins of Mediation," *Annual Review of Global Peace Operations 2008* (Boulder, CO: Lynne Rienrer, 2008).

as an explicit mandate, but arguably even those that do not have the authority to engage in good offices to try to launch, support, or sustain a political process.[18] In addition to mediation, they often engage in the promotion of good governance, support for security sector and justice sector reform, capacity-building for development, and the coordination of humanitarian aid. They are truly assistance missions in the sense that they are there to support national authorities, not substitute for them.

Political and peacebuilding missions are sometimes deployed as successors to large-scale UN missions or alongside operations deployed by other organizations. Examples of successor operations include the United Nations Integrated Peacebuilding Office in Sierra Leone (UNIPSIL) and the United Nation Office in Burundi (BNUB), both of which have now closed down. The United Nations Assistance Mission in Afghanistan (UNAMA) and the United Nations Assistance Mission in Somalia (UNSOM) are deployed alongside major NATO and AU operations respectively. The United Nations Support Mission in Libya (UNSMIL) is a mission that was deployed as an alternative to a large-scale peace operation.

After NATO's intervention in Libya in 2011 and the death of Muammar Qaddafi, fighting continued between supporters of the regime and various rebel groups, and later among the rebel groups. At the time, consideration was given to deployment of 200 UN military observers and multinational force (MNF) to protect them, whose presence would also stem the worst of the fighting. The MNF would not be a UN peacekeeping force but rather a coalition of the willing composed of Arab and European states. However, Libyan authorities (such as they existed) had no interest in a large military presence, and there was no will among contributors to deploy such a force. This dovetailed with a strategic shift in thinking among UN member states toward less expensive, lighter alternatives to multidimensional peacekeeping, run out of the Department of Political Affairs rather than Department of Peacekeeping Operations.[19] It also corresponded to a Western desire not to put boots on the ground in another Arab country, especially after being criticized for exceeding the Security Council's authorization to protect civilians in Libya by instigating regime change.

The Security Council began with a three-month mission whose main function was to consult with national leaders on what longer-term international presence they desired, and to plan for that presence. The authorizing resolution specified a substantial list of other tasks UNSMIL would be expected to perform.

---

[18] Ian Johnstone, "Emerging Doctrine for Political Missions," *Review of Political Missions 2010* (New York: Center on International Cooperation, 2010).

[19] Michael Snyder, "As Peace Talks Resume in Libya, Is the UN's 'Light Footprint' up to the Task?," IPI Global Observatory, 15 February 2015; available at: http://theglobalobservatory.org/2015/02/libya-peace-talks-resume-dialogue-unsmil/.

SECURITY COUNCIL RESOLUTION 2009 (2011)

The Security Council...

Stressing that national ownership and national responsibility are key to establishing sustainable peace and the primary responsibility of national authorities in identifying their priorities and strategies for post-conflict peace-building, ...

Recalling the letter of the Secretary-General of 7 September 2011 (S/2011/542) and welcoming his intention to dispatch, at the request of the Libyan authorities, an initial deployment of personnel, to be led by a Special Representative of the Secretary-General, ...

Acting under Chapter VII of the Charter of the United Nations ...

2. *Looks forward* to the establishment of an inclusive, representative transitional Government of Libya, and emphasises the need for the transitional period to be underpinned by a commitment to democracy, good governance, rule of law and respect for human rights; ...

12. *Decides* to establish a United Nations Support Mission in Libya (UNSMIL), under the leadership of a Special Representative of the Secretary-General for an initial period of three months, and decides further that the mandate of UNSMIL shall be to assist and support Libyan national efforts to:

(a) restore public security and order and promote the rule of law;

(b) undertake inclusive political dialogue, promote national reconciliation, and embark upon the constitution-making and electoral process;

(c) extend state authority, including through strengthening emerging accountable institutions and the restoration of public services;

(d) promote and protect human rights, particularly for those belonging to vulnerable groups, and support transitional justice;

(e) take the immediate steps required to initiate economic recovery; and

(f) coordinate support that may be requested from other mulilateral and bilateral actors.

UNSMIL was established with a core of about 250 staff in Tripoli, bolstered by a team of standby mediators. It could also call upon external civilian experts to provide technical advice as needed. Its mandate was extended for three months in December 2011 and then again for twelve months in March 2012. At that point, UNSMIL's mandate was spelled out more precisely:

SECURITY COUNCIL RESOLUTION 2040 (2012)

The Security Council, ...

6. *Decides* ... that the modified mandate of UNSMIL, in full accordance with the principles of national ownership, shall be to assist the Libyan

authorities to define national needs and priorities throughout Libya, and to match these with offers of strategic and technical advice where appropriate, and support Libyan efforts to:

(a) manage the process of democratic transition, including through technical advice and assistance to the Libyan electoral process and the process of preparing and establishing a new Libyan constitution ...

(b) promote the rule of law and monitor and protect human rights ...

(c) restore public security, including through the provision of appropriate strategic and technical advice and assistance to the Libyan government to develop capable institutions and implement a coherent national approach to the integration of ex-combatants into Libyan national security forces or their demobilization and reintegration into civilian life ...

(d) counter illicit proliferation of all arms and related materiel of all types, in particular man-portable surface-to-air missiles ...

(e) coordinate international assistance and build government capacity across all relevant sectors set out in relation to paragraphs 6 (a) to (d)

7. *Encourages* UNSMIL to continue to support efforts to promote national reconciliation, inclusive political dialogue and political processes aimed at promoting free, fair and credible elections, transitional justice and respect for human rights throughout Libya;

UNSMIL has been extended several times since then, with an evolving mandate. By mid-2014 the security situation had deteriorated so badly that it was difficult for the mission to do much other than try to mediate. Most of its personnel were relocated to Tunisia, with only a skeletal staff left behind in Tripoli.

QUESTION

18. Was a "light footprint" political mission the right instrument in Libya? Would a larger UN peacekeeping mission, or a robust multinational force alongside a smaller political mission, have been more appropriate? Were those alternatives politically realistic?

9.7 Contemporary Peace Operations Doctrine

The guiding principles for UNEF I and II, the *Agenda for Peace,* and the *Supplement to Agenda for Peace* were landmark documents in setting UN peace operations doctrine. Since then, there have been a number of important policy documents that reflect new insight into the application of the "holy trinity" of peacekeeping principles, without disavowing them.

In 2000, having decided that the time was ripe for a systematic rethinking of the whole subject of peace operations, Secretary-General Kofi Annan appointed an independent panel, under the chairmanship of Lakhdar Brahimi—a former foreign minister of Algeria and very experienced UN peacekeeper and mediator. The panel reviewed the whole gamut of UN experience, with the Srebrenica and Rwanda reports fresh in all minds and against the backdrop of ongoing developments in Southern Lebanon, Bosnia, Kosovo, East Timor, the Democratic Republic of the Congo, and Sierra Leone.

REPORT OF THE PANEL ON UN PEACE OPERATIONS (BRAHIMI REPORT), 21 AUGUST 2000[20]

3. [F]or peacekeeping to accomplish its mission, as the United Nations has discovered repeatedly over the last decade, no amount of good intentions can substitute for the fundamental ability to project credible force. However, force alone cannot create peace; it can only create a space in which peace can be built.

4. In other words, the key conditions for the success of future complex operations are political support, rapid deployment with a robust force posture and a sound peace-building strategy. Every recommendation in the present report is meant, in one way or another, to help ensure that these three conditions are met.

II. Doctrine, strategy and decision-making for peace operations

9. The United Nations system—namely the Member States, Security Council, General Assembly and Secretariat—must commit to peace operations carefully, reflecting honestly on the record of its performance over the past decade. It must adjust accordingly the doctrine upon which peace operations are established ... and summon the creativity, imagination and will required to implement new and alternative solutions to those situations into which peacekeepers cannot or should not go....

21. As the United Nations soon discovered, local parties sign peace accords for a variety of reasons, not all of them favourable to peace. "Spoilers"— groups (including signatories) who renege on their commitments or otherwise seek to undermine a peace accord by violence—challenged peace

---

[20] UN Doc. A/55/305-S/2000/809 (2000).

implementation in Cambodia, threw Angola, Somalia and Sierra Leone back into civil war, and orchestrated the murder of no fewer than 800,000 people in Rwanda. The United Nations must be prepared to deal effectively with spoilers if it expects to achieve a consistent record of success in peace-keeping or peacebuilding in situations of intrastate/transnational conflict.

E. Implications for peacekeeping doctrine and strategy

48. The Panel concurs that consent of the local parties, impartiality and use of force only in self-defence should remain the bedrock principles of peace-keeping. Experience shows, however, that in the context of modern peace operations dealing with intra-State/transnational conflicts, consent may be manipulated in many ways by the local parties. A party may give its consent to United Nations presence merely to gain time to retool its fighting forces and withdraw consent when the peacekeeping operation no longer serves its inter-ests. A party may seek to limit an operation's freedom of movement, adopt a policy of persistent non-compliance with the provisions of an agreement or withdraw its consent altogether. Moreover, regardless of faction leaders' com-mitment to the peace, fighting forces may simply be under much looser control than the conventional armies with which traditional peacekeepers work . . .

50. Impartiality for such operations must therefore mean adherence to the principles of the Charter and to the objectives of a mandate that is rooted in those Charter principles. Such impartiality is not the same as neutrality or equal treatment of all parties in all cases for all time, which can amount to a policy of appeasement. In some cases, local parties consist not of moral equals but of obvious aggressors and victims, and peacekeepers may not only be operationally justified in using force but morally compelled to do so. Genocide in Rwanda went as far as it did in part because the international community failed to use or to reinforce the operation then on the ground in that country to oppose obvious evil. The Security Council has since established, in its resolution 1296 (2000), that the targeting of civilians in armed conflict and the denial of humanitarian access to civilian populations afflicted by war may themselves constitute threats to international peace and security and thus be triggers for Security Council action. If a United Nations peace operation is already on the ground, carrying out those actions may become its responsibility, and it should be prepared.

51. This means, in turn, that the Secretariat must not apply best-case planning assumptions to situations where the local actors have historically exhibited worst-case behaviour. It means that mandates should specify an operation's authority to use force. It means bigger forces, better equipped and more costly, but able to pose a credible deterrent threat, in contrast to the symbolic and non-threatening presence that characterizes traditional peacekeeping. United Nations forces for complex operations should be sized and configured so as to leave no doubt in the minds of would-be spoilers as

to which of the two approaches the Organization has adopted. Such forces should be afforded the field intelligence and other capabilities needed to mount a defence against violent challengers. . . .

62. Finally, the desire on the part of the Secretary-General to extend additional protection to civilians in armed conflicts and the actions of the Security Council to give United Nations peacekeepers explicit authority to protect civilians in conflict situations are positive developments. Indeed, peacekeepers—troops or police—who witness violence against civilians should be presumed to be authorized to stop it, within their means, in support of basic United Nations principles and, as stated in the report of the Independent Inquiry on Rwanda, consistent with "the perception and the expectation of protection created by [an operation's] very presence" (see S/1999/1257, p. 51).

In reacting to the Brahimi Report, the Security Council requested the Secretary-General to prepare a "comprehensive operational doctrine for the military component of UN peacekeeping operations" (Security Council resolution 1327 (2000)). The Special Committee on Peacekeeping (a GA body with broader membership than the SC), on the other hand, did not encourage the Secretary-General to launch into a new doctrinal exercise. Developing countries were less enthusiastic for two reasons: first, they were concerned that the new attention being given to peace operations would distract attention (and resources) from development; and second, an unspoken fear was that more robust peacekeeping or "peace enforcement" was a Trojan horse for intervention by the global North in the South.

For that reason, the SC's request was not picked up on immediately, but later in the decade the Department of Peacekeeping Operations engaged in a review of doctrine. The outcome is the 2008 *United Nations Peacekeeping Operations: Principles and Guidelines.* It is not an official UN document, but rather an internal Secretariat document that UN member states have tacitly accepted as a guide to peacekeeping practice.

UNITED NATIONS PEACEKEEPING OPERATIONS: PRINCIPLES AND GUIDELINES (THE "CAPSTONE DOCTRINE") 2008

3.1 Applying the Basic Principles of United Nations Peacekeeping

Although the practice of United Nations peacekeeping has evolved significantly over the past six decades, three basic principles have traditionally served and continue to set United Nations peacekeeping operations apart as a tool for maintaining international peace and security:

- Consent of the parties
- Impartiality
- Non-use of force except in self-defence and defence of the mandate. . . .

Consent of the parties

United Nations peacekeeping operations are deployed with the consent of the main parties to the conflict. This requires a commitment by the parties to a political process and their acceptance of a peacekeeping operation mandated to support that process ... In the absence of such consent, a United Nations peacekeeping operation risks becoming a party to the conflict; and being drawn towards enforcement action, and away from its intrinsic role of keeping the peace. In the implementation of its mandate, a United Nations peacekeeping operation must work continuously to ensure that it does not lose the consent of the main parties, while ensuring that the peace process moves forward ... Consent, particularly if given grudgingly under international pressure, may be withdrawn in a variety of ways when a party is not fully committed to the peace process. For instance, a party that has given its consent to the deployment of a United Nations peacekeeping operation may subsequently seek to restrict the operation's freedom of action, resulting in a de facto withdrawal of consent. The complete withdrawal of consent by one or more of the main parties challenges the rationale for the United Nations peacekeeping operation and will likely alter the core assumptions and parameters underpinning the international community's strategy to support the peace process. The fact that the main parties have given their consent to the deployment of a United Nations peacekeeping operation does not necessarily imply or guarantee that there will also be consent at the local level, particularly if the main parties are internally divided or have weak command and control systems. Universality of consent becomes even less probable in volatile settings, characterized by the presence of armed groups not under the control of any of the parties, or by the presence of other spoilers ... A peacekeeping operation must have the political and analytical skills, the operational resources, and the will to manage situations where there is an absence or breakdown of local consent. In some cases this may require, as a last resort, the use of force.

Impartiality

United Nations peacekeeping operations must implement their mandate without favour or prejudice to any party. Impartiality is crucial to maintaining the consent and cooperation of the main parties, but should not be confused with neutrality or inactivity. United Nations peacekeepers should be impartial in their dealings with the parties to the conflict, but not neutral in the execution of their mandate. The need for even-handedness towards the parties should not become an excuse for inaction in the face of behavior that clearly works against the peace process. Just as a good referee is impartial, but will penalize infractions, so a peacekeeping operation should not condone actions by the parties that violate the undertakings of the peace process or the international norms and principles that a United Nations peacekeeping operation upholds ...

Non-use of force except in self-defense and defense of the mandate.

... United Nations peacekeeping operations are not an enforcement tool. However, it is widely understood that they may use force at the tactical level, with the authorization of the Security Council, if acting in self-defense and defense of the mandate. The environments into which United Nations peacekeeping operations are deployed are often characterized by the presence of militias, criminal gangs, and other spoilers who may actively seek to undermine the peace process or pose a threat to the civilian population. In such situations, the Security Council has given United Nations peacekeeping operations "robust" mandates authorizing them to "use all necessary means" to deter forceful attempts to disrupt the political process, protect civilians under imminent threat of physical attack, and/or assist the national authorities in maintaining law and order. By proactively using force in defense of their mandates, these United Nations peacekeeping operations have succeeded in improving the security situation and creating an environment conducive to longer-term peacebuilding in the countries where they are deployed.

Although on the ground they may sometimes appear similar, robust peacekeeping should not be confused with peace enforcement, as envisaged under Chapter VII of the Charter. Robust peacekeeping involves the use of force at the tactical level with the authorization of the Security Council and consent of the host nation and/or the main parties to the conflict. By contrast, peace enforcement does not require the consent of the main parties and may involve the use of military force at the strategic or international level, which is normally prohibited for Member States under Article 2(4) of the Charter, unless authorized by the Security Council.

A United Nations peacekeeping operation should only use force as a measure of last resort, when other methods of persuasion have been exhausted, and an operation must always exercise restraint when doing so. The ultimate aim of the use of force is to influence and deter spoilers working against the peace process or seeking to harm civilians; and not to seek their military defeat. The use of force by a United Nations peacekeeping operation should always be calibrated in a precise, proportional and appropriate manner, within the principle of the minimum force necessary to achieve the desired effect, while sustaining consent for the mission and its mandate.

An early draft of the Capstone Doctrine included three other guiding principles: legitimacy, credibility and local ownership. In the final version these were characterized as "success factors," because of strong reluctance of the Non-Aligned Movement and many troop-contributing countries (TCCs) to depart from the three traditional principles. Legitimacy relates to how peacekeepers conduct themselves on the ground, as well as the source of a mission's authority and its composition. Credibility is closely related to the capability of the mission, including its ability to deploy rapidly and to deter spoilers through the credible threat of force. In its conception of local ownership, *the Capstone Doctrine* suggests that it does not mean simply deferring to whoever is in power: "Partnerships with national actors would be struck with due regard to impartiality, wide representation, inclusiveness and gender considerations" (p. 39).

QUESTION

19. In what ways do the Brahimi Report and Capstone Doctrine signify an evolution in thinking about the traditional principles of peacekeeping?

The most recent document to comment on peace operations doctrine is the Report of the High Level Independent Panel on UN Peace Operations (HIPPO). Secretary-General Ban Ki-moon established the panel in October 2014, following a public announcement that he would do so, which caught many people by surprise, including the UN Secretariat. The report was released in June 2015.

UNITING OUR STRENGTHS FOR PEACE—POLITICS, PARTNERSHIP AND PEOPLE (2015)[21]

Executive Summary

First, politics must drive the design and implementation of peace operations. Lasting peace is achieved not through military and technical engagements, but through political solutions. Political solutions should always guide the design and deployment of UN peace operations . . .

---

[21] UN Doc. S/2015/446.

Second, the full spectrum of UN peace operations must be used more flexibly to respond to changing needs on the ground. The United Nations has a uniquely broad spectrum of peace operations that it can draw upon to deliver situation-specific responses. And yet, it often struggles to generate and rapidly deploy missions that are well-tailored to the context. The sharp distinctions between peacekeeping operations and special political missions should give way to a continuum of response and smoother transitions between different phases of missions. The United Nations should embrace the term "peace operations" to denote the full spectrum of responses required and invest in strengthening the underlying analysis, strategy and planning that leads to more successful design of missions. Sequenced and prioritized mandates will allow missions to develop over time rather than trying to do everything at once, and failing.

New approaches

Protection of civilians is a core obligation of the United Nations, but expectations and capability must converge. ... Significant progress has been made in promoting norms and frameworks for the protection of civilians. And yet, on the ground, the results are mixed and the gap between what is asked and what peace operations can deliver has widened in more difficult environments. The protection of civilians is a national responsibility and UN peace operations can play an important role in supporting governments to execute that responsibility. UN missions and non-governmental actors have important unarmed and civilian tools for protecting civilians, working with communities.

The United Nations must rise to the challenge of protecting civilians in the face of imminent threat, and must do so proactively and effectively, but also with recognition of its limits. Protection mandates must be realistic and linked to a wider political approach ... When a protection crisis occurs, UN personnel cannot stand by as civilians are threatened or killed. They must use every tool available to them to protect civilians under imminent threat.

Clarity is needed on the use of force and in the role of UN peace operations and others in managing armed conflict ... Where armed conflict is ongoing, missions will struggle to establish themselves, particularly if they are not perceived to be impartial ... The Panel believes that there are outer limits for UN peacekeeping operations defined by their composition, character and inherent capability limitations. Peacekeeping operations are but one tool at the disposal of the Security Council and they should perform a circumscribed set of roles. In this regard, the Panel believes that UN troops should not undertake military counterterrorism operations. Extreme caution should guide the mandating of enforcement tasks to degrade, neutralize or defeat a designated enemy. Such operations should be exceptional, time-limited and undertaken with full awareness of the risks and responsibilities for the UN mission as a whole. Where a parallel force is engaged in offensive combat operations it is important for UN peacekeeping operations to maintain a clear division of labour and distinction of roles.

The Panel has heard many views on the core principles of UN peacekeeping. The Panel is convinced of their importance in guiding successful UN peacekeeping operations. Yet, these principles must be interpreted progressively and with flexibility in the face of new challenges, and they should never be an excuse for failure to protect civilians or to defend the mission proactively.

To sustain peace, political vigilance is needed. Peace processes do not end when a peace agreement has been signed or an election held ... Peace operations have a key role to play in mobilizing political support for reforms and resources for critical gaps in state capacity, as well as supporting others to revitalize livelihoods in conflict-affected economies. Engagement with affected communities should help build confidence in political processes and responsible state structures. Missions must focus first and foremost on creating political commitment and the space for others to address important elements in sustaining peace.

The security sector must be a particular focus owing to its potential to disrupt peace in many countries, with the UN in a convening and coordinating role, if requested. A significant change in policing approaches is needed to better support national police development and reform. These efforts should be linked to the whole "justice chain", ensuring an integrated approach between human rights and rule of law capacities. ...

Counter-terrorism and enforcement tasks

116. The Panel believes that UN peacekeeping missions, due to their composition and character, are not suited to engage in military counter-terrorism operations ... Such operations should be undertaken by the host government or by a capable regional force or an *ad hoc* coalition authorized by the Security Council.

120. In situations where a UN peacekeeping operation is deployed in parallel with a non-UN force undertaking military counter-terrorism operations or other offensive operations, a clear division of labour and distinction of roles must guide their respective operations ...

Shortly after the High Level Independent Panel on Peace Operations released its report, a group of experts released a parallel report on peacebuilding.[22]

---

[22] "The Challenge of Sustaining Peace," Report of the Advisory Group of Experts for the 2015 Review of the Peacebuilding Architecture, 29 June 2015; available at: http://www.un.org/en/peacebuilding/review2015.shtml.

Shortly after that, the Secretary-General released his own report on implementation of the recommendations of the High Level Panel, in which he also made reference to the peacebuilding report.[23] A few weeks later, a landmark report on the implementation of Security Council resolution 1325 (2000) on women, peace and security was published.[24] These reports were the subject of intensive discussion in the fall of 2015—including at a summit meeting convened by US President Obama—and a range of follow-up activities were scheduled for 2016. Although none of the reports was path-breaking in themselves, some important ideas emerged, such as the "primacy of politics" in all peace operations; the challenges of peacekeeping in the context of violent extremism and terrorism; the demonstrable importance of women's participation and empowerment in efforts to create sustainable peace; and the spectrum of tools at the UN's disposal from small technical assistance missions to "special political missions" to large scale multidimensional operations. At the time of writing, it is too early to assess the impact of these reports, but they set the stage for an interesting transition from Secretary-General Ban Ki-Moon to his successor—both of whom would have to wrestle with the many proposals they contain.

9.8 Contemporary Challenges

As the policy and doctrinal documents make clear, the environment for contemporary peace operations is more challenging than ever. The United Nations has not always proved up to the task in meeting these challenges, leading some to call for a major scaling back of the number, scope, and ambition of peace operations. These calls were loudest in 2010, but the numbers did not decline between then and 2015, and new operations were launched in Somalia, South Sudan, Mali, and the Central African Republic. Combine these with ongoing missions in Afghanistan, Darfur, Haiti, Syria (on the Golan Heights), Lebanon, the DRC, and elsewhere, and it is clear that the United Nations has its hands full.

Although contemporary challenges are many and complex, four in particular stand out: the protection of civilians, the threat of violent extremism, mainstreaming gender in peace operations, and the dilemmas of state-building.

---

[23] "The future of United Nations peace operations: implementation of the recommendations of the High-level Independent Panel on Peace Operations", Report of the Secretary-General, 25 September 2015; available at http://www.un.org/en/ga/search/view_doc.asp?symbol=S/2015/682

[24] "Preventing Conflict, Transforming Justice, Securing the Peace: Implementation of Resolution 1325"; available at http://wps.unwomen.org/~/media/files/un%20women/wps/highlights/unw-global-study-1325-2015.pdf.

Protection of Civilians

More than 98 percent of uniformed personnel deployed in UN peacekeeping missions today have a mandate to protect civilians. Sierra Leone (now terminated) was one of the first; the Democratic Republic of the Congo (DRC) was the second. MONUC (UN Organization Mission in the Democratic Republic of the Congo) was originally established in November 1999 with a limited mandate under Chapter VI. By resolution 1291 (2000), its mandate was expanded to include the protection of civilians, through all necessary means, under Chapter VII, "in the areas of deployment of its battalion and as it deems it within its capabilities." This robust Chapter VII authority was progressively expanded to include not only the protection of civilians, but also to enforce MONUC's larger mandate in certain parts of the East. Nevertheless repeated instances of the failure to protect civilians led the Council to create a new Intervention Brigade in 2013 as a distinct force within MONUC's successor mission MONUSCO (UN Organization Stabilization Mission in the Democratic Republic of the Congo), though under the command of the Force Commander.

SECURITY COUNCIL RESOLUTION 2098 (2013)

The Security Council ...

9. *Decides* ... that MONUSCO shall, for an initial period of one year and within the authorized troop ceiling of 19,815, on an exceptional basis and without creating a precedent or any prejudice to the agreed principles of peacekeeping, include an "Intervention Brigade" consisting inter alia of three infantry battalions, one artillery and one Special force and Reconnaissance company with headquarters in Goma, under direct command of the MONUSCO Force Commander, with the responsibility of neutralizing armed groups as set out in paragraph 12 (b) below and the objective of contributing to reducing the threat posed by armed groups to state authority and civilian security in eastern DRC and to make space for stabilization activities;

12. *Authorizes* MONUSCO ... to take all necessary measures to perform the following tasks, through its regular forces and its Intervention Brigade as appropriate;

(a) Protection of civilians

(i) Ensure, within its area of operations, effective protection of civilians under imminent threat of physical violence, including civilians gathered in displaced and refugee camps, humanitarian personnel and human rights defenders, in the context of violence emerging from any of the parties engaged in the conflict ... ;

(b) Neutralizing armed groups through the Intervention Brigade

In support of the authorities of the DRC, on the basis of information collation and analysis, and taking full account of the need to protect civilians and mitigate risk before, during and after any military operation, carry out targeted offensive operations through the Intervention Brigade referred to in paragraph 9 and paragraph 10 above, either unilaterally or jointly with the FARDC, in a robust, highly mobile and versatile manner and in strict compliance with international law, including international humanitarian law and with the human rights due diligence policy on UN-support to non-UN forces (HRDDP), to prevent the expansion of all armed groups, neutralize these groups, and to disarm them in order to contribute to the objective of reducing the threat posed by armed groups on state authority and civilian security in eastern DRC and to make space for stabilization activities;

QUESTIONS

20. Paragraph 9 states that the Intervention Brigade shall be established without "any prejudice to the agreed principles of peacekeeping." Can the mandate of the Brigade be reconciled with those principles?
21. Is MONUSCO's mandate, including that given to the Intervention Brigade, an appropriate outer limit of robust peacekeeping? Or is it a bridge too far?

The Threat of Violent Extremism

HIPPO states unequivocally that UN peacekeepers should not be engaged in military counterterrorism operations. Indeed, none ever has. But as the line between peacekeeping and war blurs and UN peacekeeping operations and political missions are increasingly employed in environments where there is a threat of terrorism (such as Afghanistan, Somalia, and Mali), adhering to that unequivocal stance is easier said than done. If "spoilers" are associated with terrorist groups, and the United Nations is deployed alongside a mission with a mandate to engage the terrorists, the risk of getting caught in the crossfire if not drawn into a counterterrorism role is real. Mali is an example.

In mid-January 2012, a Tuareg movement known as the Mouvement national pour la libération de l'Azawad (MNLA), along with several Islamic armed groups, initiated a series of attacks against government forces in the north of the country. The MNLA was able to overrun government forces in the North and, on April 6, declared an independent state. Shortly thereafter, tensions among the armed groups emerged, and by 18 November, the Islamic groups had driven the MNLA out of the main towns of Gao, Timbuktu, and Kidal. Meanwhile a coup d'etat in Bamako produced a transitional government that requested UN assistance to build capacity for political negotiation, elections, governance, security sector reform, and humanitarian assistance. A small UN mission was deployed in January to do that and to provide support to the planning, deployment, and operations of the African-led International Support Mission in Mali (AFISMA).

The security situation deteriorated later that month, when elements of the Islamist groups advanced southward. The capture of the city of Konna led the Malian transitional authorities to request France's assistance. Military operations against terrorist and associated elements were initiated on 11 January under "Operation Serval," while the deployment of AFISMA was also accelerated, all in support of the Malian government. The security situation improved, but terrorist activities and military operations continued. The interim President of Mali requested the transformation of AFISMA into a UN stabilization and peacekeeping operation. The Security Council established a mission of 11,000 troops and 1500 police.

SECURITY COUNCIL RESOLUTION 2100 (2013)

The Security Council, . . .

Acting under Chapter VII of the Charter of the United Nations,

7. Decides to establish the United Nations Multidimensional Integrated Stabilization Mission in Mali (MINUSMA) . . . further decides that the authority be transferred from AFISMA to MINUSMA on 1 July 2013.

8. Decides that the date referred to in paragraph 7 above and MINUSMA's phased deployment shall be subject to a further review by the Council within 60 days of the adoption of this resolution of the security situation in MINUSMA's area of responsibility, specifically with respect to the cessation of major combat operations by international military forces in the immediate vicinity of and/or within MINUSMA's envisaged area of responsibility and a significant reduction in the capacity of terrorist forces to pose a major threat to the civilian population and international personnel in the immediate vicinity of and/or within MINUSMA's envisaged area of responsibility; . . .

16. Decides that the mandate of MINUSMA shall be the following:

(a) Stabilization of key population centres and support for the reestablishment of State authority throughout the country

(i) In support of the transitional authorities of Mali, to stabilize the key population centres, especially in the north of Mali and, in this context, to deter threats and take active steps to prevent the return of armed elements to those areas;

(ii) To support the transitional authorities of Mali to extend and re-establish State administration throughout the country; . . .

(c) Protection of civilians and United Nations personnel

(i) To protect, without prejudice to the responsibility of the transitional authorities of Mali, civilians under imminent threat of physical violence, within its capacities and areas of deployment;

17. Authorizes MINUSMA to use all necessary means, within the limits of its capacities and areas of deployment, to carry out its mandate as set out in paragraphs 16 (a) (i) and (ii), 16 (c) (i) ... ;

18. Authorizes French troops, within the limits of their capacities and areas of deployment, to use all necessary means, from the commencement of the activities of MINUSMA until the end of MINUSMA's mandate as authorized in this resolution, to intervene in support of elements of MINUSMA when under imminent and serious threat upon request of the Secretary-General ... ;

29. Urges Sahel and Maghreb States to enhance interregional cooperation and coordination in order to develop inclusive and effective strategies to combat in a comprehensive and integrated manner the activities of terrorist groups ...

QUESTION

22. Is the combination of Operation Serval and MINUSMA a good model for future UN operations deployed in places where there is a threat of terrorism?

Gender and Peace Operations

In 2000, the UN Security Council adopted resolution 1325. This landmark resolution was followed by six more that address "women, peace and security agenda" in UN peace operations.

SECURITY COUNCIL RESOLUTION 1325 (2000)

... and recognizing the consequent impact this has on durable peace and reconciliation,

Reaffirming the important role of women in the prevention and resolution of conflicts and in peace-building, and stressing the importance of their equal participation and full involvement in all efforts for the maintenance and promotion of peace and security, and the need to increase their role in decision-making with regard to conflict prevention and resolution,

1. Urges Member States to ensure increased representation of women at all decision-making levels in national, regional and international institutions and mechanisms for the prevention, management, and resolution of conflict;

2. Encourages the Secretary-General to implement his strategic plan of action (A/49/587) calling for an increase in the participation of women at decisionmaking levels in conflict resolution and peace processes;

3. Urges the Secretary-General to appoint more women as special representatives and envoys to pursue good offices on his behalf, and in this regard calls on Member States to provide candidates to the Secretary-General, for inclusion in a regularly updated centralized roster;

4. Further urges the Secretary-General to seek to expand the role and contribution of women in United Nations field-based operations, and especially among military observers, civilian police, human rights and humanitarian personnel;

8. Calls on all actors involved, when negotiating and implementing peace agreements, to adopt a gender perspective, including, inter alia:

(a) The special needs of women and girls during repatriation and resettlement and for rehabilitation, reintegration and post-conflict reconstruction;

(b) Measures that support local women's peace initiatives and indigenous processes for conflict resolution, and that involve women in all of the implementation mechanisms of the peace agreements;

(c) Measures that ensure the protection of and respect for human rights of women and girls, particularly as they relate to the constitution, the electoral system, the police and the judiciary;

In October 2015, a major fifteen year review of the implementation of resolution 1325 was undertaken.[25] That review covered the four pillars of Security Council resolution 1325 and its subsequent resolutions: prevention, protection, participation, and peacebuilding and recovery.

QUESTION

23. Based on your reading of the Executive Summary and Recommendations at the end of the Global Study, what are the major achievements and obstacles to further progress on the mplementation of resolution 1325?

---

[25] "Preventing Conflict, Transforming Justice, Securing the Peace: Implementation of Resolution 1325"; available at http://wps.unwomen.org/~/media/files/un%20 women/wps/highlights/unw-global-study-1325-2015.pdf.

Dilemmas of State-Building

As noted throughout this chapter, peace operations have become not only more militarily robust but more ambitious in terms of civilian tasks they are expected to perform—even small political missions such as UNSMIL. The peacebuilding agenda now encompasses support to safety and security, political processes, basic services, restoration of government functions, and economic revitalization. To some, this agenda represents a holistic vision of what it takes to build sustainable peace; to others it translates into a laundry list of desirable objectives that are impossible to fulfill. To others still it embodies a neocolonial exercise in social engineering based on liberal democratic models—the so-called liberal peacebuilding critique.[26] For all it raises questions about the appropriate role for outsiders in post-conflict societies.

In *Peacebuilding in the Immediate Aftermath of Conflict* (2009),[27] the Secretary-General describes the first two years after the main conflict ends as a window of opportunity for early peacebuilding. He states that the most "urgent and important peacebuilding objectives [are] establishing security, building confidence in a political process, delivering initial peace dividends, and expanding core national capacity." Implicitly, the provision of basic services and economic revitalization are longer-term endeavors, leadership for which should be left to others although a peace operation could provide support.[28]

The United Nations Mission in South Sudan (UNMISS) is an interesting example of an expansive state-building mission, which had to be scaled back in the face of crisis. A Comprehensive Peace Agreement (CPA) between the government of Sudan and the Sudan People's Liberation Movement (SPLM), signed in January 2005, called for a referendum to take place to determine the status of Southern Sudan. The referendum was held in January 2011, with 98.83 percent participants voting for independence. Following an interim period, South Sudan declared independence in July 2011, and the Security Council established UNMISS with an ambitious state-building mandate, parts of which are set out below.

---

[26] Oliver Richmond and Jason Franks, *Liberal Transitions: Between Statebuilding and Peacebuilding*. Edinburgh: Edinburgh University Press, 2011. Susanna Campbell, David Chandler and Meera Sabartman, *A Liberal Peace? The Problems and Practices of Peacebuilding*. London: Zed Books, 2011; Edward Newman and Roland Paris, *New Perspectives on Liberal Peacebuilding*. Tokyo: United Nations University Press, 2009.
[27] Secretary-General's Report on Peacebuilding in the Immediate Aftermath of Conflict, UN Doc. A/63/374-S/2008/620, 11 June 2009. See also subsequent Secretary-General reports on peacebuilding, UN Doc. A/67/499 (2012) and UN Doc. A/69/399, (2014).
[28] See the Department of Peacekeeping Operations and Department of Field Support in July 2009, *A New Partnership Agenda: Charting a New Horizon for UN Peacekeeping Operations*, p. 23; available at: http://www.un.org/en/peacekeeping/documents/newhorizon.pdf.

SECURITY COUNCIL RESOLUTION 1986 (2011)

The Security Council,

3. *Decides* that the mandate of UNMISS shall be to consolidate peace and security, and to help establish the conditions for development in the Republic of South Sudan, with a view to strengthening the capacity of the Government of the Republic of South Sudan to govern effectively and democratically and establish good relations with its neighbours, and accordingly authorizes UNMISS to perform the following tasks;

(a) Support for peace consolidation and thereby fostering longer-term statebuilding and economic development, through:

(i) Providing good offices, advice, and support to the Government of the Republic of South Sudan on political transition, governance, and establishment of state authority, including formulation of national policies in this regard;

(ii) Promoting popular participation in political processes, including through advising and supporting the Government of the Republic of South Sudan on an inclusive constitutional process; the holding of elections in accordance with the constitution; promoting the establishment of an independent media; and ensuring the participation of women in decision-making forums;

(c) Support the Government of the Republic of South Sudan, in accordance with the principles of national ownership, and in cooperation with the UN Country Team and other international partners, in developing its capacity to provide security, to establish rule of law, and to strengthen the security and justice sectors through:

(i) Supporting the development of strategies for security sector reform, rule of law, and justice sector development, including human rights capacities and institutions;

(ii) Supporting the Government of the Republic of South Sudan in developing and implementing a national disarmament, demobilization and reintegration strategy, in cooperation with international partners with particular attention to the special needs of women and child combatants;

(iii) Strengthening the capacity of the Republic of South Sudan Police Services through advice on policy, planning, and legislative development, as well as training and mentoring in key areas;

(iv) Supporting the Government of the Republic of South Sudan in developing a military justice system that is complementary to the civil justice system;

On 15 December 2013, violence in South Sudan's capital Juba, rooted in political friction among those sharing power within the post-independence government, spread to other locations in the country, resulting in nationwide political and security crisis. The relationship between the government and UNMISS grew tense, amid (unfounded) allegations that the Mission was aiding and abetting the antigovernment forces. The human rights and humanitarian situation deteriorated sharply throughout the country. Tens of thousands of civilians fled from areas where killings were taking place and arrived at UNMISS compounds in Juba, Malakal, and elsewhere. As many as 85,000 civilians sought and received protection in those compounds. The troop level of UNMISS was raised to 12,500 personnel and the police component to 1,323 personnel.

As a result, the Secretary-General recommended UNMISS temporarily suspend its peacebuilding and state-building activities, and adopt a posture of strict impartiality in its relations with both parties. Accepting his recommendation, the Security Council adopted resolution 2155 (2014), prioritizing protection of civilians, human rights monitoring, and support for the delivery of humanitarian assistance.

QUESTION

24. What lessons can be learned from the UNMISS experience about the United Nations' peacebuilding agenda? Has it become too ambitious? Should it be scaled back? If so, to what?

HYPOTHETICAL

You are the Special Representative of the Secretary-General of the United Nations Assistance Mission in Oritania (UNAMO)—a mission that has been deployed to support a transitional government as part of a comprehensive peace plan. The mission's mandate, among other things, is:

- To facilitate a peaceful transition in the country;
- To observe and monitor the implementation of the ceasefire agreement;
- To monitor the human rights situation;
- Acting under Chapter VII, to protect civilians under imminent threat of physical violence, within the limits of the mission's capabilities and areas of deployment.

The transition process has been difficult, with militia groups challenging the solidarity of the transitional government. There is suspicion that these groups are supported by neighboring countries, and perhaps even by political players within the transitional government. The transitional government's army (the AFO) is under-resourced and poorly disciplined. UNAMO is seen by many Oritanians as the only force in the country capable of providing stability in support of the shaky transition process.

A deployment of the AFO has fled its area of responsibility in the town of Lazula, following reports that a recently formed rebel group under the command of a mutinous ex-AFO leader General Zortan is headed for the town. Zortan and his Movement for the Liberation of Southern Oritania (MLSO) claim that the AFO discriminates against the minority Calo population living in the South and that he intends to overthrow the government forces. The UNAMO Force Commander quickly redeploys a contingent in the area, whose presence slows the MLSO advance. At the same time, several unconfirmed reports from the field contend that General Zortan is acting on instructions from a major political group within the transitional government who feel their interests are better represented by a breakdown in the transition process and siding with a neighboring country, Pangota.

In an official statement, Calo politicians in the transitional government indicate that they have tried to contain Zortan, but that he is a renegade. The MLSO forces resume their advance and, meeting with no resistance, move to occupy the town of Lazula. All remaining AFO troops flee north, engaging in systematic looting as they retreat. The small UNAMO contingent in the vicinity does not respond to a call from the Lazula city mayor for assistance. The commander claims that they must not be seen to take sides in the conflict and must be strictly neutral, and that to attack the MSLO would be to become part of the problem. The contingent pulls back to defensive positions at the Lazula airfield. Civilian UNAMO staff think the reason that the contingent is not responding is because instructions from their home country directed them not to get involved. The MLSO forces begin to engage in heavy looting and violence in Lazula, including sexual violence, targeting non-Calo populations.

You have convened your Senior Leadership Team to review the events of the past few days and to determine a way forward. One of your leadership team suggests that the guiding principles of peacekeeping might help to navigate the situation. Which of the guiding principles are at play here? What are the complexities of applying the principles? What trade-offs might be involved? How can the mission strike a balance between the principles and other practical considerations?

Further Reading

Adebajo, Adekeye. *UN Peacekeeping from the Suez Crisis to the Sudan Conflicts.* Boulder, CO: Lynne Reinner, 2002

Aoi, Chiyuki, Cedric de Coning and Ramesh Thakur. *Unintended Consequences of Peacekeeping Operations.* Tokyo: United Nations University Press, 2007.

Bellamy, Alex and Paul Williams. *Understanding Peacekeeping.* 2nd edn. Oxford: Polity Press, 2010.

Call, Charles. *Why Peace Fails: The Causes and Prevention of Civil War Recurrence.* Washington D.C.: Georgetown University Press, 2012.

Caplan, Richard. *International Governance of War-Torn Territories: Rule and Reconstruction.* Oxford: Oxford University Press, 2005.

Center on International Cooperation. *Annual Review of Global Peace Operations*. Volumes 2006–2014 Boulder, CO: Lynne Rienner.

Chesterman, Simon. *You, the People: The United Nations, Transitional Administration, and State-Building*. Oxford: Oxford University Press, 2004.

Chesterman, Simon, *Just War or Just Peace? Humanitarian Intervention and International Law*. Oxford: Oxford University Press, 2001, ch. 4.

Cockayne, James, and David M. Malone. "The Ralph Bunche Centennial: Peace Operations Then and Now." *Global Governance*, vol. 11 (2005), p. 331.

Doyle, Michael W. and Nicholas Sambanis. *Making War & Building Peace: United Nations Peace Operations*. Princeton, NJ: Princeton University Press, 2006.

Durch, William J. (ed). *Twenty-First-Century Peace Operations*. Washington, DC: USIP Press, 2006.

Einsiedel, Sebastian von, David M. Malone and Bruno Stagno Ugarte (eds). *The UN Security Council in the Twenty-First Century*, Boulder, CO and London, UK: Lynne Rienner, 2015—particularly chs. 1, 17, 18, 22, 23, 36, and 40 and the Appendices that list and categorize peace operations from the United Nations' outset until mid-2015.

Findlay, Trevor. *The Use of Force in UN Peace Operations*. Oxford: SIPRI & Oxford University Press, 2002.

Fortna, Virginia Page. *Does Peacekeeping work? Shaping Belligerents after Civil War*. Princeton, PJ: Princeton University Press, 2008.

Guehenno, Jean-Marie. *The Fog of Peace: A Memoir of International Peacekeeping in the 21st Century* Washington D.C: Brookings Institution Press, 2015.

Gray, Christine. *International Law and the Use of Force*. 3rd edn. Oxford: Oxford University Press, 2008.

Holt, Victoria and Tobias Berckman. *The Impossible Mandate? Military Preparedness, the Responsibility to Protect and Modern Peace Operations*. Washington DC: Stimson Center, 2006.

Howard, Lise Morjé, *UN Peacekeeping in Civil Wars*. Cambridge: Cambridge University Press, 2007.

Johnstone, Ian (ed). *US Peace Operations Policy: A Double-Edged Sword? London:* Routltedge, 2008.

Koops, Joachim, Norrie MacQueen, Thierry Tardy and Paul D. Williams (eds). *The Oxford Handbook of United Nations Peacekeeping Operations*. Oxford: Oxford University Press, 2015.

Mazurana, Dyan, Angela Raven-Roberst and Jane Parpart (eds). *Gender, Conflict and Peacekeeping*. Lanham MD: Rowman and Littlefield, 2005.

Newman, Edward, Roland Paris and Oliver Richmond (eds). *New Perspectives on Liberal Peacebuilding. Tokyo:* United Nations University Press, 2009.

Oswald, Bruce, Helen Durham and Adrian Bates. *Documents on the Law of UN Peace Operations*. Oxford: Oxford University Press, 2011.

Paris, Roland. *At War's End: Building Peace after Civil Conflict*. Cambridge: Cambridge University Press, 2004.

Paris, Roland and Timothy Sisk (eds). *Dilemmas of Statebuilding: Confronting the Challenges of Postwar Peace Operations*. London: Routledge, 2009.

Smith, Rupert. *The Utility of Force: The Art of War in the Modern World*. London: Allen Lane, 2005.

chapter ten
. . . .

Sanctions

Sanctions, it has often been said, stand between statements and soldiers. In situations where something more than a diplomatic dressing-down is required, but where a military response is either inappropriate or impossible, sanctions are frequently turned to as a third option. As a result, sanctions are sometimes used as a default policy option, reflecting the seriousness of a problem rather than the seriousness of engagement with it. As UN Secretary-General Kofi Annan once observed, "getting sanctions right has [often] been a less compelling goal than getting sanctions adopted."[1]

Sanctions are among the few instruments cited in the UN Charter to induce compliance with Security Council decisions. Article 41 of the Charter, under Chapter VII, envisages "complete or partial interruption of economic relations and of rail, sea, air, postal, telegraphic, radio, and other means of communication, and the severance of diplomatic relations." The Charter requires all member states to implement such sanctions.

This instrument was little used during the Cold War years. An oil embargo was adopted against break-away racist Southern Rhodesia in April 1966, widened to more comprehensive sanctions in December of that year. In 1977, under tremendous pressure from the General Assembly (which had adopted sweeping non-binding sanctions of its own), the Security Council imposed a mandatory arms embargo against apartheid South Africa.

Sanctions were not invoked again until Security Council resolution 661 of August 1990 against Iraq, discussed in Chapter 2. Swiftly, however, the imposition of sanctions became almost routine. In the early 1990s sanctions sometimes seemed to be viewed as a magic bullet that could achieve a degree of coercion without the dangers inherent in the use of force. Comprehensive and partial sanctions were imposed during this period on Iraq, the former Yugoslavia, Libya, Liberia, Somalia, parts of Cambodia, Haiti, parts of Angola, Rwanda, Sudan, Sierra Leone, and Afghanistan. (In addition, regional organizations and individual states also imposed sanctions numerous times.)

But the humanitarian consequences of comprehensive sanctions came to be seen as unacceptable. When stringent sanctions were imposed against Iraq in resolution 661 (1990) and reconfirmed in resolution 687 (1991), it was

---

[1] UN Press Release SG/SM/7360 (2000).

widely assumed that the purposes of the Security Council in Iraq—complete disarmament of weapons of mass destruction—would be achieved rapidly. There was initially little concern over "collateral damage" from sanctions. Nevertheless, growing evidence of the humanitarian impact of sanctions created pressure to address food and medical shortages on the ground. This led to the establishment of the Oil-for-Food Programme (OFFP), which provided vital support to an Iraqi civilian population caught between a hideous regime and the economic sanctions. Growing unhappiness about the continued application of the sanctions produced a rare outright split among the permanent members of the Security Council, with China, France, and Russia demanding their removal, while Britain and the United States insisted on their maintenance. The plight of Iraqi civilians, publicized by the Iraqi government, NGOs, and some UN staff, created serious hostility toward the sanctions regime in most of the UN's member states, and a degree of skepticism about the use of sanctions more generally.

Criticism of the Iraqi sanctions regime led to growing calls for sanctions to be better targeted, designed to achieve specific political ends rather than as a blunt tool with which to punish a recalcitrant state or nonstate actor. The result was a trend to embrace what became known as "smart sanctions." (Interestingly, no one saw fit to defend "dumb sanctions.")

A second aspect of the Iraq sanctions debate that had a lasting impact concerned the open-ended nature of resolutions such as resolution 661 (1990). Such resolutions impose conditions that require a further Council resolution to modify or lift them; this effectively gives any permanent member of the Council a power of veto over termination of such punishment, sometimes called a "reverse veto."[2] It was this inability to lift sanctions that set the tone for debates over Iraq policy in the early 2000s, used by Britain and the United States to sustain the "sanctions plus inspections" strategy embodied in resolution 687 (1991) until March 2003 and the US-led invasion of Iraq.[3]

Today, all sanctions regimes are targeted to a greater or lesser degree. In some cases this focuses on government officials due to their role in the policies of a recalcitrant state. In an increasingly large number of situations, however, the sanctions are targeted at an individual by name because he or she is believed to be linked to terrorist activities. The consequence of such listing is that the individual's assets are to be frozen worldwide.

Though targeting has reduced the humanitarian impact of sanctions, these moves toward selecting individuals has led to procedural concerns about the ability of those individuals to challenge the freezing of their assets—which frequently takes place without any form of due process or even, in some cases, the production of any evidence whatsoever.

This chapter first reviews the Cold War experience of sanctions against Rhodesia and South Africa, before turning to the sanctions regime imposed

---

[2] David D. Caron, "The Legitimacy of the Collective Authority of the Security Council," *American Journal of International Law*, vol. 87 (1993), p. 552.
[3] See Chapter 2, section 2.1.

on Iraq and the Oil-for-Food program. We then consider two examples of more targeted sanctions regimes being used for the purposes of exerting leverage over a recalcitrant member state: in Haiti after a coup and in Sudan after an assassination attempt in nearby Egypt. The final section discusses the freezing of assets allegedly tied to terrorism and the challenges that have been mounted in the courts of Europe in particular.

10.1 Sanctions during the Cold War

The first resolution adopted by the Security Council imposing mandatory sanctions was passed in December 1966.[4] It was not adopted against a member state as such but against a large portion of a rebellious British colony (with Britain's support). Ian Smith's white separatist regime had taken control of Southern Rhodesia in November 1965.

SECURITY COUNCIL RESOLUTION 232 (1966)

The Security Council, ...
   Deeply concerned that the Council's efforts so far and the measures taken by the administering Power have failed to bring the rebellion in Southern Rhodesia to an end, ...
   Acting in accordance with Articles 39 and 41 of the United Nations Charter,
   1. *Determines* that the present situation in Southern Rhodesia constitutes a threat to international peace and security;
   2. *Decides* that all States Members of the United Nations shall prevent:
   (a) The import into their territories of asbestos, iron ore, chrome, pig-iron, sugar, tobacco, copper, meat and meat products and hides, skins and leather originating in Southern Rhodesia and exported therefrom after the date of the present resolution;
   (b) Any activities by their nationals or in their territories which promote or are calculated to promote the export of these commodities from Southern Rhodesia ...
   (d) Any activities by their nationals or in their territories which promote or are calculated to promote the sale or shipment to Southern Rhodesia of arms, ammunition of all types, military aircraft, military vehicles, and equipment and materials for the manufacture and maintenance of arms and ammunition in Southern Rhodesia;
   (e) Any activities by their nationals or in their territories which promote or are calculated to promote the supply to Southern Rhodesia of all other

---

[4] Cf SC Res. 221 (1966), which "call[ed] upon" the United Kingdom to prevent oil being shipped into Southern Rhodesia.

aircraft and motor vehicles and of equipment and materials for the manufacture, assembly, or maintenance of aircraft and motor vehicles in Southern
Rhodesia . . .

(f) Participation in their territories or territories under their administration or in land or air transport facilities or by their nationals or vessels of their registration in the supply of oil or oil products to Southern
Rhodesia; . . .

3. *Reminds* Member States that the failure or refusal by any of them to
implement the present resolution shall constitute a violation of Article 25 of
the United Nations Charter; . . .

5. *Calls upon* all States not to render financial or other economic aid to the
illegal racist régime in Southern Rhodesia; . . .

10. *Decides* to keep this item on its agenda for further action as appropriate
in the light of developments.

The sanctions regime against Southern Rhodesia was eventually terminated
by the Security Council in 1979, when the minority regime relinquished control and Zimbabwe took its modern name.

SECURITY COUNCIL RESOLUTION 460 (1979)

The Security Council,

Noting with satisfaction that the conference held at Lancaster House in
London has produced agreement on the Constitution for a free and independent Zimbabwe providing for genuine majority rule, on arrangements for
bringing that Constitution into effect and on a cease-fire,

Noting also that the Government of the United Kingdom of Great Britain
and Northern Ireland, having resumed its responsibility as the administering Power, is committed to decolonizing Southern Rhodesia on the basis of
free and democratic elections which will lead Southern Rhodesia to genuine
independence acceptable to the international community . . . ,

2. *Decides*, having regard to the agreement reached at the Lancaster House
conference, to call upon Member States to terminate the measures taken
against Southern Rhodesia under Chapter VII of the Charter pursuant to
resolutions 232 (1966), 253 (1968) and subsequent related resolutions on the
situation in Southern Rhodesia; . . .

The only other occasion on which the Security Council imposed sanctions
during the Cold War period also concerned a racist regime, in this case South

Africa. The obduracy of the apartheid government led to growing pressure from the UN membership—much enlarged by newly independent former colonies—to punish Pretoria and to induce it to embrace majority rule. As early as 1963, the General Assembly recommended to all member states to refrain from exporting to South Africa both oil and weapons.

GENERAL ASSEMBLY RESOLUTION 1899(XVIII) (1963)

The General Assembly,
   Having considered the question of South West Africa [i.e. Namibia] . . .
   6. *Decides* to draw the attention of the Security Council to the present critical situation in South West Africa, the continuation of which constitutes a serious threat to international peace and security;
   7. *Urges* all States which have not yet done so to take, separately or collectively, the following measures with reference to the question of South West Africa:
   (a) Refrain forthwith from supplying in any manner or form any arms or military equipment to South Africa;
   (b) Refrain also from supplying in any manner or form any petroleum or petroleum products to South Africa;
   (c) Refrain from any action which might hamper the implementation of the present resolution and of the previous General Assembly resolutions on South West Africa. . .

The above resolution and others that followed had the effect of stigmatizing South Africa, but General Assembly resolutions are not binding and the Security Council declined for some years to take up the matter. The pressure continued, however, and in 1977 the Council acted to make the arms embargo—but not the oil embargo—mandatory on all member states.

SECURITY COUNCIL RESOLUTION 418 (1977)

The Security Council,
   . . . strongly condemning the South African Government for its resort to massive violence against and killings of the African people, including schoolchildren and students and others opposing racial discrimination, and calling upon that Government urgently to end violence against the African people and to take urgent steps to eliminate apartheid and racial discrimination,

Recognizing that the military build-up by South Africa and its persistent acts of aggression against the neighbouring States seriously disturb the security of those States,

Further recognizing that the existing arms embargo must be strengthened and universally applied, without any reservations or qualifications whatsoever, in order to prevent a further aggravation of the grave situation in South Africa,

Taking note of the Lagos Declaration for Action against Apartheid,

Gravely concerned that South Africa is at the threshold of producing nuclear weapons,

Strongly condemning the South African Government for its acts of repression, its defiant continuance of the system of apartheid and its attacks against neighbouring independent States,

Considering that the policies and acts of the South African Government are fraught with danger to inter-national peace and security,

Recalling ... other resolutions concerning a voluntary arms embargo against South Africa,

Convinced that a mandatory arms embargo needs to be universally applied against South Africa in the first instance,

Acting therefore under Chapter VII of the Charter of the United Nations,

1. *Determines*, having regard to the policies and acts of the South African Government, that the acquisition by South Africa of arms and related *matériel* constitutes a threat to the maintenance of international peace and security;

2. *Decides* that all States shall cease forthwith any provision to South Africa of arms and related *matériel* of all types, including the sale or transfer of weapons and ammunition, military vehicles and equipment, paramilitary police equipment, and spare parts for the afore-mentioned, and shall cease as well the provision of all types of equipment and supplies and grants of licensing arrangements for the manufacture or maintenance of the aforementioned;

3. *Calls upon* all States to review, having regard to the objectives of the present resolution, all existing contractual arrangements with and licences granted to South Africa relating to the manufacture and maintenance of arms, ammunition of all types and military equipment and vehicles, with a view to terminating them;

4. *Further decides* that all States shall refrain from any co-operation with South Africa in the manufacture and development of nuclear weapons; ...

7. *Decides* to keep this item on its agenda for further action, as appropriate, in the light of developments.

The arms embargo itself probably exerted little pressure on South Africa. But the opprobrium associated with such sanctions contributed to the isolation of South Africa, and complemented by sporting bans and other forms of shunning, put pressure on the regime. Following South Africa's first free and fair elections in April 1994, which elected President Nelson Mandela, the sanctions were duly terminated by the Security Council.

SECURITY COUNCIL RESOLUTION 919 (1994)

The Security Council, ...

Welcoming the first all-race multiparty election and the establishment of a united, democratic, non-racial government of South Africa, which was inaugurated on 10 May 1994, ...

1. *Decides*, acting under Chapter VII of the Charter of the United Nations, to terminate forthwith the mandatory arms embargo and other restrictions related to South Africa imposed by resolution 418 (1977) of 4 November 1977 ...

QUESTIONS

1. Under the UN Charter, is there a requirement to exhaust other peaceful remedies before the Council may impose sanctions? Must sanctions be tried before authorizing the use of force?
2. Did Britain require authorization to use force within Southern Rhodesia?
3. Resolution 418 (1977) was the first occasion on which the Security Council determined that the South African regime posed a threat to international peace and security. It followed riots in Soweto in which schoolchildren had been killed, and was adopted less than two months after anti-apartheid activist Steve Biko was arrested and beaten to death. Reading the text of the resolution, was it primarily intended to respond to South Africa's internal or external policies? If you think that the answer is not clear, is this because the resolution was badly drafted?
4. Sanctions in respect of Southern Rhodesia and South Africa were terminated by subsequent Security Council resolutions. What would have been the effect if those subsequent resolutions were not adopted? Would sanctions have remained mandatory even though the purpose of such sanctions had clearly been achieved?

10.2 Comprehensive Sanctions: Iraq

Days after Iraq's invasion of Kuwait, in August 1990, the Security Council adopted comprehensive sanctions intended to put pressure on Iraq to withdraw. Security Council resolution 661 (1990) is quoted at length in Chapter 2, section 2.1. Key provisions only are extracted below.

SECURITY COUNCIL RESOLUTION 661 (1990)

The Security Council, ...
   Acting under Chapter VII of the Charter of the United Nations, ...
   3. *Decides* that all States shall prevent:
   (a) The import into their territories of all commodities and products originating in Iraq or Kuwait exported therefrom after the date of the present resolution;
   (b) Any activities by their nationals or in their territories which would promote or are calculated to promote the export or trans-shipment of any commodities or products from Iraq or Kuwait; ...
   (c) The sale or supply by their nationals or from their territories or using their flag vessels of any commodities or products, including weapons or any other military equipment, whether or not originating in their territories but not including supplies intended strictly for medical purposes, and, in humanitarian circumstances, foodstuffs, to any person or body in Iraq or Kuwait ...
   4. *Decides* that all States shall not make available to the Government of Iraq or to any commercial, industrial or public utility undertaking in Iraq or Kuwait, any funds or any other financial or economic resources ... except payments exclusively for strictly medical or humanitarian purposes and, in humanitarian circumstances, foodstuffs; ...

The humanitarian dimension of the comprehensive sanctions on Iraq, maintained after Operation Desert Storm in early 1991, was immediately controversial. Early on, the Secretary-General had dispatched a team, headed by Martti Ahtisaari, to assess the humanitarian situation in Iraq. His report of 20 March 1991 described conditions in Iraq as "near-apocalyptic." There were shortages of medicine and other humanitarian supplies; Iraq's industrial infrastructure, particularly power plants, oil refineries, water treatment plants, and pumping stations, had been destroyed by Coalition bombing. The sanctions regime imposed by resolution 661 (1990) exacerbated the situation. It was clear that Iraq's humanitarian needs could not be met while the comprehensive sanctions regime remained, and that some relaxation or alteration would be necessary.[5] Independently of minor relaxations

---

[5] For a discussion of humanitarian considerations in Security Council decision-making see Thomas Weiss, "The Humanitarian Impulse" and Joanna Wechsler, "Human Rights," in David M. Malone (ed), *The UN Security Council: From the Cold War to the 21st Century* (Boulder, CO: Lynne Rienner, 2004).

contained in resolution 687 (1991), Secretary-General Pérez de Cuéllar therefore dispatched a further mission to assess Iraq's civilian needs, led by his
Executive Delegate, Sadruddin Aga Khan, in July.[6]

Prince Sadruddin's report noted the folly of seeking funds from other
states to rebuild infrastructure in one of the world's largest oil-producing
states: "With considerable oil reserves in the ground, Iraq should not have to
compete for scarce aid funds with a famine-ravaged Horn of Africa, with a
cyclone-hit Bangladesh." Instead, he proposed that "Iraq's 'essential civilian
needs' be met urgently and that rapid agreement be secured on the mechanism whereby Iraq's own resources be used to fund them to the satisfaction
of the international community."[7]

An "oil-for-food" formula (as it came to be known) was quickly adopted
by the Security Council. In resolution 706 (1991), the Council established
an elaborate program allowing Iraq to export a quota of oil and to use the
resulting export revenues to purchase humanitarian supplies, all under the
controlling eye of the United Nations. Resolution 706 (1991) established an
escrow account to hold the revenues from sales of Iraqi petroleum, and a
mechanism whereby those revenues would be spent on humanitarian
requirements, such as "the purchase of foodstuffs, medicines and materials
and supplies for essential civilian needs."[8] The Council was here taking the
unprecedented step of controlling a sovereign state's revenues and directing
its expenditures—not only to benefit its own population, but also for other
purposes including the payment of costs incurred by the United Nations
in the destruction of Iraqi arms in accordance with resolution 687 (1991), of
compensation, and of the boundary settlement process.

As the proposal depended on Iraqi cooperation for both the production of
oil and the distribution of humanitarian commodities, it could not be forced
upon Iraq. Unsurprisingly, Iraq refused to cooperate. In response, the United
States and Britain sponsored resolution 778 (1992), which authorized states
to seize revenues from Iraqi petroleum sales and transfer them to the escrow
account provided for in resolution 706 (1991), providing short-term funding
for the UN relief program in northern Iraq.[9] Following that unusual seques-
tration, the UN aid program depended from 1991 to 1995 largely on dona-
tions, beset by all of the problems of donor-funded aid programs the United
Nations has confronted before and since.

By early 1995, opposition to continuation of the sanctions regime had
expanded. Within the Council, France and Russia, and to a lesser extent
China, were opposed to sanctions. A wider constituency, particularly including Arab and some other Muslim states, were concerned by the humanitarian

---

[6] Paragraph 20 of SC Res. 687 (1991) provided for expedited import of foodstuffs on
the basis of notification to and no objection by the Sanctions Committee.

[7] See Letter dated 15 July 1991 from the Secretary-General addressed to the
President of the Security Council (Annex), UN Doc. S/22799 (1991), Annex.

[8] See SC Res. 706 (1991), paras. 1, 2.

[9] SC Res. 778 (1992), para. 1.

cost being imposed by sanctions. In addition, a growing number of voices within the United States and Britain were pushing for some kind of change.

On 14 April 1995, the Council passed resolution 986 (1995), providing a rare concession to Baghdad. It gave Iraq the primary responsibility for the distribution of humanitarian goods under the "oil-for-food" formula—except in the Kurdish-controlled north, where distribution would be kept under direct UN control. The launch of the OFFP is thus best understood as a product of the growing divide between the P-5 over the Iraq sanctions regime, balancing the desire on the part of some to maintain sanctions while mitigating their humanitarian costs.

SECURITY COUNCIL RESOLUTION 986 (1995)

The Security Council, . . .

Convinced of the need as a temporary measure to provide for the humanitarian needs of the Iraqi people until the fulfilment by Iraq of the relevant Security Council resolutions . . .

Acting under Chapter VII of the Charter of the United Nations,

1. *Authorizes* States, notwithstanding [sanctions imposed by the Council] to permit the import of petroleum and petroleum products originating in Iraq, including financial and other essential transactions directly relating thereto, sufficient to produce a sum not exceeding a total of one billion United States dollars every 90 days for the purposes set out in this resolution and subject to the following conditions:

(a) Approval by the Committee established by resolution 661 (1990), in order to ensure the transparency of each transaction and its conformity with the other provisions of this resolution, after submission of an application by the State concerned, endorsed by the Government of Iraq, for each proposed purchase of Iraqi petroleum and petroleum products, including details of the purchase price at fair market value, the export route, the opening of a letter of credit payable to the escrow account to be established by the Secretary-General for the purposes of this resolution, and of any other directly related financial or other essential transaction;

(b) Payment of the full amount of each purchase of Iraqi petroleum and petroleum products directly by the purchaser in the State concerned into the escrow account to be established by the Secretary-General for the purposes of this resolution; . . .

7. *Requests* the Secretary-General to establish an escrow account for the purposes of this resolution, to appoint independent and certified public accountants to audit it, and to keep the Government of Iraq fully informed;

8. *Decides* that the funds in the escrow account shall be used to meet the humanitarian needs of the Iraqi population and for the following other

purposes, and *requests* the Secretary-General to use the funds deposited in the escrow account:

(a) To finance the export to Iraq, in accordance with the procedures of the Committee established by resolution 661 (1990), of medicine, health supplies, foodstuffs, and materials and supplies for essential civilian needs, . . .

(b) To complement, in view of the exceptional circumstances prevailing in the three [Kurdish] Governorates . . . , the distribution by the Government of Iraq of goods imported under this resolution, in order to ensure an equitable distribution of humanitarian relief to all segments of the Iraqi population throughout the country, . . .

(d) To meet the costs to the United Nations of the independent inspection agents and the certified public accountants and the activities associated with implementation of this resolution; . . .

(f) To meet any reasonable expenses, other than expenses payable in Iraq, which are determined by the Committee established by resolution 661 (1990) to be directly related to the export by Iraq of petroleum . . .

11. *Requests* the Secretary-General to report to the Council 90 days after the date of entry into force of paragraph 1 above, and again prior to the end of the initial 180 day period, on the basis of observation by United Nations personnel in Iraq, and on the basis of consultations with the Government of Iraq, on whether Iraq has ensured the equitable distribution of medicine, health supplies, foodstuffs, and materials and supplies for essential civilian needs, financed in accordance with paragraph 8 (a) above, including in his reports any observations he may have on the adequacy of the revenues to meet Iraq's humanitarian needs, and on Iraq's capacity to export sufficient quantities of petroleum and petroleum products to produce the sum referred to in paragraph 1 above; . . .

14. *Decides* that petroleum and petroleum products subject to this resolution shall while under Iraqi title be immune from legal proceedings and not be subject to any form of attachment, garnishment or execution, and that all States shall take any steps that may be necessary under their respective domestic legal systems to assure this protection, and to ensure that the proceeds of the sale are not diverted from the purposes laid down in this resolution;

15. *Affirms* that the escrow account established for the purposes of this resolution enjoys the privileges and immunities of the United Nations;

16. *Affirms* that all persons appointed by the Secretary-General for the purpose of implementing this resolution enjoy privileges and immunities as experts on mission for the United Nations in accordance with the Convention on the Privileges and Immunities of the United Nations, and *requires* the Government of Iraq to allow them full freedom of movement and all necessary facilities for the discharge of their duties in the implementation of this resolution;

17. *Affirms* that nothing in this resolution affects Iraq's duty scrupulously to adhere to all of its obligations concerning servicing and repayment of its foreign debt, in accordance with the appropriate international mechanisms;

18. *Also affirms* that nothing in this resolution should be construed as infringing the sovereignty or territorial integrity of Iraq.

Over its lifetime, the OFFP handled $64 billion worth of Iraqi oil revenues, and served as the main source of sustenance for 60 percent of Iraq's estimated 27 million people, reducing malnutrition amongst Iraqi children by 50 percent. It underpinned national vaccination campaigns reducing child mortality and eradicating polio throughout Iraq. In addition, it employed more than 2,500 Iraqis.[10]

But it also became clear over time that sanctions were being manipulated by the Baghdad authorities to their advantage, through the creation of black markets they controlled. The main costs of sanctions therefore continued to be borne by the most vulnerable sections of Iraqi society. Years later, an inquiry led by a former Chairman of the US Federal Reserve revealed that this environment had sustained a wide variety of corruption on the part of Iraqi officials, foreign counterparts, and some members of the United Nations itself.[11]

QUESTIONS

5. Reading resolution 986 (1995), who was made responsible for oversight of the Oil-for-Food Programme?
6. If the humanitarian consequences of sanctions were unacceptable, why did the Council not simply replace comprehensive sanctions with a more targeted regime?
7. The Oil-for-Food Programme saw the Security Council making decisions requiring complex administrative machinery and management, and extensive delegation of authority and discretion to agents. Should the Council avoid such decisions in the future, or should it seek to build up its regulatory and administrative oversight capacity?

10.3 Sanctions as Leverage

After the overthrow of Haiti's President Jean-Bertrand Aristide in October 1991, the Organization of American States (OAS) imposed a trade embargo and called for his return to power. Negotiations foundered, however, and so in mid-1993 the Haiti's exiled leadership and the OAS turned to the Security

---

[10] Oil-For-Food Facts, "Oil-For-Food: FAQ," www.oilforfoodfacts.com/faq.aspx. See especially Independent Inquiry Committee into the United Nations Oil-for-Food Programme, The Impact of the Oil-for-Food Programme on the Iraqi People: Report of an Independent Working Group Established by the Independent Inquiry Committee (7 September 2005), 177, 179.
[11] See the discussion in Chapter 16, section 16.6.

Council to seek stronger, mandatory sanctions against the military regime in Haiti. Though the measures to be imposed were sweeping, they were structured in a way that was intended to encourage or compel the coup leaders to negotiate with the Secretary-General of the United Nations.

SECURITY COUNCIL RESOLUTION 841 (1993)

The Security Council,

Having received a letter dated 7 June 1993 from the Permanent Representative of Haiti to the United Nations ... requesting that the Council make universal and mandatory the trade embargo on Haiti recommended by the Organization of American States, ...

Concerned that the persistence of this situation contributes to a climate of fear of persecution and economic dislocation, which could increase the number of Haitians seeking refuge in neighbouring Member States, and convinced that a reversal of this situation is needed to prevent its negative repercussions on the region, ...

Considering that the above-mentioned request of the representative of Haiti, made within the context of the related actions previously taken by the Organization of American States and by the General Assembly of the United Nations, defines a unique and exceptional situation warranting extraordinary measures by the Council in support of the efforts undertaken within the framework of the Organization of American States,

Determining that, in these unique and exceptional circumstances, the continuation of this situation threatens international peace and security in the region,

Acting, therefore, under Chapter VII of the Charter, ...

3. *Decides* that the provisions set forth in paragraphs 5 to 14 below, which are consistent with the trade embargo recommended by the Organization of American States, shall come into force at 0001 hours eastern standard time on 23 June 1993, unless the Secretary-General, having regard for the views of the Secretary-General of the Organization of American States, has reported to the Council that, in the light of the results of the negotiations conducted by the Special Representative for Haiti of the Secretary-General of the United Nations and Secretary-General of the Organization of American States, the imposition of such measures is not warranted at that time;

4. *Decides also* that if at any time after the submission of the above-mentioned report of the Secretary-General, the Secretary-General, having regard for the views of the Secretary-General of the Organization of American States, reports to the Council that the de facto authorities in Haiti have failed to comply in good faith with their undertakings in the above-mentioned

negotiations, the provisions set forth in paragraphs 5 to 14 below shall come into force immediately;

5. *Decides further* that all States shall prevent the sale or supply, by their nationals or from their territories or using their flag vessels or aircraft, of petroleum or petroleum products or arms and related matériel of all types, including weapons and ammunition, military vehicles and equipment, police equipment and spare parts for the aforementioned, whether or not originating in their territories, to any person or body in Haiti or to any person or body for the purpose of any business carried on in or operated from Haiti, and any activities by their nationals or in their territories which promote or are calculated to promote such sale or supply;

6. *Decides* to prohibit any and all traffic from entering the territory or territorial sea of Haiti carrying petroleum or petroleum products, or arms and related matériel of all types, including weapons and ammunition, military vehicles and equipment, police equipment and spare parts for the aforementioned, in violation of paragraph 5 above;

7. *Decides* that the Committee of the Security Council established by paragraph 10 below may authorize, on an exceptional case-by-case basis under a no-objection procedure, the importation, in non-commercial quantities and only in barrels or bottles, of petroleum or petroleum products, including propane gas for cooking, for verified essential humanitarian needs, subject to acceptable arrangements for effective monitoring of delivery and use,

8. *Decides* that States in which there are funds, including any funds derived from property, (a) of the Government of Haiti or of the de facto authorities in Haiti, or (b) controlled directly or indirectly by such Government or authorities or by entities, wherever located or organized, owned or controlled by such Government or authorities, shall require all persons and entities within their own territories holding such funds to freeze them to ensure that they are not made available directly or indirectly to or for the benefit of the de facto authorities in Haiti;

9. *Calls upon* all States and all international organizations to act strictly in accordance with the provisions of the present resolution, notwithstanding the existence of any rights or obligations conferred or imposed by any international agreement or any contract entered into or any licence or permit granted prior to 23 June 1993;

10. *Decides* to establish, in accordance with rule 28 of its provisional rules of procedure, a committee of the Security Council consisting of all the members of the Council to undertake the following tasks and to report on its work to the Council with its observations and recommendations ...

16. *Expresses its readiness* to review all the measures in the present resolution with a view to lifting them if, after the provisions set forth in paragraphs 5 to 14 above have come into force, the Secretary-General, having regard for the views of the Secretary-General of the Organization of American States, reports to the Council that the de facto authorities in Haiti have signed and

have begun implementing in good faith an agreement to reinstate the legitimate Government of President Jean-Bertrand Aristide; . . .

The sanctions came into effect and pressured the de facto regime to com-
mence negotiations with Aristide later in the same month. These negotiations led to an accord that included Aristide returning to power. But violence
instigated by the de facto regime prevented the small UN peacekeeping
force from deploying. Sanctions were reimposed and strengthened with
what amounted to a naval blockade. It later took the threat of force by a
US-led "coalition of the willing," authorized by the UN Security Council
in July 1994, finally to dislodge the de facto authorities in September 1994.
Aristide resumed his office the following month, with security guaranteed
by a large-scale multilateral military deployment.

The economic sanctions, in place for little more than a year, devastated
Haiti's economy—already the poorest of the Western Hemisphere. Further,
they provided an opportunity for the Haitian military regime and its allies to
engineer a roaring black market in petroleum products across the Dominican
Republic border, frustrating the Security Council-authorized naval blockade
around Haiti's coastline. The damage proved lasting, and stands as a cau-
tionary tale. Indeed the Council has not imposed comprehensive economic
sanctions since its resolutions concerning Haiti in 1993 and 1994.

Today, sanctions regimes do not normally target entire economies. Often,
as we have already seen, the focus will be on arms and oil, but other forms
of targeting are possible also. More recent regimes have focused on specific
sectors of the economy that are believed to have the greatest leverage on the
leadership—such as diamonds and timber.

Another possibility is to confine the impact of sanctions to the realm of
diplomacy. These were invoked following an assassination attempt against
President Mubarak of Egypt while visiting Ethiopia in 1995. Investigations
into the incident suggested involvement of the Sudanese government.
Sudan had been gripped by civil war for more than a decade, with approximately 2 million deaths, but this was the first occasion on which the country
appeared on the agenda of the Security Council. That context may explain
why the measures imposed against Sudan were comparatively mild.

SECURITY COUNCIL RESOLUTION 1054 (1996)

The Security Council, . . .
   Gravely alarmed at the terrorist assassination attempt on the life of the
President of the Arab Republic of Egypt, in Addis Ababa, Ethiopia, on 26

June 1995, and convinced that those responsible for that act must be brought to justice,

Taking note that the statements of the Organization of African Unity (OAU) ... considered the attempt on the life of President Mubarak as aimed, not only at the President of the Arab Republic of Egypt, and not only at the sovereignty, integrity and stability of Ethiopia, but also at Africa as a whole,

Regretting the fact that the Government of Sudan has not yet complied with the requests of the Central Organ of the OAU set out in those statements, ...

Deeply alarmed that the Government of Sudan has failed to comply with the requests [by the Council to extradite the suspects] ...

Determining that the non-compliance by the Government of Sudan with the requests [by the Council to extradite the suspects] constitutes a threat to international peace and security,

Determined to eliminate international terrorism and to ensure effective implementation of resolution 1044 (1996) and to that end *acting* under Chapter VII of the Charter of the United Nations,

1. *Demands* that the Government of Sudan comply without further delay with the requests set out in paragraph 4 of resolution 1044 (1996) by:

(a) Taking immediate action to ensure extradition to Ethiopia for prosecution of the three suspects sheltered in Sudan and wanted in connection with the assassination attempt of 26 June 1995 on the life of the President of the Arab Republic of Egypt in Addis Ababa, Ethiopia; and

(b) Desisting from engaging in activities of assisting, supporting and facilitating terrorist activities and from giving shelter and sanctuary to terrorist elements; and henceforth acting in its relations with its neighbours and with others in full conformity with the Charter of the United Nations and with the Charter of the OAU;

2. *Decides* that the provisions set out in paragraph 3 below shall come into force at 00.01 Eastern Standard Time on 10 May 1996, and shall remain in force until the Council determines that the Government of Sudan has complied with paragraph 1 above;

3. *Decides* that all States shall:

(a) Significantly reduce the number and the level of the staff at Sudanese diplomatic missions and consular posts and restrict or control the movement within their territory of all such staff who remain;

(b) Take steps to restrict the entry into or transit through their territory of members of the Government of Sudan, officials of that Government and members of the Sudanese armed forces;

4. *Calls upon* all international and regional organizations not to convene any conference in Sudan;

5. *Calls upon* all States, including States not members of the United Nations and the United Nations specialized agencies to act strictly in conformity with this resolution, notwithstanding the existence of any rights granted or obligations conferred or imposed by any international agreement or of any

contract entered into or any licence or permit granted prior to the entry into force of the provisions set out in paragraph 3 above;

6. *Requests* States to report to the Secretary-General of the United Nations within 60 days from the adoption of this resolution on the steps they have taken to give effect to the provisions set out in paragraph 3 above;

7. *Requests* the Secretary-General to submit an initial report to the Council within 60 days of the date specified in paragraph 2 above on the implementation of this resolution;

8. *Decides* to re-examine the matter, 60 days after the date specified in paragraph 2 above and to consider, on the basis of the facts established by the Secretary-General, whether Sudan has complied with the demands in paragraph 1 above and, if not, whether to adopt further measures to ensure its compliance;

9. *Decides* to remain seized of the matter.

These measures, although far from dramatic, appear to have put some measure of pressure on Sudan. A number of steps were taken to cooperate with the particular inquiries relating to the Mubarak assassination attempt and more broadly to moderate Sudan's international behavior, notably by working with other UN member states in counterterrorism. These sanctions were lifted in September 2001, soon after the 11 September 2001 attacks on the United States.

QUESTIONS

8. Why does the preamble to resolution 841 (1993) twice refer to the situation in Haiti as "unique and exceptional"? Is this legally significant?

9. Were sanctions on Haiti intended as punishment or as a means of persuasion? What elements of resolution 841 (1993) support your answer?

10. What powers are given to the Secretary-General in paragraphs 3 and 4 of resolution 841 (1993)? Does this suggest a way of avoiding capricious resort to the veto by permanent members of the Council?

11. Why were stronger measures not imposed on Sudan? What action was required for Sudan to comply with the sanctions? How would the Security Council make the determination in paragraph 2 of resolution 1054 (1996)?

12. Compare paragraph 2 of resolution 1054 (1996) with paragraphs 3 and 4 of resolution 841 (1993) on Haiti. Which "trigger" is likely to be more effective in compelling compliance?

13. Is the "reverse veto" a problem? Why, or why not? If it is a problem, is paragraph 16 of resolution 841 a solution? Can you suggest other techniques the Council could use to address the problem?

HYPOTHETICAL A

Ruritania and Teapartistan are former French colonies. The people of Ruritania come from two religious groups: three-quarters follow the Gincha faith and almost all the rest embrace the Mo-Mo religion. The neighboring country of Teapartistan has embraced Mo-Moism as the national religion and forces all of its citizens to worship Mo-Mo. The two countries share a long and badly monitored border across which there is robust trade (legal and black market). Teapartistan exports agricultural products that are essential to the Ruritanian economy; one of its most vital imports is Mo-Mo-ite, a crystal venerated as holy that is found only in Ruritania.

Following a disputed election in Ruritania, in which a strict Gincha party has taken power, Teapartistan's citizens began a campaign to send swords to the Mo-Mo in Ruritania. This is clearly endorsed by the government of Teapartistan. Bands of sword-wielding Mo-Mo soon attacked the Ruritanian capital and drove out the elected leaders.

You are the legal adviser at the French Mission to the United Nations. The Permanent Representative (Ambassador) has asked you for options that she can take to the Security Council consultations later today. There does not appear to be any willingness to consider sending troops, but some kind of sanctions regime may be politically acceptable to the other members of the Council.

What do you advise?

10.4 Targeted Financial Sanctions

Concerns about the humanitarian consequences of comprehensive economic sanctions, in particular those imposed on Iraq from 1990, led to efforts to make them "smarter" by targeting sectors of the economy or specific individuals more likely to influence policies—or at least confining sanctions to ensure that those who bore the brunt of their consequences were also those perceived as most responsible for the situation that led to the sanctions being imposed. This utilitarian approach to minimizing suffering gave rise to different concerns, however, as the identification of individuals (and, in some cases, their immediate families)[12] for freezing of their assets suggested a shift in the way that sanctions were being used.

---

[12] · See, e.g., SC Res. 1173 (1998) (requiring the freezing of assets belonging to "senior officials of UNITA or adult members of their immediate families").

SECURITY COUNCIL RESOLUTION 1267 (1999)

The Security Council, ...

Noting the indictment of Usama [a.k.a. Osama] bin Laden and his associates by the United States of America for, *inter alia*, the 7 August 1998 bombings of the United States embassies in Nairobi, Kenya, and Dar es Salaam, Tanzania and for conspiring to kill American nationals outside the United States, and noting also the request of the United States of America to the Taliban to surrender them for trial ... ,

Determining that the failure of the Taliban authorities to respond to [Council demands that it stop providing sanctuary and training for international terrorists and their organizations, and that all Afghan factions cooperate with efforts to bring indicted terrorists to justice] constitutes a threat to international peace and security, ...

Acting under Chapter VII of the Charter of the United Nations,

1. *Insists* that the ... Taliban ... comply promptly with its previous resolutions and in particular cease the provision of sanctuary and training for international terrorists and their organizations, take appropriate effective measures to ensure that the territory under its control is not used for terrorist installations and camps, or for the preparation or organization of terrorist acts against other States or their citizens, and cooperate with efforts to bring indicted terrorists to justice;

2. *Demands* that the Taliban turn over Usama bin Laden without further delay to appropriate authorities in a country where he has been indicted, or to appropriate authorities in a country where he will be returned to such a country, or to appropriate authorities in a country where he will be arrested and effectively brought to justice; ...

4. *Decides further* that, in order to enforce paragraph 2 above, all States shall:

(a) Deny permission for any aircraft to take off from or land in their territory if it is owned, leased or operated by or on behalf of the Taliban as designated by the Committee established by paragraph 6 below, unless the particular flight has been approved in advance by the Committee on the grounds of humanitarian need, including religious obligation such as the performance of the Hajj;

(b) Freeze funds and other financial resources, including funds derived or generated from property owned or controlled directly or indirectly by the Taliban, or by any undertaking owned or controlled by the Taliban, as designated by the Committee established by paragraph 6 below, and ensure that neither they nor any other funds or financial resources so designated are made available, by their nationals or by any persons within their territory, to or for the benefit of the Taliban or any undertaking owned or controlled, directly or indirectly, by the Taliban, except as may be authorized by the Committee on a case-by-case basis on the grounds of humanitarian need; ...

6. *Decides* to establish ... a Committee of the Security Council consisting of all the members of the Council to undertake the following tasks and to report on its work to the Council with its observations and recommendations:

(a) To seek from all States further information regarding the action taken by them with a view to effectively implementing the measures imposed by paragraph 4 above;

(b) To consider information brought to its attention by States concerning violations of the measures imposed by paragraph 4 above and to recommend appropriate measures in response thereto;

(c) To make periodic reports to the Council on the impact, including the humanitarian implications, of the measures imposed by paragraph 4 above;

(d) To make periodic reports to the Council on information submitted to it regarding alleged violations of the measures imposed by paragraph 4 above, identifying where possible persons or entities reported to be engaged in such violations;

(e) To designate the aircraft and funds or other financial resources referred to in paragraph 4 above in order to facilitate the implementation of the measures imposed by that paragraph;

(f) To consider requests for exemptions from the measures imposed by paragraph 4 above as provided in that paragraph, and to decide on the granting of an exemption to these measures in respect of the payment by the International Air Transport Association (IATA) to the aeronautical authority of Afghanistan on behalf of international airlines for air traffic control services;

(g) To examine the reports submitted pursuant to paragraph 9 below; ...

8. *Calls upon* States to bring proceedings against persons and entities within their jurisdiction that violate the measures imposed by paragraph 4 above and to impose appropriate penalties;

9. *Calls upon* all States to cooperate fully with the Committee established by paragraph 6 above in the fulfilment of its tasks, including supplying such information as may be required by the Committee in pursuance of this resolution;

10. *Requests* all States to report to the Committee established by paragraph 6 above within 30 days of the coming into force of the measures imposed by paragraph 4 above on the steps they have taken with a view to effectively implementing paragraph 4 above;

11. *Requests* the Secretary-General to provide all necessary assistance to the Committee established by paragraph 6 above and to make the necessary arrangements in the Secretariat for this purpose; ...

14. *Decides* to terminate the measures imposed by paragraph 4 above once the Secretary-General reports to the Security Council that the Taliban has fulfilled the obligation set out in paragraph 2 above ...

16. *Decides* to remain actively seized of the matter.

A year later the measures had not achieved their desired effect and so they were extended to a wider range of targets.

SECURITY COUNCIL RESOLUTION 1333 (2000)

The Security Council, ...
   Acting under Chapter VII of the Charter of the United Nations,
   1. *Demands* that the Taliban comply with resolution 1267 (1999) and, in particular, cease the provision of sanctuary and training for international terrorists and their organizations, take appropriate effective measures to ensure that the territory under its control is not used for terrorist installations and camps, or for the preparation or organization of terrorist acts against other States or their citizens, and cooperate with international efforts to bring indicted terrorists to justice;
   2. *Demands also* that the Taliban comply without further delay with the demand of the Security Council in paragraph 2 of resolution 1267 (1999) that requires the Taliban to turn over Usama bin Laden to appropriate authorities in a country where he has been indicted, or to appropriate authorities in a country where he will be returned to such a country, or to appropriate authorities in a country where he will be arrested and effectively brought to justice; ...
   8. *Decides* that all States shall take further measures:
   (a) To close immediately and completely all Taliban offices in their territories;
   (b) To close immediately all offices of Ariana Afghan Airlines in their territories;
   (c) To freeze without delay funds and other financial assets of Usama bin Laden and individuals and entities associated with him as designated by the Committee, including those in the Al-Qaida organization, and including funds derived or generated from property owned or controlled directly or indirectly by Usama bin Laden and individuals and entities associated with him, and to ensure that neither they nor any other funds or financial resources are made available, by their nationals or by any persons within their territory, directly or indirectly for the benefit of Usama bin Laden, his associates or any entities owned or controlled, directly or indirectly, by Usama bin Laden or individuals and entities associated with him including the Al-Qaida organization and *requests* the Committee to maintain an updated list, based on information provided by States and regional organizations, of the individuals and entities designated as being associated with Usama bin Laden, including those in the Al-Qaida organization.

Such targeted financial sanctions intended to address terrorist financing have raised a variety of concerns. Whereas the sanctions regimes discussed earlier in this chapter had a relatively clear endpoint—Iraq's withdrawal from Kuwait, Haiti's restoration of democracy, Sudan's cooperation with an investigation—the same cannot be said of terrorist financing. If assets are frozen in order to prevent funds from being used to support a terrorist attack, it is far from clear at what point those sanctions should be lifted.

In the aftermath of the 11 September 2001 attacks, the regime was further expanded with the removal of a geographic connection to Afghanistan and any time limit on its application.[13]

The process for identifying those individuals whose assets should be frozen, meanwhile, remained opaque. Only in January 2004, with the passage of resolution 1526, were member states proposing individuals to be listed called upon to provide information demonstrating an association with al Qaida. The same resolution *"encourage[d]"* member states to inform such individuals that their assets were being frozen. In July 2005—almost six years after the listing regime was first established—resolution 1617 required that when states proposed additional names for the consolidated list they should henceforth provide to the Committee a "statement of case describing the basis of the proposal." This did not affect the more than four hundred individuals and entities that had been listed without such a formal statement of case. The resolution also *"request[ed]"* relevant States to inform, to the extent possible, and in writing where possible, individuals and entities included in the Consolidated List of the measures imposed on them, the Committee's guidelines, and, in particular, the listing and delisting procedures."

Meanwhile, the sanctions regime had been challenged in European courts on the basis that assets were being frozen without adequate legal protections.

KADI v. COUNCIL AND COMMISSION [2005] ECR II-3649 (COURT OF FIRST INSTANCE OF THE EUROPEAN COMMUNITIES, 21 SEPTEMBER 2005)

181. From the standpoint of international law, the obligations of the Member States of the United Nations under the Charter of the United Nations clearly prevail over every other obligation of domestic law or of international treaty law including, for those of them that are members of the Council of Europe, their obligations under the ECHR and, for those that are also members of the Community, their obligations under the EC Treaty.

182. As regards, first, the relationship between the Charter of the United Nations and the domestic law of the Member States of the United Nations, that rule of primacy is derived from the principles of customary international

---

[13] SC Res. 1390 (2002), para. 3.

law. Under Article 27 of the Vienna Convention on the Law of Treaties of 23 May 1969, which consolidates those principles (and Article 5 of which provides that it is to apply to "any treaty which is the constituent instrument of an international organisation and to any treaty adopted within an international organization"), a party may not invoke the provisions of its internal law as justification for its failure to perform a treaty.

183. As regards, second, the relationship between the Charter of the United Nations and international treaty law, that rule of primacy is expressly laid down in Article 103 of the Charter which provides that, "[i]n the event of a conflict between the obligations of the Members of the United Nations under the present Charter and their obligations under any other international agreement, their obligations under the present Charter shall prevail". In accordance with Article 30 of the Vienna Convention on the Law of Treaties, and contrary to the rules usually applicable to successive treaties, that rule holds good in respect of Treaties made earlier as well as later than the Charter of the United Nations. . . .

184. That primacy extends to decisions contained in a resolution of the Security Council, in accordance with Article 25 of the Charter of the United Nations, under which the Members of the United Nations agree to accept and carry out the decisions of the Security Council. . . .

189. Resolutions adopted by the Security Council under Chapter VII of the Charter of the United Nations are thus binding on all the Member States of the Community which must therefore, in that capacity, take all measures necessary to ensure that those resolutions are put into effect . . .

225. It must therefore be considered that the resolutions of the Security Council at issue fall, in principle, outside the ambit of the Court's judicial review and that the Court has no authority to call in question, even indirectly, their lawfulness in the light of Community law. On the contrary, the Court is bound, so far as possible, to interpret and apply that law in a manner compatible with the obligations of the Member States under the Charter of the United Nations.

226. None the less, the Court is empowered to check, indirectly, the lawfulness of the resolutions of the Security Council in question with regard to *jus cogens*, understood as a body of higher rules of public international law binding on all subjects of international law, including the bodies of the United Nations, and from which no derogation is possible. . . .

237. It falls therefore to be assessed whether the freezing of funds provided for by the contested regulation . . . infringes the applicant's fundamental rights.

238. The Court considers that such is not the case, measured by the standard of universal protection of the fundamental rights of the human person covered by *jus cogens*.

248. . . . [F]reezing of funds is a temporary precautionary measure which, unlike confiscation, does not affect the very substance of the right of the

persons concerned to property in their financial assets but only the use thereof. . . .

292. None of the applicant's pleas in law or arguments having been successful, the action must be dismissed.

As the months became years, however, the view that such asset freezings were a "temporary precautionary measure" became harder to sustain, and demands for some kind of due process to review the listing decisions became more strident. A focal point was created, at least establishing the contact within the UN Secretariat for those who wished to challenge a listing decision.[14] Meanwhile, Kadi appealed the decision of the Court of First Instance. In its decision, the European Court of Justice took a very different view of the relationship between the European Union and the United Nations.

KADI & AL BARAKAAT INTERNATIONAL FOUNDATION v. COUNCIL AND COMMISSION [2008] ECR I–6351 (EUROPEAN COURT OF JUSTICE, 3 SEPTEMBER 2008)

280. The Court will now consider the heads of claim in which the appellants complain that the Court of First Instance, in essence, held that it followed from the principles governing the relationship between the international legal order under the United Nations and the Community legal order that the contested regulation, since it is designed to give effect to a resolution adopted by the Security Council under Chapter VII of the Charter of the United Nations affording no latitude in that respect, could not be subject to judicial review of its internal lawfulness, save with regard to its compatibility with the norms of *jus cogens*, and therefore to that extent enjoyed immunity from jurisdiction.

281. In this connection it is to be borne in mind that the Community is based on the rule of law, inasmuch as neither its Member States nor its institutions can avoid review of the conformity of their acts with the basic constitutional charter, the EC Treaty, which established a complete system of legal remedies and procedures designed to enable the Court of Justice to review the legality of acts of the institutions . . .

282. It is also to be recalled that an international agreement cannot affect the allocation of powers fixed by the Treaties or, consequently, the autonomy of the Community legal system . . .

---

[14] SC Res. 1730 (2006).

283. In addition, according to settled case-law, fundamental rights form an integral part of the general principles of law whose observance the Court ensures. For that purpose, the Court draws inspiration from the constitutional traditions common to the Member States and from the guidelines supplied by international instruments for the protection of human rights ...

284. It is also clear from the case-law that respect for human rights is a condition of the lawfulness of Community acts ...

285. It follows from all those considerations that the obligations imposed by an international agreement cannot have the effect of prejudicing the constitutional principles of the EC Treaty, which include the principle that all Community acts must respect fundamental rights, that respect constituting a condition of their lawfulness which it is for the Court to review in the framework of the complete system of legal remedies established by the Treaty.

286. In this regard it must be emphasised that, in circumstances such as those of these cases, the review of lawfulness thus to be ensured by the Community judicature applies to the Community act intended to give effect to the international agreement at issue, and not to the latter as such.

287. With more particular regard to a Community act which, like the contested regulation, is intended to give effect to a resolution adopted by the Security Council under Chapter VII of the Charter of the United Nations, it is not, therefore, for the Community judicature ... to review the lawfulness of such a resolution adopted by an international body, even if that review were to be limited to examination of the compatibility of that resolution with *jus cogens*.

288. However, any judgment given by the Community judicature deciding that a Community measure intended to give effect to such a resolution is contrary to a higher rule of law in the Community legal order would not entail any challenge to the primacy of that resolution in international law. ...

298. It must however be noted that the Charter of the United Nations does not impose the choice of a particular model for the implementation of resolutions adopted by the Security Council under Chapter VII of the Charter, since they are to be given effect in accordance with the procedure applicable in that respect in the domestic legal order of each Member of the United Nations. The Charter of the United Nations leaves the Members of the United Nations a free choice among the various possible models for transposition of those resolutions into their domestic legal order.

299. It follows from all those considerations that it is not a consequence of the principles governing the international legal order under the United Nations that any judicial review of the internal lawfulness of the contested regulation in the light of fundamental freedoms is excluded by virtue of the

fact that that measure is intended to give effect to a resolution of the Security Council adopted under Chapter VII of the Charter of the United Nations. ...

317. The question of the Court's jurisdiction arises in the context of the internal and autonomous legal order of the Community, within whose ambit the contested regulation falls and in which the Court has jurisdiction to review the validity of Community measures in the light of fundamental rights. ...

323. In that regard, although it is now open to any person or entity to approach the Sanctions Committee directly, submitting a request to be removed from the summary list at what is called the "focal" point, the fact remains that the procedure before that Committee is still in essence diplomatic and intergovernmental, the persons or entities concerned having no real opportunity of asserting their rights and that committee taking its decisions by consensus, each of its members having a right of veto.

324. The Guidelines of the Sanctions Committee, as last amended on 12 February 2007, make it plain that an applicant submitting a request for removal from the list may in no way assert his rights himself during the procedure before the Sanctions Committee or be represented for that purpose, the Government of his State of residence or of citizenship alone having the right to submit observations on that request.

325. Moreover, those Guidelines do not require the Sanctions Committee to communicate to the applicant the reasons and evidence justifying his appearance in the summary list or to give him access, even restricted, to that information. Last, if that Committee rejects the request for removal from the list, it is under no obligation to give reasons.

326. It follows from the foregoing that the Community judicature must, in accordance with the powers conferred on it by the EC Treaty, ensure the review, in principle the full review, of the lawfulness of all Community acts in the light of the fundamental rights forming an integral part of the general principles of Community law, including review of Community measures which, like the contested regulation, are designed to give effect to the resolutions adopted by the Security Council under Chapter VII of the Charter of the United Nations.

327. The Court of First Instance erred in law, therefore, when it held, in paragraphs 212 to 231 of *Kadi* ..., that it followed from the principles governing the relationship between the international legal order under the United Nations and the Community legal order that the contested regulation, since it is designed to give effect to a resolution adopted by the Security Council under Chapter VII of the Charter of the United Nations affording no latitude in that respect, must enjoy immunity from jurisdiction so far as concerns its internal lawfulness save with regard to its compatibility with the norms of *jus cogens*. ...

352. It must, therefore, be held that the contested regulation, in so far as it concerns the appellants, was adopted without any guarantee being given as

to the communication of the inculpatory evidence against them or as to their being heard in that connection, so that it must be found that that regulation was adopted according to a procedure in which the appellants' rights of defence were not observed, which has had the further consequence that the principle of effective judicial protection has been infringed.

353. It follows from all the foregoing considerations that the pleas in law raised by Mr Kadi and Al Barakaat in support of their actions for annulment of the contested regulation and alleging breach of their rights of defence, especially the right to be heard, and of the principle of effective judicial protection, are well founded. ...

373. However, the annulment to that extent of the contested regulation with immediate effect would be capable of seriously and irreversibly prejudicing the effectiveness of the restrictive measures imposed by the regulation and which the Community is required to implement, because in the interval preceding its replacement by a new regulation Mr Kadi and Al Barakaat might take steps seeking to prevent measures freezing funds from being applied to them again.

374. Furthermore, in so far as it follows from this judgment that the contested regulation must be annulled so far as concerns the appellants, by reason of breach of principles applicable in the procedure followed when the restrictive measures introduced by that regulation were adopted, it cannot be excluded that, on the merits of the case, the imposition of those measures on the appellants may for all that prove to be justified.

375. Having regard to those considerations, the effects of the contested regulation, in so far as it includes the names of the appellants in the list forming Annex I thereto, must, by virtue of Article 231 EC, be maintained for a brief period to be fixed in such a way as to allow the Council to remedy the infringements found, but which also takes due account of the considerable impact of the restrictive measures concerned on the appellants' rights and freedoms.

376. In those circumstances, Article 231 EC will be correctly applied in maintaining the effects of the contested regulation, so far as concerns the appellants, for a period that may not exceed three months running from the date of delivery of this judgment.

In the negotiations that followed, various measures were considered by the Security Council. These included the provision of a narrative summary justifying the asset freeze and the creation of an ombudsperson in resolution 1904 (2009). Kadi's assets remained frozen, and he went back to the European courts once again.

KADI v. COMMISSION [2010] ECR II–5177 (EUROPEAN GENERAL COURT, 30 SEPTEMBER 2010)

128. .... In essence, the Security Council has still not deemed it appropriate to establish an independent and impartial body responsible for hearing and determining, as regards matters of law and fact, actions against individual decisions taken by the Sanctions Committee. Furthermore, neither the focal point mechanism nor the Office of the Ombusdperson affects the principle that removal of a person from the Sanctions Committee's list requires consensus within the committee. Moreover, the evidence which may be disclosed to the person concerned continues to be a matter entirely at the discretion of the State which proposed that he be included on the Sanctions Committee's list and there is no mechanism to ensure that sufficient information be made available to the person concerned in order to allow him to defend himself effectively (he need not even be informed of the identity of the State which has requested his inclusion on the Sanctions Committee's list). For those reasons at least, the creation of the focal point and the Office of the Ombudsperson cannot be equated with the provision of an effective judicial procedure for review of decisions of the Sanctions Committee ...

171. In the context of a judicial review which is "in principle the full review" of the lawfulness of the contested regulation in the light of the fundamental rights (judgment of the Court of Justice in *Kadi*, paragraph 326) and in the absence of any "immunity from jurisdiction" for that regulation (*Kadi*, paragraph 327), the arguments and explanations advanced by the Commission and the Council—particularly in their preliminary observations on the appropriate standard of judicial review in the present case—quite clearly reveal that the applicant's rights of defence have been "observed" only in the most formal and superficial sense, as the Commission in actual fact considered itself strictly bound by the Sanctions Committee's findings and therefore at no time envisaged calling those findings into question in the light of the applicant's observations. ....

An appeal by the Commission and Britain was dismissed with costs.[15] Note that the European Courts had technically only ruled on the implementation of UN Security Council decision through EU institutions, not on the validity of those Council decisions. Nevertheless, on 5 October 2012 the Security Council removed Kadi from the UN list, "after concluding its consideration of the delisting request submitted by this individual through the Ombudsperson."[16] The European Union soon followed suit, removing its

---

[15] European Commission and Others v Yassin Abdullah Kadi (Grand Chamber of the European Court of Justice, 18 July 2013.).
[16] UN Press Release SC/10785 (2012).

financial restrictions on Kadi. He remained on the Office of Foreign Assets Control (OFAC) counterterrorism list administered by the US Department of the Treasury but was removed from this also in November 2014.

QUESTIONS

14. The various *Kadi* judgments present distinct views about the relationship between the European Union and the United Nations, as well as concerning the legality of targeted financial sanctions. Which do you find the most persuasive? Does the time frame matter? Would your position change if the assets had been frozen for six months, or had been held for thirty years? Or if they were not released upon the death of an alleged terrorist financier?
15. Instead of freezing assets, could the Security Council authorize the detention of an individual? Can the Council authorize torture? (Compare the question of review of Council decisions, discussed in Chapter 4.)
16. What challenges do targeted financial sanctions pose for the Council as a decision-making body? Are decisions made in this context in keeping with the political character of the Council? (Compare the discussion of factors to be taken into account in the *Admissions* case in Chapter 6.)
17. Several of the sanctions regimes imposed by the Security Council produced adverse humanitarian effects, sometimes said to amount to international crimes. Who might be held responsible for these consequences? How?
18. Given the limited repertoire of Security Council instruments to encourage or coerce compliance with its decisions, sanctions are important to the Council. They tend to follow very established patterns (weapons, economic, financial, travel, diplomatic). Can you think of others that might work well? If so, what would be their strengths and weaknesses?
19. Are sanctions meant to work? That is, are they imposed because of a belief that they impact on policy choices of key actors, or because more than words but less than war is required by an international crisis? What other purposes do they serve?

Further Reading

Bailey, Sydney D. and Sam Daws. *The Procedure of the UN Security Council*. 3rd edn. Oxford: Oxford University Press, 1998, pp. 365–378 (on Security Council Sanctions Committees and some related organs).
Chesterman, Simon and Béatrice Pouligny. "Are Sanctions Meant to Work? The Politics of Creating and Implementing Sanctions through the United Nations." *Global Governance*, vol. 9 (2003), p. 503.

Cortright, David and George A. Lopez, *Sanctions and the Search for Security: Challenges to UN Action*, Boulder, CO: Lynne Rienner, 2002, particularly pp. 201–224.

Cortright, David and George A. Lopez. *The Sanctions Decade: Assessing UN Strategies in the 1990s*, Boulder, CO: Lynne Rienner, 2000.

Cortright, David, George A Lopez and Linda Gerber-Stellingwerf. "The Sanctions Era: Themes and Trends in UN Security Council Sanctions since 1990." In Vaughan Lowe, Adam Roberts, Jennifer Welsh, Dominik Zaum (eds), *The United Nations Security Council and War: The Evolution of Thought and Practice since 1945*. 1st edn. Oxford: Oxford University Press, 2010, pp. 205–225.

Drezner, Daniel W. "Sanctions Sometimes Smart: Targeted Sanctions in Theory and Practice." *International Studies Review*, vol. 13 (2011), p. 96.

Farrall, Jeremy Matam. *United Nations Sanctions and the Rule of Law*. 1st edn. Cambridge: Cambridge University Press, 2007.

Kokott, Juliane and Christoph Sobotta. "The Kadi Case—Constitutional Core Values and International Law—Finding the Balance?" *European Journal of International Law*, vol. 23 (2012), p. 1015.

Malone, David M. *Decision-Making in the UN Security Council: The Case of Haiti, 1990–1997*. Oxford: Clarendon Press, 1998, pp. 78–97 and 155–184.

Malone, David M. *The International Struggle for Iraq: Politics in the UN Security Council*. Oxford: Oxford University Press, 2006, pp. 114–151.

Tzanakopoulos, Antonios. *Disobeying the Security Council: Countermeasures against Wrongful Sanctions*. 1st edn. Oxford: Oxford University Press, 2011.

chapter eleven
. . . .

Sustainable Development

The work of the United Nations on development issues has increased significantly over the years. As we noted with respect to work on a new set of Sustainable Development Goals in Chapter 3, the UN Charter provides a solid (if not particularly focused) foundation for attention to development issues. But the United Nations' programming on development has sometimes been hampered by the sprawling nature of the UN system that evolved around this mandate, with much interagency competition for donor funding and frequent stampedes toward working on issues favored by the donors.

Examples include the emergence of humanitarian action as a principal programming vector for the United Nations, attracting billions of dollars of voluntary funding and the creation of the Office for Coordination of Humanitarian Affairs. Both wound up eating into funding available for development work—as many developing countries feared they would when key changes were introduced in 1991. Such well-meaning actions may have produced unintended adverse consequences.

So long as international humanitarian action fell clearly under the purview of the international Red Cross and Red Crescent system (altogether autonomous from the United Nations with its own constitutive treaties), it was perceived in most countries as genuinely impartial and politically neutral. But once humanitarian action started to be taken on by the UN system—with its complex strategies, mixed motives, and layers of political considerations—international humanitarian action became more open to question in its aims, notably by conflict-affected governments and local combatants. Not coincidentally, it was also more often a target of attack on the ground. The fact that Red Cross and Red Crescent personnel and operations themselves have also been attacked during the past decade suggests more the overall politicization of international humanitarian action from the perspective of local actors than any equivalency between the UN and the Red Cross system.

Competition among the many UN agencies, funds, and programs aiming to promote development—alongside other actors such as the World Bank—has been frustrating for donor and recipient countries alike. Although the development efforts of the United Nations were initially

uncontroversial, following decolonization in the 1950s and 1960s, industrialized countries became disenchanted with being potentially outvoted
on development financing in the UN General Assembly by the much
larger group of developing countries organized under the umbrella of the
"Group of 77." (Founded in 1964, the G-77 now numbers over 130 members.) Wealthy countries came to prefer channeling their development
funding through the World Bank or regional development banks, where
weighted voting ensured their control of both the agenda and approval of
proposed loans. Many developing countries have preferred the UN route.
However, except in instances where assessed contributions fund part of
the programming, the donors have called the tune.

Even following the excitement of the Millennium Summit of 2000, the
Millennium Development Goals (MDGs), and the successful Monterrey
Conference on the Financing of Development in 2002, the United Nations
still remains a junior partner in development financing—although it is frequently the lead international actor in responding to natural and man-made
humanitarian emergencies. In addition to concerns about control by donors,
the manner in which funding is provided creates its own problems. Whereas
the general running of the United Nations and its peacekeeping operations
are supported through assessed contributions (discussed in Chapter 7),
development assistance, like humanitarian relief, relies overwhelmingly
upon voluntary contributions. This undermines systematic planning and a
long-term horizon for programming.

Some UN bodies flourished for a time in the field of policy development, displaying real intellectual leadership, for example the Economic
Commission for Latin America and the Caribbean (ECLAC) in the 1960s and
still today, and UNICEF in the 1990s, the latter successfully challenging prescriptions of the World Bank and IMF that advocated structural adjustment
without any regard for social policy. But the UN system and its agencies
were simply never trusted by the donor community to the extent that the
Bank and the Fund were.

Thus, while rafts of resolutions were debated and adopted within the
United Nations on the serial debt crises afflicting many developing countries
in the 1980s and 1990s, solutions were negotiated elsewhere, often under G-7
leadership in close cooperation with the IMF, World Bank, and Paris Club
(of official creditors), which in turn operated in a degree of synchronicity
with the London Club (of private creditors). Similarly, the role of the United
Nations on trade liberalization and disputes was consistently minor, in
spite of early high hopes for the UN Conference on Trade and Development
(UNCTAD), created in 1964, that today, with the exception of often excellent
work on global investment patterns and policy, limps on alongside the more
central if also waning World Trade Organization (independent of the United
Nations). One reason for this may lie in the United Nations' often highly

ideological debates on questions involving dollars and cents, which tend to result in pragmatic compromises (leaving most parties unhappy) rather than principled strategies. Discussions in the UN's Economic and Social Council (ECOSOC) have been characterized by the heated rhetoric of skilled debaters (mostly endowed with limited economic credentials), while the real economic policy and development action unfolds elsewhere.

The United Nations' failure to matter all that much on development issues, beyond important normative efforts such as the MDGs and SDGs, has been a source of considerable unhappiness within the Organization. Efforts to expand its role include the *Global Compact*, which involved private sector companies and nongovernmental organizations in the United Nations' debates, proving controversial in its own right with some delegations. But after a flourishing start it seems to have stagnated in recent years, not so much in terms of the number of companies adhering to it, but relating more to its purposes, approaches, and results.

All of this said, the United Nations has played a tremendously important role in the normative field, creating new concepts (such as the law of the sea), focusing in a sustained way on gender inequality, and seizing on environmental challenges in successive waves of thinking and endeavor. All of these have been genuinely meaningful.

Clashing conceptions of development generated both ideological and methodological battlegrounds from the 1970s to the 1990s. The United Nations' major contributions emerging from these debates was the adoption of the concept of "human development," which was much more encompassing than simply economic growth, and saw social progress as equally important. This view, perhaps most associated with Amartya Sen, who won the 1988 Nobel Economics Prize, found expression at the United Nations through the Human Development Report (initially led by Sen's distinguished friend and colleague Mahbub ul Haq), which has appeared annually since 1991, with an influential index of country performance. Although the World Bank at first resisted the approach, it has since come around to it.

Related to it somewhat was the emergence of a "human security" agenda focused on more than prevention and resolution of war. It led, among other developments, to the creation of the International Criminal Court and a treaty to ban land mines. Through the work of an international commission sponsored by Japan, a more holistic view was articulated of human security, looping back to conceptions of security and development that saw them as intimately intertwined, an attractive approach, and one much liked in the developing world, but one hard to operationalize.

This chapter first discusses a long and contentious debate at the United Nations over a "right to development," which rich countries long feared might be, somehow, actionable, and then turns to one of the most pressing challenges of our time, developing a global strategy to address both mitigation of and adaptation to climate change, a debate that has unfolded for governments primarily within the United Nations. This debate has unfolded amidst considerable controversy, largely because the resources required to contain and combat climate change have, at times, seemed overwhelming for many of the protagonists. At heart the challenge for humanity is how to achieve economic development for all while protecting human and other forms of biological life from severe environmental degradation.

QUESTIONS

1. Some member states complain that Security Council resolutions on peace and security are binding, while General Assembly resolutions on development are not. Should development issues be addressed differently at the United Nations?
2. Is the United Nations' role in the normative field more relevant to development, and should it leave operational activities to others? Why, or why not?

11.1 The Right to Development

The language of "rights" in the area of development was long resisted by industrialized countries, concerned that its acceptance could create enormous financial obligations in order to realize that right in poor countries. In extended negotiations, stretching over many years, industrialized and developing countries came to a kind of agreement. The rhetoric was settled in a few concepts enshrined in the preambular paragraphs of the Declaration on the Right to Development, adopted in 1986, although several countries (notably the United States) withheld their formal consent until the 1993 Vienna Conference on Human Rights. Consensus was also achieved on a few important operative paragraphs in which obligations of both developed and developing states complement one another and are carefully crafted to avoid supporting expansive claims aiming for a redistributive restructuring of international economic relations. This became possible only after proponents of a New International Economic Order (NIEO) met their Waterloo in the early 1980s, when their claims-based approach ran into determined rejection from the Reagan administration and the British government under Margaret Thatcher.

DECLARATION ON THE RIGHT TO DEVELOPMENT: GENERAL ASSEMBLY RESOLUTION 41/128 (1986)

The General Assembly,

Bearing in mind the purposes and principles of the Charter of the United Nations relating to the achievement of international co-operation in solving international problems of an economic, social, cultural or humanitarian nature, and in promoting and encouraging respect for human rights and fundamental freedoms for all without distinction as to race, sex, language or religion,

Recognizing that development is a comprehensive economic, social, cultural and political process, which aims at the constant improvement of the well-being of the entire population and of all individuals on the basis of their active, free and meaningful participation in development and in the fair distribution of benefits resulting therefrom,

Considering that under the provisions of the Universal Declaration of Human Rights everyone is entitled to a social and international order in which the rights and freedoms set forth in that Declaration can be fully realized,

Recalling the provisions of the International Covenant on Economic, Social and Cultural Rights and of the International Covenant on Civil and Political Rights,

Recalling further the relevant agreements, conventions, resolutions, recommendations and other instruments of the United Nations and its specialized agencies concerning the integral development of the human being, economic and social progress and development of all peoples, including those instruments concerning decolonization, the prevention of discrimination, respect for and observance of, human rights and fundamental freedoms, the maintenance of international peace and security and the further promotion of friendly relations and co-operation among States in accordance with the Charter,

Recalling the right of peoples to self-determination, by virtue of which they have the right freely to determine their political status and to pursue their economic, social and cultural development,

Recalling also the right of peoples to exercise, subject to the relevant provisions of both International Covenants on Human Rights, full and complete sovereignty over all their natural wealth and resources,

Mindful of the obligation of States under the Charter to promote universal respect for and observance of human rights and fundamental freedoms for all without distinction of any kind such as race, colour, sex, language, religion, political or other opinion, national or social origin, property, birth or other status,

Considering that the elimination of the massive and flagrant violations of the human rights of the peoples and individuals affected by situations such as those resulting from colonialism, neo-colonialism, apartheid, all forms of racism and racial discrimination, foreign domination and occupation, aggression and threats against national sovereignty, national unity and territorial integrity and threats of war would contribute to the establishment of circumstances propitious to the development of a great part of mankind,

Concerned at the existence of serious obstacles to development, as well as to the complete fulfilment of human beings and of peoples, constituted, inter alia, by the denial of civil, political, economic, social and cultural rights, and considering that all human rights and fundamental freedoms are indivisible and interdependent and that, in order to promote development, equal attention and urgent consideration should be given to the implementation, promotion and protection of civil, political, economic, social and cultural rights and that, accordingly, the promotion of, respect for and enjoyment of certain human rights and fundamental freedoms cannot justify the denial of other human rights and fundamental freedoms,

Considering that international peace and security are essential elements for the realization of the right to development,

Reaffirming that there is a close relationship between disarmament and development and that progress in the field of disarmament would considerably promote progress in the field of development and that resources released through disarmament measures should be devoted to the economic and social development and well-being of all peoples and, in particular, those of the developing countries,

Recognizing that the human person is the central subject of the development process and that development policy should therefore make the human being the main participant and beneficiary of development,

Recognizing that the creation of conditions favourable to the development of peoples and individuals is the primary responsibility of their States,

Aware that efforts at the international level to promote and protect human rights should be accompanied by efforts to establish a new international economic order,

Confirming that the right to development is an inalienable human right and that equality of opportunity for development is a prerogative both of nations and of individuals who make up nations,

Proclaims the following Declaration on the Right to Development:

Article 1

1. The right to development is an inalienable human right by virtue of which every human person and all peoples are entitled to participate in, contribute to, and enjoy economic, social, cultural and political development, in which all human rights and fundamental freedoms can be fully realized.

2. The human right to development also implies the full realization of the right of peoples to self-determination, which includes, subject to the relevant

provisions of both International Covenants on Human Rights, the exercise of their inalienable right to full sovereignty over all their natural wealth and resources.

Article 2

1. The human person is the central subject of development and should be the active participant and beneficiary of the right to development.

2. All human beings have a responsibility for development, individually and collectively, taking in to account the need for full respect for their human rights and fundamental freedoms as well as their duties to the community, which alone can ensure the free and complete fulfilment of the human being, and they should therefore promote and protect an appropriate political, social and economic order for development.

3. States have the right and the duty to formulate appropriate national development policies that aim at the constant improvement of the well-being of the entire population and of all individuals, on the basis of their active, free and meaningful participation in development and in the fair distribution of the benefits resulting therefrom.

Article 3

1. States have the primary responsibility for the creation of national and international conditions favourable to the realization of the right to development.

2. The realization of the right to development requires full respect for the principles of international law concerning friendly relations and cooperation among States in accordance with the Charter of the United Nations.

3. States have the duty to co-operate with each other in ensuring development and eliminating obstacles to development. States should realize their rights and fulfil their duties in such a manner as to promote a new international economic order based on sovereign equality, interdependence, mutual interest and co-operation among all States, as well as to encourage the observance and realization of human rights.

Article 4

1. States have the duty to take steps, individually and collectively, to formulate international development policies with a view to facilitating the full realization of the right to development.

2. Sustained action is required to promote more rapid development of developing countries. As a complement to the efforts of developing countries, effective international co-operation is essential in providing these countries with appropriate means and facilities to foster their comprehensive development.

Article 5

States shall take resolute steps to eliminate the massive and flagrant violations of the human rights of peoples and human beings affected by situations such as those resulting from apartheid, all forms of racism and racial discrimination, colonialism, foreign domination and occupation, aggression, foreign interference and threats against national sovereignty, national unity and territorial integrity, threats of war and refusal to recognize the fundamental right of peoples to self-determination.

Article 6

1. All States should co-operate with a view to promoting, encouraging and strengthening universal respect for and observance of all human rights and fundamental freedoms for all without any distinction as to race, sex, language or religion.

2. All human rights and fundamental freedoms are indivisible and interdependent; equal attention and urgent consideration should be given to the implementation, promotion and protection of civil, political, economic, social and cultural rights.

3. States should take steps to eliminate obstacles to development resulting from failure to observe civil and political rights, as well as economic social and cultural rights.

Article 7

All States should promote the establishment, maintenance and strengthening of international peace and security and, to that end, should do their utmost to achieve general and complete disarmament under effective international control, as well as to ensure that the resources released by effective disarmament measures are used for comprehensive development, in particular that of the developing countries.

Article 8

1. States should undertake, at the national level, all necessary measures for the realization of the right to development and shall ensure, inter alia, equality of opportunity for all in their access to basic resources, education, health services, food, housing, employment and the fair distribution of income. Effective measures should be undertaken to ensure that women have an active role in the development process. Appropriate economic and social reforms should be carried out with a view to eradicating all social injustices.

2. States should encourage popular participation in all spheres as an important factor in development and in the full realization of all human rights.

Article 9

1. All the aspects of the right to development set forth in the present Declaration are indivisible and interdependent and each of them should be considered in the context of the whole.

2. Nothing in the present Declaration shall be construed as being contrary to the purposes and principles of the United Nations, or as implying that any State, group or person has a right to engage in any activity or to perform any act aimed at the violation of the rights set forth in the Universal Declaration of Human Rights and in the International Covenants on Human Rights.

Article 10

Steps should be taken to ensure the full exercise and progressive enhancement of the right to development, including the formulation, adoption and implementation of policy, legislative and other measures at the national and international levels.

QUESTIONS

3. For many activists, the debate at the United Nations on the "right to development" crystallized different visions of the United Nations' core purpose. How important has the acceptance of such a right been to actual development around the world? Does this matter?
4. Does the language of "rights" make sense in the context of development? Why, or why not? What obligations, if any, were agreed to in the Declaration on the Right to Development?
5. The declaration makes clear a number of obligations as well as rights of countries in the sphere of development. But governance is largely absent from the text. Was this a necessary but unhealthy compromise? Why or why not?
6. The "right to food" is much litigated in India. Is such a right actionable or mostly an inspiration nationally to develop better policies and achieve stronger outcomes in the field of agriculture, relative to the distribution and availability of food and even more to rational trade and investment policies?

11.2 Sustainable Development

The second part of this chapter focuses on an increasingly important sub-set of the United Nations' economic and developmental work: environmental threats. This is an area in which the United Nations became an actor quite late, beginning in earnest with the 1972 UN Conference on the Human Environment in Stockholm. The declaration adopted at that event is both sweeping and admirably brief—especially by current UN conference standards. The language captures elegantly the environmental quandaries humanity increasingly faces. Several of its preambular paragraphs and principles impart a sense of its vision and the excitement it generated, though one might question the amount of follow-through that it generated in terms of action.

DECLARATION OF THE UNITED NATIONS CONFERENCE ON THE HUMAN ENVIRONMENT (1972)[1]

Proclaims that:

1. Man is both creature and moulder of his environment, which gives him physical sustenance and affords him the opportunity for intellectual, moral, social and spiritual growth. In the long and tortuous evolution of the human race on this planet a stage has been reached when, through the rapid acceleration of science and technology, man has acquired the power to transform his environment in countless ways and on an unprecedented scale. Both aspects of man's environment, the natural and the man-made, are essential to his well-being and to the enjoyment of basic human rights-even the right to life itself.

2. The protection and improvement of the human environment is a major issue which affects the well-being of peoples and economic development throughout the world; it is the urgent desire of the peoples of the whole world and the duty of all Governments.

3. Man has constantly to sum up experience and go on discovering, inventing, creating and advancing. In our time, man's capability to transform his surroundings, if used wisely, can bring to all peoples the benefits of development and the opportunity to enhance the quality of life. Wrongly or heedlessly applied, the same power can do incalculable harm to human beings and the human environment. We see around us growing evidence of

---

[1] A/CONF.48/14/Rev.1, Report of the United Nations Conference on the Human Environment, Stockholm, 5–16 June 1972, United Nations, available at: http://www.un-documents.net/aconf48-14r1.pdf.

man-made harm in many regions of the earth: dangerous levels of pollution in water, air, earth and living beings; major and undesirable disturbances to the ecological balance of the biosphere; destruction and depletion of irreplaceable resources; and gross deficiencies, harmful to the physical, mental and social health of man, in the man-made environment, particularly in the living and working environment.

II—Principles

States the common conviction that:

Principle 1
Man has the fundamental right to freedom, equality and adequate conditions of life, in an environment of a quality that permits a life of dignity and well-being, and he bears a solemn responsibility to protect and improve the environment for present and future generations. In this respect, policies promoting or perpetuating *apartheid*, racial segregation, discrimination, colonial and other forms of oppression and foreign domination stand condemned and must be eliminated.

Principle 2
The natural resources of the earth, including the air, water, land, flora and fauna and especially representative samples of natural ecosystems, must be safeguarded for the benefit of present and future generations through careful planning or management, as appropriate.

Principle 3
The capacity of the earth to produce vital renewable resources must be maintained and, wherever practicable, restored or improved.

Principle 4
Man has a special responsibility to safeguard and wisely manage the heritage of wildlife and its habitat, which are now gravely imperilled by a combination of adverse factors. Nature conservation, including wildlife, must therefore receive importance in planning for economic development.

Principle 5
The non-renewable resources of the earth must be employed in such a way as to guard against the danger of their future exhaustion and to ensure that benefits from such employment are shared by all mankind.

Principle 6
The discharge of toxic substances or of other substances and the release of heat, in such quantities or concentrations as to exceed the capacity of the environment to render them harmless, must be halted in order to ensure that serious or irreversible damage is not inflicted upon ecosystems. The just struggle of the peoples of all countries against pollution should be supported.

Principle 7
States shall take all possible steps to prevent pollution of the seas by substances that are liable to create hazards to human health, to harm living

resources and marine life, to damage amenities or to interfere with other legitimate uses of the sea.

Principle 13

In order to achieve a more rational management of resources and thus to improve the environment, States should adopt an integrated and co-ordinated approach to their development planning so as to ensure that development is compatible with the need to protect and improve environment for the benefit of their population.

To carry the ideas forward, the conference agreed that a new body be established, the UN Environment Programme, whose headquarters are in Nairobi. Its effectiveness has waxed and waned over time somewhat, depending on the quality of its leadership, but also because it is subject to fierce competition from other UN bodies eager to expand their slice of the important and lucrative international environmental pie.

Prior to the Stockholm Conference, attention had focused above all on wildlife preservation, after several important binding conventions were reached, in this field, including: the 1973 Convention on International Trade in Endangered Species (CITES) and the 1979 Convention on the Conservation of Migratory Species of Wild Animals. However, the field of environmental or environmentally-relevant treaties was soon to expand dramatically. Perhaps the most important soon after the Stockholm Declaration was the 1982 UN Convention on the Law of the Sea (UNCLOS)—a hugely ambitious undertaking, whose Part XII provides a framework for regulating the marine environment. Among other achievements, the Convention provides for a regime relating to minerals on the seabed outside any state's territorial waters or EEZ (Exclusive Economic Zones). It establishes an International Seabed Authority (ISA) to authorize seabed exploration and mining, and collect and distribute seabed mining royalties. The Convention came into force in 1994, but the United States in particular has not yet ratified it—despite several presidents supporting doing so. Implementation of its wide-ranging provisions therefore remains inconsistent.

Another treaty that proved important, not least because it achieved concrete results, was the 1985 Convention for the Protection of the Ozone Layer. Its 1987 Montreal Protocol, relating to elimination of substances depleting the ozone layer, was at first thought too onerous to be implemented. Yet it proved highly effective at relatively low cost. In recent years, the ozone layer over the Antarctic area has been reconstituting itself, in significant part because of the Protocol's implementation.

Further activity was spurred on by the highly influential report in 1987 of the World Commission on Environment and Development (WCED). The Commission was led by Gro Harlem Brundtland, a former prime minister and environment minister of Norway, who later headed the World Health Organization. Rather than taking a catastrophist view, the Commission saw risks and opportunities as balanced, requiring very careful decision-making. Its introductory "Call to Action" is reproduced below:

REPORT OF THE WORLD COMMISSION ON ENVIRONMENT AND DEVELOPMENT: OUR COMMON FUTURE (1987)[2]

IV. A Call for Action

1. In the middle of the 20th century, we saw our planet from space for the first time. Historians may eventually find that this vision had a greater impact on thought than did the Copernican revolution of the 16th century, which upset the human self-image by revealing that the Earth is not the centre of the universe. From space, we see a small and fragile ball dominated not by human activity and edifice but by a pattern of clouds, oceans, greenery, and soils. Humanity's inability to fit its activities into that pattern is changing planetary systems, fundamentally. Many such changes are accompanied by life-threatening hazards. This new reality, from which there is no escape, must be recognized—and managed.

2. Fortunately, this new reality coincides with more positive developments new to this century. We can move information and goods faster around the globe than ever before; we can produce more food and more goods with less investment of resources; our technology and science gives us, at least, the potential to look deeper into and better understand natural systems. From space, we can see and study the Earth as an organism whose health depends on the health of all its parts. We have the power to reconcile human affairs with natural laws and to thrive in the process. In this our cultural and spiritual heritages can reinforce our economic interests and survival imperatives.

3. This Commission believes that people can build a future that is more prosperous, more just, and more secure. Our report, *Our Common Future*, is not a prediction of ever increasing environmental decay, poverty, and hardship in an ever more polluted world among ever decreasing resources. We see instead the possibility for a new era of economic growth, one that must be based on policies that sustain and expand the environmental resource base. And we believe such growth to be absolutely essential to relieve the great poverty that is deepening in much of the developing world.

---

[2] Available at: http://www.un-documents.net/our-common-future.pdf.

4. But the Commission's hope for the future is conditional on decisive political action now to begin managing environmental resources to ensure both sustainable human progress and human survival. We are not forecasting a future; we are serving a notice—an urgent notice based on the latest and best scientific evidence—that the time has come to take the decisions needed to secure the resources to sustain this and coming generations. We do not offer a detailed blueprint for action, but instead a pathway by which the peoples of the world may enlarge their spheres of cooperation. . . .

27. Humanity has the ability to make development sustainable to ensure that it meets the needs of the present without compromising the ability of future generations to meet their own needs. The concept of sustainable development does imply limits—not absolute limits but limitations imposed by the present state of technology and social organization on environmental resources and by the ability of the biosphere to absorb the effects of human activities. But technology and social organization can be both managed and improved to make way for a new era of economic growth. The Commission believes that widespread poverty is no longer inevitable. Poverty is not only an evil in itself, but sustainable development requires meeting the basic needs of all and extending to all the opportunity to fulfil their aspirations for a better life. A world in which poverty is endemic will always be prone to ecological and other catastrophes.

28. Meeting essential needs requires not only a new era of economic growth for nations in which the majority are poor, but an assurance that those poor get their fair share of the resources required to sustain that growth. Such equity would be aided by political systems that secure effective citizen participation in decision making and by greater democracy in international decision making.

29. Sustainable global development requires that those who are more affluent adopt life-styles within the planet's ecological means—in their use of energy, for example. Further, rapidly growing populations can increase the pressure on resources and slow any rise in living standards; thus sustainable development can only be pursued if population size and growth are in harmony with the changing productive potential of the ecosystem.

30. Yet in the end, sustainable development is not a fixed state of harmony, but rather a process of change in which the exploitation of resources, the direction of investments, the orientation of technological development, and institutional change are made consistent with future as well as present needs. We do not pretend that the process is easy or straightforward. Painful choices have to be made. Thus, in the final analysis, sustainable development must rest on political will.

Perhaps the greatest milestone in international discussion of and treaty making on environmental issues occurred at the Conference on Environment and Development in Rio de Janeiro in 1992, which marked the conclusion of two important international treaties: a UN Framework Convention on Climate Change (UNFCC) and a UN Convention on Biological Diversity, each spawning considerable further work and international negotiation, the former being operationalized in large part through the Kyoto Protocol of 1997.

A key contribution to the discourse on sustainable development has come from the developing world. It is sometimes argued that imposing environmental controls would unfairly prevent countries from passing through a stage of development that many industrialized countries have already attained or even graduated from, at which point it is possible to use technology and other resources to scale back the environmental consequences of development. This led to the embrace of differentiated responsibility as between developed and developing states for addressing mitigation of climate change.

UNITED NATIONS FRAMEWORK CONVENTION ON CLIMATE CHANGE (1992)[3]

Article 3: Principles

In their actions to achieve the objective of the Convention and to implement its provisions, the Parties shall be guided, *inter alia*, by the following:

1. The Parties should protect the climate system for the benefit of present and future generations of humankind, on the basis of equity and in accordance with their common but differentiated responsibilities and respective capabilities. Accordingly, the developed country Parties should take the lead in combating climate change and the adverse effects thereof.

2. The specific needs and special circumstances of developing country Parties, especially those that are particularly vulnerable to the adverse effects of climate change, and of those Parties, especially developing country Parties, that would have to bear a disproportionate or abnormal burden under the Convention, should be given full consideration.

3. The Parties should take precautionary measures to anticipate, prevent or minimize the causes of climate change and mitigate its adverse effects. Where there are threats of serious or irreversible damage, lack of full scientific certainty should not be used as a reason for postponing such measures, taking into account that policies and measures to deal with climate change should be cost-effective so as to ensure global benefits at the lowest possible cost. To achieve this, such policies and measures should take into

---

[3] Entered into Force on 21 March 1994; available at: http://unfccc.int/files/essential_background/background_publications_htmlpdf/application/pdf/conveng.pdf.

account different socio-economic contexts, be comprehensive, cover all relevant sources, sinks and reservoirs of greenhouse gases and adaptation, and comprise all economic sectors. Efforts to address climate change may be carried out cooperatively by interested Parties.

4. The Parties have a right to, and should, promote sustainable development. Policies and measures to protect the climate system against human-induced change should be appropriate for the specific conditions of each Party and should be integrated with national development programmes, taking into account that economic development is essential for adopting measures to address climate change.

5. The Parties should cooperate to promote a supportive and open international economic system that would lead to sustainable economic growth and development in all Parties, particularly developing country Parties, thus enabling them better to address the problems of climate change. Measures taken to combat climate change, including unilateral ones, should not constitute a means of arbitrary or unjustifiable discrimination or a disguised restriction on international trade.

The language of "common but differentiated responsibilities" was earlier included in the Rio Declaration.

RIO DECLARATION ON ENVIRONMENT AND DEVELOPMENT (1992)[4]

Principle 7

States shall cooperate in a spirit of global partnership to conserve, protect and restore the health and integrity of the Earth's ecosystem. In view of the different contributions to global environmental degradation, States have common but differentiated responsibilities. The developed countries acknowledge the responsibility that they bear in the international pursuit of sustainable development in view of the pressures their societies place on the global environment and of the technologies and financial resources they command.

But how might such a principle be implemented? The approach adopted was to embrace market-based mechanisms to seek efficient methods of achieving global emission reductions, such as the Kyoto Protocol's clean development mechanism (CDM). These, it was thought, would avoid exacerbating national

---

[4] UN Doc. A/CONF.151/26 (1992), Annex.

indebtedness that, during the 1980s and 1990s had proved crippling, indeed unsustainable, for many developing countries.

Concerns about debt were reflected in the first two substantive paragraphs of the conference's declaration, Agenda 21, (following its preamble) along with a strong sense of grievance over continuing gaps between rich and poor countries that might be exacerbated by any environmental commitments developing countries made.

UNITED NATIONS CONFERENCE ON ENVIRONMENT AND DEVELOPMENT, RIO DE JANEIRO (1992), AGENDA 21[5]

2.1. In order to meet the challenges of environment and development, States have decided to establish a new global partnership. This partnership commits all States to engage in a continuous and constructive dialogue, inspired by the need to achieve a more efficient and equitable world economy, keeping in view the increasing interdependence of the community of nations and that sustainable development should become a priority item on the agenda of the international community. It is recognized that, for the success of this new partnership, it is important to overcome confrontation and to foster a climate of genuine cooperation and solidarity. It is equally important to strengthen national and international policies and multinational cooperation to adapt to the new realities.

2.2. Economic policies of individual countries and international economic relations both have great relevance to sustainable development. The reactivation and acceleration of development requires both a dynamic and a supportive international economic environment and determined policies at the national level. It will be frustrated in the absence of either of these requirements. A supportive external economic environment is crucial. The development process will not gather momentum if the global economy lacks dynamism and stability and is beset with uncertainties. Neither will it gather momentum if the developing countries are weighted down by external indebtedness, if development finance is inadequate, if barriers restrict access to markets and if commodity prices and the terms of trade of developing countries remain depressed. The record of the 1980s was essentially negative on each of these counts and needs to be reversed. The policies and measures needed to create an international environment that is strongly supportive of national development efforts are thus vital. International cooperation in this area should be designed to complement and support—not to diminish or subsume—sound domestic economic policies, in both developed and developing countries, if global progress towards sustainable development is to be achieved.

---

[5] Available at: https://sustainabledevelopment.un.org/content/documents/Agenda21.pdf.

The Kyoto Protocol, which emerged in 1997 following long and difficult negotiations, was intended to operationalize the differentiated responsibilities accepted in Rio de Janeiro. It was adopted in a mood of modest euphoria. Some countries later did much to live up to their commitments, particularly on emission reduction; others did very little indeed. The clean development mechanism (CDM) was intended to channel funding, generated in industrialized countries by emission-producing economic activity, toward developing countries where it would be applied to purposes that would reduce overall global emissions while boosting economic activity.

KYOTO PROTOCOL TO THE UNITED NATIONS FRAMEWORK CONVENTION ON CLIMATE CHANGE (1997)[6]

Article 12

1. A clean development mechanism is hereby defined.

2. The purpose of the clean development mechanism shall be to assist Parties not included in Annex I [i.e., developing countries] in achieving sustainable development and in contributing to the ultimate objective of the Convention, and to assist Parties included in Annex I [i.e., developed countries] in achieving compliance with their quantified emission limitation and reduction commitments under Article 3.

3. Under the clean development mechanism:

(a) Parties not included in Annex I will benefit from project activities resulting in certified emission reductions; and

(b) Parties included in Annex I may use the certified emission reductions accruing from such project activities to contribute to compliance with part of their quantified emission limitation and reduction commitments under Article 3, as determined by the Conference of the Parties serving as the meeting of the Parties to this Protocol.

4. The clean development mechanism shall be subject to the authority and guidance of the Conference of the Parties serving as the meeting of the Parties to this Protocol and be supervised by an executive board of the clean development mechanism.

5. Emission reductions resulting from each project activity shall be certified by operational entities to be designated by the Conference of the Parties serving as the meeting of the Parties to this Protocol, on the basis of:

(a) Voluntary participation approved by each Party involved;

(b) Real, measurable, and long-term benefits related to the mitigation of climate change; and

---

[6] Entered into force 16 February 2005; available at: http://unfccc.int/resource/docs/convkp/kpeng.pdf.

(c) Reductions in emissions that are additional to any that would occur in the absence of the certified project activity.

6. The clean development mechanism shall assist in arranging funding of certified project activities as necessary.

7. The Conference of the Parties serving as the meeting of the Parties to this Protocol shall, at its first session, elaborate modalities and procedures with the objective of ensuring transparency, efficiency and accountability through independent auditing and verification of project activities.

8. The Conference of the Parties serving as the meeting of the Parties to this Protocol shall ensure that a share of the proceeds from certified project activities is used to cover administrative expenses as well as to assist developing country Parties that are particularly vulnerable to the adverse effects of climate change to meet the costs of adaptation.

9. Participation under the clean development mechanism, including in activities mentioned in paragraph 3(a) above and in the acquisition of certified emission reductions, may involve private and/or public entities, and is to be subject to whatever guidance may be provided by the executive board of the clean development mechanism.

10. Certified emission reductions obtained during the period from the year 2000 up to the beginning of the first commitment period can be used to assist in achieving compliance in the first commitment period.

QUESTIONS

7. The adoption of a framework followed by a protocol was reasonably successful in addressing ozone-depleting gases, but less so in addressing climate change. Why?

8. Is "sustainable development" sufficiently clear to be actionable in terms of concrete policies, or just sufficiently vague to be agreeable to many different countries? Which is more important?

9. If the goal of the Kyoto Protocol was to reduce emissions contributing to climate change, why does it not simply commit all countries to reducing absolute emissions?

10. "The clean development mechanism simply allows developed countries to pay for the right to pollute, while developing countries profit from threatening to pollute." Do you agree?

Within several years of the adoption of the Kyoto Protocol, it was clear that implementation was lagging seriously in some countries, while the CDM was beginning to exhibit signs of dysfunction and regional distortion (with some developing countries learning better than others how they could take advantage of it) and the pricing of permits suggested the market for them was not yet well established. By 2006, Canada, whose implementation record had been very poor, essentially dropped out of the CDM. As of 2008, the financial and economic crisis of the industrialized countries, combined with the accelerating economic growth in several emerging countries and regions (including Africa), led to a perception among some that "common but differentiated" obligations were no longer justified by economic realities, as the obligations applied only to the industrialized countries. The Executive Summary of a 2010 report by the well-regarded International Institute for Sustainable Development (IISD) gives a flavor of the mood of the times:

SUSTAINABLE DEVELOPMENT: FROM BRUNDTLAND TO RIO 2012 (2010)[7]

The term, sustainable development, was popularized in *Our Common Future*, a report published by the World Commission on Environment and Development in 1987. Also known as the Brundtland report, *Our Common Future* included the "classic" definition of sustainable development: "development which meets the needs of the present without compromising the ability of future generations to meet their own needs." Acceptance of the report by the United Nations General Assembly gave the term political salience; and in 1992 leaders set out the principles of sustainable development at the United Nations Conference on Environment and Development in Rio de Janeiro, Brazil.

It is generally accepted that sustainable development calls for a convergence between the three pillars of economic development, social equity, and environmental protection. Sustainable development is a visionary development paradigm; and over the past 20 years governments, businesses, and civil society have accepted sustainable development as a guiding principle, made progress on sustainable development metrics, and improved business and NGO participation in the sustainable development process. Yet the concept remains elusive and implementation has proven difficult. Unsustainable trends continue and sustainable development has not found the political entry points to make real progress. As a result, climate change has become the de facto proxy for implementation of the sustainable development agenda; but [...] the climate change negotiations are

---

[7] John Drexhage and Deborah Murphy, Sustainable Development: From Brundtland to Rio 2012, Background Paper prepared for consideration by the High Level Panel on Global Sustainability at its first meeting, 19 September 2010. International Institute for Sustainable Development (IISD), 2010.

not always the appropriate forum for broader strategic discussions of sustainable development.

While sustainable development is intended to encompass three pillars, over the past 20 years it has often been compartmentalized as an environmental issue. Added to this, and potentially more limiting for the sustainable development agenda, is the reigning orientation of development as purely economic growth. This has been the framework used by developed countries in attaining their unprecedented levels of wealth, and major and rapidly developing countries are following the same course. The problem with such an approach is that natural resources are in imminent peril of being exhausted or their quality being compromised to an extent that threatens current biodiversity and natural environments.

Addressing this challenge calls for changes at the consumer level in developed countries. Developed countries have the wealth and technical capacity to implement more sustainable policies and measures, yet the required level of political leadership and citizen engagement is still a long way off. The lack of action in developed countries is compounded by economic growth in developing countries that follows the resource-intensive model of developed countries. Without change and real action to address levels of consumerism and resource use in developed countries, one can hardly expect a receptive audience among developing countries when attempts are made to direct attention to their economic development practices. More sustainable development pathways are needed in both developed and developing countries, which require a level of dialogue, cooperation and, most importantly, trust that simply is not reflected in today's multilateral institutions or regimes.

There is a huge gap between the multilateral processes, with their broad goals and policies; and national action, which reflects domestic political and economic realities. A huge constituency around the world cares deeply and talks about sustainable development, but has not taken serious on-the-ground action. Deep structural changes are needed in the ways that societies manage their economic, social, and environmental affairs; and hard choices are needed to move from talk to action.

While some would argue that we have failed on sustainable development, 20 years is a relatively short time frame to implement the required changes in such a daunting area. The needed systemic changes will require a revolution in the way the world does business. This will have an impact on lifestyles and consumption patterns—especially so in developed countries, but also for the growing middle class in developing countries.

The recent financial crisis and the beginning of the decline of trust in the liberalization and globalization model could mean some renewed receptivity for a new sustainable development paradigm. A new model could chart a development path that truly is concerned with equity, poverty alleviation, reducing resource use, and integrating economic, environmental, and social issues in decision making. The opportunity is ripe to move beyond incrementalism to real systemic change.

In 2012, the *Economist* ran an editorial dramatically stating the obvious—with the price of Certified Emission Reduction Credits having fallen from $20 in early 2008 to under $5 by late 2012, although the number of such credits issued had risen from 200 million to 800 million, the CDM market was close to collapse.[8]

Although the CDM market was in deep trouble, studies have found that projects carried out under CDM provisions in developing countries (from which India and Brazil particularly benefited) had contributed to sustainable development locally and reductions in CO_2 emissions, as intended.[9] This is one of the many paradoxes of international agreements and action—local dividends but national and international disappointment.

2012 also saw an opportunity for states to develop a new model envisaged in the IISD report. On the twentieth anniversary of the 1992 Earth Summit, the "Rio+20 UN Conference on Sustainable Development" featured unprecedented participation from international organizations, the private sector, and civil society. Unfortunately, the vision articulated by world leaders in the outcome document was more hortatory than specific on what needed to be done and by whom, with few meaningful proposals for real change agreed on.

THE FUTURE WE WANT (2012)[10]

I. Our common vision

1. We, the Heads of State and Government and high-level representatives, having met at Rio de Janeiro, Brazil, from 20 to 22 June 2012, with the full participation of civil society, renew our commitment to sustainable development and to ensuring the promotion of an economically, socially and

---

[8] "Carbon Markets—Complete Disaster in the Making: The World's Only Global Carbon Market Is in Need of a Radical Overhaul," *The Economist*, 15 September 2012.
[9] See Yongfu Huana, Jingjing He and Finn Tarp. "Is the Clean Development Mechanism Effective for Emission Reductions?" *WIDER Working Paper*, Vol. 2012/73. UNU-WIDER, 2012, which examined sixty CDM host countries from 2005 to 2010 and found evidence in support of a decline in CO_2 emissions in CDM host countries; and Yongfu Huang, Jingjing He and Finn Tarp. "Is the Clean Development Mechanism Promoting Sustainable Development?" *WIDER Working Paper*, Vol. 2012/72. UNU-WIDER, 2012, which examined fifty-eight host countries from 2005 to 2010 and found CDM projects contributed to sustainable development in host countries.
[10] GA Res. 68/288 (2012), The Future We Want.

environmentally sustainable future for our planet and for present and future generations.

2. Poverty eradication is the greatest global challenge facing the world today and an indispensable requirement for sustainable development. In this regard, we are committed to freeing humanity from poverty and hunger as a matter of urgency.

3. We therefore acknowledge the need to further mainstream sustainable development at all levels, integrating economic, social and environmental aspects and recognizing their interlinkages, so as to achieve sustainable development in all its dimensions.

4. We recognize that poverty eradication, changing unsustainable and promoting sustainable patterns of consumption and production and protecting and managing the natural resource base of economic and social development are the overarching objectives of and essential requirements for sustainable development. We also reaffirm the need to achieve sustainable development by promoting sustained, inclusive and equitable economic growth, creating greater opportunities for all, reducing inequalities, raising basic standards of living, fostering equitable social development and inclusion, and promoting the integrated and sustainable management of natural resources and eco-systems that supports, inter alia, economic, social and human development while facilitating ecosystem conservation, regeneration and restoration and resilience in the face of new and emerging challenges. . . .

6. We recognize that people are at the centre of sustainable development and, in this regard, we strive for a world that is just, equitable and inclusive, and we commit to work together to promote sustained and inclusive economic growth, social development and environmental protection and thereby to benefit all. . . .

12. We resolve to take urgent action to achieve sustainable development. We therefore renew our commitment to sustainable development, assessing the progress to date and the remaining gaps in the implementation of the outcomes of the major summits on sustainable development and address-ing new and emerging challenges. We express our determination to address the themes of the United Nations Conference on Sustainable Development, namely, a green economy in the context of sustainable development and poverty eradication, and the institutional framework for sustainable development. . . .

15. We reaffirm all the principles of the Rio Declaration on Environment and Development, 3 including, inter alia, the principle of common but dif-ferentiated responsibilities, as set out in principle 7 thereof. . . .

18. We are determined to reinvigorate political will and to raise the level of commitment by the international community to move the sustainable development agenda forward, through the achievement of the internation-ally agreed development goals, including the Millennium Development Goals. We further reaffirm our respective commitments to other relevant

internationally agreed goals in the economic, social and environmental fields since 1992. We therefore resolve to take concrete measures that accelerate implementation of sustainable development commitments.

19. We recognize that the twenty years since the United Nations Conference on Environment and Development in 1992 have seen uneven progress, including in sustainable development and poverty eradication. We emphasize the need to make progress in implementing previous commitments. We also recognize the need to accelerate progress in closing development gaps between developed and developing countries, and to seize and create opportunities to achieve sustainable development through economic growth and diversification, social development and environmental protection. To this end, we underscore the continued need for an enabling environment at the national and international levels, as well as continued and strengthened international cooperation, particularly in the areas of finance, debt, trade and technology transfer, as mutually agreed, and innovation, entrepreneurship, capacity-building, transparency and accountability. We recognize the diversification of actors and stakeholders engaged in the pursuit of sustainable development. In this context, we affirm the continued need for the full and effective participation of all countries, in particular developing countries, in global decision-making.

20. We acknowledge that, since 1992, there have been areas of insufficient progress and setbacks in the integration of the three dimensions of sustainable development, aggravated by multiple financial, economic, food and energy crises, which have threatened the ability of all countries, in particular developing countries, to achieve sustainable development. In this regard, it is critical that we do not backtrack from our commitment to the outcome of the United Nations Conference on Environment and Development. We also recognize that one of the current major challenges for all countries, particularly for developing countries, is the impact from the multiple crises affecting the world today. . . .

Climate change

190. We reaffirm that climate change is one of the greatest challenges of our time, and we express profound alarm that emissions of greenhouse gases continue to rise globally. We are deeply concerned that all countries, particularly developing countries, are vulnerable to the adverse impacts of climate change and are already experiencing increased impacts, including persistent drought and extreme weather events, sea-level rise, coastal erosion and ocean acidification, further threatening food security and efforts to eradicate poverty and achieve sustainable development.
In this regard, we emphasize that adaptation to climate change represents an immediate and urgent global priority.

191. We underscore that the global nature of climate change calls for the widest possible cooperation by all countries and their participation in an

effective and appropriate international response, with a view to accelerating the reduction of global greenhouse gas emissions. We recall that the United Nations Framework Convention on Climate Change provides that parties should protect the climate system for the benefit of present and future generations of humankind on the basis of equity and in accordance with their common but differentiated responsibilities and respective capabilities. We note with grave concern the significant gap between the aggregate effect of mitigation pledges by parties in terms of global annual emissions of greenhouse gases by 2020 and aggregate emission pathways consistent with having a likely chance of holding the increase in global average temperature below 2° C, or 1.5° C above pre-industrial levels. We recognize the importance of mobilizing funding from a variety of sources, public and private, bilateral and multilateral, including innovative sources of finance, to support nationally appropriate mitigation actions, adaptation measures, technology development and transfer and capacity-building in developing countries. In this regard, we welcome the launching of the Green Climate Fund, and call for its prompt operationalization so as to have an early and adequate replenishment process.

192. We urge parties to the United Nations Framework Convention on Climate Change and parties to the Kyoto Protocol thereto to fully implement their commitments, as well as decisions adopted under those agreements. In this regard, we will build upon the progress achieved, including at the seventeenth session of the Conference of the Parties to the Convention and the seventh session of the Conference of the Parties serving as the Meeting of the Parties to the Kyoto Protocol, held in Durban, South Africa, from 28 November to 9 December 2011.

Compared to the 1992 Earth Summit, which had produced the two important agreements on climate change and biodiversity, the outcome document was criticized by civil society as inadequate, failing to make meaningful progress, lacking specific time frames and targets, and neglecting to specify funding goals.[11] Inevitably watered down due to compromises made to enable member states to reach consensus, it disappointed expectations, although unilateral commitments from the private sector did ensure that some modest progress had been made. Alert students of international conference communiques will have noted that calls for reinvigorated political will and vague imprecations for greater commitment, as in paragraph 18

---

[11] "Rio+20 Brings Hope and Solutions despite Weak Talks," National Geographic News, 21 June 2012, available at: http://news.nationalgeographic.com/news/2012/06/120621-rio-20-hope-solutions-official-talks/. See also, "Rio+20 Many ' "Mays' but Few "Musts," The Economist, 23 June, 2012.

above, generally mean that both have been signally lacking and that few ideas are being floated to achieve these lofty purposes.

One of the results of the conference was an effort to revitalize the governance machinery of the United Nations' unwieldy activities in the realm of environmental action. The Commission on Sustainable Development, created in 1992, was replaced in 2013 with a High-Level Political Forum on Sustainable Development.[12] The hopes were that high-level participation would actually occur, at least for the sessions every four years convened under the auspices of the General Assembly. (An annual meeting, also with a ministerial segment, now occurs under the aegis of ECOSOC.) Excitement over these institutional developments has, however, been restrained.

Meanwhile, the UN Framework Convention on Climate Change Office in Bonn grew to 500 staff members. It services the annual meetings of the Conference of Parties to the Convention, which also includes meetings of the Parties to the Kyoto Protocol. To a casual observer it might look like the staff sizes are inversely correlated to the credibility and effectiveness of the CDM and the standing of the wider Treaty. It became increasingly clear, after a last-minute papering over of differences at the Copenhagen Summit of 2009, that a new and different approach superseding the Kyoto Protocol would be required.

This became even more obvious following the stark findings of a report of the Intergovernmental Panel on Climate Change (IPCC) in 2013. The IPCC, created in 1988, develops its scientific assessments by drawing on a wide range of sources, with its recommendations for policymakers also subject to agreement among government representatives. It won the Nobel Peace Prize in 2007 (shared equally with former US vice president Al Gore), but has also experienced considerable controversy at times.

IPCC FIFTH ASSESSMENT REPORT, CLIMATE CHANGE (2013): THE PHYSICAL SCIENCE BASIS, SUMMARY FOR POLICYMAKERS[13]

Warming of the climate system is unequivocal, and since the 1950s, many of the observed changes are unprecedented over decades to millennia. The atmosphere and ocean have warmed, the amounts of snow and ice have diminished, sea level has risen, and the concentrations of greenhouse gases have increased.

---

[12] GA Res. 66/288 (2012), para. 84.
[13] Available at: http://www.ipcc.ch/report/ar5/wg1/.

The atmospheric concentrations of carbon dioxide, methane, and nitrous oxide have increased to levels unprecedented in at least the last 800,000 years. Carbon dioxide concentrations have increased by 40% since pre-industrial times, primarily from fossil fuel emissions and secondarily from net land use change emissions. The ocean has absorbed about 30% of the emitted anthropogenic carbon dioxide, causing ocean acidification.

Human influence on the climate system is clear. This is evident from the increasing greenhouse gas concentrations in the atmosphere, positive radiative forcing, observed warming, and understanding of the climate system.

Continued emissions of greenhouse gases will cause further warming and changes in all components of the climate system. Limiting climate change will require substantial and sustained reductions of greenhouse gas emissions.

Cumulative emissions of CO_2 largely determine global mean surface warming by the late 21st century and beyond. Most aspects of climate change will persist for many centuries even if emissions of CO_2 are stopped. This represents a substantial multi-century climate change commitment created by past, present and future emissions of CO_2.

In September 2014, the UN Secretary-General hosted a Climate Summit bringing together 100 Heads of State, and many others, including from the private sector and civil society. The aim was to generate political momentum for an ambitious agreement in Paris in December 2015 charting a new course for action to combat climate change and galvanize member states to reduce emissions and build resilience against the adverse impacts of climate change.[14] Helpfully, the summit did not aim for agreed conclusions but rather to set the tone for future negotiations

BAN KI-MOON, OPENING REMARKS AT 2014 CLIMATE SUMMIT (2014)[15]

Climate change threatens hard-won peace, prosperity, and opportunity for billions of people. Today we must set the world on a new course.

Climate change is the defining issue of our age. It is defining our present.

---

[14] IISD, Summary of Climate Summit 2014: 23 September 2014, *Climate Summit Bulletin*, vol. 172(18), 26 September 2014.
[15] Available at: http://www.un.org/apps/news/infocus/sgspeeches/print_full.asp?statID=2355.

Our response will define our future. To ride this storm we need all hands on deck. That is why we are here today. We need a clear vision.

The human, environmental and financial cost of climate change is fast becoming unbearable. We have never faced such a challenge. Nor have we encountered such great opportunity. A low-carbon, climate resilient future will be a better future. Cleaner. Healthier. Fairer. More stable. Not for some, but for all. There is only one thing in the way. Us. We.

That is why I have asked you to be here today. Thank you for your leadership. I am asking you to lead. We must cut emissions. Science says they must peak by 2020, and decline sharply thereafter. By the end of this century we must be carbon neutral. We must not emit more carbon than our planet can absorb. No one is immune from climate change.

We must invest in climate-resilient societies that protect all, especially the most vulnerable. I ask all Governments to commit to a meaningful, universal climate agreement in Paris in 2015, and to do their fair share to limit global temperature rise to less than 2 degrees Celsius. To do that, we must work together to mobilise money and move markets. Let us invest in the climate solutions available to us today.

We need all public finance institutions to step up to the challenge. And we need to bring private finance from the sidelines. We must begin to capitalize the Green Climate Fund. And we must meet the broader 100 billion dollar-a-year pledge made in Copenhagen. Let us also put a price on carbon. There is no more powerful way to drive the market transformation we need. All these actions demand collaboration, cooperation and coalitions today and all the way through to the Paris agreement next year.

The Summit was perceived as unusually successful by UN standards, almost entirely because no intergovernmental negotiations were involved.

However, movement toward serious new commitments to emission reductions essentially hinged on whether China and the United States could reach a bilateral agreement to set an example by articulating new commitments of their own. These two countries had for some time been the world's most significant atmospheric polluters in absolute rather than per capita terms (India now placing third). After intensive engagement between Washington and Beijing, this emerged as a set of voluntary commitments by each made on the occasion of a visit by President Obama to China in November 2014. Those commitments provided new impetus to a call for voluntary commitments by other countries early in 2015 to provide much of the substance underpinning the Paris Summit on Climate Change of December 2015.

US-CHINA JOINT ANNOUNCEMENT ON CLIMATE CHANGE, BEIJING CHINA, 12 NOVEMBER 2014[16]

1. The United States of America and the People's Republic of China have a critical role to play in combating global climate change, one of the greatest threats facing humanity. The seriousness of the challenge calls upon the two sides to work constructively together for the common good.

2. To this end, President Barack Obama and President Xi Jinping reaffirmed the importance of strengthening bilateral cooperation on climate change and will work together, and with other countries, to adopt a protocol, another legal instrument or an agreed outcome with legal force under the Convention applicable to all Parties at the United Nations Climate Conference in Paris in 2015. They are committed to reaching an ambitious 2015 agreement that reflects the principle of common but differentiated responsibilities and respective capabilities, in light of different national circumstances.

3. Today, the Presidents of the United States and China announced their respective post-2020 actions on climate change, recognizing that these actions are part of the longer range effort to transition to low-carbon economies, mindful of the global temperature goal of 2°C. The United States intends to achieve an economy-wide target of reducing its emissions by 26%–28% below its 2005 level in 2025 and to make best efforts to reduce its emissions by 28%. China intends to achieve the peaking of CO_2 emissions around 2030 and to make best efforts to peak early and intends to increase the share of non-fossil fuels in primary energy consumption to around 20% by 2030. Both sides intend to continue to work to increase ambition over time.

4. The United States and China hope that by announcing these targets now, they can inject momentum into the global climate negotiations and inspire other countries to join in coming forward with ambitious actions as soon as possible, preferably by the first quarter of 2015. The two Presidents resolved to work closely together over the next year to address major impediments to reaching a successful global climate agreement in Paris.

5. The global scientific community has made clear that human activity is already changing the world's climate system. Accelerating climate change has caused serious impacts. Higher temperatures and extreme weather events are damaging food production, rising sea levels and more damaging storms are putting our coastal cities increasingly at risk and the impacts of climate change are already harming economies around the world, including those of the United States and China. These developments urgently require enhanced actions to tackle the challenge.

---

[16] The White House, Office of the Press Secretary, "U.S.-China Joint Announcement on Climate Change." November 2014, available at: https://www.whitehouse.gov/the-press-office/2014/11/11/us-china-joint-announcement-climate-change.

6. At the same time, economic evidence makes increasingly clear that smart action on climate change now can drive innovation, strengthen economic growth and bring broad benefits—from sustainable development to increased energy security, improved public health and a better quality of life. Tackling climate change will also strengthen national and international security.

7. Technological innovation is essential for reducing the cost of current mitigation technologies, leading to the invention and dissemination of new zero and low-carbon technologies and enhancing the capacity of countries to reduce their emissions. The United States and China are two of the world's largest investors in clean energy and already have a robust program of energy technology cooperation. The two sides have, among other things:

- established the U.S.-China Climate Change Working Group (CCWG), under which they have launched action initiatives on vehicles, smart grids, carbon capture, utilization and storage, energy efficiency, greenhouse gas data management, forests and industrial boilers;
- agreed to work together towards the global phase down of hydrofluorocarbons (HFCs), very potent greenhouse gases;
- created the U.S.-China Clean Energy Research Center, which facilitates collaborative work in carbon capture and storage technologies, energy efficiency in buildings, and clean vehicles; and
- agreed on a joint peer review of inefficient fossil fuel subsidies under the G-20.

8. The two sides intend to continue strengthening their policy dialogue and practical cooperation, including cooperation on advanced coal technologies, nuclear energy, shale gas and renewable energy, which will help optimize the energy mix and reduce emissions, including from coal, in both countries. To further support achieving their ambitious climate goals, today the two sides announced additional measures to strengthen and expand their cooperation, using the existing vehicles, in particular the U.S.-China Climate Change Working Group, the U.S.-China Clean Energy Research Center and the U.S.-China Strategic and Economic Dialogue. These include:

- **Expanding Joint Clean Energy Research and Development:** A renewed commitment to the U.S.-China Clean Energy Research Center, including continued funding for three existing tracks on building efficiency, clean vehicles and advanced coal technology and launching a new track on the energy-water nexus;
- **Advancing Major Carbon Capture, Utilization and Storage Demonstrations:** Establishment of a major new carbon storage project based in China through an international public-private consortium led by the United States and China to intensively study and monitor carbon storage using industrial CO_2 and also work together on a new Enhanced Water

Recovery (EWR) pilot project to produce fresh water from CO_2 injection into deep saline aquifers;

- **Enhancing Cooperation on HFCs:** Building on the historic Sunnylands agreement between President Obama and President Xi regarding HFCs, highly potent greenhouse gases, the two sides will enhance bilateral cooperation to begin phasing-down the use of high global warming potential HFCs and work together in a multilateral context as agreed by the two Presidents at their meeting in St. Petersburg on 6 September 2013;
- **Launching a Climate-Smart/Low-Carbon Cities Initiative:** In response to growing urbanization and increasingly significant greenhouse gas emissions from cities and recognizing the potential for local leaders to undertake significant climate action, the United States and China will establish a new initiative on Climate-Smart/Low-Carbon Cities under the CCWG. As a first step, the United States and China will convene a Climate-Smart/Low-Carbon Cities Summit where leading cities from both countries will share best practices, set new goals and celebrate city-level leadership in reducing carbon emissions and building resilience;
- **Promoting Trade in Green Goods:** Encouraging bilateral trade in sustainable environmental goods and clean energy technologies, including through a U.S. trade mission led by Secretaries Moniz and Pritzker in April 2015 that will focus on smart low-carbon cities and smart low-carbon growth technologies; and
- **Demonstrating Clean Energy on the Ground:** Additional pilot programs, feasibility studies and other collaborative projects in the areas of building efficiency, boiler efficiency, solar energy and smart grids.

With the Kyoto Protocol now largely sidetracked and the CDM failing, much hung on whether the Paris Summit of December 2015 would restructure the international effort to combat climate change or simply graft a new approach on the old one. But a fundamental shift had occurred, with China tacitly accepting that it needed to make commitments, thus putting some pressure on other developing countries to do likewise. But India, on average much poorer than China, suffering from serious environmental degradation and levels of aerial pollution in New Delhi now the worst in any major city of the world, showed little flexibility. Speaking to the UN General Assembly on 27 September 2014, Prime Minister Modi stated: "The world had agreed on a beautiful balance of action—common but differentiated responsibilities. That should form the basis of continued action."[17]

[17] Statement by Prime Minister Modi, General Debate of the UN General Assembly, 27 September 2014, available at: http://mea.gov.in/Portal/CountryNews/3096_PM_s_speech_at_69th_UNGA_session_English.pdf.

Nevertheless, pressure was growing within India for the country to act on urgent features of its own environmental blight in its own interests.[18]

Meanwhile, en route to the Paris Summit of 2015, the UN negotiating platform for climate change touched down in Lima, Peru, in December, 2014. The hope was this might create new and more effective approaches to mitigating and adapting to climate change, with a notional $100 billion per year price tag (of which only about $10 billion per year had been pledged by governments by mid-2015).

Influenced by the China-US approach of voluntary pledges of funding and actions, including targets, to cut emissions, the discussions in Lima revolved around a dynamic that some delegates described as "pledge and chat." By the deadline the United Nations had set for pledges, 31 March 2015, many leading countries had submitted pledges or offers, but others, including Canada, Japan, and Australia, had not. Mexico was the first developing country to pledge, and others were expected to follow. Some weeks later it was difficult to evaluate how seriously pledges fell short of realistic expectations.

The United Nations, like other organizations, has difficulty facing up to concrete problems in the functioning of machinery it has set up. Decisive action does occur at times (suppression in 2013 of the Commission on Sustainable Development; creation of the Human Rights Council superseding the Commission on Human Rights), but avoidance of problems is more common. Thus, at the Lima, Peru, Conference of Parties of December 2014 (COP 20), although the dysfunction in the CDM was recognized, no way forward was identified. Rather than quoting from UN documents with little to say, we cite below an excerpt from a report of the Wuppertal Institute for Climate, Environment and Energy.

WUPPERTAL INSTITUTE FOR CLIMATE, ENVIRONMENT AND ENERGY, LIMA CLIMATE REPORT—COP20 MOVES AT SNAILS' PACE ON THE ROAD TO PARIS (2014)[19]

Carbon Markets

The negotiations on future carbon markets came to virtual standstill in Lima. A group of countries led by Brazil and China blocked any further

---

[18] See Navroz Dubash and Lavanya Rajamani, "Multilateral Diplomacy on Climate Change," *Oxford Handbook on Indian Foreign Policy*, David M. Malone, C. Raja Mohan, Srinath Raghavan, Eds. (Oxford and New York: Oxford University Press, forthcoming 2015).

[19] Hermann Ott et al. "Lima Climate Report—COP20 Moves at Snails' Pace on the Road to Paris." Wuppertal Institute for Climate, Environment and Energy, Wuppertal, 17 December 2014.

discussions on the issues of the New Market Mechanism (NMM) and the Framework for Various Approaches (FVA), arguing that negotiating concrete modalities and procedures for the NMM and defining the scope and purpose of the FVA would effectively prejudge an outcome of the [...] process on a future climate agreement. Without a clear mandate as to what role market-based mitigation instruments will play under the new agreement, these countries were not prepared to continue discussions. This position was strongly contested by others, including the EU, the Umbrella Group and the Environmental Integrity Group. In their views, the discussions on NMM and FVA historically predates the Durban process and should hence be continued independently from it.

While the position of Brazil, China and others does have some justification, it is also likely that it is motivated to some extent by tactical considerations. Brazil and China may want to hold back the market discussions in order to save it as a bargaining chip for last minute deals in Paris. Historically, the Clean Development Mechanism (CDM) had been created in just such a last minute move in Kyoto in 1997.

Parties were also not able to build on the advancements regarding CDM Modalities and Procedures that had been achieved in the intersessional meeting of the Subsidiary Bodies in June 2014. It was not possible to reach consensus on how to proceed with those issues on which disagreement prevails and discussions under this item ended with the decision to continue negotiations at the next meeting of the Subsidiary Body of Implementation in June 2015. The lack of progress further aggravates the crisis of international carbon markets in the framework of the UNFCCC.

The necessity to reform the CDM was already iterated by countries in their opening statements as well as in the CMP plenary. The annual CDM guidance document focuses mainly on streamlining standards and procedures of the CDM project cycle. For example, revisions of baseline and monitoring methodologies are now possible without reference to a concrete project activity. Also, validations of monitoring plans can now take place together with the first verification of emissions reductions. The de-registration of CDM project activities is now endorsed by the CMP. This step is necessary in order to avoid the double counting of emissions reductions for CDM projects that intend to qualify for the Chinese Certified Emissions Reductions Scheme (CCER).

Negotiations on options for building a net mitigation component into the CDM could not reach an agreement among Parties. This would have meant a departure from the current "zero-sum game" concept of the mechanism, meaning that the exact amount of GHG emissions in Annex I countries needs to be offset by GHG reductions of the same amount in non-Annex I countries. Options to go beyond this scenario, resulting in a net GHG mitigation effect, could extend to conservative baselines, shortened crediting periods, discounting and voluntary cancellation of CERs. However, though alternative text was suggested and discussed line by line various times, the issue could not be included in the final decision.

A further bone of contention centered on the monitoring of sustainable development effects of CDM projects as well as stakeholder consultation and the establishment of a grievance mechanism. Currently, the use of the Executive Board's sustainable development tool is voluntary. Although particularly the European Union and St. Lucia made a strong case for the monitoring of sustainable development effects in the beginning, their proposals met with strong opposition from China, Brazil, and India. In the end, most of the text proposed on these issues was deleted as no consensus could be found. The final decision merely requests the Executive Board "to publish its procedure for dealing with communications from stakeholders."

In part because of the relentless pressure applied to all countries by the French hosts of the climactic Summit on this issue in Paris, on 12 December 2015, agreement was reached unanimously on a new global course picking up on that of China and the US, marked by indicative voluntary commitments by virtually all countries to limit and reverse their carbon footprint over coming decades, these commitments to be reviewed every five years, with the aim of improving on them. While disappointing to many, the outcome involved commitments from all the major players, even if not in binding terms, a major improvement on the Kyoto Protocol. It is likely that pressure will only grow on capitals the world over, for domestic as well as international reasons, increasingly to curb carbon and other noxious emissions, thus validating the modest first steps taken in Paris.

QUESTIONS

11. The UN Framework Convention on Climate Change was universally welcomed. But once the Kyoto Protocol created binding obligations, following ratification by member states of the United Nations, consensus frayed, and late in the first decade of the new century, evaporated. Why?

12. Was the CDM unrealistic from the outset, or might it have worked? What factors contributed to its nadir by 2012? What might have helped it work better?

13. Might a global floor price on carbon emissions have helped, as instituted in a number of subnational settings? Would that have undermined the idea of a "market" mechanism? And would the latter have mattered less than the market dysfunction that emerged?

14. Was the path charted by China and the United States in 2014 for action against climate change a more realistic and promising one? Or did it simply make evasion of responsibility easier?

15. Is the United Nations the proper venue for negotiations on an issue such as climate change, or are agreements among smaller groups of key countries a more promising route to success?

16. Why do some states seem to find it easier to act piecemeal for their own reasons, while others find it helpful to participate in international commitments in order to carry parliamentary and public support? Is this just a fact of international life, or might it be subject to change?
17. Drawing on chapter three and the SDG negotiations described above, is the UN's intergovernmental negotiating capacity now irretrievably broken? If not, how might it be improved?
18. How do you assess the Paris Agreement on Climate Change of December 2015?

Further Reading

Alston, Philip and Mary Robinson. *Human Rights and Development: Toward Mutual Reinforcement.* Oxford: Oxford University Press, 2005.

Brohe, Arnaud. "Whither the CDM? Investment Outcomes and Future Prospects." *Environment, Development and Sustainability,* vol. 16(2) (April 2014), pp. 305–322.

Center for Development and Human Rights. *The Right to Development: A Primer.* London: Sage, 2004.

Dryzek, John S., Richard B. Norgaard and David Schlosberg. *The Oxford Handbook of Climate Change and Society.* Oxford: Oxford University Press, 2013.

Huang, Yongfu, Jingjing He and Finn Tarp. "Is the Clean Development Mechanism Effective for Emission Reductions?" WIDER Working Paper, vol. 2012/73. UNU-WIDER, 2012.

Huang, Yongfu, Jingjing He and Finn Tarp. "Is the Clean Development Mechanism Promoting Sustainable Development?" WIDER Working Paper, vol. 2012/72. UNU-WIDER, 2012.

International Panel on Climate Change. Summary for Policymakers of "Climate Change 2014," also known as the Fifth Assessment Report (AR5). Available at www.ipcc.ch.

Lomborg, Bjorn. *The Skeptical Environmentalist: Measuring the Real State of the World,* Cambridge: Cambridge University Press, 2001.

O'Hare, G, J. Sweeney and R. Wilby. *Weather, Climate and Climate Change: Human Perspectives.* London: Pearson-Prentice Hall, 2005.

Nordhaus, R. *The Climate Casino: Risk, Uncertainty, and Economics for a Warming World.* New Haven, CT: Yale University Press, 2013.

Stern, N. et al. *The Global Development of Policy Regimes to Combat Climate Change* (Tricontinental Series on Global Economic Issues), 2014.

Schwartzberg, J. *Transforming the United Nations System: Designs for a Workable World.* Tokyo: United Nations University, 2013.

The Paris Agreement on Climate Change of 12 December 2015, accessible at http://unfccc.int/resource/docs/2015/cop21/eng/l09r01.pdf.

See also the UN Development Programme's annual *Human Development Reports,* available at www.undp.org.

chapter twelve
....

Self-Determination and Democracy Promotion

The first use of the term "self-determination" in a public document is generally ascribed to President Woodrow Wilson's "Fourteen Points" issued in 1918, in which he affirmed a right of peoples to self-government.[1] Following President Wilson's proposals, the Treaty of Versailles adopted a three-pronged approach to determining the claims of statehood of territories that had been subjugated by the Triple Alliance. Under this scheme statehood was accorded to identifiable peoples, the fate of disputed border areas was to be determined by plebiscite, and ethnic groups too small or dispersed for either course of action were to be accorded the protection of special minorities regimes, supervised by the Council of the League of Nations.[2] This approach, however, was restricted to territories belonging to the defeated powers—it had no application to the colonies of the victors, and the concept did not otherwise appear in the League of Nations Covenant.

The status and content of the principle of self-determination was revisited during the drafting of the UN Charter in 1945, where a move was made to include it within Articles 1 and 55. Even after its inclusion, the debate continued on whether it was to be understood as a political principle or directly applicable law. Under Article 1(2) respect for self-determination is classified as a *principle* that advances the purpose of the United Nations to develop friendly relations among nations; under Article 55, self-determination is identified as one of the objectives to be promoted in order to create "conditions of stability" necessary for "peaceful and friendly relations among nations." Both Chapters XI and XII of the Charter—on the administration of non-self-governing territories (i.e., colonies), and a new international trusteeship system (for territories under the old League of Nations Mandate

---

[1] Frederic L Kirgis Jr., "The Degrees of Self-Determination in the United Nations Era," *American Journal of International Law*, vol. 88 (1994), p. 304.
[2] Anthony Whelan, "Wilsonian Self-Determination and the Versailles Settlement," *International & Comparative Law Quarterly*, vol. 43 (1994), p. 99.

system, territories detached from "enemy states," and others that may be placed voluntarily under the system)—include references to the principle of self-government:

CHARTER OF THE UNITED NATIONS

Article 73

Members of the United Nations which have or assume responsibilities for the administration of territories whose people have not yet attained a full measure of self-government . . . accept as a sacred trust the obligation to promote . . . the well-being of inhabitants of these territories and, to this end: . . .

b. to develop self-government, to take due account of the political aspirations of the peoples; and to assist them in the progressive development of their free political institutions, according to the particular circumstances of each territory and its peoples and their varying stages of advancement;

Article 76

The basic objectives of the trusteeship system, in accordance with the Purposes of the United Nations laid down in Article 1 of the present Charter, shall be: . . . .

b. to promote the political, economic, social, and educational advancement of the inhabitants of the trust territories, and their progressive development towards self-government or independence as may be appropriate to the particular circumstances of each territory and its peoples and the freely expressed wishes of the peoples concerned . . . ;

Over the years, the Trusteeship Council and General Assembly were active in promoting these objectives. Eleven trust territories had achieved independence by 1994, at which point the Trusteeship Council became inactive, and decolonization was one of the main areas of activity of the United Nations in the 1960s and early 1970s. That practice and subsequent normative developments embodied in General Assembly resolutions gave some precision to the concept of self-determination, but important questions remain open to this day: Is self-determination a right, who can claim it, and what is its content?

A related question is whether there is a connection between support for self-determination and democracy promotion. The UN Declaration on the

Granting of Independence to Colonial Peoples (extracts below) declares the *right* of all peoples to determine their political status. This hints at a possible link between self-determination and democracy. Has the right of "peoples" to determine their political status evolved into the right of people to have a say in the form of government that rules them? And if so, what role is there for the United Nations to facilitate that?

This chapter begins with the claim that self-determination is a right, before considering some specific cases in which that right has been asserted. It then turns to normative basis for democracy promotion by the United Nations, and various forms of operational activity that could be construed that way: advancing free and fair elections, strengthening democratic institutions in the name of development, and democratic peacebuilding in post-conflict settings.

12.1 Self-Determination as a Right

In the practice of the General Assembly, the right of self-determination came to be applied not only to the Trust Territories but also to colonies, which in the early years of the United Nations were far more numerous. Self-determination as a "right" of peoples is expressly provided for in General Assembly resolutions 1514(XV) (1960) and 1541(XV) (1960), excerpted below.

DECLARATION ON THE GRANTING OF INDEPENDENCE TO COLONIAL COUNTRIES AND PEOPLES, GA RES. 1514(XV) (1960)

1. The subjection of peoples to alien subjugation, domination and exploitation constitutes a denial of fundamental human rights, is contrary to the Charter of the United Nations and is an impediment to the promotion of world peace and co-operation.

2. All peoples have the right to self-determination; by virtue of that right they freely determine their political status and freely pursue their economic, social and cultural development.

3. Inadequacy of political, economic, social or educational preparedness should never serve as a pretext for delaying independence.

4. All armed action or repressive measures of all kinds directed against dependent peoples shall cease in order to enable them to exercise peacefully and freely their right to complete independence, and the integrity of their national territory shall be respected.

5. Immediate steps shall be taken, in Trust and Non-Self-Governing Territories or all other territories which have not yet attained independence, to transfer all powers to the peoples of those territories, without any conditions or reservations, in accordance with their freely expressed will and desire, without any distinction as to race, creed or colour, in order to enable them to enjoy complete independence and freedom.

6. Any attempt aimed at the partial or total disruption of the national unity and the territorial integrity of a country is incompatible with the purposes and principles of the Charter of the United Nations.

7. All States shall observe faithfully and strictly the provisions of the Charter of the United Nations, the Universal Declaration of Human Rights and the present Declaration on the basis of equality, non-interference in the internal affairs of all States, and respect for the sovereign rights of all peoples and their territorial integrity.

Under the guise of laying down the extent of the obligation of states to transmit information to the Secretary-General under Article 73(e) of the UN Charter, the second resolution also fleshed out the parameters against which the achievement of effective self-government must be evaluated, perhaps also asserting a right of the General Assembly to supervise this process.

PRINCIPLES WHICH SHOULD GUIDE MEMBERS IN DETERMINING WHETHER OR NOT AN OBLIGATION EXISTS TO TRANSMIT THE INFORMATION CALLED FOR UNDER ARTICLE 73(E) OF THE CHARTER, GA RES. 1541(XV) (1960)

Principle II

Chapter XI of the Charter embodies the concept of Non-Self-Governing Territories in a dynamic state of evolution and progress towards a "full measure of self-government" . . .

Principle IV

Prima facie there is an obligation to transmit information in respect of a territory which is geographically separate and is distinct ethnically and/or culturally from the country administering it.

Principle V

Once it has been established that such a *prima facie* case of geographical and ethnical or cultural distinctness of a territory exists, other elements may then be brought into consideration. These additional elements may be, *inter alia*, of an administrative, political, juridical, economic or historical nature. If they affect the relationship between the metropolitan State and the territory concerned in a manner which arbitrarily places the latter in a position or status of subordination, they support the presumption that there is an obligation to transmit information under Article 73 e of the Charter.

Principle VI

A Non-Self-Governing Territory can be said to have reached a full measure of self-government by:
   (a) Emergence as a sovereign independent State;
   (b) Free association with an independent State; or
   (c) Integration with an independent State.

Principle VII

(a) Free association should be the result of a free and voluntary choice by the peoples of the territory concerned expressed through informed and democratic processes. It should be one which respects the individuality and the cultural characteristics of the territory and its peoples, and retains for the peoples of the territory which is associated with an independent State the freedom to modify the status of that territory through the expression of their will by democratic means and through constitutional processes.

(b) The associated territory should have the right to determine its internal constitution without outside interference, in accordance with due constitutional processes and the freely expressed wishes of the people. This does not preclude consultations as appropriate or necessary under the terms of the free association agreed upon.

Principle VIII

Integration with an independent State should be on the basis of complete equality between the peoples of the erstwhile Non-Self-Governing Territory and those of the independent country with which it is integrated. The peoples of both territories should have equal status and rights of citizenship and equal guarantees of fundamental rights and freedoms without any distinction or discrimination; both should have equal rights and opportunities for representation and effective participation at all levels in the executive, legislative and judicial organs of government.

Principle IX

Integration should have come about in the following circumstances:

(a) The integrating territory should have attained an advanced stage of self-government with free political institutions so that its people should have the capacity to make a responsible choice through informed and democratic processes;

(b) The integration should be the result of the freely expressed wishes of the territory's peoples acting with full knowledge of the change in their status, their wishes having been expressed through informed and democratic processes, impartially conducted and based on universal adult suffrage. The United Nations could, when it deems necessary, supervise these processes.

The right of self-determination has since been reiterated in instruments unrelated to decolonization, such as human rights treaties,[3] the Declaration on Principles of International Law concerning Friendly Relations and Co-operation among States,[4] and the Definition of Aggression.[5]

Its invocation in practice, however, even with respect to decolonization, has been contested. This is primarily because there is a fundamental tension between the concept of self-determination—the right of "peoples"—and the right to territorial integrity of states. General Assembly resolution 1514, for example, specifically provides that "[a]ny attempt aimed at the partial or total disruption of the national unity and the territorial integrity of a country" is incompatible with the UN Charter. In some cases it is possible to interpret the right of self-determination fairly harmoniously with territorial integrity—in the case of "blue-water colonialism" or occupation by one state of another it is relatively easy to argue that the occupying state does not have a tenable territorial claim. However, in many other situations, such as where a minority seeks to separate from the state in which it is located, or where during decolonization a neighboring state claims "historic title" to the colony, the conflict between self-determination and territorial integrity is apparent.

Of course, separation or "independence" is not the only choice available to non-self-governing peoples. Resolution 1541 embodies both internal and external aspects of self-determination. It may be argued that,

---

[3] Article 1, International Covenant on Civil and Political Rights, G.A. res. 2200A (XXI), 21 UN GAOR Supp. (No. 16) at 52, UN Doc. A/6316 (1966), 999 UNTS 171, *entered into force* March 23, 1976; Article 1 International Covenant on Economic, Social and Cultural Rights, G.A. res. 2200A (XXI), 21 UNGAOR Supp. (No. 16) at 49, UN Doc. A/6316 (1966), 993 UNTS 3, *entered into force* January 3, 1976.

[4] G.A. Res. 2625 (XXV) (1970).

[5] G.A. Res. 3314(XXIX) (1974).

in the postcolonial era, self-determination can be satisfied by granting people the right to govern themselves—to freely participate on the basis of equality with all others who are citizens in the governance of a democratic state—rather than by a right of secession. This notion of internal self-determination is intertwined with human rights norms, in particular the rights of minorities and indigenous peoples. If a distinct group is systematically denied the right to participate in the government of the state, or if individuals within such a group suffer systematic violations of human rights that make their participation in that state impossible, then arguably the right of self-determination has been violated.[6] Such a definition of self-determination, although limited, may be more reconcilable with a nation's right to its "territorial integrity."

QUESTION

1. Does the right of self-determination persist into the postcolonial era? If so, does it necessarily entail a right to independence? If not, what does it entail? What is the content of the 1960 declarations?

12.2 Western Sahara

The conflict in Western Sahara began with a bid for independence by the Sahrawi people, the inhabitants of Spanish Sahara, in the late 1950s. In 1963 the territory was put on the UN General Assembly's list of countries entitled to self-determination—the so-called 73(e) list, which set out territories as to which the colonial power was obliged to report to a Committee of the General Assembly. Although Spain initially refused to make the requisite reports, two years later the UN General Assembly reaffirmed the inalienable right of self-determination by the Sahrawi people and requested Spain to end its colonial rule.[7] This was supported by Spanish Sahara's neighbors, Morocco and Mauritania, as well as by the Organization of African Unity (OAU). In 1966 the United Nations proposed a referendum to allow the Sahrawi people to choose whether they would prefer independence or Spanish rule.[8] Although some steps were taken, the referendum never occurred, and the repression of Saharan demonstrations for independence continued. In 1973,

---

[6] Hurst Hannum, "Legal Aspects of Self-Determination," in *Encyclopeida Princetoniensis: The Princeton Encyclopedia of Self-Determination*, available at: http://pesd.princeton.edu/?q=node/254.
[7] GA Res. 2072(XX) (1965).
[8] GA Res. 2229(XXI) (1966).

the Frente Polisario, the organization that has since played a major role as a representative of the Sahrawi people, was formed.

Following more than a year of attacks by the Polisario, requests by the Jema'a (the Democratic Assembly of the Sahrawi People) for greater autonomy, and calls for fulfilment of the free exercise of the right of self-determination of the Sahrawi people by the United Nations and neighboring countries, Spain finally announced that it would grant greater internal autonomy to the region. However, by this time Morocco and Mauritania had begun to put forward their own claims to parts of the Western Sahara. These claims, based on assertions of historic legal ties with the people of the Western Sahara, were confronted by another neighboring state, Algeria, which began to back the Sahrawi demand for self-determination and offered support to the Frente Polisario.

Spain, undergoing its own regime change with the ending of the long regime of dictator Francisco Franco, announced its intention of holding a referendum in the first half of 1975. The General Assembly passed resolution 3292(XXIX) (1974), presenting the following questions to the ICJ for its advisory opinion:

> I. Was Western Sahara (Río de Oro and Sakiet El Hamra) at the time of colonization by Spain a territory belonging to no one (terra nullius)?
> If the answer to the first question is in the negative,
> II. What were the legal ties between this territory and the Kingdom of Morocco and the Mauritanian entity?

The resolution also urged Spain to postpone the referendum until the General Assembly had decided on the policy to be followed in order to accelerate the decolonization process in the territory.

Spain considered that the questions were irrelevant, as the United Nations had already decided upon a referendum as the means of decolonization. Morocco and Mauritania took the view that the opinion of the Court was relevant. Morocco held that the General Assembly was free to choose from a wide range of solutions in the light of two basic principles enunciated in resolution 1514(XV): self-determination, and national unity and territorial integrity. Mauritania stated that the principle of self-determination could not be dissociated from that of respect for national unity and territorial integrity, and in several instances, the General Assembly had given priority to the latter, particularly in situations where the territory had been created by a colonizing power to the detriment of the state to which the territory had previously belonged. Algeria held that self-determination is the fundamental principle governing decolonization, and that it had been recognized as such by the General Assembly, by the administering Power, and by regional institutions, international conferences, and the neighboring countries.

WESTERN SAHARA CASE (ADVISORY OPINION) (1975)
ICJ REPORTS 12

86. The Court further observes that, inasmuch as Question II had its origin in the contentions of Morocco and Mauritania, it was for them to satisfy the Court in the present proceedings that legal ties existed between Western Sahara and the Kingdom of Morocco or the Mauritanian entity at the time of the colonization of the territory by Spain. . . .

128. Examination of the various elements adduced by Morocco in the present proceedings does not, therefore, appear to the Court to establish the international recognition by other States of Moroccan territorial sovereignty in Western Sahara at the time of the Spanish colonization. Some elements, however, more especially the material relating to the recovery of shipwrecked sailors, do provide indications of international recognition at the time of colonization of authority or influence of the Sultan . . .

162. The materials and information presented to the Court show the existence, at the time of Spanish colonization, of legal ties of allegiance between the Sultan of Morocco and some of the tribes living in the territory of Western Sahara. They equally show the existence of rights, including some rights relating to the land, which constituted legal ties between the Mauritanian entity, as understood by the Court, and the territory of Western Sahara. On the other hand, the Court's conclusion is that the materials and information presented to it do not establish any tie of territorial sovereignty between the territory of Western Sahara and the Kingdom of Morocco or the Mauritanian entity. Thus the Court has not found legal ties of such a nature as might affect the application of resolution 1514 (XV) in the decolonization of Western Sahara and, in particular, of the principle of self-determination through the free and genuine expression of the will of the peoples of the Territory.

The consequences of this opinion were twofold. First, as the following resolution indicates, it reinforced the United Nations' determination to take adequate measures to resolve the situation in the Western Sahara.

SECURITY COUNCIL RESOLUTION 377 (1975)

The Security Council, . . .

1. *Acting* in accordance with Article 34 of the Charter of the United Nations and without prejudice to any action which the General Assembly might take under the terms of its resolution 3292(XXIX) of 13 December

1974 or to negotiations that the parties concerned and interested might undertake under Article 33 of the Charter, requests the Secretary-General to enter into immediate consultations with the parties concerned and interested and to report to the Security Council as soon as possible on the results of his consultations in order to enable the Council to adopt the appropriate measures to deal with the present situation concerning Western Sahara;

2. *Appeals* to the parties concerned and interested to exercise restraint and moderation, and to enable the mission of the Secretary-General to be undertaken to satisfactory conditions.

Second, it evoked protests from Morocco and Mauritania. On 6 November 1975, on the orders of their king, 350,000 Moroccans crossed "peacefully" into Western Sahara, occupying the territory. The so-called Green March was condemned by the Security Council in a meeting convened on the same day.

SECURITY COUNCIL RESOLUTION 380 (1975)

The Security Council,

Noting with grave concern that the situation concern Western Sahara has seriously deteriorated, ...

1. *Deplores* the holding of the march;

2. *Calls upon* Morocco immediately to withdraw from the Territory of Western Sahara all the participants in the march.

3. *Calls upon* Morocco and all other parties concerned and interested, without prejudice to any action the General Assembly might take under the terms of its resolution 3292 (XXIX) of 13 December 1974 or any negotiations that the parties concerned and interested might undertake under Article 33 of the Charter, to cooperate fully with the Secretary-General in the fulfilment of the mandate entrusted to him in Security Council resolutions 377 (1975) and 379 (1975).

The General Assembly then joined the fray, explicitly invoking the right of self-determination of the Sahrawi people.

GENERAL ASSEMBLY RESOLUTION 3458(XXX) (1975): QUESTION OF SPANISH SAHARA

A

The General Assembly, ...

1. *Reaffirms* the rights of the people of the Spanish Sahara to self-determination in accordance with General Assembly resolution 1514 (XV).

2. *Reaffirms* ... its concern to see that principle applied to the inhabitants of the territory of Spanish Sahara within a framework that guarantees and permits them the free and genuine expression of their will, in accordance with the relevant resolutions of the United Nations;

3. *Reaffirms* the responsibility of the administering Power and of the United Nations with regard to the decolonization of the Territory and the guaranteeing of the free expression of the people of Spanish Sahara; ...

7. *Requests* the government of Spain, as the administering Power ... to take immediately all necessary measures, in consultation with all the parties concerned and interested, so that all Saharans originating in the Territory may exercise fully and freely, under United Nations supervision, their inalienable right to self-determination.

8. *Requests* the Secretary General, in consultation with the Government of Spain, as the administering Power, and the Special Committee on the situation with regard to the implementation of the Declaration on the Granting of Independence to Colonial Countries and Peoples, to make the necessary arrangements for the supervision of the act of self-determination referred to in paragraph 7 above.

B

The General Assembly, ...

1. *Takes note* of the tripartite agreement concluded at Madrid on 14 November 1975 by the Governments of Mauritania, Morocco and Spain, the text of which was transmitted to the Secretary-General of the United Nations on 18 November 1975; ...

3. *Requests* the parties to the Madrid Agreement to ensure respect for the freely expressed aspirations of the Saharan populations;

4. *Requests* the interim administration to take all necessary steps to ensure that all the Saharan populations originating in the Territory will be able to exercise their inalienable right to self-determination through free consultations organized with the assistance of a representative of the United Nations appointed by the Secretary-General.

What followed is forty years of effort to resolve the situation in Western Sahara. In 1990, a breakthrough appeared to have been achieved with the adoption of a UN Settlement plan, formulated by the Secretary-General and approved by the Security Council in resolution 658 (1990), which reinforced a ceasefire agreement arrived at between Morocco and the Frente Polisario, and provided for a referendum to be conducted in January 1992. To monitor the ceasefire and to assist the Secretary-General in holding the referendum, the Security Council established the United Nations Mission for the Referendum in Western Sahara (MINURSO) by resolution 690 (1991) in April 1991.

More negotiations by successive personal envoys of the Secretary-General followed. The main sticking point has been who gets to vote in the referendum. Despite strenuous diplomatic efforts, Morocco and the Polisario have not been able to agree on a voter list, and with no agreement Morocco says no referendum can take place. In a bid to break the deadlock, Envoy James Baker submitted a "Framework Agreement" 2001 that provided for autonomy for Sahrawis under Moroccan sovereignty, a referendum after a four-year transition period, and voting rights for Moroccan settlers resident in Western Sahara for over a year. This formula was rejected by Polisario and Algeria, its main backer. In July 2003, the United Nations adopted a compromise resolution proposing that Western Sahara become a semiautonomous region of Morocco for a transition period of up to five years. A referendum would then take place on independence, semiautonomy, or integration with Morocco. Polisario signaled its readiness to accept, but Morocco rejected the plan, citing security concerns. The process has remained deadlocked ever since. No immediate fulfilment of the right of self-determination of the Sahrawi people appears to be in sight.

12.3 East Timor, 1999–2002

The origins of the role played by the United Nations in East Timor lie in Indonesia's 1975 invasion of the former Portuguese colony. For decades, the UN General Assembly, Security Council, and Secretary-General sought to give effect to Timor's right to self-determination in the face of determined opposition by Indonesia. East Timor's independence only became possible following the replacement of Indonesian president Suharto by B.J. Habibie, who offered to hold a plebiscite on the territory's future. An agreement dated 5 May 1999, between Indonesia and Portugal (as the administering power of a non-self-governing territory), provided for a "popular consultation" to be held on East Timor's future on 8 August of the same year.

Crucially, the agreement left security arrangements in the hands of Indonesia's military—the very forces that had actively suppressed the East Timorese population for twenty-four years. On 11 June 1999, the Security Council established the UN Mission in East Timor (UNAMET) to organize and conduct the consultation.[9] The vote was delayed due to threats of violence, but on 30 August 1999, 98 percent of registered East Timorese voted in the referendum, with 78.5 percent choosing independence. A spasm of violence followed, under the direction of the Indonesian military, if not the government itself. Intensive diplomacy, by the Secretary-General, a UN Security Council mission to the region, ASEAN (Association of Southeast Asian Nations), and various bilateral actors (including the United States and Australia) brought the violence to an end. A 12 September statement by the Indonesian President expressed the readiness of Indonesia to accept an international peacekeeping force through the United Nations in East Timor. Australia offered to lead the force, and on 15 September the Security Council authorized the International Force in East Timor (INTERFET) to restore peace and security to the territory.[10]

Six weeks later, the Council established a transitional administration to prepare the territory for independence.

SECURITY COUNCIL RESOLUTION 1272 (1999)

The Security Council, . . .

Reiterating its welcome for the successful conduct of the popular consultation of the East Timorese people of 30 August 1999, and *taking note* of its outcome through which the East Timorese people expressed their clear wish to begin a process of transition under the authority of the United Nations towards independence, which it regards as an accurate reflection of the views of the East Timorese people,

Welcoming the decision of the Indonesian People's Consultative Assembly on 19 October 1999 concerning East Timor . . .

Welcoming the deployment of a multinational force to East Timor pursuant to resolution 1264 (1999), and *recognizing* the importance of continued cooperation between the Government of Indonesia and the multinational force in this regard, . . .

Acting under Chapter VII of the Charter of the United Nations,

1. *Decides* to establish, in accordance with the report of the Secretary-General, a United Nations Transitional Administration in East Timor (UNTAET), which will be endowed with overall responsibility for the administration of East Timor and will be empowered to exercise all legislative and executive authority, including the administration of justice;

---

[9] SC Res. 1246 (1999).
[10] SC Res. 1264 (1999).

2. *Decides also* that the mandate of UNTAET shall consist of the following elements:

(a) To provide security and maintain law and order throughout the territory of East Timor;

(b) To establish an effective administration;

(c) To assist in the development of civil and social services;

(d) To ensure the coordination and delivery of humanitarian assistance, rehabilitation and development assistance;

(e) To support capacity-building for self-government;

(f) To assist in the establishment of conditions for sustainable development; . . .

8. *Stresses* the need for UNTAET to consult and cooperate closely with the East Timorese people in order to carry out its mandate effectively with a view to the development of local democratic institutions, including an independent East Timorese human rights institution, and the transfer to these institutions of its administrative and public service functions;

These are extraordinary powers, and UNTAET quickly came in for criticism that it was an exercise in neocolonialism: a non-democratic protectorate, in which absolute power resided in the Special Representative of the Secretary-General. The most pointed criticism came from Xanana Gusmão, leader of the Timorese resistance who was imprisoned for much of the period of Indonesia's occupation of the territory.

JOSE "KAY RALA XANANA" GUSMÃO, NEW YEAR'S MESSAGE: THE RIGHT TO LIVE IN PEACE AND HARMONY, 31 DECEMBER 2000[11]

. . .

Timorese Reality

We are witnessing another phenomenon in East Timor; that of an obsessive acculturation to standards that hundreds of international experts try to convey to the East Timorese, who are hungry for values:

- democracy (many of those who teach us never practised it in their own countries because they became UN staff members);

- human rights (many of those who remind us of them forget the situation in their own countries);

---

[11] *The Guardian* (London), 31 January 2001; available at: http://www.etan.org/et2001a/january/01-06/01xanan.htm.

- gender (many of the women who attend the workshops know that in their countries this issue is no example for others);
- NGOs (numerous NGOs live off the aid "business" to poor countries);
- youth (all those who remind us of this issue know that in their countries most of the youth are unemployed and that experience is the main employment drive apart from some exceptions based on intellectual skills).

It might sound as though I am speaking against these noble values of democratic participation. I do not mind if it happens in the democratic minds of people.

What seems to be absurd is that we absorb standards just to pretend we look like a democratic society and please our masters of independence.

What concerns me is the non-critical absorption of (universal) standards given the current stage of the historic process we are building.

Old democracies are no longer like a smooth pavement or a linear social process where such standards slide along without the slightest friction.

What concerns me is that the Timorese may become detached from their reality and, above all, try to copy something which is not yet clearly understood by them.

It is necessary that we are sincere and humble so that we do not lose track of the highest interests of our People. ...

Foreigners should bear in mind that the essential condition for their operational success is to be aware that they do not come to save East Timor but rather to fulfill a mission of support; therefore, if they are not aware of this reality they will face the ungrateful mission of earning money for six months and returning to their homes, as so many have done, often revealing themselves to be less skilled than the East Timorese who cannot find a job.

As charges of "neocolonialism" grew, various mechanisms were put in place to engage Timorese authorities in the governing process. Starting in mid-2000, the mission entered into a series of power-sharing arrangements, with authority being progressively passed to the hosts: in April 2000, thirteen Timorese deputy district administrators were appointed to operate under international district administrators; in July 2000, the National Consultative Council was converted into a National Council, a 36-member body appointed by the Transitional Administrator in consultation with the Timorese, which was designed as a precursor to an East Timorese Parliament; on the same day, the Transitional Administrator also created a "Cabinet of the Transitional Government in East Timor," with eight portfolios divided evenly between Timorese leaders and UNTAET officials; the East Timorese Transitional Administration (ETTA) took over UNTAET's Governance and Public Administration pillar in mid-2000, in what was described as a "co-government" approach; starting in October 2000, all of the cabinet portfolios were handed over to Timorese, chosen by Xanana Gusmão; a Constituent Assembly was elected in August 2000 and an all-Timorese Second Transitional Government was confirmed, made up of twenty ministers; the Constituent Assembly drafted a Constitution, which was adopted in March 2002; the Constituent Assembly then transformed itself into a parliament; the first presidential election was held in April 2002, which Xanana Gusmão won by an overwhelming majority.

When East Timor attained its independence on 20 May 2002, the Council issued a statement welcoming "the attainment of independence by East Timor on 20 May 2002, which marks the culmination of a process of self-determination and transition that began in May 1999."[12] Not long afterward, the General Assembly admitted Timor-Leste as a member of the United Nations.[13]

QUESTION

2. If Morocco had been able to establish historic title to Western Sahara, would the ICJ advisory opinion have been different? See in particular paragraph 162 of the judgment. Compare the situation of Western Sahara with that of East Timor/Timor-Leste. Should the two situations have been treated similarly?

12.4 Kosovo

The fact that it took Timor-Leste twenty-five years to exercise its right to self-determination is illustrative of the lack of enthusiasm for self-determination among existing states since the end of the colonial period. The international community has responded rather coolly to bids for autonomy by literally dozens if not hundreds of separatist movements around the world, including Chechnya, Abkhazia, Quebec, Falklands/Malvinas, Basque Country, Catalonia, Kurdistan, Jammu and Kashmir, Nagorno-Karabakh, Rohingya groups in Burma/Myanmar, Somaliland, and Transnistria. The circumstances of each are unique, and not all have made explicit self-determination claims, but it is noteworthy that few have found broad international support in their efforts to become independent states. South Sudan, which achieved independence from Sudan in 2011 based on a negotiated peace agreement that provided for a referendum—driven by the two parties but with considerable African and international involvement—is

[12] UN Doc. S/PRST/2002/13 (2002).
[13] G.A. Res. 57/3 (2002).

a notable exception. The ethnic violence that broke out within South Sudan soon after independence may give further pause to international players considering support for secession elsewhere.

Kosovo is an interesting case not only for the 1999 intervention discussed in Chapter 2 and the transitional administration that followed, but also as a self-determination case. Hours after the last bomb was dropped in the course of NATO's Operation Allied Force, Security Council resolution 1244 (1999) was adopted. The resolution built upon principles adopted by the G8 Foreign Ministers a month earlier, which in turn had been elaborated in a document agreed to by Belgrade. The military aspects authorized the deployment of the Kosovo Force (KFOR)—an international security presence with "substantial" NATO participation—and UNMIK, a UN-run transitional administration. The central gap in UNMIK's mandate was that it avoided taking a position on the key political question of Kosovo's relationship to Serbia. With strongman Slobodan Milosevic still in power in Belgrade, it was long expected that Kosovo would eventually be granted independence. Nevertheless, the authorizing resolutions and official statements continued to emphasize respect for the territorial integrity and political independence of the Federal Republic of Yugoslavia.

SECURITY COUNCIL RESOLUTION 1244 (1999)

The Security Council, . . .

Reaffirming the commitment of all Member States to the sovereignty and territorial integrity of the Federal Republic of Yugoslavia and the other States of the region, as set out in the Helsinki Final Act and annex 2,

Reaffirming the call in previous resolutions for substantial autonomy and meaningful self-administration for Kosovo,

Determining that the situation in the region continues to constitute a threat to international peace and security,

Determined to ensure the safety and security of international personnel and the implementation by all concerned of their responsibilities under the present resolution, and *acting* for these purposes under Chapter VII of the Charter of the United Nations,

1. *Decides* that a political solution to the Kosovo crisis shall be based on the general principles in annex 1 and as further elaborated in the principles and other required elements in annex 2; . . .

10. *Authorizes* the Secretary-General, with the assistance of relevant international organizations, to establish an international civil presence in Kosovo in order to provide an interim administration for Kosovo under which the people of Kosovo can enjoy substantial autonomy within the Federal Republic of Yugoslavia, and which will provide transitional administration while establishing and overseeing the development of provisional

democratic self-governing institutions to ensure conditions for a peaceful and normal life for all inhabitants of Kosovo;

11. *Decides* that the main responsibilities of the international civil presence will include:

(a) Promoting the establishment, pending a final settlement, of substantial autonomy and self-government in Kosovo, taking full account of annex 2 and of the Rambouillet accords (S/1999/648); . . .

(c) Organizing and overseeing the development of provisional institutions for democratic and autonomous self-government pending a political settlement, including the holding of elections; . . .

(e) Facilitating a political process designed to determine Kosovo's future status, taking into account the Rambouillet accords (S/1999/648);

(f) In a final stage, overseeing the transfer of authority from Kosovo's provisional institutions to institutions established under a political settlement; . . .

Annex 1: Statement by the Chairman on the Conclusion of the Meeting of the G8 Foreign Ministers Held at the Petersberg Centre on 6 May 1999

The G8 Foreign Ministers adopted the following general principles on the political solution to the Kosovo crisis: . . .

- A political process towards the establishment of an interim political framework agreement providing for a substantial self-government for Kosovo, taking full account of the Rambouillet accords and the principles of sovereignty and territorial integrity of the Federal Republic of Yugoslavia and the other countries of the region, and the demilitarization of the KLA;

Annex 2: Agreement Should Be Reached on the Following Principles to Move Towards a Resolution of the Kosovo Crisis

. . .

5. Establishment of an interim administration for Kosovo as a part of the international civil presence under which the people of Kosovo can enjoy substantial autonomy within the Federal Republic of Yugoslavia, to be decided by the Security Council of the United Nations. The interim administration to provide transitional administration while establishing and overseeing the development of provisional democratic self-governing institutions to ensure conditions for a peaceful and normal life for all inhabitants in Kosovo. . . .

8. A political process towards the establishment of an interim political framework agreement providing for substantial self-government for Kosovo, taking full account of the Rambouillet accords and the principles of sovereignty and territorial integrity of the Federal Republic of Yugoslavia and the other countries of the region, and the demilitarization of UCK. Negotiations between the parties for a settlement should not delay or disrupt the establishment of democratic self-governing institutions.

Note the unusual form of this resolution, with its most substantive provisions negotiated outside UN auspices and simply annexed to the Security Council's chapeau paragraphs.

Thus the final status of Kosovo was deliberately left for subsequent negotiations, a lengthy process that bumped up against the unwavering demand of Kosovar Albanians for independence, matched by the equally strong resistance from Belgrade and the Kosovar Serbs, who insisted that the territory should remain part of Yugoslavia (now Serbia). Kosovo decided to take matters into its own hands on 17 February 2008 when its Assembly issued a unilateral declaration of independence. Serbia responded by persuading a majority in the General Assembly to put the following question to the ICJ for an Advisory Opinion: "Is the unilateral declaration of independence by the Provisional Institutions of Self-Government of Kosovo in accordance with international law?"[14]

INTERNATIONAL COURT OF JUSTICE, ACCORDANCE WITH INTERNATIONAL LAW OF THE UNILATERAL DECLARATION OF INDEPENDENCE IN RESPECT OF KOSOVO, ICJ REPORTS 2010, 423 (22 JULY 2010)

51. In the present case, the question posed by the General Assembly is clearly formulated. The question is narrow and specific; it asks for the Court's opinion on whether or not the declaration of independence is in accordance with international law. It does not ask about the legal consequences of that declaration. In particular, it does not ask whether or not Kosovo has achieved statehood. Nor does it ask about the validity or legal effects of the recognition of Kosovo by those States which have recognized it as an independent State ... Accordingly, the Court does not consider that it is necessary to address such issues as whether or not the declaration has led to the creation of a State or the status of the acts of recognition in order to answer the question put by the General Assembly

56 ... The Court is not required by the question it has been asked to take a position on whether international law conferred a positive entitlement on Kosovo unilaterally to declare its independence or, a fortiori, on whether international law generally confers an entitlement on entities situated within a State unilaterally to break away from it. Indeed, it is entirely possible for a particular act—such as a unilateral declaration of independence—not to be in violation of international law without necessarily constituting the exercise of a right conferred by it. The Court has been asked for an opinion on the first point, not the second.

---

[14] G.A Res. 63/3, 8 October 2008.

79. [S]tate practice during [the eighteenth, nineteenth and early twentieth centuries] points clearly to the conclusion that international law contained no prohibition of declarations of independence. During the second half of the twentieth century, the international law of self-determination developed in such a way as to create a right to independence for the peoples of non-self-governing territories and peoples subject to alien subjugation, domination and exploitation. A great many new States have come into existence as a result of the exercise of this right. There were, however, also instances of declarations of independence outside this context. The practice of States in these latter cases does not point to the emergence in international law of a new rule prohibiting the making of a declaration of independence in such cases. . . .

82. A number of participants in the present proceedings have claimed, although in almost every instance only as a secondary argument, that the population of Kosovo has the right to create an independent State either as a manifestation of a right to self-determination or pursuant to what they described as a right of "remedial secession" in the face of the situation in Kosovo ... Whether, outside the context of non-self-governing territories and peoples subject to alien subjugation, domination and exploitation, the international law of self-determination confers upon part of the population of an existing State a right to separate from that State is, however, a subject on which radically different views were expressed by those taking part in the proceedings and expressing a position on the question. Similar differences existed regarding whether international law provides for a right of "remedial secession" and, if so, in what circumstances ...

83. The Court considers that it is not necessary to resolve these questions in the present case ... The General Assembly has requested the Court's opinion only on whether or not the declaration of independence is in accordance with international law. Debates regarding the extent of the right of self-determination and the existence of any right of "remedial secession", however, concern the right to separate from a State ... [T]hat issue is beyond the scope of the question posed by the General Assembly.

84. For the reasons already given, the Court considers that general international law contains no applicable prohibition of declarations of independence. Accordingly, it concludes that the declaration of independence of 17 February 2008 did not violate general international law.

Thus the Court provided a very narrow basis for its ruling, avoiding any commentary on the principle of self-determination. In separate, concurring, and dissenting opinions, some of the ICJ judges regretted this.[15] They felt the Court missed an opportunity to clarify what was a confusing area of law.

---

[15] See in particular the Declaration of Judge Bruno Simma.

Meanwhile, as of May 2015, 110 states have recognized Kosovo as an independent entity. Five EU states have not—Cyprus, Greece, Romania, Slovakia, and Spain—obstructing its ability to join the European Union. It has not yet applied for UN membership, anticipating a Russian veto.

QUESTIONS

3. After GA resolutions 1514 and 1541 were adopted in 1960, there has been a good deal of state practice. What are the implications of that practice for the right of self-determination?
4. What precedent (if any) do Kosovo and Timor-Leste stand for? Is there anything that distinguishes them from other self-determination cases, apart from the fact that they were put under UN administration?
5. Has "independence" ceased to be a meaningful option in a globalized world in which so many of the prerogatives of sovereignty once exercised by independent states have been assumed by regional and international organizations and regimes such as the United Nations, the World Trade Organization, and the European Union? Should we be thinking of states in terms of degrees of independence and degrees of national sovereignty?

12.5 Normative Developments

The word "democracy" is nowhere to be found in the United Nations Charter.[16] Although it was written in the name of "we the peoples" and affirms the principle of self-determination and fundamental freedoms, the Charter does not give the United Nations an explicit mandate to engage in the promotion of democracy. Moreover democracy promotion would seem to be at odds with Article 2(7) of the Charter, which prohibits the United Nations from interfering in matters that are essentially within the domestic jurisdiction of states.

Yet, as suggested in the Introduction to this volume, some view the Charter as a living tree and the United Nations as an organization that must adapt to changing circumstances. The concept of sovereignty, or even what constitutes matters that are "essentially domestic," has evolved. Despite the absence of a clear mandate or overarching normative framework, the United Nations (like other international organizations) has responded with

---

[16] This and the next section draw on Ian Johnstone and Michael Snyder, "Democracy Promotion by International Organizations," *Oxford Handbook of International Organizations* (New York: Oxford University Press, forthcoming, 2016)

considerable ingenuity as a supporter of democratic governance—though not without resistance.

Despite the lack of explicit wording, Secretary-General Boutros-Ghali found—in a bit of creative interpretation—that the Charter "roots the sovereign authority of states and therefore the legitimacy of the UN in the will of the people."[17] *In Agenda for Democratization,* he also pointed to the right to political participation enshrined in the Universal Declaration of Human Rights (Article 21) and the International Covenant on Civil and Political Rights (Article 25). The UN Human Rights Committee clarified in one of its General Comments that Article 25 requires, inter alia, access to a free press, freedom of association, the right to form political parties, and access to judicial review.[18] The UDHR, ICCPR, and other global and regional treaties also set out a number of civil and political rights that relate to democratic governance, such as freedom of expression and of association.

From this normative starting point, the Secretary-General went on to make some bold statements about the value of democratic governance and the propriety of a UN role in promoting it.

AN AGENDA FOR DEMOCRATIZATION (1996)[19]

1. Democratization is a process which leads to a more open, more participatory, less authoritarian society. Democracy is a system of government which embodies, in a variety of institutions and mechanisms, the ideal of political power based on the will of the people. . . .

8. . . . To address the subjects of democratization and democracy does not imply a change in the respect that the United Nations vows for the sovereignty of States or in the principle of non-intervention in internal affairs set out in Article 2, para. 7, of the Charter of the United Nations . . .

10. . . . While democratization is a new force in world affairs, and while democracy can and should be assimilated by all cultures and traditions, it is not for the United Nations to offer a model of democratization or democracy or to promote democracy in a specific case. Indeed, to do so could be counter-productive to the process of democratization which, in order to take root and to flourish, must derive from the society itself. Each society must be able to choose the form, pace and character of its democratization process. . . .

12. The United Nations possesses a foundation and a responsibility to serve its Member States in democratization, yet it must receive a formal request

---

[17] Secretary-General Boutros-Ghali, *Agenda for Democratization*, para. 28.
[18] General Comment 25 of the Human Rights Committee. UN Doc. CCPR/C/21/Rev.1/Add.7. 1996.
[19] UN Doc. A/51/761 (1996), Annex.

before it can assist Member States in their democratization processes. United Nations activities and responsibilities in the area of democratization thus parallel and complement those in development: to provide and help coordinate assistance to those who request it, and to seek a strengthened context in which those requesting and those responding may achieve success. . . .

16. This is not to say that democracy is without its detractors . . . whatever evidence critics of democracy can find in support of these claims must not be allowed to conceal a deeper truth: democracy contributes to preserving peace and security, securing justice and human rights, and promoting economic and social development.

17. Democratic institutions and processes channel competing interests into arenas of discourse and provide means of compromise which can be respected by all participants in debates, thereby minimizing the risk that differences or disputes will erupt into armed conflict or confrontation . . . Democracy within States thus fosters the evolution of the social contract upon which lasting peace can be built. In this way, a culture of democracy is fundamentally a culture of peace.

18. Democratic institutions and processes within States may likewise be conducive to peace among States. The accountability and transparency of democratic Governments to their own citizens, who understandably may be highly cautious about war, as it is they who will have to bear its risks and burdens, may help to restrain recourse to military conflict with other States. The legitimacy conferred upon democratically elected Governments commands the respect of the peoples of other democratic States and fosters expectations of negotiation, compromise and the rule of law in international relations . . .

21. . . . Finally, support for democratization must be coupled with support for development in order that socio-economic as well as civil and political rights are respected. Although development can take place without democracy, there is no evidence that the breakthrough to development requires an authoritarian regime. There is, however, ample evidence suggesting that, over the long term, democracy is an ingredient for both sustainable development and lasting peace. Moreover, the globalization of economic activity and communications has generated pressures for democratization and human rights.

QUESTION

6. *Agenda for Democratization* compares democracy assistance to development assistance and claims it does not violate Article 2(7) of the UN Charter. It also draws a tight connection among peace, development, and democracy in order to justify an active UN role in democracy promotion. Are these claims persuasive?

Soft law—norms that are "formally non-binding but habitually obeyed"[20]—is also evidence of a growing normative consensus for democratic governance. Approximately every other year between 1991 and 2012, the UN General Assembly passed a resolution entitled "Strengthening the role of the United Nations in enhancing periodic and genuine elections and the promotion of democratization,"[21] In 1999, the UN Human Rights Commission adopted by a vote of fifty-one to zero (with only Cuba and China abstaining) a resolution provocatively entitled "Promotion of the Right to Democracy,"[22] These normative signposts paralleled the convening of the International Conferences of New and Restored Democracies, first held in the 1990s, which led to the creation of the UN Democracy Caucus, a body of some 100 members. Likewise, the Community of Democracies Conference, consisting of more than 100 countries, agreed to "uphold ... core democratic principles and practices" in the 2000 Warsaw Declaration.[23]

Despite these developments, the promotion of democracy in the United Nations did not come without resistance. A series of counter-resolutions on the topic of "Respect for the principle of national sovereignty and non-interference in the internal affairs of States in their electoral processes" was passed every other year beginning in 1991 until 2005.[24] Initially drafted by the Soviet Union, these counter-resolutions urged states to respect Article 2(7) of the Charter and appealed to them to abstain from supporting domestic political parties.

The 2005 World Summit deserves special note. This gathering of 191 member states unanimously declared their support for democracy. In his report leading to the World Summit, *In Larger Freedom*, Secretary-General Kofi Annan laid the groundwork by explaining that "democracy does not belong to any country or region but is a universal right."[25] Then, in a striking paragraph in the World Summit Outcome document, the General Assembly reaffirmed that democracy is a universal value.

---

[20] Kenneth W. Abbott and Duncan Snidal, "Hard Law and Soft Law in International Governance," *International Organization*, vol. 54(3), (2000), p. 421.

[21] GA Res. 66/163 (2012).

[22] UN Commission on Human Rights. "Promotion of the right to democracy." 27 April 1999, E/CN.4/RES/1999/57.

[23] Council for a Community of Democracies. Final Warsaw Declaration. 27 June 2000.

[24] GA Res. 60/164 (2005).

[25] UN Doc A/59/2005 (2005).

WORLD SUMMIT OUTCOME DOCUMENT, GA RES. 60/1 (2005)

135. We reaffirm that democracy is a universal value based on the freely expressed will of people to determine their own political, economic, social and cultural systems and their full participation in all aspects of their lives. We also reaffirm that while democracies share common features, there is no single model of democracy, that it does not belong to any country or region, and reaffirm the necessity of due respect for sovereignty and the right of self-determination. We stress that democracy, development and respect for all human rights and fundamental freedoms are interdependent and mutually reinforcing.

136. We renew our commitment to support democracy by strengthening countries' capacity to implement the principles and practices of democracy and resolve to strengthen the capacity of the United Nations to assist Member States upon their request...

Significantly, after 2005 the language in General Assembly resolutions on strengthening the role of the United Nations in enhancing periodic elections became stronger, declaring democracy to be a "universal value" based on the "freely expressed will of the people." A 2007 resolution on "Support by the United Nations system of the efforts of Governments to promote or consolidate new or restored democracies" is equally forthright, describing democracy as a "universal and indivisible" core value of the United Nations.[26]

QUESTION

7. How firm is the normative consensus on the value of democratic governance? Are we any closer to what in 1992 Tom Franck saw as an "emerging right to democracy."[27]

In 2008, Ban Ki-moon produced a "Guidance Note of the SG on Democracy." It starts by laying out the normative framework, pointing to the Charter, UDHR, World Summit, and General Assembly resolutions as key documents.

---

[26] GA Res. 62/7 (2007) on support by the United Nations system of the efforts of Governments to promote and consolidate new or restored democracies.
[27] Tom Franck, "The Emerging Right to Democratic Governance," *American Journal of International Law*, vol. 86(1), January 1992, p. 72.

Echoing *Agenda for Democratization*, he states democracy is inextricably linked with the three pillars of the United Nations: peace and security, development, and human rights. He then sets out eight principles to guide UN democracy efforts.

UNITED NATIONS, GUIDANCE NOTE OF THE SECRETARY-GENERAL ON DEMOCRACY (2008)[28]

Adopt proactive approaches to threats to democracy

The UN should develop a consistent, predictable and pragmatic framework for preventive diplomacy ... The UN framework should seek to address both immediate threats to democratic governance as well as the underlying or structural causes of such interruptions ... Also of concern are unconstitutional transfers of power. The record in past years statistically demonstrates that coups tend to worsen a State's human rights situation, do not lead to improvements in the quality of democracy and lead to poorer governance.

Do no harm

UN democracy assistance, while remaining proactive and innovative, must nevertheless "do no harm." For example, ill-timed, and in particular premature elections encouraged by the international community in fragile societies have sometimes entrenched undemocratic, nationalist or extremist groups in power, and radicalized political discourse ...

Uphold local ownership

UN democracy assistance should aim to support legitimate democratic forces, provide a platform for expression of diverse viewpoints and perspectives, connect these forces to global knowledge and expertise, including south-south collaboration, and nurture a national environment open to transparent and democratic political discourse, transition and change. Local norms and practices must be taken into consideration and weaved into emerging democratic institutions and processes to the extent possible, while at the same time promoting internationally agreed norms and principles. UN assistance should also be explicitly requested by local actors and never imposed ...

---

[28] Available at: http://www.un.org/democracyfund/guidance-note-un-secretary-general-democracy.

Broaden domestic engagement and participation in democracy-building

The UN should support a broad, inclusive approach that reaches out to all sectors of and movements in the national society to engage them in dialogue on democracy, including women, minorities, indigenous peoples, adolescents and young people, displaced persons, vulnerable and disadvantaged communities, and other poor, excluded or marginalized groups ...

Explicitly address the effects of discrimination against women

Empowering women and promoting women's rights must form an integral part of any United Nations democracy assistance, including through explicitly addressing gender discrimination that contributes to women's exclusion and the marginalization of their concerns ...

Develop democracy support strategies with a long-term horizon

UN democracy assistance needs to be premised on a long-term commitment to the society in transition, and involve realistic objectives and timeframes based on the particular context. It is also essential that capacity-building be part of the UN's activities in democracy assistance from the outset, in order to ensure long-term sustainability and local ownership ...

Invest in a comprehensive approach to democratization

UN democracy assistance should focus on building trust across various constituencies, developing the state institutions required to peacefully manage democratic transition and consolidation as well as nurturing a strong civil society and civic-engagement mechanisms ...

The Guidance Note then sets out eight areas where the United Nations has a comparative advantage and should focus its efforts:

- promote political facilitation;
- encourage popular participation and elections;
- foster development of a culture of democracy;
- support political pluralism;
- advance transparency and accountability in public affairs;
- promote the rule of law;

- encourage responsive and inclusive governance;
- support a strong and vibrant civil society.

Without using the terminology, *Agenda for Democratization* and Ban Ki-moon's Guidance Note embody "political" and "developmental" approaches to democracy promotion, a distinction drawn by Thomas Carothers.[29] The political approach underscores the importance of "elections plus rights." It includes ensuring free and fair elections, supporting political parties, and upholding core civil and political rights such as freedom of expression. In contrast, the developmental approach is guided by the conviction that transparency, accountability, inclusivity, and social and economic rights deserve more attention. Less confrontational and slower methods of promoting democracy, such as capacity-building and good governance, win out in the Carothers schema over activities that seek quick outcomes and risk easy politicization.

QUESTIONS

8. Do you agree with the Guidance Note's principles and areas of concentration?
9. Should the United Nations be leaning more toward the political or developmental approach to democracy promotion?

12.6 Operational Activities

The United Nations has not only articulated a democracy norm, it has also acted on it, experimenting with a panoply of strategies and methods: electoral assistance of various sorts, development and good governance programs to strengthen democratic institutions, conflict prevention and peacebuilding initiatives, and pro-democratic coercive intervention.

Electoral Assistance

The foray by the United Nations into democracy promotion began with electoral assistance, which remains the most common form of democracy assistance it provides. From 2011 to 2013, for instance, the United Nations provided such assistance to fifty-nine Member States, of which twelve fell under the mandate of the UN Security Council.[30] Historically, the United Nations has

---

[29] Thomas Carothers, "Democracy Assistance: Political vs. Developmental?" *Journal of Democracy*, vol. 20(1), January 2009.

[30] "Strengthening the role of the United Nations in enhancing the effectiveness of the principle of periodic and genuine elections and the promotion of democratization: Report of the Secretary General." A/68/301. 9 August 2013.

provided several different types of electoral assistance, including organizing and conducting elections, supervision and verification, election monitoring, coordination of international and domestic election monitors, and technical assistance.

The most rare, and intrusive, of these electoral support missions is when the organization assumes full responsibility for organizing elections in lieu of a sovereign government. This usually occurs under the auspices of an international transitional administration when the United Nations assumes executive authority over a territory for a transitional period. The United Nations has administered elections in Namibia (1989), Cambodia (1993), Eastern Slavonia (1997), Kosovo (2001 and 2004 with the OSCE), and Timor Leste (2001). Supervision missions, also relatively uncommon, occur when a large number of UN personnel certify each step of the electoral process, from drafting of electoral laws and the campaign period to election-day operations. These high-stakes, heavy footprint operations occurred primarily in the 1990s under the aegis of UN peace operations in post-conflict societies.

Only slightly less intrusive, verification occurs when the United Nations does not supervise every step of the process, but makes a judgment on the freeness and fairness of the election as a whole. Much less intrusive is election monitoring. On many occasions, the United Nations deployed election monitors to member states to observe and assess the integrity of election-day proceedings, as well as report on the pre-election and post-election cycle. Even less intrusive still are technical assistance missions, in which a group of technical advisers from multiple organs (such as UNDP, UNHCR, and DPKO (Department of Peacekeeping Operations)) work in conjunction with national authorities over an extended period to improve the participatory nature of electoral institutions, such as design of election laws, updates to the voter registry, and logistics and procurement. A related type of mission, known as "expert panels," consists of a handful of experts to advise informally on the electoral process.[31] With their light footprint and nimble character, expert panels keep a decidedly low profile.

Despite initial skepticism on the part of many member states, because verification and monitoring missions could give (or deny) the United Nations's stamp of approval to a country's elections—essentially conferring legitimacy on the winner—there was an increase in demand from political actors eager to receive the "blessing" of the United Nations. In fact, the number of requests for electoral assistance grew to the point where the United Nations could not accommodate it. The Electoral Assistance Division (formerly the Electoral Assistance Unit) of the Department of Political Affairs was founded

---

[31] For example, the United Nations deployed a three-member expert panel to follow Algeria's April 2014 presidential elections. "Commending Peaceful Presidential Elections, Secretary-General Reiterates Support for Democratic Reforms in Algeria." UN Press Service, 24 April 2014.

in the 1990s in part to evaluate the growing number of requests for electoral assistance from member states.

Today the United Nations is almost never given a mandate to engage in the organization or monitoring of elections. It deployed its last monitoring mission to Fiji in 2001 and has since taken a backseat role.[32] The United Nations' involvement in election monitoring tends to be limited to either technical assistance or playing a coordinating and support role for the monitoring activities of other organizations. Regional organizations such as the Organization for Security and Cooperation in Europe (OSCE), Organization of American States (OAS), African Union (AU), and the European Union (EU) have taken the lead, while the Commonwealth of Independent States (CIS) and Arab League have begun to dip their toes into the water. Nongovernmental organizations (or quasi-nongovernmental organizations) such as National Democratic Institute (NDI), the Carter Center, the Electoral Institute for Sustainable Democracy in Africa, and La Organisation Internationale de la Francophonie have also been active players.

If the United Nations served a legitimizing role in the initial stages, its retreat from election monitoring may be dirtying the waters. Although it continues to attract wide support overall, election monitoring has met resistance from various quarters in recent years. Notably, Russia placed restrictions on the OSCE's planned monitoring mission during the 2008 presidential elections, prompting the Organization to not deploy at the last minute.[33] In 2013, former Nigerian president Olusegun Obasanjo suggested that non-African monitors should be banned entirely from observing polls on the continent.[34]

More common than flat out refusal of election monitors is the tendency of some organizations to offer lenient assessments of electoral processes in pseudo-democracies, in effect condoning undemocratic elections. This occurred, for instance, during the 2008 parliamentary elections in Belarus when a delegation of monitors from the CIS called "free and democratic" the elections that led to a sweeping victory for President Alexander Lukashenko's party.[35] During Venezuela's 2004 and 2006 elections, OAS teams headed by parties "sympathetic" to the Chavez government praised the elections and

---

[32] "Overview: Electoral Assistance." UN Department of Political Affairs website, available at http://www.un.org/undpa/elections.
[33] "OSCE/ODIHR regrets that restrictions force cancellation of election observation mission to Russian Federation." OSCE. 7 February 2008.
[34] "Africa: Obasanjo Canvasses Ban on Non-African Election Observers." AllAfrica. 13 March 2013.
[35] Clifford Levy, "Electoral Rot Nearby? The Russians Don't See It." The New York Times. 16 December 2008.

glossed over a series of infractions identified by the opposition.[36] African monitoring teams from the AU, South African Development Community (SADC), and the Economic Community of Central African States released a joint statement declaring "successful" the 2011 Democratic Republic of the Congo elections that re-elected President Joseph Kabila, despite the fact that the EU, International Foundation for Electoral Systems (IFES), the Carter Center, and many citizen observers felt it "lacked credibility" and identified "significant irregularities and attempted cheating."[37]

QUESTION

10. What do these swings in the demand for and supply of electoral assistance missions tell us about the legitimating role of the United Nations? What do they tell us about the evolving nature of sovereignty?

Development and Good Governance

The expansion of technical assistance aligns closely with the United Nations' development agenda and the broader "good governance" agenda of the UNDP, the World Bank, and other development actors. UNDP democratic governance programming for example, which consumes over one-third of its budget, focuses on building more transparent and accountable government institutions, supporting anticorruption efforts, and promoting the rule of law.[38]

The idea of good governance has its roots in the policies of structural adjustment promoted by the Bretton Woods institutions. A backlash against the so-called Washington Consensus began in the early 1990s, and crystallized with the World Development Report of 1997, which focuses on state effectiveness: not less government, as the Washington Consensus called for, but better government.

---

[36] Rubin M. Perina, "The Future of Election Observation," *Americas Quarterly*, Spring 2012.
[37] Helidah Ogude, "An Appraisal of Election Monitoring and Observation in Africa: The Case of the Democratic Republic of Congo's 2011 Presidential Elections." *Consultancy Africa Intelligence*, March 2012.
[38] "Fast Facts: United Nations Development Programme." UNDP, October 2011 (accessed online July 2014), available at: www.undp.org/content/dam/undp/library/corporate/fast-facts/english/FF-Democratic-Governance-2011.pdf.

WORLD DEVELOPMENT REPORT.
THE WORLD BANK. JUNE 1997

... For human welfare to be advanced, the state's capability defined as the ability to undertake and promote collective actions efficiently must be increased. This basic message translates into a two-part strategy to make every state a more credible, effective partner in its country's development. Matching the state's role to its capability is the first element in this strategy ... [T]he second element of the strategy is to raise state capability by reinvigorating public institutions. This means designing effective rules and restraints, to check arbitrary state actions and combat entrenched corruption ... And it means making the state more responsive to people's needs, bringing government closer to the people through broader participation and decentralization ...

Giving People a Voice.

Partnership involves bringing the voice of the poor and of marginalized groups into the very center of the policymaking process. In many countries, voice is distributed as unequally as income. Greater information and transparency are vital for informed public debate and for increasing popular trust and confidence in the state whether in discussing expenditure priorities, designing social assistance programs, or managing forests and other resources ... [P]eriodic voting does not always mean the state is more responsive. Other mechanisms are needed to ensure that the concerns of minorities and the poor are reflected in public policies. Getting genuine intermediary organizations represented on policymaking councils is an important first step in articulating citizen interests in public policymaking ...

Broadening Participation.

Evidence is mounting that government programs work better when they seek the participation of potential users, and when they tap the community's reservoir of social capital rather than work against it. The benefits show up in smoother implementation, greater sustainability, and better feedback to government agencies ... In successful countries policymaking has been embedded in consultative processes, which provide civil society, labor unions, and private firms opportunities for input and oversight.

Devolving Power, Carefully

... The challenge is to find the right division of labor between the center and the other tiers of government ... Building a more responsive state requires working on mechanisms that increase openness and transparency, increase incentives for participation in public affairs, and where appropriate, lessen the distance between government and the citizens and communities it is intended to serve. This yields four broad imperatives for policymakers: Where appropriate, ensure broad-based public discussion of key policy directions and priorities. At a minimum this includes making available information in the public interest and establishing consultative mechanisms such as deliberation councils and citizen committees to gather the views and make known the preferences of affected groups. Encourage, where feasible, the direct participation of users and other beneficiaries in the design, implementation, and monitoring of local public goods and services . . . .

UNDP's s 2002 Human Development Report went further with its forthright appeal not simply for good governance, but democratic governance.

UNDP HUMAN DEVELOPMENT REPORT 2002: DEEPENING DEMOCRACY IN A FRAGMENTED WORLD (2002)

Democratic governance is valuable in its own right. But it can also advance human development, for three reasons. First, enjoying political freedom and participating in the decisions that shape one's life are fundamental human rights: they are part of human development in their own right . . . . Democracy is the only political regime that guarantees political and civil freedoms and the right to participate—making democratic rule a good in itself.

Second, democracy helps protect people from economic and political catastrophes such as famines and descents into chaos . . . Nobel Prize-winner Amartya Sen has shown how elections and a free press give politicians in democracies much stronger incentives to avert famines . . . Democracies also contribute to political stability, providing open space for political opposition and handovers of power. Between 1950 and 1990 riots and demonstrations were more common in democracies but were much more destabilizing in dictatorships. Moreover, wars were more frequent in non-democratic regimes and had much higher economic costs.

Third, democratic governance can trigger a virtuous cycle of development—as political freedom empowers people to press for policies that expand social and economic opportunities, and as open debates help communities shape their priorities. From Indonesia to Mexico to Poland, moves towards democratization and political opening have helped produce this kind of virtuous cycle,

with a free press and civil society activism giving people new ways to participate in policy decisions and debates

In the area of UN electoral assistance, the presence of UNDP and other UN
development actors is notable. As discussed, technical assistance missions
have trumped other forms of electoral assistance, but there is now a third
wave of electoral assistance that seeks to "go beyond technical advice" to
broader reform of the political process.[39] In effect, we may be witnessing a
gradual convergence of UN electoral assistance with the broader good governance agenda. The United Nations Democracy Fund, a voluntary trust
fund established in 2005, likewise promotes systemic drivers of democratization by funding civil society organizations and grassroots activism, rather
than state-centric approaches to electoral reform.

If the expansion of democratic governance projects under UNDP and
the World Bank underscored its increasing relevance to sustainable development, then the Millennium Development Goals (MDGs) were a sobering
reminder of the obstacles that remained to its complete acceptance. Although
the Millennium Declaration of September 2000 declared "democratic and
participatory governance" to be a "fundamental" value for the twenty-first
century,[40] governments refused to endorse an explicit good governance indi-
cator in the MDGs.

Debates leading to the post-2015 sustainable development goals may serve
as a bellwether of how a norm of democratic governance is converging with
the development agenda. With the MDGs slated to expire in 2015, there was a
push to include commitments relating to governance in the post-2015 development agenda. Thus one of the seventeen new sustainable development
goals is to "promote peaceful and inclusive societies for sustainable development, provide access to justice for all and build effective, accountable,
and inclusive institutions." One of the targets under this goal is "to ensure
responsive, inclusive, participatory, and representative decision-making at
all levels."[41]

---

[39] "Deepening Democracy: A Strategy for Improving the Integrity of Elections
Worldwide." Report of the Global Commission on Elections, Democracy, and
Security. Report chaired by Kofi Annan. September 2012.
[40] United Nations Millennial Declaration. UNGA Resolution 55/2. 8
September 2000.
[41] "Open Working Group proposal for Sustainable Development Goals." Outcome
Document of the Open Working Group on Sustainable Development Goals.
United Nations. July 2014, available at: https://sustainabledevelopment.un.org/
sdgsproposal.

QUESTIONS

11. Does the inclusion of this goal in the post-2015 development agenda herald a further shift in the progression of a norm of democratic governance?

12. What is the difference (if any) between democracy and good governance? Should the United Nations push for one, the other, or both?

Conflict Prevention and Peacebuilding

A final area of engagement is conflict prevention and democratic peacebuilding. As the Secretary-General explained in *An Agenda for Democratization*, democratic institutions are believed to be more effective at managing the high stakes of political competition by ensuring that conflict is resolved peacefully through the ballot box, legal system, and wider political process. This is nicely captured in an unheralded report produced in 2001, which sought to offer guidelines on exit strategies for peace operations.

NO EXIT WITHOUT STRATEGY: SECURITY COUNCIL DECISION-MAKING AND THE CLOSURE OR TRANSITION OF UNITED NATIONS PEACEKEEPING OPERATIONS (REPORT OF THE SECRETARY GENERAL, 20 APRIL 2001)[42]

. . .

10. A sustainable domestic peace presents ... complex challenges. It becomes sustainable, not when all conflicts are removed from society, but when the natural conflicts of society can be resolved peacefully through the exercise of State sovereignty and, generally, participatory governance. In many cases, an effective strategy for realizing that objective is to help warring parties to move their political or economic struggles from the battlefield and into an institutional framework where a peaceful settlement process can be engaged and future disputes can be addressed in a similar fashion. To facilitate such a transition, a mission's mandate should include peace-building and incorporate such elements as institution-building and the promotion of good governance and the rule of law, by assisting the parties to develop legitimate and broad-based institutions.

11. As discussed in the Security Council on 5 February 2001, peace-building is an attempt, after a peace has been negotiated or imposed, to address the

---

[42] UN Doc S/2001/394.

sources of present hostility and build local capacities for conflict resolution. Strengthening State institutions, increasing political participation, engaging in land reform, strengthening civil society, finding ways to respect ethnic identities: all are seen as ways to improve the prospects for peaceful governance. The aim of peace-building is to build the social, economic and political institutions and attitudes that will prevent the inevitable conflicts that every society generates from turning into violent conflicts. . . . .

20. The United Nations system has recently identified three key objectives whose fulfillment has often brought about successful, comprehensive peace-building: . . .

(b) Strengthening political institutions and good governance. This requires the creation or strengthening of national democratic institutions, political parties and other participatory mechanisms, including the media; capacity-building for government and civil society; technical assistance in human rights; civic education and training; electoral assistance, including the development of electoral law, a code of conduct, and electoral councils; and support for the fight against corruption.

The key phrase in the above extract is "participatory governance," signifying participation that may not be in the form of elections and other standard indices of democracy. But the report subscribed to the democratic peace thesis—namely that democratic states are less likely to go to war with each other and to descend into civil war. In practice, this means that UN peace operations have been active in converting rebel groups into political parties, supporting the organization of post-conflict elections, and building democratic institutions, such as an independent electoral commission and functioning judiciary. With little mincing of words, the Security Council gave the United Nations Multidimensional Integrated Stabilization Mission in Mali (MINUSMA) a mandate under Chapter VII to assist Mali toward the restoration of democracy:

UN SECURITY COUNCIL RESOLUTION 2100 (2013)

The Security Council., . . .

Acting under Chapter VII . . .

3. Urges the transitional authorities of Mali to hold free, fair, transparent and inclusive presidential and legislative elections as soon as technically possible, . . . stresses the importance of ensuring an environment conducive to the holding of elections, in particular a secure environment prior to, during and following the electoral period, equitable access to State-controlled

media and provision for all eligible persons, including internally displaced persons and refugees, to participate in the electoral process and calls upon Member States, regional and international organizations, as requested by the transitional authorities of Mali, to provide support to the electoral process, including through financial resources, electoral observation capacity and related technical assistance;

16. Decides that the mandate of MINUSMA shall be the following: . . .

(b) *Support for the implementation of the transitional road map, including the national political dialogue and the electoral process*

(i) To assist the transitional authorities of Mali to implement swiftly the transitional road map towards the full restoration of constitutional order, democratic governance and national unity in Mali; . . .

(iii) To assist the transitional authorities of Mali and communities in the north of Mali to facilitate progress towards an inclusive national dialogue and reconciliation process, notably the negotiation process referred to in paragraph 4 above, including by enhancing negotiation capacity and promoting the participation of civil society, including women's organizations;

(iv) To support the organization and conduct of inclusive, free, fair and transparent presidential and legislative elections, including through the provision of appropriate logistical and technical assistance and effective security arrangements;

Similarly, Security Council Resolution 2040 gave the UN Mission in Libya (UNSMIL) a broad mandate to "manage the process of democratic transition," not only by giving technical advice, but also through a wide variety of measures aimed at improving institutional capacity and promoting political participation.[43] The Peacebuilding Fund, managed by the UN Peacebuilding Support Office, can also "exceptionally support elections at critical junctures for peacebuilding,"[44] as it did in Guinea-Bissau in 2014.

Societies undergoing democratic transition have also become the site of conflict prevention efforts by international organizations. It is a well-known irony that although consolidated democracies are more peaceful, democratization is often a turbulent process accompanied by deep-seated social and political conflict and even violence.[45] In the wake of the protests that

---

[43] UN Security Council Resolution 2040. S/RES/2040. March 2012.

[44] "Strengthening the role of the United Nations in enhancing the effectiveness of the principle of periodic and genuine elections and the promotion of democratization: Report of the Secretary General." A/68/301. 9 August 2013.

[45] Edward Mansfield and Jack Snyder, *Electing to Fight: Why Emerging Democracies Go to War.* Cambridge, MA: MIT Press, 2005.

swept the Arab world beginning in 2010, the United Nations has taken a strong interest in supporting democratic political transitions including, inter alia, facilitating a national dialogue in Libya, support to the constitutional process in Tunisia, and deploying a standby team of mediators to Yemen. Another oft-cited example is Kenya during the 2007–2008 presidential elections. Following destabilizing election violence that left more than 1,000 people dead, UN Special Envoy Kofi Annan was called upon to broker a settlement between the opposing parties who had each claimed an election victory, preventing a deadly slide into violence in the subregion.[46]

The relationship between democracy and peacebuilding is not linear. It is a "deep and enduring dilemma" that the perpetrators of election violence in Kenya were "rewarded" with a seat at the table by the United Nations and the international community.[47] Many years earlier, in Cambodia, the United Nations endorsed a power-sharing arrangement that included Hun Sen after he threatened renewed conflict following the 1993 electoral contest. In both cases, the opposition was compensated with more political power as a result of inciting violence than had they accepted defeat. This dilemma can likewise be witnessed in the acquiescence of the international community to the flawed 2009 Afghan elections.[48]

QUESTION

13. The legacy of peace operations that have engaged in democratic peacebuilding is mixed. Does this suggest that the *No Exit Without Strategy* approach is fundamentally flawed, or simply that execution of the strategy is easier said than done?

"Pro-democratic Intervention"

The UN Security Council has on several occasions authorized the use of force to restore democratically elected regimes, starting with Haiti in 1994.

---

[46] Human Rights Watch. 2008. "Ballots to Bullets: Organized Political Violence and Kenya's Crisis of Governance." Human Rights Watch Report 20.1 (March): pp. 1–79.
[47] Timothy Sisk. "Elections in Fragile States: Between Voices and Violence." Paper Prepared for the International Studies Association Annual Meeting. March 2008.
[48] Peter W. Galbraith, "U.N. Isn't Addressing Fraud in Afghanistan." *The Washington Post*, 4 October 2009.

SECURITY COUNCIL RESOLUTION 940 (1994)

The Security Council, ...

Reaffirming that the goal of the international community remains the restoration of democracy in Haiti and the prompt return of the legitimately elected President, Jean-Bertrand Aristide ...

Determining that the situation in Haiti continues to constitute a threat to peace and security in the region, ...

3. *Determines* that the illegal de facto regime in Haiti has failed to comply with the Governors Island Agreement and is in breach of its obligations under the relevant resolutions of the Security Council;

4. *Acting* under Chapter VII of the Charter of the United Nations, *authorizes* Member States to form a multinational force under unified command and control and, in this framework, to use all necessary means to facilitate the departure from Haiti of the military leadership, consistent with the Governors Island Agreement, the prompt return of the legitimately elected President and the restoration of the legitimate authorities of the Government of Haiti ...

Under different circumstances, the Economic Community of West Africa States (ECOWAS) intervened in Sierra Leone in 1998 to remove a regime that had toppled the elected government, a decision that was approved by the UN Security Council ex post facto. ECOWAS again threatened the use of military force during Côte d'Ivoire's 2010 political crisis, in which opposition candidate Laurent Gbagbo rejected the results of democratic elections and proclaimed himself the victor. The Security Council eventually responded with resolution 1975, which referred the situation to the ICC; imposed targeted sanctions on Gbagbo, his family, and advisors; and reinforced the authorization to use force to protect civilians. Implementation of the resolution led to robust military action by UN and French forces and the eventual capture by Ouatarra forces of Gbabgo (now facing international criminal justice in The Hague, whereas his wife, Simone, was sentenced in 2015 to twenty years in prison by an Ivorian court).

SECURITY COUNCIL RESOLUTION 1975 (2011)

The Security Council,

Reiterating its strong desire that the post-electoral crisis in Côte d'Ivoire be resolved peacefully and require an overall political solution that preserves democracy and peace and promotes lasting reconciliation among Ivoirians, ...

Determining that the situation in Côte d'Ivoire continues to constitute a threat to international peace and security,

Acting under Chapter VII of the Charter of the United Nations,

1. *Urges* all the Ivorian parties and other stakeholders to respect the will of the people and the election of Alassane Dramane Ouattara as President of Côte d'Ivoire, as recognized by ECOWAS, the African Union and the rest of the international community, expresses its concern at the recent escalation of violence and demands an immediate end to the violence against civilians, including women, children and Internally displaced persons;

4. *Urges* all Ivorian State institutions, including the Defence and Security Forces of Côte d'Ivoire (FDSCI), to yield to the authority vested by the Ivorian people in President Alassane Dramane Ouattara . . .

6. *Recalls* its authorization and stresses its full support given to the UNOCI, while impartially implementing its mandate, to use all necessary means to carry out its mandate to protect civilians under imminent threat of physical violence, within its capabilities and its areas of deployment, including to prevent the use of heavy weapons against the civilian population and requests the Secretary-General to keep it urgently informed of measures taken and efforts made in this regard;

7. *Calls upon* all parties to cooperate fully in the operation of UNOCI and French forces which support it, in particular by guaranteeing their safety, security and freedom of movement with unhindered and immediate access throughout the territory of Côte d'Ivoire, to enable them to fully carry out their mandate;

QUESTIONS

14. Is resolution 1975 an example of pro-democratic intervention?
15. Should the Security Council be authorizing pro-democratic interventions? If so, in what circumstances?

A less coercive type of enforcement is the so-called "red card" principle, where regional organizations suspend states from participation in the organization for unconstitutional changes in the democratic order. This began with Western or Western-led organizations. Thus the OAS includes the 1991 Santiago Commitment and the Inter-American Democratic Charter, which calls for suspension in case of "unconstitutional interruption of the democratic order"—applied most recently in Honduras in 2009. The Andean Community and Mercosur both have language allowing for suspension of members under similar circumstances. The Commonwealth Ministerial Action Group suspended Nigeria's membership in 1995, Zimbabwe in 2002, Fiji in 2006, and Pakistan in 2007, each following a usurpation of the democratic order. The Gambia withdrew from the Commonwealth in 2013 in the context of discussions about its possible suspension.

The phenomenon spread to Africa in 1999, when the OAU adopted a declaration stating that any OAU member state whose government came to power by unconstitutional means after 1997 would be prohibited from participating in OAU meetings. This is now embodied in the Constitutive Act of the African Union.

CONSTITUTIVE ACT OF THE AFRICAN UNION (2002)

Article 4—Principles

. . .

(m) respect for democratic principles, human rights, the rule of law and good governance; . . .

(p) condemnation and rejection of unconstitutional changes of governments. . . .

Article 30—Suspension

Governments which shall come to power through unconstitutional means shall not be allowed to participate in the activities of the Union.

HYPOTHETICAL

The United Nations does not have the equivalent of the "red card" principle, in the sense that suspension for unconstitutional or undemocratic changes in government is not stated explicitly in the Charter. You are a member of a drafting committee charged with coming up with proposals on how the United Nations should deal with coups d'état. You have been asked to present the General Assembly with two options: (1) an amendment to the Charter, or (2) guidance for interpretation and application of Articles 5 and 6 of the Charter that would give effect to pro-democracy goals.

Further Reading

Cassese, Antonio. *Self-Determination of Peoples: A Legal Reappraisal.* Cambridge: Cambridge University Press, 1995.

Carothers, Thomas. *Critical Mission: Essays on Democracy Promotion.* Washington D.C.: Carnegie Endowment for International Peace 2004).

Chesterman, Simon, *Just War or Just Peace: Humanitarian Intervention and International Law.* New York:Oxford University Press, 2001.

Fox, Gregory and Brad Roth (eds), *Democratic Governance and International Law* New York: Cambridge University Press, 2000).

Franck, Thomas M. "Fairness to 'Peoples' and Their Right to Self-Determination." In *Fairness in International Law and Institutions* Oxford: Clarendon Press, 1995.

Hannum, Hurst and Eileen Babbitt (eds). *Negotiating Self-Determination.* Lanham MD: Lexington Books, 2005.

Jarstad, Anna and Timothy Sisk (eds). *From War to Democracy: Dilemmas of Peacebuilding.* Cambridge: Cambridge University Press, 2008.

Kelley, Judith G. *Monitoring Democracy: When International Election Observation Works, and Why It Often Fails.* Princeton NJ : Princeton University Press, 2012.

Knop, Karen. *Diversity and Self-Determination in International Law.* New York: Cambridge University Press, 2008.

Kumar, Khrisna (ed). *Post-Conflict Elections, Democratization and International Assistance.* Boulder, CO: Lynne Rienner, 1998.

Malone, David M. *Decision-Making in the UN Security Council: The Case of Haiti.*: Clarendon/Oxford University Press, 1998, pp. 58–118.

Mansfield, Edward and Snyder, Jack. *Electing to Fight: Why Emerging Democracies Go to War.* Cambridge MA: Belfer Center for International Science and Affairs, 2005

Newman, Edward and Rich, Roland (eds). *The UN Role in Promoting Democracy: Between Ideals and Reality.* Tokyo: United Nations University Press, 2004.

Tomuschat, Christian (ed). *Modern Law of Self-Determination.* Dordrecht: Martinus Nijhoff, 1993.

Walter, Christian, Antje von Ungern-Sternberg, and Kavus Abushov (eds). *Self-Determination and Secession in International Law.* Oxford: Oxford University Press, 2014.

chapter thirteen
....

Human Rights

The tension between sovereignty and human rights in the international legal order established after the Second World War is clear from the opening words of the UN Charter. War is to be renounced as an instrument of national policy; human rights are to be affirmed. But in its substantive provisions, the Charter appears to privilege peace over dignity: the threat or use of force is prohibited in Article 2(4); protection of human rights is limited to the more or less hortatory provisions of Articles 55 and 56.

Over time, however, human rights have come to be recognized as a core function of the United Nations. By 2005, Secretary-General Kofi Annan could argue that human rights formed one of the three core purposes of the United Nations, along with security and development.[1]

The seeds of this important change were laid elsewhere in the Charter. In the absence of agreement to incorporate a bill of rights in the Charter itself, Article 68 provided that the Economic and Social Council (ECOSOC) "shall set up commissions in economic and social fields and for the promotion of human rights." The UN Commission on Human Rights was established under this provision in 1946.

The Commission—which was abolished in 2006 and replaced by a Human Rights Council—provides a useful lens through which to view the evolution of human rights as understood within the UN system. Early successes in this area were generally attributed to its flexibility with regard to membership, and its lack of coercive powers: precisely the faults that later led to sustained criticism into the early twenty-first century.

The first major task of the Commission on Human Rights was submitting reports and proposals on an international bill of rights. Opinion was divided on whether this should take the form of a legally binding instrument that member states might ratify, or a more general declaration in the form of a recommendation by the General Assembly that would exert moral and political influence on member states. The latter path was chosen, and the

---

[1] *In Larger Freedom: Towards Development, Security, and Human Rights for All*, UN Doc. A/59/2005 (2005).

Commission proposed a draft declaration in 1948, adopted by the General Assembly as the Universal Declaration on Human Rights. Forty-eight states voted in favor;[2] eight abstained (Saudi Arabia, South Africa, and six Soviet bloc states).

The Universal Declaration was intended to form the basis of a more detailed convention with binding force. In the years that followed, however, the ideological divisions of the Cold War were reflected even in debates over human rights. In 1952 the decision was made to divide its provisions between two treaties: one elaborating civil and political rights, the other providing for economic, social, and cultural rights. Though they were negotiated and adopted in parallel, these are sometimes referred to as first generation and second generation rights respectively, or negative rights (limiting government power) and positive rights (requiring government action). A further fourteen years passed as the documents made their parallel ways through the Commission, the Third Committee of the General Assembly, and the Assembly itself.[3] In 1966 the Assembly approved the two treaties—the International Covenant on Civil and Political Rights (ICCPR) and the International Covenant on Economic, Social, and Cultural Rights (ICESCR). It took another decade to achieve sufficient ratifications for them to enter into force.[4]

These normative developments have been matched by an expanding network of bodies dedicated to the promotion and protection of human rights. Some operate under the UN Charter; others under the two covenants and other treaties.

Within the Charter regime, the Commission on Human Rights established mechanisms to address either specific country situations or thematic issues. Known as "special procedures," these typically involved the appointment of a special rapporteur, independent expert, or working group who reported back to the Commission. The mechanism was later adapted for the Human Rights Council, and in late 2015 there were forty-one thematic and fourteen country mandates.

---

[2] Afghanistan, Argentina, Australia, Belgium, Bolivia, Brazil, Burma, Canada, Chile, China, Colombia, Costa Rica, Cuba, Denmark, Dominican Republic, Ecuador, Egypt, El Salvador, Ethiopia, France, Greece, Guatemala, Haiti, Iceland, India, Iran, Iraq, Lebanon, Liberia, Luxembourg, Mexico, Netherlands, New Zealand, Nicaragua, Norway, Pakistan, Panama, Paraguay, Peru, Philippines, Siam (Thailand), Sweden, Syria, Turkey, United Kingdom, United States, Uruguay, and Venezuela.

[3] An important milestone was the International Convention on the Elimination of All Forms of Racial Discrimination, adopted and opened for signature and ratification by GA Res. 2106(XX) (1965).

[4] As of December 2015, the ICCPR had 168 parties; the ICESCR had 164 parties.

Not created under the UN Charter but part of the broader UN system, a further ten human rights treaty bodies monitor implementation of the core international human rights treaties. A key difference between the treaty bodies and the Council is that the treaty bodies are made up of independent experts, who are nominated and elected by state parties for fixed renewable terms of four years. They typically meet in Geneva and receive support from the UN Office of the High Commissioner for Human Rights. The ten bodies comprise: the Human Rights Committee (established by the ICCPR), the Committee on Economic, Social and Cultural Rights (established by the ICESCR), the Committee on the Elimination of Racial Discrimination (1965), the Committee on the Elimination of Discrimination against Women (1979), the Committee Against Torture (1984), the Committee on the Rights of the Child (1989), the Committee on Migrant Workers (1990), the Subcommittee on Prevention of Torture and other Cruel, Inhuman or Degrading Treatment or Punishment (2002), the Committee on the Rights of Persons with Disabilities (2006), and the Committee on Enforced Disappearances (2006).

Leading and coordinating many of these activities is the UN Office of the High Commissioner for Human Rights (OHCHR). At once advocate and coordinator, its mandate includes encouraging respect for human rights, preventing violations, promoting international cooperation, and coordinating activities throughout the UN system. Predictably, this requires the High Commissioner to navigate a fine line between quiet diplomacy and public advocacy—a balance struck differently by each of the High Commissioners who have held the position since it was created in 1993.

This chapter focuses on the Charter mechanisms, emphasizing the tension between sovereignty and human rights pointed out earlier. A central question is whether it is possible for an organization of states to protect human rights when the main violators of human rights are states themselves. A second set of issues concerns the restructuring of the human rights mechanisms that took place in 2006. To what extent is the United Nations now more effective in promoting and monitoring human rights? Section three turns to a relatively recent phenomenon in human rights debates: the right to digital privacy in an age of global surveillance. A final section considers the surprisingly contentious question of whether the United Nations is bound by its own human rights norms.

13.1 Sovereignty and Human Rights

The Charter provisions on human rights are far more general than those relating to peace and security. Contrast the following provisions with the adoption in 2005 of the Responsibility to Protect, discussed in Chapter 17.

UN CHARTER

Preamble

WE THE PEOPLES OF THE UNITED NATIONS DETERMINED . . .

to reaffirm faith in fundamental human rights, in the dignity and worth of the human person, in the equal rights of men and women and of nations large and small . . .

Article 1

The Purposes of the United Nations are: . . .

3. To achieve international cooperation in solving international problems of an economic, social, cultural, or humanitarian character, and in promoting and encouraging respect for human rights and for fundamental freedoms for all without distinction as to race, sex, language, or religion; . . .

Article 13

1. The General Assembly shall initiate studies and make recommendations for the purpose of: . . .

(b) promoting international cooperation in the economic, social, cultural, educational, and health fields, and assisting in the realization of human rights and fundamental freedoms for all without distinction as to race, sex, language, or religion. . . .

Article 55

With a view to the creation of conditions of stability and well-being which are necessary for peaceful and friendly relations among nations based on respect for the principle of equal rights and self-determination of peoples, the United Nations shall promote:

(a) higher standards of living, full employment, and conditions of economic and social progress and development;

(b) solutions of international economic, social, health, and related problems; and international cultural and educational cooperation; and

(c) universal respect for, and observance of, human rights and fundamental freedoms for all without distinction as to race, sex, language, or religion.

Article 56

All Members pledge themselves to take joint and separate action in co-operation with the Organization for the achievement of the purposes set forth in Article 55. . . .

Article 62

1. The Economic and Social Council may make or initiate studies and reports with respect to international economic, social, cultural, educational, health, and related matters and may make recommendations with respect to any such matters to the General Assembly, to the Members of the United Nations, and to the specialized agencies concerned.

2. It may make recommendations for the purpose of promoting respect for, and observance of, human rights and fundamental freedoms for all. ...

Article 68

The Economic and Social Council shall set up commissions in economic and social fields and for the promotion of human rights, and such other commissions as may be required for the performance of its functions.

As indicated earlier, the first major achievement of the United Nations in this area was the Universal Declaration of Human Rights. This was not intended to be a binding instrument, yet most of its provisions are now regarded as reflecting customary international law.

UNIVERSAL DECLARATION OF HUMAN RIGHTS, GENERAL ASSEMBLY RESOLUTION 217A(III) (1948)

Preamble

Whereas recognition of the inherent dignity and of the equal and inalienable rights of all members of the human family is the foundation of freedom, justice and peace in the world,

Whereas disregard and contempt for human rights have resulted in barbarous acts which have outraged the conscience of mankind, and the advent of a world in which human beings shall enjoy freedom of speech and belief and freedom from fear and want has been proclaimed as the highest aspiration of the common people,

Whereas it is essential, if man is not to be compelled to have recourse, as a last resort, to rebellion against tyranny and oppression, that human rights should be protected by the rule of law,

Whereas it is essential to promote the development of friendly relations between nations,

Whereas the peoples of the United Nations have in the Charter reaffirmed their faith in fundamental human rights, in the dignity and worth of the human person and in the equal rights of men and women and have determined to promote social progress and better standards of life in larger freedom,

Whereas Member States have pledged themselves to achieve, in cooperation with the United Nations, the promotion of universal respect for and observance of human rights and fundamental freedoms,

Whereas a common understanding of these rights and freedoms is of the greatest importance for the full realization of this pledge,

Now, therefore,

The General Assembly,

Proclaims this Universal Declaration of Human Rights as a common standard of achievement for all peoples and all nations, to the end that every individual and every organ of society, keeping this Declaration constantly in mind, shall strive by teaching and education to promote respect for these rights and freedoms and by progressive measures, national and international, to secure their universal and effective recognition and observance, both among the peoples of Member States themselves and among the peoples of territories under their jurisdiction.

Article 1

All human beings are born free and equal in dignity and rights. They are endowed with reason and conscience and should act towards one another in a spirit of brotherhood.

Article 2

Everyone is entitled to all the rights and freedoms set forth in this Declaration, without distinction of any kind, such as race, colour, sex, language, religion, political or other opinion, national or social origin, property, birth or other status.

Furthermore, no distinction shall be made on the basis of the political, jurisdictional or international status of the country or territory to which a person belongs, whether it be independent, trust, non-self-governing or under any other limitation of sovereignty.

Article 3

Everyone has the right to life, liberty and security of person.

Article 4

No one shall be held in slavery or servitude; slavery and the slave trade shall be prohibited in all their forms.

Article 5

No one shall be subjected to torture or to cruel, inhuman or degrading treatment or punishment.

Article 6

Everyone has the right to recognition everywhere as a person before the law.

Article 7

All are equal before the law and are entitled without any discrimination to equal protection of the law. All are entitled to equal protection against any discrimination in violation of this Declaration and against any incitement to such discrimination.

Article 8

Everyone has the right to an effective remedy by the competent national tribunals for acts violating the fundamental rights granted him by the constitution or by law.

Article 9

No one shall be subjected to arbitrary arrest, detention or exile.

Article 10

Everyone is entitled in full equality to a fair and public hearing by an independent and impartial tribunal, in the determination of his rights and obligations and of any criminal charge against him.

Article 11

1. Everyone charged with a penal offence has the right to be presumed innocent until proved guilty according to law in a public trial at which he has had all the guarantees necessary for his defence.

2. No one shall be held guilty of any penal offence on account of any act or omission which did not constitute a penal offence, under national or international law, at the time when it was committed. Nor shall a heavier penalty be imposed than the one that was applicable at the time the penal offence was committed.

Article 12

No one shall be subjected to arbitrary interference with his privacy, family, home or correspondence, nor to attacks upon his honour and reputation. Everyone has the right to the protection of the law against such interference or attacks.

Article 13

1. Everyone has the right to freedom of movement and residence within the borders of each State.

2. Everyone has the right to leave any country, including his own, and to return to his country.

Article 14

1. Everyone has the right to seek and to enjoy in other countries asylum from persecution.

2. This right may not be invoked in the case of prosecutions genuinely arising from non-political crimes or from acts contrary to the purposes and principles of the United Nations.

Article 15

1. Everyone has the right to a nationality.

2. No one shall be arbitrarily deprived of his nationality nor denied the right to change his nationality.

Article 16

1. Men and women of full age, without any limitation due to race, nationality or religion, have the right to marry and to found a family. They are entitled to equal rights as to marriage, during marriage and at its dissolution.

2. Marriage shall be entered into only with the free and full consent of the intending spouses.

3. The family is the natural and fundamental group unit of society and is entitled to protection by society and the State.

Article 17

1. Everyone has the right to own property alone as well as in association with others.

2. No one shall be arbitrarily deprived of his property.

Article 18

Everyone has the right to freedom of thought, conscience and religion; this right includes freedom to change his religion or belief, and freedom, either alone or in community with others and in public or private, to manifest his religion or belief in teaching, practice, worship and observance.

Article 19

Everyone has the right to freedom of opinion and expression; this right includes freedom to hold opinions without interference and to seek, receive and impart information and ideas through any media and regardless of frontiers.

Article 20

1. Everyone has the right to freedom of peaceful assembly and association.
    2. No one may be compelled to belong to an association.

Article 21

1. Everyone has the right to take part in the government of his country, directly or through freely chosen representatives.
    2. Everyone has the right to equal access to public service in his country.
    3. The will of the people shall be the basis of the authority of government; this will shall be expressed in periodic and genuine elections which shall be by universal and equal suffrage and shall be held by secret vote or by equivalent free voting procedures.

Article 22

Everyone, as a member of society, has the right to social security and is entitled to realization, through national effort and international co-operation and in accordance with the organization and resources of each State, of the economic, social and cultural rights indispensable for his dignity and the free development of his personality.

Article 23

1. Everyone has the right to work, to free choice of employment, to just and favourable conditions of work and to protection against unemployment.
    2. Everyone, without any discrimination, has the right to equal pay for equal work.

3. Everyone who works has the right to just and favourable remuneration ensuring for himself and his family an existence worthy of human dignity, and supplemented, if necessary, by other means of social protection.

4. Everyone has the right to form and to join trade unions for the protection of his interests.

Article 24

Everyone has the right to rest and leisure, including reasonable limitation of working hours and periodic holidays with pay.

Article 25

1. Everyone has the right to a standard of living adequate for the health and well-being of himself and of his family, including food, clothing, housing and medical care and necessary social services, and the right to security in the event of unemployment, sickness, disability, widowhood, old age or other lack of livelihood in circumstances beyond his control.

2. Motherhood and childhood are entitled to special care and assistance. All children, whether born in or out of wedlock, shall enjoy the same social protection.

Article 26

1. Everyone has the right to education. Education shall be free, at least in the elementary and fundamental stages. Elementary education shall be compulsory. Technical and professional education shall be made generally available and higher education shall be equally accessible to all on the basis of merit.

2. Education shall be directed to the full development of the human personality and to the strengthening of respect for human rights and fundamental freedoms. It shall promote understanding, tolerance and friendship among all nations, racial or religious groups, and shall further the activities of the United Nations for the maintenance of peace.

3. Parents have a prior right to choose the kind of education that shall be given to their children.

Article 27

1. Everyone has the right freely to participate in the cultural life of the community, to enjoy the arts and to share in scientific advancement and its benefits.

2. Everyone has the right to the protection of the moral and material interests resulting from any scientific, literary or artistic production of which he is the author.

Article 28

Everyone is entitled to a social and international order in which the rights and freedoms set forth in this Declaration can be fully realized.

Article 29

1. Everyone has duties to the community in which alone the free and full development of his personality is possible.

2. In the exercise of his rights and freedoms, everyone shall be subject only to such limitations as are determined by law solely for the purpose of securing due recognition and respect for the rights and freedoms of others and of meeting the just requirements of morality, public order and the general welfare in a democratic society.

3. These rights and freedoms may in no case be exercised contrary to the purposes and principles of the United Nations.

Article 30

Nothing in this Declaration may be interpreted as implying for any State, group or person any right to engage in any activity or to perform any act aimed at the destruction of any of the rights and freedoms set forth herein.

Human rights were initially considered within the United Nations in the context of voluntary regimes of a non-binding character. An important step toward a form of accountability was the creation of the "1235 Procedure," referring to ECOSOC resolution 1235, adopted in 1967, which provided for an annual public debate focusing on "gross violations of human rights and fundamental freedoms."

This development accompanied the adoption of the two international covenants (ICCPR and ICESCR), but reflected a desire to establish a non-treaty-based procedure to examine human rights violations as part of the struggle against racist and colonialist policies. Such a change was possible in part due to the expansion of membership of the United Nations in the course of decolonization. It was driven by Third World countries, with support from Eastern Europe, but was not limited in its application to the regimes identified in the text of the resolution.

ECOSOC RESOLUTION 1235 (XLII) OF 6 JUNE 1967

The Economic and Social Council, ...

1. *Welcomes* the decision of the Commission on Human Rights to give annual consideration to the item entitled "Question of the violation of human rights and fundamental freedoms, including policies of racial discrimination and segregation and of apartheid, in all countries, with particular reference to colonial and other dependent countries and territories," ...

2. *Authorizes* the Commission on Human Rights and the Sub-Commission on Prevention of Discrimination and Protection of Minorities, ... to examine information relevant to gross violations of human rights and fundamental freedoms, as exemplified by the policy of apartheid as practised in the Republic of South Africa and in the Territory of South West Africa ..., and to racial discrimination as practiced notably in Southern Rhodesia ...;

3. *Decides* that the Commission on Human Rights may, in appropriate cases, and after careful consideration of the information thus made available to it, in conformity with the provisions of paragraph 1 above, make a thorough study of situations which reveal a consistent pattern of violations of human rights, as exemplified by the policy of apartheid as practised in the Republic of South Africa and in the Territory of South West Africa ..., and racial discrimination as practised notably in Southern Rhodesia, and report, with recommendations thereon, to the Economic and Social Council; ...

Three years later, ECOSOC established a second procedure authorizing the examination of communications from individuals concerning "situations which appear to reveal a consistent pattern of gross and reliably attested violations of human rights requiring consideration by the Commission." The "1503 Procedure" developed more quickly than the 1235 Procedure and is frequently used as a precursor to the latter. A key difference is that discussion of 1503 communications (or complaints) is conducted in closed session. Another key difference is that this grants a right of private petition, allowing victims as well as the families and NGOs to bring complaints on behalf of the victims. By 2000 approximately 50,000 complaints were being received each year,[5] in many cases revealing patters of violations in countries that had pressed hard for the 1235 procedure.

---

[5] Henry J. Steiner and Philip Alston, *International Human Rights in Context: Law, Politics, Morals*, 2nd edn. (Oxford: Oxford University Press, 2000), p. 615.

ECOSOC RESOLUTION 1503 (XLVIII) OF 27 MAY 1970

The Economic and Social Council, ...

1. *Authorizes* the Sub-Commission on Prevention of Discrimination and Protection of Minorities to appoint a Working Group consisting of not more than five of its members, with due regard to geographical distribution, to meet once a year in private meetings for a period not exceeding ten days immediately before the sessions of the Sub-Commission to consider all communications, including replies of Governments thereon, received by the Secretary-General under Council resolution 728F (XXVIII) of 30 July 1959 with a view to bringing to the attention of the Sub-Commission those communications, together with replies of Governments, if any, which appear to reveal a consistent pattern of gross and reliably attested violations of human rights and fundamental freedoms within the terms of reference of the Sub-Commission; ...

4. *Further requests* the Secretary-General:

(a) To furnish to the members of the Sub-Commission every month a list of communications prepared by him in accordance with Council resolution 728F (XXVIII) and a brief description of them, together with the text of any replies received from Governments;

(b) To make available to the members of the working group at their meetings the originals of such communications listed as they may request ...;

5. *Requests* the Sub Commission on Prevention of Discrimination and Protection of Minorities to consider in private meetings, in accordance with paragraph 1 above, the communications brought before it in accordance with the decision of a majority of the members of the working group and any replies of Governments relating thereto and other relevant information, with a view to determining whether to refer to the Commission on Human Rights particular situations which appear to reveal a consistent pattern of gross and reliably attested violations of human rights requiring consideration by the Commission;

6. *Requests* the Commission on Human Rights after it has examined any situation referred to it by the Sub-Commission to determine:

(a) Whether it requires a thorough study by the Commission and a report and recommendations thereon to the Council in accordance with paragraph 3 of Council resolution 1235 (XLII); ...

8. *Decides* that all actions envisaged in the implementation of the present resolution by the Sub-Commission on Prevention of Discrimination and Protection of Minorities or the Commission on Human Rights shall remain confidential until such a time as the Commission may decide to make recommendations to the Economic and Social Council; ...

10. *Decides* that the procedure set out in the present resolution for dealing with communications relating to violations of human rights and fundamental freedoms should be reviewed if any new organ entitled to deal with such communications should be established within the United Nations or by international agreement.

These two procedures at least created a forum to discuss and an avenue to air human rights concerns in states. In addition, various human rights treaties include optional protocols that states may choose to adopt, allowing their nationals to put forward more formal complaints. The ICCPR, for example, allows for individuals to complain directly to the Human Rights Committee (HRC). By 1980 only 22 states had acceded to the Optional Protocol. By 1990 this number increased to 48; by 2000 it was 96. In 2015 there were a total of 115 states parties. Decisions by the HRC on these complaints, receivable only after all recourse to domestic remedies has been exhausted, have led to important changes in national legislation and administrative practice within a number of the states parties.

QUESTIONS

1. What obligations are assumed by the members of the United Nations under the Charter provisions on human rights?
2. If the Universal Declaration on Human Rights was a process chosen explicitly to avoid binding commitments, how is it that it is now seen as reflecting customary international law?
3. If the division of the rights in the Universal Declaration on Human Rights into civil and political on the one hand, and economic, social, and cultural rights on the other was a function of Cold War ideology, why do we speak of first and second generation rights? Are the latter enforceable? In which of the two divisions would you place Article 29?
4. To what extent do you regard the provisions of the UDHR as "rights"? Might some of the statements "Everyone has the right to . . ." be replaceable by "It is nice that people . . ."?
5. If one accepts that the main violators of human rights are states, is it possible to protect human rights through an organization of states such as the United Nations? Do the 1235 and 1503 procedures support or undermine your answer?

13.2 The Human Rights Council

By 2005 the Commission on Human Rights was being routinely criticized as lacking impartiality, credibility, and professionalism.[6] Identifying membership as the most difficult and sensitive issue, the High-Level Panel appointed

---

[6] A More Secure World: Our Shared Responsibility (Report of the High-Level Panel on Threats, Challenges, and Change), UN Doc. A/59/565 (1 December 2004), available at: http://www.un.org/secureworld, para. 283.

by the Secretary-General in 2003 to propose major reforms in the UN system recommended avoiding the problem through universal membership.[7]

Though it was generally accepted that the Panel's diagnosis of the problems relative to the Commission on Human Rights was correct, the Secretary-General's response took a different tack by proposing slightly more limited membership (forty-seven states versus fifty-three for the CHR) for a new Human Rights Council, whose members would be elected directly by the General Assembly by a two-thirds majority. The 2005 Summit Outcome Document endorsed the principle of establishing a Council, but left all details to the sixtieth session of the Assembly that was about to begin.

IN LARGER FREEDOM: TOWARDS DEVELOPMENT, SECURITY, AND HUMAN RIGHTS FOR ALL (REPORT OF THE SECRETARY-GENERAL), 21 MARCH 2005[8]

181. The Commission on Human Rights has given the international community a universal human rights framework, comprising the Universal Declaration on Human Rights, the two International Covenants and other core human rights treaties. During its annual session, the Commission draws public attention to human rights issues and debates, provides a forum for the development of United Nations human rights policy and establishes a unique system of independent and expert special procedures to observe and analyse human rights compliance by theme and by country. The Commission's close engagement with hundreds of civil society organizations provides an opportunity for working with civil society that does not exist elsewhere.

182. Yet the Commission's capacity to perform its tasks has been increasingly undermined by its declining credibility and professionalism. In particular, States have sought membership of the Commission not to strengthen human rights but to protect themselves against criticism or to criticize others. As a result, a credibility deficit has developed, which casts a shadow on the reputation of the United Nations system as a whole.

183. If the United Nations is to meet the expectations of men and women everywhere—and indeed, if the Organization is to take the cause of human rights as seriously as those of security and development—then Member States should agree to replace the Commission on Human Rights with a smaller standing Human Rights Council. Member States would need to decide if they want the Human Rights Council to be a principal organ of the United Nations or a subsidiary body of the General Assembly, but in

---

[7] The Report of the High-Level Panel is also discussed in Chapters 8 and 17.
[8] UN Doc. A/59/2005 (2005).

either case its members would be elected directly by the General Assembly by a two-thirds majority of members present and voting. The creation of the Council would accord human rights a more authoritative position, corresponding to the primacy of human rights in the Charter of the United Nations. Member States should determine the composition of the Council and the term of office of its members. Those elected to the Council should undertake to abide by the highest human rights standards.

Membership was the key fault line in subsequent negotiations, with the United States and a number of other countries pushing for the two-thirds requirement recommended by the Secretary-General. The United States also pressed hard for automatic exclusion of states that were the subject of coercive measures imposed by the Security Council related to human rights abuses or terrorism. (Some concerns were expressed within the US State Department that more restrictive criteria could preclude the United States itself from membership.) Failure to include these provisions led the United States to vote against the draft resolution, which was adopted on 15 March 2006 by a recorded vote of 170 in favor to 4 against (Israel, the Marshall Islands, and Palau joining the United States), with Belarus, Iran, and Venezuela abstaining. The United States also expressed opposition to the inclusion of term limits, which prevent states from serving more than six years out of every seven—apparently on the basis that this could mean that the United States would be forced to rotate off the new body every six years for at least a year.

Council members are elected directly and individually by secret ballot by a majority of members of the General Assembly. This ballot is constrained by a requirement to distribute seats among the regional groupings (thirteen from the African Group, thirteen from the Asia Pacific Group, six from the Eastern European Group, eight from the Latin American and Caribbean Group, and seven from the Western Europe and Others Group)[9]. When electing members of the Council, states are asked to "take into account the contribution of candidates to the promotion and protection of human rights and their voluntary pledges and commitments." Once on the Council, members are to uphold the highest standards and cooperate with the new body; a member that commits gross and systematic violations of human rights may be suspended by a two-thirds majority of votes in the General Assembly. The bar to expulsion is extremely high, but the key provision was thought to be the individual election of members by an absolute majority of the General Assembly (as opposed to a majority of members present and voting). It was believed that this might prevent regional slates being presented, with regional solidarity being more important than a human rights record for the

---

[9] These are the regional groups used for electoral purposes at the United Nations. See also the discussion about election to the Security Council in Chapter 1.

purposes of getting on the Council. And yet, more often than not, regions have presented full slates of candidate countries, rendering the vote in the General Assembly a formality.[10]

GENERAL ASSEMBLY RESOLUTION 60/251 (2006): THE HUMAN RIGHTS COUNCIL

The General Assembly, ...

Reaffirming that, while the significance of national and regional particularities and various historical, cultural and religious backgrounds must be borne in mind, all States, regardless of their political, economic and cultural systems, have the duty to promote and protect all human rights and fundamental freedoms, ...

Acknowledging that peace and security, development and human rights are the pillars of the United Nations system and the foundations for collective security and well-being, and recognizing that development, peace and security and human rights are interlinked and mutually reinforcing, ...

1. *Decides* to establish the Human Rights Council, based in Geneva, in replacement of the Commission on Human Rights, as a subsidiary organ of the General Assembly; the Assembly shall review the status of the Council within five years;[11]

2. *Decides* that the Council shall be responsible for promoting universal respect for the protection of all human rights and fundamental freedoms for all, without distinction of any kind and in a fair and equal manner;

3. *Decides also* that the Council should address situations of violations of human rights, including gross and systematic violations, and make recommendations thereon. It should also promote the effective coordination and the mainstreaming of human rights within the United Nations system;

4. *Decides further* that the work of the Council shall be guided by the principles of universality, impartiality, objectivity and non-selectivity, constructive international dialogue and cooperation, with a view to enhancing the promotion and protection of all human rights, civil, political, economic, social and cultural rights, including the right to development;

---

[10] Despite efforts to prevent regions fielding slates of candidates, the Africa group proposed thirteen candidates for thirteen seats in the first election to the Council. Since then, many regions have done the same. In 2011, for example, Africa, Asia, and WEOG all had full slates; in 2012, all regions but WEOG had full slates; in 2013, Asia-Pacific, GRULAC, and WEOG had full slates; in 2014, Africa, Eastern Europe, and WEOG had full slates. (For a discussion of UN electoral groups, see Chapter 1, section 1.1.)
[11] The Assembly later decided to maintain that status and review it once again in the period 2021-2026: GA Res. 65/281 (2011).

5. *Decides* that the Council shall, inter alia:

(*a*) Promote human rights education and learning as well as advisory services, technical assistance and capacity-building, to be provided in consultation with and with the consent of Member States concerned;

(*b*) Serve as a forum for dialogue on thematic issues on all human rights;

(*c*) Make recommendations to the General Assembly for the further development of international law in the field of human rights;

(*d*) Promote the full implementation of human rights obligations undertaken by States and follow-up to the goals and commitments related to the promotion and protection of human rights emanating from United Nations conferences and summits;

(*e*) Undertake a universal periodic review, based on objective and reliable information, of the fulfilment by each State of its human rights obligations and commitments in a manner which ensures universality of coverage and equal treatment with respect to all States; the review shall be a cooperative mechanism, based on an interactive dialogue, with the full involvement of the country concerned and with consideration given to its capacity-building needs; such a mechanism shall complement and not duplicate the work of treaty bodies; the Council shall develop the modalities and necessary time allocation for the universal periodic review mechanism within one year after the holding of its first session;

(*f*) Contribute, through dialogue and cooperation, towards the prevention of human rights violations and respond promptly to human rights emergencies;

(*g*) Assume the role and responsibilities of the Commission on Human Rights relating to the work of the Office of the United Nations High Commissioner for Human Rights, as decided by the General Assembly in its resolution 48/141 of 20 December 1993;

(*h*) Work in close cooperation in the field of human rights with Governments, regional organizations, national human rights institutions and civil society;

(*i*) Make recommendations with regard to the promotion and protection of human rights;

(*j*) Submit an annual report to the General Assembly;

6. *Decides also* that the Council shall assume, review and, where necessary, improve and rationalize all mandates, mechanisms, functions and responsibilities of the Commission on Human Rights in order to maintain a system of special procedures, expert advice and a complaint procedure; the Council shall complete this review within one year after the holding of its first session;

7. *Decides further* that the Council shall consist of forty-seven Member States, which shall be elected directly and individually by secret ballot by the majority of the members of the General Assembly; the membership shall be based on equitable geographical distribution, and seats shall be

distributed as follows among regional groups: Group of African States, thirteen; Group of Asian States, thirteen; Group of Eastern European States, six; Group of Latin American and Caribbean States, eight; and Group of Western European and other States, seven; the members of the Council shall serve for a period of three years and shall not be eligible for immediate re-election after two consecutive terms;

8. *Decides* that the membership in the Council shall be open to all States Members of the United Nations; when electing members of the Council, Member States shall take into account the contribution of candidates to the promotion and protection of human rights and their voluntary pledges and commitments made thereto; the General Assembly, by a two-thirds majority of the members present and voting, may suspend the rights of membership in the Council of a member of the Council that commits gross and systematic violations of human rights;

9. *Decides also* that members elected to the Council shall uphold the highest standards in the promotion and protection of human rights, shall fully cooperate with the Council and be reviewed under the universal periodic review mechanism during their term of membership;

10. *Decides further* that the Council shall meet regularly throughout the year and schedule no fewer than three sessions per year, including a main session, for a total duration of no less than ten weeks, and shall be able to hold special sessions, when needed, at the request of a member of the Council with the support of one third of the membership of the Council;

11. *Decides* that the Council shall apply the rules of procedure established for committees of the General Assembly, as applicable, unless subsequently otherwise decided by the Assembly or the Council, and also decides that the participation of and consultation with observers, including States that are not members of the Council, the specialized agencies, other intergovernmental organizations and national human rights institutions, as well as non-governmental organizations, shall be based on arrangements, including Economic and Social Council resolution 1996/31 of 25 July 1996 and practices observed by the Commission on Human Rights, while ensuring the most effective contribution of these entities;

12. *Decides also* that the methods of work of the Council shall be transparent, fair and impartial and shall enable genuine dialogue, be results-oriented, allow for subsequent follow-up discussions to recommendations and their implementation and also allow for substantive interaction with special procedures and mechanisms;

13. *Recommends* that the Economic and Social Council request the Commission on Human Rights to conclude its work at its sixty-second session, and that it abolish the Commission on 16 June 2006;

14. *Decides* to elect the new members of the Council; the terms of membership shall be staggered, and such decision shall be taken for the first election

by the drawing of lots, taking into consideration equitable geographical distribution;

15. *Decides also* that elections of the first members of the Council shall take place on 9 May 2006, and that the first meeting of the Council shall be convened on 19 June 2006;

16. *Decides further* that the Council shall review its work and functioning five years after its establishment and report to the General Assembly.

A key substantive innovation was the decision to undertake a "universal periodic review, based on objective and reliable information, of the fulfilment by each State of its human rights obligations and commitments." Intended to complement the work of other mechanisms, the universal periodic review (UPR) considers the human rights record of every member of the United Nations. States are reviewed in an order initially determined by lot, with fourteen reviewed at each of the Council's three annual sessions. This means that every member state is reviewed about every four-and-a-half years.

Each state first submits a national report of up to twenty pages that is intended to outline steps that have been taken to promote and protect human rights, including action taken since the last review.[12]

NATIONAL REPORT SUBMITTED IN ACCORDANCE WITH PARAGRAPH 5 OF THE ANNEX TO HUMAN RIGHTS COUNCIL RESOLUTION 16/21—CHINA (5 AUGUST 2013)[13]

1. The present report was compiled on the basis of the "General guidelines for the preparation of information under the universal periodic review" . . . It focuses on introducing the policies and practices undertaken to promote and protect human rights in China, including the Mainland, Hong Kong Special Administrative Region and Macao Special Administrative Region since the first-cycle universal periodic review in 2009, as well as the implementation of recommendations accepted at the time of the first-cycle review, the challenges remaining, and future goals for human rights work. . . .

2. To compile the present report, China's Ministry of Foreign Affairs took the lead in setting up a special task force comprising representatives of nearly 30 legislative, judicial and administrative organs of the national Government . . . The Ministry also solicited the oral and written opinions

---

[12] UN Doc. A/HRC/DEC/17/119 (2011).
[13] UN Doc. A/HRC/WG.6/17/CHN/1 (2013).

of nearly 20 non-governmental organizations and academic institutions ...
Broad public input on the report was sought via the website of the Ministry
of Foreign Affairs. ...

4. China respects the principle of universality of human rights, and is of
the view that all countries have a duty to take measures, commensurate with
their national conditions, continuously to promote and protect human rights
in accordance with the purposes and principles of the Charter of the United
Nations and the basic spirit of the Universal Declaration of Human Rights
and the relevant international human rights instruments. The international
community should accord equal attention to the achievement of civil and
political rights, economic, social and cultural rights, and the right to development; it should also promote the coordinated development of individual
and collective human rights. China is committed to carrying out exchanges
and cooperation on human rights with all countries, and to promoting the
resolution of human rights issues in a fair, objective and non-selective manner by the international community.

5. The Chinese Government is working to explore paths for human rights
development, establishing a robust system of human rights safeguards, and
continuously enriching the theory of human rights, all within the framework of socialism with Chinese characteristics. It strongly advocates a scientific outlook on development, emphasizes "putting people first", and takes
the furtherance and protection of the right to subsistence and the right to
development as first principles. It coordinates and promotes the safeguarding of civil, political, social, and cultural rights as well as the rights of special
groups, develops a broader, fuller and sounder people's democracy, and com-
prehensively promotes the coordinated development of rights of all kinds. It
fosters a fairer and more harmonious society, and works to ensure that every
citizen enjoys a life of ever-greater dignity, freedom and well-being. ...

23. The Chinese Government gives first priority to the realization of the
people's rights to subsistence and to development, and has achieved clear
improvements in promoting those rights for people in poverty and vulnerable groups. ...

44. Although the death penalty is retained in China, it is strictly controlled and sparingly used. In the past few years, China has further reduced
its application by taking a series of important measures to improve and per-
fect the evidence system in death penalty cases, reduce the number of capital
crimes, and codify the standards for application of the death penalty and the
procedures by which such cases are handled. ...

48. The re-education through labour system is an educational and correctional measure that is commensurate with China's national conditions; it
has examination and approval procedures, oversight mechanisms and relief
channels that are set by statute. The Government organs under whose purview it falls are presently in the process of studying specific proposals for
actively and steadily promoting reform of the system of reeducation through
labour. ...

53. China is continuously improving and perfecting its laws in order to prevent and suppress unlawful acts by individual judicial officials, such as the extraction of confessions under torture in the process of collecting evidence in a case. . . .

A second report of up to ten pages compiles information based on reports from the treaty bodies and special procedures, including observations and comments by the state concerned, and of the Office of the UN High Commissioner for Human Rights, as well as other relevant UN documents.[14]

A third document is a ten-page report compiled by the Office of the High Commissioner for Human Rights based on "[a]dditional, credible and reliable information provided by other relevant stakeholders."[15]

SUMMARY PREPARED BY THE OFFICE OF THE HIGH COMMISSIONER FOR HUMAN RIGHTS—CHINA (30 JULY 2013)[16]

22. [Human Rights in China (HRIC)] noted that since China's last UPR, it instituted a series of reforms regarding the death penalty. Dui Hua Foundation (DHF) reported that an estimated 16,500 people were executed from 2009–2012 a 39 percent decline over 2005–2008 and that the vice health minister stated that China will phase out its reliance on executed prisoners as organ donors by 2015. DHF recommended that China continue to work towards abolition including by: making public death penalty verdicts and sentencing data; and reducing the number of capital crimes, particularly non-violent and economic crimes.

23. According to [Human Rights Watch], the use of torture remained endemic in China's criminal justice system as well as by other branches of Government. . . .

24. According to HRIC, legal experts noted a resurgence of informal, extra-legal political institutions that advanced predatory and repressive government policies, including "black jails" and enforced disappearances used to target activists, petitioners and dissidents. . . .

25. HRIC observed that the current "re-education through labour" (RTL) system vested broad discretionary power in local officials, resulting in regular targeting of petitioners raising legitimate grievances. HRW stated that, in

---

[14] See, e.g., UN Doc. A/HRC/WG.6/17/CHN/2.
[15] Human Rights Council Resolution 5/1 (2007), Annex, para 15(c).
[16] UN Doc. A/HRC/WG.6/17/CHN/3 (2013) (footnotes omitted).

early 2013, the Government indicated that it was considering dismantling the administrative detention system of RTL. CHRD stated that the main reform appeared to be cosmetic—renaming RTL as "Illegal Behaviour Correction". . . .

33. [A joint submission from Dutch and Canadian lawyers] and [China Human Rights Lawyers Concern Group] reported on alleged severe repression faced by lawyers in China, particularly those working on sensitive cases, such as representing Falun Gong practitioners, Tibetan activists, land rights activists or HIV victims. [Chinese Urgent Action Working Group (CUAWG)] reported that, in 2012, the Ministry of Justice demanded that all licensed lawyers take a loyalty oath to the Communist Party, placing that loyalty above their clients. According to [a joint submission from Front Line Defenders and CUAWG], barefoot lawyers—mainly defence lawyers who did not have a license—had addressed the gap in access to legal aid left by the persecution of licensed lawyers. . . .

41. International Federation of Journalists stated that from 2009–2012 China continued to control domestic media and block international media from monitoring issues that China thinks are politically "sensitive". . . .

44. [Pen-International] alleged that there were reportedly between 20,000–50,000 employees of the "Internet police" working to maintain stability by flagging and removing content and monitoring who was posting material offensive to the Government. . . .

After these three documents have been submitted, a review takes place in the form of an "interactive session" between the state concerned and other member states. Any member state can pose questions or comments, or make recommendations. A troika of three states chosen by lot facilitate the discussion. (For China's 2013 review, the troika was Poland, Sierra Leone, and the United Arab Emirates.) "Other relevant stakeholders" are able to make "general comments" before the adoption of the outcome document.

REPORT OF THE WORKING GROUP ON THE UNIVERSAL PERIODIC REVIEW—CHINA (4 DECEMBER 2013)[17]

I. Summary of the proceedings of the review process

. . .

25. During the interactive dialogue, 137 delegations made statements. . . .

---

[17] UN Doc. A/HRC/25/5.

26. The Bolivarian Republic of Venezuela praised the universal social pension system, the wide-reaching medical insurance system and high voter turnout.

27. Viet Nam commended the informative report and noted that human rights protection was an evolving process. . . .

164. Switzerland commended reduction in the scope of the application of death penalty but expressed concern about repression towards civil society. . . .

176. The United Kingdom of Great Britain and Northern Ireland expressed concern about restrictions on freedom of expression and association and urged greater transparency over the use of the death penalty.

177. The United Republic of Tanzania welcomed economic achievement, including affordable urban-housing construction and encouraged China to share its economic experience and practices with developing countries.

178. The United States of America was concerned about suppression of freedoms of assembly, association, religion and expression, policies harmful to ethnic minorities, and harassment, detention, and punishment of activists, including Xu Zhiyong and Yang Maodong. . . .

184. China was regretful that a small number of countries labelled its crackdown on terrorism that had undermined the security of civilians as cleansing of specific ethnic groups or religions, and glorified a few criminals in China as "human rights defenders". It expressed its confidence in elevating the human rights of its people to a higher level.

185. China expressed its gratitude to most countries, developing countries in particular, who had recognized tremendous efforts and achievements made by China in human rights and had appreciated difficulties and challenges China was facing, and raised constructive ideas and recommendations. It committed to seriously studying all recommendations in light of its national conditions and giving feedback to the Human Rights Council on time.

II. Conclusions and/or recommendations

186. The following recommendations will be examined by China which will provide responses in due time, but no later than the twenty-fifth session of the Human Rights Council in March 2014:

186.1. Ratify ICCPR. . .

186.59. Establish a national human rights institution, in accordance with the Paris Principles (New Zealand); Set up a national institution in line with the Paris Principles and ensure a climate that is favourable to the activities of human rights defenders, journalists and other civil society actors (Tunisia);

186.60. Keep up its commitment to uphold its human rights treaty obligations and engage constructively with the human rights mechanisms, including the special procedures (Ghana);

186.61. Ensure that its citizens can freely engage in the UPR process (Czech Republic);

186.62. Ensure that human rights defenders can exercise their legitimate activities, including participation in international mechanisms, without being subjected to reprisals (Switzerland); . . .

186.115. End the use of harassment, detention, arrest, and extralegal measures such as enforced disappearance to control and silence human rights activists as well as their family members and friends (United States of America); . . .

186.149. Facilitate the development, in law and practice, of a safe and enabling environment in which both civil society and human rights defenders can operate free from fear, hindrance and insecurity (Ireland); . . .

186.155. Reform legislation and law enforcement in order to ensure freedom of opinion and expression, including on the internet (Germany);

186.156. Take effective measures to guarantee the freedom of expression and the media through amending existing laws and practices, including its State Secrets Law, and to release all human rights defenders and journalists (Czech Republic);..

186.159. Remove all the obstacles to freedom of information on the Internet, and guarantee freedom of expression, assembly and association for all (France);

186.160. Take steps that all persons including bloggers, journalists and human rights defenders can freely exercise their right to freedom of expression, online as well as offline, without fear from censorship or persecution (Austria);

186.161. Undertake measures enabling unrestricted use of Internet to all members of the society (Estonia); . . .

186.170. Increase transparency of its traditional and social media by guaranteeing the rights of Chinese citizens to freely critique any state organ or functionary (Australia); . . .

The state concerned finally presents its views on the conclusions and/or recommendations that have been made.

VIEWS ON CONCLUSIONS AND/OR RECOMMENDATIONS, VOLUNTARY COMMITMENTS AND REPLIES PRESENTED BY THE STATE UNDER REVIEW—CHINA (27 FEBRUARY 2014)[18]

The Chinese government has carefully examined the 252 recommendations that it received during the seventeenth session of the Working Group on the Universal Periodic Review of the Human Rights Council. The Chinese government accepts 204 recommendations, including those that have already

---

[18] UN Doc. A/HRC/25/5/Add.1.

been put into practice or are being implemented, and does not accept 48 recommendations because they are inconsistent with China's basic national conditions or contradict China's constitutional principles and spirit of its domestic laws. The specific replies are as follows: . . .

186.1. **Not Accepted.** China is now prudently carrying out its judicial and administrative reform to actively prepare for the ratification of the ICCPR. No specific timetable for the ratification of the ICCPR could be set out so far. . . .

186.59. **Not Accepted.** China has not established a national human rights institution in terms of the Paris Principles. However, many government agencies in China assume and share similar responsibilities. The issue of establishing a national human rights institution falls into China's sovereignty, and should be considered in a holistic manner in accordance with its national conditions.

186.60. **Accepted.**

186.61. **Accepted.**

186.62. **Accepted and already implemented.** There are a large number of organizations and individuals that safeguard others' rights and interests in China. Their activities are encouraged, protected and supported by the Chinese government. No one suffers reprisal for taking part in lawful activities or international mechanisms. As for the individuals or organizations engaging in illegal activities in the name of safeguarding human rights, they will be duly prosecuted by the Chinese government will enforce punishment according to law. [*sic*] . . .

186.115. **Not Accepted.** There are no arbitrary or extrajudicial detentions in China. All criminal and security detentions are decided on and implemented based on the Criminal Procedure Law and Law on Public Security Administration of China. According to China's Constitution and relevant laws, all citizens enjoy freedom of speech, the press, assembly, association and religious belief, and shall not harm the national, social and collective interests and legitimate rights of other citizens when exercising the above-mentioned rights. Illegal and criminal activities shall be prosecuted according to law. . . .

186.149. **Accepted and being implemented.** In accordance with China's Constitution and relevant national laws, citizens enjoy freedom of expression, the press, assembly, association, procession, demonstration, and religious belief. The Chinese government guarantees citizens' right to exercise these freedoms in accordance with the law. Chinese judicial organs impartially deal with all violations of citizens' personal and democratic rights according to law. There is no so-called issue of suppressing "human rights defenders". . . .

186.155. **Accepted.**

186.156. **Not Accepted.** There are specific provisions in a number of Chinese laws on the freedom of speech and the press. There is no plan to amend the State Secrets Law so far. China is a country under the rule of law. Everyone is equal before the law. Chinese judicial organs deal with people engaging in illegal and criminal activities according to law.

186.159. **Not Accepted.** See 186.115. Flow of information on the Internet is open and free in China. However, with the rapid development of the Internet, cyber security problems such as gambling, pornography, violence, and hacking are posing increasing threats to the legitimate rights and interests of the public. To ensure the safe flow of information, the Chinese government has the responsibility to prevent the flooding of harmful information and take steps to fight cybercrime.

186.160. **Not Accepted.** See 186.159.

186.161. **Not Accepted.** See 186.159.

186.170. **Accepted and being implemented.** China's Constitution stipulates that citizens have the right to criticize and make suggestions to any state organ or official. The traditional and social media in China are responsible for what and how they should report. But they must operate within the scope prescribed by law, and the content of their report should be true and credible. . . .

China will next undergo its periodic review in April 2018.

QUESTIONS

6. Is the Human Rights Council structure and mandate an improvement over the Commission on Human Rights?
7. What is your impression of the Universal Periodic Review? It focuses on obligations voluntarily undertaken by the state in question, and gives that state the last word. Is this a necessary compromise or a fundamental weakness?
8. Why do states comply with international human rights law? How effective are the UN mechanisms for inducing or trying to compel compliance?
9. How might the United Nations' monitoring of human rights be improved? How realistic is it that such improvements would be adopted by member states?

13.3 The Right to Privacy in the Digital Age

Revolutions in technology and the inexorable drive of globalization mean that people around the world are more connected and have more access to information than ever before. At the same time, however, these new forms of communication are vulnerable to surveillance and interception. Revelations by Edward Snowden and others about the extent of government and corporate spying on individuals around the world put the topic on the agenda of the High Commissioner for Human Rights.

REMARKS BY MS. NAVI PILLAY, UN HIGH COMMISSIONER FOR HUMAN RIGHTS: "HOW TO SAFEGUARD THE RIGHT TO PRIVACY IN THE DIGITAL AGE?" (GENEVA, 20 SEPTEMBER 2013)

The right to privacy is anchored firmly in international human rights law. The modern benchmarks for the right to privacy at the international level are the Universal Declaration of Human Rights and the International Covenant on Civil and Political Rights, to date ratified by 167 States around the world.

Under its article 17, the ICCPR provides, and I quote, that "No one shall be subjected to arbitrary or unlawful interference with his privacy, family, home or correspondence, nor to unlawful attacks on his honour and reputation". It further states that "Everyone has the right to the protection of the law against such interference or attacks."

The Human Rights Committee has provided important guidance in its General Comment 16 on the interpretation of article 17. According to the Committee, the term "unlawful" means that no interference can take place "except in cases envisaged by the law. Interference authorized by States can only take place on the basis of law, which itself must comply with the provisions, aims and objectives of the Covenant".

The expression "arbitrary interference", in the Committee's view, can also extend to interference provided for under the law. The introduction of this concept, the Committee has explained, "is intended to guarantee that even interference provided for by law should be in accordance with the provisions, aims and objectives of the Covenant and should be, in any event, reasonable in the particular circumstances". . . .

So what are the challenges and questions that may need to be further explored in applying this legal framework and to promoting and protecting the right to privacy in the digital age? . . .

A first challenge relates to the manner in which respect for the right to privacy is guaranteed by legislative, administrative or judicial authorities. Effective *national legal frameworks* are critical to ensuring protection against unlawful or arbitrary interference. Yet, in general, national legislation has not been adopted to match developments in communications technology and the surveillance measures these developments have facilitated. In addition, in some jurisdictions there is a lack of independent oversight to review surveillance measures, as a safeguard against abuse.

A second challenge is related to the fact that, even where adequate legislation and oversight mechanisms do exist, a *lack of effective enforcement* is bound to contribute to a lack of accountability for arbitrary or unlawful intrusions on the right to privacy.

A third challenge relates to the rapid and significant advances in communications and information technology, and a *blurring of lines between the public and private sphere*, which has prompted some to call for greater attention to the scope of the right to privacy. What is the meaning of "privacy" or "private communication", in the digital age? What are the privacy interests inherent in communications data transmitted over the internet or by mobile phone? . . .

A fourth related challenge concerns the definition of legitimate parameters for *national security surveillance*, which, increasingly, impacts on the right to privacy of individuals. In the pursuit of legitimate national security interests, governments are entitled to gather and protect certain sensitive information, as well as to restrict access of the public to certain information (such as that pertaining to operations, sources and methods of intelligence services).

In so doing, however, they must ensure full compliance with international human rights law. Serious concerns are raised over the potential for national security overreach, without adequate safeguards to protect against abuse. . . .

The last challenge I would like to draw to your attention relates to the *responsibility of businesses themselves* to respect privacy rights in the digital age. How to ensure that corporations in the communications and technology industry respect the right to privacy and other related human rights?

Again, States have an obligation to protect individuals against violations not only by their own agents, but also against acts of private persons or entities, including businesses. The Guiding Principles on Business and Human Rights, endorsed by the Human Rights Council in 2011, set out a global standard for preventing and addressing adverse impacts on human rights linked to business activity. There have been important multi-stakeholder efforts to clarify their application to the communications and information technology industry. One of the challenges, of course, lies in the transnational nature of the communications and information technology industry, which can create legal and jurisdictional hurdles to the effective protection of the right to privacy.

Three months later, the General Assembly adopted by consensus a resolution sponsored by Brazil and Germany expressing deep concern about the impact that surveillance and interception of communications was having on human rights.

GENERAL ASSEMBLY RESOLUTION 68/167 (2013): THE RIGHT TO PRIVACY IN THE DIGITAL AGE

The General Assembly, ...

Noting that the rapid pace of technological development enables individuals all over the world to use new information and communication technologies and at the same time enhances the capacity of governments, companies and individuals to undertake surveillance, interception and data collection, which may violate or abuse human rights, in particular the right to privacy, ...

Noting that while concerns about public security may justify the gathering and protection of certain sensitive information, States must ensure full compliance with their obligations under international human rights law,

Deeply concerned at the negative impact that surveillance and/or interception of communications, including extraterritorial surveillance and/or interception of communications, as well as the collection of personal data, in particular when carried out on a mass scale, may have on the exercise and enjoyment of human rights,

Reaffirming that States must ensure that any measures taken to combat terrorism are in compliance with their obligations under international law, in particular international human rights, refugee and humanitarian law,

1. *Reaffirms* the right to privacy, according to which no one shall be subjected to arbitrary or unlawful interference with his or her privacy, family, home or correspondence, and the right to the protection of the law against such interference ...

3. *Affirms* that the same rights that people have offline must also be protected online, including the right to privacy;

4. *Calls upon* all States:

(*a*) To respect and protect the right to privacy, including in the context of digital communication;

(*b*) To take measures to put an end to violations of those rights and to create the conditions to prevent such violations, including by ensuring that relevant national legislation complies with their obligations under international human rights law;

(*c*) To review their procedures, practices and legislation regarding the surveillance of communications, their interception and the collection of personal data, including mass surveillance, interception and collection, with a view to upholding the right to privacy by ensuring the full and effective implementation of all their obligations under international human rights law;

(*d*) To establish or maintain existing independent, effective domestic oversight mechanisms capable of ensuring transparency, as appropriate, and accountability for State surveillance of communications, their interception and the collection of personal data; ...

The High Commissioner subsequently presented a report on the topic, which emphasized the need for "further discussion and in-depth study of issues relating to the effective protection of the law, procedural safeguards, effective oversight, and remedies."[19]

QUESTIONS

10. Resolution 68/167 (2013) was the subject of intense negotiations. A key compromise was dropping language that had stated that domestic and international interception and collection of communications and personal data, "in particular massive surveillance," may constitute a human rights violation. Instead, the preamble expresses deep concern at "the negative impact" that such surveillance, "in particular when carried out on a mass scale, may have on the exercise and enjoyment of human rights." How significant are these changes?

11. One contentious point that remained was that the resolution does not distinguish between the privacy rights of citizens and non-citizens. This contrasts with the different legal protections that many states grant their own citizens and foreigners. Do states owe human rights obligations to noncitizens? Should they?

12. The concerns behind efforts to protect privacy are often premised on the idea that states engage in surveillance and interception of communications. In fact it is often corporations that are actually gathering the data, or individuals who are voluntarily supplying it. What impact, if any, should this have on the human rights debate over privacy in the digital age?

13.4 Is the United Nations Bound by Its Own Human Rights Norms?

The United Nations is not a party to the human rights treaties negotiated under its auspices or monitored through its agencies. In part this reflects the traditional view that only states properly enter into such treaties, a view based on the understanding that it is primarily states that violate or protect human rights. As the United Nations has assumed state-like functions, however—including administrations that ran entire territories, discussed in Chapter 9—the question of whether the United Nations is required to abide by basic human rights standards has become more pressing.[20]

---

[19] UN Doc. A/HRC/27/37 (2014), para. 51.

[20] A separate but related question is whether the United Nations and other international organizations can be responsible for internationally wrongful acts, considered in Chapter 4.

In the early 1990s, the end of the Cold War led to increased hopes that the United Nations would become a major vehicle for promoting human rights. The Vienna Declaration and Programme of Action, excerpted below, was one of the most prominent.

VIENNA DECLARATION AND PROGRAMME OF ACTION, AS ADOPTED BY THE WORLD CONFERENCE ON HUMAN RIGHTS, 25 JUNE 1993[21]

Recognizing and affirming that all human rights derive from the dignity and worth inherent in the human person, and that the human person is the central subject of human rights and fundamental freedoms, and consequently should be the principal beneficiary and should participate actively in the realization of these rights and freedoms,

Reaffirming their commitment to the purposes and principles contained in the Charter of the United Nations and the Universal Declaration of Human Rights,

Reaffirming the commitment contained in Article 56 of the Charter of the United Nations to take joint and separate action, placing proper emphasis on developing effective international cooperation for the realization of the purposes set out in Article 55, including universal respect for, and observance of, human rights and fundamental freedoms for all,

Emphasizing the responsibilities of all States, in conformity with the Charter of the United Nations, to develop and encourage respect for human rights and fundamental freedoms for all, without distinction as to race, sex, language or religion,

Recalling the Preamble to the Charter of the United Nations, in particular the determination to reaffirm faith in fundamental human rights, in the dignity and worth of the human person, and in the equal rights of men and women and of nations large and small, ...

Emphasizing that the Universal Declaration of Human Rights, which constitutes a common standard of achievement for all peoples and all nations, is the source of inspiration and has been the basis for the United Nations in making advances in standard setting as contained in the existing international human rights instruments, in particular the International Covenant on Civil and Political Rights and the International Covenant on Economic, Social and Cultural Rights. ...

Recognizing that the activities of the United Nations in the field of human rights should be rationalized and enhanced in order to strengthen the United

---

[21] UN Doc. A/Conf.157/23 (1993).

Nations machinery in this field and to further the objectives of universal respect for observance of international human rights standards, . . .

Invoking the spirit of our age and the realities of our time which call upon the peoples of the world and all States Members of the United Nations to rededicate themselves to the global task of promoting and protecting all human rights and fundamental freedoms so as to secure full and universal enjoyment of these rights, . . .

Solemnly adopts the Vienna Declaration and Programme of Action.

I

1. The World Conference on Human Rights reaffirms the solemn commitment of all States to fulfil their obligations to promote universal respect for, and observance and protection of, all human rights and fundamental freedoms for all in accordance with the Charter of the United Nations, other instruments relating to human rights, and international law. The universal nature of these rights and freedoms is beyond question.

In this framework, enhancement of international cooperation in the field of human rights is essential for the full achievement of the purposes of the United Nations.

Human rights and fundamental freedoms are the birthright of all human beings; their protection and promotion is the first responsibility of Governments. . . .

35. The full and effective implementation of United Nations activities to promote and protect human rights must reflect the high importance accorded to human rights by the Charter of the United Nations and the demands of the United Nations human rights activities, as mandated by Member States. To this end, United Nations human rights activities should be provided with increased resources.

Arguments that the United Nations should be bound sometimes proceed on the basis that such a conclusion is self-evident from the purposes and principles of the UN Charter. This argument assumes that the text of that treaty limits or defines the powers but also the obligations of the organization.

A second approach asserts that, even if it is not a party to human rights treaties, the United Nations has sufficient legal personality to be bound by customary international law. Legal personality has been discussed with respect to the *Reparations* case in Chapter 4. On the sources of law, the Statute of the International Court of Justice is commonly regarded to be an authoritative statement.[22] It provides that, in addition to treaties or conventions, international custom can also be a source of law.

---

[22] Note that the United Nations cannot be brought before the International Court of Justice; only states may be parties to contentious proceedings.

STATUTE OF THE INTERNATIONAL COURT OF JUSTICE

Article 38

1. The Court, whose function is to decide in accordance with international law such disputes as are submitted to it, shall apply:

(a) international conventions, whether general or particular, establishing rules expressly recognized by the contesting states;

(b) international custom, as evidence of a general practice accepted as law;

(c) the general principles of law recognized by civilized nations;

(d) ... judicial decisions and the teachings of the most highly qualified publicists of the various nations, as subsidiary means for the determination of rules of law.

The International Law Commission, which considers the codification and progressive development of international law, has commenced a project on the identification of customary international law. In the second report of its special rapporteur, it addressed—indirectly—the question of international organizations contributing to the creation of and being bound by custom. (See also the discussion of the responsibility of international organizations in Chapter 15, section 15.2.)

SECOND REPORT ON IDENTIFICATION OF CUSTOMARY INTERNATIONAL LAW, BY MICHAEL WOOD, SPECIAL RAPPORTEUR (22 MAY 2014)[23]

12. The debates in the Commission and in the Sixth Committee in 2013 confirmed the utility of the present topic, which aims particularly to offer practical guidance to those, in whatever capacity, called upon to identify rules of customary international law, in particular those who are not necessarily specialists in the general field of public international law. It is important that there be a degree of clarity in the practical application of this central aspect of international law, while recognizing of course that the customary process is inherently flexible. ....

13. It is not of course the object of the present topic to determine the substance of the rules of customary international law, or to address the important question of who is bound by particular rules (States, international organizations, other subjects of international law). The topic deals

---

[23] UN Doc. A/CN.4/672.

solely with the methodological question of the identification of customary international law. ...

41. Given the inevitability and pace of change, political and technological, it is neither possible nor desirable to seek to provide an exhaustive list of these "material sources" of customary international law ... The following list is therefore non-exhaustive; moreover, some of the categories below overlap, so that a particular example or type of State practice may well fall under more than one.

(a) *Physical actions of States* ...

(b) *Acts of the executive branch* ...

(c) *Diplomatic acts and correspondence* ...

(i) *Resolutions of organs of international organizations, such as the General Assembly of the United Nations, and international conferences.* This mainly concerns the practice of States in connection with the adoption of resolutions of organs of international organizations or at international conferences, namely, voting in favour or against them (or abstaining), and the explanations (if any) attached to such acts. At the same time, it must be borne in mind that "the final text of a decision of an international organization will always be incapable of reflecting all propositions and alternatives formulated by each and every party to the negotiations. ... One should, therefore, not overly rely on the shortcuts provided by the decisionmaking processes of international organizations in order to identify state practice".[24] ...

43. *The practice of international (inter-governmental) organizations.* This is an important field that will be covered in greater detail in the third report. Bearing in mind that "[t]he subjects of law in any legal system are not necessarily identical in their nature or in the extent of their rights, and their nature depends upon the needs of the community",[25] the acts of international organizations on which States have conferred authority may also contribute or attest to the formation of a general practice in the fields in which those organizations operate. In assessing the practice of such organizations one ought to distinguish between practice relating to the internal affairs of the organization on the one hand, and the practice of the organization in its relations with States, international organizations, etc., on the other. It is the latter practice that is relevant for present purposes, and which mostly consists of "operational activities", defined by one author as "the programmatic work of international organizations carried out as part of their overall mission or in fulfilment of a specific mandate".[26] Another important distinction

---

[24] J. Wouters and P. De Man, "International Organizations as Law-Makers," in J. Klabbers and A. Wallendahl (eds), *Research Handbook on the Law of International Organizations* (Cheltenham: Edward Elgar, 2011), pp. 190, 208 (reference omitted).
[25] *Reparations for injuries suffered in the service of the United Nations*, Advisory Opinion, I.C.J. Reports 1949, p. 174, at 178.
[26] I. Johnstone, "Law-Making through the Operational Activities of International Organizations," *George Washington International Law Review*, vol. 40 (2008), p. 94.

should be drawn in this context between the practice of organs or other bodies composed of the representatives of States and that of organs composed of individuals serving in their personal capacity, as the latter cannot be said to represent States. A distinction should, moreover, be made between "products of the secretariats of international organizations and products of the intergovernmental organs of international organizations. While both can provide materials that can be consulted ... the greater weight ... [is] to be given to the products of the latter, whose authors are also the primary authors of state practice." While it has been suggested that "IOs provide shortcuts to finding custom",[27] considerable caution is required in assessing their practice. Considerations that apply to the practice of States may also be relevant to the practice of international organizations, and the present report should be read in that light.

44. The practice of those international organizations (such as the European Union) to which Member States sometimes have transferred exclusive competences, may be equated with that of States, since in particular fields such organizations act in place of the Member States. This applies to the actions of such organizations, whatever forms they take, whether executive, legislative or judicial. If one were not to equate the practice of such international organizations with that of States, it would in fact mean that, not only would the organization's practice not count for State practice, but its Member States would be deprived or reduced of their ability to contribute to State practice in cases where the Member States have conferred some of their public powers to the organization.

A third approach focuses on the activities of the United Nations and the state-like functions that it is now exercising. As it is widely held that all states are subject to at least basic human rights law, it is questionable whether those states can avoid such obligations by acting through the United Nations. A key problem in this regard is Article 103 of the UN Charter, which provides that the Charter prevails over other treaty obligations—including treaties adopted subsequently. (This exception to the normal rule of treaties is specifically provided for in Article 30 of the Vienna Convention on the Law of Treaties.)

This question has been examined most thoroughly in the area of targeted financial sanctions, discussed in Chapter 10. Related questions have also arisen when the United Nations engaged in detentions without trial in Kosovo (see Chapter 14) and in the context of whether the laws of war apply to forces operating under a UN Security Council mandate.[28]

---

[27] J.E. Alvarez, *International Organizations as Law-Makers* (Oxford: Oxford University Press, 2005), p. 592.

[28] See Simon Chesterman, "The United Nations and the Law of War: Power and Sensibility in International Law," *Fordham Journal of International Law*, vol. 28 (2005), pp. 531–541.

QUESTIONS

13. Does the United Nations need to be bound by human rights norms in order to comply with those norms? How might this be different from states that are "bound" by human rights obligations that may lack any enforcement mechanism?
14. What role for the United Nations is envisaged in the treaties included in this chapter? What role is envisaged in declarations such as that which emerged from the World Conference on Human Rights in 1993?
15. In such documents, is there any indication of a wariness that the United Nations itself might have trouble living up to the standards it is espousing?
16. Can international organizations contribute to the creation of customary international law without being bound by it? Should they be able to?

HYPOTHETICAL

Imagine that you represent a state participating in a convention tasked with drafting a supplementary human rights declaration focusing on (1) the right to privacy in a digital age, and (2) the human rights obligations of the United Nations. How would you approach negotiations? What restrictions, if any, would you impose on government surveillance? What legal and policy considerations would determine your approach to the attribution of human rights responsibilities to the United Nations? If practical, convene a simulation of the convention with a variety of states represented and see what agreement (if any) is possible.

Further Reading

Alston, Philip and Ryan Goodman. *International Human Rights*. Oxford: Oxford University Press, 2012.

Alston, Philip and Frédéric Mégret (eds). *The United Nations and Human Rights: A Critical Appraisal*. 2nd edn. Oxford: Oxford University Press, 2016.

Donnelly, Jack. *International Human Rights*. 3rd edn. Boulder, CO: Westview, 2007.

Freedman, Rosa. *The United Nations Human Rights Council: A Critique and Early Assessment*. New York: Routledge, 2013.

Hannum, Hurst, S. James Anaya and Dinah Shelton. *International Human Rights: Problems of Law, Policy, and Practice*. 5th edn. New York: Aspen, 2011.

Joseph, Sarah and Adam McBeth (eds). *Research Handbook on International Human Rights Law*. Cheltenham: Edward Elgar, 2010.

Kälin, Walter and Jörg Künzli. *The Law of International Human Rights Protection*. Oxford: Oxford University Press, 2009.

Keller, Helen and Geir Ulfstein (eds). *UN Human Rights Treaty Bodies: Law and Legitimacy*. Cambridge: Cambridge University Press, 2012.

Mégrét, Fréderic and Florian Hoffman. "The UN as a Human Rights Violator? Some Reflections on the United Nations Changing Human Rights Responsibilities." *Human Rights Quarterly*, vol. 25(2) (2002), p. 314.

Morsink, Johannes. *The Universal Declaration of Human Rights: Origins, Drafting, and Intent*. Philadelphia: University of Pennsylvania Press, 2000.

chapter fourteen
....

The Rule of Law
and Transitional Justice

The United Nations was created by treaty and its Charter mentions law in both the preamble and the first article, establishing that a key purpose of the organization is to resolve disputes "in conformity with the principles of justice and international law." The Universal Declaration of Human Rights, adopted three years later in 1948, stresses in its opening lines that it is essential that "human rights should be protected by the rule of law." Half a century later, every member state of the United Nations reaffirmed "the need for universal adherence to and implementation of the rule of law at both the national and international levels" and their commitment to "an international order based on the rule of law and international law."[1]

The international dimension of these commitments—to a world in which treaties are respected and customary international law is upheld—has been far less problematic than the national dimension. Though the Charter mentions in passing the obligation to maintain law and order in the colonies designated as Trust Territories,[2] the extent to which the United Nations might affect *domestic* legal institutions quickly runs up against the obstacle of Article 2(7). If the United Nations is not meant to intervene in matters that are "essentially within the domestic jurisdiction" of member states except under Chapter VII, how much can it do to promote the rule of law?

Quite a lot, as it happens. This chapter will consider UN practice in three broad areas. First, Article 2(7) does not prohibit assistance when states invite or consent to it. Much rule of law work is conducted in the form of *development assistance*, based on the understanding that a robust legal framework supports economic progress. Similarly, the United Nations or other international actors may be requested to support *transitional justice* measures in the context of a peace process or to avoid a conflict—a key question that has arisen here is the tension between seeking justice and avoiding conflict.

---

[1] GA Res. 60/1 (2005), para. 134.
[2] UN Charter, Art 84. The last Trust Territory, Palau, became independent in 1994. See further Chapter 1, section 1.1.

Third, beginning in the 1990s, the Security Council has on occasion used its Chapter VII powers to impose rule of law measures with a view to *maintaining peace and security*. These measures have included international criminal tribunals as well as hybrid tribunals, to some extent now supplanted by the International Criminal Court that was created in 2002.

The present chapter will consider each of these areas in turn. Before we do so, however, it is necessary to highlight one of the reasons the rule of law has been so widely accepted by states with very different political traditions and interests: vagueness as to its precise meaning.

Among legal philosophers there are long-standing debates over whether the rule of law should be understood in a "thin" or "thick" sense. The "thin" conception refers only to the formal aspects of a legal system, such as its institutions and procedures. A "thick" use of the rule of law includes the content of the law, often embracing substantive goals such as the protection of specific rights or the achievement of particular economic ends.[3] Critics of a "thin" conception say that it does not distinguish between good laws and bad laws. Critics of a "thick" conception say that it smuggles concepts of human rights and democracy into the definition for political reasons.[4]

Further complications arise when one applies the rule of law to the international level. The historical origin of the rule of law within a state can be traced to efforts to regularize and limit the powers of a sovereign—the rule of law is thus distinct from "rule of man," implying power exercised at the whim of an absolute ruler, and from "rule by law," whereby a ruler exercises power in a non-arbitrary fashion but is not him- or herself bound by law in any meaningful sense. In a national legal order, the sovereign existed in a *vertical* hierarchy with other subjects of law—the modern counterpart would be a government and other institutions of the state. At the international level, however, sovereignty tends to be conceived of as remaining with states, existing in a *horizontal* plane of sovereign equality.[5]

So although there is general agreement that the rule of law is a good thing, its precise contours are open to negotiation. In 2004, UN Secretary-General Kofi Annan provided a definition that is frequently used within the United Nations. He described the rule of law as

> a principle of governance in which all persons, institutions and entities, public and private, including the State itself, are accountable to laws that are publicly promulgated, equally enforced and independently adjudicated,

---

[3] See, e.g., Paul Craig, "Formal and Substantive Conceptions of the Rule of Law: An Analytical Framework." [1997] *Public Law* 466, p. 467.

[4] The "thin" notion of the rule of law was the dominant perspective at least until the end of the nineteenth century.

[5] See further Simon Chesterman, "An International Rule of Law?" *American Journal of Comparative Law*, vol. 56 (2008), p. 331.

and which are consistent with international human rights norms and standards. It requires, as well, measures to ensure adherence to the principles of supremacy of law, equality before the law, accountability to the law, fairness in the application of the law, separation of powers, participation in decision-making, legal certainty, avoidance of arbitrariness and procedural and legal transparency.[6]

As you consider the material that follows, you may want to revisit the question of how the rule of law is defined.

14.1 The Rule of Law and Development

The rule of law has long been seen as a vehicle for promoting economic development.[7] In the 1960s, the US Agency for International Development, the Ford Foundation, and other private American donors began an ambitious program to reform the laws and judicial institutions of countries in Africa, Asia, and Latin America. The "law and development" movement generated hundreds of reports and articles, but a decade later leading academic participants and a former official at the Ford Foundation declared it a failure.[8] Among other problems, the program had assumed that it would be possible to export aspects of the US legal system, such as strategic litigation and activist judges, that were incompatible with the countries involved.

Later efforts have focused less on transplanting a specific model from one state to another, but continue to assume a close relationship between the rule of law and economic development. Whereas there are various accepted measures for economic development, however, measuring the rule of law has been trickier and more controversial. The 1992 Human Development Report, issued by the UN Development Program, suggested five possible indicators.

---

[6] UN Doc S/2004/616.

[7] See, e.g., Friedrich Hayek, *The Constitution of Liberty* (Chicago: University of Chicago Press, 1960), pp. 220–233.

[8] David M. Trubek and Marc Galanter, "Scholars in Self-Estrangement: Some Reflections on the Crisis in Law and Development," *Wisconsin Law Review*, vol. 4 (1974), p. 106, John. H. Merryman, "Comparative Law and Social Change: On the Origins, Style, Decline & Revival of the Law and Development Movement," *American Journal of Comparative Law*, vol. 25 (1977), p. 45; James Gardner, *Legal Imperialism: American Lawyers and Foreign Aid in Latin America* (Madison: University of Wisconsin Press, 1980).

HUMAN DEVELOPMENT REPORT 1992: GLOBAL DIMENSIONS OF HUMAN DEVELOPMENT[9]

An illustrative checklist of indicators of political freedom ... Rule of law:

Fair and public hearings—Are there fair and public hearings in the determination of all criminal charges? Is every person charged with an offence tried without undue delay, and with adequate time and facilities for the preparation of his or her defence?

Competent, independent, and impartial tribunal—Is the judiciary free of outside pressure or influence? Is there corruption in the judiciary? Is the procedure for selecting judges an open one in which opinions outside the executive can be heard? Do judges have security of tenure?

Legal counsel—Does everyone have the right to capable and independent defence counsel in the determination of any criminal charge against him or her? Does everyone have the right to have legal assistance assigned to him or her in any case where the interests of justice so require, and without payment by the defendant if he or she lacks the necessary means? Is there a right to consult with counsel immediately on arrest, before interrogation begins?

Review of conviction—Does everyone convicted of a crime have the right to have his or her conviction and sentence reviewed by an independent judicial tribunal?

Failure to prosecute—Do state prosecutors also prosecute government officials, or members of pro-government forces, who violate the rights and freedoms of other persons?

The World Bank also began measuring rule of law in the 1990s, though its definition was more explicitly tied to economic factors.

WORLD BANK, A DECADE OF MEASURING THE QUALITY OF GOVERNANCE: GOVERNANCE MATTERS 2007[10]

Rule of law measures the extent to which agents have confidence in and abide by the rules of society, in particular the quality of contract enforcement, the police, and the courts, as well as the likelihood of crime and violence.

---

[9] Available at http://hdr.undp.org/reports.
[10] Available at http://siteresources.worldbank.org/NEWS/Resources/wbi2007-report.pdf.

From around 1997, the development community had begun using the more general term "good governance" to refer to a set of activities that embraced participation, transparency, and accountability in government—specifically including the rule of law.[11] The term "governance" itself had emerged within the development discourse in the 1990s as a means of expanding the prescriptions of donors to embrace not merely projects and structural adjustment but government policies. Though intergovernmental organizations such as the World Bank and the International Monetary Fund are technically constrained from referring to political processes as such, "governance" provides a convenient euphemism for precisely that.[12] (See also the discussion of democracy promotion in Chapter 12.)

The international acceptance of good governance and the rule of law and their ties to economic development were reaffirmed by all UN member states in 2005.

WORLD SUMMIT OUTCOME DOCUMENT, GA RES. 60/1 (2005)

11. We acknowledge that good governance and the rule of law at the national and international levels are essential for sustained economic growth, sustainable development and the eradication of poverty and hunger. . . .

21. We further reaffirm our commitment to sound policies, good governance at all levels and the rule of law, and to mobilize domestic resources, attract international flows, promote international trade as an engine for development and increase international financial and technical cooperation for development, sustainable debt financing and external debt relief and to enhance the coherence and consistency of the international monetary, financial and trading systems. . . .

25. We resolve to encourage greater direct investment, including foreign investment, in developing countries and countries with economies in transition to support their development activities and to enhance the benefits they can derive from such investments. In this regard:

(a) We continue to support efforts by developing countries and countries with economies in transition to create a domestic environment conducive to attracting investments through, inter alia, achieving a transparent, stable and predictable investment climate with proper contract enforcement and

---

[11] UN Development Programme, Governance for Sustainable Human Development (UNDP, New York, January 1997), available at: http://magnet.undp.org/policy.
[12] Goran Hyden, "Governance and the Reconstitution of Political Order," in Richard Joseph (ed), State, Conflict and Democracy in Africa (Boulder, CO: Lynne Rienner, 1999).

respect for property rights and the rule of law and pursuing appropriate policy and regulatory frameworks that encourage business formation; . . .

134. Recognizing the need for universal adherence to and implementation of the rule of law at both the national and international levels, we:

(a) Reaffirm our commitment to the purposes and principles of the Charter and international law and to an international order based on the rule of law and international law, which is essential for peaceful coexistence and cooperation among States; . . .

(f) Recognize the important role of the International Court of Justice, the principal judicial organ of the United Nations, in adjudicating disputes among States and the value of its work, call upon States that have not yet done so to consider accepting the jurisdiction of the Court in accordance with its Statute and consider means of strengthening the Court's work, including by supporting the Secretary-General's Trust Fund to Assist States in the Settlement of Disputes through the International Court of Justice on a voluntary basis.

In 2012, a plan of action sought to offer more concrete suggestions on how the rule of law could support economic development.

DELIVERING JUSTICE: PROGRAMME OF ACTION TO STRENGTHEN THE RULE OF LAW AT THE NATIONAL AND INTERNATIONAL LEVELS (REPORT OF THE SECRETARY-GENERAL), 16 MARCH 2012[13]

3. Fostering an enabling environment for sustainable human development

26. Sustainable human development is facilitated by a strong rule of law. The provision and implementation of stable and predictable legal frameworks for businesses and labour stimulate employment by promoting entrepreneurship and the growth of small and medium-sized enterprises, and attracting public and private investment, including foreign direct investment. The link between economic development and the rule of law has long been established. Rising inequalities in wealth within and among countries are now a key concern with the potential to weaken and destabilize societies. The United Nations supports the development of a holistic sustainable human development agenda that addresses the challenges related to

---

[13] UN Doc A/66/749.

inclusive growth, social protection and the environment. In such an agenda, the rule of law must play a critical role in ensuring equal protection and access to opportunities.

(a) Fostering economic growth

27. Member States should renew their focus on the rule of law to foster enabling environments for sustainable economic growth. Such growth must be equitable, inclusive and socially responsible in order to create sufficient stability for poverty reduction and peacebuilding initiatives to take root. In this connection:

(a) Member States must resolve to develop and implement adequate legal frameworks to boost entrepreneurship and public and private sector investment, and for the development of small and medium-sized enterprises;

(b) A number of conventions and other legal texts in the domain of trade, investment and development have been developed in the context of the United Nations, and Member States should consider adopting and implementing these. Where implementation is hampered by capacity deficits, Member States must commit themselves to seeking international assistance and to providing adequate funding for such assistance;

(c) Member States must resolve to take steps to encourage employment and implement internationally agreed labour norms and standards, including for those individuals employed in the informal sectors.

(b) Fighting corruption

28. Corruption is a challenge that needs to be addressed by all Member States, particularly since there is a strong link between low levels of corruption and economic and social development. Under the auspices of the United Nations, Member States have created a strong normative framework to meet this challenge, and the focus must now be on universal adherence to the framework, and its full implementation. In this connection:

(a) Member States must consider ratifying the United Nations Convention against Corruption and fully implementing its provisions, making use of the peer review mechanism established by the Conference of the States Parties to the Convention;

(b) Bilateral and multilateral assistance providers should integrate into their rule of law budgeting and planning support for the technical assistance needs of Member States, as identified through the peer review mechanism of the United Nations Convention against Corruption.

(c) Protecting housing, land and property rights

29. The equitable and transparent administration of housing, land and property based on rule of law principles is key to economic, social and political stability. Serious deficits in this area have caused many violent conflicts and prolonged displacement. In this connection: Member States

should resolve to put in place and fully implement housing, land and property governance systems that effectively protect international social and economic rights, with particular emphasis on ensuring women's equal rights to housing, land and property, including through succession and inheritance.

The General Assembly subsequently reiterated its support for the rule of law.

GENERAL ASSEMBLY RESOLUTION 67/1 (2012)

Declaration of the high-level meeting of the General Assembly on the rule of law at the national and international levels

1. We reaffirm our solemn commitment to the purposes and principles of the Charter of the United Nations, international law and justice, and to an international order based on the rule of law, which are indispensable foundations for a more peaceful, prosperous and just world.

2. We recognize that the rule of law applies to all States equally, and to international organizations, including the United Nations and its principal organs, and that respect for and promotion of the rule of law and justice should guide all of their activities and accord predictability and legitimacy to their actions. We also recognize that all persons, institutions and entities, public and private, including the State itself, are accountable to just, fair and equitable laws and are entitled without any discrimination to equal protection of the law.

3. We are determined to establish a just and lasting peace all over the world, in accordance with the purposes and principles of the Charter of the United Nations. We rededicate ourselves to support all efforts to uphold the sovereign equality of all States, to respect their territorial integrity and political independence, to refrain in our international relations from the threat or use of force in any manner inconsistent with the purposes and principles of the United Nations, and to uphold the resolution of disputes by peaceful means and in conformity with the principles of justice and international law, the right to self-determination of peoples which remain under colonial domination and foreign occupation, non-interference in the internal affairs of States, respect for human rights and fundamental freedoms, respect for the equal rights of all without distinction as to race, sex, language or religion, international cooperation in solving international problems of an economic, social, cultural or humanitarian character, and the fulfilment in good faith of the obligations assumed in accordance with the Charter. . . .

5. We reaffirm that human rights, the rule of law and democracy are inter-linked and mutually reinforcing and that they belong to the universal and indivisible core values and principles of the United Nations. . . .

7. We are convinced that the rule of law and development are strongly interrelated and mutually reinforcing, that the advancement of the rule of law at the national and international levels is essential for sustained and inclusive economic growth, sustainable development, the eradication of poverty and hunger and the full realization of all human rights and funda-mental freedoms, including the right to development, all of which in turn reinforce the rule of law . . .

10. We recognize the progress made by countries in advancing the rule of law as an integral part of their national strategies. We also recognize that there are common features founded on international norms and standards which are reflected in a broad diversity of national experiences in the area of the rule of law. In this regard, we stress the importance of promoting the sharing of national practices and of inclusive dialogue. . . .

18. We emphasize the importance of the rule of law as one of the key ele-ments of conflict prevention, peacekeeping, conflict resolution and peace-building, stress that justice, including transitional justice, is a fundamental building block of sustainable peace in countries in conflict and post-conflict situations, and stress the need for the international community, including the United Nations, to assist and support such countries, upon their request, as they may face special challenges during their transition. . . .

21. We stress the importance of a comprehensive approach to transitional justice incorporating the full range of judicial and non-judicial measures to ensure accountability, serve justice, provide remedies to victims, promote healing and reconciliation, establish independent oversight of the security system and restore confidence in the institutions of the State and promote the rule of law. In this respect, we underline that truth-seeking processes, including those that investigate patterns of past violations of international human rights law and international humanitarian law and their causes and consequences, are important tools that can complement judicial processes.

22. We commit to ensuring that impunity is not tolerated for genocide, war crimes and crimes against humanity or for violations of international humanitarian law and gross violations of human rights law, and that such violations are properly investigated and appropriately sanctioned, includ-ing by bringing the perpetrators of any crimes to justice, through national mechanisms or, where appropriate, regional or international mechanisms, in accordance with international law, and for this purpose we encourage States to strengthen national judicial systems and institutions.

23. We recognize the role of the International Criminal Court in a multi-lateral system that aims to end impunity and establish the rule of law, and in this respect we welcome the States that have become parties to the Rome Statute of the International Criminal Court, and call upon all States that

are not yet parties to the Statute to consider ratifying or acceding to it, and emphasize the importance of cooperation with the Court. . . .

26. We reiterate our strong and unequivocal condemnation of terrorism in all its forms and manifestations, committed by whomever, wherever and for whatever purposes, as it constitutes one of the most serious threats to international peace and security; we reaffirm that all measures used in the fight against terrorism must be in compliance with the obligations of States under international law, including the Charter of the United Nations, in particular the purposes and principles thereof, and relevant conventions and protocols, in particular human rights law, refugee law and humanitarian law. . . .

31. We recognize the positive contribution of the International Court of Justice, the principal judicial organ of the United Nations, including in adjudicating disputes among States, and the value of its work for the promotion of the rule of law; we reaffirm the obligation of all States to comply with the decisions of the International Court of Justice in cases to which they are parties; and we call upon States that have not yet done so to consider accepting the jurisdiction of the International Court of Justice in accordance with its Statute. We also recall the ability of the relevant organs of the United Nations to request advisory opinions from the International Court of Justice. . . .

QUESTIONS

1. What does "the rule of law" mean? Has its use changed over time? Is it used to mean different things in developing and developed countries?
2. The idea that the rule of law facilitates development is not seriously questioned, but which aspect or aspects of the rule of law are most important? How might this affect your approach to defining the rule of law?

14.2 Transitional Justice

Almost as widely accepted as the link between law and development, law is also now generally seen as having a role to play in helping stabilize countries emerging from conflict. This role includes dealing with violations of international humanitarian law during an international or non-international armed conflict, as well as addressing the legacy of massive human rights abuses perpetrated by a state against its own population. As the term implies, "transitional" justice is intended to mark a transition toward greater order and accountability.

How that transition should take place is a question open to different answers. Some see this simply through the lens of criminal law: either wrongdoers are held accountable or they enjoy impunity. In fact the situation is more complex.

First, a useful distinction may be made between *acknowledgment*—whether to remember or forget the abuses—and *accountability*—whether to impose sanctions on the individuals who were responsible for the abuses. This helps to distinguish between four types of response. At either extreme of the spectrum are criminal prosecutions and unconditional amnesty. Criminal prosecution was the official policy toward collaborators in all Western European states occupied by Germany during the Second World War, for example. This may be contrasted with the general position of post-communist Eastern and Central Europe and the post-authoritarian regimes of Latin America, which tended to favor amnesties (although in the latter, these were often followed by considerable and growing stigmatization). Between the extremes lie policies such as "lustration" (the disqualification of certain groups of people from public office) and conditional amnesties, often in the form of a truth commission. It is also important to bear in mind that a fifth "response" is also possible: doing nothing. In some situations it might not be possible or desirable to commit to one of these paths, though that does not mean that a subsequent re-evaluation is not possible.

The best known example of a conditional amnesty is the South African Truth and Reconciliation Commission, which ran from 1995 to 2002. The goals that it embodied were expressed in the 1993 Interim Constitution: "there is a need for understanding but not for vengeance, a need for reparation but not retaliation, a need for *ubuntu*[14] but not for victimization." A person could apply to the Truth and Reconciliation Commission for amnesty for any act, omission, or offense that took place between 1 March 1960 and 11 May 1994. To be granted amnesty, the person had to satisfy the Committee on Amnesty that the act was associated with a political objective committed in the course of the conflicts of the past, and that full disclosure of all relevant facts had been made.

In the 1990s it was common for blanket amnesties to be granted as a means of encouraging abusive leaders to relinquish power without fear of prosecution for their deeds while in office. In 1994, for example, the United States actively encouraged the democratically elected government that it had helped to return to power in Haiti to grant amnesty to the junta that had been encouraged to leave the country.[15] But the atrocities that took place that decade and the realization that failure to confront past abuses can sow the seeds of future conflicts led to blanket amnesties falling from favor. The 1995 Dayton Peace Agreement included a pledge by the parties to the conflict in Bosnia and Herzegovina to cooperate with the International Criminal

---

[14] A Zulu word meaning, roughly, "humanity" or "humanness."

[15] Michael P. Scharf, "Swapping Amnesties for Peace: Was There a Duty to Prosecute International Crimes in Haiti?," *Texas International Law Journal*, vol. 31 (1996), pp. 6–8.

Tribunal for the Former Yugoslavia, as well as the exclusion of indicted fugitives from positions of authority in the new state.[16]

By the end of the decade, the Rome Statute to create an International Criminal Court had been signed,[17] "no peace without justice" had become a slogan, and blanket amnesties were generally frowned upon. In mid-1999, Secretary-General Kofi Annan sent a confidential cable to senior UN representatives attempting to establish some guidelines for how the United Nations would approach these difficult questions.

GUIDELINES FOR UNITED NATIONS REPRESENTATIVES ON CERTAIN ASPECTS OF NEGOTIATIONS FOR CONFLICT RESOLUTION, [1999][18]

In recent years, since the United Nations has become more deeply involved in efforts to resolve internal conflicts, United Nations representatives have had to grapple with the urgency of stopping the fighting, on the one hand, and the need to address punishable human rights violations, on the other, particularly when the temptation to enact hasty amnesties arises as negotiations draw to a close. This can create dilemmas for these representatives who may find themselves navigating with apparently conflicting mandates, with deep roots in the United Nations Charter and the Universal Declaration of Human Rights and other sources of international law. In order to assist them in discharging their task, the attached confidential guidelines have been prepared, having in mind the overarching goal that solutions to conflicts should be durable. They are meant as a useful practical tool for United Nations negotiators that will also serve the purpose of ensuring the consistency and quality of agreements reached in the area of human rights, under the auspices of the United Nations.

The guidelines were prepared after extensive consultations with experienced practitioners in the mediation of conflicts under the auspices of the United Nations, of other multilateral organizations, member states and non-governmental organizations on one side, and human rights experts and scholars of international law on the other. They were asked to consider, with

---

[16] UN Doc S/1995/999, art. XI. Importantly, Bosnian Serb leaders Radovan Karadžić and Ratko Mladić were excluded from negotiations, while Slobodan Milošević was not. Milošević was needed for the negotiations, but four years later he, too, was indicted. See section 14.3 of this chapter.

[17] The treaty was concluded in 1998 and came into effect in 2002.

[18] This undated document was confidential when issued in 1999, but later reprinted in the *United Nations Juridical Yearbook* (2006), pp. 495–497.

an emphasis on the practical problems faced by those who work to secure transitions from a violent past, such questions as: Is it a mediator's duty to bring human rights considerations to the attention of parties to a negotiation, and if so which? If parties to a negotiation seem to be headed towards an arrangement that would involve reciprocal impunity, ignoring internationally accepted human rights standards, what should the mediator do? and what is the mediator's responsibility with respect to addressing the past?

Finding answers to these questions will never be easy; it is not the intention of the guidelines to provide hard and fast rules for universal application. Rather, it is hoped that the existence of the guidelines ... will help alert representatives of the United Nations engaged in negotiation processes to some of the challenges they may encounter regarding human rights, including amnesties and the question of accountability and how to address the past, and encourage them to seek guidance and support from United Nations Headquarters. It goes without saying that the guidelines should at all times remain confidential to the United Nations representative; the timing with which he/she chooses to apply them within the specific process in which he/she is engaged would, as the final point of the guidelines makes clear, be entirely a question of his/her judgement and discretion.

Guidelines

1. Peace negotiations with the mediation or good offices of a Representative of the Secretary-General are deemed as taking place under the auspices of the United Nations. The Secretary-General's Representative must therefore be mindful that, as an agent of the Organization, he/she is acting within a framework of established purposes, principles and rules.

2. The purposes and principles of the United Nations Charter must be promoted and upheld. The United Nations has a record and credibility to defend and cannot condone agreements arrived at through negotiations that would violate Charter principles. Under the Charter, disputes should be settled in conformity with the principles of justice and international law.

3. Parties must be led to understand that negotiations that are conducted with an awareness of these concerns will contribute to forming the basis for a sustainable peace. . . .

4. In addition, agreements signed under the auspices of the Secretary-General must withstand the scrutiny of a variety of constituencies; the Secretary-General's representatives must therefore make every effort to make them politically defensible. . . .

7. Negotiations often take place in a context of human rights violations and violations of the laws of armed conflict. Early commitments to respect human rights and humanitarian principles should be encouraged. . . .

8. It should be borne in mind that human rights violations by state organs and acts committed by rebel groups do not fall in the same category under law, given the primary duty of the state to guarantee respect for human

rights. Violations by state organs and those by rebel groups may therefore need to be addressed in different ways. This is without prejudice to individual criminal responsibility for violations of human rights and international humanitarian law for which there is no distinction to be made as between the category of perpetrators.

9. In some circumstances the United Nations Representative may need to acquaint the parties to a conflict with the existence of a body of international law and practice regarding these issues, including those related to current human rights and humanitarian obligations, accountability and amnesties.

10. While every effort should be made to address these questions satisfactorily in the agreements, in the event that this is not possible the parties should be urged to include language that will allow for the possibility of further elaboration of any outstanding issues.

11. In the event that the negotiations are proceeding towards an agreement that may be seriously flawed from the perspective of the United Nations, the United Nations Representative should, after obtaining political and legal advice from United Nations Headquarters, in an appropriate way and at a time of his/her judgement, draw the attention of the parties to the consequences for the sustainability of the agreement and, having regard to international law and opinion, for United Nations engagement and donor assistance. He/she may even need to warn the parties that, if they cross certain lines, the United Nations might be put in a position where it would have to take a stance, on the public record, concerning aspects of the agreement.

12. The United Nations Representative should seek guidance from Headquarters should any of the following issues arise during the negotiations, in order to furnish the parties with the necessary advice and assistance:

- Allegations of serious human rights violations or violations of international humanitarian law recently committed or currently being committed that might require immediate investigation;
- Requests for investigation of allegations of serious violations of human rights or international humanitarian law committed in the past. Such demands may raise issues of prosecution of those allegedly responsible for such acts or for a comprehensive investigation into a systematic pattern of abuses that may lead to the establishment of mechanisms such as "Truth Commissions";
- Demands for amnesty may be made on behalf of different elements. It may be necessary and proper for immunity from prosecution to be granted to members of the armed opposition seeking reintegration into society as part of a national reconciliation process. Government negotiators may seek endorsement of self-amnesty proposals; however, the United Nations cannot condone amnesties regarding war crimes, crimes against humanity and genocide or foster those that violate relevant treaty obligations of the parties in this field.

Within a month of the guidelines being issued, they were put to the test in Sierra Leone. This conflict had become notorious for its brutality and its widespread use of child soldiers. On 7 July 1999, a peace agreement was concluded in which the rebel fighters agreed to a power-sharing agreement—but only in exchange for a general and unconditional amnesty for the rebel leader, Foday Sankoh, and his Revolutionary United Front (RUF).

LOMÉ EACE AGREEMENT, 7 JULY 1999[19]

... Moved by the imperative need to meet the desire of the people of Sierra Leone for a definitive settlement of the fratricidal war in their country and for genuine national unity and reconciliation;
   Committed to promoting full respect for human rights and humanitarian law; ...
   ARTICLE IX—PARDON AND AMNESTY
   1. In order to bring lasting peace to Sierra Leone, the Government of Sierra Leone shall take appropriate legal steps to grant Corporal Foday Sankoh absolute and free pardon.
   2. After the signing of the present Agreement, the Government of Sierra Leone shall also grant absolute and free pardon and reprieve to all combatants and collaborators in respect of anything done by them in pursuit of their objectives, up to the time of the signing of the present Agreement.
   3. To consolidate the peace and promote the cause of national reconciliation, the Government of Sierra Leone shall ensure that no official or judicial action is taken against any member of the [belligerents] in respect of anything done by them in pursuit of their objectives as members of those organisations, since March 1991, up to the time of the signing of the present Agreement. In addition, legislative and other measures necessary to guarantee immunity to former combatants, exiles and other persons, currently outside the country for reasons related to the armed conflict shall be adopted ensuring the full exercise of their civil and political rights, with a view to their reintegration within a framework of full legality. ...

As the twelve official copies were circulated, Special Representative for the UN Secretary-General Francis Okelo added a handwritten statement on one copy of the agreement: "The UN holds the understanding that the amnesty provisions of the Agreement shall not apply to the international crimes of genocide, crimes against humanity, war crimes and other serious violations

---

[19] UN Doc S/1999/777, Annex.

of international humanitarian law."[20] As the statement was written on only one of the twelve copies, each said to be equally authentic, it is not clear what legal status it enjoyed. The subsequent report of the Secretary-General expressed ambivalence about signing the Lomé Agreement at all.

SEVENTH REPORT OF THE SECRETARY-GENERAL ON THE UNITED NATIONS OBSERVER MISSION IN SIERRA LEONE, 30 JULY 1999[21]

54. As in other peace accords, many compromises were necessary in the Lomé Peace Agreement. As a result, some of the terms under which this peace has been obtained, in particular the provisions on amnesty, are difficult to reconcile with the goal of ending the culture of impunity, which inspired the creation of the United Nations Tribunals for Rwanda and the Former Yugoslavia, and the future International Criminal Court. Hence the instruction to my Special Representative to enter a reservation when he signed the peace agreement, explicitly stating that, for the United Nations, the amnesty cannot cover international crimes of genocide, crimes against humanity, war crimes and other serious violations of international humanitarian law. At the same time, the Government and people of Sierra Leone should be allowed this opportunity to realize their best and only hope of ending their long and brutal conflict. During my short visit to Sierra Leone on 8 July 1999, I witnessed tremendous destruction, suffering and pain, particularly on the faces of the victims of wanton and abhorrent violence. I took the opportunity to encourage all Sierra Leoneans to seize this opportunity for peace, to rally behind the agreement, seek reconciliation, and to look and work towards the future.

The Special Court for Sierra Leone was later established—a hybrid tribunal that combined a mix of national and international prosecutors and judges—with jurisdiction to try those "who bear the greatest responsibility for serious violations of international humanitarian law and Sierra Leonean law." Twenty-two persons were indicted—including Foday Sankoh, though he died from a stroke while awaiting trial. The UN prosecutor, David Crane, observed that Sankoh's death from natural causes gave him "a peaceful end that he denied to so many others."

In 2004, the Secretary-General issued another report—quoted earlier in this chapter for its definition of the rule of law—that sought to map out the normative framework within which the United Nations operated. (Note that when this was published the 1999 Guidelines were still confidential.)

---

[20] Quoted in William A. Schabas, "Amnesty, the Sierra Leone Truth and Reconciliation Commission and the Special Court for Sierra Leone," *UC Davis Journal of International Law & Policy*, vol. 11 (2004), pp. 148–149.
[21] UN Doc S/1999/836.

THE RULE OF LAW AND TRANSITIONAL JUSTICE IN CONFLICT AND POST-CONFLICT SOCIETIES (REPORT OF THE SECRETARY-GENERAL), 23 AUGUST 2004[22]

IV. Basing assistance on international norms and standards

9. The normative foundation for our work in advancing the rule of law is the Charter of the United Nations itself, together with the four pillars of the modern international legal system: international human rights law; international humanitarian law; international criminal law; and international refugee law. This includes the wealth of United Nations human rights and criminal justice standards developed in the last half-century. These represent universally applicable standards adopted under the auspices of the United Nations and must therefore serve as the normative basis for all United Nations activities in support of justice and the rule of law.

10. United Nations norms and standards have been developed and adopted by countries across the globe and have been accommodated by the full range of legal systems of Member States, whether based in common law, civil law, Islamic law, or other legal traditions. As such, these norms and standards bring a legitimacy that cannot be said to attach to exported national models which, all too often, reflect more the individual interests or experience of donors and assistance providers than they do the best interests or legal development needs of host countries. These standards also set the normative boundaries of United Nations engagement, such that, for example, United Nations tribunals can never allow for capital punishment, United Nations-endorsed peace agreements can never promise amnesties for genocide, war crimes, crimes against humanity or gross violations of human rights, and, where we are mandated to undertake executive or judicial functions, United Nations-operated facilities must scrupulously comply with international standards for human rights in the administration of justice. ...

XIX. Moving forward: conclusions and recommendations

A. Considerations for negotiations, peace agreements and Security Council mandates

64. Ensure that peace agreements and Security Council resolutions and mandates:

(a) Give priority attention to the restoration of and respect for the rule of law, explicitly mandating support for the rule of law and for transitional

---

[22] UN Doc S/2004/616.

justice, particularly where United Nations support for judicial and prosecutorial processes is required;

(b) Respect, incorporate by reference and apply international standards for fairness, due process and human rights in the administration of justice;

(c) Reject any endorsement of amnesty for genocide, war crimes, or crimes against humanity, including those relating to ethnic, gender and sexually based international crimes, ensure that no such amnesty previously granted is a bar to prosecution before any United Nations-created or assisted court;

(d) Ensure that the United Nations does not establish or directly participate in any tribunal for which capital punishment is included among possible sanctions; . . .

Though the adoption of the Rome Statute of the International Criminal Court (ICC) in 1998 played a role in rendering amnesties unacceptable, the question of how ICC prosecutions might affect a peace process was a topic of intense discussion. The International Law Commission's 1994 draft had prohibited the commencement of a prosecution if it arose from a situation that was being dealt with by the Council under Chapter VII of the Charter, unless the Council decided otherwise.[23] The consequence of such a provision was that it would effectively give each of the permanent five members of the Council a veto over prosecutions as long as the situation remained on the Council's agenda. The final version of the Rome Statute reflects the "Singapore compromise" whereby the negative veto was replaced by a positive arrangement, under which the Council may defer investigation or prosecution for a (potentially renewable) period of twelve months by adopting a Chapter VII resolution.[24] Elsewhere in the Statute, the Council is also given the power unilaterally to refer a matter to the Court.

STATUTE OF THE INTERNATIONAL CRIMINAL COURT (ROME STATUTE), 1998 (ENTERED INTO FORCE 2002)

Article 13: Exercise of jurisdiction

The Court may exercise its jurisdiction with respect to a crime referred to in article 5 in accordance with the provisions of this Statute if:

---

[23] UN Doc A/49/10 (1994).
[24] See Lionel Yee, "The International Criminal Court and the Security Council: Articles 13(b) and 16," in Roy S.K. Lee (ed), *The International Criminal Court: The Making of the Rome Statute* (The Hague: Kluwer, 1999).

(a) A situation in which one or more of such crimes appears to have been committed is referred to the Prosecutor by a State Party . . . ;

(b) A situation in which one or more of such crimes appears to have been committed is referred to the Prosecutor by the Security Council acting under Chapter VII of the Charter of the United Nations; or

(c) The Prosecutor has initiated an investigation in respect of such a crime . . .

Article 16: Deferral of investigation or prosecution

No investigation or prosecution may be commenced or proceeded with under this Statute for a period of 12 months after the Security Council, in a resolution adopted under Chapter VII of the Charter of the United Nations, has requested the Court to that effect; that request may be renewed by the Council under the same conditions.

Two situations were subsequently referred to the ICC by the Security Council: the situation in Darfur from 1 July 2002[25] and the situation in Libya from 15 February 2011.[26] No deferrals have yet been requested by the Security Council, though the African Union sought a delay in prosecution of Kenya's President and Deputy President in October 2013.

AFRICAN UNION, DECISION ON AFRICA'S RELATIONSHIP WITH THE INTERNATIONAL CRIMINAL COURT (ICC), 12 OCTOBER 2013

The Assembly . . .

2. REITERATES, in accordance with the Constitutive Act of the African Union (AU), the AU's unflinching commitment to fight impunity, promote human rights and democracy, and the rule of law and good governance in the continent;

3. REAFFIRMS its previous Decisions on the abuse of the principles of Universal Jurisdiction . . . wherein it expressed its strong conviction that the search for justice should be pursued in a way that does not impede or jeopardize efforts aimed at promoting lasting peace;

---

[25] SC Res. 1593 (2005).
[26] SC Res. 1970 (2011).

4. REITERATES AU's concern on the politicization and misuse of indictments against African leaders by ICC as well as at the unprecedented indictments of and proceedings against the sitting President and Deputy President of Kenya in light of the recent developments in that country;

5. UNDERSCORES that this is the first time that a sitting Head of State and his deputy are being tried in an international court and STRESSES the gravity of this situation which could undermine the sovereignty, stability, and peace in that country and in other Member States as well as reconciliation and reconstruction and the normal functioning of constitutional institutions;

6. RECOGNIZES that Kenya is a frontline state in the fight against terrorism at regional, continental and international levels and, in this regard, STRESSES the threat that this menace poses to the region in particular and the continent in general, and the proceedings initiated against the President and the Deputy President of the Republic of Kenya will distract and prevent them from fulfilling their constitutional responsibilities, including national and regional security affairs; ...

9. REAFFIRMS the principles deriving from national laws and international customary law by which sitting Heads of State and other senior state officials are granted immunities during their tenure of office;

10. NOW DECIDES:

(i) That to safeguard the constitutional order, stability and, integrity of Member States, no charges shall be commenced or continued before any International Court or Tribunal against any serving AU Head of State or Government or anybody acting or entitled to act in such capacity during their term of office;

(ii) That the trials of President Uhuru Kenyatta and Deputy President William Samoei Ruto, who are the current serving leaders of the Republic of Kenya, should be suspended until they complete their terms of office; ...

(ix) That Kenya should send a letter to the United Nations Security Council requesting for deferral, in conformity with Article 16 of the Rome Statute, of the proceedings against the President and Deputy President of Kenya that would be endorsed by all African States Parties; ...

The case was not dropped or deferred, and in November 2013 the ICC's Assembly of State Parties adopted a new Rule of Procedure and Evidence that allows an accused person who is subject to a summons to be excused from appearing in person if he or she is "mandated to fulfil extraordinary public duties at the highest national level," provided that he or she submits a request to the Trial Chamber to be excused and to be represented by counsel only. The request must specify that the accused explicitly waives the right to be present at the trial.[27]

---

[27] ICC Assembly of States Parties Resolution ICC-ASP/12/Res.7 (27 November 2013), available at: http://www.icc-cpi.int.

On 5 December 2014, the Office of the Prosecutor withdrew the charges against Kenya's president, Uhuru Kenyatta, stating that the "evidence has not improved to such an extent that Mr Kenyatta's alleged criminal responsibility can be proven beyond reasonable doubt." On 13 March 2015, the Trial Chamber formally terminated the proceedings against him.

Paragraph 10(i) also would have covered the case of Omar al-Bashir, the president of Sudan, indicted in July 2008 for alleged crimes in Darfur. An arrest warrant was issued in March 2009 (and a second in July 2010), though he has traveled to various African and Middle Eastern countries without this being enforced. In June 2015, he traveled to South Africa for an AU summit. While there, a South African court found that his immunity as head of state of Sudan did not preclude arrest on the basis of an ICC arrest warrant, and that he should be prevented from leaving the country. He left the country the following day, prompting the court to invite the National Director of Public Prosecutions to consider whether criminal proceedings should be commenced against the government.[28] No action was taken.

QUESTIONS

3. Why should any amnesties be granted after conflict? Combatants complying with the laws of war typically enjoy immunity for those acts—one uniformed soldier shooting a soldier from an opposing army during a battle would not normally be liable for murder. In what circumstances might the possibility of an amnesty be important?

4. If any amnesties are to be granted, why draw the line at "war crimes, crimes against humanity and genocide"? Why not all human rights violations?

5. The International Criminal Court operates according to a principle of complementarity, meaning that it exercises jurisdiction only if states are unwilling or unable to prosecute a crime. How do hybrid courts such as the one in Sierra Leone fit into this picture? In what circumstances would it be preferable to have (a) national trials, (b) a hybrid tribunal, (c) international prosecution of a crime?

6. Why were the UN Guidelines kept confidential? What would have been the consequence if they were published?

7. Paragraph 8 of the UN Guidelines states that violations by states and violations by rebel groups may need to be addressed in "different ways." Is this true? Why?

8. In General Assembly resolution 3068 (XXVIII) (1973), the United Nations declared that apartheid as practiced in South African was a crime against

---

[28] *Southern Africa Litigation Centre v Minister of Justice and Constitutional Development and Others* [2015] ZAGPPHC 402 (24 June 2015).

humanity. Should the United Nations recognize amnesties granted under South Africa's Truth and Reconciliation Commission?

9. Sitting heads of state typically enjoy immunity at home and when traveling, but their immunity is explicitly rejected in the Rome Statute. Are there reasons a sitting head of state should not be prosecuted for international crimes?

HYPOTHETICAL A

Maltopia is a fictional state in which the population is mostly drawn from two ethnic groups. The larger of the groups, the Alphas, has long dominated political and economic life in Maltopia. All cabinet and judicial posts are held by Alphas, who tend to receive better education and have rosier career prospects. The other ethnic group, the Omegas, makes up only one-quarter of the population but dominates the army and the police forces. An increasingly bitter series of protests over perceived discrimination against the Omegas eventually turned violent, involving terrorist attacks against government buildings and a brutal response from the security forces. The dispute rose to the level of a non-international armed conflict, with the Omega rebels (and a few Alpha sympathizers) controlling a significant proportion of Maltopia's territory.

You are the negotiator for the leader of the Omega rebels, a disenchanted opposition politician who reluctantly embraced terrorist tactics when she concluded that peaceful engagement was futile. The military campaign has now reached a standoff, and the United Nations has been invited in by Maltopia's government to assist in mediating a power-sharing arrangement. Assuming that your loyalty to your leader is unquestioned, what is your strategy going into the negotiations on dealing with potential criminal responsibility for violence?

14.3 The Rule of Law, International Peace, and Security

In parallel with its increased role in assisting states in transition, the United Nations also assumed a far more active role through the 1990s in imposing the rule of law in a more direct way.

The starting point was the handwringing response to the conflict in the former Yugoslavia that began in 1991. There was widespread media coverage of abuses that recalled the concentration camps of the Second World War. When political, economic, and military efforts to restrain the belligerents failed—and amidst disagreements among leading powers on an appropriate strategy—the Security Council took the unprecedented step of creating a criminal tribunal to exert legal pressure on the leaders in particular.

SECURITY COUNCIL RESOLUTION 827 (1993)

The Security Council,

Expressing once again its grave alarm at continuing reports of widespread and flagrant violations of international humanitarian law occurring within the territory of the former Yugoslavia, and especially in the Republic of Bosnia and Herzegovina, including reports of mass killings, massive, organized and systematic detention and rape of women, and the continuance of the practice of "ethnic cleansing", including for the acquisition and the holding of territory,

Determining that this situation continues to constitute a threat to international peace and security, . . .

Convinced that in the particular circumstances of the former Yugoslavia the establishment as an ad hoc measure by the Council of an international tribunal and the prosecution of persons responsible for serious violations of international humanitarian law would enable this aim to be achieved and would contribute to the restoration and maintenance of peace, . . .

Acting under Chapter VII of the Charter of the United Nations, . . .

2. *Decides* hereby to establish an international tribunal for the sole purpose of prosecuting persons responsible for serious violations of international humanitarian law committed in the territory of the former Yugoslavia between 1 January 1991 and a date to be determined by the Security Council upon the restoration of peace and to this end to adopt the Statute of the International Tribunal annexed to the above-mentioned report; . . .

4. *Decides* that all States shall cooperate fully with the International Tribunal and its organs in accordance with the present resolution and the Statute of the International Tribunal and that consequently all States shall take any measures necessary under their domestic law to implement the provisions of the present resolution and the Statute, including the obligation of States to comply with requests for assistance or orders issued by a Trial Chamber . . . ;

5. *Urges* States and intergovernmental and non-governmental organizations to contribute funds, equipment and services to the International Tribunal, including the offer of expert personnel; . . .

The use of Chapter VII powers to create an international tribunal does not appear to have been contemplated when the UN Charter was being drafted. (The Nuremberg Trials underway at the time were created by their own treaty.) In the first case that came before the new Tribunal, defense lawyers challenged the legality of its very existence. As José Alvarez framed it, the question was "whether the Council can create a denationalized body capable of depriving individuals of their liberty without national court appeal or involvement," a prescient question in light of developments in European Courts against Security Council sanctions decisions discussed in Chapter 10.[29] The following excerpt shows how the Court responded to this existential question.

PROSECUTOR v. TADIC (APPEAL ON JURISDICTION) (ICTY APPEALS CHAMBER, 2 OCTOBER 1995)

1. The Power of the Security Council to Invoke Chapter VII

28. It is clear from [Article 39 of the UN Charter] that the Security Council plays a pivotal role and exercises a very wide discretion under this Article. But this does not mean that its powers are unlimited. The Security Council is an organ of an international organization, established by a treaty which serves as a constitutional framework for that organization. The Security Council is thus subjected to certain constitutional limitations, however broad its powers under the constitution may be. Those powers cannot, in any case, go beyond the limits of the jurisdiction of the Organization at large, not to mention other specific limitations or those which may derive from the internal division of power within the Organization. In any case, neither the text nor the spirit of the Charter conceives of the Security Council as *legibus solutus* (unbound by law).

In particular, Article 24, after declaring, in paragraph 1, that the Members of the United Nations "confer on the Security Council primary responsibility for the maintenance of international peace and security", imposes on it, in paragraph 3, the obligation to report annually (or more frequently) to the General Assembly, and provides, more importantly, in paragraph 2, that:

> "In discharging these duties the Security Council shall act in accordance with the Purposes and Principles of the United Nations. The specific powers granted to the Security Council for the discharge of these duties are laid down in Chapters VI, VII, VIII, and XII."

The Charter thus speaks the language of specific powers, not of absolute fiat.

29. What is the extent of the powers of the Security Council under Article 39 and the limits thereon, if any?

The Security Council plays the central role in the application of both parts of the Article. It is the Security Council that makes the *determination*

---

[29] José Alvarez, "Nuremberg Revisited: The *Tadic* Case," *European Journal of International Law*, vol. 7 (1996), p. 252.

that there exists one of the situations justifying the use of the "exceptional powers" of Chapter VII. And it is also the Security Council that chooses the reaction to such a situation: it either makes *recommendations* (i.e., opts not to use the exceptional powers but to continue to operate under Chapter VI) or decides to use the exceptional powers by ordering measures to be taken in accordance with Articles 41 and 42 with a view to maintaining or restoring international peace and security.

The situations justifying resort to the powers provided for in Chapter VII are a "threat to the peace", a "breach of the peace" or an "act of aggression." While the "act of aggression" is more amenable to a legal determination, the "threat to the peace" is more of a political concept. But the determination that there exists such a threat is not a totally unfettered discretion, as it has to remain, at the very least, within the limits of the Purposes and Principles of the Charter.

30. . . . Appellant no longer contests the Security Council's power to determine whether the situation in the former Yugoslavia constituted a threat to the peace, nor the determination itself. . . . But he continues to contest the legality and appropriateness of the measures chosen by the Security Council to that end.

2. The Range of Measures Envisaged Under Chapter VII

31. . . . A question arises in this respect as to whether the choice of the Security Council is limited to the measures provided for in Articles 41 and 42 of the Charter (as the language of Article 39 suggests), or whether it has even larger discretion in the form of general powers to maintain and restore international peace and security under Chapter VII at large. In the latter case, one of course does not have to locate every measure decided by the Security Council under Chapter VII within the confines of Articles 41 and 42, or possibly Article 40. In any case, under both interpretations, the Security Council has a broad discretion in deciding on the course of action and evaluating the appropriateness of the measures to be taken. The language of Article 39 is quite clear as to the channelling of the very broad and exceptional powers of the Security Council under Chapter VII through Articles 41 and 42. These two Articles leave to the Security Council such a wide choice as not to warrant searching, on functional or other grounds, for even wider and more general powers than those already expressly provided for in the Charter. . . .

3. The Establishment of the International Tribunal as a Measure Under Chapter VII

32. . . . [T]he Security Council has a very wide margin of discretion under Article 39 to choose the appropriate course of action and to evaluate the

suitability of the measures chosen, as well as their potential contribution to the restoration or maintenance of peace. But here again, this discretion is not unfettered; moreover, it is limited to the measures provided for in Articles 41 and 42. . . .

In its resolution 827, the Security Council considers that "in the particular circumstances of the former Yugoslavia", the establishment of the International Tribunal "would contribute to the restoration and maintenance of peace" and indicates that, in establishing it, the Security Council was acting under Chapter VII . . . However, it did not specify a particular Article as a basis for this action. . . .

(a) What Article of Chapter VII Serves as a Basis for the Establishment of a Tribunal?

33. The establishment of an international criminal tribunal is not expressly mentioned among the enforcement measures provided for in Chapter VII, and more particularly in Articles 41 and 42.

Obviously, the establishment of the International Tribunal is not a measure under Article 42, as these are measures of a military nature, implying the use of armed force. Nor can it be considered a "provisional measure" under Article 40. These measures, as their denomination indicates, are intended to act as a "holding operation", producing a "stand-still" or a "cooling-off" effect, "without prejudice to the rights, claims or position of the parties concerned." . . .

34. *Prima facie*, the International Tribunal matches perfectly the description in Article 41 of "measures not involving the use of force." Appellant, however, has argued . . . that:"[I]t is clear that the establishment of a war crimes tribunal was not intended. The examples mentioned in this article focus upon economic and political measures and do not in any way suggest judicial measures." . . .

It has also been argued that the measures contemplated under Article 41 are all measures to be undertaken by Member States, which is not the case with the establishment of the International Tribunal.

35. The first argument does not stand by its own language. . . . It is evident that the measures set out in Article 41 are merely illustrative *examples* which obviously do not exclude other measures. All the Article requires is that they do not involve "the use of force." It is a negative definition.

That the examples do not suggest judicial measures goes some way towards the other argument that the Article does not contemplate institutional measures implemented directly by the United Nations through one of its organs but, as the given examples suggest, only action by Member States, such as economic sanctions (though possibly coordinated through an organ of the Organization). However, as mentioned above, nothing in the Article suggests the limitation of the measures to those implemented by States. The Article only prescribes what these measures cannot be. Beyond that it does not say or suggest what they have to be. . . .

36. Logically, if the Organization can undertake measures which have to be implemented through the intermediary of its Members, it can *a fortiori* undertake measures which it can implement directly via its organs, if it happens to have the resources to do so. It is only for want of such resources that the United Nations has to act through its Members. But it is of the essence of "collective measures" that they are collectively undertaken. Action by Member States on behalf of the Organization is but a poor substitute *faute de mieux*, or a "second best" for want of the first. This is also the pattern of Article 42 on measures involving the use of armed force.

In sum, the establishment of the International Tribunal falls squarely within the powers of the Security Council under Article 41.

(b) Can the Security Council Establish a Subsidiary Organ with Judicial Powers?

37. The argument that the Security Council, not being endowed with judicial powers, cannot establish a subsidiary organ possessed of such powers is untenable: it results from a fundamental misunderstanding of the constitutional set-up of the Charter.

Plainly, the Security Council is not a judicial organ and is not provided with judicial powers (though it may incidentally perform certain quasi-judicial activities such as effecting determinations or findings). The principal function of the Security Council is the maintenance of international peace and security, in the discharge of which the Security Council exercises both decision-making and executive powers.

38. The establishment of the International Tribunal by the Security Council does not signify, however, that the Security Council has delegated to it some of its own functions or the exercise of some of its own powers. Nor does it mean, in reverse, that the Security Council was usurping for itself part of a judicial function which does not belong to it but to other organs of the United Nations according to the Charter. The Security Council has resorted to the establishment of a judicial organ in the form of an international criminal tribunal as an instrument for the exercise of its own principal function of maintenance of peace and security, i.e., as a measure contributing to the restoration and maintenance of peace in the former Yugoslavia.

The General Assembly did not need to have military and police functions and powers in order to be able to establish the United Nations Emergency Force in the Middle East ("UNEF") in 1956. Nor did the General Assembly have to be a judicial organ possessed of judicial functions and powers in order to be able to establish [the UN Administrative Tribunal]. ...

4. Was the Establishment of the International Tribunal Contrary to the General Principle Whereby Courts Must Be "Established by Law"?

45. ... For a tribunal such as this one to be established according to the rule of law, it must be established in accordance with the proper international

standards; it must provide all the guarantees of fairness, justice and even-handedness, in full conformity with internationally recognized human rights instruments.

This interpretation of the guarantee that a tribunal be "established by law" is borne out by an analysis of the International Covenant on Civil and Political Rights. ... [A]t the time Article 14 of the International Covenant on Civil and Political Rights was being drafted, it was sought, unsuccessfully, to amend it to require that tribunals should be "pre-established" by law and not merely "established by law" ... if adopted, their effect would have been to prevent all *ad hoc* tribunals. ...

[T]here is wide agreement that, in most respects, the International Military Tribunals at Nuremberg and Tokyo gave the accused a fair trial in a procedural sense. ... The important consideration in determining whether a tribunal has been "established by law" is not whether it was pre-established or established for a specific purpose or situation; what is important is that it be set up by a competent organ in keeping with the relevant legal procedures, and should [*sic*] that it observes the requirements of procedural fairness. ...

46. An examination of the Statute of the International Tribunal, and of the Rules of Procedure and Evidence adopted pursuant to that Statute leads to the conclusion that it has been established in accordance with the rule of law. The fair trial guarantees in Article 14 of the International Covenant on Civil and Political Rights have been adopted almost verbatim in Article 21 of the Statute. Other fair trial guarantees appear in the Statute and the Rules of Procedure and Evidence. For example, Article 13, paragraph 1, of the Statute ensures the high moral character, impartiality, integrity and competence of the Judges of the International Tribunal, while various other provisions in the Rules ensure equality of arms and fair trial.

47. In conclusion, the Appeals Chamber finds that the International Tribunal has been established in accordance with the appropriate procedures under the United Nations Charter and provides all the necessary safeguards of a fair trial. It is thus "established by law."

Separate Opinion of Judge Li

2. The [Majority] Decision, relying on the doctrine of *competence-competence*, reviews the legality of the resolution of the Security Council on the establishment of this Tribunal. However, the said doctrine, properly understood, only allows the Tribunal to examine and determine its own jurisdiction, while here it has been improperly extended to the examination of the competence and appropriateness of the resolution of the Security Council on the establishment of this Tribunal. ...

3. Furthermore, the decision on the establishment of this Tribunal by resolution 808 (1993) of the Security Council pursuant to Article 39 of the Charter of the United Nations was grounded on its determination that the situation then existing in the former Yugoslavia constituted a threat to international

peace and security. Whether the said situation did constitute a threat to international peace and security and what measures should be taken are political questions which the Security Council as a political organ of the United Nations is well qualified to determine and of which the Judges of this Tribunal, trained only in law and having little or no experience in international political affairs, are really ignorant. Consequently, the review of the said resolution seems to be imprudent and worthless both in fact and in law.

4. In conclusion, the Decision should have dismissed the appeal on this question without examining the legality of the establishment of this Tribunal.

Soon after the creation of the ICTY, the 1994 genocide in Rwanda demonstrated even more graphically the international community's inability or unwillingness to prevent the worst human rights abuses. Inaction was untenable, and so the Security Council established a second ad hoc tribunal: the International Criminal Tribunal for Rwanda (ICTR).[30] Once again, the Council resolution asserted that the action being taken was exceptional, necessitated by the "particular circumstances in Rwanda."

Although the establishment of the ICTR was preceded by a request for a criminal tribunal from Rwanda,[31] its consent to the actually proposed structure was not required, and indeed resolution 955 (1994) was passed despite Rwanda's vote against it—cast in part because the ICTR did not have the option of imposing the death penalty on convicted offenders.

The statutes of both tribunals require states to comply without undue delay with any request for assistance or an order issued by a Trial Chamber, including the surrender or the transfer of an accused to the Tribunal. In 1996, such a request was made to the United States to surrender Elizaphan Ntakirutimana, a seventy-three-year-old Rwandan Hutu residing in Texas. As the former President of the Seventh-day Adventist Church in Rwanda, he was charged with luring several ethnic Tutsis to his church complex at Mugonero and then organizing and leading an attack to kill them. He was also accused of leading armed bands of men into the countryside of the Bisesero region to hunt down and kill those Tutsis who survived the attack at Mugonero.[32] On 26 September 1996, he was provisionally arrested on the above charges, and the US government requested his transfer to the ICTR. The District Court for the Southern District of Texas, Laredo Division, refused this request. The magistrate held surrender was not possible in the absence of an extradition treaty between the United States and the Tribunal.

---

[30] SC Res. 955 (1994).

[31] UN Doc. S/1994/1115 (1994).

[32] A letter addressed to Ntakirutimana by Tutsi Seventh-day Adventist pastors, which he showed to author Philip Gourevitch, provided the title for Gourevitch's 1998 book *We Wish to Inform You That Tomorrow We Will Be Killed with Our Families*.

He refused to accept the Agreement on Surrender of Persons between the Government of the United States and the International Tribunal, signed in January 1995, as a "treaty" of extradition, and also found the evidence insufficient to demonstrate to the Court probable cause to believe that Ntakirutimana had participated in the attacks at Mugonero and Bisesero.[33]

A second request was filed with additional declarations that satisfied the District Court. Ntakirutimana filed a petition for a writ of habeas corpus, which was denied. He appealed to the Court of Appeals for the Fifth Circuit.

ELIZAPHAN NTAKIRUTIMANA v. JANET RENO, ATTORNEY GENERAL OF THE UNITED STATES; AND OTHERS, 184 F.3D 419 (5TH CIR., 1999)

To determine whether a treaty is required to extradite Ntakirutimana, we turn to the text of the Constitution. Ntakirutimana contends that Article II, Section 2, Clause 2 of the Constitution requires a treaty to extradite ... This provision does not refer either to extradition or to the necessity of a treaty to extradite. The Supreme Court has explained, however, that "the power to surrender is clearly included within the treaty-making power and the corresponding power of appointing and receiving ambassadors and other public ministers." *Terlinden v. Ames* ... (1902).

Yet, the Court has found that the Executive's power to surrender fugitives is not unlimited. In *Valentine v. United States* ... (1936), the Supreme Court ... stated that the power to provide for extradition is a national power that "is not confided to the Executive in the absence of treaty or legislative provision." ...

Valentine indicates that a court should look to whether a treaty *or statute* grants executive discretion to extradite. Hence, *Valentine* supports the constitutionality of using the Congressional-Executive Agreement to extradite Ntakirutimana ... Thus, although some authorization by law is necessary for the Executive to extradite, neither the Constitution's text nor *Valentine* require that the authorization come in the form of a treaty. ...

Ntakirutimana next argues that historical practice establishes that a treaty is required to extradite. According to Ntakirutimana, the United States has never surrendered a person except pursuant to an Article II treaty, and the only involuntary transfers without an extradition treaty have been to "a foreign country or territory occupied by or under the control of the United States." *Valentine* ... This argument fails for numerous reasons. First, *Valentine* did not suggest that this "historical practice" limited Congress's power. Second, the Supreme Court's statements that a statute may confer the

---

[33] *In the Matter of Surrender of Elizaphan Ntakirutimana*, 988 F. Supp. 1038 (1997).

power to extradite also reflect a historical understanding of the Constitution. Even if Congress has rarely exercised the power to extradite by statute, a historical understanding exists nonetheless that it may do so. Third, in some instances in which a fugitive would not have been extraditable under a treaty, a fugitive has been extradited pursuant to a statute that "filled the gap" in the treaty. ... Thus, we are unconvinced that the President's practice of usually submitting a negotiated treaty to the Senate reflects a historical understanding that a treaty is required to extradite. ...

Finally, we turn to Ntakirutimana's remaining arguments. Ntakirutimana argues that the UN Charter does not authorize the Security Council to establish the International Criminal Tribunal for Rwanda, and that the only method for the UN to create an international criminal tribunal is by a multi-national treaty. This issue is beyond the scope of habeas review ...

Ntakirutimana contends additionally that the International Criminal Tribunal for Rwanda is incapable of protecting his rights under the United States Constitution and international law. He contends, for example, that the [Tribunal] is incapable of protecting his due process rights and that the [Tribunal] denies the right to be represented by the counsel of one's choice. Due to the limited scope of habeas review, we will not inquire into the procedures that await Ntakirutimana.

For the foregoing reasons, we AFFIRM the order of the district court denying Ntakirutimana's petition for a writ of habeas corpus, and LIFT the stay of extradition.

Special Concurrence of J. Robert M. Parker

I write separately and briefly to invite the Secretary to closely scrutinize the underlying evidence as she makes her decision regarding whether Ntakirutimana should be surrendered to the International Criminal Tribunal for Rwanda. The evidence supporting the request is highly suspect. Affidavits of unnamed Tutsi witnesses acquired during interviews utilizing questionable interpreters in a political environment that has all the earmarks of a campaign of tribal retribution raises serious questions regarding the truth of their content. ...

I fully understand that the ultimate decision in this case may well be a political one that is driven by important considerations of State that transcend the question of guilt or innocence of any single individual. I respect the political process that necessarily is implicated in this case, just as I respect the fact that adherence to precedent compels my concurrence.

Dissenting Opinion of J. Harold R. DeMoss

A structural reading of the Constitution compels the conclusion that most international agreements must be ratified according to the Treaty Clause of Article II. The history of national and international practice indicate that extradition agreements fall into this category. ...

The Constitution's treaty procedure must be followed in order to ratify an extradition agreement which contractually binds our nation to respect obligations to another nation. The intent of the framers could not be clearer on this point ... The Founders were especially concerned with the possibility that, in the conduct of foreign policy, American officials might become seduced by their foreign counterparts or a President might actually betray the country. Thus, while primary responsibility for foreign affairs was given to the President, a significant restraint and "check" on the use of the treaty power was created by requiring for treaties the advice and consent of two-thirds of the Senate. ... The decision to require approval of two-thirds of Senators was controversial and hotly debated, but it was ultimately decided that sheer importance of the treaty power merited such a treatment. Treaties cannot be accomplished by any means other than the Article II treaty ratification procedure. ...

The Attorney General and my colleagues in the majority place great reliance on *Valentine* ... *Valentine* was a case that did involve a treaty—its stray reference to "legislative provision" is pure dicta, and certainly not a plain holding that extradition may be accomplished by the President simply on the basis of congressional approval. Likewise, in *Terlinden v. Ames* ... (1902), ... there was also a valid extradition treaty, and the reference to a "legislative provision" is again dicta. ...

The extradition agreement in place between the United States and the Tribunal is unenforceable, as it has not been properly ratified. The agreement's implementing legislation is unconstitutional insofar as it purports to ratify the Surrender Agreement by a means other than that prescribed by the Treaty Clause. The two acts seek impermissibly to evade the mandatory constitutional route for implementing such an agreement. I therefore respectfully dissent.

Ntakirutimana was transferred to the ICTR, which in February 2003 found him guilty of aiding and abetting genocide. He was sentenced to ten years' imprisonment. In December 2006 he was released, after a total of ten years in custody. He died a month later.

It is now routine for UN peace operations to have rule of law components. In two situations, however—Kosovo (1999–2012) and East Timor/ Timor-Leste (1999–2002)—the United Nations assumed direct responsibility for the administration of justice, including control of police and prison services.[34] Though created as temporary operations, each was challenged

---

[34] Similar powers were exercised in Bosnia and Herzegovina through the Office of the High Representative from 1996. See also Chapters 9 and 12.

on the extent to which the rule of law applied to international officials who enjoyed personal or functional immunity from legal process, who were unaccountable to the local population through any kind of political process, and who exercised "all legislative and executive authority ... including the administration of the judiciary." Such powers, recalling the provisions of military occupation, became harder to justify as months became years and the disjunction between what international officials said and what they did continued.

SECURITY COUNCIL RESOLUTION 1244 (1999)

Reaffirming the commitment of all Member States to the sovereignty and territorial integrity of the Federal Republic of Yugoslavia ...

Reaffirming the call in previous resolutions for substantial autonomy and meaningful self-administration for Kosovo,

Determining that the situation in the region continues to constitute a threat to international peace and security,

... *acting* for these purposes under Chapter VII of the Charter of the United Nations, ...

5. *Decides* on the deployment in Kosovo, under United Nations auspices, of international civil and security presences, with appropriate equipment and personnel as required, and welcomes the agreement of the Federal Republic of Yugoslavia to such presences; ...

10. *Authorizes* the Secretary-General, with the assistance of relevant international organizations, to establish an international civil presence in Kosovo in order to provide an interim administration for Kosovo under which the people of Kosovo can enjoy substantial autonomy within the Federal Republic of Yugoslavia, and which will provide transitional administration while establishing and overseeing the development of provisional democratic self-governing institutions to ensure conditions for a peaceful and normal life for all inhabitants of Kosovo;

11. *Decides* that the main responsibilities of the international civil presence will include:

(a) Promoting the establishment, pending a final settlement, of substantial autonomy and self-government in Kosovo ...

(b) Performing basic civilian administrative functions where and as long as required;

(c) Organizing and overseeing the development of provisional institutions for democratic and autonomous self-government pending a political settlement, including the holding of elections; ...

(i) Maintaining civil law and order, including establishing local police forces and meanwhile through the deployment of international police personnel to serve in Kosovo;

(j) Protecting and promoting human rights; ...

18. *Demands* that all States in the region cooperate fully in the implementation of all aspects of this resolution;

19. *Decides* that the international civil and security presences are established for an initial period of 12 months, to continue thereafter unless the Security Council decides otherwise; ...

Shortly after the civilian authority of UNMIK was established on the ground, the first of many regulations was passed.

REGULATION 1999/1, ON THE AUTHORITY OF THE INTERIM ADMINISTRATION IN KOSOVO, 25 JULY 1999

Section 1—Authority of the Interim Administration

1.1 All legislative and executive authority with respect to Kosovo, including the administration of the judiciary, is vested in UNMIK and is exercised by the Special Representative of the Secretary-General.

1.2 The Special Representative of the Secretary-General may appoint any person to perform functions in the civil administration in Kosovo, including the judiciary, or remove such person. Such functions shall be exercised in accordance with the existing laws, as specified in section 3, and any regulations issued by UNMIK.

Section 2—Observance of Internationally Recognized Standards

In exercising their functions, all persons undertaking public duties or holding public office in Kosovo shall observe internationally recognized human rights standards and shall not discriminate against any person on any ground such as sex, race, colour, language, religion, political or other opinion, national, ethnic or social origin, association with a national community, property, birth or other status.

Section 3—Applicable Law in Kosovo

The laws applicable in the territory of Kosovo prior to 24 March 1999 shall continue to apply in Kosovo insofar as they do not conflict with standards referred to in section 2, the fulfillment of the mandate given to UNMIK under United Nations Security Council resolution 1244 (1999), or the present or any other regulation issued by UNMIK.

Section 4—Regulations Issued by UNMIK

In the performance of the duties entrusted to the interim administration under United Nations Security Council resolution 1244 (1999)), UNMIK will, as necessary, issue legislative acts in the form of regulations. Such regulations will remain in force until repealed by UNMIK or superseded by such rules as are subsequently issued by the institutions established under a political settlement, as provided for in United Nations Security Council resolution 1244 (1999).

Section 5—Entry into Force and Promulgation of Regulations Issued by UNMIK

5.1 UNMIK regulations shall be approved and signed by the Special Representative of the Secretary-General. They shall enter into force upon the date specified therein.

5.2 UNMIK regulations shall be issued in Albanian, Serbian and English. In case of divergence, the English text shall prevail. The regulations shall be published in a manner that ensures their wide dissemination by public announcement and publication.

5.3 UNMIK regulations shall bear the symbol UNMIK/REG/, followed by the year of issuance and the issuance number of that year. A register of the regulations shall indicate the date of promulgation, the subject matter and amendments or changes thereto or the repeal or suspension thereof.

Section 6—State Property

UNMIK shall administer movable or immovable property, including monies, bank accounts, and other property of, or registered in the name of the Federal Republic of Yugoslavia or the Republic

Section 7—Entry into Force

The present regulation shall be deemed to have entered into force as of 10 June 1999, the date of adoption by the United Nations Security Council of resolution 1244 (1999).

Dr. Bernard Kouchner
Special Representative of the Secretary-General

An Ombudsperson for Kosovo was established by the Organization for Security and Cooperation in Europe (OSCE) on 21 November 2000. It was intended to "promote and protect the rights and freedoms of individuals and legal entities and ensure that all persons in Kosovo are able to exercise effectively the human rights and fundamental freedoms safeguarded by international human rights standards, in particular the European Convention on Human Rights and its Protocols and the International Covenant on Civil and Political Rights." The Ombudsperson was to act independently and without charge; the office had wide jurisdiction to receive and investigate complaints from any person in Kosovo concerning human rights violations and actions constituting an abuse of authority by UNMIK or any emerging central or local institution. This jurisdiction was limited to cases within Kosovo arising after 30 June 2000, and excluded cases involving the NATO-led Kosovo Force (KFOR) and disputes between UNMIK and its staff. During or following an investigation, the Ombudsperson's powers were essentially limited to making recommendations, including recommendations that disciplinary or criminal proceedings be instituted against a person. If the officials concerned did not take appropriate measures within a reasonable time, the Ombudsperson could draw the Special Representative's attention to the matter or make a public statement.[35]

OMBUDSPERSON INSTITUTION IN KOSOVO, SECOND ANNUAL REPORT 2001–2002, 10 JULY 2002[36]

The human rights situation in Kosovo is distinct from the human rights situation in other parts of post-conflict Yugoslavia, in part due to the unique role of the United Nations Mission in Kosovo (UNMIK) as the surrogate state. As the state, however, UNMIK is not structured according to democratic principles, does not function in accordance with the rule of law, and does not respect important international human rights norms. The people of Kosovo are therefore deprived of protection of their basic rights and freedoms three years after the end of the conflict by the very entity set up to guarantee them.

On its establishment as the surrogate state in Kosovo, in 1999, UNMIK gave no cognizance to one of the founding principles of democracy, the separation of governmental powers. Amongst the earliest actions of the Special Representative of the Secretary-General of the United Nations (SRSG) was

---

[35] UNMIK Regulation 2000/38 (30 June 2000), On the Establishment of the Ombudsperson Institution in Kosovo. The Ombudsperson Institution was formally inaugurated on 21 November 2000.

[36] Available at http://www.ombudspersonkosovo.org.

the promulgation of an UNMIK Regulation vesting total executive and legislative powers in himself. In the same Regulation, he also accorded himself administrative authority over the judiciary. The SRSG can and does act outside the bounds of judicial control to restrict or deny fundamental human rights to individuals in Kosovo. For example, he has exercised this power to remove individuals from electoral lists and to override the decision of international judges and international prosecutors to release certain individuals from detention. The effects of the failure of the SRSG to respect the principle of the separation of powers continue to have extremely negative ramifications for the rule of law and human rights in the territory.

Since the establishment of the United Nations regime in Kosovo, UNMIK has both perpetuated and created obstacles to the full protection of human rights, issuing Regulations granting themselves and the international military presence (KFOR) total immunity from legal process in Kosovo, removing decision-making authority over important civil rights from the courts and placing it in administrative bodies under the direct control of UNMIK, and pursuing similar courses of action that serve to eliminate or severely restrict the rights of individuals from Kosovo. The applicable law is often unclear, with UNMIK Regulations and subsidiary legal acts declared as the supreme law of the land, prevailing over any domestic laws in force. Whatever law a court in Kosovo may apply is of little importance, however, as UNMIK will choose whether or not to permit the execution of any resulting judgment.

QUESTIONS

10. What would have been the consequence of the ICTY Appeals Chamber finding that the Tribunal had *not* been validly constituted?
11. Do member states of the United Nations have a legal obligation to surrender persons charged with an offense under the Security Council resolution establishing the Yugoslav and Rwandan tribunals? Does this obligation apply whether or not the state voted for these resolutions? Under what provision of the Charter is such an obligation made mandatory?
12. The rules of the tribunals do not permit national courts to review the indictments of the tribunals for adequacy, such power being given exclusively to a panel of the tribunals' judges charged with confirming the indictments after a review for probable cause. The duty to surrender also extends to citizens of the state from which the surrender is sought. Is this an appropriate division of power between international and national judiciaries?

13. Given the way in which the Yugoslav and Rwandan tribunals were established, why did the Security Council not simply adopt the Rome Statute (establishing the International Criminal Court and its jurisdiction) as a mandatory resolution binding on all members, thereby alleviating the problems caused by some states' reluctance to ratify that treaty?
14. Could the Security Council have simply issued a list of names of war criminals and ordered that they be arrested and detained until the end of the conflict?
15. What powers did Security Council resolution 1244 give to the Special Representative of the Secretary-General (SRSG) in Kosovo? Did the SRSG exceed these powers in passing Regulation 1999/1? If so, what remedy should be available? If not, what limits (if any) are there on the SRSG's powers?
16. Should a transitional administration such as UNMIK be democratically accountable? Should it be subject to the rule of law?

Further Reading

Bassiouni, M. Cherif. *Introduction to International Criminal Law*. The Hague: Martinus Nijhoff, 2012.

Brownlie, Ian. *The Rule of Law in International Affairs: International Law at the Fiftieth Anniversary of the United Nations*. London: Martinus Nijhoff, 1998.

Chesterman, Simon. "An International Rule of Law?" *American Journal of Comparative Law*, vol. 56 (2008), p. 331.

Gaeta, Paola, Laurel Baig, Mary Fan, Christopher Gosnell and Alex Whiting (eds). *Cassesse's International Criminal Law*. 3rd edn. Oxford: Oxford University Press, 2013.

Lee, Roy S.K. (ed). *The International Criminal Court: The Making of the Rome Statute*. The Hague: Kluwer, 1999.

McCorquodale, Robert (ed). *The Rule of Law in International and Comparative Context*. London: British Institute of International and Comparative Law, 2010.

Nollkaemper, André. *National Courts and the International Rule of Law*. Oxford: Oxford University Press, 2012.

Palombella, Gianluigi, and Neil Walker (eds). *Relocating the Rule of Law*. Oxford: Hart, 2009.

Pouligny, Béatrice, Simon Chesterman and Albrecht Schnabel (eds). *After Mass Crime: Rebuilding States and Communities*. New York: United Nations University Press, 2007.

Schabas, William. *An Introduction to the International Criminal Court*. 4th edn. Cambridge: Cambridge University Press, 2011.

Tamanaha, Brian. *On the Rule of Law: History, Politics, Theory*. Cambridge: Cambridge University Press, 2004.

Teitel, Ruti. *Transitional Justice*. Oxford: Oxford University Press, 2000.

Part Four **Accountability**

chapter fifteen
·················

Immunity and Responsibility

Norms concerning the special privileges of diplomats are among the oldest in international law. Traditionally, these were limited to the representatives of states. From the nineteenth century on, however, a gradual extension of traditional privileges and immunities began to include international organizations.[1]

Similarly, responsibility for wrongs in international law was initially limited to those entities capable of acting as full subjects: states. The law of state responsibility determines when and how a state may be held responsible for the breach of an international obligation. Because it separates the consequences of breach from the obligation itself, it is referred to as a set of "secondary" rules, as distinct from "primary" or substantive rules.[2] As with immunities and privileges, there has been a gradual, but far more recent, extension of these rules to embrace international organizations.

Both trends indicate the increasing importance of international organizations—especially, but not only, the United Nations—as actors in international affairs. The legal personality of the United Nations was discussed in Chapter 4. In this chapter, the focus is on specific issues that have arisen in relation to acts carried out in the name of the Organization.

Section 1 considers immunities and privileges. It was generally accepted when the UN Charter was being drafted that the Organization and its representatives should be granted whatever privileges and immunities were necessary to exercise the functions entrusted to them. The United Nations itself enjoys absolute immunity as a legal person and with respect to UN property. This is protected in the Convention on Privileges and Immunities and has never been a matter of serious dispute. Where no alternative form of legal recourse is available, the immunity may be waived in accordance with the Convention.

The status of officials has been more complicated. The Secretary-General and Assistant Secretaries-General (as well as the more senior Deputy

---

[1] Indeed, in some cases immunity has also been extended to nongovernmental organizations (NGOs). See Davinia Aziz, "Global Public-Private Partnerships in International Law," *Asian Journal of International Law*, vol. 2(2) (2012), p. 339.

[2] The distinction was, in larger part, a pragmatic means of avoiding contentious discussions of the content of obligations in order to focus on codifying the more technical aspects of attribution of responsibility.

Secretary-General and Under-Secretaries-General added later to the UN Secretariat's hierarchy) enjoy diplomatic privileges and immunities. Other officials receive "functional" immunity, meaning that immunity is restricted to official acts and words spoken or written in an official capacity. A key question, in such situations, is who decides whether the relevant words or deeds were indeed performed in an official capacity.

After extracting key provisions from the Charter and the Convention, the chapter looks at two groups of "officials": peacekeepers and special rapporteurs. As we will see in the next chapter on accountability, peacekeepers may present special problems of accountability for the United Nations—both because of the situations in which they operate and the terms according to which their home state sends them on mission. Here we limit ourselves to considering the manner in which the immunities and privileges of the position is presented to them. Special rapporteurs may be employed on a part-time basis, and sometimes take on mandates that are not welcomed by the territories in which they operate.

Section 2 turns to the question of responsibility. It seems axiomatic that the violation of international law entails responsibility and the obligation to make some form of reparation.[3] States, for example, are normally responsible for internationally wrongful acts that can be attributed to them.[4]

International organizations such as the United Nations raise more complicated issues concerning the attribution of acts by individuals and states to the organization. In some cases it may be unclear whether responsibility for a wrong should most appropriately be attributed to an international organization or the states that act through it. (Similar issues may arise in a corporation being punished for the wrongs of its directors.)

This was a marginal issue until the collapse of the International Tin Council in the mid-1980s, which led to much litigation in the English courts and, a decade later, the emergence of a new field of study. The present chapter will briefly consider some of the positions put forward in the Tin Council litigation, before examining efforts to codify and develop law in this area.

Establishing the legal rules for accountability is an important foundation. To be meaningful, accountability should not require the creation of new institutions or procedures but should exist as of right. In this way, it is hoped, such institutions and procedures will not merely punish abuse but encourage good behavior. As we shall see in the next chapter, however, deficits in institutions and procedures are sometimes compounded by the political context within which accountability issues arise.

---

[3] See, e.g., *Factory at Chorzów (Jurisdiction)* (1927) PCIJ, Series A, No. 9, p. 21.

[4] See generally James Crawford, *The International Law Commission's Articles on State Responsibility: Introduction, Text and Commentaries* (Cambridge: Cambridge University Press, 2002).

15.1 Privileges and Immunities

At the time of its establishment, it was recognized that the United Nations, its agents, and the representatives of states would need a status similar to that of an embassy and ambassadors.[5] The precise extent of these privileges and immunities, however, was left to later negotiations.

UN CHARTER, ARTICLE 105

1. The Organization shall enjoy in the territory of each of its Members such privileges and immunities as are necessary for the fulfilment of its purposes.

2. Representatives of the Members of the United Nations and officials of the Organization shall similarly enjoy such privileges and immunities as are necessary for the independent exercise of their functions in connection with the Organization.

3. The General Assembly may make recommendations with a view to determining the details of the application of paragraphs 1 and 2 of this Article or may propose conventions to the Members of the United Nations for this purpose.

Pursuant to Article 105(3) of the Charter, the General Assembly adopted resolution 22(I) (1946), proposing the convention to all members of the United Nations for accession. It entered into force seven months later; at the end of 2014 it had 160 states parties.

CONVENTION ON THE PRIVILEGES AND IMMUNITIES OF THE UNITED NATIONS, 13 FEBRUARY 1946, 1 UNTS 15

Whereas Article 105 of the Charter of the United Nations provides that the Organization shall enjoy in the territory of each of its Member such privileges and immunities as are necessary for the fulfilment of its purposes and that representatives of the Members of the United Nations and officials of the Organization shall similarly enjoy such privileges and immunities as are necessary for the independent exercise of their functions in connection with the Organization.

---

[5] A related requirement was legal personality, which is discussed in Chapter 4.

Consequently the General Assembly by a Resolution adopted on the 13 February 1946, approved the following Convention and proposed it for accession by each Member of the United Nations. . . .

Article II—Property, Funds and Assets

Section 2. The United Nations, its property and assets wherever located and by whomsoever held, shall enjoy immunity from every form of legal process except insofar as in any particular case it has expressly waived its immunity. It is, however, understood that no waiver of immunity shall extend to any measure of execution.

Section 3. The premises of the United Nations shall be inviolable. The property and assets of the United Nations, wherever located and by whomsoever held, shall be immune from search, requisition, confiscation, expropriation and any other form of interference, whether by executive, administrative, judicial or legislative action.

Section 4. The archives of the United Nations, and in general all documents belonging to it or held by it, shall be inviolable wherever located. . . .

Section 7. The United Nations, its assets, income and other property shall be:

(a) Exempt from all direct taxes; it is understood however, that the United Nations will not claim exemption from taxes which are, in fact, no more than charges for public utility services;

(b) Exempt from customs duties and prohibitions and restrictions on imports and exports in respect of articles imported or exported by the United Nations for its official use. It is understood, however, that articles imported under such exemption will not be sold in the country into which they were imported except under conditions agreed with the Government of that country;

(c) Exempt from customs duties and prohibitions and restrictions on imports and exports in respect of its publications.

Section 8. While the United Nations will not, as a general rule, claim exemption from excise duties and from taxes on the sale of movable and immovable property which form part of the price to be paid, nevertheless when the United Nations is making important purchases for official use of property on which such duties and taxes have been charged or are chargeable, Members will, whenever possible, make appropriate administrative arrangements for the remission or return of the amount of duty or tax.

Article III—Facilities in Respect of Communications

. . .

Section 10. The United Nations shall have the right to use codes and to dispatch and receive its correspondence by courier or in bags, which shall have the same immunities and privileges as diplomatic couriers and bags.

Article IV—The Representatives of Members

Section 11. Representatives of Members to the principal and subsidiary organs of the United Nations and to conferences convened by the United Nations, shall, while exercising their functions and during the journey to and from the place of meeting, enjoy the following privileges and immunities:

(a) Immunity from personal arrest or detention and from seizure of their personal baggage, and, in respect of words spoken or written and all acts done by them in their capacity as representatives, immunity from legal process of every kind;

(b) Inviolability for all papers and documents;

(c) The right to use codes and to receive papers or correspondence by courier or in sealed bags;

(d) Exemption in respect of themselves and their spouses from immigration restrictions, alien registration or national service obligations in the State they are visiting or through which they are passing in the exercise of their functions;

(e) The same facilities in respect of currency or exchange restrictions as are accorded to representatives of foreign governments on temporary official missions;

(f) The immunities and facilities in respect of their personal baggage as are accorded to diplomatic envoys, and also;

(g) Such other privileges, immunities and facilities not inconsistent with the foregoing as diplomatic envoys enjoy, except that they shall have no right to claim exemption from customs duties on goods imported (otherwise than as part of their personal baggage) or from excise duties or sales taxes. . . .

Section 14. Privileges and immunities are accorded to the representatives of Members not for the personal benefit of the individuals themselves, but in order to safeguard the independent exercise of their functions in connection with the United Nations. Consequently a Member not only has the right but is under a duty to waive the immunity of its representative in any case where in the opinion of the Member the immunity would impede the course of justice, and it can be waived without prejudice to the purpose for which the immunity is accorded.

Section 15. The provisions of Sections 11, 12 and 13 are not applicable as between a representative and the authorities of the state of which he is a national or of which he is or has been the representative.

Section 16. In this article the expression "representatives" shall be deemed to include all delegates, deputy delegates, advisers, technical experts and secretaries of delegations.

Article V—Officials

Section 17. The Secretary-General will specify the categories of officials to which the provisions of this Article and Article VII shall apply. He shall submit these categories to the General Assembly. Thereafter these categories shall be communicated to the Governments of all Members. The names of the officials included in these categories shall from time to time be made known to the Governments of Members.

Section 18. Officials of the United Nations shall:

(a) Be immune from legal process in respect of words spoken or written and all acts performed by them in their official capacity;

(b) Be exempt from taxation on the salaries and emoluments paid to them by the United Nations;

(c) Be immune from national service obligations;

(d) Be immune, together with their spouses and relatives dependent on them, from immigration restrictions and alien registration;

(e) Be accorded the same privileges in respect of exchange facilities as are accorded to the officials of comparable ranks forming part of diplomatic missions to the Government concerned;

(f) Be given, together with their spouses and relatives dependent on them, the same repatriation facilities in time of international crisis as diplomatic envoys;

(g) Have the right to import free of duty their furniture and effects at the time of first taking up their post in the country in question.

Section 19. In addition to the immunities and privileges specified in Section 18, the Secretary-General and all Assistant Secretaries-General shall be accorded in respect of themselves, their spouses and minor children, the privileges and immunities, exemptions and facilities accorded to diplomatic envoys, in accordance with international law.

Section 20. Privileges and immunities are granted to officials in the interests of the United Nations and not for the personal benefit of the individuals themselves. The Secretary-General shall have the right and the duty to waive the immunity of any official in any case where, in his opinion, the immunity would impede the course of justice and can be waived without prejudice to the interests of the United Nations. In the case of the Secretary-General, the Security Council shall have the right to waive immunity.

Section 21. The United Nations shall cooperate at all times with the appropriate authorities of Members to facilitate the proper administration of justice, secure the observance of police regulations and prevent the occurrence of any abuse in connection with the privileges, immunities and facilities mentioned in this Article.

Article VI—Experts on Missions for the United Nations

Section 22. Experts (other than officials coming within the scope of Article V) performing missions for the United Nations shall be accorded such privileges and immunities as are necessary for the independent exercise of their functions during the period of their missions, including the time spent on journeys in connection with their missions. In particular they shall be accorded:

(a) Immunity from personal arrest or detention and from seizure of their personal baggage;

(b) In respect of words spoken or written and acts done by them in the course of the performance of their mission, immunity from legal process of every kind. This immunity from legal process shall continue to be accorded notwithstanding that the persons concerned are no longer employed on missions for the United Nations;

(c) Inviolability for all papers and documents;

(d) For the purpose of their communications with the United Nations, the right to use codes and to receive papers or correspondence by courier or in sealed bags;

(e) The same facilities in respect of currency or exchange restrictions as are accorded to representatives of foreign governments on temporary official missions;

(f) The same immunities and facilities in respect of their personal baggage as are accorded to diplomatic envoys.

Section 23. Privileges and immunities are granted to experts in the interests of the United Nations and not for the personal benefit of the individuals themselves. The Secretary-General shall have the right and the duty to waive the immunity of any expert in any case where, in his opinion, the immunity would impede the course of justice and it can be waived without prejudice to the interests of the United Nations.

. . .

Article VIII—Settlement of Disputes

Section 29. The United Nations shall make provisions for appropriate modes of settlement of:

(a) Disputes arising out of contracts or other disputes of a private law character to which the United Nations is a party;

(b) Disputes involving any official of the United Nations who by reason of his official position enjoys immunity, if immunity has not been waived by the Secretary-General.

Section 30. All differences arising out of the interpretation or application of the present convention shall be referred to the International Court of Justice, unless in any case it is agreed by the parties to have recourse to another mode of settlement. If a difference arises between the United Nations on the one hand and a Member on the other hand, a request shall be made for an advisory opinion on any legal question involved in accordance with Article 96 of the Charter and Article 65 of the Statute of the Court. The opinion given by the Court shall be accepted as decisive by the parties.

Immunity is a very powerful tool that may easily be abused. The following is a pocket card that is given to peacekeepers and explains the behavior that is expected of UN peacekeepers.

WE ARE UNITED NATIONS PEACEKEEPERS
(POCKET CARD DISTRIBUTED TO UN PEACEKEEPERS)

The United Nations Organization embodies the aspirations of all the people of the world for peace. In this context the United Nations Charter requires that all personnel must maintain the highest standards of integrity and conduct.

We will comply with the Guidelines on International Humanitarian Law for Forces Undertaking United Nations Peacekeeping Operations and the applicable portions of the Universal Declaration of Human Rights as the fundamental basis of our standards.

We, as peace-keepers, represent the United Nations and are present in the country to help it recover from the trauma of a conflict. As a result we must consciously be prepared to accept special constraints in our public and private lives in order to do the work and to pursue the ideals of the United Nations Organization.

We will be accorded certain privileges and immunities arranged through agreements negotiated between the United Nations and the host country solely for the purpose of discharging our peacekeeping duties. Expectations of the world community and the local population will be high and our actions, behaviour and speech will be closely monitored.

We will always:

- Conduct oursel ves in a professional and disciplined manner, at all times;
- Dedicate ourselves to achieving the goals of the United Nations;
- Understand the mandate and mission and comply with their provisions;
- Respect the environment of the host country;
- Respect local customs and practices through awareness and respect for the culture, religion, traditions and gender issues;
- Treat the inhabitants of the host country with respect, courtesy and consideration;
- Act with impartiality, integrity and tact;
- Support and aid the infirm, sick and weak;
- Obey our United Nations superiors and respect the chain of command;
- Respect all other peacekeeping members of the mission regardless of status, rank, ethnic or national origin, race, gender, or creed;
- Support and encourage proper conduct among our fellow peace-keepers;
- Maintain proper dress and personal deportment at all times;
- Properly account for all money and property assigned to us as members of the mission; and
- Care for all United Nations equipment placed in our charge.

We will never:

- Bring discredit upon the United Nations, or our nations through improper personal conduct, failure to perform our duties or abuse of our positions as peace-keepers;
- Take any action that might jeopardize the mission;
- Abuse alcohol, use or traffic in drugs;
- Make unauthorized communications to external agencies, including unauthorized press statements;
- Improperly disclose or use information gained through our employment;
- Use unnecessary violence or threaten anyone in custody;
- Commit any act that could result in physical, sexual or psychological harm or suffering to members of the local population, especially women and children;
- Become involved in sexual liaisons which could affect our impartiality, or the well-being of others;
- Be abusive or uncivil to any member of the public;
- Willfully damage or misuse any United Nations property or equipment;
- Use a vehicle improperly or without authorisation;
- Collect unauthorized souvenirs;
- Participate in any illegal activities, corrupt or improper practices; or
- Attempt to use our positions for personal advantage, to make false claims or accept benefits to which we are not entitled.

We realize that the consequences of failure to act within these guidelines may:

- Erode confidence and trust in the United Nations;
- Jeopardize the achievement of the mission; and
- Jeopardize our status and security as peacekeepers.

Immunity questions have arisen on numerous occasions with respect to human rights monitoring by the United Nations.[6] In 1994 the Commission on Human Rights appointed Dato' Param Cumaraswamy, a Malaysian jurist, as the Commission's Special Rapporteur on the Independence of Judges and Lawyers. In 1995 he gave an interview to *International Commercial Litigation*, a magazine published in London, in which he commented on certain litigation in the Malaysian courts. Two Malaysian companies subsequently claimed that the published article contained defamatory words that had "brought them into public scandal, odium and contempt." This was the first of a total of four defamation suits brought against Cumaraswamy in the Malaysian courts.

---

[6] See, e.g., *Applicability of Article VI, Section 22, of the Convention on the Privileges and Immunities of the United Nations (Advisory Opinion)* (International Court of Justice, 15 December 1989), available at: www.icj-cij.org.

The Secretary-General issued a note confirming that "the words which constitute the basis of plaintiffs' complaint in this case were spoken by the Special Rapporteur in the course of his mission" and that the Secretary-General therefore maintained that Cumaraswamy was immune from legal process with respect to those words. A judge of the Malaysian High Court for Kuala Lumpur concluded that she was "unable to hold that the Defendant is absolutely protected by the immunity he claims," in part because she considered that the Secretary-General's note was merely "an opinion" with scant probative value and no binding force upon the court.

When further discussions did not produce agreement, the Economic and Social Council, at the request of the Secretary-General, sought an advisory opinion on the matter from the International Court of Justice.

ECOSOC DECISION 1998/297 (5 AUGUST 1998)

The Economic and Social Council, ...

Considering that a difference has arisen between the United Nations and the Government of Malaysia, within the meaning of Section 30 of the Convention on the Privileges and Immunities of the United Nations ...

1. *Requests* ... an advisory opinion from the International Court of Justice on the legal question of the applicability of Article VI, Section 22, of the Convention on the Privileges and Immunities of the United Nations in the case of Dato' Param Cumaraswamy as Special Rapporteur of the Commission on Human Rights on the independence of judges and lawyers, ...

2. *Calls upon* the Government of Malaysia to ensure that all judgements and proceedings in this matter in the Malaysian courts are stayed pending receipt of the advisory opinion of the International Court of Justice, which shall be accepted as decisive by the parties.

The following April the ICJ delivered its advisory opinion.

DIFFERENCE RELATING TO IMMUNITY FROM LEGAL PROCESS OF A SPECIAL RAPPORTEUR OF THE COMMISSION ON HUMAN RIGHTS (ADVISORY OPINION) (INTERNATIONAL COURT OF JUSTICE, 29 APRIL 1999)

38. The Court will initially examine the first part of the question laid before the Court by the Council, which is: "the legal question of the applicability of

Article VI, Section 22, of the Convention on the Privileges and Immunities of the United Nations in the case of Dato' Param Cumaraswamy as Special Rapporteur of the Commission on Human Rights on the independence of judges and lawyers, taking into account the circumstances set out in paragraphs 1 to 15 of the note by the Secretary-General . . ."

39. From the deliberations which took place in the Council on the content of the request for an advisory opinion, it is clear that the reference in the request to the note of the Secretary-General was made in order to provide the Court with the basic facts to which to refer in making its decision. The request of the Council therefore does not only pertain to the threshold question whether Mr. Cumaraswamy was and is an expert on mission in the sense of Article VI, Section 22, of the General Convention but, in the event of an affirmative answer to this question, to the consequences of that finding in the circumstances of the case.

40. . . . Acting in accordance with Article 105 of the Charter, the General Assembly approved the General Convention on 13 February 1946 and proposed it for accession by each Member of the United Nations. Malaysia became a party to the General Convention, without reservation, on 28 October 1957. . . .

42. In its Advisory Opinion of 14 December 1989 on the *Applicability of Article VI, Section 22, of the Convention on the Privileges and Immunities of the United Nations*, the Court examined the applicability of Section 22 *ratione personae, ratione temporis* and *ratione loci*.

In this context the Court stated: "The purpose of Section 22 is . . . evident, namely, to enable the United Nations to entrust missions to persons who do not have the status of an official of the Organization, and to guarantee them 'such privileges and immunities as are necessary for the independent exercise of their functions'. . . . The essence of the matter lies not in their administrative position but in the nature of their mission."

In that same Advisory Opinion, the Court concluded that a Special Rapporteur who is appointed by the Sub-Commission on Prevention of Discrimination and Protection of Minorities and is entrusted with a research mission must be regarded as an expert on mission within the meaning of Article VI, Section 22, of the General Convention.

43. The same conclusion must be drawn with regard to Special Rapporteurs appointed by the Human Rights Commission, of which the Sub-Commission is a subsidiary organ. It may be observed that Special Rapporteurs of the Commission usually are entrusted not only with a research mission but also with the task of monitoring human rights violations and reporting on them. But what is decisive is that they have been entrusted with a mission by the United Nations and are therefore entitled to the privileges and immunities provided for in Article VI, Section 22, that safeguard the independent exercise of their functions.

44. By a letter of 21 April 1994, the Chairman of the Commission informed the Assistant Secretary-General for Human Rights of Mr. Cumaraswamy's appointment as Special Rapporteur. The mandate of the Special Rapporteur

is contained in resolution 1994/41 of the Commission entitled "Independence and Impartiality of the Judiciary, Jurors and Assessors and the Independence of Lawyers." This resolution was endorsed by the Council in its decision 1994/251 of 22 July 1994. The Special Rapporteur's mandate consists of the following tasks:

"(a) to inquire into any substantial allegations transmitted to him or her and report his or her conclusions thereon;

(b) to identify and record not only attacks on the independence of the judiciary, lawyers and court officials but also progress achieved in protecting and enhancing their independence, and make concrete recommendations, including accommodations for the provision of advisory services or technical assistance when they are requested by the State concerned;

(c) to study, for the purpose of making proposals, important and topical questions of principle with a view to protecting and enhancing the independence of the judiciary and lawyers."

45. The Commission extended by resolution 1997/23 of 11 April 1997 the Special Rapporteur's mandate for a further period of three years.

In the light of these circumstances, the Court finds that Mr. Cumaraswamy must be regarded as an expert on mission within the meaning of Article VI, Section 22, as from 21 April 1994, that by virtue of this capacity the provisions of this Section were applicable to him at the time of his statements at issue, and that they continue to be applicable.

46. The Court observes that Malaysia has acknowledged that Mr. Cumaraswamy, as Special Rapporteur of the Commission, is an expert on mission and that such experts enjoy the privileges and immunities provided for under the General Convention in their relations with States parties, including those of which they are nationals or on the territory of which they reside. Malaysia and the United Nations are in full agreement on these points, as are the other States participating in the proceedings.

47. The Court will now consider whether the immunity provided for in Section 22 (b) applies to Mr. Cumaraswamy in the specific circumstances of the case; namely, whether the words used by him in the interview, as published in the article in *International Commercial Litigation* (November issue 1995), were spoken in the course of the performance of his mission, and whether he was therefore immune from legal process with respect to these words. . . .

50. In the process of determining whether a particular expert on mission is entitled, in the prevailing circumstances, to the immunity provided for in Section 22 (b), the Secretary-General of the United Nations has a pivotal role to play. The Secretary-General, as the chief administrative officer of the Organization, has the authority and the responsibility to exercise the necessary protection where required. This authority has been recognized by the Court when it stated: "Upon examination of the character of the functions entrusted to the Organization and of the nature of the missions of its agents, it becomes clear that the capacity of the Organization to exercise a measure

of functional protection of its agents arises by necessary intendment out of the Charter." *(Reparation for Injuries Suffered in the Service of the United Nations, Advisory Opinion, I.C.J. Reports 1949, p. 184.)*[7]

51. Article VI, Section 23, of the General Convention provides that "[p]rivileges and immunities are granted to experts in the interests of the United Nations and not for the personal benefit of the individuals themselves." In exercising protection of United Nations experts, the Secretary-General is therefore protecting the mission with which the expert is entrusted. In that respect, the Secretary-General has the primary responsibility and authority to protect the interests of the Organization and its agents, including experts on mission. As the Court held: "In order that the agent may perform his duties satisfactorily, he must feel that this protection is assured to him by the Organization, and that he may count on it. To ensure the independence of the agent, and, consequently, the independent action of the Organization itself, it is essential that in performing his duties he need not have to rely on any other protection than that of the Organization ..." *(Ibid.,* p. 183.)

52. The determination whether an agent of the Organization has acted in the course of the performance of his mission depends upon the facts of a particular case. In the present case, the Secretary-General, or the Legal Counsel of the United Nations on his behalf, has on numerous occasions informed the Government of Malaysia of his finding that Mr. Cumaraswamy had spoken the words quoted in the article in *International Commercial Litigation* in his capacity as Special Rapporteur of the Commission and that he consequently was entitled to immunity from "every kind" of legal process.

53. As is clear from the written and oral pleadings of the United Nations, the Secretary-General was reinforced in this view by the fact that it has become standard practice of Special Rapporteurs of the Commission to have contact with the media. This practice was confirmed by the High Commissioner for Human Rights who, in a letter dated 2 October 1998, included in the dossier, wrote that: "it is more common than not for Special Rapporteurs to speak to the press about matters pertaining to their investigations, thereby keeping the general public informed of their work."

54. ... Mr. Cumaraswamy was explicitly referred to several times in the article "Malaysian Justice on Trial" in *International Commercial Litigation* in his capacity as United Nations Special Rapporteur on the Independence of Judges and Lawyers. In his reports to the Commission ..., Mr. Cumaraswamy had set out his methods of work, expressed concern about the independence of the Malaysian judiciary, and referred to the civil lawsuits initiated against him. His third report noted that the Legal Counsel of the United Nations had informed the Government of Malaysia that he had spoken in the performance of his mission and was therefore entitled to immunity from legal process.

---

[7] See Chapter 3, section 3.1.

55. ... [I]n its various resolutions the Commission took note of the Special Rapporteur's reports and of his methods of work. In 1997, it extended his mandate for another three years ... The Commission presumably would not have so acted if it had been of the opinion that Mr. Cumaraswamy had gone beyond his mandate and had given the interview to *International Commercial Litigation* outside the course of his functions. Thus the Secretary-General was able to find support for his findings in the Commission's position.

56. The Court is not called upon in the present case to pass upon the aptness of the terms used by the Special Rapporteur or his assessment of the situation. In any event, in view of all the circumstances of this case, ... the Court is of the opinion that the Secretary-General correctly found that Mr. Cumaraswamy, in speaking the words quoted in the article in *International Commercial Litigation*, was acting in the course of the performance of his mission as Special Rapporteur of the Commission. Consequently, Article VI, Section 22 *(b)*, of the General Convention is applicable to him in the present case and affords Mr. Cumaraswamy immunity from legal process of every kind.

57. The Court will now deal with the second part of the Council's question, namely, "the legal obligations of Malaysia in this case."

58. Malaysia maintains that it is premature to deal with the question of its obligations. It is of the view that the obligation to ensure that the requirements of Section 22 of the Convention are met is an obligation of result and not of means to be employed in achieving that result. It further states that Malaysia has complied with its obligation under Section 34 of the General Convention, which provides that a party to the Convention must be "in a position under its own law to give effect to [its] terms," by enacting the necessary legislation; finally it contends that the Malaysian courts have not yet reached a final decision as to Mr. Cumaraswamy's entitlement to immunity from legal process.

59. The Court wishes to point out that the request for an advisory opinion refers to "the legal obligations of Malaysia in this case." The difference which has arisen between the United Nations and Malaysia originated in the Government of Malaysia not having informed the competent Malaysian judicial authorities of the Secretary-General's finding that Mr. Cumaraswamy had spoken the words at issue in the course of the performance of his mission and was, therefore, entitled to immunity from legal process ... It is as from the time of this omission that the question before the Court must be answered.

60. As the Court has observed, the Secretary-General, as the chief administrative officer of the Organization, has the primary responsibility to safeguard the interests of the Organization; to that end, it is up to him to assess whether its agents acted within the scope of their functions and, where he so concludes, to protect these agents, including experts on mission, by asserting their immunity. This means that the Secretary-General has the authority and responsibility to inform the government of a member State of his finding and, where appropriate, to request it to act accordingly and, in particular, to request it to bring his finding to the knowledge of the local courts if acts of an agent have given or may give rise to court proceedings.

61. When national courts are seized of a case in which the immunity of a United Nations agent is in issue, they should immediately be notified of any finding by the Secretary-General concerning that immunity. That finding, and its documentary expression, creates a presumption which can only be set aside for the most compelling reasons and is thus to be given the greatest weight by national courts.

The governmental authorities of a party to the General Convention are therefore under an obligation to convey such information to the national courts concerned, since a proper application of the Convention by them is dependent on such information.

Failure to comply with this obligation, among others, could give rise to the institution of proceedings under Article VIII, Section 30, of the General Convention.

62. The Court concludes that the Government of Malaysia had an obligation, under Article 105 of the Charter and under the General Convention, to inform its courts of the position taken by the Secretary-General. According to a well-established rule of international law, the conduct of any organ of a State must be regarded as an act of that State. This rule, which is of a customary character, is reflected in Article 6 of the Draft Articles on State Responsibility adopted provisionally by the International Law Commission . . .

Because the Government did not transmit the Secretary-General's finding to the competent courts, and the Minister for Foreign Affairs did not refer to it in his own certificate, Malaysia did not comply with the above-mentioned obligation.

63. Section 22 (b) of the General Convention explicitly states that experts on mission shall be accorded immunity from legal process of every kind in respect of words spoken or written and acts done by them in the course of the performance of their mission. By necessary implication, questions of immunity are therefore preliminary issues which must be expeditiously decided in limine litis [at the very outset of the proceedings]. This is a generally-recognized principle of procedural law, and Malaysia was under an obligation to respect it. The Malaysian courts did not rule in limine litis on the immunity of the Special Rapporteur . . . thereby nullifying the essence of the immunity rule contained in Section 22 (b). Moreover, costs were taxed to Mr. Cumaraswamy while the question of immunity was still unresolved. As indicated above, the conduct of an organ of a State—even an organ independent of the executive power—must be regarded as an act of that State. Consequently, Malaysia did not act in accordance with its obligations under international law.

64. In addition, the immunity from legal process to which the Court finds Mr. Cumaraswamy entitled entails holding Mr. Cumaraswamy financially harmless for any costs imposed upon him by the Malaysian courts, in particular taxed costs.

65. According to Article VIII, Section 30, of the General Convention, the opinion given by the Court shall be accepted as decisive by the parties to the dispute. Malaysia has acknowledged its obligations under Section 30.

Since the Court holds that Mr. Cumaraswamy is an expert on mission who under Section 22 *(b)* is entitled to immunity from legal process, the Government of Malaysia is obligated to communicate this advisory opinion to the competent Malaysian courts, in order that Malaysia's international obligations be given effect and Mr. Cumaraswamy's immunity be respected.

66. Finally, the Court wishes to point out that the question of immunity from legal process is distinct from the issue of compensation for any damages incurred as a result of acts performed by the United Nations or by its agents acting in their official capacity.

The United Nations may be required to bear responsibility for the damage arising from such acts. However, as is clear from Article VIII, Section 29, of the General Convention, any such claims against the United Nations shall not be dealt with by national courts but shall be settled in accordance with the appropriate modes of settlement that "[t]he United Nations shall make provisions for" pursuant to Section 29.

Furthermore, it need hardly be said that all agents of the United Nations, in whatever official capacity they act, must take care not to exceed the scope of their functions, and should so comport themselves as to avoid claims against the United Nations.

In July 2000 the Malaysian High Court ruled that Param was immune from all legal process and dismissed the lawsuits.

The United Nations itself, as we have seen earlier, enjoys immunity also. In November 2011, for example, a letter was submitted by the Institute for Justice & Democracy in Haiti alleging that UN peacekeepers were responsible for a cholera epidemic that killed at least 8,700 people since 2010. The peacekeepers were part of the UN Stabilization Mission in Haiti, MINUSTAH. The Under Secretary-General for Legal Affairs replied in February 2013.

LETTER FROM THE UNDER SECRETARY-GENERAL FOR LEGAL AFFAIRS TO BRIAN CONCANNON, DIRECTOR OF THE INSTITUTE FOR JUSTICE & DEMOCRACY IN HAITI (21 FEBRUARY 2013)

I refer to your letter of 3 November 2011 to the Secretary-General, transmitting claims against the United Nations related to the cholera outbreak in Haiti. With respect to these claims, you seek compensation for individuals affected by the cholera outbreak and an agreement with the Government of Haiti in order to establish and fund a nationwide programme for clean water, adequate sanitation and appropriate medical treatment to prevent the further spread of cholera.

The United Nations is extremely saddened by the catastrophic outbreak of cholera, and the Secretary-General has expressed his profound sympathy for the terrible suffering caused by the cholera outbreak. The cholera outbreak was not only an enormous national disaster, but was also a painful reminder of Haiti's vulnerability in the event of a national emergency.

From the very early stages of the epidemic, the United Nations, along with its partners, has expended considerable effort and resources in combating cholera and improving Haiti's water and sanitation facilities, as well as on training, logistics and early warning systems. ...

Additionally, in January 2011, the Secretary-General formed an independent panel of four independent experts (the "Panel") with a mandate to investigate and seek to determine the source of the 2010 cholera outbreak in Haiti. In its report dated 4 May 2011, the Panel concluded that the outbreak was caused by a confluence of circumstances and was not the fault of, or deliberate action of, a group or individual. ...

With respect to the claims submitted, consideration of these claims would necessarily include a review of political and policy matters. Accordingly, these claims are not receivable pursuant to Section 29 of the Convention on the Privileges and Immunities of the United Nations, adopted by the General Assembly on 13 February 1946. ...

In October 2013, three class action lawsuits were filed in US courts.

DELAMA GEORGES v. UNITED NATIONS (U.S. DISTRICT COURT, SOUTHERN DISTRICT OF NEW YORK, JUDGMENT OF 9 JANUARY 2015)[8]

Plaintiffs bring this class action diversity suit alleging various tort and contract claims against defendants the United Nations ("UN"), the United Nations Stabilization Mission in Haiti ("MINUSTAH"), United Nations Secretary-General Ban Ki-moon, and former Under-Secretary-General for MINUSTAH, Edmond Mulet. ... Specifically, Plaintiffs allege that Defendants are responsible for an epidemic of cholera that broke out in Haiti in 2010, killing over 8,000 Haitians and making over 600,000 ill. ...

---

[8] Case 1:13-cv-07146-JPO.

Plaintiffs allege that in October 2010, Defendants deployed over 1,000 UN personnel from Nepal to Haiti without screening them for cholera, a disease that is endemic to Nepal and with which some of the personnel were infected. ... Plaintiffs further allege that Defendants stationed these personnel on a base at the banks of the Meille Tributary, which flows into Haiti's primary source of drinking water, the Artibonite River. It was at this base, Plaintiffs contend, that these recently transferred personnel discharged raw untreated sewage into the tributary, causing an outbreak of cholera in Haiti. ...

Plaintiffs allege that Defendants have failed to establish any claims commission or other dispute resolution mechanism to resolve the claims of those who have been injured or who have lost family members to the cholera outbreak. This refusal, Plaintiffs contend, is in direct contravention of Defendants' responsibility under the Convention on the Privileges and Immunities of the United Nations ("CPIUN") and the Agreement Between the United Nations and the Government of Haiti Concerning the Status of the United Nations Operation in Haiti ("SOFA") to offer appropriate modes of settlement for third-party private-law claims. ...

The CPIUN provides that "[t]he United Nations, its property and assets wherever located and by whomsoever held, shall enjoy immunity from every form of legal process except insofar as in any particular case it has expressly waived its immunity." ...

Here, no party contends that the UN has expressly waived its immunity. ... Accordingly, ... the UN is immune from Plaintiffs' suit. In addition, MINUSTAH, as a subsidiary body of the UN, is also immune from suit. ...

Plaintiffs argue that the UN has materially breached the CPIUN such that it is not entitled to the "benefit of the bargain." Specifically, Plaintiffs insist that the UN has breached section 29(a), which provides that "[t]he United Nations shall make provisions for appropriate modes of settlement of ... disputes arising out of contracts or other disputes of a private law character to which the United Nations is a party." ... Because the UN has failed to provide any mode of settlement for the claims at issue here, Plaintiffs argue, it is not entitled to benefit from the CPIUN's grant of absolute immunity.

This argument is foreclosed by *Brzak*. ... Here too, construing the UN's failure to provide "appropriate modes of settlement" for Plaintiffs' claims as subjecting the UN to Plaintiffs' suit would read the strict express waiver requirement out of the CPIUN.

Moreover, nothing in the text of the CPIUN suggests that the absolute immunity of section 2 is conditioned on the UN's providing the alternative modes of settlement contemplated by section 29. ... [T]he language of section 2 of the CPIUN is clear, absolute, and does not refer to section 29: the UN is immune from suit unless it expressly waives its immunity. ... Further, the CPIUN's drafting history indicates at most the commitment that, pursuant to section 29, the UN will provide a dispute resolution mechanism for private claims; it does not, as Plaintiffs argue, indicate the intent that such a mechanism is required in order for the UN to claim immunity in any particular case. . . .

It is true that section 29 uses mandatory language, providing that the UN "shall make provisions for appropriate modes of settlement of . . . disputes . . ." This language may suggest that section 29 is more than merely aspirational—that it is obligatory and perhaps enforceable. But even if that is so, the use of the word "shall" in section 29 cannot fairly be read to override the clear and specific grant of "immunity from every form of legal process"—absent an express waiver—in section 2, as construed by the Second Circuit.

QUESTIONS

1. To whom are UN officials accountable for their conduct? What mechanisms are available to challenge the abuse of power by UN staff? Who decides whether conduct is performed in an "official capacity"?
2. Is it appropriate for UN peacekeepers to operate with immunity? Why or why not?
3. Article 19 of the Convention on the Privileges and Immunities, grants the Secretary-General and Assistant Secretaries-General (including Under-Secretaries-General) "the privileges and immunities, exemptions and facilities accorded to diplomatic envoys, in accordance with international law." Such law does not normally protect diplomats from the jurisdiction of their home state. Does the Secretary-General enjoy immunity in his or her home state?
4. In what circumstances may immunity of a UN official be waived? Is it ever required to be waived? Who determines whether the immunity of the Secretary-General should be waived?
5. Are diplomats at the United Nations required to pay parking fines?

HYPOTHETICAL A

Ruritania is a small (fictional) Southeast Asian country that recently experienced civil war. A small UN peacekeeping operation (UNMOR), consisting largely of military observers, remains in the capital to monitor implementation of a power-sharing agreement.

Ruritania has long had troubled relations with the People's Republic of China, which claims that Ruritania routinely violates intellectual property laws by selling pirated software and media developed in China, and discriminates against the small Chinese minority that live in Ruritania. Ruritania has also periodically threatened to switch diplomatic recognition from the People's Republic of China to the Republic of China (Taiwan).

Professor Jane Roe, a Ruritanian citizen, is the UN Special Rapporteur on Intellectual Property (IP) Violations and a tenured member of the National University of Singapore Faculty of Law. She lives in Singapore (on an employment pass, meaning she is not a citizen or permanent resident) but her parents live in Ruritania. Last June, she issued her annual report on IP Violations and was particularly critical of Ruritania's policy of providing government subsidies to corporations openly copying Microsoft Windows software and Hollywood movies. She also noted in her report that, although it went beyond her formal mandate, restrictions on Chinese-language media and education appeared to discriminate against the ethnically-Chinese minority in Ruritania and could be linked to the periodic violence that had been observed. Following her report there were protests that turned violent, leaving six Chinese shopkeepers dead.

The Ruritanian government disputed her claims, and on a visit to her parents last week she was arrested and charged with violations of the Ruritanian Maintenance of Ethnic Harmony Act. In particular, her comments about the treatment of Chinese Ruritanians were blamed for the six deaths.

The UN Secretary-General immediately wrote to Ruritania protesting that Professor Roe was covered by the UN Convention on the Privileges and Immunities. Ruritania responded by releasing a brief audio file in which Professor Roe could be heard saying that "My report will help resolve the Ruritania-China problem once and for all."

The People's Republic of China has protested at the treatment of Professor Roe and the Chinese minority. It has called an emergency session of the UN Security Council.

You are an independent legal consultant who has, unusually, been approached by two parties to give an opinion on the legal issues arising from this state of affairs. (For the purposes of this exercise you can ignore problems of conflict of interest or confidentiality.) Drawing in particular on materials discussed in class this semester, what legal arguments, supplemented as necessary by political strategies, can you offer to the following parties that have approached you? Also provide an assessment of the prospects for any arguments and strategies you propose.

(i) People's Republic of China
(ii) Ruritania

15.2 Responsibility of International Organizations

The International Tin Council was an organization of thirty-two members, including the European Economic Community, based on an International

Tin Agreement and headquartered in Britain. The Tin Council bought and sold tin on the world market in order to keep prices stable. In 1985 it ran out of money and defaulted on numerous contracts. A key question was whether the members could be held accountable for the sins of the organization.

INTERNATIONAL TIN COUNCIL LITIGATION (HOUSE OF LORDS, 26 OCTOBER 1989)[9]

Lord Templeman

The Sixth International Tin Agreement ("I.T.A.6") was a treaty between the United Kingdom Government, 22 other sovereign states and the European Economic Community ("the member states"). I.T.A.6 continued in existence the International Tin Council ("the I.T.C.") as an international organisation charged with regulating the worldwide production and marketing of tin in the interests of producers and consumers. By article 16 of I.T.A.6, the member states agreed that:

1. The council shall have legal personality. It shall in particular have the capacity to contract, to acquire and dispose of moveable and immoveable property and to institute legal proceedings.

Pursuant to the provisions of I.T.A.6, an Headquarters Agreement was entered into between the I.T.C. and the United Kingdom in order to define "the status, privileges and immunities of the council" in the United Kingdom. Article 3 of the Headquarters Agreement provided that:

The council shall have legal personality. It shall in particular have the capacity to contract and to acquire and dispose of movable and immovable property and to institute legal proceedings.

No part of I.T.A.6 or the Headquarters Agreement was incorporated into the laws of the United Kingdom but the International Tin Council (Immunities and Privileges) Order 1972 (S.I. 1972 No. 120) made under the International Organisations Act 1968 provided in article 5 that: "The council shall have the legal capacities of a body corporate."

The I.T.C. entered into contracts with each of the appellants. The appellants claim, and it is not disputed, that the I.T.C. became liable to pay and in breach of contract has not paid to the appellants sums amounting in the aggregate to millions of pounds. In these proceedings the appellants seek to recover the debts owed to them by the I.T.C. from the member states.

---

[9] *J.H. Rayner (Mincing Lane) Ltd. v Department of Trade and Industry; Maclaine Watson & Co. Ltd. v Department of Trade and Industry; Maclaine Watson & Co. Ltd. v International Tin Council* [1990] 2 AC 418.

The four alternative arguments adduced by the appellants in favour of the view that the member states are responsible for the debts of the I.T.C. were described throughout these appeals as submissions A, B(1), B(2) and C.

Submission A relies on the fact that the Order of 1972 did not incorporate the I.T.C. but only conferred on the I.T.C. the legal capacities of a body corporate. Therefore, it is said, under the laws of the United Kingdom the I.T.C. has no separate existence as a legal entity apart from its members; the contracts concluded in the name of the I.T.C. were contracts by the member states.

Submission A reduces the Order of 1972 to impotence. The appellants argue that the Order of 1972 was only intended to facilitate the carrying on in the United Kingdom of the activities of 23 sovereign states and the E.E.C. under the collective name of "the International Tin Council." Legislation is not necessary to enable trading to take place under a collective name. The appellants suggested that the Order of 1972 was intended to enable the member states to hold land in the United Kingdom in the name of a nominee. Legislation is not necessary for that purpose either. The appellants then suggested that the Order of 1972 was necessary to relieve the member states from a duty to register the collective name of the I.T.C. and from complying with the other provisions of the Registration of Business Names Act 1916. This trivial suggestion was confounded when, at a late stage in the hearing, the Act of 1916 (now repealed) was examined and found not to apply to an international organisation established by sovereign states. The Order of 1972 did not confer on 23 sovereign states and the E.E.C. the rights to trade under a name and to hold land in the name of the I.T.C. The Order of 1972 conferred on the I.T.C. the legal capacities of a body corporate. The appellants submitted that if Parliament had intended to do more than endow 23 sovereign states and the E.E.C. trading in this country with a collective name, then Parliament would have created the I.T.C. a body corporate. But the Government of the United Kingdom had by treaty concurred in the establishment of the I.T.C. as an international organisation. Consistently with the treaty, the United Kingdom could not convert the I.T.C. into a United Kingdom organisation. In order to clothe the I.T.C. in the United Kingdom with legal personality in accordance with the treaty, Parliament conferred on the I.T.C. the legal capacities of a body corporate. The courts of the United Kingdom became bound by the Order of 1972 to treat the activities of the I.T.C. as if those activities had been carried out by the I.T.C. as a body incorporated under the laws of the United Kingdom. The Order of 1972 is inconsistent with any intention on the part of Parliament to oblige or allow the courts of the United Kingdom to consider the nature of an international organisation. The Order of 1972 is inconsistent with any intention on the part of Parliament that creditors and courts should regard the I.T.C. as a partnership between 23 sovereign states and the E.E.C. trading in the United Kingdom like any private partnership. The Order of 1972 is inconsistent with any intention on the part of Parliament that contracts made by the I.T.C. with metal brokers, bankers, staff, landlords,

suppliers of goods and services and others, shall be treated by those creditors or by the courts of the United Kingdom as contracts entered into by 23
sovereign states and the E.E.C. The Order of 1972 conferred on the I.T.C. the
legal capacities of a body corporate. Those capacities include the power to
contract. The I.T.C. entered into contracts with the appellants.

The appellants submitted that if there had been no Order of 1972, the
courts would have been compelled to deal with the I.T.C. as though it were
a collective name for an unincorporated association. But the rights of the
creditors of the I.T.C. and the powers of the courts of the United Kingdom
must depend on the effect of the Order of 1972 and that Order cannot be
construed as if it did not exist. An international organisation might have
been treated by the courts of the United Kingdom as an unincorporated
association if the Order of 1972 had not been passed. But the Order of 1972
was passed. When the I.T.C. exercised the capacities of a body corporate,
the effect of that exercise was the same as the effect of the exercise of those
capacities by a body corporate. The I.T.C. cannot exercise the capacities of
a body corporate and at the same time be treated as if it were an unincorporated association. The Order of 1972 brought into being an entity which
must be recognised by the courts of the United Kingdom as a legal personality distinct in law from its membership and capable of entering into
contracts as principal. None of the authorities cited by the appellants were
of any assistance in construing the effect of the grant by Parliament of the
legal capacities of a body corporate to an international organisation pursuant to a treaty obligation to confer legal personality on that organisation.
In my opinion the effect is plain; the I.T.C. is a separate legal personality
distinct from its members. . . .

The third argument described as submission B(2) is that a rule of international law imposes on sovereign states, members of an international organisation, joint and several liability for the default of the organisation in the
payment of its debts unless the treaty which establishes the international
organisation clearly disclaims any liability on the part of the members. No
plausible evidence was produced of the existence of such a rule of international law before or at the time of I.T.A.6 in 1982 or thereafter. The appellants submitted that this House was bound to accept or reject such a rule
of international law and should not shrink from inventing such a law and
from publishing a precedent which might persuade other states to accept
such law.

My Lords, if there existed a rule of international law which implied in a
treaty or imposed on sovereign states which enter into a treaty an obligation (in default of a clear disclaimer in the treaty) to discharge the debts of
an international organisation established by that treaty, the rule of international law could only be enforced under international law. Treaty rights
and obligations conferred or imposed by agreement or by international law
cannot be enforced by the courts of the United Kingdom. The appellants

concede that the alleged rule of international law must imply and include a right of contribution whereby if one member state discharged the debts of the I.T.C., the other member states would be bound to share the burden. The appellants acknowledge that such right of contribution could only be enforced under international law and could not be made the subject of an order by the courts of the United Kingdom. This acknowledgement is inconsistent with the appellants' submission B(2). An international law or a domestic law which imposed and enforced joint and several liability on 23 sovereign states without imposing and enforcing contribution between those states would be devoid of logic and justice. If the present appeal succeeded the only effective remedy of the appellants in this country would be against the United Kingdom. This remedy would be fully effective so that in practice every creditor of the I.T.C. would claim to be paid, and would be paid, by the United Kingdom the full amount and any interest payable to the creditor by the I.T.C. The United Kingdom Government would then be embroiled, as a result of a decision of this House, in negotiations and possibly disagreements with other member states in order to obtain contribution. The causes of the failure of the I.T.C. and liability for its debts are disputed. Some states might continue to deny the existence of any obligation, legal or moral, municipal or international, to pay the debts of the I.T.C. or to contribute to such payment. Some states might be willing to contribute rateably with every other state, each bearing one-twenty-third. A state which under I.T.A.6 was only liable to contribute one percent of the capital of the I.T.C. might, on the other hand, only be prepared to contribute one per cent to the payment of the debts. The producing states which suffered more from the collapse of the I.T.C. than the consuming states might not be willing to contribute as much as the consuming states. Some member states might protest that I.T.A.6 shows an intention that member states should only be liable to contribute to the activities of the I.T.C. a buffer stock of metal and cash intended to be worth £500m. and lost as a result of the fall in tin prices on the metal exchanges which the I.T.C. strove to avoid and which resulted in the collapse of the I.T.C.

The courts of the United Kingdom have no power to enforce at the behest of any sovereign state or at the behest of any individual citizen of any sovereign state rights granted by treaty or obligations imposed in respect of a treaty by international law. It was argued that the courts of the United Kingdom will construe and enforce rights and obligations resulting from an agreement to which a foreign law applies in accordance with the provisions of that foreign law. For example, an English creditor of a Puerto-Rican corporation could sue and recover in the courts of the United Kingdom against the members of the corporation if, by the law of Puerto Rico, the members were liable to pay the debts of the corporation. By analogy, it was submitted, an English creditor of an international organisation should be able to sue in the courts of the United Kingdom the members of the international organisation if by international law the members are liable to pay the debts of the organisation. But there is no analogy between private international law which enables the courts of the United Kingdom to resolve differences between different laws of different states, and a rule of public international law which imposes obligations on treaty states. Public international law cannot alter the meaning and effect of United Kingdom legislation. If the suggested rule of public international law existed and imposed on a state any obligation towards the creditors of the I.T.C., then the Order of 1972 would be in breach of international law because the Order failed to confer rights on creditors against member states. It is impossible to construe the Order of 1972 as imposing any liability on the member states. The courts of the United Kingdom only have power to enforce rights and obligations which are made enforceable by the Order. . . .

Lord Griffiths

My Lords, I have had the advantage of reading the speeches of Lord Templeman and Lord Oliver of Aylmerton. I agree that for the reasons they give the appellants can obtain no redress through English law and that these appeals must be dismissed. I reach this conclusion with regret because in my view the appellants have suffered a grave injustice which Parliament never envisaged at the time legislation was first enacted to enable international organisations to operate under English law.

If during the passage of the Diplomatic Privileges (Extension) Bill through Parliament the Minister of State had been asked by a member what would happen if an international organisation refused to honour a contract on the ground that it had no money I believe that the answer would have been that such a state of affairs would be unthinkable because the governments that had set up the organisation would provide the funds necessary to honour its obligations. . . .

The rules concerning responsibility of International Organizations have been advanced through the work of the International Law Commission, a body of experts who seek to codify and progressively develop international law. In the case of the draft articles on responsibility, its work is seen largely as codifying rules that already apply as custom.[10]

---

[10] See, e.g., *Gabčíkovo-Nagymaros Project (Hungary/Slovakia) (Judgment) (International Court of Justice, 25 September 1997)*, available at: http://www.icj-cij.org, paras. 51–52. See also the Advisory Opinion on *Difference Relating to Immunity*, extracted in this chapter, at para. 62. Compare the extract from Michael Wood in Chapter 13, section 13.4.

INTERNATIONAL LAW COMMISSION, DRAFT ARTICLES ON RESPONSIBILITY OF INTERNATIONAL ORGANIZATIONS (2011)

Part One—Introduction

Article 1. *Scope of the present draft articles*

1. The present draft articles apply to the international responsibility of an international organization for an internationally wrongful act.

2. The present draft articles also apply to the international responsibility of a State for an internationally wrongful act in connection with the conduct of an international organization.

Article 2. *Use of terms*

For the purposes of the present draft articles,

(a) "international organization" means an organization established by a treaty or other instrument governed by international law and possessing its own international legal personality. International organizations may include as members, in addition to States, other entities;

(b) "rules of the organization" means, in particular, the constituent instruments, decisions, resolutions and other acts of the international organization adopted in accordance with those instruments, and established practice of the organization;

(c) "organ of an international organization" means any person or entity which has that status in accordance with the rules of the organization;

(d) "agent of an international organization" means an official or other person or entity, other than an organ, who is charged by the organization with carrying out, or helping to carry out, one of its functions, and thus through whom the organization acts.

Part Two—The Internationally Wrongful Act of an International Organization

Chapter I—*General principles*

Article 3. *Responsibility of an international organization for its internationally wrongful acts*

Every internationally wrongful act of an international organization entails the international responsibility of that organization.

Article 4. *Elements of an internationally wrongful act of an international organization*

There is an internationally wrongful act of an international organization when conduct consisting of an action or omission:

(a) is attributable to that organization under international law; and

(b) constitutes a breach of an international obligation of that organization.

Article 5. Characterization of an act of an international organization
as internationally wrongful

The characterization of an act of an international organization as internationally wrongful is governed by international law.

Chapter II—Attribution of conduct to an international organization

Article 6. Conduct of organs or agents of an international organization

1. The conduct of an organ or agent of an international organization in the performance of functions of that organ or agent shall be considered an act of that organization under international law, whatever position the organ or agent holds in respect of the organization.

2. The rules of the organization apply in the determination of the functions of its organs and agents.

Article 7. Conduct of organs of a State or organs or agents of an
international organization placed at the disposal of another
international organization

The conduct of an organ of a State or an organ or agent of an international organization that is placed at the disposal of another international organization shall be considered under international law an act of the latter organization if the organization exercises effective control over that conduct

Part Four The Implementation of the International Responsibility of an International Organization ...

Article 48. Responsibility of an international organization and
one or more States or international organizations

1. Where an international organization and one or more States or other international organizations are responsible for the same internationally wrongful act, the responsibility of each State or organization may be invoked in relation to that act.

2. Subsidiary responsibility may be invoked insofar as the invocation of the primary responsibility has not led to reparation.

3. Paragraphs 1 and 2: (a) do not permit any injured State or international organization to recover, by way of compensation, more than the damage it has suffered; (b) are without prejudice to any right of recourse that the State or international organization providing reparation may have against the other responsible States or international organizations.

The Draft Articles contain sixty-seven articles in all, but the question of attribution is one of the most interesting. Article 7, for example, highlights a problem that has arisen in UN peace operations, as the Commentary to the ILC Draft Articles discusses.

INTERNATIONAL LAW COMMISSION, COMMENTARIES ON THE DRAFT ARTICLES ON THE RESPONSIBILITY OF INTERNATIONAL ORGANIZATIONS (2011)[11]

Article 7

When an organ of a State is placed at the disposal of an international organization, the organ may be fully seconded to that organization. In this case the organ's conduct would clearly be attributable only to the receiving organization. The same consequence would apply when an organ or agent of one international organization is fully seconded to another organization. In these cases, the general rule set out in article 6 would apply. Article 7 deals with the different situation in which the seconded organ or agent still acts to a certain extent as organ of the seconding State or as organ or agent of the seconding organization. This occurs for instance in the case of military contingents that a State places at the disposal of the United Nations for a peacekeeping operation, since the State retains disciplinary powers and criminal jurisdiction over the members of the national contingent. In this situation the problem arises whether a specific conduct of the seconded organ or agent is to be attributed to the receiving organization or to the seconding State or organization. . . .

The seconding State or organization may conclude an agreement with the receiving organization over placing an organ or agent at the latter organization's disposal. The agreement may state which State or organization would be responsible for conduct of that organ or agent. For example, according to the model contribution agreement relating to military contingents placed at the disposal of the United Nations by one of its Member States, the United Nations is regarded as liable towards third parties, but has a right of recovery from the contributing State under circumstances such as "loss, damage, death or injury [arising] from gross negligence or wilful misconduct of the personnel provided by the Government". The agreement appears to deal only with distribution of responsibility and not with attribution of conduct. At any event, this type of agreement is not conclusive because it governs only the relations between the contributing State or organization and the receiving organization and could thus not have the effect of depriving a third party of any right that that party may have towards the State or organization which is responsible under the general rules. . . .

The United Nations assumes that in principle it has exclusive control of the deployment of national contingents in a peacekeeping force. This premise led the United Nations Legal Counsel to state:

"As a subsidiary organ of the United Nations, an act of a peacekeeping force is, in principle, imputable to the Organization, and if committed in violation

---

[11] Available at: http://legal.un.org/ilc/texts/instruments/english/commentaries/9_11_2011.pdf (most footnotes omitted).

of an international obligation entails the international responsibility of the Organization and its liability in compensation."

This statement sums up United Nations practice relating to the United Nations Operation in the Congo (ONUC), the United Nations Peacekeeping Force in Cyprus (UNFICYP) and later peacekeeping forces. In a recent comment, the United Nations Secretariat observed that "[f]or a number of reasons, notably political", the practice of the United Nations had been that of "maintaining the principle of United Nations responsibility vis-à-vis third parties" in connection with peacekeeping operations. . . .

As has been held by several scholars, when an organ or agent is placed at the disposal of an international organization, the decisive question in relation to attribution of a given conduct appears to be who has effective control over the conduct in question. . . .

The European Court of Human Rights considered, first in *Behrami and Behrami v. France* and *Saramati v. France, Germany and Norway,* its jurisdiction *ratione personae* in relation to the conduct of forces placed in Kosovo at the disposal of the United Nations (United Nations Interim Administration Mission in Kosovo (UNMIK)) or authorized by the United Nations (Kosovo Force (KFOR)). The Court referred to the present work of the International Law Commission and in particular to the criterion of "effective control" that had been provisionally adopted by the Commission. While not formulating any criticism to this criterion, the Court considered that the decisive factor was whether "the United Nations Security Council retained ultimate authority and control so that operational command only was delegated". While acknowledging "the effectiveness or unity of NATO command in operational matters" concerning KFOR, the Court noted that the presence of KFOR in Kosovo was based on a resolution adopted by the Security Council and concluded that "KFOR was exercising lawfully delegated Chapter VII powers of the UNSC so that the impugned action was, in principle, 'attributable' to the UN within the meaning of the word outlined [in article 4 of the present articles]". . . .

[T]he decision of the House of Lords in *Al-Jedda* contained ample references to the present work of the Commission. One of the majority opinions stated that "[i]t was common ground between the parties that the governing principle [was] that expressed by the International Law Commission in article [7] of its draft articles on Responsibility of International Organizations". The House of Lords was confronted with a claim arising from the detention of a person by British troops in Iraq. In its resolution 1546 (2004) the Security Council had previously authorized the presence of the multinational force in that country. The majority opinions appeared to endorse the views expressed by the European Court of Human Rights in *Behrami* and *Saramati,* but distinguished the facts of the case and concluded that it could not "realistically be said that US and UK forces were under the effective command and control of the UN, or that UK forces were under such command and control when they detained the appellant". This conclusion appears to be in line with the way in which the criterion of effective control was intended.

After the judgment of the House of Lords an application was made by Mr. Al-Jedda to the European Court of Human Rights. In *Al-Jedda v. United Kingdom* this Court quoted several texts concerning attribution, including the article (identical to the present article) which had been adopted by the Commission at first reading and some paragraphs of the commentary. The Court considered that "the United Nations Security Council had neither effective control nor ultimate authority and control over the acts and omissions of foreign troops within the Multi-National Force and that the applicant's detention was not, therefore, attributable to the United Nations". The Court unanimously concluded that the applicant's detention had to be attributed to the respondent State.

The question of attribution was also considered in a judgement of the District Court of The Hague concerning the attribution of the conduct of the Dutch contingent in the United Nations Protection Force (UNPROFOR) in relation to the massacre in Srebrenica. This judgment contained only a general reference to the Commission's articles. The Court found that "the reprehended acts of Dutchbat should be assessed as those of an UNPROFOR contingent" and that "these acts and omissions should be attributed strictly, as a matter of principle, to the United Nations". The Court then considered that if "Dutchbat was instructed by the Dutch authorities to ignore UN orders or to go against them, and Dutchbat behaved in accordance with this instruction from the Netherlands, this constitutes a violation of the factual basis on which the attribution to the UN rests." The Court did not find that there was sufficient evidence for reaching such a conclusion. On appeal from the judgement of the District Court the Court of Appeal of The Hague referred to the draft article (identical to the present article) which had been adopted by the Commission at first reading. The Court applied the criterion of "effective control" to the circumstances of the case and reached the conclusion that the respondent State was responsible for its involvement in the events at Srebrenica which had led to the killing of three Bosnian Muslim men after they had been evicted from the compound of Dutchbat.

In a subsequent decision on Dutchbat's activites in Srebrenica, the Dutch Supreme Court drew on Article 48 to conclude that the same conduct could, in principle, be attributed both to the United Nations and to the Netherlands ("dual attribution"). In the case of the impugned conduct, the state did in fact exercise "effective control," and it was therefore attributable to the Netherlands. It was not necessary for the Court to determine whether the conduct was also attributable to the United Nations itself, which was not party to the proceedings.[12]

---

[12] *Netherlands v. Hasan Nuhanović* (Supreme Court of the Netherlands, decision of 6 September 2013).

As the *Commentary* makes clear, attribution will often depend on a close examination of the legal and factual circumstances. The European Court of Human Rights decision in *Al-Jedda*, to which the ILC *Commentary* refers, provides a good example of how this might be done.

Hilal Abdul-Razzaq Ali Al-Jedda was a joint Iraqi/British national who flew to Iraq in September 2004. Two weeks later he was detained by US soldiers, apparently on the basis of intelligence provided by British authorities, and transferred to a detention center in Basra that was run by the British. He remained in the facility until December 2007, with his ongoing internment justified on the basis that he was recruiting terrorists from outside Iraq and facilitating attacks on Coalition forces inside the country. He was never charged with a criminal offense. Prior to his release in December 2007 he was stripped of his British citizenship, a decision later upheld by the Special Immigration Appeals Commission.

AL-JEDDA v. UNITED KINGDOM (2011) 35 EHRR 23

76. When examining whether the applicant's detention was attributable to the United Kingdom or, as the Government submit, the United Nations, it is necessary to examine the particular facts of the case. These include the terms of the United Nations Security Council resolutions which formed the framework for the security regime in Iraq during the period in question. In performing this exercise, the Court is mindful of the fact that it is not its role to seek to define authoritatively the meaning of provisions of the Charter of the United Nations and other international instruments. It must nevertheless examine whether there was a plausible basis in such instruments for the matters impugned before it ... The principles underlying the Convention cannot be interpreted and applied in a vacuum and the Court must take into account relevant rules of international law ... It relies for guidance in this exercise on the statement of the International Court of Justice in paragraph 114 of its Advisory Opinion *Legal Consequences for States of the Continued Presence of South Africa in Namibia, notwithstanding Security Council Resolution 276 (1970)* (hereinafter "*Namibia*") ..., indicating that a United Nations Security Council resolution should be interpreted in the light not only of the language used but also the context in which it was adopted.

77. The Court takes as its starting point that, on 20 March 2003, the United Kingdom together with the United States of America and their Coalition partners, through their armed forces, entered Iraq with the aim of displacing the Ba'ath regime then in power. At the time of the invasion, there was no United Nations Security Council resolution providing for the allocation of roles in Iraq in the event that the existing regime was displaced. Major combat

operations were declared to be complete by 1 May 2003 and the United States of America and the United Kingdom became Occupying Powers within the meaning of Article 42 of the Hague Regulations . . .

78. The first United Nations Security Council resolution after the invasion was Resolution 1483, adopted on 22 May 2003 . . . In the Preamble, the Security Council noted the letter of 8 May 2003 from the Permanent Representatives of the United States of America and the United Kingdom and recognised that the United States of America and the United Kingdom were Occupying Powers in Iraq, under unified command (the CPA), and that specific authorities, responsibilities, and obligations applied to them under international humanitarian law. The Security Council noted further that other States that were not Occupying Powers were working or might in the future work under the CPA, and welcomed the willingness of member States to contribute to stability and security in Iraq by contributing personnel, equipment and other resources "under the Authority". Acting under Chapter VII of the Charter of the United Nations, the Security Council called upon the Occupying Powers, through the CPA, "to promote the welfare of the Iraqi people through the effective administration of the territory, including in particular working towards the restoration of conditions of security and stability". The United Kingdom and the United States of America were encouraged "to inform the Council at regular intervals of their efforts under this Resolution". The Preamble to Resolution 1483 recognised that the United Nations were to "play a vital role in humanitarian relief, the reconstruction of Iraq and the restoration and establishment of national and local institutions for representative governance". The Secretary-General of the United Nations was requested to appoint a Special Representative for Iraq, whose independent responsibilities were to include, *inter alia*, reporting regularly to the Security Council on his activities under this Resolution, coordinating activities of the United Nations in post-conflict processes in Iraq and coordinating among United Nations and international agencies engaged in humanitarian assistance and reconstruction activities in Iraq. Resolution 1483 did not assign any security role to the United Nations. The Government does not contend that, at this stage in the invasion and occupation, the acts of its armed forces were in any way attributable to the United Nations.

79. In Resolution 1511, adopted on 16 October 2003, the United Nations Security Council, again acting under Chapter VII of the Charter, underscored the temporary nature of the exercise by the CPA of the authorities and responsibilities set out in Resolution 1483, which would cease as soon as an internationally recognised, representative Iraqi government could be sworn in. In paragraphs 13 and 14, the Security Council authorised "a Multinational Force under unified command to take all necessary measures to contribute to the maintenance of security and stability in Iraq" and urged member States "to contribute assistance under this United Nations mandate, including military forces, to the Multinational Force referred to in paragraph 13" . . . The United States of America, on behalf of the Multinational Force, was requested periodically to report on the efforts and progress of the Force. The Security Council

also resolved that the United Nations, acting through the Secretary-General, his Special Representative, and the United Nations Assistance Mission for Iraq, should strengthen its role in Iraq, including by providing humanitarian relief, promoting the economic reconstruction of and conditions for sustainable development in Iraq, and advancing efforts to restore and establish national and local institutions for representative government.

80. The Court does not consider that, as a result of the authorisation contained in Resolution 1511, the acts of soldiers within the Multinational Force became attributable to the United Nations or—more importantly, for the purposes of this case—ceased to be attributable to the troop-contributing nations. The Multinational Force had been present in Iraq since the invasion and had been recognised already in Resolution 1483, which welcomed the willingness of member States to contribute personnel. The unified command structure over the Force, established from the start of the invasion by the United States of America and the United Kingdom, was not changed as a result of Resolution 1511. Moreover, the United States of America and the United Kingdom, through the CPA which they had established at the start of the occupation, continued to exercise the powers of government in Iraq. Although the United States of America was requested to report periodically to the Security Council about the activities of the Multinational Force, the United Nations did not, thereby, assume any degree of control over either the Force or any other of the executive functions of the CPA.

81. The final resolution of relevance to the present issue was Resolution 1546 ... It was adopted on 8 June 2004, twenty days before the transfer of power from the CPA to the Iraqi interim government and some four months before the applicant was taken into detention. Annexed to the Resolution was a letter from the Prime Minister of the interim government of Iraq, seeking from the Security Council a new resolution on the Multinational Force mandate. There was also annexed a letter from the US Secretary of State to the President of the United Nations Security Council, confirming that "the Multinational Force [under unified command] [wa]s prepared to continue to contribute to the maintenance of security in Iraq" and informing the President of the Security Council of the goals of the Multinational Force and the steps which its Commander intended to take to achieve those goals. It does not appear from the terms of this letter that the US Secretary of State considered that the United Nations controlled the deployment or conduct of the Multinational Force. In Resolution 1546 the Security Council, acting under Chapter VII of the Charter of the United Nations, reaffirmed the authorisation for the Multinational Force established under Resolution 1511. There is no indication in Resolution 1546 that the Security Council intended to assume any greater degree of control or command over the Multinational Force than it had exercised previously.

82. In Resolution 1546 the Security Council also decided that, in implementing their mandates in Iraq, the Special Representative of the Secretary-General and the United Nations Assistance Mission for Iraq (UNAMI) should play

leading roles in assisting in the establishment of democratic institutions, economic development and humanitarian assistance. The Court notes that the Secretary-General and UNAMI, both clearly organs of the United Nations, in their quarterly and bi-monthly reports to the Security Council for the period during which the applicant was detained, repeatedly protested about the extent to which security internment was being used by the Multinational Force ... It is difficult to conceive that the applicant's detention was attributable to the United Nations and not to the United Kingdom when United Nations organs, operating under the mandate of Resolution 1546, did not appear to approve of the practice of indefinite internment without trial and, in the case of UNAMI, entered into correspondence with the United States embassy in an attempt to persuade the Multinational Force under American command to modify the internment procedure.

83. In the light of the foregoing, the Court agrees with the majority of the House of Lords that the United Nations' role as regards security in Iraq in 2004 was quite different from its role as regards security in Kosovo in 1999. The comparison is relevant, since in its decision in *Behrami and Saramati* ... the Court concluded, *inter alia*, that Mr Saramati's detention was attributable to the United Nations and not to any of the respondent States. It is to be recalled that the international security presence in Kosovo was established by United Nations Security Council Resolution 1244, adopted on 10 June 1999, in which, "determined to resolve the grave humanitarian situation in Kosovo", the Security Council "decide[d] on the deployment in Kosovo, under United Nations auspices, of international civil and security presences". The Security Council therefore authorised "member States and relevant international organisations to establish the international security presence in Kosovo" and directed that there should be "substantial North Atlantic Treaty Organization participation" in the Force, which "must be deployed under unified command and control". In addition, Resolution 1244 authorised the Secretary-General of the United Nations to establish an international civil presence in Kosovo in order to provide an interim administration for Kosovo. The United Nations, through a Special Representative appointed by the Secretary-General in consultation with the Security Council, was to control the implementation of the international civil presence and coordinate closely with the international security presence ... On 12 June 1999, two days after the Resolution was adopted, the first elements of the NATO-led Kosovo Force (KFOR) entered Kosovo.

84. It would appear from the opinion of Lord Bingham in the first set of proceedings brought by the applicant that it was common ground between the parties before the House of Lords that the test to be applied in order to establish attribution was that set out by the International Law Commission in Article 5 of its Draft Articles on the Responsibility of International Organisations and in its commentary thereon, namely that the conduct of an organ of a State placed at the disposal of an international organisation should be attributable under international law to that organisation if the

organisation exercises effective control over that conduct . . . For the reasons set out above, the Court considers that the United Nations Security Council had neither effective control nor ultimate authority and control over the acts and omissions of troops within the Multinational Force and that the applicant's detention was not, therefore, attributable to the United Nations.

85. The internment took place within a detention facility in Basra City, controlled exclusively by British forces, and the applicant was therefore within the authority and control of the United Kingdom throughout . . . The decision to hold the applicant in internment was made by the British officer in command of the detention facility. Although the decision to continue holding the applicant in internment was, at various points, reviewed by committees including Iraqi officials and non-United Kingdom representatives from the Multinational Force, the Court does not consider that the existence of these reviews operated to prevent the detention from being attributable to the United Kingdom.

86. In conclusion, the Court agrees with the majority of the House of Lords that the internment of the applicant was attributable to the United Kingdom and that during his internment the applicant fell within the jurisdiction of the United Kingdom for the purposes of Article 1 of the Convention.

The Court subsequently found that there had indeed been a violation of Al-Jedda's right to liberty under the European Convention on Human Rights, but the monetary compensation awarded for more than three years' detention was limited to €25,000.

QUESTIONS

6. In the Tin Council case, Lord Griffiths agreed that the appeals must be dismissed, and yet went on to say that he did so with "much regret," because the appellants had "suffered a grave injustice which Parliament never envisaged at the time legislation was first enacted to enable international organizations to operate under English law." What does he mean? Do you agree?
7. If an international organization is composed by and acts through member states, should responsibility for a wrong committed by the organization be attributed to the organization or its members?
8. Can the United Nations be held internationally responsible for wrongful acts by a state acting pursuant to an authorization, such as an enforcement action authorized by the Security Council?
9. What should be the test for attribution of conduct to an international organization: "effective control" or "ultimate authority and control," or some combination of the two?

10. Given the ambiguity that may arise in complex operations involving states and international organizations, some authors have argued that a notion of shared attribution would be more appropriate. Do you agree? Why or why not?

Further Reading

Amerasinghe, C.F. *Principles of the Institutional Law of International Organizations.* Cambridge: Cambridge University Press, 1996.

Bekker, Pieter H.F. *The Legal Position of Intergovernmental Organizations—A Functional Necessity Analysis of Their Legal Status and Immunities.* The Hague: Martinus Nijhoff, 1994.

Crawford, James, Alain Pellet, Simon Olleson and Kate Parlett (eds). *The Law of International Responsibility.* Oxford: Oxford University Press, 2010.

Crawford, James. *The International Law Commission's Articles on State Responsibility: Introduction, Text and Commentaries.* Cambridge: Cambridge University Press, 2002.

Denza, Eileen. *Diplomatic Law: A Commentary on the Vienna Convention on Diplomatic Relations.* 2nd edn. Oxford: Clarendon Press, 1998.

Direk, Ömer Faruk. "Responsibility in Peace Support Operations: Revisiting the Proper Test for Attribution Conduct and the Meaning of the 'Effective Control' Standard". *Netherlands International Law Review*, vol. 61 (2014), p. 1.

Klabbers, Jan. *An Introduction to International Institutional Law.* Cambridge: Cambridge University Press, 2002.

Larsen, Kjetil Mujezinović. *The Human Rights Treaty Obligations of Peacekeepers.* Cambridge: Cambridge University Press, 2012.

Ragazzi, Maurizio (ed). *International Responsibility Today: Essays in Memory of Oscar Schachter.* The Hague: Martinus Nijhoff, 2005.

Ragazzi, Maurizio (ed). *Responsibility of International Organizations: Essays in Memory of Sir Ian Brownlie.* The Hague: Martinus Nijhoff, 2013.

Reinisch, August (ed). *The Privileges and Immunities of International Organizations in Domestic Courts.* Oxford: Oxford University Press, 2013.

Reinisch, August. *International Organizations before National Courts.* Cambridge: Cambridge University Press, 2000.

Sands, Philippe and Pierre Klein. *Bowett's Law of International Institutions.* London: Sweet & Maxwell, 2001.

Schermers, Henry G. and Niels M. Blokker. *International Institutional Law: Unity within Diversity.* 4th edn. Leiden: Brill, 2004.

Verdirame, Guglielmo. *The UN and Human Rights: Who Guards the Guardians?* Cambridge: Cambridge University Press, 2011.

Wellens, Karel. *Remedies against International Organisations.* Cambridge: Cambridge University Press, 2002.

chapter sixteen
....

Accountability in Practice

Several UN bodies possess sweeping jurisdiction under the UN Charter, notably the power to determine the limits of their own jurisdiction— *kompetenz-kompetenz* as the Germans say. None of these bodies (the Security Council, the General Assembly, the International Court of Justice) is directly accountable to any other. This facilitates decision-making, but also creates an apparent accountability deficit. To whom are these bodies accountable?

In theory, the answer may appear to be no one.[1] This chapter tests that theory by examining some high-profile UN failures and abuses that happened in the course of UN operations. The chapter focuses on six situations. The first connects with Chapter 3, examining the UN Secretary-General's response to the "Petrie Report" (excerpted in that chapter) documenting systemic failures of the UN in the run-up to the slaughter of civilians that attended the final days of Sri Lanka's civil war in 2009.

The next two are the inability of the United Nations to prevent widespread killing in Rwanda in 1994 and Srebrenica (Bosnia and Herzegovina) in 1995, briefly discussed in Chapter 9. The fourth is the questionable use of authority in the UN Interim Administration in Kosovo, where individuals were detained at length without trial. The fifth concerns allegations against UN peacekeepers of sexual exploitation. The sixth is the management (or mismanagement) of the Oil-for-Food Programme touched on in Chapters 2 and 10, which allowed a humanitarian exemption from embargoes on the sale of Iraqi oil from 1995 to 2003 but was the subject of great criticism.

There are various ways of holding power to account, some more or less effective than others. The tendency through each of these incidents has been to rely primarily on a public airing of the facts, though the terms of reference of such an airing are typically selective. The United Nations, for example, opened itself to significant criticism over its action and inaction in Rwanda and Srebrenica. Without diminishing the justified nature of that criticism, it is clear that a number of member states also bore responsibility for what happened—or did not happen—in Rwanda in particular.

---

[1] For more on this question, see the discussion of "indirect judicial review" in Chapter 4.

Unusually, Kosovo had an institutionalized reporting capacity in the person of the Ombudsperson Institution, established by the OSCE as part of the UN Mission. This is typically more effective than after-the-fact reporting, but the Ombudsperson lacked any power to do more than publicize his findings. Sexual abuse in the Congo operation (MONUC) was merely the most prominent and widespread example of a problem that affects many peace operations, particularly those with large military deployments. It also highlights some of the problems with immunity regimes discussed in the previous chapter. Finally, the Oil-for-Food scandal demonstrates the problem with narrowly construing the terms of reference of an inquiry—poor performance by the Secretariat should not be excused, but neither should it be used to excuse poor oversight by member states.

There are occasional exceptions. US president Bill Clinton is alone among the leaders of the permanent five members of the Security Council in having made a serious effort to apologize for the disastrous inaction during Rwanda's genocide. On Srebrenica, member states engaged in a degree of finger-pointing, but only the Netherlands, which issued a scathing report on the performance of its peacekeeping contingent in Srebrenica and whose Supreme Court on 16 July 2014 found the Netherlands "responsible" for the deaths at Srebrenica (partly in light of a European Court of Justice determining UN immunity relative to any responsibility), opening the way to compensation claims from the Dutch government for families of the victims. Nevertheless, as discussed earlier, poor decision-making in the Security Council, in the UN Secretariat, by the headquarters of the UN peacekeeping operation in Bosnia, and within NATO actively contributed to the loss of thousands of lives.

No state has a particular interest in having its own peacekeepers investigated for allegations of sexual abuse—leading to the suppression of even the names of the countries involved in the incident described here, with the result that the abuse was attributed to "the United Nations" generally. And, as we shall see, the Oil-for-Food Programme was a deeply politicized institution from its very creation.

16.1 Sri Lanka

Chapter 3 excerpted significant portions of an independent expert report on the UN's performance in protecting several hundred thousand civilians in Sri Lanka during the final days of the civil war there. Many of these managed to flee, leaving perhaps 50,000 trapped in the last stages, corralled by the Tamil Tiger (LTTE) leadership into a very limited territory. The LTTE presumably adopted this strategy to deflect or to make more difficult a final assault on their rebel forces by the Sri Lankan army (or possibly as a gesture of "mass suicide" rather than surrender, even though the civilians had no voice in the decision.) This report, quite critical of overall UN inaction to prevent humanitarian disaster (while nevertheless recognizing the efforts of individual UN teams on the ground) recommended to the Secretary-General a comprehensive review of the United Nations' performance in the humanitarian and protection spheres. The Secretary-General duly constituted a senior-level internal review panel that in November 2012 submitted a report detailing multiple UN failures (while recognizing the reluctance of member states to confront the crisis) and formulated a number of very detailed recommendations to avert a recurrence of these events. Before reading the Secretary-General's response to this fairly searing indictment of the UN bureaucracy's actions and equivocations both in Sri Lanka itself and at UN Headquarters, please review excerpts of the Independent Review Panel report (more widely known as the Petrie report, after the chair of the panel), the final official text cited in Chapter 3. A year later, on 17 December 2013, the Secretary-General's rejoinder, entitled "Rights Up Front," which had several iterations in 2013 and 2014, was articulated by the Deputy Secretary-General in New York as follows:

INFORMAL REMARKS AT BRIEFING OF THE GENERAL ASSEMBLY ON RIGHTS UP FRONT, 17 DECEMBER 2013[2]

Promoting and encouraging respect for human rights is a core purpose of the United Nations and defines its identity as an organization for people around the world.

Member States have mandated the Secretary-General and the UN System, through the Charter and successive General Assembly resolutions to help them meet the standards expressed in the Universal Declaration of Human Rights. In carrying out these responsibilities, the UN System is to use all the resources at its disposal, including its moral authority, diplomatic creativity and operational reach.

Member States have the primary responsibility to protect their populations against massive and widespread violations of human rights. Yet, they have sometimes been unable or unwilling to meet these obligations. At times, the UN System has also failed to meet its responsibilities.

The consequences of failing to prevent serious violations of international human rights and humanitarian law are all too evident, whether for individuals, countries, or regions. In terms of lost lives and people displaced, the

---

[2] The Deputy Secretary-General, "Informal remarks at briefing of the General Assembly on Rights up Front," 17 December 2013, available at: http://www.un.org/sg/rightsupfront/doc/DSG-rights-up-front-GA-statement.htm.

price paid due to these failures has been staggering. The legacy may reverberate for generations.

Protecting human rights can help prevent armed conflict and mass atrocities. Deterioration in respect for human rights can be a telling sign of impending crisis. Success in promoting and protecting rights and in ensuring accountability for the violation of human rights, can offer effective means to de-escalate conflict and to forestall the human and financial cost of humanitarian crises. Once conflict erupts, the imperative becomes to use all practical means to protect civilians. At these times, respect for international humanitarian law is critical, as is respect for human rights.

The challenges to ensuring effective protection have existed for many years and in a range of diverse situations. In some cases the Secretariat has failed to effectively communicate evidence of impending crises. The UN's Secretariat, Agencies, Funds and Programmes have sometimes lacked a sufficiently coherent agreed internal strategy to address serious violations. They have not always deployed and empowered UN staff swiftly to address rapidly changing circumstances, or backed them up when they take risks. And Member States have not always been able to reach agreement on concerted action, thereby weakening the impact of their expressions of concern over ongoing violations.

Many recommendations for improving UN action have been made over the years—most importantly those from the 1999 Independent Inquiry on UN Action in Rwanda and the 1999 review on the fall of Srebrenica. While the UN System has become better at anticipating and responding to crises affecting civilian populations, the lessons have not always been adequately learned and implemented.

In 2012, the Internal Review Panel (IRP) on UN Action in Sri Lanka characterized UN efforts in the last stages of the war as a "systemic failure". Today the agony of the Syrian people provides a further test—not just of Member States' political will to fulfil their responsibilities, but of the UN's ability to use the full breadth of its mandates and activities to protect the people it is meant to serve.

In the follow-up action to the IRP report, the Secretary-General saw an opportunity to ensure that the lessons of the past are fully acted upon. There are limits to what the broader UN System can do if a government is not protecting its population, shuts the UN out, or when disagreements among Member States delay UN action. But the UN System must still do its utmost to meet its responsibilities.

The actions outlined below to implement the IRP's recommendations place "Rights Up Front." They are focused primarily on what the UN Secretariat, Agencies, Funds and Programmes can do to improve their response to future crises. Several elements are intended to complement Member States' action to meet their responsibilities in the General Assembly, the Security Council and the Human Rights Council. These actions endeavour to place people, wherever they may be, at the heart of UN strategies and operational activities.

Six actions, in particular, can make a qualitative difference in the way the UN System meets its responsibilities:

Action 1: Integrating human rights into the lifeblood of staff so that they understand what the UN's mandates and commitments to human rights mean for their Department, Agency, Fund or Programme and for them personally.

Action 2: Providing Member States with candid information with respect to peoples at risk of, or subject to, serious violations of international human rights or humanitarian law.

Action 3: Ensuring coherent strategies of action on the ground and leveraging the UN System's capacities in a concerted manner.

Action 4: Adopting at Headquarters a "One-UN approach" to facilitate early coordinated action.

Action 5: Achieving, through better analysis, greater impact in the UN's human rights protection work.

Action 6: Supporting all these activities through an improved system of information management on serious violations of human rights and humanitarian law.

The actions proposed form part of the responsibilities of the UN as set out by the Charter and Member States. Implementation will require different ways of doing things, including some re-prioritization of existing resources which will need to be approved by Member States, as appropriate. More important than resources, however, will be the multiplier effect of the change in institutional culture these actions will bring about.

Above all, success requires leadership at every level to encourage teamwork and collaboration and to ensure that the diverse mandates of the UN System are harnessed to the achievement of the UN System's core purposes. It demands the courage and confidence to speak up and to support staff that live up to the values enshrined in the Charter and the Universal Declaration of Human Rights.

People, who are at risk of suffering massive and widespread violations of their human rights, look to the UN for action to protect their rights. They must know and be assured that the UN System is doing everything in its power to assist them and to mobilize the efforts of those who can protect them.

A "Plan of Action" for the UN circulated on the internet in mid-2013, but seems not to have been presented to UN member States officially, for example in the General Assembly. It is easy to see why it might have proved quite controversial in such a political forum of sovereign (and often prickly) states. States prefer not to think of themselves as fragile and many would be loath to countenance in their own countries UN contingency planning of the sort outlined below—which would confirm that their civilian populations were judged at risk by UN staff. The plan's status, at the time of writing, remains publicly vague, but one can speculate that it is invoked as a guide within the Secretariat and within UN teams in fragile countries and ones at risk of deteriorating political circumstances, acute humanitarian distress or civil war.

RIGHTS UP FRONT. A PLAN OF ACTION TO STRENGTHEN THE UN'S ROLE IN PROTECTING PEOPLE IN CRISES. FOLLOW-UP TO THE REPORT OF THE SECRETARY-GENERAL'S INTERNAL REVIEW PANEL ON UN ACTION IN SRI LANKA[3]

II. The Plan of Action

UN VISION AND RESPONSIBILITIES

All UN staff will be aware of the UN's responsibilities with respect to serious violations of international human rights and humanitarian law and will be held accountable for fulfilling them.

1. Renew the vision of the UN's responsibilities: renew a vision of the UN's responsibilities with respect to serious violations; communicate it to staff, Member States and the general public; define UN entities' responsibilities in this respect.

2. Embed the vision into human resources management processes: embed the vision into relevant human resources practices; roll out mandatory human rights induction and training.

3. Hold staff and institutions accountable: hold accountable staff, particularly at senior levels; appraise RCs on human rights and political acumen; conduct real-time reviews of UN response to serious violations.

UN ENGAGEMENT WITH MEMBER STATES AND OTHER STAKEHOLDERS

In situations of serious violations, Member States and other influential stakeholders will be actively mobilized by the UN. Member States will receive full and timely information from the UN.

4. Engage more pro-actively, strategically and creatively with Member States and other stakeholders: implement strategies of engagement; partner with regional actors and civil society; upgrade and expand the repertoire of tools for engagement; better use the Protection of Civilians process.

5. Provide comprehensive and timely briefings: conduct 'horizon scanning' briefings for the Security Council; when situations of serious violations are not on the Security Council's agenda, the Deputy Secretary-General to brief Member States; use Article 99 when needed.

---

[3] "Rights Up Front, A Plan of Action to strengthen the UN's role in protecting people in crises. Follow-up to the report of the Secretary-General's Internal Review Panel on UN Action in Sri Lanka" 9 July 2013, available at: http://www.innercitypress.com/sriban1rightsupfronticp.pdf.

UN ACTION AT COUNTRY LEVEL

RCs and UN Country Teams (UNCTs) will have the right profile for crisis contexts and will be adequately supported. The UN will have a strategy to address serious violations and its footprint will match its human rights responsibilities.

6. Ensure that UNCTs respond to the human rights context: provide UNCTs with human rights and protection analysis; reflect human rights and protection objectives in UN plans.

7. Develop a strategy to address potential or actual serious violations: spell out what UN political, human rights, humanitarian and development entities will do at country, regional and global level to address the specific country situation.

8. Ensure that RCs and UNCTs in crisis contexts have a suitable profile: attract the best candidates to the RC track; assess their ability to uphold human rights responsibilities; improve application and shortlisting for RC posts; provide RCs with political and human rights training; review the level and profile of RCs and UNCTs in crisis countries.

9. Provide RCs and UNCTs with the support they require: on human rights and political issues and for their leadership role; reinforce protection capacity in crisis countries.

10. Deploy human rights and political capacity: identify "light" models of UN deployment with political and human rights expertise; work with the concerned State and other Member States to ensure early deployment for prevention.

11. Ensure that the UN is able to operate in crises: roll out the Programme Criticality Framework to stay and deliver in high risk situations; respond more effectively to violations of UN privileges and immunities; publicize such violations; equip RCs with secure telecommunications.

UN HEADQUARTERS COORDINATION

The UN will have a whole-of-UN approach to non-mission settings under the auspices of the Executive Office of the Secretary-General (EOSG).

12. Establish coordination mechanisms for early warning and early action: hold quarterly inter-agency meetings to review situations of concern and decide on concerted action.

13. Streamline coordination mechanisms for situations of concern: establish Inter-Agency Task Forces to coordinate implementation of the country-specific strategies (see 7) and provide consolidated guidance to the RC/HC; if required appoint a Situation Response Coordinator to pull the system together and convene a Situation Response Cabinet chaired by the Deputy Secretary-General; eliminate duplicative platforms.

14. Strengthen the capacity of EOSG to ensure a whole-of-UN approach: second additional senior staff to EOSG.

UN HUMAN RIGHTS CAPACITY

Human rights entities will have greater influence and impact thanks to better coordination.

15. Strengthen UN human rights capacity and coordination: step up coordination and collaboration among UN human rights entities on information management, joint analysis, advocacy and field support; UN human rights entities to co-locate; OHCHR to strengthen capacity in New York.

COMMON UN INFORMATION MANAGEMENT SYSTEM ON VIOLATIONS

The UN will have at its disposal credible, timely and joined-up information on violations of international human rights and humanitarian law and broader threats to populations.

16. Establish a common UN information management system on violations of human rights and international humanitarian law: review current UN monitoring and reporting mechanisms on violations, and recommend ways to establish a common system; recommend how to join up analysis of human rights and humanitarian information; establish a small joint team at headquarters to monitor violations where this cannot be done at country level.

It is important to note that, unlike Rwanda and Bosnia, the United Nations had only a modest number of civilian, international, and local staff deployed in Sri Lanka, mostly focused on economic and social development, and, to some degree, on relieving humanitarian distress. (This is the reverse of the situation in Kosovo discussed below, where the United Nations enjoyed sweeping powers, backed up by a significant multinational military force on the ground and a large number of civilian administrators, many of them quite expert.)

In spite of the Plan of Action reproduced above that was developed internally by the Secretariat, some UN staff remained sceptical. They recalled several cases from the past that inspired caution, notably that of one UN Resident Coordinator, Dr. Mukesh Kapila, a senior British aid official who had become the United Nations' lead actor on the ground in Khartoum in 2003. On 19 March 2004, after considerable efforts to rouse New York to action, he sharply raised the alarm, in an interview with the BBC, about a diplomatically inconvenient but massive humanitarian disaster in the making in Darfur, Sudan, conscious he might be committing professional suicide, an assessment soon confirmed when he found himself without a job. (The gripes about him in New York were the usual ones—not a team player, jumping the gun, preempting the decision-making hierarchy—but they ignored the fact that up until then UN Headquarters had done very little to confront the Khartoum government with the Darfur situation, for which Sudanese president Omar Bashir would subsequently be indicted by the International Criminal Court.) Kapila writes in his 2013 memoir *Against a Tide of Evil* that although he was sure to lose his job, none of those who failed to act did—indeed, a number, he suggests, were subsequently promoted.

QUESTIONS

1. To what extent did the Secretary-General seek to respond in detail to the Petrie Report, and what aspects of the recommendations appear to be elided in the summary of "Rights Up Front" provided above?
2. UN staff were intended to be galvanized by "Rights Up Front." Mostly they agreed with its sentiments, but found little in it to reassure them that activism by UN field staff to promote human rights and to protect civilian lives at risk in politically delicate situations would be positively appreciated by higher-ups in the UN system—in the face of inevitable complaints by government (and rebel) officials involved. How might the Secretary-General have preempted such worries?
3. Does the draft Plan of Action reproduced above appear to be a good one in fragile states?
4. Having read the excoriating extracts of the Petrie Report and the Secretary-General's response in "Rights up Front," is it likely the United Nations will perform better in the next such crisis? How, even now, could this be made more likely?
5. Some UN staffers commented with respect to Sri Lanka that invocation of the Responsibility to Protect (R2P) principle had been an unnecessary irritant with local authorities and also within the UN Security Council. How would you react to such views?

16.2 Rwanda

The report by the UN Panel established by Secretary-General Annan to inquire into the failure to prevent or react to the genocide in Rwanda is a long and still quite controversial document.[4] In order to provide a flavor of some of the panel's further findings, the following summary is from the *UN Yearbook*.

SUMMARY OF THE INDEPENDENT INQUIRY INTO THE ACTIONS OF THE UNITED NATIONS DURING THE 1994 GENOCIDE IN RWANDA, *UN YEAR BOOK* 1999[5]

The Secretary-General ... informed the Security Council of his intention to set up an independent inquiry into the actions taken by the United Nations at the time of the 1994 genocide in Rwanda. In view of the enormity

---

[4] UN Doc. S/1999/12571 (1999).
[5] See also excerpts from the report in Chapter 7 of this volume.

of the genocide, he stated, questions continued to surround the actions of the United Nations immediately before and during the period of the crisis. The primary purpose of the inquiry would be to establish the facts and to draw conclusions as to the UN response to the tragedy. The President of the Council stated ... that the members supported the Secretary-General's proposed course of action.

The Independent Inquiry, which was chaired by Ingvar Carlsson, former Prime Minister of Sweden, and included Han Sung-Joo, former Foreign Minister of the Republic of Korea, and Lieutenant-General Rufus M. Kupolati of Nigeria, submitted its report to the Secretary-General on 15 December. On the same date, the Secretary-General forwarded the report to the Council. The Inquiry's terms of reference were to establish a chronology of key events pertaining to UN involvement in Rwanda from October 1993 to July 1994; to evaluate the mandate and resources of the United Nations Assistance Mission for Rwanda (UNAMIR) and how they affected the UN response to the events relating to the massacres; and to draw conclusions and identify the lessons to be learned from the tragedy. The Inquiry had unrestricted access to all UN documentation and persons involved.

The report stated that approximately 800,000 people were killed during the 1994 genocide in Rwanda. The systematic slaughter of men, women and children took place over the course of about 100 days between April and July 1994, during which atrocities were committed by militia and the armed forces, but also by civilians against other civilians. The international community did not prevent the genocide, nor did it stop the killing once the genocide had begun. The failure by the United Nations to prevent and subsequently to stop the genocide was a failure by the UN system as a whole. The fundamental failure was the lack of resources and political commitment devoted to the situation in Rwanda and to the UN presence there. There was a persistent lack of political will by Member States to act, or to act with enough assertiveness, thus affecting the response by the Secretariat and decision-making by the Security Council; it was also evident in the difficulties in obtaining sufficient troops for UNAMIR. Despite the Mission's chronic lack of resources and political priority, serious mistakes were made with the resources that were at the disposal of the United Nations.

The Inquiry noted that the 1948 Convention on the Prevention and Punishment of the Crime of Genocide established the criteria for determining genocide and the Security Council had used the same criteria in outlining the mandate of the International Criminal Tribunal for Rwanda, which had determined that the mass killings of Tutsi in Rwanda in 1994 constituted genocide. The Inquiry concluded that the genocide was planned and incited by Hutu extremists against the Tutsi.

The Inquiry found that the UN response before and during the genocide failed in a number of respects. The responsibility for the failure to prevent and stop the genocide lay with a number of different actors, in particular the

Secretary-General, the Secretariat, the Security Council, UNAMIR and the broader membership of the United Nations. The Organization and Member States concerned owed a clear apology to the Rwandan people. In addition, efforts should be made to bring to justice those Rwandans who planned, incited and carried out the genocide against their countrymen. The overriding failure in the UN response before and during the genocide was summarized by the Inquiry as a lack of resources and a lack of will.

UNAMIR, the main component of the UN presence in Rwanda, was not planned, dimensioned, deployed or instructed in a way that provided for a proactive and assertive role in dealing with a peace process in serious trouble. The Mission's mandate was based on an analysis of the peace process that proved erroneous and that was never corrected, despite significant warning signs that the original mandate had become inadequate. In the time of deepest crisis, the Mission experienced a lack of political leadership, lack of military capacity, severe problems of command and control and lack of coordination and discipline. Despite facing a deteriorating security situation that should have motivated a more assertive and preventive UN role, no steps were taken to adjust the mandate to the reality of the needs in Rwanda.

The Inquiry addressed the matter of the 11 January 1994 cable sent by UNAMIR Force Commander Brigadier-General Roméo A. Dallaire to the Secretary-General's Military Adviser, Major-General Maurice Baril, stating that Dallaire had received information regarding a strategy to provoke the killing of Belgian soldiers and the Belgian battalion's withdrawal from Rwanda. He had also been informed that trained men were scattered throughout Kigali, that all Tutsi in Kigali were to be registered, probably for their extermination, and that there was a major arms cache for that purpose. In response to Dallaire's request to take military action, senior Secretariat officials responded that such an operation went beyond UNAMIR's mandate. The Inquiry believed that serious mistakes were made in dealing with the cable, both in UNAMIR and in the Secretariat. The leadership of the Department of Peacekeeping Operations did not brief the Secretary-General and the Security Council was not informed. The Inquiry also found it incomprehensible that more was not done to follow up on the information received. However, it saw no reason to criticize the Secretariat's decision on the mandate issue but felt that the matter should have been raised with the Council. Further, the threat against the Belgian contingent should have been followed up more clearly.

Regarding failure to respond to the genocide, the Inquiry noted that UNAMIR was in disarray. It was also under rules of engagement not to use force except in self-defence. The operation was prevented from performing its political mandate, incapable of protecting the civilian population or civilian UN staff and at risk itself. Further, UNAMIR was sidelined in relation to the national evacuation operations conducted by Belgium, France, Italy and the United States. The responsibility for that situation, said the Inquiry, had to be shared between the leadership of UNAMIR, the Secretariat and troop-contributing countries.

As to the withdrawal of the Belgian contingent following the killing of 10 of its members, the Inquiry believed it was essential to preserve the unity of UN command and control and that troop-contributing countries, despite domestic political pressures, should refrain from unilateral withdrawal to the detriment and even risk of ongoing peacekeeping operations. The subsequent Council decision to reduce UNAMIR to a minimal force rather than make every effort to muster the political will to stop the killing led to widespread bitterness in Rwanda; it was a decision that the Inquiry found difficult to justify and it felt that the Council bore a responsibility for its lack of political will to do more.

Rwanda was to prove a turning point in UN peacekeeping, and came to symbolize a lack of will to commit to peacekeeping and, above all, to take risks in the field, said the Inquiry. From its inception, UNAMIR suffered from a lack of resources and logistics. During the massacres, the Mission and the Secretariat continued to focus on achieving a ceasefire and too little attention was given to the massacres. Furthermore, there was a weakness in the capacity for political analysis, in particular within UNAMIR but also at Headquarters. The Mission also failed to protect civilians, political leaders and Rwandan UN staff members who expected or sought protection.

The Inquiry believed that there were institutional lessons to be learned from the Rwandan crisis with regard to the capacity and willingness of the United Nations to conduct peacekeeping operations, and there were lessons to be learned relating to the relationship between the United Nations and Rwanda. The aftermath of the genocide was still a reality—in the suffering, in the efforts to build reconciliation, in bringing those responsible to justice, and in the continued problems of those displaced and the needs of the survivors. It was also a reality in the continued existence of the Interahamwe as an armed force in the Great Lakes region, and in the continued instability in that region.

The Inquiry made a number of recommendations for future peacekeeping efforts:

(1) the Secretary-General should initiate an action plan to prevent genocide involving the whole UN system;

(2) efforts should be made to improve UN peacekeeping capacity, including the availability of resources and clarity as to which rules of engagement should apply;

(3) the United Nations—and in particular the Security Council and troop-contributing countries—should be prepared to prevent acts of genocide or gross violations of human rights;

(4) the UN early warning capacity should be improved, both with outside actors and within the Secretariat;

(5) protection of civilians in conflict situations should be improved;

(6) the security of UN and associated personnel, including local staff, needed to be improved;

(7) cooperation between officials responsible for the security of different categories of staff in the field needed to be ensured;

(8) an effective flow of information needed to be ensured;

(9) improvements should be made in the flow of information to the Council;

(10) the flow of information on human rights issues should be improved;

(11) national evacuation operations should be coordinated with UN missions on the ground;

(12) further study should be given to suspending participation of a Member State on the Security Council in exceptional circumstances, such as the Rwandan crisis;

(13) the international community should support efforts in Rwanda to rebuild the society; and

(14) the United Nations should acknowledge its part of the responsibility for not having done enough to prevent or stop the genocide in Rwanda.

These very significant failings at the United Nations occurred at a time when parallel problems in other UN peacekeeping operations were inspiring a degree of reticence on the part of potential troop contributors. The UN operation in the former Yugoslavia, UNPROFOR, was bogged down between belligerents engaged in a war of attrition and was saddled with mandates not much clearer or more useful than that of UNAMIR. Similarly, the United Nations' setbacks in Somalia, along with crucial US military losses there, had created a fear in Washington of African "quagmires." Without US leadership, any international response was always likely to be meek. French involvement in Rwanda had produced—to say the least—complex and not always helpful policy responses from Paris. Belgium, the former colonial power in Rwanda, was effectively intimidated by the slaughter of ten of its UNAMIR peacekeepers and withdrew. In this context, the lack of political will in the Council is more readily understandable, however deplorable.

Several Council members, notably its President in April 1994, New Zealand, and Nigeria argued for more forceful action to counter the genocide, but they were overridden by those with the means to make a difference on the ground. That Rwanda happened at the time also to hold one of the elected seats on the Council is one of the ironies of this sad chapter in Council history. The recommendations of the Panel outlined above were all sensible. But it is not clear that either the Security Council or the Secretariat took them entirely to heart.

The same might be said of the report by the Organization of African Unity (OAU), though it was more biting about the failures by Western powers, the United Nations, the Rwanda Patriotic Front, and indeed the OAU itself.

RWANDA: THE PREVENTABLE GENOCIDE: THE REPORT OF THE INTERNATIONAL PANEL OF EMINENT PERSONALITIES TO INVESTIGATE THE 1994 GENOCIDE IN RWANDA AND THE SURROUNDING EVENTS (ORGANIZATION OF AFRICAN UNITY, 7 JULY 2000)

9.16. An unforgivable tragedy for the Tutsi of Rwanda was that the international community failed to take a single step to halt the genocide once it began, even though everyone knew it was in progress. . . . The interpretation of the countless individual incidents recorded is surely inescapable: There were a thousand early warnings that something appalling was about to occur in Rwanda. If not a genocide, it was at least a catastrophe of so great a magnitude that it should command international intervention. As we shall see, that intervention was utterly inadequate, largely owing to the political interests of the Americans and the French. . . .

10.11. Rather than respond with appropriate force, the opposite happened, spurred by the murders of the Belgian Blue Berets and Belgium's withdrawal of its remaining troops. Exactly two weeks after the genocide began—following strenuous lobbying for total withdrawal led by Belgium and Britain, and with American UN Ambassador Madeleine Albright advocating the most token of forces and the United States adamantly refusing to accept publicly that a full-fledged, Convention-defined genocide was in fact taking place—the Security Council made the astonishing decision to reduce the already inadequate UNAMIR force to a derisory 270 men.

10.12. Today, it seems barely possible to believe. The international community actually chose to abandon the Tutsi of Rwanda at the very moment when they were being exterminated. Even that was not the end of it. The UN Secretariat officials then instructed General Dallaire that his rump force was not to take an active role in protecting Rwandan citizens. To his great credit, Dallaire manoeuvered to keep the force at almost twice the size authorized, and UNAMIR was still able to save the lives of an estimated 20,000 to 25,000 Rwandans during the course of the genocide. . . .

13.37. . . . To use a phrase that became commonplace after the genocide, the failure of the international community to stand up to Hutu Power reinforced the culture of impunity that further empowered the radicals. In a terrible irony, as UNAMIR's commanders perfectly well understood, the very feebleness of the UN's intervention emboldened the Hutu radicals, persuading them that they had nothing to fear from the outside world regardless of what they did. This assessment, of course, proved to be accurate. . . .

15.34. [T]he UN Secretariat went far beyond being merely neutral bureaucrats carrying out the wishes of their political masters in the Security Council. Time and again, they imposed on UNAMIR the tightest constraints imaginable, refusing it the slightest flexibility even when lives were directly at stake. The sole exception to this rigid position was when the lives at stake were those of expatriates as they were being frantically evacuated from the country after April 6.

15.35. The Secretariat did not exercise its right to function as an advocate with the Security Council by attempting to persuade members of the urgent need to take more positive action. Indeed, the non-permanent members of the Council were at times kept largely in the dark. The Czech ambassador at the time, for example, complained that, "The Secretariat was not giving us the full story. It knew much more than it was letting on, so members like us did not appreciate the distinction between civil war and genocide." Their record is a dark stain on the United Nations and themselves, as Secretary-General Kofi Annan, Boutros-Ghali's successor, acknowledged in his response to the Carlsson Inquiry report: "I fully accept their conclusions, including those which reflect on officials of the UN Secretariat, of whom I myself was one."

15.36. It is not entirely clear what conclusions Secretary-General Annan accepts. About 18 months earlier, he had, like President Clinton, travelled to Kigali and apologized that "in their greatest hour of need, the world failed the people of Rwanda.... All of us who cared about Rwanda, who witnessed its suffering, fervently wish that we could have prevented the genocide." Kofi Annan's explanation was remarkably similar to President Clinton's: "Looking back now," he told the Rwandan Parliament, "we see the signs which then were not recognized. Now we know that what we did was not nearly enough, not enough to save Rwanda from itself." Rwandan officials, who had no doubt whatsoever about the signs that had been available, were furious with the Secretary-General's performance. . . .

15.87. Under the circumstances of the time, this Panel finds that the silence of the OAU and a large majority of African Heads of State constituted a shocking moral failure. The moral position of African leaders in the councils of the world would have been strengthened had they unanimously and unequivocally labelled the war against the Tutsi a genocide and called on the world to treat the crisis accordingly. Whether their actual influence would have been any greater we will, of course, never know. . . .

QUESTIONS

6. Although "the United Nations" is widely blamed for the failure to forestall genocide in Rwanda in 1994, how would you assess and assign legal and political responsibility to different actors within the United Nations (Security Council members, UN Secretariat officials, UN staff—including UNAMIR peacekeepers)—on the ground)? Have any of these actors paid a price for their mistakes?

7. Were a Rwanda-like situation to recur in Africa or elsewhere, are you confident the UN's reaction would be any different. Why?

16.3 Srebrenica

The disaster at Srebrenica remains a terrible stain on the record of UN peacekeeping and an indictment of strategies in the UN Security Council premised as much on wishful thinking and the "art of the possible" as on realistic planning for harsh realities on the ground. Around 7,000 men and boys were killed after the "safe area" fell to Serb forces despite the presence of a Dutch battalion of peacekeepers intended to deter attack. NATO was also involved due to the "air cover" (through air strikes) it was providing for the UN mission. (See Chapter 9 for more on the so-called "dual key" formula.) The NATO strikes requested by the local UN commander failed to materialize after squabbling among UN, NATO, and national officials. The UN report on these sorry events—also commissioned by Secretary-General Kofi Annan—was widely praised as the frankest document of its sort to have been published by the United Nations.[6] Again, a sense of the report is provided by the summary from the UN Year Book.

SUMMARY OF THE REPORT OF THE SECRETARY-GENERAL PURSUANT TO GENERAL ASSEMBLY RESOLUTION 53/35: THE FALL OF SREBRENICA, UN YEAR BOOK 1999

In response to General Assembly resolution 53/35, the Secretary-General submitted a comprehensive report [A/54/549] on the events dating from the establishment of the safe area of Srebrenica on 16 April 1993 until the endorsement of the Peace Agreement by the Security Council in resolution 1031 (1995).

The Secretary-General said the tragedy that occurred after the fall of Srebrenica was shocking for the magnitude of the crimes committed and because the enclave's inhabitants believed that the Council's authority, the presence of the United Nations Protection Force (UNPROFOR) peacekeepers and the might of NATO's air power would ensure their safety. Instead, the Bosnian Serb forces ignored the Council, pushed aside UNPROFOR troops and overran the safe area of Srebrenica, assessing correctly that air power would not be used against them. They proceeded to depopulate the territory within 48 hours and executed and buried thousands of men and boys within a matter of days, while their leaders negotiated with the international community.

The Secretary-General said that many of the errors the United Nations made flowed from its well-intentioned effort to keep the peace and apply the rules of peacekeeping when there was no peace to keep. Knowing that any

---

[6] UN Doc. A/54/549 (1999).

other course of action would jeopardize the lives of the troops, the Council and Member States tried to create or imagine an environment in which the tenets of peacekeeping could be upheld, to stabilize the situation on the ground through ceasefire agreements and to eschew the use of force, except in self-defence. The international community's response to the war in Bosnia and Herzegovina, comprising an arms embargo, humanitarian aid and the deployment of a peacekeeping force, was a poor substitute for more decisive and forceful action to prevent the unfolding horror, the Secretary-General stated.

None of the conditions for the deployment of peacekeepers had been met: there was no peace agreement, not even a functioning ceasefire, and there was no clear will to peace and no clear consent by the belligerents. It had become clear that the ability to adapt mandates to the reality on the ground was of critical importance to ensuring that the appropriate force under the appropriate structure was deployed. None of that flexibility was present in the management of UNPROFOR.

There was neither the will to use decisive air power against Serb attacks on the safe areas, nor the means on the ground to repulse them.

Two of the safe areas, Srebrenica and Zepa, were demilitarized to a far greater extent than any of the others. However, instead of enhancing their security, it only made them easier targets for the Serbs. The failure to fully comprehend the extent of the Serb war aims might explain in part why the Secretariat and the peacekeeping mission did not react more quickly and decisively when the Serbs initiated their attack on Srebrenica. In fact, the Council was given the impression that the situation was under control and many believed that to be the case. Some instances of incomplete and inaccurate information being given to the Council could be attributed to problems with reporting from the field, but in other instances the reporting might have been illustrative of a more general tendency to assume that the parties were equally responsible for the transgressions that occurred. It was not clear, in any event, that the provision of more fully accurate information to the Council would have led to appreciably different results.

In the end, the Bosnian Serb war aims were repulsed on the battlefield and not at the negotiating table, yet the Secretariat had convinced itself that the broader use of force by the international community was beyond its mandate and undesirable.

The fall of Srebrenica was replete with lessons for the Organization and its Member States: when peacekeeping operations were used as a substitute for political consensus they were likely to fail; and peacekeepers should never be deployed where there was no ceasefire or peace agreement, or told to use their peacekeeping tools—lightly armed soldiers in scattered positions—to impose the ill-defined wishes of the international community by military means. If the necessary resources were not provided, and the political, military and moral judgements were not made, the job simply could not be done. Protected zones and safe areas should be demilitarized and established by the agreement of the belligerents, as in the case of the "protected zones" and "safe havens" recognized by international humanitarian law, or they should be truly safe areas, fully defended by a credible military deterrent.

The responsibility for allowing that tragic course of events by its prolonged refusal to use force in the early stages of the war was shared by the Council, the Contact Group and other Governments, which contributed to that delay, as well as by the Secretariat and the mission in the field. Clearly, however, the primary and most direct responsibility lay with the architects and implementers of the attempted genocide in Bosnia. The cardinal lesson of Srebrenica was that a deliberate and systematic attempt to terrorize, expel or murder an entire people should be met decisively with all necessary means, and with the political will to carry the policy through to its logical conclusion.

The Secretary-General concluded that through error, misjudgement and an inability to recognize the scope of the evil, the United Nations failed to help save the people of Srebrenica from the Serb campaign of mass murder, crystallizing a truth understood only too late by the United Nations and the world at large: that Bosnia was as much a moral cause as a military conflict.

Importantly, the report identifies a mismatch between Security Council strategies (peacekeeping) and the situation on the ground (no peace to keep). The summary above rather underplays the Secretariat's attempts in 1993 and 1994 to secure the larger numbers of peacekeepers for UNPROFOR that might have deterred the Serb attack on Srebrenica, but it rightly points to the determination of the Serb military leadership and strategies largely discouraging the use of force by the United Nations and NATO. There was either reprehensible confusion or doubly reprehensible finessing of what UN "safe areas" were meant to represent. They certainly did not have the deterrent military capacity that would have made them truly safe.

Were any lessons learned from this episode? Importantly, did the United Nations subsequently insist on peace agreements before deploying peacekeepers? Did peacekeepers subsequently deploy in sufficient numbers and so equipped as to be able to defend their mandates? Too often they did not. The case of Sierra Leone, discussed in Chapter 9, is one of several in which UN peacekeepers were easily overrun by local combatants. By 2005, the UN Secretariat (eventually supported by the Security Council), clearly fed up with the United Nations' own frequent military incapacity and ineffectiveness, adopted tougher strategies on the ground in the Democratic Republic of the Congo after a French-led EU "coalition of the willing," Operation Artemis, had restored order. Perhaps as a consequence, MONUC also absorbed larger casualties there in 2005 and 2006 than had earlier been the case. It remains the case that UN peacekeeping operations are frequently caught between demanding situations on the ground and the expediency with which members of the Security Council are all too often driven to adopt mandates seriously under-resourced relative to their objectives.

QUESTION

8. How would you contrast the responsibility of the United Nations for action or inaction in Srebrenica, in comparison with the responsibility of the United Nations for events in Rwanda?

16.4 Kosovo

We have seen in Chapter 2 and again in Chapters 9 and 14 how extensive were the powers conferred on the UN Special Representative of the Secretary-General (SRSG) in Kosovo by Security Council resolution 1244 (1999). Considerable unease grew not only over these powers, but also over the virtually unlimited nature of such powers available to the international community's High Representative in Bosnia under the Dayton agreements and to the SRSG in East Timor during the United Nations' period of transitional administration there. The ability to "check and balance" local political actors engaged in irresponsible pandering to their own communities was seen internationally as a positive feature of robust mandates for the leading international actor in such theaters of operation. Nevertheless, the local effects of prolonged undemocratic rule by international fiat have been less discussed. In a case in point, the international ombudsperson in Kosovo (an office created by the Organization for Security and Cooperation in Europe, OSCE, one of several organizations charged with implementing resolution 1244) sought to rein in the SRSG, on legal and human rights grounds.

One of the consequences of the diminished credibility of UNMIK and its own lack of faith in the local judiciary was recourse to detention on executive orders. On 28 May 2000, Afrim Zeqiri, a Kosovar Albanian and former Kosovo Liberation Army (KLA) fighter, was arrested on suspicion of murdering three Serbs in the village of Cernica, including the shooting of a four-year-old boy. An Albanian prosecutor ordered him released for lack of evidence, raising suspicions of judicial bias. The decision was upheld by an international judge, but SRSG Bernard Kouchner nevertheless ordered that Zeqiri continue to be detained under an "executive hold," claiming that the authority to issue such orders derived from "security reasons" and Security Council resolution 1244 (1999).

Similar orders were made by Kouchner's successor, Hans Haekkerup. In February 2001, a bus carrying Serbs from Nis into Kosovo was bombed, killing eleven. British KFOR troops arrested Florim Ejupi, Avdi Behluli, Çelë Gashi, and Jusuf Veliu in mid-March on suspicion of being involved, but on 27 March a panel of international judges of the District Court of Pristina ordered that Behluli, Gashi, and Veliu be released. The following day, Haekkerup issued an executive order extending their detention for thirty days, later extended by six more such orders. (Ejupi was subsequently reported to have "escaped" from the high-security detention facility at Camp Bondsteel.)[7]

SPECIAL REPORT NO. 3, ON THE CONFORMITY OF DEPRIVATIONS OF LIBERTY UNDER "EXECUTIVE ORDERS" WITH RECOGNISED INTERNATIONAL STANDARDS, 29 JUNE 2001

[Addressed to Mr. Hans Haekkerup, Special Representative of the Secretary-General of the United Nations]

Pursuant to his authority under Sections 1.1 and 4.1 of UNMIK Regulation No. 2000/38 on the Establishment of the Ombudsperson Institution in Kosovo and Rule 22, paras. 3 and 4 of the Rules of Procedure of the Ombudsperson Institution, the Ombudsperson has issued the above Special Report.

The Ombudsperson found that deprivations of liberty imposed under "Executive Orders" or any other form of executive instruction, decree or decision issued by the Special Representative of the Secretary-General of the United Nations (SRSG) do not conform with recognised international standards. He found that any such deprivation of liberty cannot be considered to be lawful in the sense of para. 1 of Article 5 of the European Convention on Human Rights, that the absence of judicial control over deprivations of liberty imposed under Executive Orders constitutes a violation of paras. 3 and 4 of Article 5 of the Convention and that the lack of an enforceable right to compensation for unlawful deprivations of liberty constitutes a violation of para. 5 of Article 5.

The Ombudsperson recommended that the SRSG immediately cease the practice of issuing Executive Orders imposing on any individual in Kosovo a deprivation of liberty. The Ombudsperson further recommended that the SRSG, no later than 20 July 2001, convene one or more panels composed of international judges to review, on an urgent basis, the lawfulness of detentions of individuals currently deprived of their liberty under Executive Orders, such review to conform with the requirements of Article 5 of the European Convention on Human Rights. The Ombudsperson also recommended that the SRSG should undertake to comply with decisions on deprivations of liberty taken by the judicial panels convened in accordance with the recommendations.

The Ombudsperson also recommended that the SRSG, no later than 31 August 2001, promulgate a Regulation setting forth the legal bases for compensation claims for unlawful deprivations of liberty and proper judicial proceedings in this respect and, on the date of its entry into force, disseminate it through all appropriate channels in all languages widely used in Kosovo. The Ombudsperson further recommended that the new Regulation

---

[7] Simon Chesterman, *You, the People: The United Nations, Transitional Administration and State-Building* (Oxford: Oxford University Press, 2004), pp. 167–168.

should be distributed to all persons who have been deprived of their liberty under Executive Orders issued by the SRSG and to all judges, judicial officers or others exercising judicial authority in Kosovo.

Following criticism by the OSCE Ombudsperson, as well as international human rights organizations such as Human Rights Watch and Amnesty International, a Detention Review Commission of international experts was established by UNMIK in August 2001 to make final decisions on the legality of administrative detentions. The Commission approved extension of the detentions of the alleged Nis bombers until 19 December 2001—a few weeks after Kosovo's first provincial elections—ruling that "there are reasonable grounds to suspect that each of the detained persons has committed a criminal act." At the end of that period, the three-month mandate of the Commission had not been renewed; in its absence, the Kosovo Supreme Court ordered the release of the three detainees. The last person held under an Executive Order, Afrim Zeqiri, was released by a judge on bail in early February 2002 after approximately twenty months in detention.

QUESTIONS

9. The Kosovo case outlined above relates to the special (and potentially unlimited) powers of UN representatives in territories under UN rule. Are there judicial or other international processes that should be set in place to serve as checks on such powers whenever they are established? How could this be done practically, without creating cumbersome and expensive bureaucracies?
10. Are you more worried about UN representatives in such situations doing too much (relative to their mandate) or too little in situations such as Kosovo? Why?

16.5 Sexual Exploitation by UN Peacekeepers

The issue of sexual exploitation across borders grew in prominence during the 1990s, and early in the 2000s attention started to focus on the conduct of UN and other international personnel, in light of complaints that the UN peacekeepers in the Balkans and in Africa had engaged in sexual exploitation of those they were meant to protect. Concern crystallized in 2004 over reports of widespread sexual exploitation by troops and civilian staff of MONUC, the United Nations' large peacekeeping operation in the Democratic Republic of the Congo. The Secretary-General, acknowledging the gravity of the allegations, commissioned a report from a panel led by the Jordanian ambassador to the United Nations, Prince Zeid Ra'ad Zeid Al-Hussein, himself a former civilian peacekeeper in Bosnia, and in 2014 appointed the UN's High Commissioner for Human Rights.

A COMPREHENSIVE STRATEGY TO ELIMINATE FUTURE SEXUAL EXPLOITATION AND ABUSE IN UNITED NATIONS PEACEKEEPING OPERATIONS, 24 MARCH 2005[8]

3. United Nations peacekeeping has a distinguished history of helping many States and peoples to emerge from conflict with the hope of a better future. Many peacekeeping personnel have given their lives to realize that goal, and their achievements and sacrifices must not be forgotten. But despite the distinguished role that United Nations peacekeeping personnel have played over the last half-century, there regrettably will always be those who violate codes of conduct and thereby dishonour the many who have given their lives in the cause of peace. Sexual exploitation and abuse by military, civilian police and civilian peacekeeping personnel is not a new phenomenon. Such acts cover a wide spectrum of behaviour, from breaches of the Organization's standards of conduct, such as solicitation of adult prostitutes, which may be legal in some countries, to acts that would be considered a criminal offence in any national jurisdiction, for example rape and paedophilia. . . .

6. The reality of prostitution and other sexual exploitation in a peacekeeping context is profoundly disturbing to many because the United Nations has been mandated to enter into a broken society to help it, not to breach the trust placed in it by the local population. Moreover, the Organization should not in any way increase the suffering of vulnerable sectors of the population, which has often been devastated by war or civil conflict. For example, in the Democratic Republic of the Congo, it would appear that sexual exploitation and abuse mostly involves the exchange of sex for money (on average $1–$3 per encounter), for food (for immediate consumption or to barter later) or for jobs (especially affecting daily workers). Some young girls whom I spoke within the Democratic Republic of the Congo talked of "rape disguised as prostitution," in which they said they were raped and given money or food afterwards to give the rape the appearance of a consensual transaction. Once young girls are in this situation, a situation of dependency is created which tends to result in a continued downward spiral of further prostitution, with its attendant violence, desperation, disease and further dependency. A consequence of sexual exploitation and abuse is the presence of abandoned "peacekeeper babies," children fathered and abandoned by peacekeeping personnel. The absence of a functioning legal system means that the protections afforded to citizens of most countries against this type of abuse are absent. . . .

---

[8] UN Doc. A/59/710 (2005).

II. The Rules

15. United Nations staff have the status and the privileges and immunities of officials under the Convention on the Privileges and Immunities of the United Nations (the General Convention), which also sets out the conditions under which their immunity may be waived by the Secretary-General. . . .

16. United Nations Volunteers are also employed in peacekeeping missions. Recent status-of-forces agreements extend to them the privileges and immunities of officials granted under the General Convention. . . .

17. Individual contractors and consultants are also employed by peacekeeping missions. They are subject to local law and are bound by the standards set out in the Organization's standard conditions of contract for individual contractors and consultants.

18. Civilian police and military observers have the status and the privileges and immunities of experts on mission granted under the General Convention (military liaison officers and military staff officers are also considered experts on mission). . . .

19. Military members of national contingents have the privileges and immunities specified in the status-of-forces agreement or, if none has been concluded, in the model status-of-forces agreement, which the Security Council makes applicable to peacekeeping operations pending the conclusion of a status-of-forces agreement with the host State. The model status-of-forces agreement provides that the troop-contributing country has criminal and disciplinary jurisdiction over military members of the contingents (A/45/594, annex, para. 47 (b)). However, as an administrative measure, the Secretary-General may order the repatriation of any military member of a contingent who has been found culpable of serious misconduct in a mission investigation. Troop-contributing countries have over the years universally accepted the general standards of conduct set out in the publications entitled "Ten Rules: Code of Personal Conduct for Blue Helmets" and "We Are United Nations Peacekeepers." . . .

21. The basic standards of conduct and integrity required of the various categories of peacekeeping personnel—set out in the Staff Regulations and Rules, the Ten Rules and We Are United Nations Peacekeepers—are similar because they are all derived from principles established in Article 101, paragraph 3, of the Charter, which requires the highest standards of integrity of United Nations officials. But those documents are general in nature; they do not give specific instructions on precisely what acts of sexual exploitation and abuse are prohibited. The 2003 bulletin fills that gap by setting out such detailed prohibitions. The bulletin was welcomed by the Special Committee on Peacekeeping Operations (Special Committee) and by the General Assembly in its resolution 58/315 of 1 July 2004, but it must be noted that the bulletin applies of its own force only to United Nations staff.

22. There is thus an extensive mosaic of provisions drafted at varying points in time and with varying degrees of legal force dealing with sexual exploitation and abuse that apply to the various categories of peacekeeping personnel. As noted above, only United Nations staff members are unquestionably

bound by the prohibitions set out in the 2003 Secretary-General's bulletin. Civilian police and military observers agree to be bound by directives, which, since approximately mid-2004, have included a summary of those prohibitions. The situation of military members of contingents is unclear. Rules can be made binding on military members of contingents only with the agreement of and action by the troop-contributing country concerned. . . .

27. The General Assembly should reiterate its approval of the standards set out in the 2003 bulletin and make them applicable to all categories of peacekeeping personnel, without exception. It should also request the Secretary-General to ensure that all civilian personnel are bound by them. Furthermore, the Assembly should decide that those standards and the standards contained in Ten Rules and We Are United Nations Peacekeepers be included in the model memorandums of understanding, and the troop-contributing countries should undertake to issue the standards in a form binding on their personnel. The Secretary-General and troop-contributing countries should cooperate to issue the standards set out in the 2003 bulletin, as well as those contained in Ten Rules and We Are United Nations Peacekeepers, to troop-contributing country personnel in convenient card form in the languages of those personnel, with the troop-contributing country providing the translation and the mission arranging for publication of the cards at its cost. . . .

V. Individual Disciplinary, Financial and Criminal Accountability

67. Some of the difficulties faced by troop-contributing countries in acting on what they perceived to be flawed preliminary investigations and board of inquiry reports were explained earlier in the present report. Also examined were the difficulties faced by the Department of Peacekeeping Operations in investigating allegations of sexual exploitation and abuse where traditional methods of identification through witnesses proved difficult if not impossible. Underlying such problems of investigative technique are two more fundamental problems that are more difficult to resolve:

(a) In respect of military members of national contingents, troop-contributing countries are often reluctant to admit publicly to acts of wrong doing and consequently lack the will to court-martial alleged offenders;

(b) In respect of staff and experts on mission, the lack of a legal system in some peacekeeping areas that meets minimum international human rights standards makes it difficult for the Secretary-General to waive the immunity of staff accused of serious crimes in the mission area. . . .

68. Personnel who violate the standards established in the 2003 Secretary-General's bulletin ought to be subjected to disciplinary action unless, in the case of staff or experts on mission, the Secretary-General, in lieu of such action, accepts an immediate resignation and a designation that

the individual is never to be re-employed by the United Nations is placed in his or her file. . . .

71. It is recommended that the model memorandum of understanding be amended to provide that troop-contributing countries undertake to institute disciplinary action against military members of their contingents found to have violated the standards set out in the 2003 bulletin by means of an investigation conducted in accordance with the recommendations set out in section II above.

Financial Accountability

72. Many victims, especially those who have "peacekeeper babies" and who have been abandoned by the fathers, are in a desperate financial situation. There is a need to try to ensure that fathers, who can be identified, perhaps through blood or DNA testing, bear some financial responsibility for their actions. . . .

Individual Criminal Accountability

Military Members of Contingents

78. Under the model status-of-forces agreement, military members are subject to the criminal authority of the troop-contributing country concerned. Because military members of national contingents are not subject to the criminal jurisdiction of the host State, the model status-of-forces agreement, which has been repeatedly endorsed by the Security Council, specifically envisaged that the Secretary-General would obtain formal assurances from the troop-contributing country concerned that it would exercise jurisdiction with respect to crimes that might be committed by their forces in the mission area (see A/45/594, annex, para. 48). In a footnote to that provision, it was noted that such formal assurances would be inserted into the country-specific memorandum of understanding. The practice of the Organization no longer follows that understanding, but it should. . . .

79. . . . The model memorandum of understanding should also provide that if those authorities conclude that prosecution is not appropriate, the troop-contributing country will submit a report to the Secretary-General explaining why prosecution was not appropriate. The model memorandum of understanding also ought to require the troop-contributing country to agree to inform the Secretary-General within 120 days after a case has been referred to it of measures it has taken under its national law and to inform him of progress achieved every 120 days thereafter until the case is finalized.

80. It must be emphasized that the provisions outlined above do not obligate a troop-contributing country to prosecute. A decision whether or not to prosecute is an act of sovereignty. However, these provisions will require a troop-contributing country to submit the case to the appropriate authorities, who must decide whether or not to prosecute in the same way

as they would for an offence of a similar grave nature under their laws in their own jurisdiction. The suggested provisions would also obligate the troop-contributing country to report the outcome of the case in its jurisdiction. ...

82. The Secretary-General, in his annual report to the Special Committee, should describe in general terms the actions taken by troop-contributing countries in response to cases referred to them. The Secretary-General should, in a separate section of the report, set out the details of cases in which a troop-contributing country failed to inform him of the action taken as a result of the mission's investigation. In such cases the report shall name the troop-contributing country and provide details of the alleged conduct, of course without revealing the identity of the member of the contingent alleged to have committed those acts. ...

United Nations Staff and Experts on Mission

84. The 1945 United Nations Conference on International Organization decided that personnel of the Organization would be immune from national jurisdiction only with respect to acts performed by them in their official capacity unless that immunity were waived by the United Nations. ...

85. ... It further provides that the Secretary-General shall have the right and the duty to waive the immunity of any official in any case where, in his opinion, the immunity would impede the course of justice and can be waived without prejudice to the interests of the United Nations. ...

86. The practice of the Secretary-General in implementing this provision is clear. If staff or experts on mission commit criminal acts in their duty station and the host State seeks to prosecute, the Secretary-General will first make a determination as to whether the acts in question were performed in the course of official duties. If the acts were not performed in the course of official duties, the Secretary-General will inform the local authorities that no functional immunity exists. ... If the acts in question have some connection to official duties, such as driving of a United Nations vehicle, while drunk, or if the official enjoys the immunity of a diplomatic envoy and the host State seeks to prosecute, the Secretary-General must waive that immunity if ... continued immunity would impede the course of justice and where immunity can be waived without prejudice to the interests of the United Nations. This policy, of course, must be rigorously applied in peacekeeping operations to acts of sexual exploitation and abuse that constitute crimes under the laws of the host State. But it must be remembered that not all the acts of sexual exploitation and abuse specified in the 2003 Secretary-General's bulletin constitute crimes under national law; for example, in many jurisdictions purchasing sex from prostitutes over the age of 18 is not a crime.

87. In the great majority of cases the application of the tests in the Convention is clear. What was not anticipated at the time the General

Convention was drafted was that the United Nations would, on occasion, be operating in areas where there was no functioning legal system or where the legal system was so devastated by conflict that it no longer satisfied minimum international human rights standards. In such cases it would not be in the interests of the United Nations to waive immunity because its Charter requires it to uphold, promote and respect human rights. In other words, it would not be in the interest of the Organization for the Secretary-General to permit a staff member to be subjected to a criminal process that did not respect basic international human rights standards.

88. In such cases, making United Nations personnel criminally accountable depends upon whether another State has jurisdiction under its laws to prosecute. A number of States assert criminal jurisdiction over their nationals, but whether an effective prosecution can be launched depends on whether the offence is a crime under the law of the prosecuting State, whether sufficient evidence for prosecution under the applicable substantive and procedural law can be obtained and whether the prosecuting State can obtain custody of the accused. Whether those factors combine to enable prosecution is fortuitous. This is unsatisfactory. The intention of the Organization's founders to make United Nations personnel criminally accountable for their misdeeds may be thwarted.

89. It is not easy to devise a solution. It may be possible to develop an international convention that would subject United Nations personnel to the jurisdiction of States parties for specified crimes committed *by* such personnel (the Convention on the Safety of United Nations and Associated Personnel does this for specified crimes *against* United Nations personnel). The difficulty with this alternative is that it would apply only to the parties to the convention. Another possibility, at least for peacekeeping operations with a rule-of-law mandate from the Security Council, might be to try to get agreement with the host State when negotiating the status-of-forces agreement for the United Nations to provide assistance to the host State to ensure that criminal proceedings against United Nations personnel satisfied international human rights standards. The difficulty with this alternative is that it would be seen as instituting two standards of justice: one for local inhabitants and one for international officials. This is not an attractive proposition. But at least there would be criminal accountability for acts of sexual exploitation and abuse committed by officials and experts on mission that constituted crimes under local law.

As often happens at the United Nations, these recommendations point to the diffusion of responsibility when failure to meet minimal standards of behavior involves "UN" staff. In this instance, peacekeeping troops supplied by member states were primarily involved. Ultimately, poor behavior of such staff needs to be corrected (and prosecuted) by the troop-contributing nations rather than the United Nations itself.

Beginning in 2015, the Secretary-General released a report containing data on allegations of sexual exploitation and abuse, and measures being taken to prevent and respond to such charges. In 2014, these included fifty-one allegations in nine peacekeeping and one special political mission, and twenty-eight allegations against UN staff members and related personnel in other locations (headquarters and other UN offices).[9] Later in the same year, the UN Office of Internal Oversight Services (OIOS) released its own report, which concluded that the United Nations' "enforcement architecture involves multiple actors having distributed responsibilities, with each considering the other as causing performance deficits. Enforcement delays are common and confusion is often apparent on the ground."[10]

QUESTIONS

11. In cases where sexual abuse is perpetrated by UN peacekeeping personnel provided by member states, what measures can the United Nations take to ensure punishment of guilty parties? What policy should be adopted with respect to UN civilian officials?
12. How might the United Nations do its best to ensure that UN peacekeeping personnel are conditioned to avoid sexual abuse on arrival in the UN's theatre of operations and remain so? Are Prince Zeid's recommendations sufficient?

16.6 The Iraq Oil-for-Food Programme Inquiry

The Oil-for-Food Programme (OFFP) was created as a humanitarian exemption to the comprehensive sanctions imposed on Iraq from 1990. The program was authorized by Security Council resolution 986 (1995), but only became operational in December 1996, seven months after a long-delayed Memorandum of Understanding was concluded between the United Nations and the government of Iraq. During the seven years of the program, $64 billion of Iraqi oil was exported, of which $37 billion was spent in Iraq on humanitarian relief. ($18 billion was allocated for Iraqi compensation of claims arising from Iraq's invasion of Kuwait; a further 2.2 percent—about $1.4 billion—was reserved for funding UN administration of the program.)

---

[9] UN Doc A/69/779 (2015).
[10] UN Office of Internal Oversight Services, Assignment No.: IED-15-001, 15 May 2015.

Although a degree of leakage and sanctions-busting was anticipated, wholesale flouting of the program's parameters was not. In late 2003 and early 2004, media reports increasingly drew attention not only to possible mismanagement of the OFFP, but also to alleged corruption of UN officials. In response, Kofi Annan in April 2004 created an Independent Inquiry Committee into the OFFP, a decision endorsed by the Security Council in resolution 1534 (2004). The Committee comprised Paul Volcker (former Chair of the US Federal Reserve), Richard Goldstone (a former South African justice and International Criminal Tribunal Prosecutor), and Mark Pieth (an international expert on money laundering).

The Committee released a series of reports, the most important of which was the third, published in September 2005. This extensive report was covered by a press release, the contents of which were shaped by discussions among the Committee's members themselves and with UN Secretary-General Kofi Annan and his deputy Louise Fréchette.

PRESS RELEASE—IRAQ OIL-FOR-FOOD PROGRAMME: INDEPENDENT INQUIRY COMMITTEE FINDS MISMANAGEMENT AND FAILURE OF OVERSIGHT[11]

The Independent Inquiry Committee today issues its definitive Report on the overall management and oversight of the "temporary" Oil-for-Food Programme, a programme which stretched to seven years with more than $100 billion in transactions (over $64 billion in oil sales and approximately $37 billion for food). In preceding interim reports and briefing papers, the Committee has reported the results of its investigations on specific aspects of the Oil-for-Food Programme.

This very large and very complex Programme accomplished many vital goals in Iraq. It reversed a serious and deteriorating food crisis, preventing widespread hunger and probably reducing deaths due to malnutrition. While there were problems with the sporadic delivery of equipment and medical supplies, undoubtedly many lives were saved. At the same time, things went wrong, damaging the reputation and credibility of the United Nations.

With respect to the Programme as a whole, the Committee's central conclusion is that the United Nations requires stronger executive leadership, thoroughgoing administrative reform, and more reliable controls and auditing.

---

[11] This press release can be found at: http://reliefweb.int/report/iraq/iraq-oil-food-programme-independent-inquiry-committee-finds-mismanagement-and-failure. For the full report, dated 7 September 2005, see http://www.isn.ethz.ch/Digital-Library/Publications/Detail/?ots591=0c54e3b3-1e9c-be1e-2c24-a6a8c7060233&lng=en&id=13545.

However, responsibility for what went wrong with the Programme cannot be laid exclusively at the door of the Secretariat. Members of the Security Council and its 661 Committee must shoulder their share of the blame in providing uneven and wavering direction in the implementation of the Programme.

What Went Wrong

However well-conceived the Programme was, in principle, the Security Council failed to clearly define the broad parameters, policies and administrative responsibilities for the Programme. This lack of clarity was exacerbated by permitting the Iraqi regime to exercise too much initiative in the Programme design and its subsequent implementation. Compounding that difficulty, the Security Council, in contrast to most past practice, retained through its 661 Committee, substantial elements of administrative control. As a result, neither the Security Council nor the Secretariat leadership was in overall control.

For all that uncertainty, the Secretariat had significant responsibilities in implementing and administering the Programme. As the Chief Administrative Officer of the United Nations, the Secretary-General, in turn, carried oversight and management responsibilities for the entire Secretariat. That included auditing and controls functions that had demonstrable problems with respect to the Programme.

Within the Programme itself, problems arose almost from the start. This report records the reluctance of both the Secretary-General and the Deputy Secretary-General to recognize their own responsibility for the Programme's shortcomings, their failure to ensure that critical evidence was brought to the attention of the Security Council and the 661 Committee, and their minimal efforts to address sanctions violations with Iraqi officials; altogether there was a lack of oversight concerning OIP's administration of the $100 billion Oil-for-Food Programme, and, above all a failure shared by them both to provide oversight of the Programme's Executive Director, Benon Sevan.

In sum, in light of these circumstances, the cumulative management performance of the Secretary-General and the Deputy Secretary-General fell short of the standards that the United Nations Organization should strive to maintain. In making these findings, the Committee has recognized the difficult administrative demands imposed upon the Secretariat and the Secretary-General, both by the design of the Programme and the overlapping Security Council responsibilities.

The Committee's investigation clearly makes the point that, as the Programme expanded and continued, Saddam Hussein found ways and means of turning it to his own advantage, primarily through demands for surcharges and kickbacks from companies doing business with the Programme. For UN agencies, the work went beyond their core competencies of overseeing the distribution of humanitarian goods—from monitoring, planning, and consulting—to infrastructure rebuilding, thus multiplying problems. Nor was there much success in coordinating so large a programme among UN Agencies accustomed to zealously defending their institutional autonomy.

Illicit Income

To put the Programme's flaws and the manipulation by the Saddam Hussein regime into perspective, it is important to note that the regime derived far more revenues from smuggling oil *outside* the Programme than from its demands for surcharges and kickbacks from companies that contracted *within* the Programme. Thousands of vehicles and trucks carried smuggled goods—in both directions across the Iraqi border—with limited, if any, kind of inspection or oversight by the United Nations or, for that matter, member states involved. By the Programme's design, these inspectors were charged only with the inspection of oil and goods that were financed under the Programme. The value of oil smuggled outside of the Programme is estimated by the Committee to be USD 10.99 billion as opposed to an estimated USD 1.8 billion of illicit revenue from Saddam Hussein's manipulation of the Programme.

Kofi and Kojo Annan

In the light of new information relating to *Kojo* Annan's activities to assist Cotecna win the humanitarian goods inspection contract, and a document suggesting that the Secretary-General may have been informed of Cotecna's bid, the Committee reviewed its findings concerning the Secretary-General in its Second Interim Report. After a careful examination of the new information, the Committee has affirmed its prior finding that, weighing all of the information and the credibility of witnesses, the evidence is not reasonably sufficient to conclude that the Secretary-General knew that Cotecna had submitted a bid on the humanitarian inspection contract in 1998.

The Committee also affirms its prior finding that no evidence exists that the Secretary-General influenced, or attempted to influence, the procurement process in 1998 leading to the selection of Cotecna.

As to the adequacy of the Secretary-General's response to press reports in January 1999 of a possible conflict of interest, the Committee re-emphasizes its earlier conclusion that the Secretary-General was not diligent and effective in pursuing an investigation of the procurement of Cotecna. What is now known about *Kojo* Annan's efforts to intervene in the procurement process, underscores the Committee's prior finding that a thorough and independent investigation of the allegations regarding *Kojo* Annan's relationship with Cotecna was required in 1999. A resolution of the questions much earlier would likely have resolved the issues arising from the Cotecna bid process and the consequent conflict of interest concerns.

The "Backchannel" and the MOU Negotiations

This Report deals with the negotiations that resulted in the Memorandum of Understanding between the UN and Saddam Hussein. It also records Iraqi attempts to pass money to former Secretary-General Boutros Boutros-Ghali, principally through an Iraqi-American businessman, Samir Vincent, and a Korean lobbyist, Tongsun Park. The Iraqi leadership hoped that Secretary-General Boutros-Ghali would be "more flexible" and would take steps to "ease the conclusion" in the oil-for-food negotiations. The Committee has determined that well over $1 million was paid to Mr. Vincent and Mr. Park. However, the Committee has not found evidence that Secretary-General Boutros-Ghali received or agreed to receive monies from Mr. Park and Mr. Vincent.

Also reported are Iraq's efforts to secure another high-level contact at the United Nations in 1997 when Mr. Park introduced his Iraqi contacts to a Canadian, Maurice Strong—Secretary-General Annan's newly-appointed Executive Coordinator for United Nations Reform. In the course of Mr. Park's relationship with Mr. Strong, he obtained $1 million in cash from his Iraqi contacts which he used to consummate a stock purchase in a company controlled by Strong's family. While there is an indication that Iraqi officials tried to establish a relationship with Mr. Strong, the Committee has found no evidence that Mr. Strong was involved in Iraqi affairs or matters relating to the Programme.

Reform Proposals

On the central matter of United Nations reform, the Committee's investigation leads it to make six major recommendations:

- Create the position of Chief Operating Officer ("COO"). The COO would have authority over all aspects of administration and would be appointed by the General Assembly on the recommendation of the Security Council. The position would report to the Secretary-General and the United Nations Charter should be amended as appropriate.
- Establish an Independent Oversight Board (IOB) with a majority of independent members. In discharging its mandate, the IOB should have functional responsibility for all independent audit, investigation and evaluation activities, both internal and external, across the United Nations Secretariat and those agencies receiving funds from the United Nations and for which the Secretary-General appoints the executive heads.

- Improve the coordination and the oversight framework for cross-Agency programs.
- Strengthen the quality of the United Nations management and management practices.
- Extend the financial disclosure requirement well below the current assistant secretary-general level within the organization and specifically include the Secretary-General and the Deputy Secretary-General as well as all UN staff who have any decision-making role in the disbursement or award of UN funds (e.g. Procurement Department, Office of the Controller).
- Expand and better define the United Nations conflict of interest rules so that they encompass actual, potential and apparent conflicts of interest.
- Agencies involved in a United Nations programme are entitled to reasonable support for "overhead" as well as direct expenses. In the context of the Oil-for-Food Programme, those charges were excessive and the Agencies involved should return up to $ 50 million in excess compensation secured as a result of work performed under Security Council Resolution 1483.

Emphasizing points expressed in the Report's Preface, the Committee's Chairman, Paul A Volcker, stated, "The inescapable conclusion from the Committee's work is that the United Nations Organization needs thoroughgoing reform—and it needs it urgently. What is important—*what has been recognized by one investigation after another*—is that real change must take place, and change over a wide area. Clear benchmarks for measuring progress must be set. The General Assembly should insist, in its forthcoming meeting, that key reforms be put in place no later than the time of its regular meeting in 2006. To settle for less, to permit delay and dilution, would be to invite failure. It would, in reality, further erode public support, undercut effectiveness, and dishonor the ideals upon which the United Nations is built."

He added, "Before concluding its work, the Committee also intends a more comprehensive listing of firms participating in the Programme, either in the purchase of oil or the sale of humanitarian goods, as well as a more detailed analysis of the manner in which Iraq and its vendors and oil purchasers unlawfully manipulated the Programme."

The Committee members were not intimately involved in the drafting of the report but did, as noted above, influence the terms of this press release and some of the report's prefatory paragraphs, placing the responsibility of the Secretary-General and Deputy Secretary-General in a degree of context, and, in particular, weighing it against that of the Security Council. The Committee's staff, adopting a more prosecutorial tone and mode, had largely elided the issue of Security Council oversight of its own Iraq Sanctions Committee (the so-called 661 Committee), in which the widely known sanctions-busting by Turkey and Jordan was supported by the avowed policy of several Council members. Further, the 661 Committee had approved many contracts widely thought to be of dubious compliance with OFFP terms. Sticking narrowly to the mandate set for the IIC, the staff avoided issues of political responsibility and focused instead on bureaucratic responsibility, financial accountability, and corruption, which led to, apparently, some corrective drafting at the request of Committee members. Nevertheless, the media focused overwhelmingly on the sins of omission and commission by UN Secretariat members, including Annan and Fréchette, mostly providing the Security Council with a "free pass."

The Report, in its preface, did point to a particular challenge faced by the Secretary-General.

The Management of the United Nations Oil-for-Food Programme. Volume I—The Report of the Committee.[12]

The reality is that the Secretary-General has come to be viewed as chief diplomatic and political agent of the United Nations. The present Secretary-General is widely respected for precisely those qualities. In these turbulent times, those responsibilities tend to be all consuming. The record amply reflects consequent administrative failings.

Although the appointment of a Chief Operating Officer, leaving the Secretary-General free to devote himself full-time to his diplomatic responsibilities, could serve to improve accountability at the top, the Charter and most member states do not appear to regard the Secretary-General's diplomatic and administrative responsibilities as quite so severable.

Subsequently, in national courts of, for example, the United States and France, individuals, including a former French ambassador to the United Nations and a former most senior official of the French Foreign ministry, were convicted of corruption in relation to their relations with the Iraqi government. These cases attracted very little media attention, even in their own countries.

Kofi Annan (and the United Nations in general) came under intense attack in some US media over the Oil-for-Food debacle, threatening his ability to marshal on at the United Nations. However, he persevered, and ended tenure on 31 January 2006 as one of the most admired individuals to have held that office. His stature in retirement has continued to grow, particularly in Africa, and he has several times agreed to take on challenging mediation missions, including for the United Nations, notably in Syria in 2012.

---

[12] Independent Inquiry Committee into the United Nations Oil-for-Food-Programme, Volume I—The Report of the Committee, 2005 available at: http://news.bbc.co.uk/2/shared/bsp/hi/pdfs/08_09_05_volume1.pdf

QUESTIONS

13. The IIC convincingly held Secretary-General Annan, his deputy, and several other officials to account for their failures of oversight of the Iraq OFFP. How might member states, particularly those in the Security Council, also be held accountable for their parallel failures of oversight or in some cases for their active collusion with sanctions-busting?

14. Might you speculate why the media was not as alert to the responsibility of UN member states in various UN bodies overseeing activity on Iraq as they were to the accusations against UN staff members?

HYPOTHETICAL

You are the head of the UN Staff Association, and believe you need to articulate a position for your membership with respect to the Secretary-General's "Rights up Front" report of 17 December 2013. Can you do so in no more than 1,000 words?

Further Reading

Annan, Kofi with Nader Mousavizadeh, *Interventions: A Life in War and Peace*, New York: Penguin, 2013, pp. 81–134 and 315–372.

Byers, Michael, and Simon Chesterman, "Changing the Rules about Rules? Unilateral Humanitarian Intervention and the Future of International Law." In J.L. Holzgrefe and Robert O. Keohane (eds), *Humanitarian Intervention: Ethical, Legal and Political Dilemmas*. Cambridge: Cambridge University Press, 2003, pp. 177–203.

Chesterman, Simon. *You, the People: The United Nations, Transitional Administration, and State-Building*. Oxford: Oxford University Press, 2004, pp. 126–153.

Franck, Thomas M. *Recourse to Force: State Action against Threats and Armed Attacks*. Cambridge: Cambridge University Press, 2002, pp. 1–19.

Kapila, Mukesh, *Against a Tide of Evil: How One Man Became the Whistleblower to the First Mass Murder Of the Twenty-First Century;* New York: Pegasus Books, 2013.

Malone, David M. *The International Struggle for Iraq: Politics in the UN Security Council, 1980–2005*. Oxford: Oxford University Press, 2006, pp. 114–151.

Meyer, Jeffrey A. and Mark G. Califano. *Good Intentions Corrupted: The Oil-for-Food Scandal and the Threat to the UN*. New York: Public Affairs, 2006.

Power, Samantha. *A Problem from Hell: America and the Age of Genocide*. New York: Basic Books, 2002, pp. 247–327.

Roberts, Adam and Richard Guelff. *Documents on the Laws of War*. 3rd edn. Oxford: Oxford University Press, 2000, pp. 1–46.

Subramanian, Samanth, *This Divided Island: Stories from the Sri Lankan War*. New York: Atlantic Books, 2015.

Wheeler, Nicholas J. *Saving Strangers: Humanitarian Intervention in International Society*. Oxford: Oxford University Press, 2000, pp. 208–241.

Zwanenburg, Marten. *Accountability of Peace Support Operations: International Humanitarian Law*. Heidelberg: Springer Books, 2005.

chapter seventeen
....

Reform

Many organizations tend to resist change. Those that operate in a competitive environment, with economic imperatives and the threat of failure, are often forced to change, and may have oversight structures designed to encourage change. Others, such as the United Nations, are set up in a manner that reinforces the resistance to change.

This is not merely institutional. Nearly every part of the United Nations Organization has one or more member states that care deeply about that part—or claim to do so. These vested interests make change difficult, even in efforts to retire agenda items that have long lost their relevance. The path of least resistance is to allow established structures, methods of work, and patterns of staffing to carry on, with new priorities grafted on to old ones. "Creative destruction" has never been the United Nations' mantra.

The result has been the accumulation of structures and overlap of mandates, leading to duplication and unproductive competition. Against this, there have been growing calls for reform—or at least a halt to expansion. Member states have insisted that core budgets cannot be further increased, or in some agencies must be cut back significantly (notably UNDP and UNESCO).

This is not limited to the United Nations. When Jim Yong Kim took over as President of the World Bank in 2013, he initiated plans to reduce the Bank's operational budget by US$400 million (approximately 8 percent of the Bank's annual expenses),[1] inaugurating an era of unprecedented staff protest that, unsurprisingly, did not elicit much sympathy elsewhere.

At the United Nations, budget rigor has generated considerable ill humor among the member states and, if anything, even greater resistance to meaningful reform than was the case earlier. Virtually all of Secretary-General Ban Ki-moon's ambitious reform agenda that envisaged, for example, a degree of consolidation of the UN system, greater mobility of staff, and an enhanced role for partnerships between the United Nations and others, was eviscerated by the UN General Assembly. The mood has remained sour among member states deeply suspicious of whose interests are served by reform initiatives.

---

[1] Anna Yukhananov, "Exclusive: World Bank to Cut $400 Million from Budget Reorganization," *Reuters*, 7 October 2013, available at: http://www.reuters.com/article/2013/10/08/us-worldbank-cuts-idUSBRE99700320131008.

Budgetary pressures are only one reason for reform, of course. And even they can produce perverse results. The budget of the World Health Organization (WHO) was reduced by approximately 20 percent between 2009–2010 and 2014–2015, with funding for its outbreak and emergency response team reduced by 35 percent over the same period.[2] The emergence of new global funding arrangements over the last decade has shifted money away from WHO into separately governed, so-called "vertical" funds,[3] leaving a major gap in the organization's capacity to respond to emergencies, as evidenced by its inadequate response to the Ebola crisis of 2014.

This chapter considers efforts to reform different aspects of the United Nations, ranging from the way member states conceive of its role in the international order to efforts to reform the Security Council and the right to veto. First, it examines efforts to articulate new visions of international order by UN officials and representatives of member states, dating back over a decade. It then considers efforts to give equality of the rights of UN staff members, followed by an examination of proposed reforms of the United Nations' approach to conflict.

17.1 Visions of Order

The United States is still the most powerful of the member states of the United Nations. In September 2002 US president George W. Bush used his address to the General Assembly to call on the United Nations to help confront what he described as the threat then posed by Iraq.

US PRESIDENT GEORGE W. BUSH'S ADDRESS TO THE UNITED NATIONS GENERAL ASSEMBLY, 12 SEPTEMBER 2002

Mr. Secretary-General, Mr. President, distinguished delegates, and ladies and gentlemen: We meet one year and one day after a terrorist attack brought grief to my country, and brought grief to many citizens of our world.

---

[2] For 2009–2010 the total WHO budget was almost US$5 billion, down to US$3.98 billion for the 2014–2015 budget: CFR Backgrounders, Council of Foreign Relations, available at: http://www.cfr.org/public-health-threats-and-pandemics/world-health-organization-/p20003.

[3] *Ibid.* Global health funding has grown from US$5.6 billion in the 1990s to more than US$31 billion in funding in 2013. See also CFR Global Governance Monitor, Issue Brief, available at: http://www.cfr.org/global-governance/global-governance-monitor/p18985.

Yesterday, we remembered the innocent lives taken that terrible morning. Today, we turn to the urgent duty of protecting other lives, without illusion and without fear.

The United Nations was born in the hope that survived a world war—the hope of a world moving toward justice, escaping old patterns of conflict and fear. The founding members resolved that the peace of the world must never again be destroyed by the will and wickedness of any man. We created the United Nations Security Council, so that, unlike the League of Nations, our deliberations would be more than talk, our resolutions would be more than wishes. After generations of deceitful dictators and broken treaties and squandered lives, we dedicated ourselves to standards of human dignity shared by all, and to a system of security defended by all.

Today, these standards, and this security, are challenged. Our commitment to human dignity is challenged by persistent poverty and raging disease. The suffering is great, and our responsibilities are clear. The United States is joining with the world to supply aid where it reaches people and lifts up lives, to extend trade and the prosperity it brings, and to bring medical care where it is desperately needed. . . .

Above all, our principles and our security are challenged today by outlaw groups and regimes that accept no law of morality and have no limit to their violent ambitions. In the attacks on America a year ago, we saw the destructive intentions of our enemies. This threat hides within many nations, including my own. In cells and camps, terrorists are plotting further destruction, and building new bases for their war against civilization. And our greatest fear is that terrorists will find a shortcut to their mad ambitions when an outlaw regime supplies them with the technologies to kill on a massive scale.

In one place—in one regime—we find all these dangers, in their most lethal and aggressive forms, exactly the kind of aggressive threat the United Nations was born to confront.

Twelve years ago, Iraq invaded Kuwait without provocation. And the regime's forces were poised to continue their march to seize other countries and their resources. Had Saddam Hussein been appeased instead of stopped, he would have endangered the peace and stability of the world. Yet this aggression was stopped—by the might of coalition forces and the will of the United Nations.

To suspend hostilities, to spare himself, Iraq's dictator accepted a series of commitments. The terms were clear, to him and to all. And he agreed to prove he is complying with every one of those obligations. . . .

Delegates to the General Assembly, we have been more than patient. We've tried sanctions. We've tried the carrot of oil for food, and the stick of coalition military strikes. But Saddam Hussein has defied all these efforts and continues to develop weapons of mass destruction. The first time we may be completely certain he has nuclear weapons is when, God forbid, he uses one. We owe it to all our citizens to do everything in our power to prevent that day from coming.

The conduct of the Iraqi regime is a threat to the authority of the United Nations, and a threat to peace. Iraq has answered a decade of UN demands with a decade of defiance. All the world now faces a test, and the United Nations a difficult and defining moment. Are Security Council resolutions to be honored and enforced, or cast aside without consequence? Will the United Nations serve the purpose of its founding, or will it be irrelevant?

The United States helped found the United Nations. We want the United Nations to be effective, and respectful, and successful. We want the resolutions of the world's most important multilateral body to be enforced. And right now those resolutions are being unilaterally subverted by the Iraqi regime. Our partnership of nations can meet the test before us, by making clear what we now expect of the Iraqi regime. . . .

My nation will work with the UN Security Council to meet our common challenge. If Iraq's regime defies us again, the world must move deliberately, decisively to hold Iraq to account. We will work with the UN Security Council for the necessary resolutions. But the purposes of the United States should not be doubted. The Security Council resolutions will be enforced—the just demands of peace and security will be met—or action will be unavoidable. And a regime that has lost its legitimacy will also lose its power.

The failure to agree on a strategy with respect to Iraq has been discussed in Chapter 2. The High-Level Panel on Threats, Challenges, and Change was set up in response to the political crisis that followed the March 2003 invasion of Iraq. Speaking to the General Assembly a year after President Bush's address quoted above, Secretary-General Annan was blunt about the challenges confronting the United Nations.

SECRETARY-GENERAL'S ADDRESS TO THE UNITED NATIONS GENERAL ASSEMBLY, 23 SEPTEMBER 2003[4]

Excellencies, we have come to a fork in the road. This may be a moment no less decisive than 1945 itself, when the United Nations was founded. At that time, a group of far-sighted leaders, led and inspired by President Franklin

---

[4] Reprinted with permission of the United Nations.

D. Roosevelt, were determined to make the second half of the 20th century different from the first half. They saw that the human race had only one world to live in, and that unless it managed its affairs prudently, all human beings may perish. So they drew up rules to govern international behaviour, and founded a network of institutions, with the United Nations at its centre, in which the peoples of the world could work together for the common good.

Now we must decide whether it is possible to continue on the basis agreed then, or whether radical changes are needed. And we must not shy away from questions about the adequacy, and effectiveness, of the rules and instruments at our disposal.

In 2006, Mark Malloch Brown, following a crisis of confidence in the United Nations in the wake of the "oil for food" scandal which had been given great play in Washington, gave a speech that he later said had been intended to encourage greater involvement by the United States in the United Nations.

SPEECH BY DEPUTY SECRETARY-GENERAL MARK MALLOCH BROWN AT THE CENTURY FOUNDATION, 6 JUNE 2006

My underlying message, which is a warning about the serious consequences of a decades-long tendency by US Administrations of both parties to engage only fitfully with the UN, is not one a sitting United Nations official would normally make to an audience like this.

But I feel it is a message that urgently needs to be aired. And as someone who has spent most of his adult life in this country, only a part of it at the UN, I hope you will take it in the spirit in which it is meant: as a sincere and constructive critique of US policy towards the UN by a friend and admirer. Because the fact is that the prevailing practice of seeking to use the UN almost by stealth as a diplomatic tool while failing to stand up for it against its domestic critics is simply not sustainable. You will lose the UN one way or another. . . .

Americans complain about the UN's bureaucracy, weak decision-making, the lack of accountable modern management structures and the political divisions of the General Assembly here in New York. And my response is, "guilty on all counts."

But why?

In significant part because the US has not stuck with its project—its professed wish to have a strong, effective United Nations—in a systematic way.

Secretary Albright and others here today have played extraordinary leadership roles in US-UN relations, for which I salute them. But in the eyes of the rest of the world, US commitment tends to ebb much more than it flows. And in recent years, the enormously divisive issue of Iraq and the big stick of financial withholding have come to define an unhappy marriage. . . .

Exacerbating matters is the widely held perception, even among many US allies, that the US tends to hold on to maximalist positions when it could be finding middle ground.

We can see this even on apparently non-controversial issues such as renovating the dilapidated UN Headquarters in New York. While an architectural landmark, the building falls dangerously short of city codes, lacks sprinklers, is filled with asbestos and is in most respects the most hazardous workplace in town. But the only Government not fully supporting the project is the US. Too much unchecked UN-bashing and stereotyping over too many years—manifest in a fear by politicians to be seen to be supporting better premises for overpaid, corrupt UN bureaucrats—makes even refurbishing a building a political hot potato.

Making Reform Work

One consequence is that, like the building itself, the vital renewal of the Organization, the updating of its mission, its governance and its management tools, is addressed only intermittently. And when the US does champion the right issues like management reform, as it is currently doing, it provokes more suspicion than support. . . .

One day soon we must address the massive gap between the scale of world issues and the limits of the institutions we have built to address them. However, today even relatively modest proposals that in any other organization would be seen as uncontroversial, such as providing more authority and flexibility for the Secretary-General to shift posts and resources to organizational priorities without having to get direct approval from Member States, have been fiercely resisted by the G-77, the main group of developing countries, on the grounds that this weakens accountability. Hence the current deadlock.

What lies behind this?

It is not because most developing countries don't want reform. To be sure, a few spoilers do seem to be opposed to reform for its own sake, and there is no question that some countries are seeking to manipulate the process for their own ends with very damaging consequences. But in practice, the vast majority is fully supportive of the principle of a better run, more effective UN; indeed they know they would be the primary beneficiaries, through more peace, and more development.

So why has it not so far been possible to isolate the radicals and build a strong alliance of reform-minded nations to push through this agenda?

I would argue that the answer lies in questions about motives and power.

Motives, in that, very unfortunately, there is currently a perception among many otherwise quite moderate countries that anything the US supports must have a secret agenda aimed at either subordinating multilateral processes to Washington's ends or weakening the institutions, and therefore, put crudely, should be opposed without any real discussion of whether they make sense or not.

And power, that in two different ways revolves around perceptions of the role and representativeness of the Security Council.

First, in that there has been a real, understandable hostility by the wider membership to the perception that the Security Council, in particular the five permanent members, is seeking a role in areas not formally within its remit, such as management issues or human rights.

Second, an equally understandable conviction that those five, veto-wielding permanent members who happen to be the victors in a war fought 60 years ago, cannot be seen as representative of today's world—even when looking through the lens of financial contributions. Indeed, the so-called G-4 of Security Council aspirants—Japan, India, Brazil and Germany—contribute twice as much as the P-4, the four permanent members excluding the US. . . .

The very reasonable concerns of the full UN membership that the fundamental multilateral principle that each Member State's vote count equally in the wider work of the UN needs to be acknowledged and accommodated within a broader framework of reform. If the multilateral system is to work effectively, all States need to feel they have a real stake.

New Global Challenges

But a stake in what system?

The US—like every nation, strong and weak alike—is today beset by problems that defy national, inside-the-border solutions: climate change, terrorism, nuclear proliferation, migration, the management of the global economy , the internationalization of drugs and crime, the spread of diseases such as HIV and avian flu. Today's new national security challenges basically thumb their noses at old notions of national sovereignty. Security has gone global, and no country can afford to neglect the global institutions needed to manage it.

For many developing countries, however, reform of the United Nations is less about whether the United States participates or not, than it is about how decisions are made and resources allocated.

STATEMENT BY DUMISANI KUMALO, PERMANENT REPRESENTATIVE OF SOUTH AFRICA TO THE UNITED NATIONS, ON BEHALF OF THE GROUP OF 77 AND CHINA, TO GENERAL ASSEMBLY, 8 MAY 2006

The Group of 77 and China has been supportive of a number of major reforms. We supported the approval of the resources needed for the Human Rights Council. It was the Group of 77 and China that fought to have a peace-building support office be funded from predictable new resources and not from within existing budget levels or through establishing temporary posts. It is the Group of 77 and China that wants to ensure that we deal with development challenges in more concrete and tangible ways. As it is, we are still awaiting our negotiating partners to join in a consensus that will build on the global partnership that was confirmed by the September Summit.

We were instrumental in the approval of an amount of $100 million that the Secretary-General urgently needed to proceed with the Capital Master Plan. It was the developing countries that have always insisted that the Secretary-General should receive adequate and predictable resources to undertake effectively the numerous tasks of this Organization. It was also the Group of 77 and China that supported the budget level requested by the Secretary-General in 2005 and opposed the spending cap. . . .

The Group of 77 and China has supported the creation of an ethics office, the finalization of the whistle-blower policy and increasing the investigation and auditing capacity of the Office of Internal Oversight Services.

Clearly, the suggestion that the Group of 77 and China is somehow blocking or delaying reform is at best misleading or at worst absolutely untrue.

We want to reassure all Member States that the resolution we have just adopted does not in any way delay or prevent the reform of the United Nations. In fact, a careful reading of this resolution will show that many of the proposals in it are meant to make this a better Organization. A large part of this resolution captures areas in which there is general agreement among Member States about their importance and necessity. The exceptions are those proposals that would have amended the oversight role of Member States, through the General Assembly.

In addition to the governance issues, the elements in the resolution that we differed on with our negotiating partners were on the enforcement of gender targets in the Secretariat, ensuring equitable geographical representation in the recruitment of the Secretariat, in particular at senior levels, and increasing procurement opportunities for developing countries. These elements are important to developing countries and to suggest that fighting for them would detract from the reform initiatives of the Secretary-General is misleading.

Everyone in this Assembly knows that this Organization does not reflect the international character of its Membership, in particular at senior levels that seem to be monopolized by nationals from a few countries. This is despite repeated calls on this matter by the General Assembly. The suggestion that nationals from developing countries are somehow less qualified and not able to meet the standards that we have set for our international civil servants in the Charter of the United Nations is untrue.

The Secretariat must stop paying more than just lip service to the calls to ensure a greater gender balance and equitable geographical representation in the recruitment and promotion of its staff. Our resolution is merely asking for proposals on gender targets and geographical distribution to be included in the September 2006 report. To suggest that these requests will delay the proposals of the Secretary-General or halt the reform exercise is false. . . .

The Group of 77 and China supports the Secretary-General as chief administrative officer of the United Nations. The Secretary-General is elected by the Member States and therefore we believe that he is accountable to the General Assembly. For this reason, we did not understand, or even accept, that in order for the Secretary-General to carry out his duties, this should be accompanied by denying the majority of Member States the right to pronounce on the administration of the United Nations. The Group of 77 and China has continued to maintain that for a "small but representative group of Members States" to replace the role of all Member States in carrying out the oversight responsibilities of the General Assembly, is an attempt to deny every Member of the United Nations the role due to them.

QUESTIONS

1. US president Bush said the response of the United Nations to Iraq would determine whether the organization would be relevant or not. What might this mean? Did the United Nations pass the test? Did it pass some other form of "test"? And how did US authority internationally emerge from this episode?
2. The June 2006 speech by the Deputy Secretary-General was greeted with apoplexy by various US officials. Was giving such a speech wise? Could it be construed as helpful?
3. How should concerns relating to legitimacy, such as those expressed by the Permanent Representative of South Africa, be balanced against the desire for an effective and efficient United Nations?
4. Although these speeches are a decade or more old, can you think of contemporary examples that illustrate the key points of each? And how have changes in the global balance of power since these speeches reinforced or undermined their power, with respect to law, principle, and leadership in the world today?

5. The powerful will always seek to concentrate privileges among their own hands and to corral weaker actors in international relations in ways that reinforce the already considerable power of those largely controlling the game. Without any reforms to the Security Council, how might nonpermanent members force the permanent ones to pay heed to their views and to acquiesce in reform using their own not inconsiderable powers under the Charter?

17.2 Individual Rights at the United Nations

The Secretary-General has relative freedom with respect to human resources policies governing the personnel. In 2014, for example, Ban Ki-moon responded to the growing support for marriage equality, in particular the need to ensure that same-sex civil partnerships or marriages were recognized by the United Nations. He promulgated, through the Secretary-General's Bulletin, a new approach to allocation of staff benefits:

SECRETARY-GENERAL'S BULLETIN: PERSONAL STATUS FOR PURPOSES OF UNITED NATIONS ENTITLEMENTS (26 JUNE 2014)[5]

The Secretary-General, in consultation with the executive heads of separately administered organs and programmes of the United Nations, hereby promulgates the following:

1. The personal status of staff members for the purpose of entitlements under the Staff Rules and Staff Regulations of the United Nations will be determined by reference to the law of the competent authority under which the personal status has been established.

2. Requests relating to the determination of the personal status of staff members in connection with their entitlements may be submitted by the Secretariat for verification by the Permanent Mission to the United Nations of the country of that competent authority. Once the Permanent Mission has verified that the status in question is legally recognized for the purposes of granting benefits and entitlements, the Secretariat will take action in accordance with that verification.

3. Secretary-General's bulletin ST/SGB/2004/13 is hereby superseded.

4. The present bulletin shall enter into force on the date of its issuance.

---

[5] UN Doc ST/SGB/2004/13/Rev.1.

This approach superseded that which had been adopted by Kofi Annan in 2004 in the following Bulletin entry:

SECRETARY-GENERAL'S BULLETIN: PERSONAL STATUS FOR PURPOSES OF UNITED NATIONS ENTITLEMENTS (24 SEPTEMBER 2004)[6]

1. The practice of the Organization when determining the personal status of staff members for the purpose of entitlements under the Staff Regulations and Rules has been done, and will continue to be done, by reference to the law of nationality of the staff member concerned. When a staff member has more than one nationality, and in accordance with applicable rules, the Organization recognizes the nationality of the State with which the staff member is most closely associated.

2. Requests relating to the determination of the personal status of staff members in connection with their entitlements will be submitted by the Secretariat for verification by the Permanent Mission to the United Nations of the country of nationality of the staff member concerned. Once the Mission has verified that the status in question is legally recognized under the law of that country for the purposes of granting benefits and entitlements, the Secretariat will take action in accordance with that verification.

3. Secretary-General's bulletin ST/SGB/2004/4 is hereby abolished.

4. The present bulletin shall enter into force on 1 October 2004.

Can you spot the vital difference?

The Secretariat had faced difficulties in seeking to implement the provisions of document ST/SGB/2004/13 particularly as, by nature of its international character, it employed many international staff members who married at their duty station or in a country other than their country of nationality, and often to spouses of different nationalities. Under the former policy, determination of personal status for entitlements purposes required the Secretariat to request the employee's country of nationality to determine this status under its legal system, whether or not such determination was based on documentation supplied by the authorities of another country. Because some member states were unfamiliar with the legal systems of other countries, this approach often led to delays and incomplete responses. As a result, employees with identical documentation of one member state had

---

[6] UN Doc ST/SGB/2004/13.

their personal status determined differently by the Secretariat. By practicing this differential treatment, the United Nations was treating some of its employees in a discriminatory manner. Other inequities related to international organizations (some within the UN system) that had amended their procedures by conferring personal status recognition on the basis of the law of the competent authority rather than of the employee's country of nationality thus causing problems with inter-organizational transfers for some.

The Secretary-General's decision followed, by four years, a judgment of the UN Appeals Tribunal (an administrative tribunal of the organization, discussed in Chapter 5) on the El-Zaim case relating to a divorce, in which the Tribunal moved in the direction of recognizing the law of the country in which family status had originally been established, rather than that of the employee's nationality.[7]

Soon after the Secretary-General promulgated the new approach to family status for the purposes of the calculation and allocation of UN benefits, the Permanent Mission of the Russian Federation sought through a resolution of the UN General Assembly to countermand the Secretary-General's approach. This was met by a determined campaign (led by the US delegation), and Russia was not able to bring its proposal to a vote during the fall session of the UN General Assembly in 2014. It did manage to force a vote on a draft resolution expressing its position in March 2015. The following document describes the resolution, the vote, and some of the debate among member states surrounding it.

BUDGET COMMITTEE REJECTS DRAFT DECISION TO WITHDRAW CURRENT PERSONAL STATUS RULES FOR DETERMINING STAFF BENEFITS AND ENTITLEMENTS (24 MARCH 2015)[8]

The Fifth Committee (Administrative and Budgetary) today rejected a draft decision that would have had the Secretary-General withdraw his bulletin laying out the United Nations current rules for the personal status of staff members used to determine their benefits and entitlements.

The proposal by the Russian Federation generated discussions that revolved around such principles as the Secretary-General's prerogatives in organizational matters, equality of United Nations employees, national sovereignty, and transparency, culminating in a recorded vote of 43 in favour and 80 against, with 37 abstentions.

---

[7] See UN Appeals Tribunal Judgment 2010-UNAT-007 (*El Zaim v. United Nations Joint Staff Pension Board*).
[8] GA/AB/4150 of 24 March 2015.

Under the current rule in effect since July 2014, set forth in document ST/SGB/2004/13/Rev.1, the personal status of staff members is determined by the laws established by the competent authority where the status was established. Prior to that, the status was determined by the laws of the staff members' country of origin.

Speaking prior to the vote on the draft, titled "Human resources management" (document A/C.5/69/L.9), Yukio Takasu, Under-Secretary-General for Management, said the Secretary-General had the responsibility to see that the Organization's values were maintained at all times through staff regulations promulgated. Tens of thousands of men and women of different backgrounds, ethnicities, sexual orientations and religions worked for the Organization and were entitled to equal treatment. The previous way of determining entitlements, based strictly on nationality, had created some discrepancies and had led to lawsuits at cost to the United Nations.

The representative of Mexico, who voted against the draft decision, said the bulletin did not establish an international standard for marriages, domestic partnerships, or similar types of unions, or the legal arrangements in which people participated in the exercise of their freedom. The Secretary-General's actions did not encroach upon the competencies of national laws regulating those types of acts.

In a similar vein, the representative of the United States said the draft undermined the Secretary-General's authority and would create legal uncertainty about the extent of that authority, as well as uncertainty on future administrative change.

The representative of Australia, also speaking for Canada and New Zealand, said the decision was not just about process or the Secretary-General's authority but was also about the broader issue of discrimination against people because of their sexual orientation.

Countering those views, the Russian Federation's representative said his country was not challenging the Secretary-General's role. However, the changes under consideration must be made in consultation with Member States, and usually had financial implications. A staff member's nationality should be taken into account when determining entitlements. The past arrangement had achieved a delicate balance, in that regard, which the relevant United Nations bodies had found to be non-discriminatory. On the other hand, the new arrangement discriminated against several Member States, as it did not consider their legislative and judicial systems, and denied the General Assembly the opportunity to discuss its substance.

Saudi Arabia's representative said he supported the draft on moral grounds, as the Kingdom held that same-sex marriage was immoral.

Explaining his delegation's abstention, the representative of Indonesia said he supported the Secretary-General's prerogative on administrative matters but felt the need for greater consultations among Member States on matters of such importance.

Defeat in this initiative can hardly have taken the Permanent Mission of the Russian Federation by surprise. The mood favoring equal treatment for those of varying sexual preferences had changed decisively in many countries of the world over the preceding decade. But the fact that the Permanent Mission was so dogged in pressing its text to a vote suggests that Moscow attached importance to the initiative (perhaps at the level of the president himself), possibly ignoring the tactical advice of its team on the ground, as it reportedly did in the case of its disastrous Security Council draft resolution of 26 March 1999 seeking to condemn NATO's military intervention in Kosovo.[9] Nevertheless, the surprisingly lopsided outcome and the number of abstentions (and absent delegations) suggests poor "floor management" by the normally very accomplished Russian delegation. Or perhaps their heart simply was not in the initiative.

QUESTIONS

6. In what ways does the apparently innocuous administrative decision under Secretary-General Kofi Annan provided above differ from that on the same issue taken by Ban Ki-moon in 2014? Might this decision have wider resonance within the organization and beyond?

7. Piecing together this particular saga on employee status for purposes of staff benefits, what is the significance of the UN Appeals Tribunal decision dealing with divorce (rather than civil partnerships and same-sex marriage)?

8. What were the most salient points raised by member states in the debate on the Russian Federation's draft resolution? And did the outcome of the vote reflect them? Might you speculate why?

9. Is it appropriate for the UN Secretary-General to introduce administratively into the UN recognition and acceptance of practices that many member states would regard as abhorrent? Or might it simply be necessary rather than provocative? What do the facts of the case suggest to you?

17.3 How the United Nations Approaches Conflict

In addition to the perennial problems of complex institutions, including often inadequate resources and ephemeral political will, the United Nations has always faced crises of expectations. At the beginning of the 1990s the United States, while proclaiming itself the victor of the Cold War,

---

[9] See Chapter 2, section 2.2.

asserted that this provided an opportunity for the United Nations to fulfill its long-promised role as the guardian of international peace and security. The Security Council saw new possibilities for action without the paralyzing veto, and Secretary-General Boutros Boutros-Ghali laid out grand plans with *An Agenda for Peace*. In the words of US president George H.W. Bush the rule of law would supplant "the rule of the jungle."[10]

The rhetoric was euphoric, utopian, and short-lived. International security issues continued to be resolved by reference to Great Power interests; economic development attracted more speeches than resources. (Indeed, global development assistance levels dropped sharply in the 1990s.) Rhetoric has its own significance, however, and the language of human rights and the rule of law became more accepted through this period, as was the principle of greater international engagement in areas previously considered to lie solely within the domestic jurisdiction of member states. Whether such principles should be supported by action remained a bone of some contention.

In this context, discussion of reform has always begged the question of whether that reform must take place primarily in the structures, procedures, and personnel that make up the United Nations, or in the willingness of member states to use them. Past efforts at creating and reshaping the international institutions to promote peace and security have tended to be driven by political will, which is most plentiful in a time of crisis. The First World War was the backdrop for establishment of the League of Nations; the League's failure to prevent the Second World War led to its replacement by the United Nations. Importantly, US president Franklin Roosevelt pushed for the negotiation of the UN Charter to be held in San Francisco while the bombs of the Second World War were still falling. Unlike the Covenant of the League of Nations, which was negotiated as one agreement among many at Versailles in 1919, debate on and adoption of the UN Charter was the main event in San Francisco, and its references to "the scourge of war" were reinforced by daily reports of final battles in the worldwide conflict.

For some, the US-led invasion of Iraq in March 2003 represented a similar challenge not merely to the institutions but to the very idea of international order. The war split the Security Council, divided NATO and the European Union, and prompted the creation of a high-level panel to rethink the very idea of collective security in a world dominated by US military power.[11] In the wake of the Iraq war, anxiety concerning the role and relevance of the United Nations was widespread. But leadership on the reform agenda came, unusually, from the Secretary-General. It was Kofi Annan who appointed the High-Level Panel on Threats, Challenges, and Change, which attempted to grapple with legitimate US security concerns while broadening discussion

---

[10] George H.W. Bush, "Address Before a Joint Session of the Congress on the Persian Gulf Crisis and the Federal Budget Deficit," 11 September 1990.

[11] The Report of the High-Level Panel is also discussed in Chapters 1, 4, 9, and 13.

of international threats beyond its counterterrorism and nonproliferation agenda. He had already commissioned Jeffrey Sachs's UN Millennium Project to propose strategies for achieving the Millennium Development Goals.[12] And in March 2005 these security and development agendas were joined by a third, human rights, in a Secretary-General's report unusual for its ambition.

That report, *In Larger Freedom*, was intended to set both the tone and the substantive agenda for the sixtieth General Assembly, which included a Summit of Heads of State on 14–16 September 2005. The report was broad in scope, seeking to define a new security consensus based on the interdependence of threats and responses, and narrow in detail, setting specific targets for official development assistance, calling for the creation of a Peacebuilding Commission, and outlining a long-awaited definition of terrorism. However, on the most contested political question, on Security Council expansion, the report endorsed the fence-sitting position of the High-Level Panel, laying out options but not choosing among them, while urging member states to take a decision on Council expansion even if consensus was not possible.[13] Such discretion did not detract from larger anomalies in this approach: that the Secretary-General was trying to use reform to generate political will rather than reflect it, and that he was taking a lead role just when his political and moral credibility was being called into question by allegations of corruption and mismanagement in the Oil-for-Food Programme.

This chapter now moves on to examine the context within which reform of the United Nations takes place, examining first the Charter and two commonly bemoaned constraints: the membership of the Security Council and the veto power of its permanent members. It then turns to the larger question of political will, looking at efforts to articulate new visions of international cooperation.

17.4 The Charter

As suggested in the Introduction, the Charter bears many similarities to a constitution. And, like most constitutions, it is designed to be difficult to amend.[14]

---

[12] Investing in Development: A Practical Plan to Achieve the Millennium Development Goals (Report of the UN Millennium Project to the Secretary-General) (17 January 2005), available at: http://www.unmillenniumproject.org/reports.

[13] In Larger Freedom: Towards Development, Security, and Human Rights for All, UN Doc. A/59/2005 (21 March 2005), available at http://www.un.org/largerfreedom.

[14] See the discussion of whether the Charter might be considered a constitution in the Introduction to this volume.

UN CHARTER (1945 TEXT)

Article 108

Amendments to the present Charter shall come into force for all Members of the United Nations when they have been adopted by a vote of two thirds of the members of the General Assembly and ratified in accordance with their respective constitutional processes by two thirds of the Members of the United Nations, including all the permanent members of the Security Council.

Article 109

1. A General Conference of the Members of the United Nations for the purpose of reviewing the present Charter may be held at a date and place to be fixed by a two-thirds vote of the members of the General Assembly and by a vote of any seven members of the Security Council. Each Member of the United Nations shall have one vote in the conference.

2. Any alteration of the present Charter recommended by a two-thirds vote of the conference shall take effect when ratified in accordance with their respective constitutional processes by two thirds of the Members of the United Nations including all the permanent members of the Security Council.

3. If such a conference has not been held before the tenth annual session of the General Assembly following the coming into force of the present Charter, the proposal to call such a conference shall be placed on the agenda of that session of the General Assembly, and the conference shall be held if so decided by a majority vote of the members of the General Assembly and by a vote of any seven members of the Security Council.

The three Charter amendments to date all took place between 1963 and 1973. The first expanded Security Council membership from eleven to fifteen and increased the number of votes necessary to pass a resolution from seven to nine; it also expanded the membership of the Economic and Social Council (ECOSOC) from eighteen to twenty-seven. The second corrected the amendment procedures themselves, in line with the increased size of the Security Council, requiring that nine (rather than seven) members be required to support a call for a General Conference of member states for the purposes of reviewing the Charter. The third further increased the membership of ECOSOC from twenty-seven to fifty-four.

QUESTIONS

10. Do the permanent members of the Security Council have a veto over amending the Charter?

11. It is sometimes said that debate over UN reform is intractable because, as with academic politics, the stakes are so small. Does UN reform matter?

12. ECOSOC's expansion did not lead to greater effectiveness of the body—quite to the contrary. Might a similar fate attend the Security Council were its membership to be significantly expanded?

17.5 Institutions: The Security Council

As the Security Council is widely seen as the most influential part of the UN system, much discussion of reform focuses on its membership. In 1993, the General Assembly established an open-ended working group (that is, open to all members of the United Nations) to consider, among other things, the question of increasing Council membership.[15] More than two decades into its deliberations there is still no agreement on an appropriate formula for Security Council representation, and the body is jokingly referred to as the "never-ending working group." Issues of general consensus are that the Council should be expanded and probably include new permanent members—but probably without granting newcomers the coveted veto, currently held by only the P-5.

In March 1997, Razali Ismail, chairman of the working group, presented a paper synthesizing the majority view on expansion of the Security Council. Now known as the "Razali Plan," it proposed increasing Council membership from fifteen to twenty-four by adding five permanent members (one each from the developing continents of Africa, Asia, and Latin America and the Caribbean, and two from the industrialized states—generally seen as Germany and Japan) and four nonpermanent members (one each from Africa, Asia, Eastern Europe, and Latin America and the Caribbean). Though unable to generate much enthusiasm, the Razali Plan became the benchmark for other reform proposals.[16]

---

[15] GA Res. 48/26 (1993).

[16] Paper by the Chairman of the Open-ended Working Group on the Question of Equitable Representation on and Increase in the Membership of the Security Council and Other Matters Related to the Security Council, 20 March 1997.

REPORT OF THE HIGH-LEVEL PANEL ON THREATS, CHALLENGES, AND CHANGE: A MORE SECURE WORLD: OUR SHARED RESPONSIBILITY, 1 DECEMBER 2004[17]

244. The founders of the United Nations conferred primary responsibility on the Security Council for the maintenance of international peace and security. The Security Council was designed to enable the world body to act decisively to prevent and remove threats. It was created to be not just a representative but a responsible body, one that had the capacity for decisive action. The five permanent members were given veto rights but were also expected to shoulder an extra burden in promoting global security. Article 23 of the Charter of the United Nations established that membership in the Council as a whole was explicitly linked not just to geographical balance but also to contributions to maintaining peace and security.

245. Since the Council was formed the threats and challenges to international peace and security have changed, as has the distribution of power among members. But the Security Council has been slow to change. Decisions cannot be implemented just by members of the Security Council but require extensive military, financial and political involvement by other States. Decisions taken and mandates given have often lacked the essential components of realism, adequate resources and the political determination to see them through. The Secretary-General is frequently holding out a begging bowl to implement Security Council decisions. Moreover, the paucity of representation from the broad membership diminishes support for Security Council decisions.

246. Since the end of the Cold War, the effectiveness of the Council has improved, as has its willingness to act; but it has not always been equitable in its actions, nor has it acted consistently or effectively in the face of genocide or other atrocities. This has gravely damaged its credibility. The financial and military contributions to the United Nations of some of the five permanent members are modest compared to their special status, and often the Council's non-permanent members have been unable to make the necessary contribution to the work of the Organization envisaged by the Charter. Even outside the use of a formal veto, the ability of the five permanent members to keep critical issues of peace and security off the Security Council's agenda has further undermined confidence in the body's work.

247. Yet recent experience has also shown that the Security Council is the body in the United Nations most capable of organizing action and responding rapidly to new threats.

248. Thus, the challenge for any reform is to increase both the effectiveness and the credibility of the Security Council and, most importantly,

---

[17] UN Doc. A/59/565 (2004).

to enhance its capacity and willingness to act in the face of threats. This requires greater involvement in Security Council decision-making by those who contribute most; greater contributions from those with special decision-making authority; and greater consultation with those who must implement its decisions. It also requires a firm consensus on the nature of today's threats, on the obligations of broadened collective security, on the necessity of prevention, and on when and why the Council should authorize the use of force.

249. We believe that reforms of the Security Council should meet the following principles:

(a) They should, in honouring Article 23 of the Charter of the United Nations, increase the involvement in decision-making of those who contribute most to the United Nations financially, militarily and diplomatically—specifically in terms of contributions to United Nations assessed budgets, participation in mandated peace operations, contributions to voluntary activities of the United Nations in the areas of security and development, and diplomatic activities in support of United Nations objectives and mandates. Among developed countries, achieving or making substantial progress towards the internationally agreed level of 0.7 per cent of GNP for ODA should be considered an important criterion of contribution;

(b) They should bring into the decision-making process countries more representative of the broader membership, especially of the developing world;

(c) They should not impair the effectiveness of the Security Council;

(d) They should increase the democratic and accountable nature of the body.

250. The Panel believes that a decision on the enlargement of the Council, satisfying these criteria, is now a necessity. The presentation of two clearly defined alternatives, of the kind described below as models A and B, should help to clarify—and perhaps bring to resolution—a debate which has made little progress in the last 12 years.

251. Models A and B both involve a distribution of seats as between four major regional areas, which we identify respectively as "Africa," "Asia and Pacific," "Europe" and "Americas." We see these descriptions as helpful in making and implementing judgements about the composition of the Security Council, but make no recommendation about changing the composition of the current regional groups for general electoral and other United Nations purposes. Some members of the Panel, in particular our Latin American colleagues, expressed a preference for basing any distribution of seats on the current regional groups.

252. Model A provides for six new permanent seats, with no veto being created, and three new two-year term non-permanent seats, divided among the major regional areas as follows:

Model A

Regional area	No. of States	Permanent seats (continuing)	Proposed new permanent seats	Proposed two-year seats (non-renewable)	Total
Africa	53	0	2	4	6
Asia and Pacific	56	1	2	3	6
Europe	47	3	1	2	6
Americas	35	1	1	4	6
Totals model A	**191**	**5**	**6**	**13**	**24**

253. Model B provides for no new permanent seats but creates a new category of eight four-year renewable-term seats and one new two-year non-permanent (and non-renewable) seat, divided among the major regional areas as follows:

Model B

Regional area	No. of States	Permanent seats (continuing)	Proposed four-year renewable seats	Proposed two-year seats (non-renewable)	Total
Africa	53	0	2	4	6
Asia and Pacific	56	1	2	3	6
Europe	47	3	2	1	6
Americas	35	1	2	3	6
Totals model B	**191**	**5**	**8**	**11**	**24**

254. In both models, having regard to Article 23 of the Charter of the United Nations, a method of encouraging Member States to contribute more to international peace and security would be for the General Assembly, taking into account established practices of regional consultation, to elect Security Council members by giving preference for permanent or longer-term seats to those States that are among the top three financial contributors in their relevant regional area to the regular budget, or the top three voluntary contributors from their regional area, or the top three troop contributors from their regional area to United Nations peacekeeping missions.

255. The Panel was strongly of the view that no change to the composition of the Security Council should itself be regarded as permanent or unchallengeable in the future. Therefore, there should be a review of the composition of the Security Council in 2020, including, in this context, a review of the contribution (as defined in para. 249 above) of permanent and non-permanent members from the point of view of the Council's effectiveness in taking collective action to prevent and remove new and old threats to international peace and security.

Germany, Japan, India, and Brazil swiftly constituted themselves as a candidate group (known as the G-4) for permanent seats, initially with South Africa, but Pretoria withdrew when it became clear there was no consensus on its candidacy within the African Union. Indeed, both Nigeria and Egypt are also "aspirants" for permanent seats, with Ethiopia not far behind. Combined with resistance from other members—both permanent members wary of diluting their powers, and other members suspicious of the value to them of neighbors receiving permanent seats—this meant that agreement was impossible and has remained beyond reach.

The case for each of India and Brazil has strengthened in recent years with their status as "emerging" powers widely recognized. Germany, despite being part of the European Union—represented already by Britain and France—has emerged as a key player economically but also politically, including the novel P5+1 formula that included Germany in negotiations with Iran. Japan, although still boasting the world's third largest economy, remains beset by economic difficulties; its candidacy is also complicated by a tense relationship with China.

Kishore Mahbubani, the Singaporean scholar-diplomat and twice former ambassador to the United Nations (representing it during its only term on the Security Council to date in 2001–2002), attempted to cut this Gordian knot in his 2013 book *The Great Convergence.* He proposed a "7-7-7" scheme that would see an increase to seven permanent seats for the United States, the European Union, China, Russia, India, Brazil, and Nigeria. There would also be seven semipermanent seats of eight years in duration for twenty-eight "middle power" countries (such as Japan, Indonesia, Pakistan, South Africa, Egypt, Turkey, Mexico, Argentina, South Africa and Ethiopia). Finally, there would be seven elected seats along the model of the existing ones, for two-year terms, available to the rest of the membership.[18]

As pointed out by India's experienced Chinmaya Gharekhan, the proposal, although creative, would run into stiff headwinds if debated officially at the United Nations.[19] Why would either France or the United Kingdom agree to give up their seat and how credible would a common European seat be at a time of considerable disunity within the European Union, even on foreign policy questions? Why would the majority of member states be prepared to see their theoretical access to the Council reduced from ten to seven regular elected seats (even if these are, in practice, often occupied currently by those countries that Mahbubani sees as the constituency for semipermanent

---

[18] Kishore Mahbubani, *The Great Convergence: Asia, the West, and the Logic of One World* (New York: Public Affairs, 2013), "Keeping the Ship on Course", *The World Today*, December 2012–January 2013, p. 7. See also Kishore Mahbubani, "To the New Order, Strategically", *The Indian Express*, 2 April 2015.

[19] Chinmaya Gharekhan, "Why Security Council Reform Is an Uphill Task", *The Indian Express*, 11 April 2015.

seats). Would Japan, still a major funder of the United Nations, including its agencies, funds, and programs, gracefully accept being relegated to a secondary category, or might it retaliate by cutting back on its funding for the Organization?

Meanwhile, a group of highly regarded small member states—Costa Rica, Jordan, Liechtenstein, Singapore, and Switzerland—in 2011 advanced their own proposals for reform of the Council's working methods. The proposals centered on its relationship with the General Assembly and other principal organs, the effectiveness of its decisions, its subsidiary bodies, operations mandated and missions carried out by the Council, its governance and accountability, the process for appointing the UN Secretary-General, and the use of the veto. Virtually all of their ideas were useful, but would have constrained the power of the Council, and at its heart, the P-5. The proposals had considerable resonance among the United Nations' membership, but the "S5" effort ended in a rout, as a result of P-5 maneuvers among the membership and an opinion from the UN's Legal Counsel, Patricia O'Brien, that the proposals would require a two-thirds majority to pass in a vote in the UN General Assembly—a very high hurdle.[20]

The United Nations therefore faces a quandary. Reform is difficult but vital. Resistance is strong from the P-5, though often not made public. And there is no generally acceptable scheme around which the wider UN membership can currently rally within the General Assembly. The cost of continuing with the current system could be greater marginalization of the body as international security migrates to other institutions or flexible coalitions. The perverse consequence could be that P-5 intransigence will bring about what they fear most: dilution of their own authority. Nevertheless, in the short- to medium-term they have little incentive to compromise.

QUESTIONS

13. Should the Council be more representative of the membership of the United Nations? Why, or why not—and what reform might best achieve this goal?
14. Would making the Council more representative make it more effective? Should a trade-off be considered? Can it be avoided?

---

[20] See an entertaining chapter on the epic defeat of the S5 mainly due to P-5 machinations in 2012 by Liechtenstein's Permanent Representative to the United Nations, Christian Wenaweser, in "Working Methods: The Ugly Duckling of Security Council Reform", in Sebastian von Einsiedel, David M. Malone and Bruno Stagno Ugarte (eds), *The UN Security Council in the Twenty First Century* (Boulder, CO and London: Lynne Rienner 2015).

17.6 Procedures: The Veto

The veto power of the five permanent members of the Security Council is sometimes cited as a barrier to the effectiveness of the United Nations. As Article 108 makes clear, however, any proposal to abolish or modify it would require endorsement by those five permanent members. Various efforts have been made to circumvent this requirement—or at least limit its impact.

One noteworthy example was the report that coined the term "responsibility to protect." Less noticed was an effort to reduce the impact of the veto on humanitarian crises.

INTERNATIONAL COMMISSION ON INTERVENTION AND STATE SOVEREIGNTY, THE RESPONSIBILITY TO PROTECT, DECEMBER 2001

6.20 An issue which we cannot avoid addressing, . . ., is that of the veto power enjoyed by the present Permanent Five. Many of our interlocutors regarded capricious use of the veto, or threat of its use, as likely to be the principal obstacle to effective international action in cases where quick and decisive action is needed to stop or avert a significant humanitarian crisis. As has been said, it is unconscionable that one veto can override the rest of humanity on matters of grave humanitarian concern. Of particular concern is the possibility that needed action will be held hostage to unrelated concerns of one or more of the permanent members—a situation that has too frequently occurred in the past. There is another political problem. Those states who insist on the right to retaining permanent membership of the UN Security Council and the resulting veto power, are in a difficult position when they claim to be entitled to act outside the UN framework as a result of the Council being paralyzed by a veto cast by another permanent member. That is, those who insist on keeping the existing rules of the game unchanged have a correspondingly less compelling claim to rejecting any specific outcome when the game is played by those very rules.

6.21 For all these reasons, the Commission supports the proposal put to us in an exploratory way by a senior representative of one of the Permanent Five countries, that there be agreed by the Permanent Five a "code of conduct" for the use of the veto with respect to actions that are needed to stop or avert a significant humanitarian crisis. The idea essentially is that a permanent member, in matters where its vital national interests were not claimed to be involved, would not use its veto to obstruct the passage of what would otherwise be a majority resolution. The expression "constructive abstention" has been used in this context in the past. It is unrealistic to imagine any amendment of the Charter happening any time soon so far as the veto power and its distribution are concerned. But the adoption by the permanent members of a more formal, mutually agreed practice to govern these situations in the future would be a very healthy development.

In addition to voluntarily restraining the use of the veto, a second possible check would be to raise the costs of exercising it. For in reality, these days the threat of the veto has far more impact than actual vetoes—and routinely the threat can be exercised behind closed doors.

REPORT OF THE HIGH-LEVEL PANEL ON THREATS, CHALLENGES, AND CHANGE: A MORE SECURE WORLD: OUR SHARED RESPONSIBILITY, 1 DECEMBER 2004[21]

256. ... We recognize that the veto had an important function in reassuring the United Nations most powerful members that their interests would be safeguarded. We see no practical way of changing the existing members' veto powers. Yet, as a whole the institution of the veto has an anachronistic character that is unsuitable for the institution in an increasingly democratic age and we would urge that its use be limited to matters where vital interests are genuinely at stake. We also ask the permanent members, in their individual capacities, to pledge themselves to refrain from the use of the veto in cases of genocide and large-scale human rights abuses. We recommend that under any reform proposal, there should be no expansion of the veto.

257. We propose the introduction of a system of "indicative voting," whereby members of the Security Council could call for a public indication of positions on a proposed action. Under this indicative vote, "no" votes would not have a veto effect, nor would the final tally of the vote have any legal force. The second formal vote on any resolution would take place under the current procedures of the Council. This would, we believe, increase the accountability of the veto function.

258. In recent years, many informal improvements have been made to the transparency and accountability of the Security Council's deliberative and decision-making procedures. We also remind the Security Council that troop contributors have rights under Article 44 of the Charter to be fully consulted concerning the deployment of troops to Council-mandated operations. We recommend that processes to improve transparency and accountability be incorporated and formalized in the Council's rules of procedure.

259. Many delegations on the Security Council lack access to professional military advice. Yet they are frequently called upon to take decisions with far-ranging military implications. We recommend therefore that the

---

[21] UN Doc. A/59/565 (2004).

Secretary-General's Military Adviser and the members of his staff be available on demand by the Security Council to offer technical and professional advice on military options.

260. We welcome greater civil society engagement in the work of the Security Council.

None of these reforms was adopted, and the Council continues to operate under "provisional" rules of procedure.

QUESTIONS

15. Is it possible to abolish the veto? What other mechanisms might limit its impact on Council decision-making? What lessons, if any, may be drawn from the acceptance that abstention by a permanent member is not regarded as a failure to "concur" within the meaning of Article 27(3) of the UN Charter?

16. Is reform most needed in the institutions and procedures of the United Nations, or in the willingness of states to use them? Which type of change is more difficult?

HYPOTHETICAL A

You work for the newly appointed Chairman of the Open-ended Working Group,[22] who wants to reinvigorate the stalled process of Security Council Reform. You are asked to prepare a concise overview of current ideas (and roadblocks) on the topic, highlighting any realistic opportunities for progress, in a paper not exceeding three pages.

17.7 Political Will: Interdependence of Threats

Underlying questions of reform of the United Nations are different visions of its role in addressing distinct species of threat. In 2004 the High-Level Panel explored the possibility that the United Nations could bridge these distinct threats.

---

[22] The Open-ended Working Group on the Question of Equitable Representation on and Increase in the Membership of the Security Council and Other Matters related to the Security Council.

REPORT OF THE HIGH-LEVEL PANEL ON THREATS, CHALLENGES, AND CHANGE: A MORE SECURE WORLD: OUR SHARED RESPONSIBILITY, 1 DECEMBER 2004[23]

II. The Case for Comprehensive Collective Security

A. Threats Without Boundaries

17. Today, more than ever before, threats are interrelated and a threat to one is a threat to all. The mutual vulnerability of weak and strong has never been clearer.

18. Global economic integration means that a major terrorist attack any-where in the developed world would have devastating consequences for the well-being of millions of people in the developing world. The World Bank estimates that the attacks of 11 September 2001 alone increased the number of people living in poverty by 10 million; the total cost to the world economy probably exceeded 80 billion dollars. These numbers would be far surpassed by an incident involving nuclear terrorism.

19. Similarly, the security of the most affluent State can be held hostage to the ability of the poorest State to contain an emerging disease. Because international flight times are shorter than the incubation periods for many infectious diseases, any one of 700 million international airline passengers every year can be an unwitting global disease-carrier. Severe acute respiratory syndrome (SARS) spread to more than 8,000 people in 30 countries in three months, killing almost 700. The influenza pandemic of 1919 killed as many as 100 million people, far more than the First World War, over a period of a little more than a year. Today, a similar virus could kill tens of millions in a fraction of the time.

20. Every threat to international security today enlarges the risk of other threats. Nuclear proliferation by States increases the availability of the mate-riel and technology necessary for a terrorist to acquire a nuclear weapon. The ability of non-State actors to traffic in nuclear material and technology is aided by ineffective State control of borders and transit through weak States.

21. International terrorist groups prey on weak States for sanctuary. Their recruitment is aided by grievances nurtured by poverty, foreign occupation and the absence of human rights and democracy; by religious and other intol-erance; and by civil violence—a witch's brew common to those areas where civil war and regional conflict intersect. In recent years, terrorists have helped to finance their activities and moved large sums of money by gaining access to such valuable commodities as drugs in countries beset by civil war.

22. Poverty, infectious disease, environmental degradation and war feed one another in a deadly cycle. Poverty (as measured by per capita gross

---

[23] UN Doc. A/59/565 (2004).

domestic product (GDP)) is strongly associated with the outbreak of civil war. Such diseases as malaria and HIV/AIDS continue to cause large numbers of deaths and reinforce poverty. Disease and poverty, in turn, are connected to environmental degradation; climate change exacerbates the occurrence of such infectious disease as malaria and dengue fever. Environmental stress, caused by large populations and shortages of land and other natural resources, can contribute to civil violence.

23. Transnational organized crime facilitates many of the most serious threats to international peace and security. Corruption, illicit trade and money-laundering contribute to State weakness, impede economic growth and undermine democracy. These activities thus create a permissive environment for civil conflict. The prospect of organized criminal groups providing nuclear, radiological, chemical or biological weapons to terrorists is particularly worrying. Increasing drug trade partly accounts for rapidly increasing levels of HIV/AIDS infections, especially in Eastern Europe and parts of Asia. And organized criminal activities undermine peacebuilding efforts and fuel many civil wars through illicit trade in conflict commodities and small arms.

B. The Limits of Self-Protection

24. No State, no matter how powerful, can by its own efforts alone make itself invulnerable to today's threats. Every State requires the cooperation of other States to make itself secure. It is in every State's interest, accordingly, to cooperate with other States to address their most pressing threats, because doing so will maximize the chances of reciprocal cooperation to address its own threat priorities.

25. Take, as one example, the threat of nuclear terrorism. Experts estimate that terrorists with 50 kilograms of highly enriched uranium (HEU), an amount that would fit into six one-litre milk cartons, need only smuggle it across borders in order to create an improvised nuclear device that could level a medium-sized city. Border controls will not provide adequate defence against this threat. To overcome the threat of nuclear terrorism requires the cooperation of States, strong and weak, to clean up stockpiles of HEU, better protect shipping containers at ports and agree on new rules regulating the enrichment of uranium. Cooperation in the sharing of intelligence by States is essential for stopping terrorism.

26. Similarly, in order to stop organized crime States must cooperate to fight money-laundering, trafficking in drugs and persons, and corruption. International efforts to stem the problem are only as strong as the weakest link. Ineffective collective security institutions diminish the security of every region and State.

27. The most robust defence against the possible terrorist use of nuclear, chemical or biological weapons would seek to control dangerous materials, deter and capture terrorists, and address the broader threats that increase

the risk of terrorist action. Civil war, disease and poverty increase the likelihood of State collapse and facilitate the spread of organized crime, thus
also increasing the risk of terrorism and proliferation due to weak States and
weak collective capacity to exercise the rule of law. Preventing mass-casualty
terrorism requires a deep engagement to strengthen collective security systems, ameliorate poverty, combat extremism, end the grievances that flow
from war, tackle the spread of infectious disease and fight organized crime.

28. Thus all States have an interest in forging a new comprehensive collective security system that will commit all of them to act cooperatively in the
face of a broad array of threats.

C. Sovereignty and Responsibility

29. In signing the Charter of the United Nations, States not only benefit from
the privileges of sovereignty but also accept its responsibilities. Whatever
perceptions may have prevailed when the Westphalian system first gave rise
to the notion of State sovereignty, today it clearly carries with it the obligation of a State to protect the welfare of its own peoples and meet its obligations to the wider international community. But history teaches us all too
clearly that it cannot be assumed that every State will always be able, or
willing, to meet its responsibilities to protect its own people and avoid harming its neighbours. And in those circumstances, the principles of collective
security mean that some portion of those responsibilities should be taken
up by the international community, acting in accordance with the Charter of
the United Nations and the Universal Declaration of Human Rights, to help
build the necessary capacity or supply the necessary protection, as the case
may be.

30. What we seek to protect reflects what we value. The Charter of the
United Nations seeks to protect all States, not because they are intrinsically
good but because they are necessary to achieve the dignity, justice, worth
and safety of their citizens. These are the values that should be at the heart
of any collective security system for the twenty-first century, but too often
States have failed to respect and promote them. The collective security we
seek to build today asserts a shared responsibility on the part of all States
and international institutions, and those who lead them, to do just that.

D. Elements of a Credible Collective Security System

31. To be credible and sustainable a collective security system must be effective, efficient and equitable. In all these respects, the multilateral system as
we now know it, in responding to the major security threats which the world
has confronted in recent decades, has shown that it can perform. But it must
be strengthened to perform better—in all the ways we spell out in the present report.

1. Effectiveness

32. Whether by reducing the demand for nuclear weapons, mediating inter-State conflict or ending civil wars, collective security institutions have made critical contributions to the maintenance of international peace and security, although those contributions are often denigrated, both by those who would have the institutions do more and by those who would have them do less.

33. Collective security institutions are rarely effective in isolation. Multilateral institutions normally operate alongside national, regional and sometimes civil society actors, and are most effective when these efforts are aligned to common goals. This is as true of mediation as it is of post-conflict reconstruction, poverty-reduction strategies and non-proliferation measures.

34. States are still the front-line responders to today's threats. Successful international actions to battle poverty, fight infectious disease, stop transnational crime, rebuild after civil war, reduce terrorism and halt the spread of dangerous materials all require capable, responsible States as partners. It follows that greater effort must be made to enhance the capacity of States to exercise their sovereignty responsibly. For all those in a position to help others build that capacity, it should be part of *their* responsibility to do so.

35. Collective action often fails, sometimes dramatically so. Collective instruments are often hampered by a lack of compliance, erratic monitoring and verification, and weak enforcement. Early warning is only effective when it leads to early action for prevention. Monitoring and verification work best when they are treated as complements to, not substitutes for, enforcement.

36. Collective security institutions have proved particularly poor at meeting the challenge posed by large-scale, gross human rights abuses and genocide. This is a normative challenge to the United Nations: the concept of State and international responsibility to protect civilians from the effects of war and human rights abuses has yet to truly overcome the tension between the competing claims of sovereign inviolability and the right to intervene. It is also an operational challenge: the challenge of stopping a Government from killing its own civilians requires considerable military deployment capacity.

2. Efficiency

37. Some collective security instruments have been efficient. As the institutional embodiment of the Treaty on the Non-Proliferation of Nuclear Weapons and of considerable long-term success in preventing widespread proliferation of nuclear weapons, the International Atomic Energy Agency (IAEA)—with its regular budget of less than $275 million—stands out as an extraordinary bargain. Similarly, the Secretary-General's mediation efforts, though grossly underresourced, have helped reduce international tensions.

38. But more collective security instruments have been inefficient. Post-conflict operations, for example, have too often been characterized by countless ill-coordinated and overlapping bilateral and United Nations programmes, with inter-agency competition preventing the best use of scarce resources.

39. The biggest source of inefficiency in our collective security institutions has simply been an unwillingness to get serious about preventing deadly violence. The failure to invest time and resources early in order to prevent the outbreak and escalation of conflicts leads to much larger and deadlier conflagrations that are much costlier to handle later.

3. Equity

40. The credibility of any system of collective security also depends on how well it promotes security for all its members, without regard to the nature of would-be beneficiaries, their location, resources or relationship to great Powers.

41. Too often, the United Nations and its Member States have discriminated in responding to threats to international security. Contrast the swiftness with which the United Nations responded to the attacks on 11 September 2001 with its actions when confronted with a far more deadly event: from April to mid-July 1994, Rwanda experienced the equivalent of three 11 September 2001 attacks every day for 100 days, all in a country whose population was one thirty-sixth that of the United States. Two weeks into the genocide, the Security Council withdrew most of its peacekeepers from the country. It took almost a month for United Nations officials to call it a genocide and even longer for some Security Council members. When a new mission was finally authorized for Rwanda, six weeks into the genocide, few States offered soldiers. The mission deployed as the genocide ended.

42. Similarly, throughout the deliberation of the High-level Panel on Threats, Challenges and Change, we have been struck once again by the glacial speed at which our institutions have responded to massive human rights violations in Darfur, Sudan.

43. When the institutions of collective security respond in an ineffective and inequitable manner, they reveal a much deeper truth about which threats matter. Our institutions of collective security must not just assert that a threat to one is truly a threat to all, but perform accordingly.

QUESTIONS

17. Member states of the United Nations perceive threats differently. Should a state concerned with, say, terrorism, be prepared to compromise on action in response to threats perceived as more pressing by another state, such as underdevelopment?
18. If a "grand bargain" that recognized and addressed the different threats facing different countries were possible, who would be the most likely broker of such an agreement?

17.8 Security and Justice

In mid-2015, an international Commission on Global Security, Justice and Governance tabled its report, reaffirming a number of recommendations of earlier such panels. Its most appealing innovation relates to its arguments in favor of "just security," at the heart of the report, as quoted below. The cochairs of the commission, former US Secretary of State (and previously US Ambassador to the United Nations) Madeleine Albright and former Nigerian foreign minister (and later ambassador to the United Nations) Ibrahim Gambari, because of their hands-on experience with the United Nations' challenge in wrestling with laws and norms while simultaneously seeking to deliver on security and other outcomes on the ground, may provide this particular concept with added weight in the UN setting.

CONFRONTING THE CRISIS OF GLOBAL GOVERNANCE, REPORT OF THE COMMISSION ON GLOBAL SECURITY, JUSTICE AND GOVERNANCE (2015)[24]

2.5 Toward Just Security

The quest for international security (and the related notion of order) is not new, though its full realization remains aspirational. Before the UN Charter, its pursuit was enshrined in the Covenant of the League of Nations and earlier in the Concert of Europe. The notion of justice emerged more resolutely in deliberations at the global level with the Charter, a result of the insight that to truly "save succeeding generations from the scourge of war," collective or common security alone is not enough, that global justice—as the effective pursuit of "larger freedom" on a global scale—is equally important.

Security is merely the appearance of order in a framework of structural violence unless tempered or leavened by concepts of justice that include human rights, human dignity, legitimate government, and other normative limits on the use of power. Vice versa, the pursuit of justice is crippled if not backed up by the requisite means to sustain security and order.

In a world at peace, which provides all its inhabitants with the chance of a decent and safe life, security and justice are visibly complementary. Concerns for one entail concerns for the other. Indeed, history has shown

---

[24] *Confronting the Crisis of Global Governance*, Report of the Commission on Global Security, Justice and Governance, The Hague and Washington, DC: The Hague Institute for Global Justice and the Stimson Center, 2015, available at: http://www.globalsecurityjusticegovernance.org/publications-resources/report/.

time and again the futility of attempts to instill—worse, impose—security with no consideration for justice. That simply creates the manifestation of order underpinned by the use or threat of violence. At the same time, endeavors to impart justice without security are all too easily undone. Security and justice are both needed if humanity is to not only survive but also thrive with dignity.

For this Report and its reform agenda, we view the joint pursuit of security and justice in global governance as a quest for just security. Just security aims to forge a mutually supportive system of accountable, fair, and effective governance and sustainable peace globally. It further recognizes that both security and justice are indispensable to human development.

For good global governance and a resilient global order that empowers people and nations, security and justice must prevail across governance levels; global actors, including those within civil society and the business community, need to promote these linkages actively. Lack of either security or justice on any level, from local to global, not only contributes to instability, but produces destabilizing spillovers both horizontally (to neighboring regions) and vertically (to higher or lower levels of governance).

Advocating Justice and Security Together (AdJuST), discussed in Part IV of this Report, is critical to implementing the vision of just security and its associated policy goals. The AdJuST initiative encourages the reconciling of views on security and justice among emerging powers, developing and developed states, and increasingly powerful nonstate actors. The twin pursuit of security and justice is an essential element of any new global governance architecture or reform enterprise.

Government, though important, is not the totality of governance, let alone human experience. Governments may provide a considerable amount of security and justice for their citizens. However, in an age of globalization, international organizations as well as nongovernmental actors found within civil society and the business community are significant contributors and, indeed, may be global actors in their own right, with the potential to contribute to security and justice across the globe.

The growing connectivity between security and justice in global affairs exhibits both short term trade-offs and tensions but can also reveal ways in which they are mutually reinforcing (for instance, security can lend urgency and fresh perspectives to long-standing climate justice concerns). Their intersection provides a framework for understanding and responding to today's most pressing global governance challenges in this project's three spaces. It connotes the central importance of institutions and policy innovations—at global, regional, national, and subnational levels—in promoting security and justice effectively, equitably, democratically, and accountably.

Moreover, the notion of just security places justice and legitimate forms of governance at the center of twenty-first century conceptions of security. Applied to challenges facing global governance today, an approach that emphasizes security and justice simultaneously would aim to refashion global institutions and their policy instruments to strike a more effective balance between security and justice that does not privilege one major concept over the other.

In highly unstable environments, short-term trade-offs favoring security may be necessary, but always with the goal of returning to balance, and with justice—as embodied in military law codes, International Humanitarian Law, International Human Rights Law, and mission rules of engagement—as a constant "governor" of security and stabilization actions. Lastly, just security encourages the reconciling of perceptions of security and justice of emerging powers and lesser developed countries of the Global South with actors in the Global North. Both concepts, however, need not be pursued equally at all times and in each conceivable setting.

The interplay of security and justice can strengthen global governance and improve the quality of life for all people. But it can also generate tensions, risks, and pitfalls for global governance. Skillful, cooperative, and innovative leadership among a range of state and nonstate actors sensitive to historical context and current global realities can, by insisting on the pursuit of justice and security simultaneously, help ready global governance for twenty-first-century challenges

QUESTION

19. Does the concept of "just security" represent a potential breakthrough for the United Nations? Or does it advocate more than the United Nations is likely to be able to deliver, setting it up to fail? Why?

Further Reading

www.un.org/en/strengtheningtheun
www.globalpolicy.org/un-reform.
Chhabra Tarun, Sebastian von Einsiedel and Heiko Nitzschke. "Evolution of the United Nations Security Concept: Role of the High-Level Panel on Threats, Challenges, and Change." In H.-G. Brauch et al. (eds), *Globalisation and Environmental Challenges: Reconceptualising Security in the 21st Century* (Berlin: Springer, 2008).
Chesterman, Simon (ed). Secretary or General? *The UN Secretary-General in World Politics.* Cambridge: Cambridge University Press, 2007.
Einsiedel, Sebastian von, David M. Malone and Bruno Stagno Ugarte (eds). *The UN Security Council in the 21st Century.* Boulder, CO and London: Lynne Rienner,

2015, particularly the following chapters: Colin Keating, "Power Dynamics between Permanent and Elected Council Members"; Edward C. Luck, "The Security Council at 70: Ever Changing or Never Changing?".

Gowan, Richard and Nora Gordon. "Pathways to Security Council Reform". New York: Center on International Cooperation, New York University, May 2014.

Johnstone, Ian. "Normative Evolution at the UN: Impact on Operational Activities". In Bruce Jones, Shepard Forman and Richard Gowan (eds), *Cooperating for Peace and Security: Evolving Institutions and Arrangements in a Context of Changing US Security Policy* (Cambridge: Cambridge University Press, 2010).

Luck, Edward C. *UN Security Council: Practice and Promise.* London and New York: Routledge, 2006, pp. 111–126.

Malone, David M. "The High Level Panel and the Security Council". *Security Dialogue,* vol. 36(3) (September 2005), pp. 370–372.

Stedman, Stephen J. "UN Transformation in an Era of Soft Balancing". In Bruce Jones, Shepard Forman and Richard Gowan (eds), *Cooperating for Peace and Security: Evolving Institutions and Arrangements in a Context of Changing US Security Policy.* Cambridge: Cambridge University Press, 2010.

Thant Myint-U and Amy Scott, *The UN Secretariat: A Brief History,* New York: International Peace Institute, 2007.

Thakur, Ramesh. *The United Nations, Peace and Security: From Collective Security to the Responsibility to Protect.* Cambridge: Cambridge University Press, 2006.

Weiss, Thomas G., *What's Wrong with the United Nations and How to Fix It,* Cambridge: Polity Press, 2012.

Weiss, Thomas G. and Sam Daws (eds), *The Oxford Handbook on the United Nations* (Oxford: Oxford University Press, 2007). Specifically please see the chapters by Edward C. Luck ("Principal Organs"), Jeff Laurenti ("Financing"), and Chadwick Alger ("Widening Participation").

Appendices

Appendix A
. . . .

Charter of the United Nations[1]

WE THE PEOPLES OF THE UNITED NATIONS DETERMINED

to save succeeding generations from the scourge of war, which twice in our lifetime has brought untold sorrow to mankind, and

to reaffirm faith in fundamental human rights, in the dignity and worth of the human person, in the equal rights of men and women and of nations large and small, and

to establish conditions under which justice and respect for the obligations arising from treaties and other sources of international law can be maintained, and

to promote social progress and better standards of life in larger freedom,

AND FOR THESE ENDS

to practice tolerance and live together in peace with one another as good neighbours, and

to unite our strength to maintain international peace and security, and

to ensure by the acceptance of principles and the institution of methods, that armed force shall not be used, save in the common interest, and

to employ international machinery for the promotion of the economic and social advancement of all peoples,

HAVE RESOLVED TO COMBINE OUR EFFORTS TO ACCOMPLISH THESE AIMS

Accordingly, our respective Governments, through representatives assembled in the city of San Francisco, who have exhibited their full powers found to be in good and due form, have agreed to the present Charter of the United Nations and do hereby establish an international organization to be known as the United Nations.

CHAPTER I—PURPOSES AND PRINCIPLES

Article 1

The Purposes of the United Nations are:

1. To maintain international peace and security, and to that end: to take effective collective measures for the prevention and removal of threats to the peace, and for the suppression of acts of aggression or other breaches of the peace, and to bring about by peaceful means, and in conformity with the principles of justice and international law, adjustment or settlement of international disputes or situations which might lead to a breach of the peace;

2. To develop friendly relations among nations based on respect for the principle of equal rights and self-determination of peoples, and to take other appropriate measures to strengthen universal peace;

---

[1] Signed at San Francisco on 26 June 1945. Entered into force 24 October 1945.

3. To achieve international cooperation in solving international problems of an economic, social, cultural, or humanitarian character, and in promoting and encouraging respect for human rights and for fundamental freedoms for all without distinction as to race, sex, language, or religion; and

4. To be a centre for harmonizing the actions of nations in the attainment of these common ends.

Article 2

The Organization and its Members, in pursuit of the Purposes stated in Article 1, shall act in accordance with the following Principles.

1. The Organization is based on the principle of the sovereign equality of all its Members.

2. All Members, in order to ensure to all of them the rights and benefits resulting from membership, shall fulfil in good faith the obligations assumed by them in accordance with the present Charter.

3. All Members shall settle their international disputes by peaceful means in such a manner that international peace and security, and justice, are not endangered.

4. All Members shall refrain in their international relations from the threat or use of force against the territorial integrity or political independence of any state, or in any other manner inconsistent with the Purposes of the United Nations.

5. All Members shall give the United Nations every assistance in any action it takes in accordance with the present Charter, and shall refrain from giving assistance to any state against which the United Nations is taking preventive or enforcement action.

6. The Organization shall ensure that states which are not Members of the United Nations act in accordance with these Principles so far as may be necessary for the maintenance of international peace and security.

7. Nothing contained in the present Charter shall authorize the United Nations to intervene in matters which are essentially within the domestic jurisdiction of any state or shall require the Members to submit such matters to settlement under the present Charter; but this principle shall not prejudice the application of enforcement measures under Chapter VII.

CHAPTER II—MEMBERSHIP

Article 3

The original Members of the United Nations shall be the states which, having participated in the United Nations Conference on International Organization at San Francisco, or having previously signed the Declaration by United Nations of January 1, 1942, sign the present Charter and ratify it in accordance with Article 110.

Article 4

1. Membership in the United Nations is open to all other peace-loving states which accept the obligations contained in the present Charter and, in the judgment of the Organization, are able and willing to carry out these obligations.

2. The admission of any such state to membership in the United Nations will be effected by a decision of the General Assembly upon the recommendation of the Security Council.

Article 5

A member of the United Nations against which preventive or enforcement action has been taken by the Security Council may be suspended from the exercise of the rights and privileges of membership by the General Assembly upon the recommendation of the Security Council. The exercise of these rights and privileges may be restored by the Security Council.

Article 6

A Member of the United Nations which has persistently violated the Principles contained in the present Charter may be expelled from the Organization by the General Assembly upon the recommendation of the Security Council.

CHAPTER III—ORGANS

Article 7

1. There are established as the principal organs of the United Nations: a General Assembly, a Security Council, an Economic and Social Council, a Trusteeship Council, an International Court of Justice, and a Secretariat.

2. Such subsidiary organs as may be found necessary may be established in accordance with the present Charter.

Article 8

The United Nations shall place no restrictions on the eligibility of men and women to participate in any capacity and under conditions of equality in its principal and subsidiary organs.

CHAPTER IV—THE GENERAL ASSEMBLY

Composition

Article 9

1. The General Assembly shall consist of all the Members of the United Nations.

2. Each member shall have not more than five representatives in the General Assembly.

Functions and Powers

Article 10

The General Assembly may discuss any questions or any matters within the scope of the present Charter or relating to the powers and functions of any organs provided for in the present Charter, and, except as provided in Article 12, may make recommendations to the Members of the United Nations or to the Security Council or to both on any such questions or matters.

Article 11

1. The General Assembly may consider the general principles of cooperation in the maintenance of international peace and security, including the principles governing disarmament and the regulation of armaments, and may make recommendations with regard to such principles to the Members or to the Security Council or to both.

2. The General Assembly may discuss any questions relating to the maintenance of international peace and security brought before it by any Member of the United Nations, or by the Security Council, or by a state which is not a Member of the United Nations in accordance with Article 35, paragraph 2, and, except as provided in Article 12, may make recommendations with regard to any such questions to the state or states concerned or to the Security Council or to both. Any such question on which action is necessary shall be referred to the Security Council by the General Assembly either before or after discussion.

3. The General Assembly may call the attention of the Security Council to situations which are likely to endanger international peace and security.

4. The powers of the General Assembly set forth in this Article shall not limit the general scope of Article 10.

Article 12

1. While the Security Council is exercising in respect of any dispute or situation the functions assigned to it in the present Charter, the General Assembly shall not make any recommendation with regard to that dispute or situation unless the Security Council so requests.

2. The Secretary-General, with the consent of the Security Council, shall notify the General Assembly at each session of any matters relative to the maintenance of international peace and security which are being dealt with by the Security Council and shall similarly notify the General Assembly, or the Members of the United Nations if the General Assembly is not in session, immediately the Security Council ceases to deal with such matters.

Article 13

1. The General Assembly shall initiate studies and make recommendations for the purpose of:

a. promoting international cooperation in the political field and encouraging the progressive development of international law and its codification;

b. promoting international cooperation in the economic, social, cultural, educational, and health fields, and assisting in the realization of human rights and fundamental freedoms for all without distinction as to race, sex, language, or religion.

2. The further responsibilities, functions and powers of the General Assembly with respect to matters mentioned in paragraph 1(b) above are set forth in Chapters IX and X.

Article 14

Subject to the provisions of Article 12, the General Assembly may recommend measures for the peaceful adjustment of any situation, regardless of origin, which it deems likely to impair the general welfare or friendly relations among nations, including situations resulting from a violation of the provisions of the present Charter setting forth the Purposes and Principles of the United Nations.

Article 15

1. The General Assembly shall receive and consider annual and special reports from the Security Council; these reports shall include an account of the measures that the Security Council has decided upon or taken to maintain international peace and security.

2. The General Assembly shall receive and consider reports from the other organs of the United Nations.

Article 16

The General Assembly shall perform such functions with respect to the international trusteeship system as are assigned to it under Chapters XII and XIII, including the approval of the trusteeship agreements for areas not designated as strategic.

Article 17

1. The General Assembly shall consider and approve the budget of the Organization.

2. The expenses of the Organization shall be borne by the Members as apportioned by the General Assembly.

3. The General Assembly shall consider and approve any financial and budgetary arrangements with specialized agencies referred to in Article 57 and shall examine the administrative budgets of such specialized agencies with a view to making recommendations to the agencies concerned.

Voting

Article 18

1. Each member of the General Assembly shall have one vote.

2. Decisions of the General Assembly on important questions shall be made by a two-thirds majority of the members present and voting. These questions shall include: recommendations with respect to the maintenance of international peace and security, the election of the non-permanent members of the Security Council, the election of the members of the Economic and Social Council, the election of members of the Trusteeship Council in accordance with paragraph 1(c) of Article 86, the admission of new Members to the United Nations, the suspension of the rights and privileges of membership, the expulsion of Members, questions relating to the operation of the trusteeship system, and budgetary questions.

3. Decisions on other questions, including the determination of additional categories of questions to be decided by a two-thirds majority, shall be made by a majority of the members present and voting.

Article 19

A Member of the United Nations which is in arrears in the payment of its financial contributions to the Organization shall have no vote in the General Assembly if the amount of its arrears equals or exceeds the amount of the contributions due from it for the preceding two full years. The General Assembly may, nevertheless, permit such a Member to vote if it is satisfied that the failure to pay is due to conditions beyond the control of the Member.

Procedure

Article 20

The General Assembly shall meet in regular annual sessions and in such special sessions as occasion may require. Special sessions shall be convoked by the Secretary-General at the request of the Security Council or of a majority of the Members of the United Nations.

Article 21

The General Assembly shall adopt its own rules of procedure. It shall elect its President for each session.

Article 22

The General Assembly may establish such subsidiary organs as it deems necessary for the performance of its functions.

CHAPTER V—THE SECURITY COUNCIL

Article 23

[1945 text]

1. The Security Council shall consist of eleven Members of the United Nations. The Republic of China, France, the Union of Soviet Socialist Republics, the United Kingdom of Great Britain and Northern Ireland, and the United States of America shall be permanent members of the Security Council. The General Assembly shall elect six other Members of the United Nations to be non-permanent members of the Security Council, due regard being specially paid, in the first instance to the contribution of Members of the United Nations to the maintenance of international peace and security and to the other purposes of the Organization, and also to equitable geographical distribution.

2. The non-permanent members of the Security Council shall be elected for a term of two years. In the first election of the non-permanent members, however, three shall be chosen for a term of one year. A retiring member shall not be eligible for immediate re-election.

[1963 text]²

1. The Security Council shall consist of fifteen Members of the United Nations. The Republic of China, France, the Union of Soviet Socialist Republics, the United Kingdom of Great Britain and Northern Ireland, and the United States of America shall be permanent members of the Security Council. The General Assembly shall elect ten other Members of the United Nations to be non-permanent members of the Security Council, due regard being specially paid, in the first instance to the contribution of Members of the United Nations to the maintenance of international peace and security and to the other purposes of the Organization, and also to equitable geographical distribution.

2. The non-permanent members of the Security Council shall be elected for a term of two years. In the first election of the non-permanent members after the increase of the membership of the Security Council from eleven to fifteen, two of the four additional members shall be chosen for a term of one year. A retiring member shall not be eligible for immediate re-election.

3. Each member of the Security Council shall have one representative.

Functions and Powers

Article 24

1. In order to ensure prompt and effective action by the United Nations, its Members confer on the Security Council primary responsibility for the maintenance of international peace and security, and agree that in carrying out its duties under this responsibility the Security Council acts on their behalf.

---

² Amendment adopted by the General Assembly on 17 December 1963, and entered into force on 31 August 1965.

2. In discharging these duties the Security Council shall act in accordance with the Purposes and Principles of the United Nations. The specific powers granted to the Security Council for the discharge of these duties are laid down in Chapters VI, VII, VIII, and XII.

3. The Security Council shall submit annual and, when necessary, special reports to the General Assembly for its consideration.

Article 25

The Members of the United Nations agree to accept and carry out the decisions of the Security Council in accordance with the present Charter.

Article 26

In order to promote the establishment and maintenance of international peace and security with the least diversion for armaments of the world's human and economic resources, the Security Council shall be responsible for formulating, with the assistance of the Military Staff Committee referred to in Article 47, plans to be submitted to the Members of the United Nations for the establishment of a system for the regulation of armaments.

Voting

Article 27

1. Each member of the Security Council shall have one vote.

[1945 text]

2. Decisions of the Security Council on procedural matters shall be made by an affirmative vote of seven members.

3. Decisions of the Security Council on all other matters shall be made by an affirmative vote of seven members including the concurring votes of the permanent members; provided that, in decisions under Chapter VI, and under paragraph 3 of Article 52, a party to a dispute shall abstain from voting.

[1963 text][3]

2. Decisions of the Security Council on procedural matters shall be made by an affirmative vote of nine members.

3. Decisions of the Security Council on all other matters shall be made by an affirmative vote of nine members including the concurring votes of the permanent members; provided that, in decisions under Chapter VI, and under paragraph 3 of Article 52, a party to a dispute shall abstain from voting.

Procedure

Article 28

1. The Security Council shall be so organized as to be able to function continuously. Each member of the Security Council shall for this purpose be represented at all times at the seat of the Organization.

2. The Security Council shall hold periodic meetings at which each of its members may, if it so desires, be represented by a member of the government or by some other specially designated representative.

---

[3] Amendment adopted by the General Assembly on 17 December 1963 and entered into force on 31 August 1965.

3. The Security Council may hold meetings at such places other than the seat of the Organization as in its judgment will best facilitate its work.

Article 29

The Security Council may establish such subsidiary organs as it deems necessary for the performance of its functions.

Article 30

The Security Council shall adopt its own rules of procedure, including the method of selecting its President.

Article 31

Any Member of the United Nations which is not a member of the Security Council may participate, without vote, in the discussion of any question brought before the Security Council whenever the latter considers that the interests of that Member are specially affected.

Article 32

Any Member of the United Nations which is not a member of the Security Council or any state which is not a Member of the United Nations, if it is a party to a dispute under consideration by the Security Council, shall be invited to participate, without vote, in the discussion relating to the dispute. The Security Council shall lay down such conditions as it deems just for the participation of a state which is not a Member of the United Nations.

CHAPTER VI—PACIFIC SETTLEMENT OF DISPUTES

Article 33

1. The parties to any dispute, the continuance of which is likely to endanger the maintenance of international peace and security, shall, first of all, seek a solution by negotiation, enquiry, mediation, conciliation, arbitration, judicial settlement, resort to regional agencies or arrangements, or other peaceful means of their own choice.

2. The Security Council shall, when it deems necessary, call upon the parties to settle their dispute by such means.

Article 34

The Security Council may investigate any dispute, or any situation which might lead to international friction or give rise to a dispute, in order to determine whether the continuance of the dispute or situation is likely to endanger the maintenance of international peace and security.

Article 35

1. Any Member of the United Nations may bring any dispute, or any situation of the nature referred to in Article 34, to the attention of the Security Council or of the General Assembly.

2. A state which is not a Member of the United Nations may bring to the attention of the Security Council or of the General Assembly any dispute to which it is a party if it accepts in advance, for the purposes of the dispute, the obligations of pacific settlement provided in the present Charter.

3. The proceedings of the General Assembly in respect of matters brought to its attention under this Article will be subject to the provisions of Articles 11 and 12.

Article 36

1. The Security Council may, at any stage of a dispute of the nature referred to in Article 33 or of a situation of like nature, recommend appropriate procedures or methods of adjustment.

2. The Security Council should take into consideration any procedures for the settlement of the dispute which have already been adopted by the parties.

3. In making recommendations under this Article the Security Council should also take into consideration that legal disputes should as a general rule be referred by the parties to the International Court of Justice in accordance with the provisions of the Statute of the Court.

Article 37

1. Should the parties to a dispute of the nature referred to in Article 33 fail to settle it by the means indicated in that Article, they shall refer it to the Security Council.

2. If the Security Council deems that the continuance of the dispute is in fact likely to endanger the maintenance of international peace and security, it shall decide whether to take action under Article 36 or to recommend such terms of settlement as it may consider appropriate.

Article 38

Without prejudice to the provisions of Articles 33 to 37, the Security Council may, if all the parties to any dispute so request, make recommendations to the parties with a view to a pacific settlement of the dispute.

CHAPTER VII—ACTION WITH RESPECT TO THREATS TO THE PEACE, BREACHES OF THE PEACE, AND ACTS OF AGGRESSION

Article 39

The Security Council shall determine the existence of any threat to the peace, breach of the peace, or act of aggression and shall make recommendations, or decide what measures shall be taken in accordance with Articles 41 and 42, to maintain or restore international peace and security.

Article 40

In order to prevent an aggravation of the situation, the Security Council may, before making the recommendations or deciding upon the measures provided for in Article 39, call upon the parties concerned to comply with such provisional measures as it deems necessary or desirable. Such provisional measures shall be without prejudice to the rights, claims, or position of the parties concerned. The Security Council shall duly take account of failure to comply with such provisional measures.

Article 41

The Security Council may decide what measures not involving the use of armed force are to be employed to give effect to its decisions, and it may call upon the Members of the United Nations to apply such measures. These may include complete or partial interruption of economic relations and of rail, sea, air, postal, telegraphic, radio, and other means of communication, and the severance of diplomatic relations.

Article 42

Should the Security Council consider that measures provided for in Article 41 would be inadequate or have proved to be inadequate, it may take such action by air, sea, or land forces as may be necessary to maintain or restore international peace and security. Such action may include demonstrations, blockade, and other operations by air, sea, or land forces of Members of the United Nations.

Article 43

1. All Members of the United Nations, in order to contribute to the maintenance of international peace and security, undertake to make available to the Security Council, on its call and in accordance with a special agreement or agreements, armed forces, assistance, and facilities, including rights of passage, necessary for the purpose of maintaining international peace and security.

2. Such agreement or agreements shall govern the numbers and types of forces, their degree of readiness and general location, and the nature of the facilities and assistance to be provided.

3. The agreement or agreements shall be negotiated as soon as possible on the initiative of the Security Council. They shall be concluded between the Security Council and Members or between the Security Council and groups of Members and shall be subject to ratification by the signatory states in accordance with their respective constitutional processes.

Article 44

When the Security Council has decided to use force it shall, before calling upon a Member not represented on it to provide armed forces in fulfilment of the obligations assumed under Article 43, invite that Member, if the Member so desires, to participate in the decisions of the Security Council concerning the employment of contingents of that Member's armed forces.

Article 45

In order to enable the United Nations to take urgent military measures, Members shall hold immediately available national air-force contingents for combined international enforcement action. The strength and degree of readiness of these contingents and plans for their combined action shall be determined within the limits laid down in the special agreement or agreements referred to in Article 43, by the Security Council with the assistance of the Military Staff Committee.

Article 46

Plans for the application of armed force shall be made by the Security Council with the assistance of the Military Staff Committee.

Article 47

1. There shall be established a Military Staff Committee to advise and assist the Security Council on all questions relating to the Security Council's military requirements for the maintenance of international peace and security, the employment and command of forces placed at its disposal, the regulation of armaments, and possible disarmament.

2. The Military Staff Committee shall consist of the Chiefs of Staff of the permanent members of the Security Council or their representatives. Any Member of the United Nations not permanently represented on the Committee shall be invited by the Committee to be associated with it when the efficient discharge of the Committee's responsibilities requires the participation of that Member in its work.

3. The Military Staff Committee shall be responsible under the Security Council for the strategic direction of any armed forces placed at the disposal of the Security Council. Questions relating to the command of such forces shall be worked out subsequently.

4. The Military Staff Committee, with the authorization of the Security Council and after consultation with appropriate regional agencies, may establish regional sub-committees.

Article 48

1. The action required to carry out the decisions of the Security Council for the maintenance of international peace and security shall be taken by all the Members of the United Nations or by some of them, as the Security Council may determine.

2. Such decisions shall be carried out by the Members of the United Nations directly and through their action in the appropriate international agencies of which they are members.

Article 49

The Members of the United Nations shall join in affording mutual assistance in carrying out the measures decided upon by the Security Council.

Article 50

If preventive or enforcement measures against any state are taken by the Security Council, any other state, whether a Member of the United Nations or not, which finds itself confronted with special economic problems arising from the carrying out of those measures shall have the right to consult the Security Council with regard to a solution of those problems.

Article 51

Nothing in the present Charter shall impair the inherent right of individual or collective self-defence if an armed attack occurs against a Member of the United Nations, until the Security Council has taken measures necessary to maintain international peace and security. Measures taken by Members in the exercise of this right of self-defence shall be immediately reported to the Security Council and shall not in any way affect the authority and responsibility of the Security Council under the present Charter to take at any time such action as it deems necessary in order to maintain or restore international peace and security.

CHAPTER VIII—REGIONAL ARRANGEMENTS

Article 52

1. Nothing in the present Charter precludes the existence of regional arrangements or agencies for dealing with such matters relating to the maintenance of international peace and security as are appropriate for regional action, provided that such arrangements or agencies and their activities are consistent with the Purposes and Principles of the United Nations.

2. The Members of the United Nations entering into such arrangements or constituting such agencies shall make every effort to achieve pacific settlement of local disputes through such regional arrangements or by such regional agencies before referring them to the Security Council.

3. The Security Council shall encourage the development of pacific settlement of local disputes through such regional arrangements or by such regional agencies either on the initiative of the states concerned or by reference from the Security Council.

4. This Article in no way impairs the application of Articles 34 and 35.

Article 53

1. The Security Council shall, where appropriate, utilize such regional arrangements or agencies for enforcement action under its authority. But no enforcement action shall be taken under regional arrangements or by regional agencies without the authorization of the Security Council, with the exception of measures against any enemy state, as defined in paragraph 2 of

this Article, provided for pursuant to Article 107 or in regional arrangements directed against renewal of aggressive policy on the part of any such state, until such time as the Organization may, on request of the Governments concerned, be charged with the responsibility for preventing further aggression by such a state.

2. The term enemy state as used in paragraph 1 of this Article applies to any state which during the Second World War has been an enemy of any signatory of the present Charter.

Article 54

The Security Council shall at all times be kept fully informed of activities undertaken or in contemplation under regional arrangements or by regional agencies for the maintenance of international peace and security.

CHAPTER IX—INTERNATIONAL ECONOMIC AND SOCIAL CO-OPERATION

Article 55

With a view to the creation of conditions of stability and well-being which are necessary for peaceful and friendly relations among nations based on respect for the principle of equal rights and self-determination of peoples, the United Nations shall promote:

a. higher standards of living, full employment, and conditions of economic and social progress and development;

b. solutions of international economic, social, health, and related problems; and international cultural and educational co-operation; and

c. universal respect for, and observance of, human rights and fundamental freedoms for all without distinction as to race, sex, language, or religion.

Article 56

All Members pledge themselves to take joint and separate action in co-operation with the Organization for the achievement of the purposes set forth in Article 55.

Article 57

1. The various specialized agencies, established by intergovernmental agreement and having wide international responsibilities, as defined in their basic instruments, in economic, social, cultural, educational, health, and related fields, shall be brought into relationship with the United Nations in accordance with the provisions of Article 63.

2. Such agencies thus brought into relationship with the United Nations are hereinafter referred to as specialized agencies.

Article 58

The Organization shall make recommendations for the coordination of the policies and activities of the specialized agencies.

Article 59

The Organization shall, where appropriate, initiate negotiations among the states concerned for the creation of any new specialized agencies required for the accomplishment of the purposes set forth in Article 55.

Article 60

Responsibility for the discharge of the functions of the Organization set forth in this Chapter shall be vested in the General Assembly and, under the authority of the General Assembly, in the Economic and Social Council, which shall have for this purpose the powers set forth in Chapter X.

CHAPTER X—THE ECONOMIC AND SOCIAL COUNCIL

Composition

Article 61

[1945 text]

1. The Economic and Social Council shall consist of eighteen Members of the United Nations elected by the General Assembly.

2. Subject to the provisions of paragraph 3, six members of the Economic and Social Council shall be elected each year for a term of three years. A retiring member shall be eligible for immediate re-election.

3. At the first election, eighteen members of the Economic and Social Council shall be chosen. The term of office of six members so chosen shall expire at the end of one year, and of six other members at the end of two years, in accordance with arrangements made by the General Assembly.

[1971 text][4]

1. The Economic and Social Council shall consist of fifty-four Members of the United Nations elected by the General Assembly.

2. Subject to the provisions of paragraph 3, eighteen members of the Economic and Social Council shall be elected each year for a term of three years. A retiring member shall be eligible for immediate re-election.

3. At the first election after the increase in the membership of the Economic and Social Council from twenty-seven[5] to fifty-four members, in addition to the members elected in place of the nine members whose term of office expires at the end of that year, twenty-seven additional members shall be elected. Of these twenty-seven additional members, the term of office of nine members so elected shall expire at the end of one year, and of nine other members at the end of two years, in accordance with arrangements made by the General Assembly.

4. Each member of the Economic and Social Council shall have one representative.

---

[4] Amendment adopted by the General Assembly on 17 December 1963 and entered into force on 31 August 1965. A further amendment was adopted by the General Assembly on 20 December 1971, and entered into force on 24 September 1973.

[5] Text reflects the earlier amendment, which expanded membership of the Economic and Social Council from eighteen to twenty-seven.

Functions and Powers

Article 62

1. The Economic and Social Council may make or initiate studies and reports with respect to international economic, social, cultural, educational, health, and related matters and may make recommendations with respect to any such matters to the General Assembly, to the Members of the United Nations, and to the specialized agencies concerned.

2. It may make recommendations for the purpose of promoting respect for, and observance of, human rights and fundamental freedoms for all.

3. It may prepare draft conventions for submission to the General Assembly, with respect to matters falling within its competence.

4. It may call, in accordance with the rules prescribed by the United Nations, international conferences on matters falling within its competence.

Article 63

1. The Economic and Social Council may enter into agreements with any of the agencies referred to in Article 57, defining the terms on which the agency concerned shall be brought into relationship with the United Nations. Such agreements shall be subject to approval by the General Assembly.

2. It may coordinate the activities of the specialized agencies through consultation with and recommendations to such agencies and through recommendations to the General Assembly and to the Members of the United Nations.

Article 64

1. The Economic and Social Council may take appropriate steps to obtain regular reports from the specialized agencies. It may make arrangements with the Members of the United Nations and with the specialized agencies to obtain reports on the steps taken to give effect to its own recommendations and to recommendations on matters falling within its competence made by the General Assembly.

2. It may communicate its observations on these reports to the General Assembly.

Article 65

The Economic and Social Council may furnish information to the Security Council and shall assist the Security Council upon its request.

Article 66

1. The Economic and Social Council shall perform such functions as fall within its competence in connection with the carrying out of the recommendations of the General Assembly.

2. It may, with the approval of the General Assembly, perform services at the request of Members of the United Nations and at the request of specialized agencies.

3. It shall perform such other functions as are specified elsewhere in the present Charter or as may be assigned to it by the General Assembly.

Article 67

1. Each member of the Economic and Social Council shall have one vote.

2. Decisions of the Economic and Social Council shall be made by a majority of the members present and voting.

Procedure

Article 68

The Economic and Social Council shall set up commissions in economic and social fields and for the promotion of human rights, and such other commissions as may be required for the performance of its functions.

Article 69

The Economic and Social Council shall invite any Member of the United Nations to participate, without vote, in its deliberations on any matter of particular concern to that Member.

Article 70

The Economic and Social Council may make arrangements for representatives of the specialized agencies to participate, without vote, in its deliberations and in those of the commissions established by it, and for its representatives to participate in the deliberations of the specialized agencies.

Article 71

The Economic and Social Council may make suitable arrangements for consultation with non-governmental organizations which are concerned with matters within its competence. Such arrangements may be made with international organizations and, where appropriate, with national organizations after consultation with the Member of the United Nations concerned.

Article 72

1. The Economic and Social Council shall adopt its own rules of procedure, including the method of selecting its President.

2. The Economic and Social Council shall meet as required in accordance with its rules, which shall include provision for the convening of meetings on the request of a majority of its members.

CHAPTER XI—DECLARATION REGARDING NON-SELF-GOVERNING TERRITORIES

Article 73

Members of the United Nations which have or assume responsibilities for the administration of territories whose peoples have not yet attained a full measure of self-government recognize the principle that the interests of the inhabitants of these territories are paramount, and accept as a sacred trust the obligation to promote to the utmost, within the system of international peace and security established by the present Charter, the well-being of the inhabitants of these territories, and, to this end:

a. to ensure, with due respect for the culture of the peoples concerned, their political, economic, social, and educational advancement, their just treatment, and their protection against abuses;

b. to develop self-government, to take due account of the political aspirations of the peoples, and to assist them in the progressive development of their free political institutions, according to the particular circumstances of each territory and its peoples and their varying stages of advancement;

c. to further international peace and security;

d. to promote constructive measures of development, to encourage research, and to co-operate with one another and, when and where appropriate, with specialized international bodies with a view to the practical achievement of the social, economic, and scientific purposes set forth in this Article; and

e. to transmit regularly to the Secretary-General for information purposes, subject to such limitation as security and constitutional considerations may require, statistical and other information of a technical nature relating to economic, social, and educational conditions in the territories for which they are respectively responsible other than those territories to which Chapter XII and XIII apply.

Article 74

Members of the United Nations also agree that their policy in respect of the territories to which this Chapter applies, no less than in respect of their metropolitan areas, must be based on the general principle of good-neighborliness, due account being taken of the interests and well-being of the rest of the world, in social, economic, and commercial matters.

CHAPTER XII—INTERNATIONAL TRUSTEESHIP SYSTEM

Article 75

The United Nations shall establish under its authority an international trusteeship system for the administration and supervision of such territories as may be placed thereunder by subsequent individual agreements. These territories are hereinafter referred to as trust territories.

Article 76

The basic objectives of the trusteeship system, in accordance with the Purposes of the United Nations laid down in Article 1 of the present Charter, shall be:

a. to further international peace and security;

b. to promote the political, economic, social, and educational advancement of the inhabitants of the trust territories, and their progressive development towards self-government or independence as may be appropriate to the particular circumstances of each territory and its peoples and the freely expressed wishes of the peoples concerned, and as may be provided by the terms of each trusteeship agreement;

c. to encourage respect for human rights and for fundamental freedoms for all without distinction as to race, sex, language, or religion, and to encourage recognition of the interdependence of the peoples of the world; and

d. to ensure equal treatment in social, economic, and commercial matters for all Members of the United Nations and their nationals and also equal treatment for the latter in the administration of justice without prejudice to the attainment of the foregoing objectives and subject to the provisions of Article 80.

Article 77

1. The trusteeship system shall apply to such territories in the following categories as may be placed thereunder by means of trusteeship agreements:

a. territories now held under mandate;

b. territories which may be detached from enemy states as a result of the Second World War; and

c. territories voluntarily placed under the system by states responsible for their administration.

2. It will be a matter for subsequent agreement as to which territories in the foregoing categories will be brought under the trusteeship system and upon what terms.

Article 78

The trusteeship system shall not apply to territories which have become Members of the United Nations, relationship among which shall be based on respect for the principle of sovereign equality.

Article 79

The terms of trusteeship for each territory to be placed under the trusteeship system, including any alteration or amendment, shall be agreed upon by the states directly concerned, including the mandatory power in the case of territories held under mandate by a Member of the United Nations, and shall be approved as provided for in Articles 83 and 85.

Article 80

1. Except as may be agreed upon in individual trusteeship agreements, made under Articles 77, 79, and 81, placing each territory under the trusteeship system, and until such agreements have been concluded, nothing in this Chapter shall be construed in or of itself to alter in any manner the rights whatsoever of any states or any peoples or the terms of existing international instruments to which Members of the United Nations may respectively be parties.

2. Paragraph 1 of this Article shall not be interpreted as giving grounds for delay or postponement of the negotiation and conclusion of agreements for placing mandated and other territories under the trusteeship system as provided for in Article 77.

Article 81

The trusteeship agreement shall in each case include the terms under which the trust territory will be administered and designate the authority which will exercise the administration of the trust territory. Such authority, hereinafter called the administering authority, may be one or more states or the Organization itself.

Article 82

There may be designated, in any trusteeship agreement, a strategic area or areas which may include part or all of the trust territory to which the agreement applies, without prejudice to any special agreement or agreements made under Article 43.

Article 83

1. All functions of the United Nations relating to strategic areas, including the approval of the terms of the trusteeship agreements and of their alteration or amendment, shall be exercised by the Security Council.

2. The basic objectives set forth in Article 76 shall be applicable to the people of each strategic area.

3. The Security Council shall, subject to the provisions of the trusteeship agreements and without prejudice to security considerations, avail itself of the assistance of the Trusteeship Council to perform those functions of the United Nations under the trusteeship system relating to political, economic, social, and educational matters in the strategic areas.

Article 84

It shall be the duty of the administering authority to ensure that the trust territory shall play its part in the maintenance of international peace and security. To this end the administering authority may make use of volunteer forces, facilities, and assistance from the trust territory in carrying out the obligations towards the Security Council undertaken in this regard by the administering authority, as well as for local defense and the maintenance of law and order within the trust territory.

Article 85

1. The functions of the United Nations with regard to trusteeship agreements for all areas not designated as strategic, including the approval of the terms of the trusteeship agreements and of their alteration or amendment, shall be exercised by the General Assembly.

2. The Trusteeship Council, operating under the authority of the General Assembly, shall assist the General Assembly in carrying out these functions.

CHAPTER XIII—THE TRUSTEESHIP COUNCIL

Composition

Article 86

1. The Trusteeship Council shall consist of the following Members of the United Nations:

a. those Members administering trust territories;

b. such of those Members mentioned by name in Article 23 as are not administering trust territories; and

c. as many other Members elected for three-year terms by the General Assembly as may be necessary to ensure that the total number of members of the Trusteeship Council is equally divided between those Members of the United Nations which administer trust territories and those which do not.

2. Each member of the Trusteeship Council shall designate one specially qualified person to represent it therein.

Functions and Powers

Article 87

The General Assembly and, under its authority, the Trusteeship Council, in carrying out their functions, may:

a. consider reports submitted by the administering authority;

b. accept petitions and examine them in consultation with the administering authority;

c. provide for periodic visits to the respective trust territories at times agreed upon with the administering authority; and

d. take these and other actions in conformity with the terms of the trusteeship agreements.

Article 88

The Trusteeship Council shall formulate a questionnaire on the political, economic, social, and educational advancement of the inhabitants of each trust territory, and the administering authority for each trust territory within the competence of the General Assembly shall make an annual report to the General Assembly upon the basis of such questionnaire.

Voting

Article 89

1. Each member of the Trusteeship Council shall have one vote.

2. Decisions of the Trusteeship Council shall be made by a majority of the members present and voting.

Procedure

Article 90

1. The Trusteeship Council shall adopt its own rules of procedure, including the method of selecting its President.

2. The Trusteeship Council shall meet as required in accordance with its rules, which shall include provision for the convening of meetings on the request of a majority of its members.

Article 91

The Trusteeship Council shall, when appropriate, avail itself of the assistance of the Economic and Social Council and of the specialized agencies in regard to matters with which they are respectively concerned.

CHAPTER XIV—THE INTERNATIONAL COURT OF JUSTICE

Article 92

The International Court of Justice shall be the principal judicial organ of the United Nations. It shall function in accordance with the annexed Statute which is based upon the Statute of the Permanent Court of International Justice and forms an integral part of the present Charter.

Article 93

1. All Members of the United Nations are ipso facto parties to the Statute of the International Court of Justice.

2. A state which is not a Member of the United Nations may become a party to the Statute of the International Court of Justice on conditions to be determined in each case by the General Assembly upon the recommendation of the Security Council.

Article 94

1. Each Member of the United Nations undertakes to comply with the decision of the International Court of Justice in any case to which it is a party.

2. If any party to a case fails to perform the obligations incumbent upon it under a judgment rendered by the Court, the other party may have recourse to the Security Council, which may, if it deems necessary, make recommendations or decide upon measures to be taken to give effect to the judgment.

Article 95

Nothing in the present Charter shall prevent Members of the United Nations from entrusting the solution of their differences to other tribunals by virtue of agreements already in existence or which may be concluded in the future.

Article 96

1. The General Assembly or the Security Council may request the International Court of Justice to give an advisory opinion on any legal question.

2. Other organs of the United Nations and specialized agencies, which may at any time be so authorized by the General Assembly, may also request advisory opinions of the Court on legal questions arising within the scope of their activities.

CHAPTER XV—THE SECRETARIAT

Article 97

The Secretariat shall comprise a Secretary-General and such staff as the Organization may require. The Secretary-General shall be appointed by the General Assembly upon the recommendation of the Security Council. He shall be the chief administrative officer of the Organization.

Article 98

The Secretary-General shall act in that capacity in all meetings of the General Assembly, of the Security Council, of the Economic and Social Council, and of the Trusteeship Council, and shall perform such other functions as are entrusted to him by these organs. The Secretary-General shall make an annual report to the General Assembly on the work of the Organization.

Article 99

The Secretary-General may bring to the attention of the Security Council any matter which in his opinion may threaten the maintenance of international peace and security.

Article 100

1. In the performance of their duties the Secretary-General and the staff shall not seek or receive instructions from any government or from any other authority external to the Organization. They shall refrain from any action which might reflect on their position as international officials responsible only to the Organization.

2. Each Member of the United Nations undertakes to respect the exclusively international character of the responsibilities of the Secretary-General and the staff and not to seek to influence them in the discharge of their responsibilities.

Article 101

1. The staff shall be appointed by the Secretary-General under regulations established by the General Assembly.

2. Appropriate staffs shall be permanently assigned to the Economic and Social Council, the Trusteeship Council, and, as required, to other organs of the United Nations. These staffs shall form a part of the Secretariat.

3. The paramount consideration in the employment of the staff and in the determination of the conditions of service shall be the necessity of securing the highest standards of efficiency, competence, and integrity. Due regard shall be paid to the importance of recruiting the staff on as wide a geographical basis as possible.

CHAPTER XVI—MISCELLANEOUS PROVISIONS

Article 102

1. Every treaty and every international agreement entered into by any Member of the United Nations after the present Charter comes into force shall as soon as possible be registered with the Secretariat and published by it.

2. No party to any such treaty or international agreement which has not been registered in accordance with the provisions of paragraph I of this Article may invoke that treaty or agreement before any organ of the United Nations.

Article 103

In the event of a conflict between the obligations of the Members of the United Nations under the present Charter and their obligations under any other international agreement, their obligations under the present Charter shall prevail.

Article 104

The Organization shall enjoy in the territory of each of its Members such legal capacity as may be necessary for the exercise of its functions and the fulfillment of its purposes.

Article 105

1. The Organization shall enjoy in the territory of each of its Members such privileges and immunities as are necessary for the fulfillment of its purposes.

2. Representatives of the Members of the United Nations and officials of the Organization shall similarly enjoy such privileges and immunities as are necessary for the independent exercise of their functions in connection with the Organization.

3. The General Assembly may make recommendations with a view to determining the details of the application of paragraphs 1 and 2 of this Article or may propose conventions to the Members of the United Nations for this purpose.

CHAPTER XVII—TRANSITIONAL SECURITY ARRANGEMENTS

Article 106

Pending the coming into force of such special agreements referred to in Article 43 as in the opinion of the Security Council enable it to begin the exercise of its responsibilities under Article 42, the parties to the Four-Nation Declaration, signed at Moscow October 30, 1943, and France, shall, in accordance with the provisions of paragraph 5 of that Declaration, consult with one another and as occasion requires with other Members of the United Nations with a view to such joint action on behalf of the Organization as may be necessary for the purpose of maintaining international peace and security.

Article 107

Nothing in the present Charter shall invalidate or preclude action, in relation to any state which during the Second World War has been an enemy of any signatory to the present Charter, taken or authorized as a result of that war by the Governments having responsibility for such action.

CHAPTER XVIII—AMENDMENTS

Article 108

Amendments to the present Charter shall come into force for all Members of the United Nations when they have been adopted by a vote of two thirds of the members of the General Assembly and ratified in accordance with their respective constitutional processes by two thirds of the Members of the United Nations, including all the permanent members of the Security Council.

Article 109

[1945 text]

1. A General Conference of the Members of the United Nations for the purpose of reviewing the present Charter may be held at a date and place to be fixed by a two-thirds vote of the members of the General Assembly and by a vote of any seven members of the Security Council. Each Member of the United Nations shall have one vote in the conference.

[1965 text][6]

1. A General Conference of the Members of the United Nations for the purpose of reviewing the present Charter may be held at a date and place to be fixed by a two-thirds vote of the members of the General Assembly and by a vote of any nine members of the Security Council. Each Member of the United Nations shall have one vote in the conference.

2. Any alteration of the present Charter recommended by a two-thirds vote of the conference shall take effect when ratified in accordance with their respective constitutional processes by two thirds of the Members of the United Nations including all the permanent members of the Security Council.

3. If such a conference has not been held before the tenth annual session of the General Assembly following the coming into force of the present Charter, the proposal to call such a conference shall be placed on the agenda of that session of the General Assembly, and the conference shall be held if so decided by a majority vote of the members of the General Assembly and by a vote of any seven members of the Security Council.

CHAPTER XIX—RATIFICATION AND SIGNATURE

Article 110

1. The present Charter shall be ratified by the signatory states in accordance with their respective constitutional processes.

2. The ratifications shall be deposited with the Government of the United States of America, which shall notify all the signatory states of each deposit as well as the Secretary-General of the Organization when he has been appointed.

3. The present Charter shall come into force upon the deposit of ratifications by the Republic of China, France, the Union of Soviet Socialist Republics, the United Kingdom of Great Britain and Northern Ireland, and the United States of America, and by a majority of the other signatory states. A protocol of the ratifications deposited shall thereupon be drawn up by the Government of the United States of America which shall communicate copies thereof to all the signatory states.

---

[6] Amendment adopted by the General Assembly on 20 December 1965 and entered into force on 12 June 1968.

4. The states signatory to the present Charter which ratify it after it has come into force will become original Members of the United Nations on the date of the deposit of their respective ratifications.

Article 111

The present Charter, of which the Chinese, French, Russian, English, and Spanish texts are equally authentic, shall remain deposited in the archives of the Government of the United States of America. Duly certified copies thereof shall be transmitted by that Government to the Governments of the other signatory states.

IN FAITH WHEREOF the representatives of the Governments of the United Nations have signed the present Charter.

DONE at the city of San Francisco the twenty-sixth day of June, one thousand nine hundred and forty-five.

Statute of the International Court of Justice

Article 1

The International Court of Justice established by the Charter of the United Nations as the principal judicial organ of the United Nations shall be constituted and shall function in accordance with the provisions of the present Statute.

CHAPTER I—ORGANIZATION OF THE COURT

Article 2

The Court shall be composed of a body of independent judges, elected regardless of their nationality from among persons of high moral character, who possess the qualifications required in their respective countries for appointment to the highest judicial offices, or are jurisconsults of recognized competence in international law.

Article 3

1. The Court shall consist of fifteen members, no two of whom may be nationals of the same state.

2. A person who for the purposes of membership in the Court could be regarded as a national of more than one state shall be deemed to be a national of the one in which he ordinarily exercises civil and political rights.

Article 4

1. The members of the Court shall be elected by the General Assembly and by the Security Council from a list of persons nominated by the national groups in the Permanent Court of Arbitration, in accordance with the following provisions.

2. In the case of Members of the United Nations not represented in the Permanent Court of Arbitration, candidates shall be nominated by national groups appointed for this purpose by their governments under the same conditions as those prescribed for members of the Permanent Court of Arbitration by Article 44 of the Convention of The Hague of 1907 for the pacific settlement of international disputes.

3. The conditions under which a state which is a party to the present Statute but is not a Member of the United Nations may participate in electing the members of the Court shall, in the absence of a special agreement, be laid down by the General Assembly upon recommendation of the Security Council.

Article 5

1. At least three months before the date of the election, the Secretary-General of the United Nations shall address a written request to the members of the Permanent Court of Arbitration belonging to the states which are parties to the present Statute, and to the members of the national groups appointed under Article 4, paragraph 2, inviting them to undertake, within a given time, by national groups, the nomination of persons in a position to accept the duties of a member of the Court.

2. No group may nominate more than four persons, not more than two of whom shall be of their own nationality. In no case may the number of candidates nominated by a group be more than double the number of seats to be filled.

Article 6

Before making these nominations, each national group is recommended to consult its highest court of justice, its legal faculties and schools of law, and its national academies and national sections of international academies devoted to the study of law.

Article 7

1. The Secretary-General shall prepare a list in alphabetical order of all the persons thus nominated. Save as provided in Article 12, paragraph 2, these shall be the only persons eligible.

2. The Secretary-General shall submit this list to the General Assembly and to the Security Council.

Article 8

The General Assembly and the Security Council shall proceed independently of one another to elect the members of the Court.

Article 9

At every election, the electors shall bear in mind not only that the persons to be elected should individually possess the qualifications required, but also that in the body as a whole the representation of the main forms of civilization and of the principal legal systems of the world should be assured.

Article 10

1. Those candidates who obtain an absolute majority of votes in the General Assembly and in the Security Council shall be considered as elected.

2. Any vote of the Security Council, whether for the election of judges or for the appointment of members of the conference envisaged in Article 12, shall be taken without any distinction between permanent and non-permanent members of the Security Council.

3. In the event of more than one national of the same state obtaining an absolute majority of the votes both of the General Assembly and of the Security Council, the eldest of these only shall be considered as elected.

Article 11

If, after the first meeting held for the purpose of the election, one or more seats remain to be filled, a second and, if necessary, a third meeting shall take place.

Article 12

1. If, after the third meeting, one or more seats still remain unfilled, a joint conference consisting of six members, three appointed by the General Assembly and three by the Security Council, may be formed at any time at the request of either the General Assembly or the Security Council,

for the purpose of choosing by the vote of an absolute majority one name for each seat still vacant, to submit to the General Assembly and the Security Council for their respective acceptance.

2. If the joint conference is unanimously agreed upon any person who fulfills the required conditions, he may be included in its list, even though he was not included in the list of nominations referred to in Article 7.

3. If the joint conference is satisfied that it will not be successful in procuring an election, those members of the Court who have already been elected shall, within a period to be fixed by the Security Council, proceed to fill the vacant seats by selection from among those candidates who have obtained votes either in the General Assembly or in the Security Council.

4. In the event of an equality of votes among the judges, the eldest judge shall have a casting vote.

Article 13

1. The members of the Court shall be elected for nine years and may be re-elected; provided, however, that of the judges elected at the first election, the terms of five judges shall expire at the end of three years and the terms of five more judges shall expire at the end of six years.

2. The judges whose terms are to expire at the end of the above-mentioned initial periods of three and six years shall be chosen by lot to be drawn by the Secretary-General immediately after the first election has been completed.

3. The members of the Court shall continue to discharge their duties until their places have been filled. Though replaced, they shall finish any cases which they may have begun.

4. In the case of the resignation of a member of the Court, the resignation shall be addressed to the President of the Court for transmission to the Secretary-General. This last notification makes the place vacant.

Article 14

Vacancies shall be filled by the same method as that laid down for the first election subject to the following provision: the Secretary-General shall, within one month of the occurrence of the vacancy, proceed to issue the invitations provided for in Article 5, and the date of the election shall be fixed by the Security Council.

Article 15

A member of the Court elected to replace a member whose term of office has not expired shall hold office for the remainder of his predecessor's term.

Article 16

1. No member of the Court may exercise any political or administrative function, or engage in any other occupation of a professional nature.

2. Any doubt on this point shall be settled by the decision of the Court.

Article 17

1. No member of the Court may act as agent, counsel, or advocate in any case.

2. No member may participate in the decision of any case in which he has previously taken part as agent, counsel, or advocate for one of the parties, or as a member of a national or international court, or of a commission of enquiry, or in any other capacity.

3. Any doubt on this point shall be settled by the decision of the Court.

Article 18

1. No member of the Court can be dismissed unless, in the unanimous opinion of the other members, he has ceased to fulfill the required conditions.

2. Formal notification thereof shall be made to the Secretary-General by the Registrar.

3. This notification makes the place vacant.

Article 19

The members of the Court, when engaged on the business of the Court, shall enjoy diplomatic privileges and immunities.

Article 20

Every member of the Court shall, before taking up his duties, make a solemn declaration in open court that he will exercise his powers impartially and conscientiously.

Article 21

1. The Court shall elect its President and Vice-President for three years; they may be re-elected.

2. The Court shall appoint its Registrar and may provide for the appointment of such other officers as may be necessary.

Article 22

1. The seat of the Court shall be established at The Hague. This, however, shall not prevent the Court from sitting and exercising its functions elsewhere whenever the Court considers it desirable.

2. The President and the Registrar shall reside at the seat of the Court.

Article 23

1. The Court shall remain permanently in session, except during the judicial vacations, the dates and duration of which shall be fixed by the Court.

2. Members of the Court are entitled to periodic leave, the dates and duration of which shall be fixed by the Court, having in mind the distance between The Hague and the home of each judge.

3. Members of the Court shall be bound, unless they are on leave or prevented from attending by illness or other serious reasons duly explained to the President, to hold themselves permanently at the disposal of the Court.

Article 24

1. If, for some special reason, a member of the Court considers that he should not take part in the decision of a particular case, he shall so inform the President.

2. If the President considers that for some special reason one of the members of the Court should not sit in a particular case, he shall give him notice accordingly.

3. If in any such case the member Court and the President disagree, the matter shall be settled by the decision of the Court.

Article 25

1. The full Court shall sit except when it is expressly provided otherwise in the present Statute.

2. Subject to the condition that the number of judges available to constitute the Court is not thereby reduced below eleven, the Rules of the Court may provide for allowing one or more judges, according to circumstances and in rotation, to be dispensed from sitting.

3. A quorum of nine judges shall suffice to constitute the Court.

Article 26

1. The Court may from time to time form one or more chambers, composed of three or more judges as the Court may determine, for dealing with particular categories of cases; for example, labour cases and cases relating to transit and communications.

2. The Court may at any time form a chamber for dealing with a particular case. The number of judges to constitute such a chamber shall be determined by the Court with the approval of the parties.

3. Cases shall be heard and determined by the chambers provided for in this article if the parties so request.

Article 27

A judgment given by any of the chambers provided for in Articles 26 and 29 shall be considered as rendered by the Court.

Article 28

The chambers provided for in Articles 26 and 29 may, with the consent of the parties, sit and exercise their functions elsewhere than at The Hague.

Article 29

With a view to the speedy dispatch of business, the Court shall form annually a chamber composed of five judges which, at the request of the parties, may hear and determine cases by summary procedure. In addition, two judges shall be selected for the purpose of replacing judges who find it impossible to sit.

Article 30

1. The Court shall frame rules for carrying out its functions. In particular, it shall lay down rules of procedure.

2. The Rules of the Court may provide for assessors to sit with the Court or with any of its chambers, without the right to vote.

Article 31

1. Judges of the nationality of each of the parties shall retain their right to sit in the case before the Court.

2. If the Court includes upon the Bench a judge of the nationality of one of the parties, any other party may choose a person to sit as judge. Such person shall be chosen preferably from among those persons who have been nominated as candidates as provided in Articles 4 and 5.

3. If the Court includes upon the Bench no judge of the nationality of the parties, each of these parties may proceed to choose a judge as provided in paragraph 2 of this Article.

4. The provisions of this Article shall apply to the case of Articles 26 and 29. In such cases, the President shall request one or, if necessary, two of the members of the Court forming the chamber to give place to the members of the Court of the nationality of the parties concerned, and, failing such, or if they are unable to be present, to the judges specially chosen by the parties.

5. Should there be several parties in the same interest, they shall, for the purpose of the preceding provisions, be reckoned as one party only. Any doubt upon this point shall be settled by the decision of the Court.

6. Judges chosen as laid down in paragraphs 2, 3, and 4 of this Article shall fulfill the conditions required by Articles 2, 17 (paragraph 2), 20, and 24 of the present Statute. They shall take part in the decision on terms of complete equality with their colleagues.

Article 32

1. Each member of the Court shall receive an annual salary.

2. The President shall receive a special annual allowance.

3. The Vice-President shall receive a special allowance for every day on which he acts as President.

4. The judges chosen under Article 31, other than members of the Court, shall receive compensation for each day on which they exercise their functions.

5. These salaries, allowances, and compensation shall be fixed by the General Assembly. They may not be decreased during the term of office.

6. The salary of the Registrar shall be fixed by the General Assembly on the proposal of the Court.

7. Regulations made by the General Assembly shall fix the conditions under which retirement pensions may be given to members of the Court and to the Registrar, and the conditions under which members of the Court and the Registrar shall have their travelling expenses refunded.

8. The above salaries, allowances, and compensation shall be free of all taxation.

Article 33

The expenses of the Court shall be borne by the United Nations in such a manner as shall be decided by the General Assembly.

CHAPTER II—COMPETENCE OF THE COURT

Article 34

1. Only states may be parties in cases before the Court.

2. The Court, subject to and in conformity with its Rules, may request of public international organizations information relevant to cases before it, and shall receive such information presented by such organizations on their own initiative.

3. Whenever the construction of the constituent instrument of a public international organization or of an international convention adopted thereunder is in question in a case before the Court, the Registrar shall so notify the public international organization concerned and shall communicate to it copies of all the written proceedings.

Article 35

1. The Court shall be open to the states parties to the present Statute.

2. The conditions under which the Court shall be open to other states shall, subject to the special provisions contained in treaties in force, be laid down by the Security Council, but in no case shall such conditions place the parties in a position of inequality before the Court.

3. When a state which is not a Member of the United Nations is a party to a case, the Court shall fix the amount which that party is to contribute towards the expenses of the Court. This provision shall not apply if such state is bearing a share of the expenses of the Court.

Article 36

1. The jurisdiction of the Court comprises all cases which the parties refer to it and all matters specially provided for in the Charter of the United Nations or in treaties and conventions in force.

2. The states parties to the present Statute may at any time declare that they recognize as compulsory ipso facto and without special agreement, in relation to any other state accepting the same obligation, the jurisdiction of the Court in all legal disputes concerning:

a. the interpretation of a treaty;

b. any question of international law;

c. the existence of any fact which, if established, would constitute a breach of an international obligation;

d. the nature or extent of the reparation to be made for the breach of an international obligation.

3. The declarations referred to above may be made unconditionally or on condition of reciprocity on the part of several or certain states, or for a certain time.

4. Such declarations shall be deposited with the Secretary-General of the United Nations, who shall transmit copies thereof to the parties to the Statute and to the Registrar of the Court.

5. Declarations made under Article 36 of the Statute of the Permanent Court of International Justice and which are still in force shall be deemed, as between the parties to the present Statute, to be acceptances of the compulsory jurisdiction of the International Court of Justice for the period which they still have to run and in accordance with their terms.

6. In the event of a dispute as to whether the Court has jurisdiction, the matter shall be settled by the decision of the Court.

Article 37

Whenever a treaty or convention in force provides for reference of a matter to a tribunal to have been instituted by the League of Nations, or to the Permanent Court of International Justice, the matter shall, as between the parties to the present Statute, be referred to the International Court of Justice.

Article 38

1. The Court, whose function is to decide in accordance with international law such disputes as are submitted to it, shall apply:

a. international conventions, whether general or particular, establishing rules expressly recognized by the contesting states;

b. international custom, as evidence of a general practice accepted as law;

c. the general principles of law recognized by civilized nations;

d. subject to the provisions of Article 59, judicial decisions and the teachings of the most highly qualified publicists of the various nations, as subsidiary means for the determination of rules of law.

2. This provision shall not prejudice the power of the Court to decide a case *ex aequo et bono*, if the parties agree thereto.

CHAPTER III—PROCEDURE

Article 39

1. The official languages of the Court shall be French and English. If the parties agree that the case shall be conducted in French, the judgment shall be delivered in French. If the parties agree that the case shall be conducted in English, the judgment shall be delivered in English.

2. In the absence of an agreement as to which language shall be employed, each party may, in the pleadings, use the language which it prefers; the decision of the Court shall be given in French and English. In this case the Court shall at the same time determine which of the two texts shall be considered as authoritative.

3. The Court shall, at the request of any party, authorize a language other than French or English to be used by that party.

Article 40

1. Cases are brought before the Court, as the case may be, either by the notification of the special agreement or by a written application addressed to the Registrar. In either case the subject of the dispute and the parties shall be indicated.

2. The Registrar shall forthwith communicate the application to all concerned.

3. He shall also notify the Members of the United Nations through the Secretary-General, and also any other states entitled to appear before the Court.

Article 41

1. The Court shall have the power to indicate, if it considers that circumstances so require, any provisional measures which ought to be taken to preserve the respective rights of either party.

2. Pending the final decision, notice of the measures suggested shall forthwith be given to the parties and to the Security Council.

Article 42

1. The parties shall be represented by agents.

2. They may have the assistance of counsel or advocates before the Court.

3. The agents, counsel, and advocates of parties before the Court shall enjoy the privileges and immunities necessary to the independent exercise of their duties.

Article 43

1. The procedure shall consist of two parts: written and oral.

2. The written proceedings shall consist of the communication to the Court and to the parties of memorials, counter-memorials and, if necessary, replies; also all papers and documents in support.

3. These communications shall be made through the Registrar, in the order and within the time fixed by the Court.

4. A certified copy of every document produced by one party shall be communicated to the other party.

5. The oral proceedings shall consist of the hearing by the Court of witnesses, experts, agents, counsel, and advocates.

Article 44

1. For the service of all notices upon persons other than the agents, counsel, and advocates, the Court shall apply direct to the government of the state upon whose territory the notice has to be served.

2. The same provision shall apply whenever steps are to be taken to procure evidence on the spot.

Article 45

The hearing shall be under the control of the President or, if he is unable to preside, of the Vice-President; if neither is able to preside, the senior judge present shall preside.

Article 46

The hearing in Court shall be public, unless the Court shall decide otherwise, or unless the parties demand that the public be not admitted.

Article 47

1. Minutes shall be made at each hearing and signed by the Registrar and the President.

2. These minutes alone shall be authentic.

Article 48

The Court shall make orders for the conduct of the case, shall decide the form and time in which each party must conclude its arguments, and make all arrangements connected with the taking of evidence.

Article 49

The Court may, even before the hearing begins, call upon the agents to produce any document or to supply any explanations. Formal note shall be taken of any refusal.

Article 50

The Court may, at any time, entrust any individual, body, bureau, commission, or other organization that it may select, with the task of carrying out an enquiry or giving an expert opinion.

Article 51

During the hearing any relevant questions are to be put to the witnesses and experts under the conditions laid down by the Court in the rules of procedure referred to in Article 30.

Article 52

After the Court has received the proofs and evidence within the time specified for the purpose, it may refuse to accept any further oral or written evidence that one party may desire to present unless the other side consents.

Article 53

1. Whenever one of the parties does not appear before the Court, or fails to defend its case, the other party may call upon the Court to decide in favour of its claim.

2. The Court must, before doing so, satisfy itself, not only that it has jurisdiction in accordance with Articles 36 and 37, but also that the claim is well founded in fact and law.

Article 54

1. When, subject to the control of the Court, the agents, counsel, and advocates have completed their presentation of the case, the President shall declare the hearing closed.

2. The Court shall withdraw to consider the judgment.

3. The deliberations of the Court shall take place in private and remain secret.

Article 55

1. All questions shall be decided by a majority of the judges present.

2. In the event of an equality of votes, the President or the judge who acts in his place shall have a casting vote.

Article 56

1. The judgment shall state the reasons on which it is based.

2. It shall contain the names of the judges who have taken part in the decision.

Article 57

If the judgment does not represent in whole or in part the unanimous opinion of the judges, any judge shall be entitled to deliver a separate opinion.

Article 58

The judgment shall be signed by the President and by the Registrar. It shall be read in open court, due notice having been given to the agents.

Article 59

The decision of the Court has no binding force except between the parties and in respect of that particular case.

Article 60

The judgment is final and without appeal. In the event of dispute as to the meaning or scope of the judgment, the Court shall construe it upon the request of any party.

Article 61

1. An application for revision of a judgment may be made only when it is based upon the discovery of some fact of such a nature as to be a decisive factor, which fact was, when the judgment was given, unknown to the Court and also to the party claiming revision, always provided that such ignorance was not due to negligence.

2. The proceedings for revision shall be opened by a judgment of the Court expressly recording the existence of the new fact, recognizing that it has such a character as to lay the case open to revision, and declaring the application admissible on this ground.

3. The Court may require previous compliance with the terms of the judgment before it admits proceedings in revision.

4. The application for revision must be made at latest within six months of the discovery of the new fact.

5. No application for revision may be made after the lapse of ten years from the date of the judgment.

Article 62

1. Should a state consider that it has an interest of a legal nature which may be affected by the decision in the case, it may submit a request to the Court to be permitted to intervene.

2 It shall be for the Court to decide upon this request.

Article 63

1. Whenever the construction of a convention to which states other than those concerned in the case are parties is in question, the Registrar shall notify all such states forthwith.

2. Every state so notified has the right to intervene in the proceedings; but if it uses this right, the construction given by the judgment will be equally binding upon it.

Article 64

Unless otherwise decided by the Court, each party shall bear its own costs.

CHAPTER IV—ADVISORY OPINIONS

Article 65

1. The Court may give an advisory opinion on any legal question at the request of whatever body may be authorized by or in accordance with the Charter of the United Nations to make such a request.

2. Questions upon which the advisory opinion of the Court is asked shall be laid before the Court by means of a written request containing an exact statement of the question upon which an opinion is required, and accompanied by all documents likely to throw light upon the question.

Article 66

1. The Registrar shall forthwith give notice of the request for an advisory opinion to all states entitled to appear before the Court.

2. The Registrar shall also, by means of a special and direct communication, notify any state entitled to appear before the Court or international organization considered by the Court, or, should it not be sitting, by the President, as likely to be able to furnish information on the question, that the Court will be prepared to receive, within a time limit to be fixed by the President, written statements, or to hear, at a public sitting to be held for the purpose, oral statements relating to the question.

3. Should any such state entitled to appear before the Court have failed to receive the special communication referred to in paragraph 2 of this Article, such state may express a desire to submit a written statement or to be heard; and the Court will decide.

4. States and organizations having presented written or oral statements or both shall be permitted to comment on the statements made by other states or organizations in the form, to the extent, and within the time limits which the Court, or, should it not be sitting, the President, shall decide in each particular case. Accordingly, the Registrar shall in due time communicate any such written statements to states and organizations having submitted similar statements.

Article 67

The Court shall deliver its advisory opinions in open court, notice having been given to the Secretary-General and to the representatives of Members of the United Nations, of other states and of international organizations immediately concerned.

Article 68

In the exercise of its advisory functions the Court shall further be guided by the provisions of the present Statute which apply in contentious cases to the extent to which it recognizes them to be applicable.

CHAPTER V—AMENDMENT

Article 69

Amendments to the present Statute shall be effected by the same procedure as is provided by the Charter of the United Nations for amendments to that Charter, subject however to any provisions which the General Assembly upon recommendation of the Security Council may adopt concerning the participation of states which are parties to the present Statute but are not Members of the United Nations.

Article 70

The Court shall have power to propose such amendments to the present Statute as it may deem necessary, through written communications to the Secretary-General, for consideration in conformity with the provisions of Article 69.

Index

Page references followed by *f*, *t* and *n* refer to figures, tables, and notes respectively; page references in bold refer to document excerpts.

CPSIA information can be obtained
at www.ICGtesting.com
Printed in the USA
BVHW031015101222
653908BV00001B/1